Timeline

A HISTORY O
A BRIEF OVERVIEW

	1500	1600	1700
Africa	Portugal dominates East Africa, ca. 1500–1650 Height of Kanem-Bornu, 1571–1603	Dutch West India Co. supplants Portuguese in West Africa, ca. 1630 Dutch settle Cape Town, 1651	Rise of Ashanti Empire, ca. 1700  **Oba of Benin:** Museum für Völkerkunde, Kunsthistorisches Museum, Vienna
The Americas	Mesoamerican and South American holocaust, ca. 1500–1600 First African slaves brought to Americas, ca. 1510 Cortés arrives in Mexico, 1519; Aztec Empire falls, 1521 Pizarro reaches Peru, conquers Incas, 1531	British settle Jamestown, 1607; first plantations established Champlain founds Quebec, 1608 Dutch found New Amsterdam, 1624	Silver production quadruples in Mexico and Peru, ca. 1700–1800 Spain's defeat in War of the Spanish Succession results in colonial dependence on Spanish goods, ca. 1700–1800
Asia and Oceania	Babur defeats Delhi sultanate, 1526–1527; founds Mughal Empire Christian missionaries active in China and Japan, ca. 1550–1650 Akbar expands Mughal Empire, 1556–1605 Unification of Japan, 1568–1600 Spain conquers Philippines, 1571	Tokugawa Shogunate, 1600–1867 Height of Mughal Empire, 1628–1658 Japan expels all Europeans, 1637 Manchus establish Qing Dynasty, 1644–1911 British found Calcutta, 1690	Height of Edo urban culture in Japan, ca. 1700 Decline of Mughal Empire, ca. 1700–1800 Persian invaders loot Delhi, 1739 French and British fight for control of India, 1740–1763
Europe	Luther's Ninety-five Theses, 1517 Charles V elected Holy Roman emperor, 1519 English Reformation begins, 1532 Council of Trent, 1545–1563 Dutch declare independence, 1581 Spanish Armada, 1588	Thirty Years' War, 1618–1648 English civil war, 1642–1649 Growth of absolutism in central and eastern Europe, ca. 1680–1790 The Enlightenment, ca. 1680–1800 Ottomans besiege Vienna, 1683 Revocation of Edict of Nantes, 1685 Glorious Revolution in England, 1688	War of the Spanish Succession, 1701–1713 Peace of Utrecht, 1713 Cabinet system develops in England, 1714–1742
Middle East	Safavid Empire in Persia, 1501–1722 Peak of Ottoman power under Suleiman, 1520–1566 Battle of Lepanto, 1571 Height of Safavid Empire under Shah Abbas, 1587–1629	**Turkish coffeehouse:** Reproduced by kind permission of the Trustees of the Chester Beatty Library, Dublin, Ms 439, folio 9	Decline of Safavid Empire under Nadir Shah, 1737–1747

1000 C.E.	1200 C.E.	1300 C.E.	1400 C.E.
Islam penetrates sub-Saharan Africa, ca. 1000–1100 Great Zimbabwe built, flourishes, ca. 1100–1400 Kingdom of Benin, ca. 1100–1897	Kingdom of Mali, ca. 1200–1450 Mongols conquer Baghdad, 1258; fall of Abbasid Dynasty	Rise of Yoruba states, West Africa, ca. 1300 Height of Swahili (East African) city-states, ca. 1300–1500 Mansa Musa rules Mali, 1312–1337	Arrival of Portuguese in Benin, ca. 1440 Songhay Empire, ca. 1450–1591 Atlantic slave trade, ca. 1450–1850 Da Gama reaches East Africa, 1498
Inca civilization in South America, ca. 1000–1500 Toltec state collapses, 1174		Aztecs arrive in Valley of Mexica, found Tenochtitlán (Mexico City), ca. 1325	Height of Inca Empire, 1438–1493 Reign of Montezuma I, 1440–1468; height of Aztec culture Columbus reaches Americas, 1492
Vietnam gains independence from China, ca. 1000 Construction of Angkor Wat, ca. 1100–1150 China divided into Song, Jin empires, 1127 Kamakura Shogunate, 1185–1333 Muslim conquerors end Buddhism in India, 1192	Peak of Khmer Empire, ca. 1200 Turkish sultanate at Delhi, 1206–1526 Mongols invade China, 1215 Yuan (Mongol) Dynasty, 1271–1368 Mongols invade Japan, 1274, 1281 Marco Polo arrives at Kublai Khan's court, ca. 1275	Ashikaga Shogunate, 1336–1408 Hong Wu defeats Mongols, 1368; founds Ming Dynasty, 1368–1644 Tamerlane conquers the Punjab, 1398	Ming policy encourages foreign trade, ca. 1400–1500 Ming maritime expeditions to India, Middle East, Africa, 1405–1433 Sultan Mehmed II, 1451–1481 Da Gama reaches India, 1498
Yaroslav the Wise, 1019–1054; peak of Kievan Russia Latin, Greek churches split, 1054 Norman Conquest of England, 1066 Investiture struggle, 1073–1122 Crusades, 1096–1270 Growth of trade and towns, ca. 1100–1400 Barbarossa invades Italy, 1154–1158	Magna Carta, 1215 Nevsky recognizes Mongol overlordship of Moscow, 1252 Aquinas, *Summa Theologica*, 1253	Babylonian Captivity of papacy, 1307–1377 Tver revolt in Russia, 1327–1328 Hundred Years' War, 1337–1453 Bubonic plague, 1347–1700 Beginnings of representative government, ca. 1350–1500	Italian Renaissance, ca. 1400–1530 Voyagers of discovery, ca. 1450–1600 Ottomans capture Constantinople, 1453; end of Byzantine Empire Wars of the Roses in England, 1453–1471 Unification of Spain completed, 1492
Seljuk Turks take Baghdad, 1055	Mongol invasion of Middle East, ca. 1220	Ottomans invade Europe, 1356	Ottoman Empire, 1453–1918

Great Mosque at Kilwa: Karen Samson Photography

Manco Capac, first Inca king, ca. 1200

Mongol horse and groom National Palace Museum, Taipei, Taiwan

OF WORLD SOCIETIES:

McKay • Hill • Buckler • Ebrey • Beck • Crowston • Wiesner-Hanks

1750	1800	1850	1900
British seize Cape Town, 1795 Napoleon's campaign in Egypt, 1798	Muhammad Ali founds dynasty in Egypt, 1805–1848 Slavery abolished in British Empire, 1807 Peak year of African transatlantic slave trade, 1820	Suez Canal opens, 1869 European "scramble for Africa," 1880–1900 Battle of Omdurman, 1898 South African War, 1899–1902	Union of South Africa formed, 1910 French annex Morocco, 1912 Ottoman Empire dissolved, 1919; Kemal's nationalist struggle in Turkey
"French and Indian Wars," 1756–1763 Quebec Act, 1774 American Revolution, 1775–1783 Comunero revolution, New Granada, 1781	Latin American wars of independence, 1806–1825 Brazil wins independence, 1822 Monroe Doctrine, 1823 Political instability in most Latin American countries, 1825–1870 U.S.-Mexican War, 1846–1848	U.S. Civil War, 1861–1865 British North America Act, 1867, for Canada Diaz controls Mexico, 1876–1911 Immigration from Europe and Asia to the Americas, 1880–1914 U.S. practices "dollar diplomacy" in Latin America, 1890–1920s Spanish-American War, 1898	Mexican Revolution, 1910 Panama Canal opens, 1914 Mexico adopts constitution, 1917
Height of Qing Empire, 1759 Treaty of Paris gives French colonies in India to Britain, 1763 Cook in Australia, 1768–1771 East India Act, 1784 First British convict-settlers arrive in Australia, 1788	British found Singapore, 1819 Java War, 1825–1830 Opium War, 1839–1842 Treaty of Nanjing, 1842: Manchus surrender Hong Kong to British British defeat last independent native state in India, 1848	Taiping Rebellion, 1850–1864 Perry opens Japan to trade, 1853 Great Rebellion in India, 1857–1858 Meiji Restoration in Japan, 1867 Indian National Congress, 1885 Japanese constitution, 1890 French acquire Indochina, 1893 Sino-Japanese War, 1894–1895 U.S. gains Philippines, 1898	Commonwealth of Australia, 1900 Boxer Rebellion, 1900–1903 Russo-Japanese War, 1904–1905 Muslim League formed, 1906 First calls for Indian independence, 1907 Chinese revolution; fall of Qing Dynasty, 1911 Chinese Republic, 1912–1949
Watt produces first steam engine, 1769 Outbreak of French Revolution, 1789 National Convention declares France a republic, 1792	Napoleonic Empire, 1804–1814 Congress of Vienna, 1814–1815 European economic penetration of non-Western countries, ca. 1816–1880 Greece wins independence, 1830 Revolution of 1848	Second Empire and Third Republic in France, 1852–1914 Unification of Italy, 1859–1870 Bismarck controls Germany, 1862–1890 Second Reform Bill, Great Britain, 1867 Franco-Prussian War, 1870–1871; foundation of the German Empire	Revolution in Russia; Tsar Nicholas II issues October Manifesto, 1905 Triple Entente (Britain, Russia, France), 1914–1918 World War I, 1914–1918 Treaty of Versailles, 1919
Selim III introduces administrative and military reforms, 1761–1808	Ottoman Empire launches Tanzimat reforms, 1839	Crimean War, 1853–1856	

Pasha Halim: Miramare Palace
Trieste/Dagli Orti/The Art Archive

200 C.E.	300 C.E.	500 C.E.	700 C.E.
Camel first used for trans-Saharan transport, ca. 200	Axum accepts Christianity, ca. 300–400	Political and commercial ascendancy of Axum, ca. 500–700	Berbers control trans-Saharan trade, ca. 700–900
Axum (Ethiopia) controls Red Sea trade, ca. 250		African Mediterranean slave trade, ca. 600–1900	Decline of Ethiopia, ca. 800–900
			Kingdom of Ghana, ca. 900–1300

	Maya civilization in Central America, ca. 300–1500	Maya civilization reaches peak, ca. 600–900	Teotihuacán, Monte Alban destroyed, ca. 700
	Classic period of Teotihuacán civilization in Mexico, ca. 300–900	Tiahuanaco civilization in South America, ca. 600–1000	"Time of Troubles" in Mesoamerica, 800–1000
			Toltec hegemony, ca. 980–1000

Creation of Yamato state in Japan, ca. 200–300	Three Kingdoms Period in Korea, 313–668	Sui Dynasty restores order in China, 581–618	Nara era, creation of Japan's first capital, 710–794
Buddhism gains popularity in China and Japan, ca. 220–590	China divides into northern, southern regimes, 316	Sanskrit drama, ca. 600–1000	Islam reaches India, 713
Fall of Han Dynasty, 220; Period of Division, 220–589	Chandragupta I founds Gupta Dynasty in India, ca. 320–480	Shotoku's "Constitution" in Japan, 604	Heian era in Japan, 794–1185
Fall of the Parthian empire, rise of the Sasanids, ca. 225	Gupta expansion, trade with Middle East and China, ca. 400	Tang Dynasty, 618–907; cultural flowering	Khmer Empire (Kampuchea) founded, 802
	Huns invade India, ca. 450	Taika Reforms in Japan, 646	Era of the Five Dynasties in China, 907–960
		Korea unified, 668	Song Dynasty, 960–1279

Reforms by Diocletian, 284–305	Constantine, 306–337; Edict of Milan, 313; founding of Constantinople, 324; Council of Nicaea, 325	*Rule* of Saint Benedict, 529	Charles Martel defeats Muslims at Tours, 732
		Code of Justinian, 529	Charlemagne rules, 768–814
	Christianity official state religion of Roman Empire, 380	Synod of Whitby, 664	Viking, Magyar invasions, 845–90
	Germanic raids on western Europe, 400s		Treaty of Verdun divides Carolingian Empire, 843
	Clovis rules Gauls, 481–511		Cluny monastery founded, 909

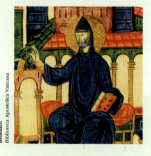

Sassanid Empire in Persia, 226–650		Muhammad, 570–632; the *hijra*, 622	Abbasid Dynasty, 750–1258; Islamic capital moved to Baghdad
		Umayyad Dynasty, 661–750; continued expansion of Islam	Golden age of Muslim learning, ca. 900–1100

1920	1940	1950	1960
Cultural nationalism in Africa, 1920s African farmers organize first "cocoa holdups," 1930–1931	Apartheid system in South Africa, 1948–1991	Egypt declared a republic; Nasser named premier, 1954 Morocco, Tunisia, Sudan, and Ghana gain independence, 1956–1957 French-British Suez invasion, 1956	Mali, Nigeria, and the Congo gain independence, 1960 Biafra declares independence from Nigeria, 1967
U.S. "consumer revolution," 1920s Stock market crash in U.S.; Great Depression begins, 1929 Revolutions in six South American countries, 1930 New Deal begins in United States, 1933	Surprise attack by Japan on Pearl Harbor, 1941 United Nations established, 1945 Perón rules Argentina, 1946–1953	Castro takes power in Cuba, 1959	Cuban missile crisis, 1962 Military dictatorship in Brazil, 1964–1985 United States escalates war in Vietnam, 1964
Kita Ikki advocates ultranationalism in Japan, 1923 Jiang Jieshi unites China, 1928 Gandhi's Salt March, 1930 Japan invades China, 1931 Mao Zedong's Long March, 1934 Sino-Japanese War, 1937–1945 Japan conquers Southeast Asia, 1939–1942	United States drops atomic bombs on Hiroshima and Nagasaki, 1945 Chinese civil war, 1945–1949; Communists win Philippines gain independence, 1946 India (Hindu) and Pakistan (Muslim) gain independence, 1947	Japan begins long period of rapid economic growth, 1950 Korean War, 1950–1953 Vietnamese Nationalists defeat French; Vietnam divided, 1954 Islamic Republic of Pakistan declared, 1956 Mao Zedong announces Great Leap Forward, 1958	Sino-Soviet split becomes apparent, 1960 Great Proletarian Cultural Revolution in China, 1965–1969 Indira Gandhi prime minister of India, 1966–1977, 1980–1984
Mussolini seizes power in Italy, 1922 Stalin takes power in U.S.S.R., 1927 Great Depression, 1929–1933 Hitler gains power, 1933 Civil war in Spain, 1936–1939 World War II, 1939–1945	Marshall Plan, 1947 NATO formed, 1949 Soviet Union and Communist China sign 30-year alliance, 1949	Death of Stalin, 1953 Warsaw Pact, 1955 Revolution in Hungary, 1956 Common Market formed, 1957	Student revolution in France, 1968 Soviet invasion of Czechoslovakia, 1968 Brandt's Ostpolitik, 1969–1973
Turkish Republic recognized, 1923 Reza Shah leads Iran, 1925–1941 Iraq gains independence, 1932	Yalta. F.D.R. Library Arabs and Jews at war in Palestine; Israel created, 1948	Suez crisis, 1956	Czechs protest Soviet invasion: Bettmann/Corbis OPEC founded, 1960 Arab-Israeli Six-Day War, 1967

OF WORLD SOCIETIES:

McKay • Hill • Buckler • Ebrey • Beck • Crowston • Wiesner-Hanks

1000 B.C.E.	500 B.C.E.	250 B.C.E.	1 C.E.
Political fragmentation of Egypt; rise of small kingdoms, ca. 1100–700 Ironworking spreads throughout Africa, ca. 1000 B.C.E.–300 C.E. Persians conquer Egypt, 525	Death of Alexander, 323; Ptolemy conquers Egypt, Seleucus rules Asia	Scipio Africanus defeats Hannibal at Zama, 202 Meroë becomes iron-smelting center, 1st century B.C.E.	Expansion of Bantu-speaking peoples, ca. 100–900
Chavin civilization in Andes, ca. 1000–200 Olmec center at San Lorenzo destroyed, ca. 900; power passes to La Venta	Fall of La Venta, 300; Tres Zapotes becomes leading Olmec site	Andean peoples intensify agriculture, ca. 200	Moche civilization flourishes in Peru, ca. 100–800
Zhou Dynasty, ca. 1027–256 Later Vedic Age, solidification of caste system, ca. 1000–500 Upanishads; foundation of Hinduism, 700–500 Confucius, 551–479 Siddhartha Gautama (Buddha), 528–461 Persians conquer parts of India, 513	Warring States Period in China, 403–221 Zhuangzi and development of Daoism, 369–268 Alexander invades India, 327–326 Chandragupta founds Mauryan Dynasty, 322–ca. 185 Ashoka, 269–232	Qin Dynasty unifies China; Great Wall begun, 221–210 Han Dynasty, 206 B.C.E.–220 C.E. Greeks invade India, ca. 183–145 Silk Road opens to Parthia, Rome; Buddhism enters China, ca. 104 Bhagavad Gita, ca. 100 B.C.E.–100 C.E.	First (Chinese) written reference to Japan, 45 C.E. Shakas and Kushans invade eastern Parthia and India, 1st century C.E. Kushan rule in northwestern India, ca. 100–300 Chinese invent paper, 105 Roman attacks on Parthian empire, 115–211
Greek Lyric Age; rise of Sparta and Athens, 800–500 Origin of Greek polis, ca. 700 Roman Republic founded, 509	Persian Wars, 499–479 Athenian Empire, flowering of art and philosophy, 5th century Peloponnesian War, 431–404 Roman expansion, 390–146 Conquests of Alexander the Great, 334–323 Punic Wars, destruction of Carthage, 264–146	Late Roman Republic, 133–27 Julius Caesar killed, 44 Octavian seizes power, rules imperial Rome as Augustus, 27 B.C.E.–14 C.E.	Roman Empire at greatest extent, 117 Breakdown of pax Romana, ca. 180–284
Assyrian Empire, 900–612 Zoroaster, ca. 600 Babylonian captivity of Hebrews, 586–539 Cyrus the Great founds Persian Empire, 550 Darius and Xerxes complete Persian conquest of Middle East, 521–464	Alexander the Great extends empire, 334–331	Arsaces of Parthia begins conquest of Persia, ca. 250–137 Pompey conquers Syria and Palestine, 63	Jesus Christ, ca. 4 B.C.E.–30 C.E. Jews revolt; Romans destroy temple in Jerusalem: end of Hebrew state, 70

Nok woman: National Museum, Lagos, Nigeria/Werner Forman Archive, Art Resource, NY

Alexander: National Museum, Naples/Alinari/Art Resource, NY

1970	1980	1990	2000

Nelson Mandela. Mohamed Lounes/Gamma

1970	1980	1990	2000
	South African president Frederik de Klerk legalizes African National Congress, 1989 Nelson Mandela freed, 1990	Growth of Islamic fundamentalism, 1990 to present Nelson Mandela elected president of South Africa, 1994 Rwandan genocide, 1994	AIDS epidemic, 2000 to present Civil war and genocide in Darfur, 2003 to present Zimbabwean President Robert Mugabe increases violence against opponents after losing election, 2008
Military coup in Chile, 1973 U.S. Watergate scandal, 1974 Revolutions in Nicaragua and El Salvador, 1979	U.S. military buildup, 1980–1988 Argentina restores civilian rule, 1983	Canada, Mexico, and United States form free-trade area (NAFTA), 1994 Haiti establishes democratic government, 1994 Permanent extension of Treaty on the Non-Proliferation of Nuclear Weapons, 1995	Terrorist attack on United States, September 11, 2001 Space shuttle *Columbia* explodes, 2003 Hurricanes Katrina and Rita ravage Gulf Coast of U.S., 2005 Raúl Castro succeeds his ailing brother Fidel as president of Cuba, 2008
India-Pakistan war, 1971 Communist victory in Vietnam War, 1975 China pursues modernization, 1976 to present Chinese invade Vietnam, 1979	Japanese foreign investment surge, 1980–1992 Sikh nationalism in India, 1984 to present China crushes democracy movement, 1989	Economic growth and political repression in China, 1990 to present Vietnam embraces foreign investment, 1990 to present U.S. military bases closed in Philippines, 1991 Hong Kong returns to Chinese rule, 1997	China joins WTO, 2001 India and Pakistan come close to all-out war, 2002 Tsunami in Southeast Asia, 2004 North Korea dismantles nuclear facilities, 2007 Cyclone Nargis in Myanmar (Burma), 2008 8.0 magnitude earthquake in Sichuan Province, China, 2008
Helsinki Accord on human rights, 1975 Soviet invasion of Afghanistan, 1979	 Chinese students in 1989. Erika Lansner/stockphoto.com Soviet reform under Gorbachev, 1985–1991 Communism falls in eastern Europe, 1989–1990	Maastricht treaty proposes monetary union, 1990 Conservative economic policies, 1990s End of Soviet Union, 1991 Civil war in Bosnia, 1991–1995 Creation of European Union, 1993	Euro note enters circulation, 2002 Madrid train bombing, 2004 Chechen terrorists take Russian schoolchildren hostage, 2004 London subway and bus bombing, 2005
"Yom Kippur War," 1973 Islamic revolution in Iran, 1979 Camp David Accords, 1979	Iran-Iraq War, 1980–1988	Growth of Islamic fundamentalism, 1990 to present Iraq driven from Kuwait by United States and allies, 1991 Israel and Palestinians sign peace agreement, 1993 Assassination of Israeli prime minister Yitzak Rabin, 1995	Israel begins construction of West Bank barrier, 2003 Wars in Iraq and Afghanistan, 2003 to present Iran advances nuclear energy program, 2004 to present Benazir Bhutto assassinated, 2007

A HISTORY O
A BRIEF OVERVIEW

	10,000 B.C.E.	2500 B.C.E.	1500 B.C.E.
Africa	New Stone Age culture, ca. 10,000–3500 Farming begins in Nile River Valley, ca. 6000 Unification of Egypt, 3100–2660	Bantu migrations throughout western Africa, ca. 2000–500 Egypt's Old Kingdom, 2660–2180 Egypt's Middle Kingdom, 2080–1640 Hyksos "invade" Egypt, 1640–1570	Egypt's New Kingdom; Egyptian empire, ca. 1570–1075 Akhenaten institutes worship of Aton, ca. 1360
The Americas	Migration into Americas begins, ca. 20,000 Maize domesticated in Mexico, ca. 5000 First pottery in Americas, Ecuador, ca. 3000	First metalworking in Peru, ca. 2000	Olmec civilization, Mexico ca. 1500 B.C.E.–300 C.E.
Asia and Oceania	Farming begins in Yellow River Valley, ca. 4000 Indus River Valley civilization, ca. 2800–1800; capitals at Mohenjo-daro and Harappa	Horse domesticated in China, ca. 2500	Shang Dynasty, first writing in China, ca. 1500–ca. 1050 Aryans arrive in India; Early Vedic Age, ca. 1500–1000 Vedas, oldest Hindu sacred texts, ca. 1500–500
Europe	New Stone Age culture, ca. 10,000–3500	Greek Bronze Age, 2000–1100 Height of Minoan culture, 1700–1450 Arrival of Greeks in peninsular Greece, ca. 1650	Mycenaeans conquer Minoan Crete, ca. 1450 Mycenaean Age, 1450–120 Trojan War, ca. 1180 Greek Dark Age, ca. 1100–800
Middle East	Farming begins in Tigris-Euphrates River Valley, ca. 6000 First writing in Sumeria; city-states emerge, ca. 3500	Akkadian empire, ca. 2331–2200 Hammurabi, 1792–1750 Hebrew monotheism, ca. 1700	Hittite Empire, ca. 1475–1200 Moses leads Hebrews out of Egypt, ca. 1300–1200 United Hebrew kingdom, 1020–922

Neolithic jade plaque: Zhejiang Provincial Institute of Archaeology/ Cultural Relics Publishing House

A·HISTORY·OF
WORLD·SOCIETIES

A·HISTORY·OF WORLD·SOCIETIES

Volume B
From 800 to 1815

eighth edition

John P. McKay
University of Illinois at Urbana-Champaign

Bennett D. Hill
Late of Georgetown University

John Buckler
University of Illinois at Urbana-Champaign

Patricia Buckley Ebrey
University of Washington

Roger B. Beck
Eastern Illinois University

Clare Haru Crowston
University of Illinois at Urbana-Champaign

Merry E. Wiesner-Hanks
University of Wisconsin–Milwaukee

BEDFORD / ST. MARTIN'S
Boston • New York

FOR BEDFORD/ST. MARTIN'S

Publisher for History: Mary Dougherty
Executive Editor for History: Traci Mueller
Director of Development for History: Jane Knetzger
Executive Marketing Manager: Jenna Bookin Barry
Copyeditor: Sybil Sosin
Proofreader: Angela Hoover Morrison
Text Design and Page Layout: Janet Theurer
Photo Research: Carole Frohlich
Indexer: Leoni McVey
Cover Design: Donna Lee Dennison
Cover Art: Yamamoto Shurei, Portrait of two young women, Edo period, Japan, late 18th century.
  Photograph: British Museum, London/Erich Lessing/Art Resource, NY.
Cartography: Charlotte Miller/GeoNova
Composition: NK Graphics
Printing and Binding: R.R. Donnelley & Sons Company

President: Joan E. Feinberg
Editorial Director: Denise B. Wydra
Director of Marketing: Karen R. Soeltz
Director of Editing, Design, and Production: Marcia Cohen
Assistant Director of Editing, Design, and Production: Elise S. Kaiser
Managing Editor: Elizabeth M. Schaaf

Library of Congress Control Number: 2008933879

Manufactured in the United States of America.

3   2   1   0   9   8
f   e   d   c   b   a

For information, write: Bedford/St. Martin's, 75 Arlington Street, Boston, MA 02116 (617-399-4000)

ISBN-10: 0–312–68293–X   ISBN-13: 978–0–312–68293–4   (combined edition)
ISBN-10: 0–312–68294–8   ISBN-13: 978–0–312–68294–1   (Vol. I)
ISBN-10: 0–312–68295–6   ISBN-13: 978–0–312–68295–8   (Vol. II)
ISBN-10: 0–312–68296–4   ISBN-13: 978–0–312–68296–5   (Vol. A)
ISBN-10: 0–312–68297–2   ISBN-13: 978–0–312–68297–2   (Vol. B)
ISBN-10: 0–312–68298–0   ISBN-13: 978–0–312–68298–9   (Vol. C)

Preface

In this age of a global environment and global warming, of a global economy and global banking, of global migration and rapid global travel, of global sports and global popular culture, the study of world history becomes more urgent. Surely, an appreciation of other, and earlier, societies helps us to understand better our own and to cope more effectively in pluralistic cultures worldwide. The large numbers of Turks living in Germany, of Italians, Hungarians, and Slavic peoples living in Australia, of Japanese living in Peru and Argentina, and of Arabs, Mexicans, Chinese, and Filipinos living in the United States—to mention just a few obvious examples—represent diversity on a global scale. The movement of large numbers of peoples from one continent to another goes back thousands of years, at least as far back as the time when peoples migrated from Asia into the Americas. Swift air travel and the Internet have accelerated these movements, and they testify to the incredible technological changes the world has experienced in the last half of the twentieth century and beginning of the twenty-first.

For most peoples, the study of history has traditionally meant the study of their own national, regional, and ethnic pasts. Fully appreciating the great differences among various societies and the complexity of the historical problems surrounding these cultures, we have wondered if the study of local or national history is sufficient for people who will spend their lives in the twenty-first century on one small interconnected planet. The authors of this book believe the study of world history in a broad and comparative context is an exciting, important, and highly practical pursuit. It is our conviction, based on considerable experience in introducing large numbers of students to the broad sweep of world history, that a book reflecting current trends can excite readers and inspire an enduring interest in the long human experience. Our strategy has been twofold.

First, we have made social history the core element of our work. We not only incorporate recent research by social historians but also seek to re-create the life of ordinary people in appealing human terms. A strong social element seems especially appropriate in a world history text, for identification with ordinary men and women of the past allows today's reader to reach an empathetic understanding of different cultures. At the same time we have been mindful of the need to give great economic, political, intellectual, and cultural developments the attention they deserve. We want to give individual students and instructors a balanced, integrated perspective so that they can pursue on their own or in the classroom those themes and questions that they find particularly exciting and significant.

Second, we have made every effort to strike an effective global balance. We are acutely aware of the great drama of our times—the passing of the era of Western dominance and the increasing complexity in lines of political, economic, and cultural power and influence. Today the whole world interacts, and to understand that interaction and what it means for today's citizens, we must study the whole world's history. Thus we have adopted a comprehensive yet manageable global perspective. We study all geographical areas, conscious of the separate histories of many parts of the world, particularly in the earliest millennia of human development. We also stress the links among cultures, political units, and economic systems, for it is these connections and interactions that have made the world what it is today.

Changes in the Eighth Edition

In preparing the Eighth Edition of this book, we have worked hard to keep our book up-to-date and to strengthen our distinctive yet balanced approach.

Organizational Changes

Responding to the wishes of many of the faculty who use this book, we have shortened the text significantly. The narrative has been tightened in each chapter, and the consolidations improve the overall global balance of our work.

In addition, several chapters have been extensively reorganized. Merry Wiesner-Hanks from the University of Wisconsin-Milwaukee and Clare Crowston from the University of Illinois joined the author team with this edition, taking responsibility for Chapters 7, 10, 13, and 14 and Chapters 15–17 and 21, respectively. Chapter 7, "Europe and Western Asia, ca. 350–850," has a broader geographic focus, with more material on the Byzantine Empire and the various migrating peoples. Former Chapter 13 on the Americas has been brought into the story earlier as new Chapter 10, and the chapter has been rewritten to reflect the newest scholarship on early cultures of North America, Mesoamerica, and South America. Discussion of the Thirty Years' War has been integrated into Chapter 16, allowing a better assessment of its impact on state-building, along with broader coverage of economic and demographic trends. Other chapters have been restructured as well. Chapter 19, "The Islamic World Powers, ca. 1400–1800," has been completely reorganized to highlight parallels among the Ottoman, Safavid, and Mughal Empires in terms of political, cultural, and economic developments. Reflecting current understandings of the connections around the Atlantic world, Chapter 21 includes extensive discussion of the Haitian Revolution along with the American and French Revolutions. Chapter 26, "Nation Building in the Western Hemisphere and Australia," contains a new section that places the nations in comparative perspective. In addition, former chapters 33 and 34 are now combined as a new and streamlined Chapter 33, "A New Era in World History." The new chapter focuses on global political and economic issues (such as the United Nations, terrorism, globalization and its consequences, and vital resources), plus global issues that affect individuals (such as poverty, disease, urbanization, and education), and shows how they evolved over the course of the twentieth century. "The Middle East in Today's World," a supplement to later printings of the seventh edition, has been updated to reflect recent developments in the Middle East, and is now the Epilogue.

Geographical and Gender Issues

In previous editions we added significantly more discussion of groups and regions that are often shortchanged in the general histories of world civilizations, and we have continued to do so in this new revision. This expanded scope reflects the renewed awareness within the historical profession of the enormous diversity of the world's peoples. Examples include more material on the Etruscans in Chapter 5, the Huns in Chapter 7, and the Turks in Chapter 8. Chapter 10 includes increased discussion of the Hohokam, Hopewell, and Mississippian peoples in North America and of pre-Inca cultures in Peru. Study of the Mongols and other peoples of Central Asia has exploded in the past several years, which has shaped the changes in Chapter 11. Chapter 17 includes a new discussion of new ideas about race during the Enlightenment. Chapter 21 has considerable new material on the Haitian Revolution. Overall, an expanded treatment of non-European societies and cultures has been achieved.

In addition, we have continued to include updated and expanded material relating to gender in nearly every chapter, incorporating insights from women's history, the history of sexuality, the history of the family, and the new history of masculinities. Chapter 4 includes revised coverage of Greek sexuality and the family, with new focus in Chapter 7 on the role of women in barbarian society, Chapter 8 on women in classical Islamic society, Chapter 12 on women's lives in Song China, Chapter 14 on gender hierarchies in Renaissance Europe and on the Reformation and marriage, Chapter 18 on women, marriage, and work in early modern Africa, Chapter 22 on the sexual division of labor in the Industrial Revolution, and Chapter 33 on women's rights and feminist movements. In addition to "Individuals in Society" features from previous editions that focus on the lives of specific women, several new ones have been added: the feature in Chapter 1 focuses on the Egyptian monarch Nefertiti, in Chapter 7 on Empress Theodora of Constantinople, in Chapter 13 on the Christian abbess Hildegard of Bingen, and in Chapter 16 on the Jewish merchant and diarist Glückel of Hameln. Chapter 8 includes a new "Listening to the Past" feature on the etiquette of marriage in the Islamic world.

Cross-Cultural Comparisons and Connections

In this edition we have continued to expand our comparative coverage to help students see and understand the cross-cultural connections of world history. Chapter 2 offers expanded discussion of trading networks in early India, and both Chapters 5 and 6 provide enhanced discussion of the Silk Road. Chapter 7 includes a reframed discussion of the barbarian migrations into Europe. Chapter 8 addresses new questions such as "How were the Muslim lands governed and what new challenges did they face?" and "What social distinctions were important in Muslim society?" Updated treatment of the trans-Saharan trade appears in Chapter 9, and Chapter 10 now discusses trade along the rivers and lakes of North America. Chapter 15 has been extensively rewritten, with a new section on global economies, forced migrations, and cultural encounters. Chapter 24 addresses the important question "What were the global consequences of European industrialization between 1800 and 1914?"

Incorporation of Recent Scholarship

As in previous revisions we have made a serious effort to keep our book fresh and up-to-date by incorporating new and important scholarship throughout the Eighth Edition. Chapter 4 includes new findings about the role of women in religious movements in the ancient world, including Christianity. Chapter 7 highlights the continuing significance of the Byzantines and the transformations brought through barbarian migrations. Chapter 10 features innovative research on agricultural communities in the Americas and the connections among them. New sections on popular religion and social hierarchies appear in Chapters 13 and 14. Chapters 14 and 17 include sections derived from the new scholarship on changing conceptions of race. Chapter 17 also draws upon new work about the emergence of the public sphere in Enlightenment Europe to discuss the political and social implications of intellectual change. Chapter 20 features new treatment of maritime East Asia. Chapter 26 includes a new comparative discussion of the incorporation of the nations of the Americas into the world economy. Material in the final three chapters and the Epilogue has been updated to ensure a clear account of contemporary world history. Thus, the text includes discussion of such events as the unfolding war in Iraq, the worsening crisis in Afghanistan, Hezbollah's revival in Lebanon, moves toward peace in Israel, elections in Zimbabwe, charges of genocide against the Sudanese president, China and Tibet and the 2008 Olympics, and North Korea's dismantling of its nuclear facilities. In sum, we have tried hard to bring new research and interpretation into our global history, believing it essential to keep our book stimulating, accurate, and current for students and instructors.

Revised Full-Color Art and Map Program

Finally, the illustrative component of our work has been carefully revised. We have added many new illustrations to our extensive art program, which includes over three hundred color reproductions, thus highlighting the connections among art, material culture, events, and social changes. Illustrations have been selected to support and complement the text, and, wherever possible, illustrations are contemporaneous with the textual material discussed. Considerable research went into many of the captions in order to make them as informative as possible. We have reflected on the observation that "there are more valid facts and details in works of art than there are in history books," and we would modify it to say that art is "a history book." Artwork remains an integral part of our book; the past can speak in pictures as well as in words. The maps have been completely redesigned and revised in this edition to be more dynamic, engaging, and relevant than ever before. The use of full color serves to clarify the maps and graphs and to enrich the textual material. The maps and map captions have been updated to correlate directly to the text.

Distinctive Features

Distinctive features from earlier editions guide the reader in the process of historical understanding. Many of these features also show how historians sift through and evaluate evidence. Our goal is to suggest how historians actually work and think. We want the reader to think critically and to realize that history is neither a list of cut-and-dried facts nor a senseless jumble of conflicting opinions.

"Individuals in Society" Feature

The Eighth Edition presents eight new short studies of a fascinating woman or man, which are carefully integrated into the main discussion of the text. This "Individuals in Society" feature grew out of our long-standing focus on people's lives and the varieties of historical experience, and we believe that readers will empathize with these flesh-and-blood human beings as they themselves seek to define their own identities today. The spotlighting of individuals, both famous and obscure, carries forward the greater attention to cultural and intellectual developments that we have used to invigorate our social history, and it reflects changing interests within the historical profession as well as the development of "micro history."

The men and women included in the Eighth Edition represent a wide range of careers and personalities. Several are renowned historical or present-day figures, such as Plutarch, the Greek historian and biographer (Chapter 5); Amda Siyon, probably the most important ruler of Ethiopia's Solomonic dynasty (Chapter 9); Giuseppe Garibaldi, the flamboyant, incorruptible popular hero of Italy's national unification (Chapter 23); and the Dalai Lama, exiled spiritual leader of a captive nation (Chapter 33). Two individuals were brilliant writers who testified to tragedy and calamitous destruction: Vera Brittain, an English nurse on the frontlines in World War I (Chapter 27); and Primo Levi, an Italian Jewish chemist who survived the Holocaust and probed the horrors of the death camps (Chapter 30). Others are lesser-known individuals, yet highly accomplished in their own societies and time, such as the Ban family from China, who were influential in the military, government, and literary fields (Chapter 6); Bhaskara, the Indian astronomer and mathematician who published many books in those fields (Chapter 11); Tan Yunxian, a Chinese female doctor who devoted her practice to the treatment of women (Chapter 20); and José Rizal, a Philippine nationalist and author (Chapter 25).

"Listening to the Past" Feature

A two-page excerpt from a primary source concludes each chapter. This signature feature, entitled "Listening to the Past," extends and illuminates a major historical issue considered in the chapter. Each primary source opens with a problem-setting introduction and closes with "Questions for Analysis" that invite students to evaluate the evidence as historians would. Drawn from a range of writings addressing a variety of social, cultural, political, and intellectual issues, these sources promote active involvement and critical interpretation. Selected for their interest and importance and carefully fitted into their historical context, these sources do indeed allow the student to "listen to the past" and to observe how history has been shaped by individual men and women, some of them great aristocrats, others ordinary folk.

"Global Trade" Feature

In the form of two-page essays that focus on a particular commodity, this popular feature explores the world trade, social and economic impact, and cultural influence of that commodity. Each essay is accompanied by a detailed map showing the trade routes of the commodity. Retaining the seven essays of the previous edition on pottery, silk, tea, slaves, indigo, oil, and arms, we added one on spices in Chapter 11. We believe that careful attention to all of these essays will enable the student to appreciate the complex ways in which trade has connected and influenced the various parts of the world.

Improved Pedagogy

To help make the narrative accessible to students, we have put a number of pedagogical features in the text. At the start of each chapter, an outline of the major section titles provides students with a brief preview of the chapter coverage. Also at the beginning of each chapter, we pose specific historical questions to help guide the reader toward understanding. These questions are then answered in the course of the chapter, and each chapter concludes with a concise summary of its findings. All of the questions and summaries have been re-examined and frequently revised in order to maximize their usefulness.

Throughout the chapter we have highlighted in boldface the major terms with which a student should become familiar. These Key Terms are then listed at the conclusion of the chapter. The student may use these terms to test his or her understanding of the chapter's material. A complete list of the Key Terms and definitions is also provided on the student website, along with electronic flashcards that allow students to quiz themselves on their mastery of the terms.

In addition to posing chapter-opening questions and presenting more problems in historical interpretation, we have quoted extensively from a wide variety of primary sources in the narrative, demonstrating in our use of these quotations how historians evaluate evidence. Thus primary sources are examined as an integral part of the narrative as well as presented in extended form in the "Listening to the Past" chapter feature. We believe that such an extensive program of both integrated and separate primary source excerpts will help readers learn to interpret and think critically.

Each chapter concludes with a Summary section and carefully selected suggestions for further reading. These suggestions are briefly described to help readers know where to turn to continue thinking and learning about the world. Also, chapter bibliographies have been thoroughly revised and updated to keep them current with the vast amount of new work being done in many fields.

Revised Timelines

To better present the flow of critical developments, the comparative timelines of earlier editions have been converted into chapter chronologies in each chapter. The extended comparative timeline has been moved to the front of the book and is now a perforated foldout poster. Comprehensive and easy to locate, this useful timeline poster allows students to compare simultaneous political, economic, social, cultural, intellectual, and scientific developments over the centuries.

Flexible Format

World history courses differ widely in chronological structure from one campus to another. To accommodate the various divisions of historical time into intervals that fit a two-quarter, three-quarter, or two-semester period, *A History of World Societies* is published in three versions that embrace the complete work:

- One-volume hardcover edition: *A History of World Societies* (Chapters 1–33 and Epilogue)
- Two-volume paperback edition: *Volume I: To 1715* (Chapters 1–16); and *Volume II: Since 1500* (Chapters 15–33 and Epilogue)
- Three-volume paperback edition: *Volume A: From Antiquity to 1500* (Chapters 1–13); *Volume B: From 800 to 1815* (Chapters 10–21); and *Volume C: From 1775 to the Present* (Chapters 21–33 and Epilogue)

Overlapping chapters in two-volume and three-volume editions facilitate matching the appropriate volume with the opening and closing dates of a specific course. In addition, this title is available as an e-Book.

Ancillaries

We are pleased to introduce a full ancillary package that will help students in learning and instructors in teaching:

- *Student website*
- *Instructor website*
- *Electronic Testing (powered by Diploma™)*
- *Online Instructor's Resource Manual*
- *PowerPoint maps and images*
- *PowerPoint questions for personal response systems*
- *Blackboard® and WebCT® course cartridges*

The student website features a wide array of resources to help students master the subject matter including learning objectives, chapter outlines, pre-class quizzes and other self-testing material like interactive flashcards, chronological ordering exercises, and more. Students can also find additional text resources such as an online glossary, audio chapter summaries, and an audio pronunciation guide.

The instructor website features all of the material on the student site plus additional password-protected resources for teaching the course such as an electronic version of the *Instructor's Resource Manual* and *PowerPoint* slides.

Electronic Testing (powered by *Diploma*) offers instructors a flexible and powerful tool for test generation and test management. Supported by the Brownstone Research Group's market-leading *Diploma* software, this new version of *Electronic Testing* significantly improves on functionality and ease of use by offering all of the tools needed to create, author, deliver, and customize multiple types of tests. *Diploma* is currently in use at thousands of college and university campuses throughout the United States and Canada.

The online *Instructor's Resource Manual,* prepared by John Reisbord of Vassar College and updated for the Eighth Edition by Jason Stratton of Bakersfield College, contains advice on teaching the world history course, instructional objectives, chapter outlines, lecture suggestions, paper and class activity topics, primary source and map activities, and suggestions for cooperative learning.

We are pleased to offer a collection of world history *PowerPoint* maps and images for use in classroom presentations. This collection includes all of the photos and maps in the text, as well as numerous other images from our world history titles. *PowerPoint* questions and answers for use with personal response system software are also offered to adopters free of charge.

Graded homework questions have been developed to work with the *Blackboard* and *WebCT* course management systems. Instructors can choose to use the content as is, modify it, or even add their own.

In addition, instructors have numerous options for packaging Bedford/St. Martin's titles with *A History of World Societies.* Based on the popular "World History Matters" websites produced by the Center for History and New Media at George Mason University, the print resource *World History Matters: A Student Guide to World History Online* provides an illustrated and annotated guide to 150 of the most useful and reliable websites for student research in world history as well as advice on evaluating and using Internet sources. This title, edited by Kristin Lehner, Kelly Schrum, and T. Mills Kelly, is available free when packaged with the textbook. Over 100 titles in the *Bedford Series in History and Culture* combine first-rate scholarship, historical narrative, and important primary documents for undergraduate courses. Each book is brief, inexpensive, and focused on a specific topic or period. Package discounts are available. Trade books published by sister companies Farrar, Straus and Giroux; Henry Holt and Company; Hill and Wang;

Picador; St. Martin's Press; and Palgrave Macmillan are available at a 50 percent discount when packaged with Bedford/St. Martin's textbooks. For more information, visit **bedfordstmartins.com/tradeup**.

Acknowledgments

It is a pleasure to thank the many instructors who have read and critiqued the manuscript throughout its development:

Wayne Ackerson
Salisbury University

Edward M. Anson
University of Arkansas at Little Rock

Beau Bowers
Central Piedmont Community College

Eric Dorn Brose
Drexel University

Erwin F. Erhardt III
Thomas More College

Dolores Grapsas
New River Community College

Candace Gregory-Abbott
California State University, Sacramento

Roger Hall
Allan Hancock College

John Jovan Markovic
Andrews University

Christopher E. Mauriello
Salem State College

Michael G. Murdock
Brigham Young University

Phyllis E. Pobst
Arkansas State University

Thomas Saylor
Concordia University

Jason M. Stratton
Bakersfield College

Ruth Smith Truss
University of Montevallo

Claude Welch
State University of New York at Buffalo

It is also a pleasure to thank our editors for their efforts over many years. To Christina Horn, who guided production, and to Tonya Lobato, our development editor, we express our admiration and special appreciation. And we thank Carole Frohlich for her contributions in photo research and selection.

Many of our colleagues at the University of Illinois, University of Washington, Eastern Illinois University, and the University of Wisconsin–Milwaukee continue to provide information and stimulation, often without even knowing it. We thank them for it.

Each of us has benefited from the criticism of his or her coauthors, although each of us assumes responsibility for what he or she has written. John Buckler has written Chapters 1, 4, and 5. Patricia Buckley Ebrey has written or updated Chapters 2–3, 6, 8, 11–12, 19–20, and 25–26. Bennett Hill originally conceived the narrative for Chapters 7–9, 12–15, 18–20, and 26; since his untimely death his coauthors have taken on his chapters. In this edition new coauthor Merry Wiesner-Hanks handled Chapters 7, 10, 13, and 14; and new coauthor Clare Crowston handled Chapters 15–17 and 21. Roger Beck contributed to Chapters 9 and 18 and handled Chapters 27–33 in this edition. Roger Beck also wrote the Epilogue. John McKay originally wrote the narrative for Chapters 16–17, 21–24, and 27–30, and he continues to take responsibility for Chapters 22–24 in this edition. Finally, we continue to welcome the many comments and suggestions that have come from our readers, for they have helped us greatly in this ongoing endeavor.

J.P.M.

J.B.

P.B.E.

R.B.B.

C.H.C.

M.W-H.

Brief Contents

Contents

Chapter 13

EUROPE IN THE MIDDLE AGES, 850–1400   350

Chapter 14

EUROPE IN THE RENAISSANCE AND REFORMATION, 1350–1600   386

Chapter 15

THE ACCELERATION OF GLOBAL CONTACT   426

Maps

Listening to the Past

Individuals in Society

About the Authors

JOHN P. McKAY   Born in St. Louis, John P. McKay received his B.A. from Wesleyan University (1961), his M.A. from the Fletcher School of Law and Diplomacy (1962), and his Ph.D. from the University of California, Berkeley (1968). He began teaching history at the University of Illinois in 1966 and became a Professor there in 1976. John won the Herbert Baxter Adams Prize for his book *Pioneers for Profit: Foreign Entrepreneurship and Russian Industrialization, 1885–1913* (1970). He has also written *Tramways and Trolleys: The Rise of Urban Mass Transport in Europe* (1976) and has translated Jules Michelet's *The People* (1973). His research has been supported by fellowships from the Ford Foundation, the Guggenheim Foundation, the National Endowment for the Humanities, and IREX. He has written well over a hundred articles, book chapters, and reviews, which have appeared in numerous publications, including *The American Historical Review, Business History Review, The Journal of Economic History,* and *Slavic Review.* He contributed extensively to C. Stewart and P. Fritzsche, eds., *Imagining the Twentieth Century* (1997).

BENNETT D. HILL   A native of Philadelphia, Bennett D. Hill earned an A.B. from Princeton (1956) and advanced degrees from Harvard (A.M., 1958) and Princeton (Ph.D., 1963). He taught history at the University of Illinois, where he was department chair from 1978 to 1981. He published *English Cistercian Monasteries and Their Patrons in the Twelfth Century* (1968), *Church and State in the Middle Ages* (1970), and articles in *Analecta Cisterciensia, The New Catholic Encyclopaedia, The American Benedictine Review,* and *The Dictionary of the Middle Ages.* His reviews appeared in *The American Historical Review, Speculum, The Historian,* the *Journal of World History,* and *Library Journal.* He was one of the contributing editors to *The Encyclopedia of World History* (2001). He was a Fellow of the American Council of Learned Societies and served on the editorial board of *The American Benedictine Review,* on committees of the National Endowment for the Humanities, and as vice president of the American Catholic Historical Association (1995–1996). A Benedictine monk of St. Anselm's Abbey in Washington, D.C., he was also a Visiting Professor at Georgetown University.

JOHN BUCKLER   Born in Louisville, Kentucky, John Buckler received his Ph.D. from Harvard University in 1973. In 1980 Harvard University Press published his *Theban Hegemony, 371–362 B.C.* He published *Philip II and the Sacred War* (Leiden 1989) and also edited *BOIOTIKA: Vorträge vom 5. Internationalen Böotien-Kolloquium* (Munich 1989). In 2003 he published *Aegean Greece in the Fourth Century B.C.* In the following year appeared his editions of W. M. Leake, *Travels in the Morea* (three volumes), and Leake's *Peloponnesiaca.* Cambridge University Press published his *Central Greece and the Politics of Power in the Fourth Century BC,* edited by Hans Beck, in 2008.

PATRICIA BUCKLEY EBREY   Born in Hasbrouck Heights, New Jersey, Patricia Ebrey received her A.B. from the University of Chicago in 1968 and her Ph.D. from Columbia University in 1975. She taught Asian history and culture at the University of Illinois for twenty years before moving to the University of Washington in 1997. Her research has been supported by fellowships from the American Council of Learned Societies, the National Endowment for the Humanities, the Guggenheim Foundation, and the Chiang Ching-Kuo Foundation. Probably the best known of her many books are *Chinese Civilization: A Sourcebook* (1981, 1993), *The Inner Quarters: Marriage and the Lives of Chinese Women in the Sung Period* (1993) (which won the Levenson Prize of the Association for Asian Studies), and *The Cambridge Illustrated History of China* (1996). *East Asia: A Cultural, Social, and Political History,* coauthored with Anne Walthall and James Palais, is now in its second edition.

ROGER B. BECK   An Indiana native, Roger B. Beck received his B.A. from the University of Evansville (1969), and an M.S. in social studies education (1977), M.A. in history (1979), and Ph.D. in African history (1987) from Indiana University. He taught history at international schools in Paris, Tokyo, and London for six years and was a visiting lecturer at the University of Cape Town in 1981. He has taught at Eastern Illinois University since 1987, where he is Distinguished Professor of African, World, and Twentieth-century World History. His publications include *The History of South Africa* (2000), a translation of P. J. van der Merwe's *The Migrant Farmer in the History of the Cape Colony, 1657–1842,* and more than seventy-five articles, book chapters, and reviews. He is a senior consultant to McDougal Littell's widely used high school text *World History: Patterns of Interaction,* now in its third edition. He is the recipient of two Fulbright fellowships. He has been an active member of the World Hisvtory Association for nearly twenty years, including serving a term on the executive council and as treasurer for six years.

CLARE HARU CROWSTON Born in Cambridge, Massachusetts, and raised in Toronto, Clare Haru Crowston received her B.A. in 1985 from McGill University and her Ph.D. in 1996 from Cornell University. Since 1996, she has taught at the University of Illinois, where she has served as associate chair and Director of Graduate Studies, and is currently Associate Professor of history. She is the author of *Fabricating Women: The Seamstresses of Old Regime France, 1675–1791* (Duke University Press, 2001), which won two awards, the Berkshire Prize and the Hagley Prize. She edited two special issues of the *Journal of Women's History* (vol. 18, nos. 3 and 4) and has published numerous articles and reviews in journals such as *Annales: Histoire, Sciences Sociales, French Historical Studies, Gender and History,* and the *Journal of Economic History.* Her research has been supported with grants from the National Endowment for the Humanities, the Mellon Foundation, and the Bourse Châteaubriand of the French government. She is a past president of the Society for French Historical Studies and a former chair of the Pinkney Prize Committee.

MERRY E. WIESNER-HANKS Having grown up in Minneapolis, Merry E. Wiesner-Hanks received her B.A. from Grinnell College in 1973 (as well as an honorary doctorate some years later), and her Ph.D. from the University of Wisconsin–Madison in 1979. She taught first at Augustana College in Illinois, and since 1985 at the University of Wisconsin–Milwaukee, where she is currently UWM Distinguished Professor in the department of history. She is the co-editor of the *Sixteenth Century Journal* and the author or editor of nineteen books and many articles that have appeared in English, German, Italian, Spanish, and Chinese. These include *Early Modern Europe, 1450–1789* (Cambridge, 2006), *Women and Gender in Early Modern Europe* (Cambridge, 3d ed., 2008), and *Gender in History* (Blackwell, 2001). She currently serves as the Chief Reader for Advanced Placement World History and has also written a number of source books for use in the college classroom, including *Discovering the Western Past* (Houghton Mifflin, 6th ed, 2007) and *Discovering the Global Past* (Houghton Mifflin, 3d. ed., 2006), and a book for young adults, *An Age of Voyages, 1350–1600* (Oxford 2005).

ARCTIC OCEAN

Arctic

ALASKA RANGE

60°N

ROCKY MOUNTAINS

CANADIAN SHIELD

NORTH
AMERICA

40°N

NORTH PACIFIC OCEAN

NORTH
ATLANTIC
OCEAN

Mississippi R.

APPALACHIAN MTS.

Rio Grande R.

Tropic of Cancer

20°N

0° — Equator

Amazon R.

SOUTH
AMERICA

ANDES MOUNTAINS

20°S

Tropic of Capricorn

SOUTH PACIFIC OCEAN

SOUTH
ATLANTIC
OCEAN

40°S

Cape Horn

60°S

Antarctic Circle

80°S

Sea ice
Ice cap
Tundra
Forest
Grassland
Desert
Mountains

180°   160°W   140°W   120°W   100°W   80°W   60°W   40°W   20°W

ALASKA
(U.S.)

CANADA

GREENLAND
(DENMARK)

ICELAND

80°N

60°N

UN
KIN
IRELAND

UNITED STATES

40°N

PORTUGAL

Azores
(Port.)

Bermuda
(U.K.)

ATLANTIC OCEAN

MORO

Midway Is.
(U.S.)

Hawaiian Is.
(U.S.)

MEXICO

BAHAMAS

CUBA
JAMAICA HAITI
BELIZE Puerto Rico
HONDURAS (U.S.)

DOMINICAN REP.
Virgin Is.

ST. KITTS AND NEVIS
ANTIGUA AND BARBUDA
DOMINICA
BARBADOS
ST. VINCENT AND
THE GRENADINES

WESTERN
SAHARA
(MOROCCO)

20°N

MAURITANIA

CAPE
VERDE

SENEGAL
GAMBIA
GUINEA-BISSAU

GUATEMALA
EL SALVADOR

NICARAGUA

COSTA RICA

PANAMA

ST. LUCIA
GRENADA

VENEZUELA

TRINIDAD AND TOBAGO
GUYANA

FR. GUIANA
(FRANCE)

GUINEA

SIERRA
LEONE

IVO
COA

LIBERIA

GH
EQUAT

PACIFIC OCEAN

COLOMBIA

SURINAM

SÃO TOMÉ A

Equator

Galapagos Is.
(Ecuador)

ECUADOR

0°

PERU

BRAZIL

SAMOA

French Polynesia
(France)

BOLIVIA

TONGA

PARAGUAY

20°S

Easter Is.
(Chile)

CHILE

URUGUAY

ARGENTINA

40°S

0   1,000   2,000 Km.

0   1,000   2,000 Mi.

Falkland Is.
(U.K.)

60°S

160°W   140°W   120°W   100°W   80°W   60°W   40°W   20°W

80°S

TIC OCEAN

PACIFIC OCEAN

NORWAY
SWEDEN
FINLAND
ESTONIA
DEN.
LATVIA
LITHUANIA
BELARUS
GERMANY POLAND
CZ.
SLK.
AUS. HUNG.
ITALY
SLN. CR.
B. H. SE.
MO.
ALBANIA MAC.
GREECE
MALTA
TUNISIA

UKRAINE
MOLDOVA
ROMANIA
K.
BULGARIA
TURKEY
CYPRUS
LEBANON
ISRAEL

RUSSIA

KAZAKHSTAN

MONGOLIA

N. KOREA

S. KOREA JAPAN

PACIFIC OCEAN

GEORGIA
ARMENIA
AZERBAIJAN
SYRIA
IRAQ
JORDAN
KUWAIT
IRAN
BAHRAIN
QATAR

UZBEKISTAN

TURKMENISTAN
TAJIKISTAN

KYRGYZSTAN

AFGHANISTAN

PEOPLE'S REPUBLIC OF CHINA

LIBYA
EGYPT

SAUDI
ARABIA
UNITED
ARAB EMIRATES
OMAN

PAKISTAN

NEPAL

BHUTAN

BANGLADESH

TAIWAN

Mariana
Islands
(U.S.)

Wake I.
(U.S.)

NIGER
CHAD
SUDAN

ERITREA
DJIBOUTI

YEMEN

INDIA

MYANMAR
(BURMA)

LAOS

Guam
(U.S.)

MARSHALL
ISLANDS

BENIN
NIGERIA
CENTRAL
AFRICAN REP.
CAMEROON

ETHIOPIA

THAILAND

VIETNAM

PHILIPPINES

FEDERATED STATES
OF MICRONESIA

KIRIBATI

CAMBODIA
(KAMPUCHEA)

SRI LANKA

MALDIVES

SOMALIA

BRUNEI
DARUSSALAM

PALAU

GABON
CONGO
RWANDA
DEM. REP.
OF CONGO
BURUNDI

UGANDA KENYA

SEYCHELLES

INDIAN OCEAN

SINGAPORE

MALAYSIA

NAURU

TANZANIA

INDONESIA

PAPUA
NEW
GUINEA

SOLOMON IS.

TUVALU

ANGOLA

COMOROS

TIMOR LESTE

VANUATU

ZAMBIA
MALAWI

MADAGASCAR

FIJI

NAMIBIA
ZIMBABWE
MAURITIUS

New Caledonia
(France)

BOTSWANA

ABBREVIATIONS

AUS.   AUSTRIA
BEL.   BELGIUM
B. H.   BOSNIA AND HERZEGOVINA
CR.   CROATIA
CZ.   CZECH REPUBLIC
DEN.   DENMARK
HUNG.   HUNGARY
K.   KOSOVO
LUX.   LUXEMBOURG
MAC.   MACEDONIA
MO.   MONTENEGRO
NETH.   NETHERLANDS
SE.   SERBIA
SLK.   SLOVAKIA
SLN.   SLOVENIA
SWITZ. SWITZERLAND

AUSTRALIA

MOZAMBIQUE
SWAZILAND
SOUTH
AFRICA
LESOTHO

NEW
ZEALAND

20°E   40°E   60°E   80°E   100°E   120°E   140°E   160°E

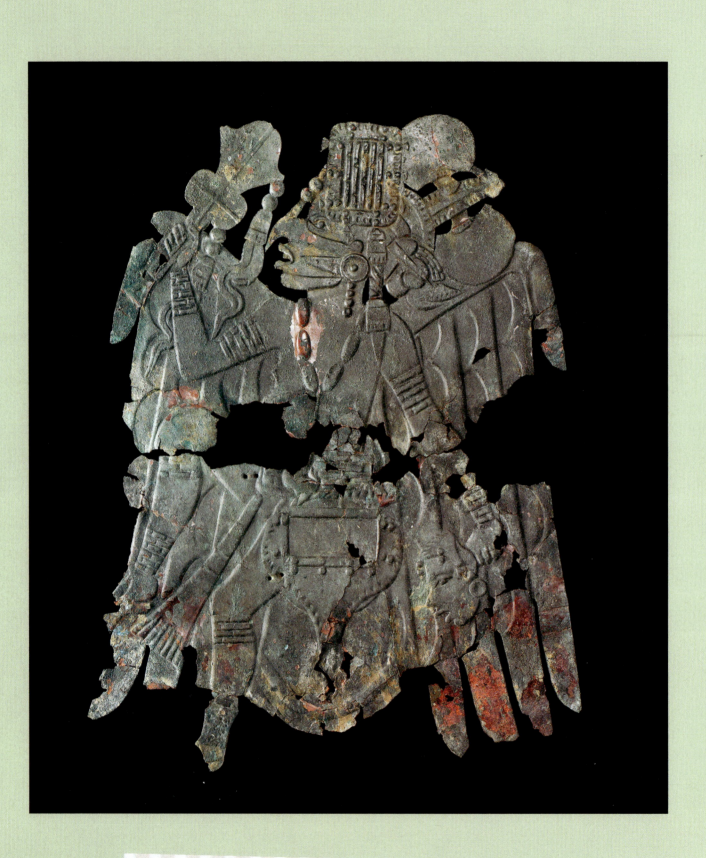

Engraved Mississippian Copper Plate. This ornamental copper plate was excavated in Etowah Mound, Georgia, a Mississippian site first settled in about 1000 C.E. The copper may have been mined along the shore of Lake Superior in what is now northern Michigan, the largest source of copper in North America. *(National Museum of American History, Smithsonian Institution, Washington, D.C.)*

chapter

10

CIVILIZATIONS OF THE AMERICAS, 2500 B.C.E.—1500 C.E.

Chapter Preview

The Early Peoples of the Americas
• *How did early peoples in the Americas adapt to their environment as they created economic and political systems?*

Early Civilizations
• *What physical, social, and intellectual features characterized early civilizations in the Americas?*

Classical Era Mesoamerica and North America
• *How did Mesoamerican and North American peoples develop prosperous and stable societies in the classical era?*

The Aztecs
• *How did the Aztecs both build on the achievements of earlier Mesoamerican cultures and develop new traditions to create their large empire?*

The Incas
• *What were the sources of strength and prosperity, and of problems, for the Incas as they created their enormous empire?*

From the beginning of recorded history—that is, from the earliest invention of writing systems—the Eastern and Western Hemispheres developed in isolation from one another. In both areas people initially gathered and hunted their food, and then some groups began to plant crops, adapting plants that were native to the areas they settled. Techniques of plant domestication spread, allowing for greater density of population because harvested crops provided a more regular food supply than did gathered food. In certain parts of both hemispheres, efficient production and transportation of food supplies allowed for the development of cities, with monumental buildings constructed to honor divine and human power, specialized production of a wide array of products, and marketplaces where those products were exchanged. New products included improved military equipment, which leaders used to enhance their power and build up the large political entities we call "kingdoms" and "empires." The power of those leaders also often rested on religious ideas, in which providing service to a king was viewed as a way to honor divine power. These large political units did not develop everywhere in either hemisphere, however, nor was settled agriculture the only economic system. In many places, particularly where the climate or environment made growing crops difficult or impossible, gathering and hunting, sometimes combined with raising animals for food, continued to provide for human sustenance.

The separate but parallel paths of the two hemispheres were radically changed by Columbus's voyage and the events that followed. The greater availability of metals, especially iron, in the Eastern Hemisphere meant that the military technology of the Europeans who came to the Western Hemisphere was more deadly than anything indigenous peoples had developed. Even more deadly, however, were the germs Europeans brought with them: measles, mumps, bubonic plague, influenza, and smallpox. Because the two hemispheres had been out of contact for so long, indigenous people had no resistance, and they died in astounding numbers. Population estimates of the Western Hemisphere in the 1400s vary,

MAP 10.1 **The Peoples of Mesoamerica and South America** The major indigenous peoples of Mesoamerica and South America represented a great variety of languages and cultures adapted to a wide range of environments. (*Source: Adapted from* The Times Atlas of World History, *3d ed., p. 149. Reprinted by permission of HarperCollins Publishers Ltd.*)

but many demographers place the total population at about 70 million people. They also estimate that in many parts of the Western Hemisphere, 90 percent of the population died within the first decades of European contact.

Disease often spread ahead of actual groups of conquerors or settlers, when a few or even one native person came into contact with a European landing party and then returned to the village. Germs spread to other people as they did normal things like preparing food, carrying children, or talking about what they had seen. People became sick and died quickly, so that when Europeans got to an area several weeks or months later, they found people who were already weak and fewer in number.

The history of the Western Hemisphere *after* Columbus shapes all the words we use to describe it. About a decade after Columbus's first voyage, another Italian explorer and adventurer, Amerigo Vespucci, wrote a letter to his old employers, the Medici rulers in Italy, trumpeting the wonders of the "new world" he had seen. He claimed to have been the first to see what is now Venezuela on a voyage in 1497, a year before Columbus got there. This letter was published many times in many different languages, and the phrase "New World" began to show up on world maps around 1505. Shortly after that the word *America,* meaning "the land of Amerigo," also appeared, because mapmakers read and believed Vespucci's letter. By just a few years later, mapmakers and others knew that Columbus had been the first to this new world. They wanted to omit the label "America" from future maps, but the name had already stuck.

Our use of the word *Indian* for the indigenous peoples of the Americas stems from another mistake. Columbus was trying to reach Asia by sailing west and thought he was somewhere in the East Indies when he landed, which is why he called the people he met "Indians." They apparently called themselves "Tainos," and people who lived on nearby islands called themselves other things. In many cases people died so fast that we have no idea now what they actually called themselves, so the words we use for various indigenous groups come from other indigenous groups or from European languages and were sometimes originally insulting or derogatory nicknames. Many indigenous groups today are returning to designations from their own languages, and scholars are attempting to use terminology that is historically accurate, so certain groups are known by multiple names. The use of the word *Indian* is itself highly controversial, and various other terms are often used, including Native Americans, Amerindians, and (in Canada) First Peoples. Each of these substitutes has supporters and opponents, including people who are themselves of indigenous background. There is no term for all the inhabitants of the Western Hemisphere that is universally accepted, though in the United States "American Indians" is now preferred. The many peoples of the Americas did not think of themselves as belonging to a single group, any more than the peoples living in sixteenth-century Europe thought of themselves as Europeans (see Map 10.1).

All these issues were in the future in 1492, of course. Columbus's voyage resulted in a devastating chain of events for the inhabitants of the Western Hemisphere and determined the language we use to talk about them. In fact, even Western Hemisphere is a post-Columbus concept, as it requires setting an arbitrary line that divides the two halves of the world. Many different points were proposed over the centuries, and only in the nineteenth century was the current prime meridian at Greenwich—a suburb of London—agreed on.

This huge area had a highly complex history for millennia before Columbus, however, and a great diversity of peoples, cultures, and linguistic groups. New information about these cultures is emerging every year, provoking vigorous debates among scholars. In no other chapter of this book are the basic outlines of what most people agree happened changing as fast as they are for this chapter.

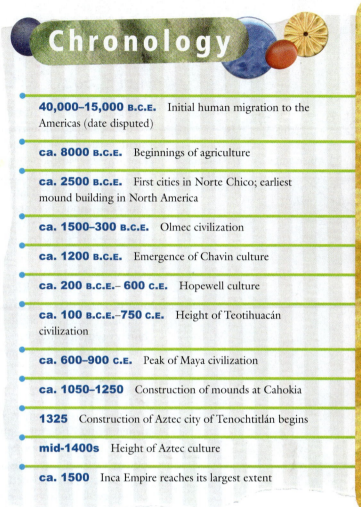

Chronology

40,000–15,000 B.C.E.   Initial human migration to the Americas (date disputed)

ca. 8000 B.C.E.   Beginnings of agriculture

ca. 2500 B.C.E.   First cities in Norte Chico; earliest mound building in North America

ca. 1500–300 B.C.E.   Olmec civilization

ca. 1200 B.C.E.   Emergence of Chavin culture

ca. 200 B.C.E.– 600 C.E.   Hopewell culture

ca. 100 B.C.E.–750 C.E.   Height of Teotihuacán civilization

ca. 600–900 C.E.   Peak of Maya civilization

ca. 1050–1250   Construction of mounds at Cahokia

1325   Construction of Aztec city of Tenochtitlán begins

mid-1400s   Height of Aztec culture

ca. 1500   Inca Empire reaches its largest extent

THE EARLY PEOPLES OF THE AMERICAS

How did early peoples in the Americas adapt to their environment as they created economic and political systems?

Mesoamerica *The term used by scholars to designate the area of present-day Mexico and Central America.*

As in the development of early human cultures in Afroeurasia (Chapter 1), the environment shaped the formation of human settlements in the Americas. North America includes arctic tundra, dry plains, coastal wetlands, woodlands, deserts, and temperate rain forests. Mesoamerica, a term scholars use to designate the area of present-day Mexico and Central America, is dominated by high plateaus with a temperate climate and good agricultural land bounded by coastal plains. The Caribbean coast of Central America—modern Belize, Guatemala, Honduras, Nicaragua, El Salvador, Costa Rica, and Panama—is characterized by thick jungle lowlands, heavy rainfall, and torrid heat. South America is a continent of extremely varied terrain. The entire western coast is edged by the Andes, the highest mountain range in the Western Hemisphere. Three-fourths of South America—almost the entire interior of the continent—is lowland plains. The Amazon River, at four thousand miles the second-longest river in the world, is bordered by tropical lowland rain forests with dense growth and annual rainfall in excess of eighty inches. All these environments have supported extensive human settlement at various times, though it is easier to learn about those in dryer areas because artifacts survive longer there.

Settling the Americas

The traditions of many American Indian peoples teach that the group originated independently, often through the actions of a divine figure. Many creation accounts, including that of the book of Genesis in the Bible, begin with people who are created out of earth and receive assistance from supernatural beings—who set out certain ways people are supposed to behave. Both Native American and biblical creation accounts continue to have deep spiritual importance for many people.

Archaeological and DNA evidence indicates that the earliest humans came to the Americas from Siberia and East Asia, but exactly when and how this happened is currently being hotly debated. The traditional account is that people crossed the Bering Strait from what is now Russian Siberia to what is now Alaska about fifteen thousand years ago, mostly by walking. This was the end of the last Ice Age, so that more of the world's water was frozen and ocean levels were much lower than they are today. (This situation is the opposite of what is occurring today; global warming is melting polar ice, which will raise water levels around the world.) The people migrated southward through North America between two large ice sheets that were slowly melting and retreating, and relatively quickly they spread through the entire hemisphere. They lived by gathering and hunting, using spears with stone tips that archaeologists term *Clovis points* after the town in New Mexico where they were first discovered.

Clovis points have been found widely throughout the Americas, and many archaeologists see the Clovis people as the ancestors of most indigenous people in the Western Hemisphere. There is some difference of opinion about exactly when the Clovis culture flourished, for various methods of carbon-14 dating produce slightly different results, with some scholars accepting 11,000 B.C.E. as the height of Clovis technology and others 9000 B.C.E. (Carbon-14 dating uses the rate at which the radioactive isotope of carbon—present in all living things—breaks down into a nonradioactive form to determine how old things are.)

Disagreements regarding the age of the Clovis culture are significant because they are part of a much broader debate about the traditional account of migration to the Americas. Archaeologists working at Monte Verde along the coast of Chile have excavated a site that they date to about 9000 B.C.E., and perhaps much earlier. This site is ten thousand miles from the Bering Land bridge, which would have meant a very fast walk. Monte Verde and a few other sites are leading increasing numbers of archaeologists to conclude that migrants over the land bridge were preceded by people who traveled along the coast in skin boats, perhaps as early as forty thousand years ago. They lived by fishing and gathering rather than hunting big game, and they slowly worked their way southward. The coasts that they traveled along are today far under water, so archaeological evidence is difficult to obtain, but DNA and other genetic evidence has lent support to this idea. (DNA evidence has generally not supported various other theories of early migrations from Europe or Australia.)

However and whenever people got to the Western Hemisphere—and a consensus about this may emerge in the next decade—they lived by gathering, fishing, and hunting, as did everyone throughout the world at that point. Some groups were nomadic and followed migrating game, while others did not have to travel to be assured of a regular food supply. Coastal settlements from the Pacific Northwest to the southern end of South America relied on fish and shellfish, and some also hunted seals and other large marine mammals.

The Development of Agriculture

About 8000 B.C.E., people in some parts of the Americas began raising crops as well as gathering wild produce. As in the development of agriculture in Afroeurasia, people initially planted the seeds of native plants. Pumpkins and other members of the gourd family were one of the earliest crops, as were chilies, beans, and avocados. At some point, people living in what is now southern Mexico also began raising what would become the most important crop in the Americas—maize, which we generally call "corn." Exactly how this happened is not clear. In contrast to other grain crops such as wheat and rice, the kernels of maize—which are the seeds as well as the part that is eaten for food—are wrapped in a husk, so that the plant cannot propagate itself easily. In addition, no wild ancestor of maize has been found. What many biologists now think happened is that a related grass called *teosinte* developed mutant forms with large kernels enclosed in husks, and people living in the area quickly realized its benefits. They began to intentionally plant these kernels and crossbred the results to get a better crop each year.

People bred various types of maize for different purposes and for different climates, making it the staple food throughout the highlands of Mesoamerica. They often planted maize along with squash, beans, and other crops in a field called a **milpa;** the beans use the maize stalks for support as they both grow and also fix nitrogen in the soil, acting as a natural fertilizer. Crops can be grown in milpas year after year, in contrast to single-crop planting in which rotation is needed so as not to exhaust the soil. Maize came to have a symbolic and religious meaning; it was viewed as the source of human life and was a prominent feature in sculptures of kings and gods.

In central Mexico, along with milpas, people also built *chinampas,* floating gardens. They dredged soil from the bottom of a lake or pond, placed the soil on mats of woven twigs, and then planted crops in the soil. Chinampas were enormously productive, yielding up to three harvests a year.

Knowledge of maize cultivation, and maize seeds themselves, spread out from Mesoamerica into both North and South America. By 3000 B.C.E. farmers in what is now Peru and Uruguay were planting maize, and by 2000 B.C.E. farmers in southwest North America were as well. The crop then spread into the Mississippi Valley and to northeastern North America, where farmers bred slightly different variants for the different growing conditions. After 1500 C.E. maize cultivation spread to Europe, Africa, and Asia as well, becoming an essential food crop there. (In the twentieth century maize became even more successful; about one-quarter of the nearly fifty thousand items in the average American supermarket now contain corn.)

milpa   *A system of effective agriculture used throughout Mesoamerica that relies on crop rotation and the planting of multiple crops in a single field. The term is derived from a Nahuatl word meaning "field."*

The expansion of maize was the result of contacts between different groups that can be traced through trade goods as well. Copper from the Great Lakes was a particularly valuable item and was traded throughout North America, reaching Mexico by 3000 B.C.E. Obsidian from the Rocky Mountains, used for blades, was traded widely, as were shells and later pottery.

Different cultivars of maize could be developed for many different climates, but maize was difficult to grow in high altitudes. Thus in the high Andes, people relied on potatoes, terracing the slopes with stone retaining walls to keep the hillsides from sliding. High-altitude valleys were connected to mountain life and vegetation to form a single interdependent agricultural system called "vertical archipelagoes" capable of supporting large communities. Such vertical archipelagoes often extended more than thirty-seven miles from top to bottom. The terraces were shored up with earthen walls to retain moisture, enabling the production of bumper crops of many different types of potatoes. Potatoes ordinarily cannot be stored for long periods, but Andean

● **Inca Terraces** In order to create more land for farming and limit soil erosion, Andean peoples built terraces up steep slopes. Later the Incas built systems of aqueducts and canals to bring water to terraced fields. *(Wolfgang Kaehler/Corbis)*

peoples developed a product called *chuñu,* freeze-dried potatoes made by subjecting potatoes alternately to nightly frosts and daily sun. Chuñu will keep unspoiled for several years. Coca (the dried leaves of a plant native to the Andes from which cocaine is derived), chewed in moderation as a dietary supplement, enhanced people's stamina and their ability to withstand the cold.

Maize will also not grow in hot, wet climates very well. In Amazonia, manioc, a tuber that can be cooked in many ways, became the staple food. It was planted along with other crops, including fruits, nuts, and various types of palm trees. People domesticated peach palms, for example, which produce fruit, pulp that is made into flour, heart of palm that is eaten raw, and juice that can be fermented into beer. Just how many people Amazonian agriculture supported before the introduction of European diseases is an issue hotly debated by anthropologists, but increasing numbers see the original tropical rain forest not as a pristine wilderness, but as an ecosystem managed effectively by humans for thousands of years. The oldest known pottery in the Americas has been found along the Amazon River, as well as in the Andes.

Farming in the Americas was not limited to foodstuffs. Beginning about 2500 B.C.E., people living along the coast of Peru used irrigation to raise cotton, and textiles became an important part of Peruvian culture. Agriculture in the Americas was extensive, though it was limited by the lack of an animal that could be harnessed to pull a plow. People throughout the Americas domesticated dogs, and in the Andes they domesticated llamas and alpacas to carry loads through the mountains. But no native species allowed itself to be harnessed as horses, oxen, and water buffalo did in Asia and Europe, which meant that all agricultural labor was human-powered.

● **Colombian Lime Container** The use of coca in rituals and to withstand bodily discomfort is an ancient tradition in South America. Pieces of coca leaves were placed in the mouth with small amounts of powdered lime made from seashells. The lime helped release the hallucinogens in the coca. This 9-inch gold bottle for holding lime shows a seated figure with rings in the ears and beads across the forehead and at the neck, wrists, knees, and ankles. A tiny spatula would be used to secure the lime through the bottle's narrow neck. *(The Metropolitan Museum of Art, Jan Mitchell and Sons Collection, Gift of Jan Mitchell, 1991 [1991.419.22]. Photograph © 1992 The Metropolitan Museum of Art)*

EARLY CIVILIZATIONS

What physical, social, and intellectual features characterized early civilizations in the Americas?

Agricultural advancement had definitive social and political consequences. Careful cultivation of the land brought a reliable and steady food supply, which contributed to a relatively high fertility rate and in turn to a population boom. Population in the Americas grew steadily and may have been about 15 million people by the first century B.C.E. This growth in population allowed for greater concentrations of people and the creation of the first urban societies.

Mounds, Towns, and Trade in North and South America

In North America by 2500 B.C.E., some groups began to build massive earthworks, mounds of earth and stone. The mounds differed in shape, size, and purpose: some were conical, others elongated or wall-like, others pyramidical, and still others, called effigy mounds, in serpentine, bird, or animal form. The Ohio and Mississippi Valleys

● **Inca Khipu, ca. 1400 C.E.** This khipu, a collection of colored, knotted strings, recorded numeric information and allowed Inca administrators to keep track of the flow of money, goods, and people in their large empire. Every aspect of the khipu—the form and position of the knots, the colors and spin of the string—may have provided information. Administrators read them visually and by running their hands through them, as Braille text is read today. *(Museo Arqueologico Rafael Larco Herrera, Lima, Peru)*

Norte Chico *A region along the coast of Peru that possessed a highly developed urban culture characterized by massive stepped pyramids and extensive use of cotton as early as 2500 B.C.E.*

khipu *A intricate system of knotted and colored strings used by early Peruvian cultures to store information such as census and tax records.*

contain the richest concentration of mounds, but they have been found from the Great Lakes down to the Gulf of Mexico (see Map 10.3 on page 273). One early large mound at Poverty Point, Louisiana, on the banks of the Mississippi, dates from about 1300 B.C.E. and consists of six octagonal ramparts, one within the other, that measure 6 feet high and more than 400 yards across. The area was home to perhaps five thousand people and was inhabited for hundreds of years, with trade goods brought in by canoe and carved stone beads exported.

Large structures for political and religious purposes began to be built earlier in South America than in North America. By about 2500 B.C.E. cities grew along river valleys on the coast of Peru in the region called **Norte Chico.** Stepped pyramids, some more than ten stories high, dominated these settlements, which were built at about the same time the pyramids were being constructed in Egypt. Cities in Norte Chico often used irrigation to produce crops of squash, beans, cotton, and other crops. Those along the coast relied extensively on fish and shellfish, which they traded with inland cities for the cotton needed to make nets. The largest city, Caral, had many plazas, houses, and temples, built with quarried stone using woven cotton and grass bags filled with smaller stones for support. Cotton was used in Norte Chico for many things, including the earliest example yet discovered of a **khipu** (also spelled *quipu*), a collection of knotted strings that was used to record information. Later Peruvian cultures, including the Incas, developed ever more complex khipu, using the colors of the string and the style and position of the knots to represent tax obligations, census records, and other numeric data.

Along with khipu, Norte Chico culture also developed religious ideas that may have been adopted by later Andean cultures. The oldest religious image yet found in the Americas, a piece of gourd with a drawing of a fanged god holding a staff, comes from Norte Chico, dating about 2250 B.C.E. This Staff God became a major deity in many Andean cultures, one of a complex pantheon of deities. Religious ceremonies, as well as other festivities, in Norte Chico involved music, as a large number of bone flutes have been discovered.

The earliest cities in the Andes were built by the **Chavin** people beginning about 1200 B.C.E. They built pyramids and other types of monumental architecture, quarrying and trimming huge blocks of stone and assembling them without mortar. They worked gold and silver into human and animal figurines, trading these and other goods to coastal peoples.

Chavin *A culture that developed in the Andes Mountains of Peru around 1200 B.C.E. and was responsible for the earliest cities in the region.*

The Olmecs

The **Olmecs** created the first society with cities in Mesoamerica. The word *Olmec* comes from an Aztec term for the peoples living in southern Veracruz and western Tabasco, Mexico, between about 1500 and 300 B.C.E. They did not call themselves Olmecs or consider themselves a unified group, but their culture penetrated and influenced all parts of Mesoamerica. Until 1993 knowledge of the Olmecs rested on archaeological evidence—pyramids, jade objects, axes, figurines, and stone monuments—but that year two linguists deciphered Olmec writing. Since then, understanding of Olmec and other contemporary Mesoamerican cultures such as the Zapotecs also comes from the written records they left.

Olmecs *The oldest of the early advanced Amerindian civilizations.*

The Olmecs cultivated maize, squash, beans, and other plants and supplemented that diet with wild game and fish. Originally they lived in egalitarian societies that had no distinctions based on status or wealth. After 1500 B.C.E. more complex, hierarchical societies evolved. Most peoples continued to live in small villages along the rivers of the region, while the leaders of the societies resided in the large cities today known as San Lorenzo, La Venta, Tres Zapotes, and Laguna de los Cerros. These cities contained palaces (large private houses) for the elite, large plazas, temples (ritual centers), ball courts, water reservoirs, and carved stone drains for the disposal of wastes. Like the Chavin (with whom they had no contact), the Olmecs created large pyramid-shaped buildings. They also carved huge stone heads of rulers or gods, beginning a tradition of monumental stone sculptures adopted by later Mesoamerican civilizations. In order to trace celestial phenomena—which they believed influenced human life—they developed a complex calendar involving three different ways of counting time. The need to record time led to the development of a writing system. Whereas the earliest written records from Mesopotamia are tax records for payments to the temple (see page 4), the earliest written records from Mesoamerica, dating from about 700 B.C.E., are dates. Many early records also record the deeds of kings, so that the political history of Mesoamerica is becoming more detailed as scholars learn to read various writing systems.

The Olmecs had sacred ceremonial sites where they sometimes practiced human sacrifice, another tradition adopted by later Mesoamerican cultures. They erected special courts on which men played a game with a hard rubber ball that was both religious ritual and sport. Finally, the Olmecs engaged in long-distance trade, exchanging rubber, cacao (from which chocolate is made), pottery, figurines, jaguar pelts, and the services of painters and sculptors for obsidian (a hard, black volcanic glass from which paddle-shaped weapons were made), basalt, iron ore, shells, and various perishable goods. Commercial networks extended as far away as central and western Mexico and the Pacific coast.

Around 900 B.C.E. San Lorenzo, the center of early Olmec culture, was destroyed, probably by migrating peoples from the north, and power passed to La Venta in Tabasco. Archaeological excavation at La Venta has uncovered a huge volcano-shaped pyramid. Standing 110 feet high at an inaccessible site on an island in the Tonala River, the so-called Great Pyramid was the center of the Olmec religion. The upward thrust of this monument, like ziggurats in Mesopotamia or cathedrals of medieval Europe, may have represented the human effort to get closer to the gods. Built of huge stone slabs, the Great Pyramid required, scholars estimated, some eight hundred thousand man-hours of labor. It testifies to the region's bumper harvests, which were able to support a labor force large enough to build such a monument.

CLASSICAL ERA MESOAMERICA AND NORTH AMERICA

How did Mesoamerican and North American peoples develop prosperous and stable societies in the classical era?

The urban culture of the Olmecs and other Mesoamerican peoples influenced subsequent Mesoamerican societies. Especially in what became known as the classical era (300–900 C.E.), various groups developed large states centered on cities, with high levels of technological and intellectual achievement. Of these, the **Maya** were the most long-lasting, but other city-states were significant as well. Peoples living in North America built communities that were smaller than those in Mesoamerica, but many also used irrigation techniques to enhance agricultural production and built earthwork mounds for religious purposes.

Maya *A highly developed Mesoamerican culture centered in the Yucatán peninsula of Mexico. The Maya created the most intricate writing system in the Western Hemisphere.*

● **Palace Doorway Lintel at Yaxchilan, Mexico**
Lady Xoc, principal wife of King Shield-Jaguar, who holds a torch over her, pulls a thorn-lined rope through her tongue to sanctify with her blood the birth of a younger wife's child—reflecting the importance of blood sacrifice in Maya culture. The elaborate headdresses and clothes of the couple show their royal status. (© Justin Kerr 1985)

Maya Technology and Trade

The word *Maya* seems to derive from *Zamna,* the name of a Maya god. Linguistic evidence leads scholars to believe that the first Maya were a small North American Indian group that emigrated from the area that is now southern Oregon and northern California to the western highlands of Guatemala. Between the third and second millennia B.C.E., various groups, including the Cholans and Tzeltalans, broke away from the parent group and moved north and east into the Yucatán peninsula. The Cholan-speaking Maya, who occupied the area during the time of great cultural achievement, apparently created the culture.

Maya culture rested on agriculture. The staple crop in Mesoamerica was maize, often raised in multiple-crop milpas with other foodstuffs, including beans, squash, chili peppers, some root crops, and fruit trees. The Maya also practiced intensive agriculture in raised, narrow, rectangular plots that they built above the low-lying, seasonally flooded land bordering rivers.

The raised-field and milpa systems of intensive agriculture yielded food sufficient to support large population centers. The entire Maya region could have had as many as 14 million inhabitants. At Uxmal, Uaxactún, Copán, Piedras Negras, Tikal, Palenque, and Chichén Itzá (see Map 10.2), archaeologists have uncovered the palaces of nobles, elaborate pyramids where nobles were buried, engraved *steles* (stone-slab monuments), masonry temples, altars, sophisticated polychrome pottery, and courts for games played with a rubber ball. The largest site, Tikal, may have had forty thousand people and served as a religious and ceremonial center.

Public fairs for trading merchandise accompanied important religious festivals. Jade, obsidian, beads of red spiny oyster shell, lengths of cloth, and cacao beans—all in high demand in the

Mesoamerican world—served as media of exchange. The extensive trade among Maya communities, plus a common language, promoted the union of the peoples of the region and gave them a common sense of identity. Merchants trading beyond Maya regions, such as with the Zapotecs of the Valley of Oaxaca and the Teotihuacános of the central valley of Mexico, were considered state ambassadors bearing "gifts" to royal neighbors, who reciprocated with their own "gifts." Since this long-distance trade played an important part in international relations, the merchants conducting it were high nobles or even members of the royal family.

The extensive networks of rivers and swamps in the area ruled by the Maya were the main arteries of transportation; over them large canoes carved out of hardwood trees carried cargoes of cloth and maize. Wide roads also linked Maya centers; on the roads merchants and lords were borne in litters, goods and produce on human backs. Trade produced considerable wealth that seems to have been concentrated in a noble class, for the Maya had no distinctly mercantile class. They did have a sharply defined hierarchical society. A hereditary elite owned private land, defended society, carried on commercial activities, exercised political power, and directed religious rituals. Artisans and scribes made up the next social level. The rest of the people were workers, farmers, and slaves, the latter including prisoners of war.

Wars were fought in Maya society for a variety of reasons. Long periods without rain caused crop failure, which led to famine and then war with other centers for food. Certain cities, such as Tikal, extended their authority over larger areas through warfare with neighboring cities. Within the same communities, domestic strife between factions over the succession to the kingship or property led to violence.

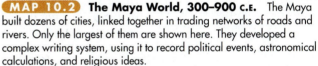

MAP 10.2   **The Maya World, 300–900 C.E.**   The Maya built dozens of cities, linked together in trading networks of roads and rivers. Only the largest of them are shown here. They developed a complex writing system, using it to record political events, astronomical calculations, and religious ideas.

Maya Science and Religion

The Maya developed the most complex writing system in the Americas, a script with nearly a thousand characters that represent concepts and sounds. They used it to record chronology, religion, and astronomy in books made of bark paper and deerskin, on stone pillars archaeologists term "steles," on pottery, and on the walls of temples and other buildings. The deciphering of this writing over the last fifty years has demonstrated that inscriptions on steles are historical documents recording the births, accessions, marriages, wars, and deaths of Maya kings. The writing and pictorial imagery often represent the same events and have allowed for a fuller understanding of Maya dynastic history.

Learning about Maya religion through written records is more difficult. In the sixteenth century Spanish religious authorities ordered all books of Maya writing to be destroyed, viewing them as demonic. Only three (and part of a fourth) survived, because they were already in Europe. These texts do provide information about religious rituals and practices, as well as astronomical calculations. Further information comes from the **Popul Vuh,** or Book of Council, a book of mythological narratives and dynastic history written in the Maya language but in Roman script in the middle of the sixteenth century. Like the Bible in Judeo-Christian tradition, the *Popul Vuh* gives

Popul Vuh   *The Book of Council, a collection of mythological narratives and dynastic histories that constitutes the primary record of the Maya civilization.*

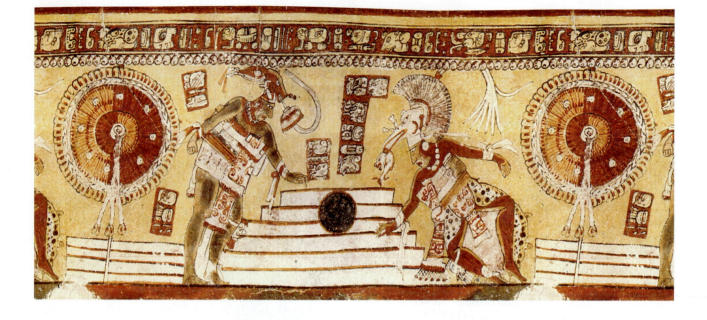

● **Maya Ballplayers** Two teams of two players each face off in this lively scene on a painted ceramic vessel. Note that the ballplayers are wearing deer and vulture headdresses, Maya symbols of hunting and war. War was sometimes called the "hunting of men." *(Chrysler Museum of Art, Norfolk, Va., © Justin Kerr)*

the Maya view of the creation of the world, concepts of good and evil, and the entire nature and purpose of the living experience. Because almost all religious texts from Mesoamerica—not just Maya texts, but those from other cultures as well—were destroyed by Spanish Christian authorities, its significance is enormous.

Maya religious practice emphasized performing rituals at specific times, which served as an impetus for further refinements of the calendar. From careful observation of the earth's movements around the sun, the Maya devised a calendar of eighteen 20-day months and one 5-day month, for a total of 365 days. Their religious calendar, like that of the Olmecs, was a cycle of 260 days based perhaps on the movement of the planet Venus. When these two calendars coincided, which happened once every fifty-two years, the Maya celebrated a period of feasting, ballgame competitions, and religious observance. These observances—and those at other times as well—included human sacrifice to honor the gods and demonstrate the power of earthly kings.

Using a system of bars (— = 5) and dots (○ = 1), the Maya devised a form of mathematics based on the vigesimal (20) rather than the decimal (10) system. More unusual was their use of the number zero, which allows for more complex calculations than are possible in number systems without it. The zero may have actually been "discovered" by the Olmecs, who used it in figuring their calendar, but the Maya used it mathematically as well. (At about the same time, mathematicians in India also began using zero.) They proved themselves masters of abstract knowledge—notably in astronomy, mathematics, calendric development, and the recording of history.

Maya civilization lasted about a thousand years, reaching its peak between approximately 600 and 900 C.E., the period when the Tang Dynasty was flourishing in China, Islam was spreading in the Middle East, and Carolingian rulers were extending their sway in Europe. Between the eighth and tenth centuries, the Maya abandoned their cultural and ceremonial centers, and Maya civilization collapsed. Archaeologists and historians attribute the decline to a combination of agricultural failures due to land exhaustion and drought; overpopulation; disease; and constant wars fought as an extension of economic and political goals. These wars brought widespread destruction, which aggravated agrarian problems. Maya royal ideology also played a role in their decline: just as in good times kings attributed moral authority and prosperity to themselves, so in bad times, when military, economic, and social conditions deteriorated, they became the objects of blame.

Teotihuacán and the Toltecs

The Maya were not alone in creating a complex culture in Mesoamerica during the classic period. In the isolated valley of Oaxaca at modern-day Monte Albán in southern Mexico, Zapotecan-speaking peoples established a great religious center whose temples and elaborately decorated tombs testify to the wealth of the nobility. To the north of Monte Albán, **Teotihuacán** in central Mexico witnessed the flowering of a remarkable civilization built by a new people from regions east and south of the Valley of Mexico. The city of Teotihuacán had a population of over two hundred thousand—larger than any European city at the time. The inhabitants were stratified into distinct social classes. The rich and powerful resided in houses of palatial splendor in a special precinct. Ordinary working people, tradespeople, artisans, and obsidian craftsmen lived in apartment compounds, or *barrios,* on the edge of the city. Agricultural laborers lived outside the city. Teotihuacán was a great commercial center, the entrepôt for trade and culture for all of Mesoamerica. It was also the ceremonial center, a capital filled with artworks, a mecca that attracted thousands of pilgrims a year.

In the center of the city stood the Pyramids of the Sun and the Moon. The Pyramid of the Sun is built of sun-dried bricks and faced with stone. Each of its sides is seven hundred feet long and two hundred feet high. The smaller Pyramid of the Moon is similar in construction. In lesser temples, natives and outlanders worshiped the rain-god and the feathered serpent later called Quetzalcoatl. These gods were associated with the production of corn, the staple of the people's diet.

Around 750 C.E. less-developed peoples from the southwest burned Teotihuacán, and the city-state fell apart. This collapse, plus that of the Maya, marks the end of the classical period in Mesoamerica for most scholars, just as the end of the Roman Empire in the west marks the end of the classical era in Europe. As in Europe, a period characterized by disorder, militarism, and domination by smaller states followed.

Whereas nature gods and their priests seem to have governed the great cities of the earlier period, militant gods and warriors dominated the petty states that now arose. Among these states, the most powerful heir to Teotihuacán was the Toltec confederation, a weak union of strong states. The **Toltecs** admired the culture of their predecessors and sought to absorb and preserve it. Through intermarriage, they assimilated with the Teotihuacán people. In fact, every new Mesoamerican confederation became the cultural successor of earlier confederations.

Under Topiltzin (r. ca. 980–1000), the Toltecs extended their hegemony over most of central Mexico. Topiltzin established his capital at Tula. Its splendor and power became legendary during his reign. After the reign of Topiltzin, troubles beset the Toltec state. Drought led to crop failure. Northern peoples, the Chichimecas, attacked the borders in waves. Weak, incompetent rulers could not quell domestic uprisings. When the last Toltec king committed suicide in 1174, the Toltec state collapsed.

Teotihuacán *A city in central Mexico that became a great commercial center during the classic period.*

Toltecs *An heir to Teotihuacán, this confederation extended its hegemony over most of central Mexico under the reign of Topiltzin.*

● **Maya Burial Urn** After tightly wrapping the bodies of royal and noble persons in cloth, the K'iché Maya people of Guatemala placed them in urns and buried them in pyramids or sacred caves. The lid represents a divine being through whose mouth gifts may have been offered to the deceased. The figure with corncobs on top of the lid is the maize-god, a sacred figure to all Mesoamerican peoples. *(Museum of Fine Arts, Boston, Gift of Landon T. Clay [1988.1290]. © 2008 Museum of Fine Arts, Boston)*

● **Zapotec Deity**   This Zapotec image of a god was found at Monte Albán, the primary Zapotec religious center. Made to be worn as a breast ornament, it was created through lost-wax casting, in which a mold is made from a wax model, and molten gold poured in to replace the wax. *(Giraudon/The Bridgeman Art Library)*

Hohokam   *A Native American culture that emerged around 300 B.C.E. and was centered around the Gila River in Arizona. The Hohokam practiced a system of agriculture that relied on irrigation trenches, dams, and terraces to cultivate their arid land.*

Anasazi   *A Native American culture that dominated the Four Corners region of the southwestern United States; remarkable for their construction of numerous cliff-dwellings in the region.*

Hopewell   *An important mound-building Native American culture that thrived between 200 B.C.E. and 600 C.E. The culture was centered near the town of Hopewell, Ohio, and was noted for extensive canals and a trade network that extended from the Caribbean to Illinois.*

Hohokam, Hopewell, and Mississippian

Mesoamerican trading networks extended into southwestern North America, where by 300 B.C.E. the **Hohokam** people and other groups were using irrigation canals, dams, and terraces to enhance their farming of the arid land (see Map 10.3). The Hohokam built platforms for ceremonial purposes and played ballgames with rubber balls similar to those of the Olmecs and other Mesoamerican people. The rubber balls themselves were imported, for rubber trees do not grow in the desert, with turquoise and other precious stones exported in return. Religious ideas came along with trade goods, as the feathered serpent god became important to desert peoples. Other groups, including the **Anasazi,** Yuma, and later Pueblo, also built settlements in this area, using large sandstone blocks and masonry to construct thick-walled houses that offered protection from the heat. Mesa Verde, the largest Anasazi town, had a population of about twenty-five hundred living in houses built into and on cliff walls. Roads connected Mesa Verde to other Anasazi towns, allowing timber and other construction materials to be brought in more easily. Drought, deforestation, and soil erosion led to decline in both the Hohokam and Anasazi cultures, increasing warfare between towns.

To the east, the mound building that had first been developed at settlements along the Mississippi around 2000 B.C.E. spread more widely along many river basins. The most important mound-building culture in the first several centuries B.C.E. was the **Hopewell** culture, named for a town in Ohio near where the most extensive mounds were built. Some mounds were burial chambers for priests, leaders, and other high-status individuals, or for thousands of more average people. Others were platforms for the larger houses of important people. Still others were simply huge mounds of earth shaped like animals or geometric figures. Mound building thus had many purposes: it was a way to honor the gods, to remember the dead, and to make distinctions between leaders and common folk

Hopewell earthwork construction also included canals that enabled trading networks to expand, bringing products from the Caribbean far into the interior. Those

MAP 10.3 **Major North American Agricultural Societies, 600–1500 c.e.** Many North American groups used agriculture to increase the available food supply and allow for greater population density and the development of urban centers. Shown here are three of these cultures: the Mississippian, Anasazi, and Hohokam. Most mound-building cultures raised crops, and many were connected in an extensive trading network.

trading networks also carried maize, allowing more intensive agriculture to spread throughout the eastern woodlands of North America.

At Cahokia, near the confluence of the Mississippi and Missouri Rivers in Illinois, archaeologists have uncovered the largest mound of all. Begun about 1050 C.E. and completed about 1250 C.E., the complex at Cahokia covered five and a half square miles and was the ceremonial center for perhaps thirty-eight thousand people. A fence of wooden posts surrounded the core. More than five hundred rectangular mounds or houses, inside and outside the fence, served as tombs and as the bases for temples and palaces. Within the fence, the largest mound rose in four stages to a height of one hundred feet and was more than one thousand feet long, larger than the largest Egyptian pyramid. At its top, a small conical platform supported a wooden fence and a rectangular temple. The mounds at Cahokia represent the culture of the **Mississippian** mound builders.

What do the mounds tell us about Mississippian societies? The largest mounds served as burial chambers for leaders and, in many cases, the women and retainers who were sacrificed in order to assist the leader in the afterlife. Mounds also contain valuable artifacts, such as jewelry made from copper from Michigan, mica (a mineral used in building) from the Appalachians, obsidian from the Rocky Mountains, conch shells from the Caribbean, and pipestone from Minnesota.

From these burial items, archaeologists have deduced that mound culture was hierarchical. The leader had religious responsibilities and also managed long-distance trade and gift-giving. The exchange of goods was not perceived as a form of commerce, but as a means of showing respect and of establishing bonds among diverse groups. Large towns housed several thousand inhabitants and served as political and ceremonial centers. They controlled surrounding villages of a few hundred people, but did not grow into politically unified city-states the way Tikal or Teotihuacán did.

Pottery in the form of bowls, jars, bottles, and effigy pipes in various shapes best reveals Mississippian peoples' art and religious ideas. Designs showing eagles, plumed serpents, warriors decapitating victims, and ceremonially ornamented priests suggest a strong Mesoamerican influence. At its peak, about 1150, Cahokia and its environs probably housed between thirty thousand and fifty thousand people, the largest city north of Mesoamerica. Building the interior wooden fence had denuded much of the

Mississippian *An important mound-building culture that thrived between 800 and 1500 C.E. in a territory that extended from the Mississippi River to the Appalachian Mountains. The largest mound produced by this culture is found at Cahokia, Illinois.*

● **Great Serpent Mound, Adams County, Ohio** Made by people in the Hopewell culture, this 1,254-foot-long mound in the form of a writhing snake has its "head" at the highest point, suggesting an open mouth ready to swallow a huge egg formed by a heap of stones. *(Georg Gerster/ Photo Researchers, Inc.)*

MAP 10.4 **The Aztec (Mexica) Empire** The Mexica migrated into the central valley of what is now Mexico from the north, conquering other groups and establishing an empire, later called the Aztec Empire. The capital of the Aztec Empire was Tenochtitlán, built on islands in Lake Texcoco.

surrounding countryside of trees, however, which made spring floods worse and destroyed much of the city. An earthquake at the beginning of the thirteenth century knocked down more, and the city never recovered. Thus ecological crises appear to have played a part in bringing an end to various North American cultures, though their technologies and religious ideas were often maintained by those that developed later in the same areas.

Mississippian mound builders relied on agriculture to support their complex cultures, and by the time Cahokia was built, maize agriculture had spread to the Atlantic coast. Particularly along riverbanks and the coastline, fields of maize, beans, and squash surrounded large, permanent villages. Hunting provided meat protein, but the bulk of people's foodstuffs came from farming. The earliest European reports from Virginia and New England describe these villages and sometimes show illustrations of rows of houses within walls. By several decades after contact, disease had destroyed village life.

THE AZTECS

How did the Aztecs both build on the achievements of earlier Mesoamerican cultures and develop new traditions to create their large empire?

The **Aztecs** provide a spectacular example of a culture that adopted many things from earlier peoples and also adapted them to create an even more powerful state. Around 1300, a group of **Nahuatl**-speaking people are believed to have migrated southward from what is now northern Mexico, settling on the shores and islands in Lake Texcoco in the central valley of Mexico (see Map 10.4). Here they built the twin cities of Tenochtitlán and Tlatelolco, which by 1500 were probably larger than any city in Europe except Istanbul. As they migrated, these people conquered many neighboring city-states and established an empire. This empire was later termed the "Aztec" Empire and the people called the "Aztecs." This was not a word used at the time,

Aztec *A term coined by nineteenth-century historians to describe the Mexica people.*

Nahuatl *The language of both the Toltecs and the Aztecs.*

Mexica *Another term for Aztec; it is a pre-Columbian term designating the dominant ethnic people of the island capital of Tenochtitlán-Tlatelolco.*

however, and now most scholars prefer the term **Mexica** to refer to the empire and its people; we use both terms here.

Religion and War in Aztec Society

In Mexica society, religion was the dynamic factor that transformed other aspects of the culture: economic security, social mobility, education, and especially war. War was an article of religious faith. The state religion of the Aztecs initially gave them powerful advantages over other groups in central Mexico; it inspired them to conquer vast territories in a remarkably short time. War came to be seen as a religious duty to the Mexicas, through which nobles, and occasionally commoners, honored the gods, gained prestige, and often acquired wealth.

The Mexicas worshiped a number of gods and goddesses as well as some deities that had dual natures as both male and female. The basic conflict in the world was understood as one between order and disorder, though the proper life balances these two, as disorder could never be completely avoided. Disorder was linked to dirt and uncleanness, so temples, shrines, and altars were kept very clean; rituals of purification often involved sweeping or bathing. Like many polytheists, Mexicas took the deities of people they encountered into their own pantheon, or mixed their attributes with those of existing gods. Quetzalcoatl, for example, the feathered serpent god found among many Mesoamerican groups, was generally revered by the Mexicas as a creator deity and source of knowledge.

Huitzilopochtli *The chief among the Aztecs' many gods, who symbolized the sun blazing at high noon.*

Among the deities venerated by Mexica and other Mesoamerican groups was **Huitzilopochtli,** a young warrior god whose name translates fully as "Blue Hummingbird of the South" (or "on the Left") and who symbolized the sun blazing at high noon. The sun, the source of all life, had to be kept moving in its orbit if darkness was not to overtake the world. To keep it moving, Aztecs believed, the sun had to be frequently fed precious fluids—that is, human blood. Human sacrifice was a sacred duty, essential for the preservation and prosperity of humankind. (See the feature "Individuals in Society: Tlacaélel.")

Most victims were war captives, for the Aztecs controlled their growing empire by sacrificing prisoners seized in battle, by taking hostages from among defeated peoples as ransom against future revolt, and by demanding from subject states an annual tribute of people to be sacrificed to Huitzilopochtli. Unsuccessful generals, corrupt judges, and careless public officials, even people who accidentally entered forbidden precincts of the royal palaces, were routinely sacrificed. In some years it was difficult to provide enough war captives, so other types of people, including criminals, slaves, and people supplied as tribute, were sacrificed as well. Such victims did not have the same status as captives, however, and Mexicas engaged in special wars simply to provide victims for sacrifices, termed "flower (or flowery) wars." Flowers were frequently associated metaphorically with warfare in Mexica culture, with blood described as a flower of warfare, swords and banners as blooming like flowers, and a warrior's life as fleeting like a flower's blooming. The objective of flower wars was capturing warriors from the other side, not killing them.

The Mexica state religion required constant warfare for two basic reasons. One was to meet the gods' needs for human sacrifice; the other was to acquire warriors for the next phase of imperial expansion. The sacred campaigns of Huitzilopochtli were synchronized with the political and economic needs of the Mexica nation as a whole. Moreover, defeated peoples had to pay tribute in foodstuffs to support rulers, nobles, warriors, and the imperial bureaucracy. The vanquished supplied laborers for agriculture, the economic basis of Mexica society. Likewise, conquered peoples had to produce workers for the construction and maintenance of the entire Aztec infrastructure—roads, dike systems, aqueducts, causeways, and the royal palaces. Finally, merchants also benefited, for war opened new markets for traders' goods in subject territories.

Tlacaélel

The hummingbird god Huitzilopochtli was originally a somewhat ordinary god of war and of young men, but in the fifteenth century he was elevated in status among the Mexica. He became increasingly associated with the sun and gradually became the Mexicas' most important deity. This change was primarily the work of Tlacaélel, the very long-lived chief adviser to the emperors Itzcóatl (r. 1427–1440), Montezuma I (r. 1440–1469), and Axayacatl (r. 1469–1481). Tlacaélel first gained influence during wars in the 1420s in which the Mexicas defeated the rival Tepanecs, after which he established new systems of dividing military spoils and enemy lands. At the same time, he advised the emperor that new histories were needed in which the destiny of the Mexica people was made clearer. Older historical texts were destroyed, and in these new chronicles the fate of the Mexicas was directly connected to Huitzilopochtli. Mexica writing was primarily pictographic, drawn and then read by specially trained scribes, who used written records as an aid to oral presentation, especially for legal issues, historical chronicles, religious and devotional poetry, and astronomical calculations.

According to these new texts, the Mexicas had been guided to Lake Texcoco by Huitzilopochtli; there they saw an eagle perched on a cactus, which a prophecy had told would mark the site of their new city. Huitzilopochtli kept the world alive by bringing the sun's warmth, but to do this he required the Mexicas, who increasingly saw themselves as the "people of the sun," to provide a steady offering of human blood.

The worship of Huitzilopochtli became linked to cosmic forces as well as daily survival. In Nahua tradition, the universe was understood to exist in a series of five suns, or five cosmic ages. Four ages had already passed, and their suns had been destroyed; the fifth sun, the age in which the Mexicas were now living, would also be destroyed unless the Mexicas fortified the sun with the energy found in blood. Warfare thus not only brought new territory under Mexica control, but also provided sacrificial victims for their collaboration with divine forces. With these ideas, Tlacaélel created what Miguel León-Portilla, a leading contemporary scholar of Nahuatl religion and philosophy, has termed a "mystico-militaristic" conception of Aztec destiny.

Human sacrifice was practiced in many cultures of Mesoamerica, including the Olmec and the Maya as well as the Mexica, before the changes introduced by Tlacaélel, but the number of victims is believed to have

Tlacaélel emphasized human sacrifice as one of the Aztecs' religious duties. *(Scala/Art Resource, NY)*

increased dramatically during the last period of Mexica rule. A huge pyramid-shaped temple in the center of Tenochtitlán, dedicated to Huitzilopochtli and the water god Tlaloc, was renovated and expanded many times, the last in 1487. Each expansion was dedicated by priests sacrificing war captives. Similar ceremonies were held regularly throughout the year on days dedicated to Huitzilopochtli and were attended by many observers, including representatives from neighboring states as well as masses of Mexicas. According to many accounts, victims were placed on a stone slab and their hearts cut out with an obsidian knife; the officiating priest then held the heart up as an offering to the sun. Sacrifices were also made to other gods at temples elsewhere in Tenochtitlán, and perhaps in other cities controlled by the Mexicas.

Estimates about the number of people sacrificed to Huitzilopochtli and other Mexica gods vary enormously and are impossible to verify. Both Mexica and later Spanish accounts clearly exaggerated the numbers, but most historians today assume that between several hundred and several thousand people were killed each year.

Questions for Analysis

1. How did the worship of Huitzilopochtli contribute to Aztec expansion? To hostility toward the Aztecs?
2. Why might Tlacaélel have seen it as important to destroy older texts as he created this new Aztec mythology?

Sources: León-Portilla, Miguel. *Pre-Columbian Literatures of Mexico* (Norman: University of Oklahoma Press, 1969); Clendinnen, Inga. *Mexicas: An Interpretation* (Cambridge: Cambridge University Press, 1991).

278 **CHAPTER 10** Civilizations of the Americas, 2500 B.C.E.–1500 C.E.

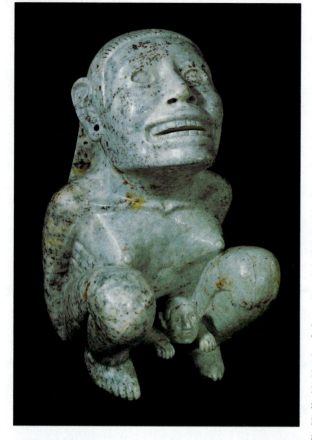

● **The Goddess Tlazolteotl** The Aztecs believed that cleanliness was a way to honor the gods, and that Tlazolteotl (sometimes called "Mother of the Gods") consumed the sins of humankind by eating refuse. She was also the goddess of childbirth. Notice the squatting position for childbirth, then common all over the world. (Dumbarton Oaks, Pre-Columbian Collection, Washington, D.C.)

tecuhtli *Provincial governors who exercised full political, judicial, and military authority on the Aztec emperor's behalf.*

The Life of the People

A wealth of information has survived about fifteenth- and sixteenth-century Mexico. The Aztecs wrote many books recounting their history, geography, and religious practices. They loved making speeches, which scribes wrote down. The Aztecs also preserved records of their legal disputes, which alone amounted to vast files. The Spanish conquerors subsequently destroyed much of this material. But enough documents remain to construct a picture of the Mexica people at the time of the Spanish intrusion.

No sharp social distinctions existed among the Aztecs during their early migrations. All were equally poor. The head of a family was both provider and warrior, and a sort of tribal democracy prevailed in which all adult males participated in important decision making. By the early sixteenth century, however, Aztec society had changed. A stratified social structure had come into being, and the warrior aristocracy exercised great authority.

Scholars do not yet understand precisely how this change occurred. According to Aztec legend, the Mexica admired the Toltecs and chose their first king, Acamapichti, from among them. The many children he fathered with Mexica women formed the nucleus of the noble class. At the time of the Spanish intrusion into Mexico, men who had distinguished themselves in war occupied the highest military and social positions in the state. Generals, judges, and governors of provinces were appointed by the emperor from among his servants who had earned reputations as war heroes. These great lords, or **tecuhtli,** dressed luxuriously and lived in palaces. The provincial governors exercised full political, judicial, and military authority on the emperor's behalf. In their territories they maintained order, settled disputes, and judged legal cases; oversaw the cultivation of land; and made sure that tribute—in food or gold—was paid. The governors also led troops in wartime. These functions resembled those of feudal lords in western Europe during the Middle Ages (see pages 367–368). Just as only nobles in France and England could wear fur and carry swords, just as gold jewelry and elaborate hairstyles for women distinguished royal and noble classes in African kingdoms, so in Mexica societies only the tecuhtli could wear jewelry and embroidered cloaks. The growth of a strong mercantile class as the empire expanded led to an influx of tropical wares and luxury goods: cotton, feathers, cocoa, skins, turquoise jewelry, and gold. The upper classes enjoyed an elegant and extravagant lifestyle.

Beneath the great nobility of soldiers and imperial officials was the class of warriors. Theoretically every free man could be a warrior, and parents dedicated their male children to war, burying a male child's umbilical cord with some arrows and a shield on the day of his birth. In actuality the sons of nobles enjoyed advantages deriving from their fathers' position and influence in the state. At the age of six, boys entered a school that trained them for war. Future warriors were taught to fight with a *macana,* a paddle-shaped wooden club edged with bits of obsidian. Youths were also trained in the use of spears, bows and arrows, and lances fitted with obsidian points. They learned to live on little food and sleep and to accept pain without complaint. At about age eighteen, a warrior fought his first campaign. If he captured a prisoner for ritual sacrifice, he acquired the title *iyac,* or warrior. If in later campaigns he succeeded in killing or capturing four of the enemy, he became a *tequiua*—one who shared in the booty and thus was a member of the nobility. If a young man failed in several campaigns to capture the required four prisoners, he joined the **maceualtin,** the plebeian or working class.

The maceualtin were the ordinary citizens—the backbone of Aztec society and the vast majority of the population. The word *maceualti* means "worker" and implies boorish speech and vulgar behavior. Members of this class performed all sorts of agricultural, military, and domestic services and carried heavy public burdens not required of noble warriors. Government officials assigned the maceualtin work on the temples, roads, and bridges. Army officers called them up for military duty, but Mexica considered this an honor and a religious rite, not a burden. Unlike nobles, priests, orphans, and slaves, maceualtin paid taxes. Maceualtin in the capital, however, possessed certain rights: they held their plots of land for life, and they received a small share of the tribute paid by the provinces to the emperor.

Beneath the maceualtin were the *tlalmaitl,* the landless workers or serfs. Some social historians speculate that this class originated during the period of migrations and upheavals following the end of the classical period (see page 271), when weak and defenseless people placed themselves under the protection of strong warriors, just as European peasants had become serfs after the end of the Roman Empire (see page 126). The tlalmaitl provided agricultural labor, paid rents in kind, and were bound to the soil—they could not move off the land. The tlalmaitl resembled in many ways the serfs of western Europe, but unlike serfs they performed military service when called on to do so. They enjoyed some rights as citizens and generally were accorded more respect than slaves.

Slaves were the lowest social class. Like Asian, European, and African slaves, most were prisoners captured in war or kidnapped from enemy tribes. But Aztecs who stole from a temple or private house or plotted against the emperor could also be enslaved, and people in serious debt sometimes voluntarily sold themselves into slavery. Female

maceualtin   *The vast majority of the Aztec population; the ordinary citizens or members of the working class.*

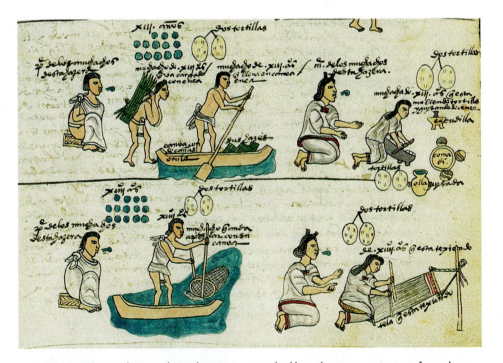

● **Aztec Youth**   As shown in this codex, Aztec society had basic learning requirements for each age (indicated by dots) of childhood and youth. In the upper panel, boys of age thirteen gather firewood and collect reeds and herbs in a boat, while girls learn to make tortillas on a terra-cotta grill. At fourteen (*lower panel*), boys learn to fish from a boat, and girls are taught to weave. (*The Bodleian Library, University of Oxford, MS Arch. Selden. A,1, fol. 60r*)

slaves often became their masters' concubines. Mexica slaves, however, differed fundamentally from European ones, for they could possess goods, save money, buy land and houses and even slaves for their own service, and purchase their freedom. If a male slave married a free woman, their offspring were free, and a slave who escaped and managed to enter the emperor's palace was automatically free. Most slaves eventually gained their freedom. Mexica slavery, therefore, had some humane qualities and resembled slavery in Islamic societies (see pages 205–207).

Women of all social classes played important roles in Mexica society, but those roles were restricted entirely to the domestic sphere. As the little hands of the newborn male child were closed around a tiny bow and arrow indicating his warrior destiny, so the infant female's hands were wrapped around miniature weaving instruments and a small broom: weaving was a sacred and exclusively female art; the broom signaled a female's responsibility for the household shrines and for keeping the household swept and free of contamination. Almost all of the Mexica people married, a man at about twenty when he had secured one or two captives, a woman a couple of years earlier. As in premodern Asian and European societies, parents selected their children's spouses, using neighborhood women as go-betweens. Save for the few women vowed to the service of the temple, marriage and the household were a woman's fate; marriage represented social maturity for both sexes. Pregnancy became the occasion for family and neighborhood feasts, and a successful birth launched celebrations lasting from ten to twenty days.

Women were expected to pray for their husbands' success in battle while they were gone. As one prayer to Huitzilopochtli went:

O great Lord of All Things, remember your servant
Who has gone to exalt your honor and the greatness of your name.
He will offer blood in that sacrifice that is war.
Behold, Lord, that he did not go out to work for me
Or for his children . . . He went for your sake,
In your name, to obtain glory for you . . .
Give him victory in this war so that he may return
To rest in his home and so that my children and I may see
His countenance again and feel his presence."[1]

Alongside the secular social classes stood the temple priests. Huitzilopochtli and each of the numerous lesser gods had many priests to oversee the upkeep of the temple, assist at religious ceremonies, and perform ritual sacrifices. The priests also did a brisk business in foretelling the future from signs and omens. Aztecs consulted priests on the selection of wives and husbands, on the future careers of newborn babies, and before leaving on journeys or for war. Temples possessed enormous wealth in gold and silver ceremonial vessels, statues, buildings, and land. From the temple revenues and resources, the priests supported schools, aided the poor, and maintained hospitals. The chief priests had the ear of the emperor and often exercised great power and influence.

At the peak of the social pyramid stood the emperor. The various Aztec historians contradict one another about the origin of the imperial dynasty, but modern scholars tend to accept the verdict of one sixteenth-century authority that the "custom has always been preserved among the Mexicans (that) the sons of kings have not ruled by right of inheritance, but by election."[2] A small oligarchy of the chief priests, warriors, and state officials made the selection. If none of the sons proved satisfactory, a brother or nephew of the emperor was chosen, but election was always restricted to the royal family.

The Aztec emperor was expected to be a great warrior who had led Mexica and allied armies into battle. All his other duties pertained to the welfare of his people. It was up to the emperor to see that justice was done—he was the final court of appeal. He also held ultimate responsibility for ensuring an adequate food supply. The emperor Montezuma I (r. 1440–1467) distributed twenty thousand loads of stock-piled grain when a flood hit Tenochtitlán. The records show that the Aztec emperors took their public duties seriously.

The Cities of the Aztecs

When the Spanish entered **Tenochtitlán** (which they called Mexico City) in November 1519, they could not believe their eyes. According to Bernal Díaz, one of Cortés's companions:

when we saw all those cities and villages built in the water, and other great towns on dry land, and that straight and level causeway leading to Mexico, we were astounded. These great towns and cues (temples) and buildings rising from the water, all made of stone, seemed like an enchanted vision. . . . Indeed, some of our soldiers asked whether it was not all a dream.[3]

Tenochtitlán had about sixty thousand households. The upper class practiced polygamy and had many children, and many households included servants and slaves. The total population probably numbered around 250,000. At the time, no European city and few Asian ones could boast a population even half that size. The total Aztec Empire has been estimated at around 5 million inhabitants, with the total population of Mesoamerica estimated at between 20 and 30 million.

Originally built on salt marshes, Tenochtitlán was approached by four great highways that connected it with the mainland. Bridges stood at intervals (comparable to modern Paris). Stone and adobe walls surrounded the city itself, making it (somewhat like medieval Constantinople; see page 169) highly defensible and capable of resisting

Tenochtitlán *A large and prosperous Aztec city that was admired by the Spanish when they entered in 1519.*

● **Tenochtitlán** The great Mexican archaeologist Ignacio Marquina designed this reconstruction of the central plaza of the Mexica city as it looked in 1519. The temple precinct, an area about 500 square yards, contained more than eighty structures, pyramids, pools, and homes of gods and of the men and women who served them. Accustomed to the clutter and filth of Spanish cities, the Spaniards were amazed by the elegance and cleanliness of Tenochtitlán. *(Enrique Franco-Torrijos)*

a prolonged siege. Wide, straight streets and canals crisscrossed the city. Boats and canoes plied the canals. Lining the roads and canals stood thousands of rectangular one-story houses of mortar faced with stucco. Although space was limited, many small gardens and parks were alive with the colors and scents of flowers.

A large aqueduct whose sophisticated engineering astounded Cortés carried pure water from distant springs and supplied fountains in the parks. Streets and canals opened onto public squares and marketplaces. Tradespeople offered every kind of merchandise. Butchers hawked turkeys, ducks, chickens, rabbits, and deer; grocers sold kidney beans, squash, avocados, corn, and all kinds of peppers. Artisans sold intricately designed gold, silver, and feathered jewelry. Seamstresses offered sandals, loincloths and cloaks for men, and blouses and long skirts for women—the clothing customarily worn by ordinary people—and embroidered robes and cloaks for the rich. Slaves for domestic service, wood for building, herbs for seasoning and medicine, honey and sweets, knives, jars, smoking tobacco, even human excrement used to cure animal skins—all these wares made a dazzling spectacle.

At one side of the central square of Tenochtitlán stood the great temple of Huitzilopochtli. Built as a pyramid and approached by three flights of 120 steps each, the temple was about one hundred feet high and dominated the city's skyline. According to Cortés, it was "so large that within the precincts, which are surrounded by a very high wall, a town of some five hundred inhabitants could easily be built. All round inside this wall there are very elegant quarters with very large rooms and corridors where their priests live."[4]

Travelers, perhaps inevitably, compare what they see abroad with what is familiar to them at home. Tenochtitlán thoroughly astounded Cortés, and in his letter to the emperor Charles V, he describes the city in comparison to his homeland: "the market square," where sixty thousand people a day came to buy and sell, "was twice as big as Salamanca"; the beautifully constructed "towers," as the Spaniards called the pyramids, rose higher "than the cathedral at Seville"; Montezuma's palace was "so marvelous that it seems to me to be impossible to describe its excellence and grandeur[;] . . . in Spain there is nothing to compare with it." Accustomed to the squalor and filth of Spanish cities, the cleanliness of Tenochtitlán dumbfounded the Spaniards, as did all the evidence of its ordered and elegant planning.[5]

THE INCAS

What were the sources of strength and prosperity, and of problems, for the Incas as they created their enormous empire?

Incas *The Peruvian empire that was at its peak from 1438 until 1532.*

In the center of Peru rise the cold highlands of the Andes. Six valleys of fertile and wooded land at altitudes ranging from eight thousand to eleven thousand feet punctuate highland Peru. The largest of these valleys are the Huaylas, Cuzco, and Titicaca. It was there that Inca civilization developed and flourished. Like the Aztecs, the **Incas** were a small militaristic group that came to power, conquered surrounding groups, and established one of the most extraordinary empires in the world. Gradually, Inca culture spread throughout Peru.

Earlier Peruvian Cultures

Moche *A Native American culture that thrived along Peru's northern coast between 100 and 800 C.E. The culture existed as a series of city-states rather than a single empire and is distinguished by an extraordinarily rich and diverse pottery industry.*

Inca achievements built on those of cultures that preceded them in the Andes and the Peruvian coast. These included the Chavin and the **Moche** civilization, which flourished along a 250-mile stretch of Peru's northern coast between 100 and 800 C.E. Rivers that flowed out of the Andes into the valleys allowed the Moche people to develop complex irrigation systems for agricultural development. Each Moche valley contained a large ceremonial center with palaces and pyramids surrounded by settlements of up to ten thousand people. The dazzling gold and silver artifacts, elaborate headdresses, and ceramic vessels display a remarkable skill in metalwork and pottery.

Politically, Moche culture was a series of small city-states rather than one unified state, which increased warfare. As in Aztec culture, war provided victims for human sacrifice, frequently portrayed on Moche pottery. Beginning about 500, the Moche suffered several severe *El Niños,* the change in ocean current patterns in the Pacific that brings both searing drought and flooding. Their leaders were not able to respond effectively, and the cities lost population.

In the Andes, various states developed after Chavin that were each able to carve out a slightly larger empire. They built cities around large public plazas, with temples, palaces, and elaborate stonework. Using terraces and other means to increase the amount of arable soil, they grew potatoes and other crops, even at very high altitudes. Enough food was harvested to feed not only the farmers themselves but also massive armies and administrative bureaucracies and thousands of industrial workers. These cultures were skilled at using fibers for a variety of purposes, including building boats to use on Lake Titicaca and bridges for humans and pack llamas to cross steep valleys.

Inca Imperialism

Who were the Incas? *Inca* was originally the name of the governing family of an Amerindian group that settled in the basin of Cuzco (see Map 10.5). From that family, the name was gradually extended to all peoples living in the Andes valleys. The Incas themselves used the word to identify their ruler or emperor. Here the term is used for both the ruler and the people. As with the Aztecs, so with the Incas: religious ideology was the force that transformed the culture. Religious concepts created pressure for imperialist expansion.

The Incas believed their ruler descended from the sun-god and that the health and prosperity of the state depended on him. Dead rulers were thought to link the people to the sun-god. When the ruler died, his corpse was preserved as a mummy in elaborate clothing and housed in a sacred and magnificent chamber. His royal descendants as a group managed his lands and sources of income for him and used the revenues to care for his mummy, maintain his cult, and support themselves. New rulers did not inherit these riches, so they had to win their own possessions by means of war and imperial expansion.

Around 1000 C.E. the Incas were one of many small groups fighting among themselves for land and water. The cult of royal mummies provided the impetus for expansion. The desire for conquest provided incentives for courageous (or ambitious) nobles: those who were victorious in battle and gained new territories for the state could expect lands, additional wives, servants, herds of llamas, gold, silver, fine clothes, and other symbols of high status. Even common soldiers who distinguished themselves in battle could be rewarded with booty and raised to noble status. The imperial interests of the emperor paralleled those of other social groups. Under Pachacuti Inca (1438–1471) and his successors, Inca domination was gradually extended by warfare to the frontier of present-day Ecuador and Colombia in the north and to the Maule River in present-day Chile in the south (see Map 10.5), an area of about 350,000 square miles. Eighty provinces, scores of ethnic groups, and 16 million people came under Inca control. A remarkable system of roads held the empire together.

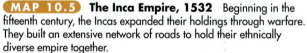

MAP 10.5 **The Inca Empire, 1532** Beginning in the fifteenth century, the Incas expanded their holdings through warfare. They built an extensive network of roads to hold their ethnically diverse empire together.

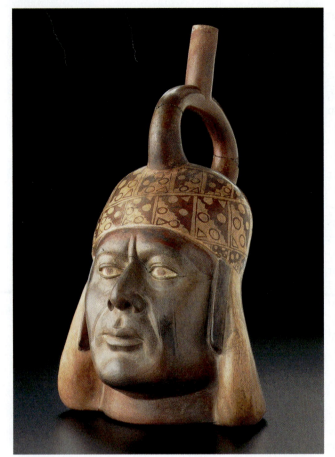

● **Portrait Vessel of a Ruler**   Artisans of the Moche culture on the northern coast of Peru produced objects representing many aspects of their world, including this flat-bottomed stirrup-spout jar with a ruler's face. The commanding expression conveys a strong sense of power, as does the elaborate headdress with the geometric designs of Moche textiles worn only by elite persons. (*South America, Peru, North Coast, Moche Culture, Portrait Vessel of a Ruler, earthenware with pigmented clay slip, 300–700, 35.6 x 24.1, Kate S. Buckingham Endowment, 1955.2338, 3/4 view. Photograph by Robert Hashimoto. Photograph © 1999, The Art Institute of Chicago*)

Quechua   *First deemed the official language of the Incas under Pachacuti, it is still spoken by most Peruvians today.*

Primary Source: Chronicles
Learn how the Incas used the elaborate knotted ropes called khipus as record-keeping devices that helped them govern a vast and prosperous empire.

Before Inca civilization, each group that entered the Andes valleys had its own distinct language. These languages were not written and have become extinct. Scholars will probably never understand the linguistic condition of Peru before the fifteenth century when Pachacuti made the Inca language, which the Spanish called **Quechua** (pronounced "keshwa"), the official language of his people and administration. Conquered peoples were forced to adopt the language, and Quechua spread the Inca way of life throughout the Andes. Though not written until the Spanish in Peru adopted it as a second official language, Quechua had replaced local languages by the seventeenth and eighteenth centuries and is still spoken by most Peruvians today.

Both the Aztecs and the Incas ruled very ethnically diverse peoples. Whereas the Aztecs tended to control their subject peoples through terror, the Incas governed by means of imperial unification. They imposed not only their language but also their entire panoply of gods. Magnificent temples scattered throughout the expanding empire housed images of these gods. Priests led prayers and elaborate rituals, and on such occasions as a terrible natural disaster or a great military victory, they sacrificed human beings to the gods. Subject peoples were required to worship the state gods.

Imperial unification was also achieved through the forced participation of local chieftains in the central bureaucracy and through a policy of colonization. To prevent rebellion in newly conquered territories, Pachacuti Inca and subsequent rulers transferred all their inhabitants to other parts of the empire, replacing them with workers who had lived longer under Inca rule. They drafted local men for distant wars, breaking up kin groups that had existed in Andean society for centuries.

An excellent system of roads—averaging three feet in width, some paved and others not—facilitated the transportation of armies and the rapid communication of royal orders by runners. The roads followed straight lines wherever possible but also crossed pontoon bridges and tunneled through hills. This great feat of Inca engineering bears striking comparison with Roman roads, which also linked an empire.

Ruling an empire requires a bureaucracy as well as an army, and Inca officials, tax collectors, and accountants traveled throughout the empire. They made increasingly elaborate khipus (see page 266) to record financial and labor obligations, the output of fields, population levels, land transfers, and other numerical records. Scholars have deciphered the way numbers were recorded on khipus, finding a base-ten system. Khipus may also have been used to record narrative history, but this is more speculative, as knowledge of how to read them died out after the Spanish conquest. Just as the Spanish destroyed books in Mesoamerica, they destroyed khipus in the Andes because they thought they might contain religious messages and encourage people to resist Spanish authority. About 750 Inca khipus survive today, more than half in museums in Europe.

Rapid Inca expansion, however, produced stresses. Although the pressure for growth remained unabated, open lands began to be scarce. Attempts to penetrate the tropical Amazon forest east of the Andes led to repeated military disasters. The Incas waged wars with highly trained armies drawn up in massed formation and fought pitched battles on level ground, often engaging in hand-to-hand combat. But in dense jungles, the troops could not maneuver or maintain order against enemies using guerrilla tactics and sniping at them with deadly blowguns. Another source of stress was revolts among subject peoples in conquered territories. Even the system of roads and trained runners eventually caused administrative problems. The average runner could cover about 50 leagues, or 175 miles, per day—a remarkable feat of physical endurance, especially at high altitude—but the larger the empire became, the greater the distances to be covered. The roundtrip from the capital at Cuzco to Quito in Ecuador, for example, took from ten to twelve days, so that an emperor might have to base urgent decisions on incomplete or out-of-date information. The empire was overextended.

When the Inca Huayna Capac died in 1525, his throne was bitterly contested by two of his sons, Huascar and Atauhualpa. Huascar's threat to do away with the cult of royal mummies led the nobles—who often benefited from managing land and wealth for a deceased ruler—to throw their support behind Atauhualpa. In the civil war that began in 1532, Atauhualpa's veteran warriors easily defeated Huascar's green recruits, but the conflict weakened the Incas. On his way to his coronation at Cuzco, Atauhualpa encountered Pizarro and 168 Spaniards who had recently entered the kingdom. The Spaniards quickly became the real victors in the Inca kingdom (see pages 442–443).

● **Machu Picchu**   The Inca city of Machu Picchu, surrounded by mountains in the clouds, clings to a spectacular crag in upland Peru. It was built around 1450, at the point that the Inca Empire was at its height, and abandoned about a century later. (Will McIntyre/Photo Researchers, Inc.)

● **An Inca Cape** Inca artisans could produce gorgeous textiles, and on ceremonial occasions nobles proudly paraded in brightly colored feathers or in garments made of luxurious alpaca wool. This exquisite cape is fashioned from the feathers of a blue and yellow macaw; the pattern, befitting aristocratic tastes, features lordly pelicans carried on litters by less exalted birds. *(The Textile Museum, Washington, D.C., 91.395. Acquired by George Hewitt Myers in 1941)*

Inca Society

ayllu *A clan; it served as the fundamental social unit of Inca society.*

curacas *The headman of the Inca clan; he was responsible for conducting relations with outsiders.*

mita *A draft rotary system that determined when men of a particular hamlet performed public works.*

The **ayllu**, or clan, served as the fundamental social unit of Inca society. All members of the ayllu owed allegiance to the **curacas**, or headman, who conducted relations with outsiders. The ayllu held specific lands, granted it by village or provincial authorities on a long-term basis, and individual families tended to work the same plots for generations. Cooperation in the cultivation of the land and intermarriage among members of the ayllu wove people there into a tight web of connections.

In return for the land, all men had to perform public duties and pay tribute to the authorities. Their duties included building and maintaining palaces, temples, roads, and irrigation systems. Tribute consisted of potatoes, corn, and other vegetables paid to the village head, who in turn paid them to the provincial governor. A draft rotary system called **mita** (turn) determined when men of a particular village performed public works. As the Inca Empire expanded, this pattern of social and labor organization was imposed on other, newly conquered indigenous peoples. After the conquest, the Spaniards adopted and utilized the Incas' ways of organizing their economy and administration, just as the Incas (and, in Mesoamerica, the Aztecs) had built on earlier cultures.

The Incas had well-established mechanisms for public labor drafts and tribute collection. The emperors sometimes gave newly acquired lands to victorious generals, distinguished civil servants, and favorite nobles. These lords subsequently exercised authority previously held by the native curacas. Whether long-time residents or new colonists, common people had the status of peasant farmers, which entailed heavy agricultural or other obligations. Just as in medieval Europe peasants worked several days each week on their lord's lands, so the Inca people had to work on state lands (that is, the emperor's lands) or on lands assigned to the temple. Peasants also labored on roads and bridges; terraced and irrigated new arable land; served on construction crews for royal palaces, temples, and public buildings such as fortresses; acted as runners on the post roads; and excavated in the imperial gold, silver, and copper mines. The imperial government annually determined the number of laborers needed for these various undertakings, and each district had to supply an assigned quota. The government also made an ayllu responsible for the state-owned granaries and for the production of cloth for army uniforms.

The state required everyone to marry and even decided when and sometimes whom a person should marry. Men married around the age of twenty, women a little younger. The Incas did not especially prize virginity; premarital sex was common. The marriage ceremony consisted of the joining of hands and the exchange of a pair of sandals. This ritual was followed by a large wedding feast at which the state presented the bride and groom with two sets of clothing, one for everyday wear and one for festive occasions. If a man or woman did not find a satisfactory mate, the provincial governor selected one for him or her. Travel was forbidden, so couples necessarily came from the same region. Like most warring societies with high male death rates, the Incas practiced polygamy, though the cost of supporting many wives restricted it largely to the upper classes.

The Incas relied heavily on local authorities and cultural norms for day-to-day matters. In some ways, however, the common people were denied choice and initiative and led regimented lives. The Incas did, however, take care of the poor and aged, distribute grain in times of shortage and famine, and supply assistance in natural disasters. Scholars have debated whether Inca society was socialistic, totalitarian, or a forerunner of the welfare state; it may be merely a matter of definition. Although the Inca economy was strictly regulated, there certainly was not an equal distribution of wealth. Everything above and beyond the masses' basic needs went to the emperor and the nobility.

The backbreaking labor of ordinary people in the fields and mines made possible the luxurious lifestyle of the great Inca nobility. The nobles—called *oregones,* or "big ears," by the Spanish because they pierced their ears and distended the lobes with heavy jewelry—were the ruling Inca's kinsmen. Lesser nobles included the curacas, royal household servants, public officials, and entertainers.

In the fifteenth century Inca rulers superimposed imperial institutions on those of kinship. They ordered allegiance to be paid to the ruler at Cuzco rather than to the curacas and relocated the entire populations of certain regions. Entirely new ayllus were formed, based on residence rather than kinship. As the empire expanded, there arose a noble class of warriors, governors, and local officials whose support the ruling Inca secured with gifts of land, precious metals, and llamas and alpacas (llamas were used as beasts of burden; alpacas were raised for their long fine wool). The nobility was exempt from agricultural work and from other kinds of public service.

Chapter Summary

Key Terms

Mesoamerica
milpa
Norte Chico
khipu
Chavin
Olmecs
Maya
Popul Vuh
Teotihuacán
Toltecs
Hohokam
Anasazi
Hopewell
Mississippian
Aztec
Nahuatl
Mexica
Huitzilopochtli
tecuhtli
maceualtin
Tenochtitlán
Incas
Moche
Quechua
ayllu
curacas
mita

To assess your mastery of this chapter, go to
bedfordstmartins.com/mckayworld

• How did early peoples in the Americas adapt to their environment as they created economic and political systems?

The environment shaped the formation of human settlements in the Americas, which began when people crossed into the Western Hemisphere from Asia. All the highly varied environments, from polar tundra to tropical rain forests, came to support human settlement. About 8000 B.C.E., people in some parts of the Americas began raising crops as well as gathering wild produce. Maize became the most important crop, with knowledge about its cultivation spreading out from Mesoamerica into North and South America.

• What physical, social, and intellectual features characterized early civilizations in the Americas?

Agricultural advancement led to an increase in population, which allowed for greater concentrations of people and the creation of the first urban societies. In certain parts of North and South America, towns dependent on agriculture flourished, especially in coastal areas and river valleys. Some in North America began to build large earthwork mounds, while those in South America practiced irrigation. The Olmecs created the first society with cities in Mesoamerica, with large ceremonial buildings, an elaborate and accurate calendar, and a system of writing.

• How did Mesoamerican and North American peoples develop prosperous and stable societies in the classical era?

The urban culture of the Olmecs and other Mesoamerican peoples influenced subsequent societies. Especially in what became known as the classical era (300–900 C.E.), various groups developed large states centered on cities, with high levels of technological and intellectual achievement. Of these, the Maya were the most long-lasting, creating a complex written language and elegant art. Peoples living in North America built communities that were smaller than those in Mesoamerica, but many also used irrigation techniques to enhance agricultural production and continued to build earthwork mounds for religious purposes.

• How did the Aztecs both build on the achievements of earlier Mesoamerican cultures and develop new traditions to create their large empire?

The Aztecs, also known as the Mexica, built a unified culture based heavily on the heritage of earlier Mesoamerican societies and distinguished by achievements in engineering, sculpture, and architecture. In Mexica society, religion was the dynamic factor that transformed other aspects of the culture: economic security, social mobility, education, and especially war. War was an article of religious faith, providing riches and land, and also sacrificial victims for ceremonies honoring the Aztec gods. Aztec society was hierarchical, with nobles and priests having special privileges. The Aztec empire centered on Tenochtitlán, the most spectacular and one of the largest cities in the world in 1500.

• **What were the sources of strength and prosperity, and of problems, for the Incas as they created their enormous empire?**

The Peruvian coast and Andean highlands were home to a series of cultures that cultivated cotton as well as food crops. Of these, the largest empire was created by the Incas, who began as a small militaristic group and conquered surrounding groups. The Incas established a far-flung empire that stretched along the Andes, keeping this together through a system of roads, along which moved armies and administrators. Andean society was dominated by clan groups, and Inca measures to disrupt these and move people great distances created resentment.

Suggested Reading

Clendinnen, I. *Aztecs: An Interpretation.* 1992. Pays particular attention to the role that rituals and human sacrifice played in Aztec culture.

Coe, M. *The Mayas.* 2005. A new edition of a classic survey that incorporates the most recent scholarship.

Conrad, G. W., and A. A. Demarest. *Religion and Empire: The Dynamics of Aztec and Inca Expansionism.* 1993. Compares the two largest American empires.

D'Altroy, T. *The Incas.* 2003. Examines the ways in which the Incas drew on earlier traditions to create their empire; by a leading scholar.

Freidel, D. *A Forest of Kings: The Untold Story of the Ancient Maya.* 1990. A splendidly illustrated work providing expert treatment of the Maya world.

Kehoe, Alice Beck. *America Before the European Invasion.* 2002. An excellent survey of North America before the coming of the Europeans, by an eminent anthropologist.

Knight, A. *Mexico: From the Beginnings to the Spanish Conquest.* 2002. Provides information on many Mesoamerican societies.

León-Portilla, M. *The Aztec Image of Self and Society: An Introduction to Nahua Culture.* 1992. The best appreciation of Aztec religious ritual and symbolism.

Mann, Charles C. *1491: New Revelations of the Americas Before Columbus.* 2005. A thoroughly researched overview of all the newest scholarship, written for a general audience.

Milner, G. *The Moundbuilders: Ancient Peoples of Eastern North America.* 2005. Beautifully illustrated book that discusses the mounds and the societies that built them; could also be used as a tourist guide.

Wright, R. *Time Among the Mayas.* 1989. A highly readable account of Maya agricultural and religious calendars.

Notes

1. Fray Diego Durán, *Mexicas: The History of the Indies of New Spain,* translated, with notes, by Doris Heyden and Fernand Horcasitas (New York: Orion Press, 1964), p. 203.

2. Quoted in J. Soustelle, *Daily Life of the Aztecs on the Eve of the Spanish Conquest,* trans. P. O'Brian (Stanford, Calif.: Stanford University Press, 1970), p. 89.

3. B. Díaz, *The Conquest of New Spain,* trans. J. M. Cohen (New York: Penguin Books, 1978), p. 214.

4. Quoted in J. H. Perry, *The Discovery of South America* (New York: Taplinger, 1979), pp. 161–163.

5. Quoted in I. Clendinnen, *Aztecs: An Interpretation* (New York: Cambridge University Press, 1992), pp. 16–17.

The Death of Inca Yupanque (Pachacuti Inca) in 1471

In 1551 the Spaniard Juan de Betanzos began to write Narrative of the Incas. *Although Betanzos had only the Spanish equivalent of a grade school education when he arrived in Peru, and although he lacked dictionaries and grammar books, he had two powerful assets. First, he learned Quechua and earned a reputation for being the best interpreter and translator in postconquest Peru. Second, Betanzos had married Angelina Yupanque, an Inca noblewoman (her Inca name was Cuxirimay Ocllo) who was the widow of Atahualpa. Through her, Betanzos gained immediate and firsthand access to the Inca oral tradition. When he finished his book six years later, modern scholars believe he had produced "the most authentic chronicle that we have."*

Narrative of the Incas *provides a gold mine of information about Inca customs and social history. There is so much description of marriage, childbirth, and raising children—activities that were seen as the realm of women in both Inca and Spanish society—that scholars suspect Angelina Yupanque provided her husband with much of his information. Here is his account of the death of Inca Yupanque (Pachacuti Inca) in 1471.*

Since there were instructions for the idolatries and activities that you have heard about, Inca Yupanque ordered that immediately after he died these activities and sacrifices should be done. In addition, as soon as this was done, word should be sent to all the land, and from all the provinces and towns they should bring again all that was necessary for the service of the new lord, including gold, silver, livestock, clothing, and the rest of the things needed to replenish all the storehouses that, because of his death, had been emptied for the sacrifices and things he ordered to be done, and it should be so abundant because he realized that the state of the one who was thus Inca was growing greater.

While Inca Yupanque was talking and ordering what was to be done after he died, he raised his voice in a song that is still sung today in his memory by those of his generation. This song went as follows: "Since I bloomed like the flower of the garden, up to now I have given order and justice in this life and world as long as my strength lasted. Now I have turned into earth." Saying these words of his song, Inca Yupanque Pachacuti expired, leaving in all the land justice and order, as already stated. And his people were well supplied with idols, idolatries, and activities. After he was dead, he was taken to a town named Patallacta, where he had ordered some houses built in which his body was to be entombed. He was buried by putting his body in the earth in a large new clay urn, with him very well dressed. Inca Yupanque ordered that a golden image made to resemble him be placed on top of his tomb. And it was to be worshiped in place of him by the people who went there. Soon it was placed there. He ordered that a statue be made of his fingernails and hair that had been cut in his lifetime. It was made in that town where his body was kept. They very ceremoniously brought this statue on a litter to the city of Cuzco for the fiestas in the city. This statue was placed in the houses of Topa Inca Yupanque. When there were fiestas in the city, they brought it out for them with the rest of the statues. What is more laughable about this lord Inca Yupanque is that, when he wanted to make some idol, he entered the house of the Sun [the temple to the sun in Cuzco] and acted as though the Sun spoke to him, and he himself answered the Sun to make his people believe that the Sun ordered him to make those idols and *guacas** and so that they would worship them as such.

When the statue was in the city, Topa Inca Yupanque ordered those of his own lineage to bring this statue out for the feasts that were held in Cuzco. When they brought it out like this, they sang about the things that the Inca did in his life, both in the wars and in his city. Thus they served and revered him, changing its garments as he used to do, and serving it as he was served when he was alive. All of which was done thus.

This statue, along with the gold image that was on top of his tomb, was taken by Manco Inca from

---

*Any object, place, or person worshiped as a deity.

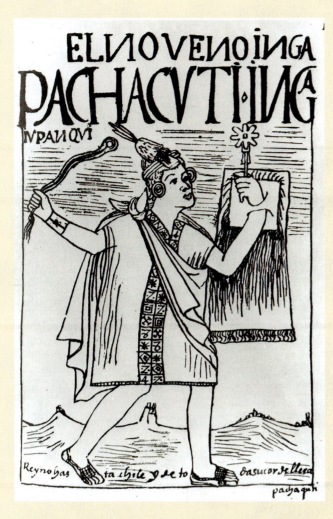

EL NOVENO INGA
PACHACVTI ING A
IVPANQVI

Reyno has ta chile y... de... to

pachacuti

dasucor de lleca

Revered as a great conqueror and lawgiver, Pachacuti Inca here wears the sacred fringed headband symbolizing his royal authority and the large earrings of the *oregones*, the nobility. (Pachacuti Inca, from Nueva Coronica & Buen Gobierno, by Guaman Poma de Ayala. Courtesy, Musée du Quai Branly/ Scala Picture Library)

the city when he revolted. On the advice that Doña Angelina Yupanque gave to the Marquis Don Francisco Pizarro, he got it and the rest of the wealth with it. Only the body is in Patallacta at this time, and judging by it, in his lifetime he seems to have been a tall man. They say that he died at the age of one hundred twenty years. After his father's death, Topa Inca Yupanque ordered that none of the descendants of his father, Inca Yupanque, were to settle the area beyond the rivers of Cuzco. From that time until today the descendants of Inca Yupanque were called *Capacaillo Ynga Yupanque haguaynin,* which means "lineage of kings," "descendants and grandchildren of Inca Yupanque." These are the most highly regarded of all the lineages of Cuzco. These are the ones who were ordered to wear two feathers on their heads.

As time passed, this generation of *orejones* [*oregones*]† multiplied. There were and are today many who became heads of families and renowned as firstborn. Because they married women who were not of their lineage, they took a variety of family names. Seeing this, those of Inca Yupanque ordered that those who had mixed with other people's blood should take

†Nobles.

new family names and extra names so that [only] those of his lineage could clearly be called *Capacaillo* and descendants of Inca Yupanque.

Questions for Analysis

1. Juan de Betanzos clearly shows his disapproval of the cult of the royal mummies through his choice of words, but he also includes details that help explain its power. Judging by his description, why did people honor deceased rulers? Why did rulers (or at least Inca Yupanque) think they deserved such honors?

2. In the last paragraph, Inca Yupanque's descendants seek to limit their special title of *Capacaillo.* Why might they have done this? What effect might this have on marriage patterns among the descendants of an Inca king?

Source: Narrative of the Incas by Juan de Betanzos, trans. and ed. Roland Hamilton and Dana Buchanan from the Palma de Mallorca manuscript (Austin: University of Texas Press, 1996), pp. 138–139. Copyright © 1996. Used by permission of the University of Texas Press.

Mongol Army Attacking a Walled City, from a Persian manuscript. Note the use of catapults on both sides. *(Bildarchiv Preussischer Kulturbesitz/Art Resource, NY)*

11 CENTRAL AND SOUTHERN ASIA, TO 1400

Chapter Preview

The large chunks of Asia treated in this chapter underwent profound changes during the centuries examined here. The Central Asian grasslands gave birth to nomadic confederations capable of dominating major states—first the Turks, then later, even more spectacularly, the Mongols. In the Indian subcontinent regional cultures flourished and the area had its first encounter with Islam. Southeast Asia developed several distinct cultures, most of them adopting Buddhism and other ideas and techniques from India.

Ancient India is covered in Chapter 2. This is the first chapter to treat Southeast Asia and to look at Central Asia on its own terms rather than as a problem for nearby agricultural societies.

CENTRAL ASIAN NOMADS

What gave the nomadic pastoralists of Central Asia military advantages over nearby settled civilizations?

One experience Rome, Persia, India, and China all shared was conflict with **nomads** who came from the very broad region referred to as Central Asia. This broad region was dominated by the arid **grasslands** (also called the **steppe**) that stretched from Hungary, through southern Russia and across Central Asia (today's Tajikistan, Turkmenistan, Kazakhstan, Kyrgyzstan, and Uzbekistan) and adjacent parts of China, to Mongolia and parts of north China. Easily crossed by horses but too dry for crop agriculture, the grasslands could support only a thin population of nomadic herders who lived off their flocks of sheep, goats, camels, horses, or other animals. At least twice a year they would break camp and move their animals to new pastures, in the spring moving north, in the fall south.

In their search for water and good pastures, nomadic groups often came into conflict with other nomadic groups pursuing the same resources,

nomads *Groups of people who move from place to place in search of food, water, and pasture for their animals, usually following the seasons.*

grasslands *Also called the* steppe, *these lands are too dry for crops but support pasturing animals.*

steppe *Another name for the* grasslands *that are common across much of the center of Eurasia.*

which the two would then fight over, as there was normally no higher political authority able to settle disputes. Groups on the losing end, especially if they were small, faced the threat of extermination or slavery, which prompted them to make alliances with other groups or move far away. Thus, over the centuries, the ethnic groups living in particular sections of the grasslands would change. Groups on the winning end of intertribal conflicts could exact tribute from those they defeated, sometimes so much that they could devote themselves entirely to war, leaving to their slaves and vassals the work of tending herds.

To get the products of nearby agricultural societies, especially grain, woven textiles, iron, tea, and wood, nomadic herders would trade their own products, such as horses and furs. When trade was difficult, they would turn to raiding to seize what they needed. Much of the time nomadic herders raided other nomads, but nearby agricultural settlements were common targets as well. The nomads' skill as horsemen and archers made it difficult for farmers and townsmen to defend against them. It was largely to defend against the raids of the Xiongnu nomads, for example, that the Chinese built the Great Wall (see page 134).

Political organization among nomadic herders was generally very simple. Clans had chiefs, as did tribes (which were coalitions of clans, often related to each other). Leadership within a group was based on military prowess and was often settled by fighting. Occasionally a charismatic leader would emerge who was able to extend alliances to form confederations of tribes. From the point of view of the settled societies, which have left most of the records about these nomadic groups, large confederations were much more of a threat, since they could plan coordinated attacks on cities and towns. Large confederations rarely lasted more than a century or so, however, and when they broke up, tribes again spent much of their time fighting with each other, relieving some of the pressure on their settled neighbors.

The three most wide-ranging and successful confederations were those of the Xiongnu/Huns, who emerged in the third century B.C.E. in the area near China; the Turks, who had their origins in the same area in the fourth and fifth centuries C.E.; and the Mongols, who did not become important until the late twelfth century. In all three cases, the entire steppe region was eventually swept up in the movement of peoples and armies.

The Turks

The Turks are the first of the Inner Asian peoples to have left a written record in their own language; the earliest Turkish documents date from the eighth century. Turkic languages may have already been spoken in dispersed areas of the Eurasian steppe when the Turks first appeared; today these languages are spoken by the Uighurs in western China, the Uzbeks, Kazakhs, Kyrghiz, and Turkmens of Central Asia, and the Turks of modern Turkey. The original religion of the Turks was shamanistic and involved worship of Heaven, making it similar to the religions of many other groups in the steppe region.

In 552 a group called Turks who specialized in metalworking rebelled against their overlords, the Rouruan, whose empire then dominated the region from the eastern Silk Road cities of Central Asia through Mongolia. The Turks quickly supplanted the Rouruan as overlords. When the first Turkish khagan (ruler) died a few years later, the Turkish Empire was divided between his younger brother, who took the western part (modern Central Asia), and his son, who took the eastern part (modern Mongolia). Sogdians working for the Western Turks convinced them to send embassies to both the Persian and the Byzantine courts. Repeat embassies in both directions did not prevent hostilities, however, and in 576 the Western Turks captured the Byzantine city of Bosporus in the Crimea.

The Eastern Turks frequently raided into China and just as often fought among themselves. The Chinese history of the Sui Dynasty records that "The Turks prefer to destroy each other rather than to live side-by-side. They have a thousand, nay ten thousand clans who are hostile to and kill one another. They mourn their dead with much grief and swear vengeance."[1] In the early seventh century the empire of the Eastern Turks ran up against the growing military might of the Tang Dynasty in China and soon broke apart. In the eighth century a Turkic people called the Uighurs formed a new empire based in Mongolia that survived about a century. It had close ties to Tang China, providing military aid but also extracting large payments in silk. During this period many Uighurs adopted religions then current along the Silk Road, notably Buddhism, Nestorian Christianity, and Manichaeism. In the ninth century this Uighur empire was destroyed by another Turkic people from north of Mongolia called the Kyrgyz. Some fled to what is now western China (Kansu and Xinjiang provinces). Setting up their capital city in Kucha, these Uighurs created a remarkably stable and prosperous kingdom that lasted four centuries (ca. 850–1250). Because of the dry climate of the region, many buildings, wall paintings, and manuscripts written in a variety of languages have been preserved from this era. They reveal a complex, urban civilization in which Buddhism, Manichaeism, and Christianity existed side by side, practiced by Turks as well as by Tokharians, Sogdians, and other Iranian peoples.

Farther west in Central Asia other groups of Turks, such as the Karakhanids, Ghaznavids, and Seljuks, rose to prominence. Often local Muslim forces would try to capture them, convert them, and employ them as slave soldiers (see pages 206–207). By the mid- to late tenth century many were serving in the Abbasid armies. It was also in the tenth century that Central Asian Turks began converting to Islam (which protected them from being abducted as slaves). Then they took to raiding unconverted Turks.

In the mid-eleventh century the Turks had gained the upper hand in the caliphate, and the caliphs became little more than figureheads. From there Turkish power was extended into Syria, Palestine, and other parts of the realm. (Asia Minor is now called Turkey because Turks migrated there by the thousands over several centuries.) In 1071 Seljuk Turks inflicted a devastating defeat on the Byzantine army in eastern Anatolia and even took the Byzantine emperor captive. Other Turkish confederations established themselves in Afghanistan and extended their control into north India (see page 312).

In India, Persia, and Anatolia, the formidable military skills of nomadic Turkish warriors made it possible for them to become overlords of settled societies. By the end of the thirteenth century nomad power prevailed through much of Eurasia. Just as the Uighurs developed a hybrid urban culture along the eastern end of the Silk Road, adopting many elements from the mercantile Sogdians, the Turks of Central and Western Asia created an Islamic culture that drew from both Turkish and Iranian sources. Often Persian was used as the administrative language of the states they formed. Nevertheless, despite the presence of Turkish overlords all along the southern fringe of the steppe, no one group of Turks was able to unite them all into a single

Chronology

ca. 320–480 Gupta Empire in India

ca. 380–450 Life of India's greatest poet, Kalidasa

ca. 450 White Huns invade India

ca. 500–1400 India's medieval age; caste system reaches its mature form

552 Turks rebel against Rouruan and rise to power

ca. 780 Borobudur temple complex begun in Srivijaya (modern Java)

802–1432 Khmer Empire of Cambodia

ca. 850–1250 Kingdom of the Uighurs

870–1030 Turks raid north India

939 Vietnamese gain independence from China

12th century Buddhism declines in India

1206 Chinggis proclaimed Great Khan; Mongol language recorded

ca. 1240 *The Secret History of the Mongols*

1276 Mongol conquest of China

ca. 1300 Plague spreads throughout Mongol Empire

1405 Death of Tamerlane

political unit. That feat had to wait for the next major power on the grasslands, the Mongols.

The Mongols

In Mongolia in the twelfth century ambitious Mongols did not aspire to match the Turks or other groups that had migrated west, but rather the groups that had stayed in the east and mastered ways to extract resources from China, the largest and richest country in the region. In the tenth and eleventh centuries the Khitans had accomplished this; in the twelfth century the Jurchens had overthrown the Khitans and extended their reach even deeper into China. The Khitans and Jurchens formed hybrid nomadic-urban states, with northern sections where tribesmen continued to live in the traditional way and southern sections politically controlled by the non-Chinese rulers but settled largely by tax-paying Chinese. The Khitans and Jurchens had scripts created to record their languages and adopted many Chinese governing practices. They built cities in pastoral areas as centers of consumption and trade. In both cases, their elite became culturally dual, adept in Chinese ways as well as in their own traditions.

The Mongols lived north of these hybrid nomadic-settled societies and maintained their traditional ways. Chinese, Persian, and European observers have all left descriptions of the daily life of the Mongols, which they found strikingly different from their own. The daily life of the peasants of China, India, Vietnam, and Japan had much more in common with each other than with the Mongol pastoralists. Before considering the military conquests of the Mongols, it is useful to look more closely at their way of life.

Daily Life

Before their great conquests the Mongols did not have cities, towns, or villages. Rather, they moved with their animals between winter and summer pastures. They had to keep their belongings to a minimum because they had to be able to pack up and move everything they owned when it was time to move.

yurts *Tents in which the pastoral nomads lived; they could be quickly dismantled and loaded onto animals or carts.*

To make their settlements portable, the Mongols lived in tents called **yurts** rather than in houses. The yurts, about twelve to fifteen feet in diameter, were constructed of light wooden frames covered by layers of wool felt, greased to make them waterproof. The yurts were always round, since this shape held up better against the strong winds that blew across the treeless grasslands. They could be dismantled and loaded onto pack animals or carts in a short time. The floor of the yurt would be covered with dried grass or straw, then felt, skins, or rugs. In the center would be the hearth, directly under the smoke hole. Usually the yurt was set up with the entrance facing south. The master's bed would be on the north. Goat horns would be attached to the frame of the yurt and used as hooks to hang joints of meat, cooking utensils, bows, quivers of arrows, and the like. A group of families traveling together would set up their yurts in a circle open to the south and draw up their wagons in a circle around the yurts for protection.

For food the Mongols ate mostly animal products. Without granaries to store food for years of famine, the Mongols' survival was endangered whenever weather or diseases of their animals threatened their food supply. The most common meat was mutton, supplemented with wild game. When grain or vegetables could be obtained through trade, they were added to the diet. Wood was scarce, so the common fuel for the cook fires was dried animal dung or grasses.

The Mongols milked sheep, goats, cows, and horses and made cheese and fermented alcoholic drinks from the milk. A European visitor to Mongolia in the 1250s described how they milked mares, a practice unfamiliar to Europeans:

They fasten a long line to two posts standing firmly in the ground, and to the line they tie the young colts of the mares which they mean to milk. Then come the mothers who stand by their foals, and allow themselves to be milked. And if any of them be too unruly, then one takes her colt and puts it under her, letting it suck a while, and presently taking it away again, and the milker takes its place.[2]

He also described how they made the alcoholic drink kumiss from the milk, a drink that "goes down very pleasantly, intoxicating weak brains."[3]

Because of the intense cold of the grasslands in the winter, the Mongols made much use of furs and skins for clothing. Both men and women usually wore silk trousers and tunics (the silk obtained from China). Over these they wore robes of fur, for the very coldest times in two layers—an inner layer with the hair on the inside and an outer layer with the hair on the outside. Hats were of felt or fur, boots of felt or leather. Men wore leather belts to which their bows and quivers could be attached. Women of high rank wore elaborate headdresses decorated with feathers.

Mongol women had to work very hard and had to be able to care for the animals when the men were away hunting or fighting. They normally drove the carts and set up and dismantled the yurts. They were also the ones who milked the sheep, goats, and cows and made the butter and cheese. In addition, they made the felt, prepared the skins, and sewed the clothes. Because water was scarce, clothes were not washed with water, nor were dishes. Women, like men, had to be expert riders, and many also learned to shoot. Women participated actively in family decisions, especially as wives and mothers. In *The Secret History of the Mongols,* a work written in Mongolian in the mid-thirteenth century, Chinggis Khan's mother and wife frequently make impassioned speeches on the importance of family loyalty. (See the feature "Listening to the Past: The Abduction of Women in *The Secret History of the Mongols*" on pages 324–325.)

Mongol men kept as busy as the women. They made carts and wagons and the frames for the yurts. They also made harnesses for the horses and oxen, leather saddles, and the equipment needed for hunting and war, such as bows and arrows. Men

● **Mongol Yurt** A Chinese artist captured the essential features of a Mongol yurt to illustrate the story of a Chinese woman who married a nomad. *(The Metropolitan Museum of Art, Ex coll.: C. C. Wang Family, Gift of The Dillon Fund, 1973 [1973.120.3]. Photograph © 1994 The Metropolitan Museum of Art)*

also had charge of the horses, and they milked the mares. Young horses were allowed to run wild until it was time to break them in. Catching them took great skill in the use of a long springy pole with a noose at the end. One specialist among the nomads was the blacksmith, who made stirrups, knives, and other metal tools.

Kinship underlay most social relationships among the Mongols. Normally each family occupied a yurt, and groups of families camping together were usually related along the male line (brothers, uncles, nephews, and so on). More distant patrilineal relatives were recognized as members of the same clan and could call on each other for aid. People from the same clan could not marry each other, so men had to get wives from other clans. When a woman's husband died, she would be inherited by another male in the family, such as her husband's brother or his son by another woman. Tribes were groups of clans, often distantly related. Both clans and tribes had recognized chiefs who would make decisions on where to graze and when to retaliate against another tribe that had stolen animals or people. Women were sometimes abducted for brides. When tribes stole men from each other, they normally made them into slaves, and slaves were forced to do much of the heavy work. They would not necessarily remain slaves their entire lives, however, as their original tribes might be able to recapture them or make exchanges for them, or their masters might free them.

Even though population was sparse in the regions where the Mongols lived, conflict over resources was endemic, and each camp had to be on the alert for attacks. Defending against attacks and retaliating against raids was as much a part of the Mongols' daily life as caring for their herds and trading with nearby settlements.

Mongol children learned to ride at a young age, first riding on goats. The horses they later rode were short and stocky, almost like ponies, but nimble and able to endure long journeys and bitter cold. Even in the winter they survived by grazing, foraging beneath the snow. The prime weapon boys had to learn to use was the compound bow, which had a pull of about 160 pounds and a range of more than 200 yards. Other commonly used weapons were small battle-axes and lances fitted with hooks to pull enemies off their saddles.

From their teenage years Mongol men participated in battles, and among the Mongols courage in battle was essential to male self-esteem. Hunting was a common form of military training. Each year there would be one big hunt when mounted hunters would form a vast ring perhaps ten or more miles in circumference, then gradually shrink it down, trapping all the animals before killing them. On military campaigns a Mongol soldier had to be able to ride for days without stopping to cook food; he had to carry a supply of dried milk curd and cured meat, which could be supplemented by blood let from the neck of his horse. When time permitted, the soldiers would pause to hunt, adding to their food dogs, wolves, foxes, mice, and rats.

A common specialist among the Mongols was the shaman, a religious expert able to communicate with the gods. The high god of the Mongols was Heaven, but they recognized many other gods as well. Some groups of Mongols, especially those closer to settled communities, converted to Buddhism, Nestorian Christianity, or Manichaeism.

CHINGGIS KHAN AND THE MONGOL EMPIRE

How was the world changed by the Mongol conquests of much of Eurasia?

In the mid-twelfth century the Mongols were just one of many peoples in the eastern grasslands, neither particularly numerous nor especially advanced. Why did the Mongols suddenly emerge on the historical stage? One explanation is ecological. A drop in the mean annual temperature created a subsistence crisis. As pastures shrank, the Mongols and other nomads had to get more of their food from the agricultural world.

But the Mongols ended up getting much more than enough to eat. A second reason for their sudden rise is the appearance of a single individual, the brilliant but utterly ruthless Temujin (ca. 1162–1227), later called Chinggis.

Chinggis's early career was recorded in *The Secret History of the Mongols,* written within a few decades of his death. In Chinggis's youth his father had built up a modest following. When Chinggis's father was poisoned by a rival, his followers, not ready to follow a boy of twelve, drifted away, leaving Chinggis and his mother and brothers in a vulnerable position. In 1182 Chinggis was captured and carried in a cage to a rival's camp. After a daring midnight escape, he led his followers to join a stronger chieftain whom his father had once aided. With the chieftain's help, Chinggis began avenging the insults he had received.

As Chinggis subdued the Tartars, Kereyids, Naimans, Merkids, and other Mongol and Turkish tribes, he built up an army of loyal followers. He mastered the art of winning allies through displays of personal courage in battle and generosity to his followers. He also was willing to turn against former allies who proved troublesome. To those who opposed him, he could be merciless. He once asserted that nothing gave more pleasure than massacring one's enemies, seizing their horses and cattle, and ravishing their women. Sometimes Chinggis would kill all the men in a defeated tribe to prevent any later vendettas. At other times he would take them on as soldiers in his own armies. Courage impressed him. One of his leading generals, Jebe, first attracted his attention when he held his ground against overwhelming opposition and shot Chinggis's horse out from under him. Another prominent general, Mukhali, became Chinggis's personal slave at age twenty-seven after his tribe was defeated by Chinggis in 1197. Within a few years he was leading a corps of a thousand men from his own former tribe.

In 1206, at a great gathering of tribal leaders, Chinggis was proclaimed the **Great Khan.** He decreed that Mongol, until then an unwritten language, be written down in the script used by the Uighur Turks. With this script a record was made of the Mongol laws and customs, ranging from the rules for the annual hunt to punishments of death for robbery and adultery. Another measure adopted at this assembly was a postal relay system to send messages rapidly by mounted courier.

Great Khan *The title given to the Mongol ruler Chinggis in 1206 and later to his successors.*

With the tribes of Mongolia united, the energies previously devoted to infighting and vendettas were redirected to exacting tribute from the settled populations nearby, starting with the Jurchen (Jin) state that extended into north China (see Map 12.2 on page 334). In this Chinggis was following the precedent of the Jurchens, who had defeated the Khitans to get access to China's wealth a century earlier.

After Chinggis subjugated a city, he would send envoys to cities farther out to demand submission and threaten destruction. Those who opened their city gates and submitted without fighting could become allies and retain local power, but those who resisted faced the prospect of mass slaughter. He despised city dwellers and would sometimes use them as living shields in the next battle. After the Mongol armies swept across north China in 1212–1213, ninety-odd cities lay in rubble. Beijing, captured in 1215, burned for more than a month. Not surprisingly many governors of cities and rulers of small states hastened to offer submission.

Chinggis preferred conquest to administration and did not stay in north China to set up an administrative structure. He left that to subordinates and turned his attention westward, to Central Asia and Persia, then dominated by different groups of Turks. In 1218 Chinggis proposed to the Khwarizm shah of Persia that he accept Mongol overlordship and establish trade relations. The shah, to show his determination to resist, ordered the envoy and the merchants who had accompanied him killed. The next year Chinggis led an army of one hundred thousand soldiers west to retaliate. Mongol forces destroyed the shah's army and sacked one Persian city after another, demolishing buildings and massacring hundreds of thousands of people.

After returning from Central Asia, Chinggis died in 1227 during the siege of a city in northwest China. Before he died, he instructed his sons not to fall out among themselves but instead to divide the spoils.

Chinggis's Successors

khanates *The states ruled by a khan; the four units into which Chinggis divided the Mongol Empire.*

Although Mongol tribal leaders traditionally had had to win their positions, after Chinggis died the empire was divided into four **khanates,** with one of the lines of his descendants taking charge of each one. Chinggis's third son, Ögödei, became Great Khan, and he directed the next round of invasions.

In 1237 representatives of all four lines led 150,000 Mongol, Turkish, and Persian troops into Europe. During the next five years they gained control of Moscow and Kievan Russia and looted cities in Poland and Hungary. They were poised to attack deeper into Europe when they learned of the death of Ögödei in 1241. To participate in the election of a new khan, the army returned to the Mongols' new capital city, Karakorum.

Once Ögödei's son was certified as his successor, the Mongols turned their attention to Persia and the Middle East. In 1256 a Mongol army took northwest Iran, then pushed on to the Abbasid capital of Baghdad. When it fell in 1258, the last Abbasid caliph was murdered, and the population was put to the sword. The Mongol onslaught was successfully resisted, however, by both the Delhi sultanate (see page 312) and the Mamluk rulers in Egypt (see page 203).

Under Chinggis's grandson Khubilai (r. 1260–1294) the Mongols completed their conquest of China. South China had never been captured by non-Chinese, in large part because horses were of no strategic advantage in a land of rivers and canals. Perhaps because they were entering a very different type of terrain, the Mongols proceeded deliberately. First they surrounded the Song empire by taking its westernmost province in 1252, destroying the Nanzhao kingdom in modern Yunnan in 1254, and then continuing south and taking Annam (northern Vietnam) in 1257. A surrendered Song commander advised them to build a navy to attack the great Song cities located on rivers. During the five-year siege of a central Chinese river port, both sides used thousands of boats and tens of thousands of troops. The Mongols employed experts in naval and siege warfare from all over their empire—Chinese, Korean, Jurchen, Uighur, and Persian. Catapults designed by Muslim engineers launched a barrage of rocks weighing up to a hundred pounds each. During their advance toward the Chinese capital of Hangzhou, the Mongols ordered the total slaughter of the people of the major city of Changzhou, and in 1276 the Chinese empress dowager surrendered in hopes of sparing the people of the capital a similar fate.

Having overrun China and Korea, Khubilai turned his eyes toward Japan. In 1274 a force of 30,000 soldiers and support personnel sailed from Korea to Japan. In 1281 a combined Mongol and Chinese fleet of about 150,000 made a second attempt to conquer Japan. On both occasions the Mongols managed to land but were beaten back by Japanese samurai armies. Each time fierce storms destroyed the Mongol fleets. The Japanese claimed that they had been saved by the *kamikaze,* the "divine wind" (which later lent its name to the thousands of Japanese aviators who crashed their airplanes into American warships during World War II). A decade later, in 1293, Khubilai tried sending a fleet to the islands of Southeast Asia, including Java, but it met with no more success than the fleets sent to Japan.

Why were the Mongols so successful against so many different types of enemies? Even though their population was tiny compared to the populations of the large agricultural societies they conquered, their tactics, their weapons, and their organization all gave them advantages. Like other nomads before them, they were superb horsemen and excellent archers. Their horses were extremely nimble, able to change direction quickly, thus allowing the Mongols to maneuver easily and ride through infantry forces armed with swords, lances, and javelins. Usually the only armies that could stand up well against the Mongols were other nomadic ones like the Turks.

Marco Polo left a vivid description of the Mongol soldiers' endurance and military skill:

Mongol Conquests

1206	Chinggis made Great Khan
1215	Fall of Beijing (Jurchens)
1219–1220	Fall of Bukhara and Samarkand in Central Asia
1227	Death of Chinggis
1237–1241	Raids into eastern Europe
1257	Conquest of Annam (northern Vietnam)
1258	Conquest of Abbasid capital of Baghdad Conquest of Korea
1260	Accession of Khubilai
1274	First attempt at invading Japan
1276	Surrender of Song Dynasty (China)
1281	Second attempt at invading Japan
1293	Expedition to Java
mid-14th century	Decline of Mongol power; ouster or absorption

They are brave in battle, almost to desperation, setting little value upon their lives, and exposing themselves without hesitation to all manner of danger. Their disposition is cruel. They are capable of supporting every kind of privation, and when there is a necessity for it, can live for a month on the milk of their mares, and upon such wild animals as they may chance to catch. The men are habituated to remain on horseback during two days and two nights, without dismounting, sleeping in that situation whilst their horses graze. No people on earth can surpass them in fortitude under difficulties, nor show greater patience under wants of every kind.[4]

The Mongols were also open to new military technologies and did not insist on fighting in their traditional ways. To attack walled cities, they learned how to use catapults and other engines of war. At first they employed Chinese catapults, but when they later learned that those used by the Turks in Afghanistan were half again as powerful, they quickly adopted the better model. The Mongols also used exploding arrows and gunpowder projectiles developed by the Chinese.

Because of his early experiences with intertribal feuding, Chinggis mistrusted traditional Mongol tribal loyalties, and as he fashioned a new army, he gave it a new, nontribal structure. Chinggis also created an elite bodyguard of ten thousand sons and brothers of commanders, which served directly under him. Chinggis allowed commanders to pass their posts to their sons, but he could remove them at will. Marco Polo explained the decimal hierarchy of his armies this way:

When one of the great Tartar chiefs proceeds on an expedition, he puts himself at the head of an army of a hundred thousand horses, and organizes them in the following manner. He appoints an officer to the command of every ten men, and others to command a hundred, a thousand, and ten thousand men, respectively. Thus ten of the officers commanding ten men take their orders from him who commands a hundred; of these, each ten, from him who

Primary Source:
Description of the World
Follow Marco Polo, and hear him relate the natural—and sometimes supernatural—wonders he encountered on his journey to Khubilai Khan.

commands a thousand; and each ten of these latter, from him who commands ten thousand. By this arrangement each officer has only to attend to the management of ten men or ten bodies of men.[5]

The Mongols also made good use of intelligence and tried to exploit internal divisions in the countries they attacked. Thus, in north China they appealed to the Khitans, who had been defeated by the Jurchens a century earlier, to join them in attacking the Jurchens. In Syria they exploited the resentment of Christians against their Muslim rulers.

The Mongols as Rulers

The success of the Mongols in ruling vast territories was due in large part to their willingness to incorporate other ethnic groups into their armies and governments. Whatever their original country or religion, those who served the Mongols loyally were rewarded and given important posts. Uighurs, Tibetans, Persians, Chinese, and Russians came to hold powerful positions in the Mongol government. Chinese helped breach the walls of Baghdad in the 1250s, and Muslims operated the catapults that helped reduce Chinese cities in the 1270s. Mongol armies incorporated the armies they vanquished and in time had large numbers of Turkish troops.

Since, in Mongol eyes, the purpose of fighting was to gain riches, they regularly would loot the settlements they conquered, taking whatever they wanted, including the residents. Land would be granted to military commanders, nobles, and army units, to be governed and exploited as the recipients wished. Those who had worked on the land would be given to them as serfs. The Mongols built a capital city called Karakorum in modern Mongolia, and to bring it up to the level of the cities they

● **Gold-Decorated Saddle**   The Mongols, like earlier nomads, prized fine metalwork. The gold panels that decorate this saddle were found in the tomb of a Mongol girl of about eighteen. The central motif of the front arch is a reclining deer; surrounding it are peonies. *(Collection of Inner Mongolia Autonomous Region Museum, Hohhot City, China)*

conquered, they transported skilled workers from those cities. For instance, after Bukhara and Samarkand were captured in 1219–1220, some thirty thousand artisans were seized and transported to Mongolia (see Map 11.1). Sometimes these slaves gradually improved their status. A French goldsmith working in Budapest named Guillaume Boucher was captured by the Mongols in 1242 and taken to Karakorum, where he lived for at least the next fifteen years. He gradually won favor and was put in charge of fifty workers to make gold and silver vessels for the Mongol court.

The traditional nomad disdain for farmers led some commanders to suggest turning north China into a gigantic pasture after it was conquered. In time, though, the Mongols came to realize that simply appropriating the wealth and human resources of the settled lands was not as good as extracting regular revenue from them. A Sinified Khitan who had been working for the Jurchens in China explained to the Mongols that collecting taxes from farmers would be highly profitable: they could extract a revenue of 500,000 ounces of silver, 80,000 bolts of silk, and more than 20,000 tons of grain from the region by taxing it. The Mongols gave this a try, but soon political rivals convinced the khan that he would gain even more by letting Central Asian Muslim merchants bid against each other for licenses to collect taxes any way they could, a system called **tax-farming.** Ordinary Chinese found this method of tax collecting much more oppressive than traditional Chinese methods, since there was little to keep the tax collectors from seizing everything they could.

tax-farming *Assigning the collection of taxes to whoever bids the most for the privilege.*

By the second half of the thirteenth century there was no longer a genuine pan-Asian Mongol Empire. Much of Asia was in the hands of Mongol successor states, but these were generally hostile to each other. Khubilai was often at war with the khanate of Central Asia, then held by his cousin Khaidu, and he had little contact with the khanate of the Golden Horde in south Russia. The Mongols adapted their methods of government to the existing traditions of each place they ruled, and the regions now went their separate ways.

In China the Mongols resisted assimilation and purposely avoided many Chinese social and political practices. The rulers conducted their business in the Mongol language and spent their summers in Mongolia. Khubilai discouraged Mongols from marrying Chinese and took only Mongol women into the palace. Some Mongol princes preferred to live in yurts erected on the palace grounds rather than in the grand palaces constructed at Beijing. Chinese were treated as legally inferior not only to the Mongols but also to all other non-Chinese.

In Central Asia, Persia, and Russia the Mongols tended to merge with the Turkish groups already there and like them converted to Islam. Russia in the thirteenth century was not a strongly centralized state, and the Mongols were satisfied to see Russian princes and lords continue to rule their territories as long as they turned over adequate tribute (which, of course, added to the burden on peasants). The city of Moscow became the center of Mongol tribute collection and grew in importance at the expense of Kiev. In the Middle East the Mongol Il-khans were more active as rulers, again continuing the traditions of the caliphate. In Mongolia itself, however, Mongol traditions were maintained.

Mongol control in each of the khanates lasted about a century. In the mid-fourteenth century the Mongol dynasty in China deteriorated into civil war, and in the 1360s the Mongols withdrew back to Mongolia. There was a similar loss of Mongol power in Persia and Central Asia. Only on the south Russian steppe was the Golden Horde able to maintain its hold for another century. As Mongol rule in Central Asia declined, a new conqueror emerged, known as Tamerlane (Timur the Lame). Not a nomad but a highly civilized Turkish noble, Tamerlane in the 1360s struck out from his base in Samarkand into Persia, north India, southern Russia, and beyond. His armies used the terror tactics that the Mongols had perfected, massacring the citizens of cities that resisted. With his death in 1405, however, Tamerlane's empire fell apart.

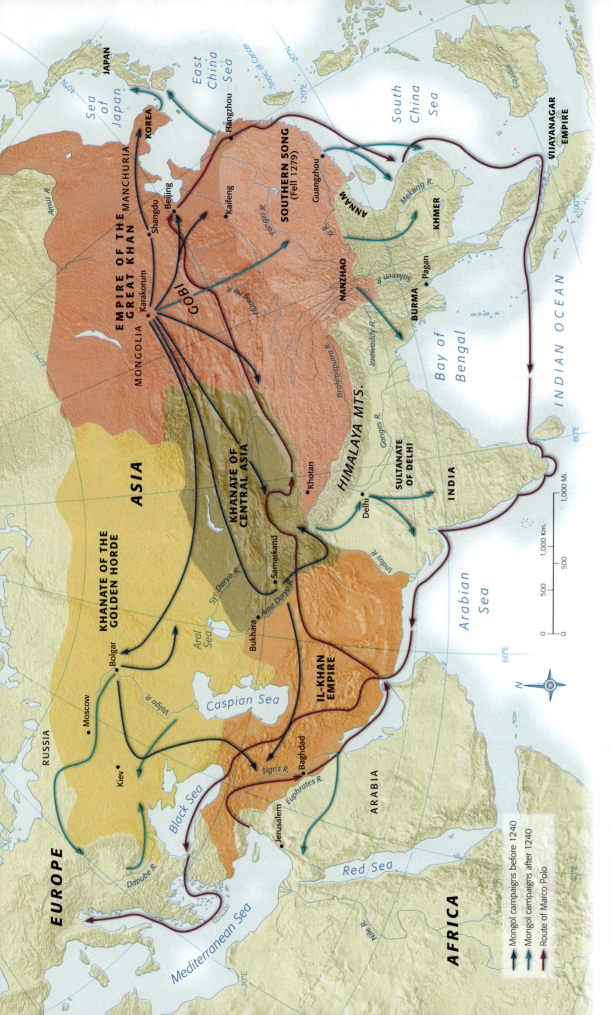

MAP 11.1 **The Mongol Empire** The creation of the vast Mongol Empire facilitated communication across Eurasia and led to both the spread of deadly plagues and the transfer of technical and scientific knowledge. After the death of Chinggis in 1227, the empire was divided into four khanates, ruled by different lines of his successors. In the 1270s the Mongols conquered southern China, but most of their subsequent campaigns did not lead to further territorial gains.

→ Mongol campaigns before 1240
→ Mongol campaigns after 1240
→ Route of Marco Polo

EUROPE

ASIA

AFRICA

RUSSIA
• Moscow
• Kiev

KHANATE OF THE
GOLDEN HORDE
• Bolgar

Caspian Sea

Aral Sea

KHANATE OF
CENTRAL ASIA

MONGOLIA

EMPIRE OF THE
GREAT KHAN

MANCHURIA

KOREA

JAPAN

Karakorum •

Shangdu •

Beijing •

Kaifeng •

Hangzhou •

SOUTHERN SONG
(Fell 1279)

Guangzhou •

GOBI

Khotan •

HIMALAYA MTS.

NANZHAO

ANNAM

KHMER

BURMA
• Pagan

Delhi •

SULTANATE
OF DELHI

INDIA

VIJAYANAGAR
EMPIRE

Samarkand •
Bukhara •

IL-KHAN
EMPIRE

Baghdad •

Jerusalem •

ARABIA

Tigris R.
Euphrates R.

Red Sea

Nile R.

Mediterranean Sea

Black Sea

Danube R.

Volga R.

Syr Darya R.
Amu Darya R.

Indus R.

Ganges R.

Brahmaputra R.

Huang He R.

Yangzi R.

Xi R.

Mekong R.

Salween R.

Irrawaddy R.

Amur R.

Arabian Sea

Bay of
Bengal

INDIAN OCEAN

East China Sea

Sea of Japan

South China Sea

Tropic of Cancer

Equator

N

0   500   1,000 Mi.
0   500   1,000 Km.

40°E   60°E   80°E   100°E   120°E

20°N   40°N

EAST-WEST COMMUNICATION DURING THE MONGOL ERA

How did the Mongol conquests facilitate the spread of ideas, religions, inventions, and diseases?

The Mongol governments did more than any earlier political entities to encourage the movement of people and goods across Eurasia. The Mongols had never looked down on merchants the way the elites of many traditional states did, and they welcomed the arrival of merchants from distant lands. Even when different groups of Mongols were fighting among themselves, they usually allowed caravans to pass unharassed.

The Mongol practice of transporting skilled people from the lands they conquered also brought people into contact with each other in new ways. Besides those forced to move, the Mongols recruited administrators from all over. Chinese, Persians, and Arabs served the Mongols, and the Mongols often sent them far from home. Especially prominent were the Uighur Turks of Chinese Central Asia, whose familiarity with Chinese civilization and fluency in Turkish were extremely valuable in facilitating communication. Literate Uighurs were many of the clerks and administrators running the Mongol administration.

One of the most interesting of those who served the Mongols was Rashid al-Din (ca. 1247–1318). A Jew from Persia and the son of an apothecary, Rashid al-Din converted to Islam at the age of thirty and entered the service of the Mongol Il-khan of Persia as a physician. He rose in government service, traveled widely, and eventually became prime minister. Rashid al-Din became friends with the ambassador from China, and together they arranged for translations of Chinese works on medicine, agronomy, and statecraft. He had ideas on economic management that he communicated to Mongol officials in Central Asia and China. Aware of the great differences between cultures, he believed that the Mongols should try to rule in accord with the moral principles of the majority in each land. On that basis he convinced the Mongol khan of Persia to convert to Islam. Rashid al-Din undertook to explain the great variety of cultures by writing a history of the world that was much more comprehensive than any previously written.

The Mongols were remarkably open to religious experts from all the lands they encountered. More Europeans made their way as far as Mongolia and China in the Mongol period than ever before. Popes and kings sent envoys to the Mongol court in the hope of enlisting the Mongols on their side in their long-standing conflict with Muslim forces over the Holy Land. These and other European visitors were especially interested in finding Christians who had been cut off from the West by the

● **Depictions of Europeans** The Mongol Empire, by facilitating travel across Asia, increased knowledge of faraway lands. Rashid al-Din's *History of the World* included a history of the Franks, illustrated here with images of Western popes (*left*) conferring with Byzantine emperors (*right*). *(Topkapi Saray Museum, Ms. H.1654, fol. 303a)*

spread of Islam, and in fact there were considerable numbers of Nestorian Christians in Central Asia. In 1245 Pope Innocent IV wrote two letters to the "King and people of the Tartars" that were delivered to a Mongol general in Armenia. The next year another envoy, Giovanni di Pian de Carpine, reached the Volga River and the camp of Batu, the khan of the Golden Horde. Batu sent him on to the new Great Khan in Karakorum with two Mongol guides, riding so fast that they had to change horses five to seven times a day. Their full journey of more than three thousand miles took five and a half months. Carpine spent four months at the Great Khan's court but never succeeded in convincing the Great Khan to embrace Christianity or drop his demand that the pope appear in person to tender his submission. When Carpine returned, he wrote a report that urged preparation for a renewed Mongol attack on Europe. The Mongols had to be resisted "because of the harsh, indeed intolerable, and hitherto unheard-of slavery seen with our own eyes, to which they reduce all peoples who have submitted to them."[6]

A few years later, in 1253, Flemish friar William of Rubruck set out with the permission of King Louis IX of France as a missionary to convert the Mongols. He too made his way to Karakorum, where he found many Europeans. At Easter, Hungarians, Russians, Georgians, Armenians, and Alans all took communion in a Nestorian church. Rubruck also gathered some information about China while in Mongolia, such as the Chinese use of paper money and practice of writing with a brush.

The most famous European visitor to the Mongol lands was the Venetian Marco Polo. In his famous *Travels,* Marco Polo described all the places he visited or learned about during his seventeen years away from home. He reported being warmly received by Khubilai, who impressed him enormously. He was also awed by the wealth and splendor of Chinese cities and spread the notion of Asia as a land of riches. Even in Marco Polo's lifetime, some skeptics did not believe his tale, and today some scholars speculate that he may have learned about China from Persian merchants he met in the Middle East without actually going to China. But Marco Polo also has staunch

● **Horse and Groom** Zhao Mengfu (1254–1322), the artist of this painting and a member of the Song imperial family, took up service under the Mongol emperor Khubilai. The Mongol rulers, great horsemen themselves, would likely have appreciated this depiction of a horse buffeted by the wind. *(National Palace Museum, Taipei, Taiwan)*

defenders, even though they admit that he stretched the truth in more than one place to make himself look good. One leading Mongol scholar titled his review of the controversy "Marco Polo Went to China."[7] Regardless of the final verdict on Marco Polo's veracity, there is no doubt that the great popularity of his book contributed to European interest in finding new routes to Asia.

The more rapid transfer of people and goods across Central Asia spread more than ideas and inventions. It also spread diseases, the most deadly of which was the plague known in Europe as the Black Death. Scholars once thought that this plague was the bubonic plague, transmitted through rats and fleas, but some scholars now question that supposition. What is known is that it spread from Central Asia into West Asia, the Mediterranean, and western Europe. When the Mongols were assaulting the city of Kaffa in the Crimea in 1346, they themselves were infected by the plague and had to withdraw. They purposely spread the disease to their enemy by catapulting the bodies of victims into the city. Soon the disease was carried from port to port throughout the Mediterranean by ship. The confusion of the mid-fourteenth century that led to the loss of Mongol power in China, Iran, and Central Asia undoubtedly owes something to the effect of the spread of the plague and other diseases.

Traditionally, the historians of each of the countries conquered by the Mongols portrayed them as a scourge. Russian historians, for instance, saw this as a period of bondage that set Russia back and cut it off from western Europe. Today it is more common to celebrate the genius of the Mongol military machine and treat the spread of ideas and inventions as an obvious good, probably because we see global communication as a good in our own world. There is no reason to assume, however, that every person or every society benefited equally from the improved communications and the new political institutions of the Mongol era. Merchants involved in long-distance trade prospered, but those enslaved and transported hundreds or thousands of miles from home would have seen themselves not as the beneficiaries of opportunities to encounter cultures different from their own, but rather as the most pitiable of victims.

The places that were ruled by Mongol governments for a century or more—China, Central Asia, Persia, and Russia—do not seem to have advanced at a more rapid rate during that century than they did in earlier centuries, either economically or culturally. By Chinese standards Mongol imposition of hereditary status distinctions was a step backward from a much more mobile and open society, and placing Persians, Arabs, or Tibetans over Chinese did not arouse interest in foreign cultures. Much more foreign music and foreign styles in clothing, art, and furnishings were integrated into Chinese civilization in Tang times than in Mongol times.

In terms of the spread of technological and scientific ideas, Europe seems to have been by far the main beneficiary of increased communication, largely because in 1200 it lagged farther behind than the other areas. Chinese inventions such as printing, gunpowder, and the compass spread westward. Persian and Indian expertise in astronomy and mathematics also spread. In terms of the spread of religions, Islam

● **Kalyan Minaret** The Silk Road city of Bukhara (in today's Uzbekistan) is still graced by a 48-meter-tall minaret completed in 1127. Made of baked bricks laid in ornamental patterns, it is topped by a rotunda with sixteen arched windows, from which local Muslims were called to prayer five times a day. In times of war, the minaret could also serve as a watchtower. *(C. Rennie/Robert Harding World Imagery)*

probably gained the most. It spread into Chinese Central Asia, which had previously been Buddhist.

Perhaps because it was not invaded itself, Europe also seems to have been energized by the Mongol-imposed peace in ways that the other major civilizations were not. The goods from China and elsewhere in the East brought by merchants like Marco Polo to Europe whetted the appetites of Europeans for increased contacts with the East, and the demand for Asian goods eventually culminated in the great age of European exploration and expansion (see Chapter 15). By comparison, in areas the Mongols had directly attacked, protecting their own civilization became a higher priority than drawing from the outside to enrich or enlarge it.

INDIA (300–1400)

How did India respond to its encounters with Turks, Mongols, and Islam?

South Asia, far from the heartland of the steppe, still felt the impact of developments there. Over the course of many centuries, the Shakas, Huns, Turks, and Mongols all sent armies south to raid or invade north India.

Chapter 2 traces the early development of Indian civilization, including the emergence of the principal religious traditions of Hinduism, Buddhism, and Jainism; the impact of the Persian and Greek invasions; and the Mauryan Empire, with its great pro-Buddhist king, Ashoka. As discussed at the end of that chapter, after the Mauryan Empire broke apart in 184 B.C.E., India was politically divided into small kingdoms for several centuries.

The Gupta Empire (ca. 320–480)

In the early fourth century a state emerged in the Ganges plain that was able to bring large parts of north India under its control. The rulers of this Indian empire, the Guptas, consciously modeled their rule after that of the Mauryan Empire, and the founder took the name of the founder of that dynasty, Chandragupta. Although the Guptas never controlled as much territory as the Mauryans had, they united north India and received tribute from states in Nepal and the Indus Valley, thus giving large parts of India a period of peace and political unity.

The Guptas' administrative system was not as centralized as that of the Mauryans. In the central regions they drew their revenue from a tax on agriculture of one-quarter of the harvest and maintained monopolies on key products such as metals and salt (reminiscent of Chinese practice). They also exacted labor service for the construction and upkeep of roads, wells, and irrigation systems. More distant areas were assigned to governors who were allowed considerable leeway, and governorships often became hereditary. Areas still farther away were encouraged to become vassal states, able to participate in the splendor of the capital and royal court in subordinate roles and to engage in profitable trade, but not required to turn over much in the way of revenue.

The Gupta kings were patrons of the arts. Poets composed epics for the courts of the Gupta kings, and other writers experimented with prose romances and popular tales. India's greatest poet, Kalidasa (ca. 380–450), like Shakespeare, wrote poems as well as plays in verse. His most highly esteemed play, *Shakuntala*, concerns a daughter of a hermit who enthralls a king out hunting. The king sets up house with her, then returns to his court and owing to a curse forgets her. Only much later does he acknowledge their child as his true heir. Equally loved is Kalidasa's one-hundred-verse poem "The Cloud Messenger," about a demigod who asks a passing cloud to carry a message to his wife, from whom he has long been separated. At one point he instructs the cloud to tell her:

● **Wall Painting at Ajanta**   Many of the best surviving examples of Gupta period painting are found at the twenty-nine Buddhist cave temples at Ajanta in central India. The walls of these caves were decorated in the fifth and sixth centuries with scenes from the former lives of the Buddha. These two scenes, showing a royal couple on the right and a princess and her attendants on the left, offer us glimpses of what the royal courts of the period must have looked like. *(Benoy K. Behl)*

I see your body in the sinuous creeper, your gaze in the startled eyes of deer,
your cheek in the moon, your hair in the plumage of peacocks,
and in the tiny ripples of the river I see your sidelong glances,
but alas, my dearest, nowhere do I see your whole likeness.[8]

In mathematics, too, the Gupta period could boast of impressive intellectual achievements. The so-called Arabic numerals were actually of Indian origin. Indian mathematicians developed the place-value notation system, with separate columns for ones, tens, and hundreds, as well as a zero sign to indicate the absence of units in a given column. This system greatly facilitated calculation and spread as far as Europe by the seventh century.

The Gupta rulers were Hindus but tolerated all faiths. Buddhist pilgrims from other areas of Asia reported that Buddhist monasteries with hundreds or even thousands of monks and nuns flourished in the cities.

The great crisis of the Gupta Empire was the invasion of the Huns. The migration of these nomads from Central Asia shook much of Eurasia. Around 450 a group of them known as the White Huns thundered into India. Mustering his full might, the ruler Skandagupta (r. ca. 455–467) threw back the invaders. Although the Huns failed to uproot the Gupta Empire, they dealt the dynasty a fatal blow.

India's Medieval Age (ca. 500–1400) and the First Encounter with Islam

After the decline of the Gupta Empire, India once again broke into separate kingdoms that were frequently at war with each other. Most of the dynasties were short-lived, but a balance of power was maintained between the four major regions of India, with none gaining enough of an advantage to conquer the others. Particularly notable are

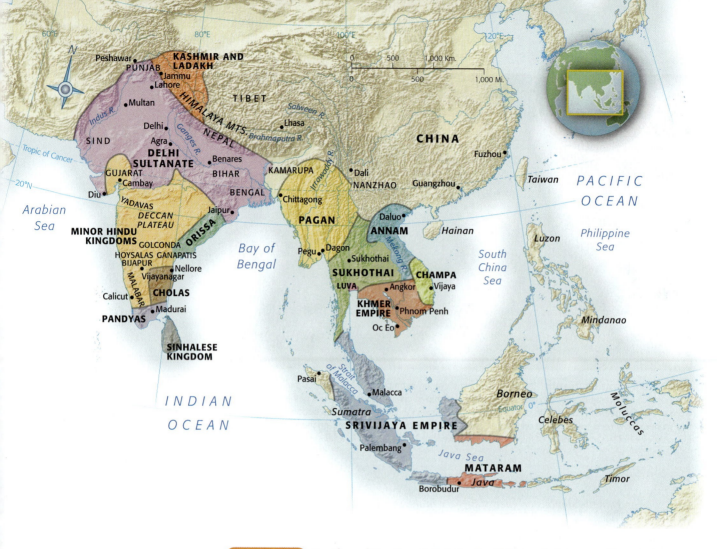

MAP 11.2 **South and Southeast Asia in the Thirteenth Century** The extensive coastlines of South and Southeast Asia and the predictable monsoon winds aided seafaring in this region. Note the Strait of Malacca, through which most east-west sea trade passed.

the Cholas, who dominated the southern tip of the peninsula, Sri Lanka, and much of the eastern Indian Ocean to the twelfth century (see Map 11.2).

Political division fostered the development of regional cultures. Literature came to be written in regional languages, among them Marathi, Bengali, and Assamese. Commerce continued as before, and the coasts of India remained important in the sea trade of the Indian Ocean.

The first encounters with Islam occurred in this period. In 711, after pirates had plundered a richly laden Arab ship near the mouth of the Indus, the Umayyad governor of Iraq sent a force with six thousand horses and six thousand camels to seize the Sind area. The western part of India remained a part of the caliphate for centuries, but Islam did not spread much beyond this foothold. During the ninth and tenth centuries Turks from Central Asia moved into the region of today's northeastern Iran and western Afghanistan, then known as Khurasan. Converts to Islam, they first served as military forces for the caliphate in Baghdad, but as its authority weakened (see pages 200–203), they made themselves rulers of an effectively independent Khurasan and frequently sent raiding parties into north India. Beginning in 997, Mahmud of Ghazni (r. 997–1030) led seventeen annual forays into India from his base in modern Afghanistan. His goal was plunder to finance his wars against other Turkish rulers in

Central Asia. Toward this end, he systematically looted Indian palaces and temples, viewing religious statues as infidels' idols. Eventually even the Arab conquerors of the Sind fell to the Turks. By 1030 the Indus Valley, the Punjab, and the rest of northwest India were in the grip of the Turks.

The new rulers encouraged the spread of Islam, but the Indian caste system made it difficult to convert higher-caste Indians. Al-Biruni (d. 1048), a Persian scholar who spent much of his later life at the court of Mahmud and learned Sanskrit, gave some thought to the obstacles to Hindu-Muslim communication. The most basic barrier, he wrote, was language, but the religious gulf was also fundamental:

They totally differ from us in religion, as we believe in nothing in which they believe, and vice versa. On the whole, there is very little disputing about theological topics among them; at the utmost they fight with words, but they will never stake their soul or body or property on religious controversy. . . . They call foreigners impure and forbid having any connection with them, be it by intermarriage or any kind of relationship, or by sitting, eating, and drinking with them, because thereby, they think, they would be polluted.[9]

After the initial period of raids and destruction of temples, the Muslim Turks came to an accommodation with the Hindus, who were classed as a **protected people,** like the Christians and Jews, and allowed to follow their religion. They had to pay a special tax but did not have to perform military service. Local chiefs and rajas were often allowed to remain in control of their domains as long as they paid tribute. Most Indians looked on the Muslim conquerors as a new ruling caste, capable of governing and taxing them but otherwise peripheral to their lives. The myriad castes largely governed themselves, isolating the newcomers. Nevertheless, over the course of several centuries Islam gained a strong hold on north India, especially in the Indus Valley (modern Pakistan) and in Bengal at the mouth of the Ganges River (modern Bangladesh). Moreover, the sultanate seems to have had a positive effect on the economy. Much of the wealth confiscated from temples was put to more productive use, and India's first truly large cities emerged. The Turks also were eager to employ skilled workers, giving new opportunities to low-caste manual and artisan labor.

The Muslim rulers were much more hostile to Buddhism than to Hinduism, seeing Buddhism as a competitive proselytizing religion. In 1193 a Turkish raiding party destroyed the great Buddhist university at Nalanda in Bihar. Buddhist monks were killed or forced to flee to Buddhist centers in Southeast Asia, Nepal, and Tibet. Buddhism, which had thrived for so long in peaceful and friendly competition with Hinduism, was forced out of its native land.

Hinduism, however, remained as strong as ever. South India was largely unaffected by these invasions, and traditional Hindu culture flourished

protected people *The Muslim classification used for Hindus, Christians, and Jews; they were allowed to follow their religions but had to pay a special tax.*

● **Hindu Temple** Medieval Hindu temples were frequently decorated with scenes of sexual passion. Here Vishnu caresses Lakshami at the Parshvinath Temple. *(Richard Ashworth/Robert Harding World Imagery)*

there under native kings ruling small kingdoms (see the feature "Individuals in Society: Bhaskara the Teacher"). Temple-centered Hinduism flourished, as did devotional cults and mystical movements. This was a great age of religious art and architecture in India. Extraordinary temples covered with elaborate bas-relief were built in many areas. Sexual passion and the union of men and women were frequently depicted, symbolically representing passion for and union with the temple god.

In the twelfth century a new line of Turkish rulers arose in Afghanistan, led by Muhammad of Ghur (d. 1206). Muhammad captured Delhi and extended his control nearly throughout north India. When Muhammad of Ghur fell to an assassin in 1206, one of his generals, the former slave Qutb-ud-din, seized the reins of power and established a government at Delhi, separate from the government in Afghanistan. This sultanate of Delhi lasted for three centuries, even though dynasties changed several times.

The North African Muslim world traveler Ibn Battuta (1304–1368) (see page 213), who journeyed through Africa and Asia from 1325 to 1354, served for several years as a judge at the court of one of the Delhi sultans. He praised the sultan for his insistence on the observance of ritual prayers and many acts of generosity to those in need, but he also considered the sultan overly violent. Here is just one of many examples he offered of how quick the sultan was to execute:

During the years of the famine, the Sultan had given orders to dig wells outside the capital, and have grain crops sown in those parts. He provided the cultivators with the seed, as well as with all that was necessary for cultivation in the way of money and supplies, and required them to cultivate these crops for the [royal] grain-store. When the jurist 'Afif al-Din heard of this, he said, "This crop will not produce what is hoped for." Some informer told the Sultan what he had said, so the Sultan jailed him, and said to him, "What reason have you to meddle with the government's business?" Some time later he released him, and as 'Afif al-Din went to his house he was met on the way by two friends of his, also jurists, who said to him, "Praise be to God for your release," to which our jurist replied, "Praise be to God who has delivered us from the evildoers." They then separated, but they had not reached their houses before this was reported to the Sultan, and he commanded all three to be fetched and brought before him. "Take out this fellow," he said, referring to 'Afif al-Din, "and cut off his head baldrickwise," that is, the head is cut off along with an arm and part of the chest, "and behead the other two." They said to him, "He deserves punishment, to be sure, for what he said, but in our case for what crime are you killing us?" He replied, "You heard what he said and did not disavow it, so you as good as agreed with it." So they were all put to death, God Most High have mercy on them.[10]

A major accomplishment of the Delhi sultanate was holding off the Mongols. Chinggis Khan and his troops entered the Indus Valley in 1221 in pursuit of the shah of Khurasan. The sultan wisely kept out of the way, and when Chinggis left some troops in the area, the sultan made no attempt to challenge them. Two generations later, in 1299, a Mongol khan launched a campaign into India with two hundred thousand men, but the sultan of the time was able to defeat them. Two years later the Mongols returned and camped at Delhi for two months, but they eventually left without taking the sultan's fort. Another Mongol raid in 1306–1307 also was successfully repulsed.

Although the Turks by this time were highly cosmopolitan, they had retained their martial skills and understanding of steppe warfare. They were expert horsemen, and horses thrived in northwest India. The south and east of India, like the south of China, were less hospitable to raising horses and generally had to import them. In India's case, though, the climate of the south and east was well suited to elephants, which had been used as weapons of war in India since early times. Rulers in the northwest imported elephants from more tropical regions. The Delhi sultanate is said to have had as many as one thousand war elephants at its height.

During the fourteenth century, however, the Delhi sultanate was in decline and proved unable to ward off the armies of Tamerlane (see page 303), who took Delhi in

Bhaskara the Teacher

In India, as in many other societies, astronomy and mathematics were closely linked, and many of the most important mathematicians served their rulers as astronomers. Bhaskara (1114–ca. 1185) was such an astronomer-mathematician. For generations his Brahman family had been astronomers at the Ujjain astronomical observatory in north-central India, and his father had written a popular book on astrology.

Bhaskara was a highly erudite man. A disciple wrote that he had thoroughly mastered eight books on grammar, six on medicine, six on philosophy, five on mathematics, and the four Vedas. Bhaskara eventually wrote six books on mathematics and mathematical astronomy. They deal with solutions to simple and quadratic equations and show his knowledge of trigonometry, including the sine table and relationships between different trigonometric functions, and even some of the basic elements of calculus. Earlier Indian mathematicians had explored the use of zero and negative numbers. Bhaskara developed these ideas further, in particular improving on the understanding of division by zero.

A court poet who centuries later translated Bhaskara's book titled *The Beautiful* explained its title by saying Bhaskara wrote it for his daughter named Beautiful (Lilavati) as consolation when his divination of the best time for her to marry went awry. Whether or not Bhaskara wrote this book for his daughter, many of the problems he provides in it have a certain charm:

On an expedition to seize his enemy's elephants, a king marched two yojanas the first day. Say, intelligent calculator, with what increasing rate of daily march did he proceed, since he reached his foe's city, a distance of eighty yojanas, in a week?*

Out of a heap of pure lotus flower, a third part, a fifth, and a sixth were offered respectively to the gods Siva, Vishnu, and the Sun; and a quarter was presented to Bhavani. The remaining six lotuses were given to the venerable preceptor. Tell quickly the whole number of lotus.†

If eight best variegated silk scarfs, measuring three cubits in breadth and eight in length, cost a hundred nishkas, say quickly, merchant, if thou understand trade, what a like scarf, three and a half cubits long and half a cubit wide will cost.‡

In the conclusion to *The Beautiful,* Bhaskara wrote:

Joy and happiness is indeed ever increasing in this world for those who have The Beautiful *clasped to their throats, decorated as the members are with neat reduction of fractions, multiplication, and involution, pure and perfect as are the solutions, and tasteful as is the speech which is exemplified.*

The observatory where Bhaskara worked in Ujjain today stands in ruins. *(Dinodia Picture Agency)*

Bhaskara had a long career. His first book on mathematical astronomy, written in 1150 when he was thirty-six, dealt with such topics as the calculation of solar and lunar eclipses or planetary conjunctions. Thirty-three years later he was still writing on the subject, this time providing simpler ways to solve problems encountered before. Bhaskara wrote his books in Sanskrit, already a literary language rather than a vernacular language, but even in his own day some of them were translated into other Indian languages.

Within a couple of decades of his death, a local ruler endowed an educational institution to study Bhaskara's works, beginning with his work on mathematical astronomy. In the text he had inscribed at the site, the ruler gave the names of Bhaskara's ancestors for six generations, as well as of his son and grandson, who had continued in his profession.

Questions for Analysis

1. What are the advantages of making occupations like astronomer hereditary?
2. Do you think there are connections between Bhaskara's broad erudition and his accomplishments as a mathematician?

*Quotations from Haran Chandra Banerji, *Colebrooke's Translation of the Lilanvanti,* 2d ed. (Calcutta: The Book Co., 1927), pp. 80–81, 30, 51, 200. The answer is that each day he must travel 22/7 yojanas farther than the day before.
†The answer is 120.
‡The answer, from the formula $x = (1 \times 7 \times 1 \times 100) / (8 \times 3 \times 8 \times 2 \times 2)$, is given in currencies smaller than the nishka: 14 drammas, 9 panas, 1 kakini, and 6⅔ cowry shells. (20 cowry shells = 1 kakini, 4 kakini = 1 pana, 16 panas = 1 dramma, and 16 drammas = 1 nishka.)

● **The God Ganesha** Known as the Destroyer of Obstacles, the elephant-headed Ganesha is one of the best-loved gods in the Hindu pantheon, invoked by those in need of a solution to a difficult situation. This stone sculpture was carved in southern India in the thirteenth century and is 37 inches tall. *(Gift of the de Young Museum Society Auxiliary, B68S4. © Asian Art Museum of San Fransisco. Used by permisson)*

1398. Tamerlane's chronicler reported that when the troops drew up for battle outside Delhi, the sultanate had 10,000 horsemen, 20,000 foot soldiers, and 120 war elephants with archers riding on them. Though alarmed at the sight of the elephants, Tamerlane's men dug trenches to trap them and also shot at their drivers. The sultan fled, leaving the city to surrender. Tamerlane took as booty all the elephants, loading them with treasures seized from the city. Ruy Gonzalez de Clavijo, an ambassador from the king of Castile who arrived in Samarkand in 1403, was greatly impressed by these well-trained elephants. "When all the elephants together charged abreast, it seemed as though the solid earth itself shook at their onrush," he observed, noting that he thought each elephant was worth a thousand foot soldiers in battle.[11]

Daily Life in Medieval India

To the overwhelming majority of people in medieval India, the size of the territory controlled by their king did not matter much. Local institutions played a much larger role in their lives than did the state. Guilds oversaw conditions of work and trade; local councils handled law and order at the town or village level; local castes gave members a sense of belonging and identity.

Like peasant societies elsewhere, including in China, Japan, and Southeast Asia, agricultural life in India ordinarily meant village life. The average farmer worked a small plot of land outside the village. All the family members pooled their resources—human, animal, and material—under the direction of the head of the family. Joint struggles strengthened family solidarity.

The agricultural year began with spring plowing. The ancient plow, drawn by two oxen wearing yokes and collars, had an iron-tipped share and a handle with which the farmer guided it. Rice, the most important and popular grain, was sown at the beginning of the long rainy season. Beans, lentils, and peas were the farmer's friends, for they grew during the cold season and were harvested in the spring when fresh food was scarce. Cereal crops such as wheat, barley, and millet provided carbohydrates and other nutrients. Sugar cane was another important crop. Some families cultivated vegetables, spices, fruit trees, and flowers in their gardens.

Cattle were raised for plowing and milk, hides, and horns, but Hindus did not slaughter them for meat. Like the Islamic and Jewish prohibition on the consumption of pork, the eating of beef was forbidden among Hindus.

Local craftsmen and tradesmen lived and worked in specific parts of a town or village. They were frequently organized into guilds, with guild heads and guild rules. The textile industries were particularly well developed. Silk (which had entered India from China), linen, wool, and cotton fabrics were produced in large quantities and traded throughout India and beyond. The cutting and polishing of precious stones was another industry associated closely with foreign trade.

In the cities shops were open to the street; families lived on the floors above. The busiest tradesmen dealt in milk and cheese, oil, spices, and perfumes. Equally prominent but disreputable were tavern keepers. Indian taverns were haunts of criminals and con artists, and in the worst of them fighting was as common as drinking. In addition to these tradesmen and merchants, a host of peddlers shuffled through towns and villages selling everything from needles to freshly cut flowers.

The Chinese Buddhist pilgrim Faxian, during his six years in Gupta India, described India as a peaceful land where people could move about freely without needing passports and where the upper castes were vegetarians. He was the first to make explicit reference to "untouchables," remarking that they hovered around the margins of Indian society, carrying gongs to warn upper-caste people of their polluting presence.

Villages were often walled, as in north China and the Middle East. The streets were unpaved, and the rainy season turned them into a muddy soup. Cattle and sheep roamed as freely as people. Some families kept pets, such as cats or parrots. Half-wild mongooses served as effective protection against snakes. The pond outside the village was its main source of water and also a spawning ground for fish, birds, and mosquitoes. Women drawing water frequently encountered water buffalo wallowing in the shallows. After the farmers returned from the fields in the evening, the village gates were closed until morning.

In this period the caste system reached its mature form. Within the broad division into the four *varna* (strata) of Brahman, Kshatriya, Vaishya, and Shudra, the population was subdivided into numerous castes, or **jati.** Each caste had a proper occupation. In addition, its members married only within the caste and ate only with other members. Members of high-status castes feared pollution from contact with lower-caste individuals and had to undertake rituals of purification to remove the taint. Eventually Indian society comprised perhaps as many as three thousand castes. Each caste had its own governing body, which enforced the rules of the caste. Those incapable of living up to the rules were expelled, becoming outcastes. These unfortunates lived hard lives, performing tasks that others considered unclean or lowly.

jati *Indian castes.*

The life of the well-to-do is described in the *Kamasutra* (Book on the Art of Love). Comfortable surroundings provided a place for men to enjoy poetry, painting, and music in the company of like-minded friends. Well-trained courtesans added to the pleasures of the wealthy. A man who had more than one wife was advised not to let one speak ill of the other and to try to keep each of them happy by taking them to gardens, giving them presents, telling them secrets, and loving them well.

For all members of Indian society, regardless of caste, marriage and the family were the focus of life. As in China, the joint family was under the authority of the eldest male, who might take several wives. The family affirmed its solidarity by the religious ritual of honoring its dead ancestors—a ritual that linked the living and the dead, much like ancestor worship in China. People commonly lived in extended families: grandparents, uncles and aunts, cousins, and nieces and nephews all lived together in the same house or compound.

Children were viewed as a great source of happiness. The poet Kalidasa depicts children as the greatest joy of their father's life:

With their teeth half-shown in causeless laughter,
and their efforts at talking so sweetly uncertain,
when children ask to sit on his lap
a man is blessed, even by the dirt on their bodies.[12]

Children in poor households worked as soon as they were able. Children in wealthier households faced the age-old irritations of reading, writing, and arithmetic. Less attention was paid to daughters, though in more prosperous families they were often literate. Because girls who had lost their virginity could seldom hope to find good husbands and thus would become financial burdens and social disgraces to their families, daughters were customarily married as children, with consummation delayed until they reached puberty.

Wives' bonds with their husbands were so strong that it was felt a wife should have no life apart from her husband. A widow was expected to lead the hard life of the ascetic, sleeping on the ground; eating only one simple meal a day, without meat, wine, salt, or honey; wearing plain undyed clothes without jewelry; and shaving her head. She was viewed as inauspicious to everyone but her children, and she did not attend family festivals. Among high-caste Hindus, a widow would be praised for throwing herself on her husband's funeral pyre. Buddhist sects objected to this practice, called **sati,** but some writers declared that by self-immolation a widow could expunge both her own and her husband's sins, so that both would enjoy eternal bliss in Heaven.

Within the home the position of a wife often depended chiefly on her own intelligence and strength of character. Wives were traditionally supposed to be humble, cheerful, and diligent even toward worthless husbands. As in other patriarchal societies, however, occasionally a woman ruled the roost. For women who did not want to accept the strictures of married life, the main way out was to join a Buddhist or Jain religious community.

sati *A practice whereby a high-caste Hindu woman would throw herself on her husband's funeral pyre.*

SOUTHEAST ASIA, TO 1400

How did states develop along the maritime trade routes of Southeast Asia?

Much as Roman culture spread to northern Europe and Chinese culture spread to Korea, Japan, and Vietnam, in the first millennium C.E. Indian learning, technology, and material culture spread to Southeast Asia, both mainland and insular.

Southeast Asia is a tropical region that is more like India than China, with temperatures hovering around 80°F and rain falling dependably throughout the year. The topography of mainland Southeast Asia is marked by north-south mountain ranges separated by river valleys. It was easy for people to migrate south along these rivers but harder for them to cross the heavily forested mountains that divided the region into areas that had limited contact with each other. The indigenous population was originally mostly Malay, but migrations over the centuries brought many other peoples, including speakers of Austro-Asiatic, Austronesian, and Sino-Tibetan-Burmese languages, some of whom moved on to the islands offshore.

● **Bayan Relief, Angkor Wat**   Among the many relief sculptures at the amazing complex of Angkor Wat are depictions of royal processions, armies at war, trade, cooking, cockfighting, and other scenes of everyday life. In the relief shown here, the boats and fish convey something of the significance of the sea to life in Southeast Asia. *(Robert Wilson, photographer)*

The northern part of modern Vietnam was under Chinese political control off and on from the second century B.C.E. to the tenth century C.E. (see pages 153–154), but for the rest of Southeast Asia, Indian influence was of much greater significance. The first state to appear in Southeast Asia, called Funan by Chinese visitors, had its capital in southern Vietnam. In the first to sixth centuries C.E. Funan extended its control over much of Indochina and the Malay Peninsula. Merchants from northwest India would offload their goods and carry them across the narrowest part of the Malay Peninsula. The ports of Funan offered food and lodging to the merchants as they waited for the winds to shift to continue their voyages. Brahman priests and Buddhist monks from India settled along with the traders, serving the Indian population and attracting local converts. Rulers often invited Indian priests and monks to serve under them, using them as foreign experts knowledgeable about law, government, architecture, and other fields.

Sixth-century Chinese sources report that the Funan king lived in a multistory palace and the common people lived in houses built on piles with roofs of bamboo leaves. The king rode about on an elephant, but narrow boats measuring up to ninety feet long were a more important means of transportation. The people enjoyed both cockfighting and pig fighting. Instead of drawing water from wells, as the Chinese did, they made pools, from which dozens of nearby families would draw water.

After the decline of Funan, maritime trade continued to grow, and petty kingdoms appeared in many places. Indian traders frequently established small settlements, generally located on the coast. Contact with the local populations led to intermarriage and the creation of hybrid cultures. Local rulers often adopted Indian customs and values, embraced Hinduism and Buddhism, and learned **Sanskrit,** India's classical

Sanskrit   *India's classical literary language.*

GLOBAL TRADE

SPICES

From ancient times on, for both Europeans and Chinese, a major reason to trade with South and Southeast Asia was to acquire spices, especially pepper, nutmeg, cloves, and cinnamon. These and other spices were in high demand not only because they could be used to flavor food but also because they were thought to have positive pharmacological properties. Unlike other highly desired products of India and farther east—such as sugar, cotton, rice, and silk—no way was found to produce the spices close to where they were in demand. Because of the location where

these spices were produced, this trade was from earliest times largely a maritime trade conducted through a series of middlemen. The spices were transported from where they were grown to nearby ports, and from there to major entrepôts, where merchants would take them in many different directions.

Two types of pepper grew in India and Southeast Asia. Black pepper is identical to our familiar pepper corns. "Long pepper," from a related plant, was hotter. The Mediterranean world imported its pepper from India; China imported it from Southeast Asia. After the discovery of the New World the importation of long pepper declined, as the chili pepper found in

The Spice Trade

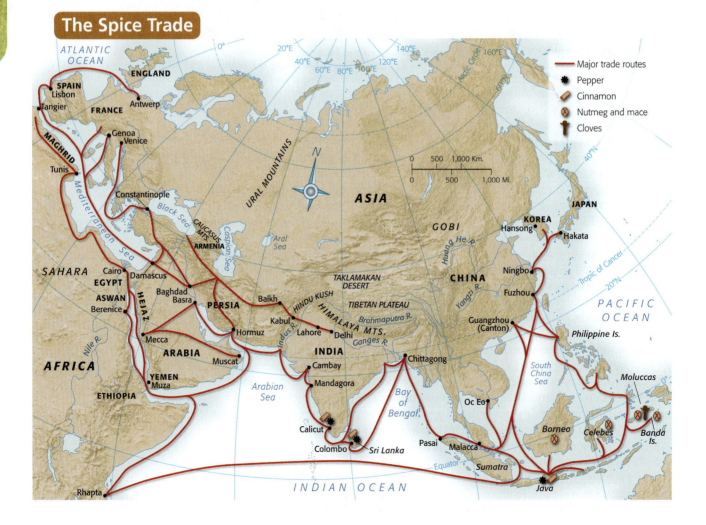

Legend:
— Major trade routes
❋ Pepper
Cinnamon
Nutmeg and mace
Cloves

Mexico was at least as spicy and grew well in Europe and China.

Already in Greek and Roman times trade in pepper was substantial. According to the Greek geographer Strabo (64 B.C.E.–24 C.E.), 120 ships a year made the trip to India to acquire pepper, the round trip taking a year because they had to wait for the monsoon winds to be blowing in the right direction. Pliny in about 77 C.E. complained that the Roman Empire wasted fifty million sesterces per year on long pepper and white and black pepper combined.

Cloves and nutmeg entered the repertoire of spices somewhat later than pepper. They are interesting because they could be grown in only a handful of small islands in the eastern part of the Indonesian archipelago. Merchants in China, India, Arab lands, and Europe got them through intermediaries and did not know where they were grown. An Arab source from about 1000 C.E. reported that cloves came from an island near India that had a Valley of Cloves, and that they were acquired by a silent barter. The sailors would lay out on the beach the items they were willing to trade, and the next morning they would find cloves in their place.

The demand for these spices in time encouraged Chinese, Indian, and Arab seamen to make the trip to the Straits of Malacca or east Java. Malay seamen in small craft such as outrigger canoes would bring the spices the thousand or more miles to the major ports where foreign merchants would purchase them. This trade was important to the prosperity of the Srivijaya kingdom. The trade was so profitable, however, that it also attracted pirates.

In the Mongol era travelers like Marco Polo, Ibn Battuta, and Odoric of Pordenone reported on the cultivation and marketing of spices in the various places they visited. Ibn Battuta described pepper plants as vines planted to grow up coconut palms. He also reported seeing the trunks of cinnamon trees floated down rivers in India. Odoric reported that pepper was picked like grapes from groves so huge it would take eighteen days to walk around them. Marco Polo referred to the 7,459 islands in the China Sea that local mariners could navigate and that produced a great variety of spices as well as aromatic wood. He also reported that spices could be acquired at the great island of Java, including pepper, nutmeg, and cloves, perhaps not understanding that these had often been shipped from the innumerable small islands to Java.

Gaining direct access to the spices of the East was one of the motivations behind Christopher Columbus's voyages. Not long after, Portuguese sailors did reach India by sailing around Africa, and soon the Dutch were competing with them for control of the spice trade and setting up rival trading posts. Pepper was soon successively planted in other tropical places, including Brazil. India, however, has remained the largest exporter of spices to this day.

literary language. Sanskrit gave different peoples a common mode of written expression, much as Chinese did in East Asia and Latin did in Europe.

When the Indians entered mainland Southeast Asia, they encountered both long-settled peoples and migrants moving southward from the frontiers of China. As in other such extensive migrations, the newcomers fought one another as often as they fought the native populations. In 939 the Vietnamese finally became independent of China and extended their power southward along the coast of present-day Vietnam. The Thais had long lived in what is today southwest China and north Burma. In the eighth century the Thai tribes united in a confederacy and even expanded northward against Tang China. Like China, however, the Thai confederacy fell to the Mongols in 1253. Still farther west another tribal people, the Burmese, migrated to the area of modern Burma in the eighth century. They also established a state, which they ruled from their capital, Pagan, and came into contact with India and Sri Lanka.

The most important mainland state was the Khmer Empire of Cambodia (802–1432), which controlled the heart of the region. The Khmers were indigenous to the area. Their empire, founded in 802, eventually extended south to the sea and the northeast Malay Peninsula. Indian influence was pervasive; the impressive temple complex at Angkor Wat was dedicated to the Hindu god Vishnu. Social organization, however, was modeled not on the Indian caste system but on indigenous traditions. A large part of the population was of servile status, many descended from non-Khmer mountain tribes defeated by the Khmers. Generally successful in a long series of wars with the Vietnamese, the Khmers reached the peak of their power in 1219 and then gradually declined.

Srivijaya *A maritime empire that held the Strait of Malacca and the waters around Sumatra, Borneo, and Java.*

Far different from these land-based states was the maritime empire of **Srivijaya,** based on the island of Sumatra. From the sixth century on, it held the important Strait of Malacca, through which most of the sea traffic between China and India passed. (See the feature "Global Trade: Spices" on pages 318–319.) This state, held together as much by alliances as by direct rule, was in many ways like the Gupta state in India, securing its prominence and binding its vassals and allies through its splendor and the promise of riches through trade.

Much as the Korean and Japanese rulers adapted Chinese models (see page 157), the Srivijayan rulers drew on Indian traditions to justify their rule and organize their state. The Sanskrit writing system was used for government documents, and Indians were often employed as priests, scribes, and administrators. Using Sanskrit overcame the barriers raised by the many different native languages of the region. Indian mythology took hold, as did Indian architecture and sculpture. Kings and their courts, the first to embrace Indian culture, consciously spread it to their subjects. The Chinese Buddhist monk Yixing (d. 727) stopped at Srivijaya for six months in 671 on his way to India and for four years on his return journey. He found a thousand monks there, some of whom helped him translate Sanskrit texts.

Borobudur, the magnificent Buddhist temple complex, was begun around 780. This stone monument depicts the ten tiers of Buddhist cosmology. When pilgrims made the three-mile-long winding ascent, they passed numerous sculpted reliefs depicting the journey from ignorance to enlightenment.

After several centuries of prosperity, Srivijaya suffered a stunning blow in 1025. The Chola state in south India launched a large naval raid and captured the Srivijayan king and capital. Unable to hold their gains, the Indians retreated, but the Srivijaya Empire never regained its vigor.

Buddhism became progressively more dominant in Southeast Asia after 800. Mahayana Buddhism became important in Srivijaya and Vietnam, but Theravada Buddhism, closer to the original Buddhism of early India, became the dominant form in the rest of mainland Southeast Asia. Buddhist missionaries from India and Sri Lanka played a prominent role in these developments. Local converts continued the process by making pilgrimages to India and Sri Lanka to worship and to observe Indian life for themselves.

The Spread of Indian Culture in Comparative Perspective

The social, cultural, and political systems developed in India, China, and Rome all had enormous impact on neighboring peoples whose cultures were originally not as advanced. Some of the mechanisms for cultural spread were similar in all three cases, but differences were important as well.

In the case of Rome and both Han and Tang China, strong states directly ruled outlying regions, bringing their civilizations with them. India's states, even its largest empires, such as the Mauryan and Gupta, did not have comparable bureaucratic reach. Outlying areas tended to be in the hands of local lords who had consented to recognize the overlordship of the stronger state. Moreover, most of the time India was politically divided.

The expansion of Indian culture into Southeast Asia thus came not from conquest and extending direct political control, but from the extension of trading networks, with missionaries following along. This made it closer to the way Japan adopted features of Chinese culture, often through the intermediary of Korea. In both cases, the cultural exchange was largely voluntary, as the Japanese or Southeast Asians sought to adopt more up-to-date technologies (such as writing) or were persuaded of the truth of religious ideas they learned from foreigners.

Chapter Summary

To assess your mastery of this chapter, go to **bedfordstmartins.com/mckayworld**

Key Terms
nomads
grasslands
steppe
yurts
Great Khan
khanates
tax-farming
protected people
jati
sati
Sanskrit
Srivijaya

• **What gave the nomadic pastoralists of Central Asia military advantages over nearby settled civilizations?**

The nomadic pastoral societies that stretched across Eurasia had the great military advantage of being able to raise horses in large numbers and support themselves from their flocks. Their mastery of the horse and mounted archery allowed them repeatedly to overawe or conquer their neighbors. Nomadic pastoralists generally were organized on the basis of clans and tribes that selected chiefs for their military talent. Much of the time these tribes fought with each other, but several times in history leaders rose who formed larger confederations capable of coordinated attacks on cities and towns. From the fifth to the twelfth centuries, the most successful nomadic groups on the Eurasian grasslands were Turks of one sort or another.

• **How was the world changed by the Mongol conquests of much of Eurasia?**

The greatest of the nomadic military leaders was the Mongol Chinggis Khan. In the early thirteenth century, through his charismatic leadership and military genius, he was able to lead victorious armies from one side of Eurasia to another. The initial conquests were quite destructive, with the inhabitants of many cities enslaved or killed. After the empire was divided into four khanates ruled by different lines of Chinggis's descendants, more stable forms of government were developed. The Mongols rewarded loyalty and gave important positions to those willing to serve them faithfully. The Mongols did not try to change the cultures or religions of the countries they conquered. In Mongolia and China the Mongol rulers welcomed those learned in all religions. In Central Asia and Persia the Mongol khans converted to Islam and gave it the support earlier rulers there had done.

• How did the Mongol conquests facilitate the spread of ideas, religions, inventions, and diseases?

For a century Mongol hegemony fostered unprecedented East-West trade and contact. The Mongols encouraged trade and often moved craftsmen and other specialists from one place to another. More Europeans made their way east than ever before, and Chinese inventions such as printing and the compass made their way west. Because Europe was further behind in 1200, it benefited most from the spread of technical and scientific ideas. Diseases also spread, including, it seems, the plague referred to as the Black Death in Europe.

• How did India respond to its encounters with Turks, Mongols, and Islam?

India was invaded by the Mongols, but not conquered. After the fall of the Gupta Empire in about 480, India was for the next millennium ruled by small kingdoms, which allowed regional cultures to flourish. The north and northwest were frequently raided by Turks from Afghanistan or Central Asia, and for several centuries Muslim Turks ruled a state in north India called the Delhi Sultanate. Over time Islam gained adherents throughout South Asia. Hinduism continued to flourish, but Buddhism went into decline.

• How did states develop along the maritime trade routes of Southeast Asia?

Throughout the medieval period India continued to be the center of a very active seaborne trade, and this trade helped carry Indian ideas and practices to Southeast Asia. Local rulers used experts from India to establish strong states, such as the Khmer kingdom in Cambodia and the Srivijaya kingdom in Malaysia and Indonesia. Buddhism became the dominant religion throughout the region, though Hinduism also played an important role.

Suggested Reading

Abu-Lughod, Janet L. *Before European Hegemony: The World System A.D. 1250–1350.* 1989. Examines the period of Mongol domination from a global perspective.

Ali, Daud. *Courtly Culture and Political Life in Early Medieval India.* 2004. Explores the growth of royal households and the development of a courtly worldview in India from 350 to 1200.

Chaudhuri, K. N. *Asia Before Europe.* 1990. Discusses the economy and civilization of cultures within the basin of the Indian Ocean.

Findley, Carter Vaughn. *The Turks in World History.* 2005. Covers both the early Turks and the connections between the Turks and the Mongols.

Franke, Herbert, and Denis Twitchett, eds. *The Cambridge History of China,* vol. 6, *Alien Regimes and Border States.* 1994. Clear and thoughtful accounts of the Mongols and their predecessors in East Asia.

Jackson, Peter. *The Delhi Sultanate.* 2003. Provides a close examination of north India in the thirteenth and fourteenth centuries.

Jackson, Peter. *The Mongols and the West, 1221–1410.* 2005. A close examination of many different types of connections between the Mongols and both Europe and the Islamic lands.

Ratchnevsky, Paul. *Genghis Khan: His Life and Legacy.* 1992. A reliable account by a major Mongolist.

Rossabi, Morris. *Khubilai Khan: His Life and Times.* 1988. Provides a lively account of the life of one of the most important Mongol rulers.

Shaffer, Lynda. *Maritime Southeast Asia to 1500.* 1996. A short account of early Southeast Asia from a world history perspective.

Notes

1. Trans. in Denis Sinor, "The Establishment and Dissolution of the Türk Empire," in *The Cambridge History of Early Inner Asia,* ed. Denis Sinor (Cambridge: Cambridge University Press, 1990), p. 307.

2. Manuel Komroff, ed., *Contemporaries of Marco Polo* (New York: Dorset Press, 1989), p. 65.

3. Ibid.

4. *The Travels of Marco Polo, the Venetian,* ed. Manuel Komroff (New York: Boni and Liveright, 1926), p. 93.

5. Ibid., pp. 93–94.

6. Cited in John Larner, *Marco Polo and the Discovery of the World* (New Haven, Conn.: Yale University Press, 1999), p. 22.

7. Igor de Rachewiltz, "Marco Polo Went to China," *Zentralasiatische Studien* 27(1997): 34–92. See also Larner, *Marco Polo and the Discovery of the World.*

8. Quoted in A. L. Basham, *The Wonder That Was India,* 2d ed. (New York: Grove Press, 1959), p. 420. All quotations from this work are reprinted by permission of Pan Macmillan, London.

9. Edward C. Sachau, *Alberuni's India,* vol. 1 (London: Kegan Paul, 1910), pp. 19–20, slightly modified.

10. H. A. R. Gibb, *The Travels of Ibn Battuta* (Cambridge: Cambridge University Press for the Hukluyt Society, 1971), pp. 700–701.

11. Guy le Strang, trans., *Clavijo, Embassy to Tamerlane, 1403–1406* (London: Routledge, 1928), pp. 265–266.

12. Quoted in Basham, *The Wonder That Was India,* p. 161.

Listening to the
PAST

The Abduction of Women in *The Secret History of the Mongols*

Within a few decades of Chinggis Khan's death, oral traditions concerning his rise were written down in the Mongolian language. They begin with the cycles of revenge among the tribes in Mongolia, many of which began when women were abducted for wives. These passages relate how Temujin's (Chinggis's) father Yesugei seized Hogelun, Temujin's future mother, from a passing Merkid; how twenty years later three Merkids in return seized women from Temujin; and Temujin's revenge.

That year Yesugei the Brave was out hunting with his falcon on the Onan. Yeke Chiledu, a nobleman of the Merkid tribe, had gone to the Olkhunugud people to find himself a wife, and he was returning to the Merkid with the girl he'd found when he passed Yesugei hunting by the river. When he saw them riding along Yesugei leaned forward on his horse. He saw it was a beautiful girl. Quickly he rode back to his tent and just as quick returned with his two brothers, Nekun Taisi and Daritai Odchigin. When Chiledu saw the three Mongols coming he whipped his dun-colored horse and rode off around a nearby hill with the three men behind him. He cut back around the far side of the hill and rode to Lady Hogelun, the girl he'd just married, who stood waiting for him at the front of their cart. "Did you see the look on the faces of those three men?" she asked him. "From their faces it looks like they mean to kill you. As long as you've got your life there'll always be girls for you to choose from. There'll always be women to ride in your cart. As long as you've got your life you'll be able to find some girl to marry. When you find her, just name her Hogelun for me, but go now and save your own life!" Then she pulled off her shirt and held it out to him, saying: "And take this to remember me, to remember my scent." Chiledu reached out from his saddle and took the shirt in his hands. With the three Mongols close behind him he struck his dun-colored horse with his whip and took off down the Onan River at full speed.

The three Mongols chased him across seven hills before turning around and returning to Hogelun's cart. Then Yesugei the Brave grasped the reins of the cart, his elder brother Nekun Taisi rode in front to guide them, and the younger brother Daritai Odchigin rode along by the wheels. As they rode her back toward their camp, Hogelun began to cry, . . . and she cried till she stirred up the waters of the Onan River, till she shook the trees in the forest and the grass in the valleys. But as the party approached their camp Daritai, riding beside her, warned her to stop: "This fellow who held you in his arms, he's already ridden over the mountains. This man who's lost you, he's crossed many rivers by now. You can call out his name, but he can't see you now even if he looks back. If you tried to find him now you won't even find his tracks. So be still now," he told her. Then Yesugei took Lady Hogelun to his tent as his wife. . . .

[Some twenty years later] one morning just before dawn Old Woman Khogaghchin, Mother Hogelun's servant, woke with a start, crying: "Mother! Mother! Get up! The ground is shaking, I hear it rumble. The Tayichigud must be riding back to attack us. Get up!"

Mother Hogelun jumped from her bed, saying: "Quick, wake my sons!" They woke Temujin and the others and all ran for the horses. Temujin, Mother Hogelun, and Khasar each took a horse. Khachigun, Temuge Odchigin, and Belgutei each took a horse. Bogorchu took one horse and Jelme another. Mother Hogelun lifted the baby Temulun onto her saddle. They saddled the last horse as a lead and there was no horse left for [Temujin's wife] Lady Borte. . . .

Old Woman Khogaghchin, who'd been left in the camp, said: "I'll hide Lady Borte." She made her get into a black covered cart. Then she harnessed the cart to a speckled ox. Whipping the ox, she drove the cart away from the camp down the Tungelig. As the first light of day hit them, soldiers rode up and told them to stop. "Who are you?" they asked her, and Old Woman Khogaghchin answered: "I'm a servant of Temujin's. I've just come from shearing his sheep. I'm on my way back to my own tent to make felt

This portrait of Chinggis's wife, Borte, is found in a shrine to her in Mongolia. *(Courtesy of Genghis Khan Shrine, Yijinhuoluo Banner)*

from the wool." Then they asked her: "Is Temujin at his tent? How far is it from here?" Old Woman Khogaghchin said: "As for the tent, it's not far. As for Temujin, I couldn't see whether he was there or not. I was just shearing his sheep out back." The soldiers rode off toward the camp, and Old Woman Khogaghchin whipped the ox. But as the cart moved faster its axletree snapped. "Now we'll have to run for the woods on foot," she thought, but before she could start the soldiers returned. They'd made [Temujin's half brother] Belgutei's mother their captive, and had her slung over one of their horses with her feet swinging down. They rode up to the old woman shouting: "What have you got in that cart!" "I'm just carrying wool," Khogaghchin replied, but an old soldier turned to the younger ones and said, "Get off your horses and see what's in there." When they opened the door of the cart they found Borte inside. Pulling her out, they forced Borte and Khogaghchin to ride on their horses, then they all set out after Temujin. . . .

The men who pursued Temujin were the chiefs of the three Merkid clans, Toghtoga, Dayin Usun, and Khagatai Darmala. These three had come to get their revenge, saying: "Long ago Mother Hogelun was stolen from our brother, Chiledu." When they couldn't catch Temujin they said to each other: "We've got our revenge. We've taken their wives from them," and they rode down from Mount Burkhan Khaldun back to their homes. . . .

Having finished his prayer Temujin rose and rode off with Khasar and Belgutei. They rode to [his father's sworn brother] Toghoril Ong Khan of the Kereyid camped in the Black Forest on the Tula River. Temujin spoke to Ong Khan, saying: "I was attacked by surprise by the three Merkid chiefs. They've stolen

my wife from me. We've come to you now to say, 'Let my father the Khan save my wife and return her.'" . . .

[Temujin and his allies] moved their forces from Botoghan Bogorjin to the Kilgho River where they built rafts to cross over to the Bugura Steppe, into [the Merkid] Chief Toghtoga's land. They came down on him as if through the smoke-hole of his tent, beating down the frame of his tent and leaving it flat, capturing and killing his wives and his sons. They struck at his door-frame where his guardian spirit lived and broke it to pieces. They completely destroyed all his people until in their place there was nothing but emptiness. . . .

As the Merkid people tried to flee from our army running down the Selenge with what they could gather in the darkness, as our soldiers rode out of the night capturing and killing the Merkid, Temujin rode through the retreating camp shouting out: "Borte! Borte!"

Lady Borte was among the Merkid who ran in the darkness and when she heard his voice, when she recognized Temujin's voice, Borte leaped from her cart. Lady Borte and Old Woman Khogaghchin saw Temujin charge through the crowd and they ran to him, finally seizing the reins of his horse. All about them was moonlight. As Temujin looked down to see who had stopped him he recognized Lady Borte. In a moment he was down from his horse and they were in each other's arms, embracing. . . .

Questions for Analysis

1. What do you learn from these stories about the Mongol way of life?

2. "Marriage by capture" has been practiced in many parts of the world. Can you infer from these stories why such a system would persist? What was the impact of such practices on kinship relations?

3. Can you recognize traces of the oral origins of these stories?

Source: Paul Kahn, trans., *The Secret History of the Mongols: The Origin of Chinghis Khan,* © Paul Kahn (Boston: Cheng & Tsui Company, 1998) Permission granted by Cheng & Tsui Company.

City Life. A well-developed system of river and canal transport kept the Song capital well supplied with goods from across China. *(The Palace Museum, Beijing)*

chapter

12 EAST ASIA, CA. 800–1400

Chapter Preview

The Medieval Chinese Economic Revolution (800–1100)
• What allowed China to become a world leader economically and intellectually in this period?

China During the Song Dynasty (960–1279)
• How did the civil service examinations and the scholar-official class shape Chinese society and culture?

Japan's Heian Period (794–1185)
• How did the Heian form of government contribute to the cultural flowering of the period?

The Samurai and the Kamakura Shogunate (1185–1333)
• What were the causes and consequences of military rule in Japan?

During the six centuries between 800 and 1400, East Asia was the most advanced region of the world. For several centuries the Chinese economy had grown spectacularly, and in fields as diverse as rice cultivation, the production of iron and steel, and the printing of books, China's methods of production were highly advanced. Its system of government was also advanced for its time. In the Song period the principle that the government should be in the hands of highly educated scholar-officials, selected through competitive written civil service examinations, became well established.

During the previous millennium basic elements of Chinese culture had spread beyond China's borders, creating a large cultural sphere centered on the use of Chinese as the language of civilization. Beginning around 800, however, the pendulum shifted toward cultural differentiation in East Asia, as Japan, Korea, and Vietnam developed in distinctive ways. This is particularly evident in the case of Japan, which in the samurai developed a military elite that was radically different from the Chinese scholar-official class.

THE MEDIEVAL CHINESE ECONOMIC REVOLUTION (800–1100)

What allowed China to become a world leader economically and intellectually in this period?

Chinese historians traditionally viewed dynasties as following a standard pattern. Founders were vigorous men able to recruit able followers to serve as officials and generals. Externally they would extend China's borders; internally they would bring peace. They would collect low but fairly assessed taxes. Over time, however, emperors born in the palace would get used to luxury and lack the founders' strength and wisdom. Entrenched interests would find ways to avoid taxes, forcing the government to impose heavier taxes on the poor. Impoverished peasants would flee; the morale of those in the government and armies would decline; and the dynasty would find itself able neither to maintain internal peace nor to defend its borders.

Viewed in terms of this theory of the **dynastic cycle,** by 800 the Tang Dynasty was in decline. It had ruled China for nearly two centuries, and its high point was in the past. A massive rebellion had wracked it in the mid-eighth century, and the Uighur Turks and Tibetans were menacing its borders. Many of the centralizing features of the government had been abandoned, with power falling more and more to regional military governors.

Chinese political theorists always made the assumption that a strong, centralized government was better than a weak one or political division, but if anything the late Tang period seems to have been both intellectually and economically more vibrant than the early Tang. Less control from the central government seems to have stimulated trade and economic growth.

In 742 China's population was still approximately 50 million, very close to what it had been in 2 C.E. Over the next three centuries, with the expansion of rice cultivation in central and south China, the country's food supply steadily increased, and so did its population, which reached 100 million by 1100. China was certainly the largest country in the world at the time; its population probably exceeded that of all of Europe (as it has ever since).

Agricultural prosperity and denser settlement patterns aided commercialization of the economy. Peasants in Song China did not aim at self-sufficiency. They had found that producing for the market made possible a better life. Peasants sold their surpluses and bought charcoal, tea, oil, and wine. In many places, farmers specialized in commercial crops, such as sugar, oranges, cotton, silk, and tea. (See the feature "Global Trade: Tea" on pages 330–331.) The need to transport the products of interregional trade stimulated the inland and coastal shipping industries, providing employment for shipbuilders and sailors and business opportunities for enterprising families with enough capital to purchase a boat. Marco Polo, the Venetian merchant who wrote of his visit to China in the late thirteenth century, was astounded at the boat traffic on the Yangzi River. He claimed to have seen no fewer than fifteen thousand vessels at one city on the river, "and yet there are other towns where the number is still greater."[1]

As marketing increased, demand for money grew enormously, leading eventually to the creation of the world's first **paper money.** The late Tang government's decision to abandon the use of bolts of silk as supplementary currency had increased the demand for copper coins. By 1085 the output of coins had increased tenfold to more than 6 billion coins a year. To avoid the weight and bulk of coins for large transactions, local merchants in late Tang times started trading receipts from deposit shops where they had left money or goods. The early Song authorities awarded a small set of shops a monopoly on the issuing of these certificates of deposit, and in the 1120s the government took over the system, producing the world's first government-issued paper money. Marco Polo was amazed:

The coinage of this paper money is authenticated with as much form and ceremony as if it were actually of pure gold or silver; for to each note a number of officers, specially appointed, not only subscribe their names, but affix their signets also; and when this

dynastic cycle *The theory that Chinese dynasties go through a predictable cycle, from early vigor and growth to subsequent decline as administrators become lax and the well-off find ways to avoid paying taxes, cutting state revenues.*

> **Primary Source:**
> **The Craft of Farming**
> *Look inside a twelfth-century Chinese treatise on farming, with advice on when to plow, which crops to plant, and how to use compost as fertilizer.*

paper money *Legal currency issued on paper; it developed in China as a convenient alternative to metal coins.*

● **Chinese Paper Money** Chinese paper currency indicated the unit of currency and the date and place of issue. The Mongols continued the use of paper money; this note dates from the Mongol period. *(DNP Archives)*

has been regularly done by the whole of them, the principal officer . . . having dipped into vermilion the royal seal committed to his custody, stamps with it the piece of paper, so that the form of the seal tinged with the vermilion remains impressed upon it.[2]

With the intensification of trade, merchants became progressively more specialized and organized. They set up partnerships and joint stock companies, with a separation of owners (shareholders) and managers. In the large cities merchants were organized into guilds according to the type of product sold, and they arranged sales from wholesalers to shop owners and periodically set prices. When government officials wanted to requisition supplies or assess taxes, they dealt with the guild heads.

Foreign trade also flourished in the Song period. In 1225 the superintendent of customs at the coastal city of Quanzhou wrote an account of the foreign places Chinese merchants visited. It includes sketches of major trading cities from Srivijaya to Malabar, Cairo, and Baghdad. Pearls were said to come from the Persian Gulf, ivory from Aden, pepper from Java and Sumatra, and cotton from the various kingdoms of India. In this period Chinese ships began to displace Indian and Arab merchants in the South Seas. Ship design was improved in several ways. Watertight bulkheads improved buoyancy and protected cargo. Stern-mounted rudders improved steering. Some of the ships were powered by both oars and sails and were large enough to hold several hundred men.

Also important to oceangoing travel was the perfection of the **compass.** The way a magnetic needle would point north had been known for some time, but in Song times the needle was reduced in size and attached to a fixed stem (rather than floated in water). In some cases it was put in a small protective case with a glass top, making it suitable for sea travel. The first reports of a compass used in this way date to 1119.

The Song also witnessed many advances in industrial techniques. Heavy industry, especially iron, grew astoundingly. With advances in metallurgy, iron production reached around 125,000 tons per year in 1078, a sixfold increase over the output in 800. At first charcoal was used in the production process, leading to deforestation of parts of north China. By the end of the eleventh century, however, bituminous coke had largely taken the place of charcoal. Much of this iron was put to military purposes. Mass-production methods were used to make iron armor in small, medium, and large sizes. High-quality steel for swords was made through high-temperature metallurgy. Huge bellows, often driven by water wheels, were used to superheat the molten ore. The needs of the army also brought Chinese engineers to experiment with the use of gunpowder. In the wars against the Jurchens, those defending a besieged city used gunpowder to propel projectiles at the enemy.

The quickening of the economy fueled the growth of cities. Dozens of cities had fifty thousand or more residents, and quite a few had more than a hundred thousand. Both the capitals, Kaifeng and Hangzhou, are estimated to have had in the vicinity of

Chronology

794–1185	Heian period in Japan
804	Two Japanese Buddhist monks, Saichō and Kūkai, travel to China
960–1279	Song Dynasty in China; emergence of scholar-official class; invention of movable type
995–1027	Fujiwara Michinaga is dominant at Heian court
ca. 1010	*The Tale of Gengi,* world's first novel
1069	Wang Anshi introduces sweeping political and economic reforms
1100–1400	Zen Buddhism flourishes in Japan
1119	First reported use of compass
1120s	First government-issued paper money introduced by Song
1126	Loss of north China to the Jurchens; capital relocated to Hangzhou
1130–1200	Zhu Xi, Neo-Confucian philosopher
1185–1333	Kamakura Shogunate in Japan
ca. 1275–1292	Marco Polo travels in China

compass *A tool developed in Song times to aid in navigation at sea; it consisted of a magnetic needle that would point north in a small protective case.*

TEA

Tea is made from the young leaves and leaf buds of *Camellia sinensis*, a plant native to the hills of southwest China. As an item of trade, tea has a very long history. Already by Han times (206 B.C.E.–220 C.E.), tea was being grown and drunk in southwest China, and for several centuries thereafter it was looked on as a local product of the region with useful pharmacologic properties, such as countering the effects of wine. By Tang times (608–907) it was being widely cultivated in the Yangzi River valley and was a major item of interregional trade. Tea was common enough in Tang life that poets often mentioned it in their poems. In the eighth century Lu Yu wrote an entire treatise on the wonders of tea.

During the Tang Dynasty tea was a major commercial crop, especially in the southeast. The most intensive time for tea production was the harvest season, since young leaves were of much more value than mature ones. Mobilized for about a month each year, women would come out to help pick the tea. Not only were tea merchants among the wealthiest merchants, but from the late eighth century on, taxes on tea became a major source of government revenue.

Tea circulated in several forms, loose and compressed (brick), powder and leaf. The cost of tea varied both by form and by region of origin. In Song times (960–1279), the cheapest tea could cost as little as 18 cash per catty, the most expensive 275. In Kaifeng in the 1070s the most popular type was loose tea

The Tea Trade

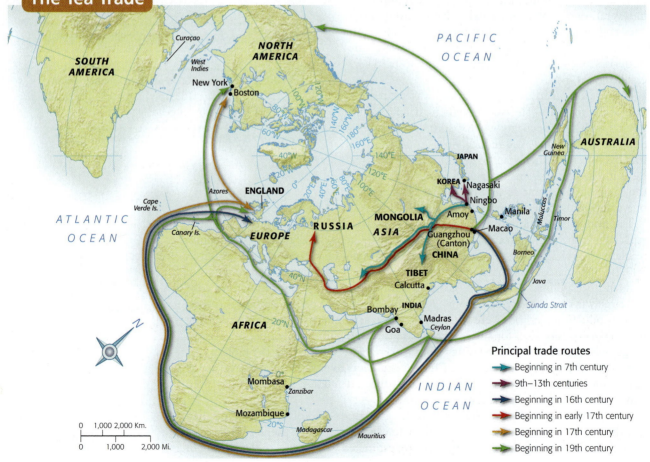

Principal trade routes

→ Beginning in 7th century
→ 9th–13th centuries
→ Beginning in 16th century
→ Beginning in early 17th century
→ Beginning in 17th century
→ Beginning in 19th century

Tea-leaf jar, fourteenth century, south China. This 42-centimeter-tall jar (about 16½ inches) was imported to Japan, where it was treasured as an art object and used by tea masters. In the sixteenth century it came into the possession of the first Tokugawa shogun, Ieyasu. (Tokugawa Art Museum, Nagoya)

powdered at water mills. The tea exported from Sichuan to Tibet, however, was formed into solid bricks.

The Song Dynasty established a government monopoly on tea. Only those who purchased government licenses could legally trade in tea. The dynasty also used its control of tea to ensure a supply of horses, needed for military purposes. The government could do this because the countries on its borders that produced the best horses—Tibet, Central Asia, Mongolia, and so on—were not suitable for growing tea. Thus the Song government insisted on horses for tea.

Tea reached Korea and Japan as a part of Buddhist culture. Buddhist monks drank it to help them stay awake during long hours of recitation or meditation. The priest Saichō, patriarch of Tendai Buddhism, visited China in 804–805 and reportedly brought back tea seeds. Tea drinking did not become widespread in Japan, however, until the twelfth century, when Zen monasteries popularized its use. By the fourteenth century tea imported from China was still prized, but the Japanese had already begun to appreciate the distinctive flavors of teas from different regions of Japan. With the development of the tea ceremony, tea drinking became an art in Japan, with much attention to the selection and handling of tea utensils. In both Japan and Korea, offerings of tea became a regular part of offerings to ancestors.

Tea did not become important in Europe until the seventeenth century. Tea first reached Russia in 1618, when a Chinese embassy presented some to the tsar. Under agreements between the Chinese and Russian governments, camel trains would arrive in China laden with furs and would return carrying tea, taking about a year for the round trip.

By 1700 Russia was receiving more than 600 camel loads of tea annually. By 1800 it was receiving more than 6,000 loads, amounting to more than 3.5 million pounds. Tea reached western Europe in the sixteenth century, both via Arabs and via Jesuit priests traveling on Portuguese ships.

In Britain, where tea drinking would become a national institution, tea was first drunk in coffeehouses. In his famous diary Samuel Pepys recorded having his first cup of tea in 1660. By the end of the seventeenth century tea made up more than 90 percent of China's exports to England. In the eighteenth century tea drinking spread to homes and tea gardens. Queen Anne (r. 1702–1714) was credited with starting the custom of drinking tea instead of ale for breakfast. In the nineteenth century afternoon tea became a central feature of British social life.

Already by the end of the eighteenth century Britain imported so much tea from China that it worried about the outflow of silver to pay for it. Efforts to balance trade with China involved promoting the sale of Indian opium to China and efforts to grow tea in British colonies. Using tea seeds collected in China and a tea plant indigenous to India's Assam province, both India and Sri Lanka eventually grew tea successfully. By the end of the nineteenth century huge tea plantations had been established in India, and India surpassed China as an exporter of tea.

The spread of the popularity of drinking tea also stimulated the desire for fine cups to drink it from. Importation of Chinese ceramics, therefore, often accompanied adoption of China's tea customs.

**Primary Source:
A Description of
Foreign Peoples**
*Discover the rich commodities
and exotic customs of Arabia
and southern Spain, as seen by a
thirteenth-century Chinese trade
official.*

a million residents. Marco Polo described Hangzhou as the finest and most splendid city in the world. He reported that it had ten marketplaces, each half a mile long, where forty thousand to fifty thousand people would go to shop on any given day. There were also bathhouses; permanent shops selling things such as spices, drugs, and pearls; and innumerable courtesans—"adorned in much finery, highly perfumed, occupying well-furnished houses, and attended by many female domestics."[3]

The medieval economic revolution shifted the economic center of China south to the Yangzi River drainage area. This area had many advantages over the north China plain. Rice, which grew in the south, provides more calories per unit of land and therefore allows denser settlement. The milder temperatures often allowed two crops to be grown on the same plot of land, a summer and then a winter crop. The abundance of rivers and streams facilitated shipping, which reduced the cost of transportation and thus made regional specialization economically more feasible. In the first half of the Song Dynasty, the capital was still in the north, but on the Grand Canal, which linked it to the rich south.

The economic revolution of Song times cannot be attributed to intellectual change, as Confucian scholars did not reinterpret the classics to defend the morality of commerce. But neither did scholar-officials take a unified stand against economic development. As officials they had to work to produce revenue to cover government expenses such as defense, and this was much easier to do when commerce was thriving.

Ordinary people benefited from the Song economic revolution in many ways. There were more opportunities for the sons of farmers to leave agriculture and find work in cities. Those who stayed in agriculture had a better chance to improve their situations by taking up sideline production of wine, charcoal, paper, or textiles. Energetic farmers who grew cash crops such as sugar, tea, mulberry leaves (for silk), and cotton (recently introduced from India) could grow rich. Greater interregional trade led to the availability of more goods at the rural markets held every five or ten days.

Of course, not everyone grew rich. Poor farmers who fell into debt had to sell their

● **City Life** In Song times many cities in China grew to fifty thousand or more people, and the capital, Kaifeng, reached over a million. The bustle of a commercial city is shown here in a detail from a 17-foot-long handscroll painted in the twelfth century. *(The Palace Museum, Beijing)*

● **Transplanting Rice** To get the maximum yield per plot and to make it possible to grow two crops in the same field, Chinese farmers grew rice seedlings in a seed bed and then, when a field was free, transplanted the seedlings into the flooded field. Because the Song government wanted to promote up-to-date agricultural technology, in the twelfth century it commissioned a set of twelve illustrations of the steps to be followed. This painting comes from a later version of those illustrations. *(Courtesy of the Freer Gallery of Art, Smithsonian Institution, Washington, D.C. [54.21])*

land, and if they still owed money, they could be forced to sell their daughters as maids, concubines, or prostitutes. The prosperity of the cities created a huge demand for women to serve the rich in these ways, and Song sources mention that criminals would kidnap girls and women to sell in distant cities at huge profits.

CHINA DURING THE SONG DYNASTY (960–1279)

How did the civil service examinations and the scholar-official class shape Chinese society and culture?

In the tenth century Tang China broke up into separate contending states, some of which had non-Chinese rulers. The two states that proved to be long lasting were the Song, which came to control almost all of China proper south of the Great Wall, and the Liao, whose ruling house was Khitan and who held the territory of modern Beijing and areas north (see Map 12.1). Although the Song Dynasty had a much larger population, the Liao was militarily the stronger of the two.

The founder of the Song Dynasty, Taizu (r. 960–976), was a general whose troops elevated him to emperor (somewhat reminiscent of Roman practice). Taizu worked to make sure that such an act could not happen in the future by placing the armies under central government control. He retired or rotated his own generals and assigned civil officials to supervise them. In time civil bureaucrats came to dominate every aspect of Song government and society. The civil service examination system was greatly expanded to provide the dynasty with a constant flow of men trained in the Confucian classics.

Curbing the generals ended warlordism but did not solve the military problem of defending against the Khitans to the north. After several attempts to push them back beyond the Great Wall, the Song concluded a peace treaty with them. The Song agreed to make huge annual payments of gold and silk to the Khitans, in a sense paying them

MAP 12.1 **East Asia in 1000** The Song Empire did not extend as far as its predecessor, the Tang, and faced powerful rivals to the north—the Liao Dynasty of the Khitans and the Xia Dynasty of the Tanguts. Korea under the Koryo Dynasty maintained regular contact with Song China, but Japan, by the late Heian period, was no longer deeply involved with the mainland.

MAP 12.2 **East Asia in 1200** By 1200 military families dominated both Korea and Japan, but their borders were little changed. On the mainland, the Liao Dynasty had been overthrown by the Jurchens' Jin Dynasty, which also seized the northern third of the Song Empire. Because the Song relocated its capital to Hangzhou in the south, this period is called the Southern Song period.

not to invade. Even so, the Song rulers had to maintain a standing army of more than a million men. By the middle of the eleventh century military expenses consumed half the government's revenues. Song had the industrial base to produce swords, armor, and arrowheads in huge quantities, but had difficulty maintaining enough horses and well-trained horsemen. Even though China was the economic powerhouse of the region with by far the largest population, in this period, when the horse was a major weapon of war, it was not easy to convert wealth to military advantage.

In the early twelfth century the military situation rapidly worsened when the Khitan state was destroyed by another tribal confederation led by the Jurchens. Although the Song allied with the Jurchens, the Jurchens quickly realized how easy it would be to defeat the Song. When they marched into the Song capital in 1126, they captured the emperor and took him and his entire court hostage. Song forces rallied around a prince who reestablished a Song court in the south at Hangzhou (see Map 12.2). This Southern Song Dynasty controlled only about two-thirds of the former Song territories, but the social, cultural, and intellectual life there remained vibrant until the Song fell to the Mongols in 1279.

The Scholar-Officials and Neo-Confucianism

The Song period saw the full flowering of one of the most distinctive features of Chinese civilization, the scholar-official class certified through highly competitive civil service examinations. This elite was both broader and better educated than the elites of earlier periods in Chinese history. Once the **examination system** was fully developed, aristocratic habits and prejudices largely disappeared.

The invention of printing should be given some credit for this development. Tang craftsmen developed the art of carving words and pictures into wooden blocks, inking the blocks, and then pressing paper onto them. Each block held an entire page of text and illustrations. Such whole-page blocks were used for printing as early as the middle of the ninth century, and in the eleventh century **movable type** (one piece of type for each character) was invented. Movable type was never widely used in China because whole-block printing was cheaper. In China as in Europe, the introduction of printing dramatically lowered the price of books, thus aiding the spread of literacy.

Among the upper class the availability of cheaper books enabled scholars to amass their own libraries. Song publishers printed the classics of Chinese literature in huge editions to satisfy scholarly appetites. Works on philosophy, science, and medicine also were avidly consumed, as were Buddhist texts. Han and Tang poetry and historical works became the models for Song writers. One popular literary innovation was the encyclopedia, which first appeared in the Song period, at least five centuries before publication of a European encyclopedia.

The examination system came to carry such prestige that the number of scholars entering each competition escalated rapidly, from fewer than 30,000 early in the eleventh century, to nearly 80,000 by the end of that century, to about 400,000 by the dynasty's end. To prepare for the examinations, men had to memorize the classics in order to be able to recognize even the most obscure passages. They also had to master specific forms of composition, including poetry, and be ready to discuss policy issues, citing appropriate historical examples. Those who became officials this way had usually tried the exams several times and were on average a little over thirty years of age when they succeeded. The great majority of those who devoted years to preparing for the exams, however, never became officials.

The life of the educated man involved more than study for the civil service examinations. Many took to refined pursuits such as collecting antiques or old books and

examination system *A system of selecting officials based on competitive written examinations.*

movable type *A system of printing in which one piece of type was used for each unique character.*

● **On a Mountain Path in Spring** With spare, sketchy strokes, the court painter Ma Yuan (ca. 1190–1225) depicts a scholar on an outing accompanied by his boy servant carrying a lute. The scholar gazes into the mist, his eyes attracted by a bird in flight. The poetic couplet was inscribed by Emperor Ningzong (r. 1194–1124), at whose court Ma Yuan served. *(National Palace Museum, Taipei, Taiwan)*

practicing the arts—especially poetry writing, calligraphy, and painting. For many individuals these cultural interests overshadowed any philosophical, political, or economic concerns; others found in them occasional outlets for creative activity and aesthetic pleasure. In the Song period the engagement of the elite with the arts led to extraordinary achievement in calligraphy and painting, especially landscape painting. A large share of the informal social life of upper-class men was centered on these refined pastimes, as they gathered to compose or criticize poetry, to view each other's treasures, and to patronize young talents.

The new scholar-official elite produced some extraordinary men, able to hold high court offices while pursuing diverse intellectual interests. (See the feature "Individuals in Society: Shen Gua.") Ouyang Xiu spared time in his busy official career to write love songs, histories, and the first analytical catalogue of rubbings of ancient stone and bronze inscriptions. Sima Guang, besides serving as prime minister, wrote a narrative history of China from the Warring States Period (403–221 B.C.E.) to the founding of the Song Dynasty. Su Shi wrote more than twenty-seven hundred poems and eight hundred letters while active in opposition politics. He was also an esteemed painter, calligrapher, and theorist of the arts. Su Song, another high official, constructed an eighty-foot-tall mechanical clock. He adapted the water-powered clock invented in the Tang period by adding a chain-driven mechanism. The clock told not only the time of day but also the day of the month, the phase of the moon, and the position of certain stars and planets in the sky. At the top was a mechanically rotated armillary sphere.

These highly educated men accepted the Confucian responsibility to aid the ruler in the governing of the country. In this period, however, this commitment tended to embroil them in unpleasant factional politics. In 1069 the chancellor Wang Anshi proposed a series of sweeping reforms designed to raise revenues and help small farmers. Many well-respected scholars and officials thought that Wang's policies would do more harm than good and resisted enforcing them. Animosities grew as critics were assigned far from the capital. Those sent away later got the chance to retaliate, escalating the conflict.

Besides politics, scholars also debated issues in ethics and metaphysics. For several centuries Buddhism had been more vital than Confucianism. Beginning in the late Tang period Confucian teachers began claiming that the teachings of the Confucian sages contained all the wisdom one needed and a true Confucian would reject Buddhist teachings. During the eleventh century many Confucian teachers gathered around them students whom they urged to set their sights not on exam success but on the higher goals of attaining the wisdom of the sages. Metaphysical theories about the workings of the cosmos in terms of *li* (principle) and *qi* (vital energy) were developed in response to the challenge of the sophisticated metaphysics of Buddhism.

Neo-Confucianism *The revival of Confucian thinking that began in the eleventh century.*

Neo-Confucianism, as this movement is generally termed, was more fully developed in the twelfth century by the immensely learned Zhu Xi (1130–1200). Besides serving in office, he wrote, compiled, or edited almost a hundred books; corresponded with dozens of other scholars; and still regularly taught groups of disciples, many of whom stayed with him for years at a time. Although he was treated as a political threat during his lifetime, within decades of his death his writings came to be considered orthodox, and in subsequent centuries candidates for the examinations had to be familiar with his commentaries on the classics.

Women's Lives

With the spread of printing, more books and more types of books survive from the Song period than from earlier periods, letting us catch more glimpses of women's lives. Song stories, documents, and legal cases show us widows who ran inns, maids sent out by their mistresses to do errands, midwives who delivered babies, pious women who spent their days chanting Buddhist sutras, nuns who called on such

Shen Gua

In the eleventh century it was not rare for Chinese men of letters to have broad interests, but few could compare to Shen Gua (1031–1095), a man who tried his hand at everything from mathematics, geography, economics, engineering, medicine, divination, and archaeology to military strategy and diplomacy.

In his youth Shen Gua traveled widely with his father, who served as a provincial official. His own career as an official, which started when he was only twenty, also took him to many places, adding to his knowledge of geography. He received a post in the capital in 1066, just before Wang Anshi's rise to power, and he generally sided with Wang in the political disputes of the day. He eventually held high astronomical, ritual, and financial posts and became involved in waterworks and the construction of defense walls. He was sent as an envoy to the Khitans in 1075 to try to settle a boundary dispute. When a military campaign that he advised failed in 1082, he was demoted and later retired to write.

It is from his book of notes that we know the breadth of his interests. In one note Shen describes how, on assignment to inspect the frontier, he made a relief map of wood and glue-soaked sawdust to show the mountains, roads, rivers, and passes. The emperor was so impressed when he saw it that he ordered all the border prefectures to make relief maps. Elsewhere Shen describes the use of petroleum and explains how to make movable type from clay. Shen Gua often applied a mathematical approach to issues that his contemporaries did not think of in those terms. He once computed the total number of possible situations on a go board, and another time he calculated the longest possible military campaign given the limits of human carriers, who had to carry their own food as well as food for the soldiers.

Shen Gua is especially known for what might be called scientific explanations. In one place, he explains the deflection of the compass from due south. In another, he identifies petrified bamboo and from its existence argues that the region where it was found must have been much warmer and more humid in ancient times. He argued against the theory that tides are caused by the rising and setting of the sun, demonstrating that they correlate rather with the cycles of the moon. He proposed switching from a lunar calendar to a solar one of 365 days, saying that even though his contemporaries would reject his idea, "surely in the fu-

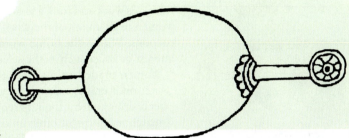

Among the advances of the Song period was the development of gunpowder. An eleventh-century manual on military technology illustrated this "thunderbolt ball," filled with gunpowder and iron scraps and hurled at the enemy with a catapult. (*Zeng Gongliang and Ding Du*, Wujing zongyao [Zhong-guo bingshu jicheng, 1988 ed.], 12:59, p. 640)

ture some will adopt my idea." To convince his readers that the sun and the moon were spherical, not flat, he suggested that they cover a ball with fine powder on one side and then look at it obliquely. The powder was the part of the moon illuminated by the sun, and as the viewer looked at it obliquely, the white part would be crescent shaped, like a waxing moon. Shen Gua, however, did not realize that the sun and moon had entirely different orbits, and he explained why they did not collide by positing that both were composed of *qi* (vital energy) and had form but not substance.

Shen Gua also wrote on medicine and criticized his contemporaries for paying more attention to old treatises than to clinical experience. Yet he, too, was sometimes stronger on theory than on observation. In one note he argues that longevity pills could be made from cinnabar. He reasoned that if cinnabar could be transformed in one direction, it ought to be susceptible to transformation in the opposite direction as well. Therefore, since melted cinnabar causes death, solid cinnabar should prevent death.

Questions for Analysis

1. Do you think Shen Gua's wide travels added to his curiosity about the material world?

2. In what ways could Shen Gua have used his scientific interests in his work as an official?

3. How does Shen Gua's understanding of the natural world compare to that of the early Greeks?

women to explain Buddhist doctrine, girls who learned to read with their brothers, farmers' daughters who made money by weaving mats, childless widows who accused their nephews of stealing their property, wives who were jealous of the concubines their husbands brought home, and women who used part of their own large dowries to help their husbands' sisters marry well.

Families who could afford it usually tried to keep their wives and daughters at home, where there was plenty for them to do. Not only was there the work of tending children and preparing meals, but spinning, weaving, and sewing also were considered women's work and took a great deal of time. Families that raised silkworms also needed women to do much of the work of coddling the worms and getting them to spin their cocoons. Within the home women generally had considerable say and took an active interest in issues such as the selection of marriage partners for their children.

Women tended to marry between the ages of sixteen and twenty. The husbands were, on average, a couple of years older than they were. The marriage would have been arranged by their parents, who would have either called on a professional matchmaker (most often an older woman) or turned to a friend or relative for suggestions. Before the wedding took place, written agreements would be exchanged, which would list the prospective bride's and groom's birth dates, parents, and grandparents; the gifts that would be exchanged; and the dowry the bride would bring. The goal was to match families of approximately equal status, but a young man who had just passed the civil service exams would be considered a good prospect even if his family had little wealth.

A few days before the wedding the bride's family would send to the groom's family her dowry, which at a minimum would contain boxes full of clothes and bedding. In better-off families, the dowry also would include items of substantial value, such as gold jewelry or deeds to land. On the day of the wedding the groom and some of his friends and relatives would go to the bride's home to get her. She would be elaborately dressed and would tearfully bid farewell to everyone in her family. She would be carried to her new home in a fancy sedan chair to the sound of music, alerting everyone on the street that a wedding was taking place. Meanwhile the groom's family's friends and relatives would have gathered at his home, and when the bridal party arrived, they would be there to greet them. The bride would have to kneel and bow to her new parents-in-law and later also to the tablets representing her husband's ancestors. A classical ritual still practiced was for the new couple to drink wine from the same cup. A ritual that had become popular in Song times was to attach a string to both of them, literally tying them together. Later they would be shown to their new bedroom, where the bride's dowry had already been placed, and people would toss beans or rice on the bed, symbolizing the desired fertility. After teasing them, the guests would leave them alone and go out to the courtyard for a wedding feast.

The young bride's first priority was to try to win over her mother-in-law, since everyone knew that mothers-in-law were hard to please. One way to do this was to quickly bear a son for the family. Within the patrilineal system, a woman fully secured her position in the family by becoming the mother of one of the men. Every community had older women skilled in midwifery who could be called to help when a woman went into labor. If the family was well-to-do, arrangements might be made for a wet nurse to help her take care of the newborn.

Women frequently had four, five, or six children, but likely one or more would die in infancy. If a son reached adulthood and married before the woman herself was widowed, she would be considered fortunate, for she would have always had an adult man who could take care of business for her—first her husband, then her grown son. But in the days when infectious diseases took many

● **Woman Attendant** The Song emperors were patrons of a still-extant temple in northern China that enshrined a statue of the "holy mother," the mother of the founder of the ancient Zhou Dynasty. The forty-two maids who attend her, one of whom is shown here, seem to have been modeled on the palace ladies who attended Song emperors. (© *Cultural Relics Press*)

people in their twenties and thirties, it was not uncommon for a woman to be widowed while in her twenties, when her children were still very young.

A woman with a healthy and prosperous husband faced another challenge in middle age: her husband could bring home a **concubine** (more than one if he could afford it). Moralists insisted that it was wrong for a wife to be jealous of her husband's concubines, but everyone agreed that jealousy was very common. Wives outranked concubines and could give them orders in the house, but a concubine had her own ways of getting back through her hold on the husband. The children born to a concubine were considered just as much children of the family as the wife's children, and if the wife had had only daughters and the concubine had a son, the wife would find herself dependent on the concubine's son in her old age.

As a woman's children grew up, she would start thinking of suitable marriage partners. Many women liked the idea of bringing a woman from her natal family—perhaps her brother's daughter—to be her daughter-in-law. No matter who was selected, her life became easier once she had a daughter-in-law to do the cooking and cleaning. Many found more time for religious devotions at this stage of their lives. Their sons, still living with them, could be expected to look after them and do their best to make their late years comfortable.

Neo-Confucianism is sometimes blamed for a decline in the status of women in Song times, largely because one of the best known of the Neo-Confucian teachers, Cheng Yi, once told a follower that it would be better for a widow to die of starvation than to lose her virtue by remarrying. In later centuries this saying was often quoted to justify pressuring widows, even very young ones, to stay with their husbands' families and not remarry. In Song times, however, widows frequently remarried.

It is true that **foot binding** began during the Song Dynasty, but it was not recommended by Neo-Confucian teachers; rather it was associated with the pleasure quarters and with women's efforts to beautify themselves. Mothers bound the feet of girls aged five to eight with long strips of cloth to keep them from growing and to bend the four smaller toes under to make the foot narrow and arched. The hope was that the girl would be judged more beautiful. Foot binding spread gradually during Song times but was probably still largely an elite practice. In later centuries it became extremely common in north and central China, eventually spreading to all classes. Women with bound feet were less mobile than women with natural feet, but only those who could afford servants bound their feet so tightly that walking was difficult.

concubine *A woman contracted to a man as a secondary spouse; although subordinate to the wife, her sons were considered legitimate heirs.*

foot binding *The practice of binding the feet of girls with long strips of cloth to keep them from growing large.*

JAPAN'S HEIAN PERIOD (794–1185)

How did the Heian form of government contribute to the cultural flowering of the period?

As discussed in Chapter 6, during the seventh and eighth centuries the Japanese ruling house pursued a vigorous policy of adopting useful ideas, techniques, and policies from the more advanced civilization of China. The rulers built a splendid capital along Chinese lines in Nara and fostered the growth of Buddhism. Monasteries grew so powerful in Nara, however, that in less than a century the court decided to move away from them and encourage other sects of Buddhism.

The new capital was built not far away at Heian (modern Kyoto). Heian was, like Nara, modeled on the Tang capital of Chang'an (although neither of the Japanese capitals had walls, a major feature of Chinese cities), and for the first century at Heian the government continued to follow Chinese models. With the decline of the Tang Dynasty in the late ninth century, the Japanese turned away from dependence on Chinese models. The last official embassy to China made the trip in 894.

Fujiwara Rule

Only the first two Heian emperors were activists. Thereafter political management was taken over by a series of regents from the Fujiwara family, who supplied most of the empresses in this period. The emperors continued to be honored, even venerated, because of their presumed divine descent, but it was the Fujiwaras who ruled. Fujiwara dominance represented the privatization of political power and a reversion to clan politics. Political history thus took a very different course in Japan than in China, where political contenders sought the throne and successful contenders deposed the old emperor and founded new dynasties. In Japan for the next thousand years, political contenders sought to manipulate the emperors rather than supplant them.

The Fujiwaras reached the apogee of their glory under Fujiwara Michinaga (966–1027). Like many aristocrats of the period, he was learned in Buddhism, music, poetry, and Chinese literature and history. He dominated the court for more than thirty years as the father of four empresses, the uncle of two emperors, and the grandfather of three emperors. He acquired great landholdings and built fine palaces for himself and his family. After ensuring that his sons could continue to rule, he retired to a Buddhist monastery, all the while continuing to maintain control himself.

By the end of the eleventh century several emperors who did not have Fujiwara mothers found a device to counter Fujiwara control: they abdicated but continued to exercise power by controlling their young sons on the throne. This system of rule has been called **cloistered government** because the retired emperors took Buddhist orders. Thus for a time the imperial house was a contender for political power along with other aristocratic groups.

cloistered government
A system in which an emperor retired to a Buddhist monastery, but continued to exercise power by controlling his young son on the throne.

Aristocratic Culture

A brilliant aristocratic culture developed in the Heian period. It was strongly focused on the capital, where nobles, palace ladies, and imperial family members lived a highly refined and leisured life. Their society was one in which niceties of birth, rank, and breeding counted for everything. From their diaries we know of the pains aristocratic women took in selecting the color combinations of the kimonos they wore, layer upon layer. Even among men, knowing how to dress tastefully was more important than skill with a horse or sword. The elegance of one's calligraphy and the allusions in one's poems were matters of intense concern to both men and women at court. Courtiers did not like to leave the capital, and some like the court lady Sei Shonagon shuddered at the sight of ordinary working people. In her *Pillow Book,* she wrote of encountering a group of commoners on a pilgrimage: "They looked like so many basket-worms as they crowded together in their hideous clothes, leaving hardly an inch of space between themselves and me. I really felt like pushing them all over sideways."[4] (See the feature "Listening to the Past: *The Pillow Book* of Sei Shonagon" on pages 348–349.)

In this period a new script was developed for writing Japanese phonetically. Each symbol, based on a simplified Chinese character, represented one of the syllables used in Japanese (such as *ka, ki, ku, ke, ko*). Although "serious" essays, histories, and government documents continued to be written in Chinese, less formal works such as poetry and memoirs were written in Japanese. Mastering the new writing system took much less time than mastering writing in Chinese and aided the spread of literacy, especially among women in court society.

In Heian, women played important roles at all levels of society. Women educated in the arts and letters could advance at court as attendants to the rulers' consorts. Women could inherit property from their parents, and they would compete with their brothers for shares of the family property. In political life, marrying a daughter to an emperor or shogun was one of the best ways to gain power, and women often became major players in power struggles.

The literary masterpiece of this period is *The Tale of Genji,* written in Japanese by Lady Murasaki over several years (ca. 1000–1010). This long narrative depicts a cast of characters enmeshed in court life, with close attention to dialogue and personality. Murasaki also wrote a diary that is similarly revealing of aristocratic culture. In one passage she tells of an occasion when word got out that she had read the Chinese classics:

Worried what people would think if they heard such rumors, I pretended to be unable to read even the inscriptions on the screens. Then Her Majesty asked me to read to her here and there from the collected works of [the Tang Chinese poet] Bo Juyi, and, because she evinced a desire to know much more about such things, we carefully chose a time when other women would not be present and, amateur that I was, I read with her the two books of Bo Juyi's New Ballads *in secret; we started the summer before last.*[5]

Despite the reluctance of Murasaki and the lady she served to let others know of their learning, there were, in fact, quite a few women writers in this period. The wife of a high-ranking court official wrote a poetic memoir of her unhappy twenty-year marriage to him and his rare visits. One woman wrote both an autobiography that related her father's efforts to find favor at court and a love story of a hero who travels to China. Another woman even wrote a history that concludes with a triumphal biography of Fujiwara Michinaga.

Buddhism remained very strong throughout the Heian period. A mission sent to China in 804 included two monks in search of new texts. Saichō spent time at Mount Tiantai and brought back Tendai teachings. Tendai's basic message is that all living beings share the Buddha nature and can be brought to salvation. Tendai practices include strict monastic discipline, prayer, textual study, and meditation. Once back in Japan, Saichō established a monastery on Mount Hiei, outside Kyoto, which grew to be one of the most important monasteries in Japan. By the twelfth century this monastery and its many branch temples had vast lands and a powerful army of monk-soldiers to protect its interests. Whenever the monastery felt that its interests were at risk, it sent the monk-soldiers into the capital to parade its sacred symbols in an attempt to intimidate the civil authorities.

Kūkai, the other monk on the 804 mission to China, came back with texts from another school of Buddhism—Shingon, "True Word," a form of **Esoteric Buddhism.** Esoteric Buddhism is based on the idea that teachings containing the secrets of enlightenment had been secretly transmitted from the Buddha. An adept can gain access to these mysteries through initiation into the mandalas (cosmic diagrams), mudras (gestures), and mantras (verbal formulas). On his return to Japan, Kūkai attracted many followers and was allowed to establish a monastery at Mount Kōya, south of Osaka. The popularity of Esoteric Buddhism proved a great stimulus to art.

The Tale of Genji *A Japanese literary masterpiece written by Lady Murasaki about court life.*

Esoteric Buddhism *A sect of Buddhism that maintains that the secrets of enlightenment have been secretly transmitted from the Buddha and can be accessed through initiation into the mandalas, mudras, and mantras.*

THE SAMURAI AND THE KAMAKURA SHOGUNATE (1185–1333)

What were the causes and consequences of military rule in Japan?

The rise of a warrior elite finally brought an end to the domination of the Fujiwaras and other Heian aristocratic families. In 1156 civil war broke out between the Taira and Minamoto clans, warrior clans with bases in western and eastern Japan, respectively. Both clans relied on skilled warriors, later called samurai, who were rapidly becoming a new social class. A samurai and his lord had a double bond: in return for the samurai's loyalty and service, the lord granted him land or income. From 1159 to 1181 a Taira named Kiyomori dominated the court, taking the position of prime minister and marrying his daughter to the emperor. His relatives became governors of more than thirty provinces, managed some five hundred tax-exempt estates, and amassed a fortune in the trade with Song China and Koryŏ Korea. Still, the Minamoto clan managed to defeat them, and the Minamoto leader, Yoritomo, became shogun, or general-in-chief. With him began the Kamakura Shogunate (1185–1333). This period is often referred to as Japan's feudal period because it was dominated by a military class whose members were tied to their superiors by bonds of loyalty and supported by landed estates rather than salaries.

Military Rule

The similarities between military rule in Japan and feudalism in medieval Europe have fascinated scholars, as have the very significant differences. In Europe feudalism emerged out of the fusion of Germanic and Roman social institutions and flowered under the impact of Muslim and Viking invasions. In Japan military rule evolved from a combination of the native warrior tradition and Confucian ethical principles of duty to superiors.

Bushido *Literally, the "Way of the Warrior," this was the code of conduct by which samurai were expected to live.*

military land stewards *Officials placed in charge of overseeing estates.*

military governors *Officials appointed to enforce the law in the provinces and oversee the samurai there.*

The emergence of the samurai was made possible by the development of private landholding. The government land allotment system, copied from Tang China, began breaking down in the eighth century (much as it did in China). By the ninth century local lords began escaping imperial taxes and control by formally giving (commending) their land to tax-exempt entities such as monasteries, the imperial family, and certain high-ranking officials. The local lord then received his land back as a tenant and paid his protector a small rent. The monastery or privileged individual received a steady income from the land, and the local lord escaped imperial taxes and control. By the end of the thirteenth century most land seems to have been taken off the tax rolls this way. Each plot of land could thus have several people with rights to shares of its produce, ranging from the cultivator, to a local lord, to an estate manager working for him, to a regional strongman, to a noble or temple in the capital. Unlike peasants in medieval Europe, where similar practices of commendation occurred, the cultivators in Japan never became serfs. Moreover, Japanese lords rarely lived on the lands they had rights in, unlike English or French lords who lived on their manors.

Samurai resembled European knights in several ways. Both were armed with expensive weapons, and both fought on horseback. Just as the knight was supposed to live according to the chivalric code, so Japanese samurai were expected to live according to **Bushido,** or "Way of the Warrior," a code that stressed military honor, courage, stoic acceptance of hardship, and, above all, loyalty. Physical hardship was accepted as routine, and soft living was despised as weak and unworthy. Disloyalty brought social disgrace, which the samurai could avoid only through *seppuku,* ritual suicide by slashing his belly.

The Kamakura Shogunate derives its name from Kamakura, a city near modern Tokyo that was the seat of the Minamoto clan. The founder, Yoritomo, ruled the country much the way he ran his own estates, appointing his retainers to newly created offices. To cope with the emergence of hard-to-tax estates, he put **military land stewards** in charge of seeing to the estates' proper operation. To bring order to the lawless countryside, he appointed **military governors** to oversee the military and enforce the law in the provinces. They supervised the conduct of the land stewards in peacetime and commanded the provincial samurai in war.

● **Samurai Armor** A member of the Taira clan once wore this twelfth-century set of armor. Armor had to serve the practical purpose of defense, but as in medieval Europe and medieval Islam, it was often embellished, turning armor into works of art. *(Suzanne Perrin/Japan Interlink)*

Yoritomo's wife Masako protected the interests of her own family, the Hōjōs, especially after Yoritomo died. She went so far as to force her first son to abdicate when he showed signs of preferring the family of his wife to the family of his mother. She later helped her brother take power away from her father. Thus the process of reducing power holders to figureheads went one step further in 1219 when the Hōjō family reduced the shogun to a figurehead. The Hōjō family held the reins of power until 1333.

The Mongols' two massive seaborne invasions in 1274 and 1281 (see page 300) were a huge shock to the shogunate. The Kamakura government was hard-pressed to gather adequate resources for its defense. Temples were squeezed, farmers taken away from their fields to build walls, and warriors promised generous rewards. Although the Hōjō regents, with the help of a "divine wind" (*kamikaze*), repelled the Mongols, they were unable to reward their vassals in the traditional way because little booty was found among the wreckage of the Mongol fleets. Discontent grew among the samurai, and by the fourteenth century the entire political system was breaking down. Both the imperial and the shogunate families were fighting among themselves. As land grants were divided, samurai became impoverished and took to plunder and piracy, or shifted their loyalty to local officials who could offer them a better living.

The factional disputes among Japan's leading families remained explosive until 1331, when the emperor Go-Daigo tried to recapture real power. His attempt sparked an uprising by the great families, local lords, samurai, and even Buddhist monasteries, which had thousands of samurai retainers. Go-Daigo destroyed the Kamakura Shogunate in 1333 but soon lost the loyalty of his followers. By 1338 one of his most important military supporters, Ashikaga Takauji, had turned on him and established the Ashikaga Shogunate, which lasted until 1573. Takauji's victory was also a victory for the samurai, who took over civil authority throughout Japan.

Cultural Trends

The cultural distance between the elites and the commoners narrowed a little during the Kamakura period. In this period Buddhism was vigorously spread to ordinary Japanese by energetic preachers. Hōnen propagated the Pure Land teaching (see page 152), preaching that paradise could be reached through simple faith in the Buddha and repeating the name of the Buddha Amitabha. Neither philosophical understanding of Buddhist scriptures nor devotion to rituals was essential. His follower Shinran taught that monks should not shut themselves off in monasteries but should marry and have children. Nichiren, a fiery and intolerant preacher, proclaimed that to be saved people had only to invoke sincerely the Lotus Sutra. These lay versions of Buddhism found a receptive audience among ordinary people in the countryside.

It was also during the Kamakura period that **Zen** (Chan) came to flourish in Japan. As mentioned in Chapter 6, Zen teachings originated in Tang China. Rejecting the authority of the sutras, Zen teachers claimed the superiority of mind-to-mind transmission of Buddhist truth. When Japanese monks went to

Zen *A school of Buddhism that emphasized meditation and truths that could not be conveyed in words.*

● **The Shogun Minamoto Yoritomo in Court Dress** This wooden sculpture, 27.8 inches tall (70.6 cm), was made about a half century after Yoritomo's death for use in a shrine dedicated to his memory. The bold shapes convey Yoritomo's dignity and power. *(Tokyo National Museum/image: TNM Image Archives; http://TnmArchives.jp/)*

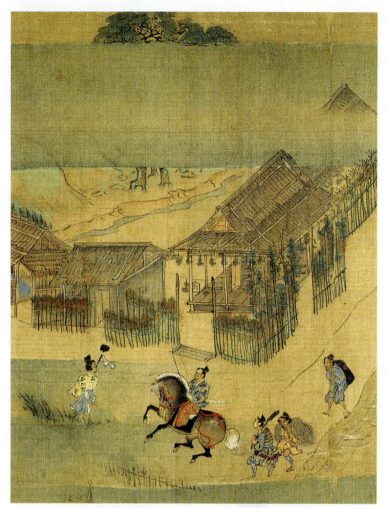

● **The Itinerant Preacher Ippen** The monk Ippen traveled through Japan urging people to call on the Amida Buddha through song and dance. This detail from a set of twelve paintings done in 1299, a decade after his death, shows him with his belongings on his back as he approaches a village. *(Tokyo National Museum/ image: TNM Image Archives; http://TnmArchives.jp/)*

China in the twelfth century looking for ways to revitalize Japanese Buddhism, they were impressed by the rigorous monastic life of the Chan/Zen monasteries. One school of Zen held that enlightenment could be achieved suddenly through insight into one's own true nature. This school taught rigorous meditation and the use of kōan riddles to unseat logic and free the mind for enlightenment. This teaching found eager patrons among the samurai, who were attracted to its discipline and strong master-disciple bonds.

Buddhism remained central to the visual arts. Many temples in Japan still house fine sculptures done in this period. In painting, narrative handscrolls brought to life the miracles that faith could bring and the torments of Hell awaiting unbelievers. All forms of literature could be depicted in these scrolls, including *The Tale of Genji,* war stories, and humorous anecdotes.

During the Kamakura period the tradition of long narrative prose works was continued with the war tale. *The Tale of the Heike,* written by a courtier in the early thirteenth century, tells the story of the fall of the Taira family and the rise of the Minamoto clan. The tale reached a large audience because blind minstrels would chant sections of the tale to the accompaniment of the lute. The story is suffused with the Buddhist idea of the transience of life and the illusory nature of glory. Yet it also celebrates strength, courage, loyalty, and pride. The Minamoto warriors from the east are portrayed as the toughest. In one scene one of them dismisses his own prowess with the bow, claiming that other warriors from his region could pierce three sets of armor with their arrows. He then brags about the martial spirit of warriors from the east: "They are bold horsemen who never fall, nor do they let their horses stumble on the roughest road. When they fight they do not care if even their parents or children are killed; they ride over their bodies and continue the battle."[6] In this they stood in contrast to the warriors of the west who in good Confucian fashion would retire from battle to mourn their parents.

After stagnating in the Heian period, agricultural productivity began to improve in the Kamakura period, and the population grew, reaching perhaps 8.2 million by 1333. Much like farmers in contemporary Song China, Japanese farmers in this period adopted new strains of rice, often double-cropped in warmer regions, made increased use of fertilizers, and improved irrigation for paddy rice. Besides farming, ordinary people could make their livings as artisans, traders, fishermen, and entertainers. Although trade in human beings was banned, those who fell into debt might sell themselves or their children, and professional slave traders kidnapped women and children. A vague category of outcastes occupied the fringes of society. Buddhist strictures against killing and Shinto ideas of pollution probably account for the exclusion of butchers, leatherworkers, morticians, and lepers, but other groups, such as bamboo whisk makers, were also traditionally excluded for no obvious reason.

● **Zen Rock Garden**   Rock gardens, such as this one at Ryoanji in Kyoto, capture the austere aesthetic of Zen Buddhism. *(Ryoanji Temple/DNP Archives)*

Chapter Summary

To assess your mastery of this chapter, go to
bedfordstmartins.com/mckayworld

● **What allowed China to become a world leader economically and intellectually in this period?**

In the period from 800 to 1100, China's population doubled to 100 million, and its economy became increasingly commercialized. There was a huge increase in the use of money and even the introduction of paper money. Cities grew, and the economic center of China shifted from the north China plain to the south, the region drained by the Yangzi River.

● **How did the civil service examinations and the scholar-official class shape Chinese society and culture?**

China's great wealth could not be easily converted to military supremacy, and Song had to pay tribute to its northern neighbors. The booming economy and the invention of printing did allow a great expansion in the size of the educated class in the Song period, which came to dominate the government. The

Key Terms

dynastic cycle
paper money
compass
examination system
movable type
Neo-Confucianism
concubine
foot binding
cloistered government
The Tale of Genji
Esoteric Buddhism
Bushido
military land stewards
military governors
Zen

life of the educated class in Song times was strongly shaped by the civil service examinations, which most educated men spent a decade or more studying for, often unsuccessfully. Their high levels of education fostered interests in literature, antiquities, philosophy, and art, but may well have been a disadvantage when the times called for military leadership. Because there were more educated men, more books were written, and because of the spread of printing, a much greater share of them have survived to the present, making it possible to see dimensions of life poorly documented for earlier periods, such as the lives of women.

• How did the Heian form of government contribute to the cultural flowering of the period?

In marked contrast to Song China, in Heian Japan a tiny aristocracy dominated government and society. More important than the emperors were a series of regents, most of them from the Fujiwara family and fathers-in-law of the emperors. The aristocratic court society put great emphasis on taste and refinement. Women were influential at the court and wrote much of the best literature of the period. The Heian aristocrats had little interest in life in the provinces, which gradually came under the control of military clans.

• What were the causes and consequences of military rule in Japan?

After a civil war between the two leading military clans, a military government, called the shogunate, was established in the east. Emperors were still placed on the throne, but they had little power. During this period of military rule, culture was no longer so capital-centered, and Buddhism was vigorously spread to ordinary people. Arts that appealed to the samurai, such as war stories and Zen Buddhism, all flourished.

Suggested Reading

Bol, Peter K. *"This Culture of Ours": Intellectual Transitions in T'ang and Sung China.* 1992. A challenging inquiry into how intellectuals evaluated learning and culture.

Chaffee, John W. *The Thorny Gates of Learning in Sung China: A Social History of Examinations.* 1985. Documents the wide-ranging impact of the examination system and the ways men could improve their chances.

Ebrey, Patricia Buckley. *The Inner Quarters: Marriage and the Lives of Chinese Women in the Sung Period.* 1993. Overview of the many facets of women's lives, from engagements to dowries, childrearing, and widowhood.

Egan, Ronald. *Word, Image, and Deed in the Life of Su Shi.* 1994. A sympathetic portrait of one of the most talented men of the age.

Farris, Wayne W. *Heavenly Warriors.* 1992. Argues against Western analogies in explaining the dominance of the samurai.

Friday, Karl F. *Hired Swords.* 1992. Treats the evolution of state military development in connection with the emergence of the samurai.

Gernet, Jacques. *Daily Life in China on the Eve of the Mongol Invasion, 1250–76.* 1962. An accessible, lively introduction to the Song period.

Hansen, Valerie. *Changing the Gods in Medieval China, 1127–1276.* 1990. A portrait of the religious beliefs and practices of ordinary people in Song times.

Morris, Ivan. *The World of the Shining Prince: Court Life in Ancient Japan.* 1964. An engaging portrait of Heian culture based on both fiction and nonfiction sources.

Souyri, Pierre François. *The World Turned Upside Down: Medieval Japanese Society.* 2001. A thought-provoking analysis of both the social system and the mentalities of Japan's Middle Ages.

Notes

1. *The Travels of Marco Polo, the Venetian,* ed. Manuel Komroff (New York: Boni and Liveright, 1926), p. 227.
2. Ibid., p. 159.
3. Ibid., p. 235.
4. Ivan Morris, trans., *The Pillow Book of Sei Shonagon* (New York: Penguin Books, 1970), p. 258.
5. Quoted in M. Collcott, M. Jansen, and I. Kumakura, *Cultural Atlas of Japan* (New York: Facts on File, 1988), p. 82, slightly modified.
6. Ibid., p. 101.

Listening to the PAST

The Pillow Book of Sei Shonagon

Beginning in the late tenth century, Japan produced a series of great women writers. At the time women were much freer than men to write in vernacular Japanese, giving them a large advantage. Lady Murasaki, author of the novel The Tale of Genji, *is the most famous of the women writers of the period, but her contemporary Sei Shonagon is equally noteworthy. Sei Shonagon served as a lady in waiting to Empress Sadako during the last decade of the tenth century (990–1000). Her only known work is* The Pillow Book, *a collection of notes, character sketches, anecdotes, descriptions of nature, and eccentric lists such as boring things, awkward things, hateful things, and things that have lost their power.*

The Pillow Book portrays the lovemaking/marriage system among the aristocracy more or less as it is depicted in The Tale of Genji. *Marriages were arranged for family interests, and men could have more than one wife. Wives and their children commonly stayed in their own homes, where their husbands and fathers would visit them. But once a man had an heir by his wife, there was nothing to prevent him from establishing relations with other women. Some relationships were long-term, but many were brief, and men often had several lovers at the same time. Some women became known for their amorous conquests, others as abandoned women whose husbands ignored them. The following passage from* The Pillow Book *looks on this lovemaking system with amused detachment.*

It is so stiflingly hot in the Seventh Month that even at night one keeps all the doors and lattices open. At such times it is delightful to wake up when the moon is shining and to look outside. I enjoy it even when there is no moon. But to wake up at dawn and see a pale sliver of a moon in the sky—well, I need hardly say how perfect that is.

I like to see a bright new straw mat that has just been spread out on a well-polished floor. The best place for one's three-foot curtain of state is in the front of the room near the veranda. It is pointless to put it in the rear of the room, as it is most unlikely that anyone will peer in from that direction.

It is dawn and a woman is lying in bed after her lover has taken his leave. She is covered up to her head with a light mauve robe that has a lining of dark violet; the colour of both the outside and the lining is fresh and glossy. The woman, who appears to be asleep, wears an unlined orange robe and a dark crimson skirt of stiff silk whose cords hang loosely by her side, as if they have been left untied. Her thick tresses tumble over each other in cascades, and one can imagine how long her hair must be when it falls freely down her back.

Nearby another woman's lover is making his way home in the misty dawn. He is wearing loose violet trousers, an orange hunting costume, so lightly coloured that one can hardly tell whether it has been dyed or not, a white robe of still silk, and a scarlet robe of glossy, beaten silk. His clothes, which are damp from the mist, hang loosely about him. From the dishevelment of his side locks one can tell how negligently he must have tucked his hair into the black lacquered headdress when he got up. He wants to return and write his next-morning letter before the dew on the morning glories has had time to vanish; but the path seems endless, and to divert himself he hums "the sprouts in the flax fields."

As he walks along, he passes a house with an open lattice. He is on his way to report for official duty, but cannot help stopping to lift up the blind and peep into the room. It amuses him to think that a man has probably been spending the night here and has only recently got up to leave, just as happened to himself. Perhaps that man too had felt the charm of the dew.

Looking around the room, he notices near the woman's pillow an open fan with a magnolia frame and purple paper; and at the foot of her curtain of state he sees some narrow strips of Michinoku paper and also some other paper of a faded colour, either orange-red or maple.

The woman senses that someone is watching her and, looking up from under her bedclothes, sees a gentleman leaning against the wall by the threshold, a smile on his face. She can tell at once that he is the

During the Heian period, noblewomen were fashion-conscious. Wearing numerous layers of clothing gave women the opportunity to choose different designs and colors for their robes. The layers also kept them warm in drafty homes. *(The Museum Yamato Bunkakan)*

sort of man with whom she need feel no reserve. All the same, she does not want to enter into any familiar relations with him, and she is annoyed that he should have seen her asleep.

"Well, well, Madam," says the man, leaning forward so that the upper part of his body comes behind her curtains, "what a long nap you're having after your morning adieu! You really are a lie-abed!"

"You call me that, Sir," she replied, "only because you're annoyed at having had to get up before the dew had time to settle."

Their conversation may be commonplace, yet I find there is something delightful about the scene.

Now the gentleman leans further forward and, using his own fan, tries to get hold of the fan by the woman's pillow. Fearing his closeness, she moves further back into her curtain enclosure, her heart pounding. The gentleman picks up the magnolia fan and, while examining it, says in a slightly bitter tone, "How standoffish you are!"

But now it is growing light; there is a sound of people's voices, and it looks as if the sun will soon be up. Only a short while ago this same man was hurrying home to write his next-morning letter before the mists had time to clear. Alas, how easily his intentions have been forgotten!

While all this is afoot, the woman's original lover has been busy with his own next-morning letter, and

now, quite unexpectedly, the messenger arrives at her house. The letter is attached to a spray of bush-clover, still damp with dew, and the paper gives off a delicious aroma of incense. Because of the new visitor, however, the woman's servants cannot deliver it to her.

Finally it becomes unseemly for the gentleman to stay any longer. As he goes, he is amused to think that a similar scene may be taking place in the house he left earlier that morning.

Questions for Analysis

1. What sorts of images does Sei Shonagon evoke to convey an impression of a scene?

2. What can you learn from this passage about the material culture of Japan in this period?

3. Why do you think Sei Shonagon was highly esteemed as a writer?

Source: Ivan Morris, trans., *The Pillow Book of Sei Shonagon* (New York: Penguin Books, 1970), pp. 60–62. Copyright © 1970. Reprinted by permission of Oxford University Press.

Scenes of Agricultural Work, ca. 1190, from a German manuscript, *Speculum Virginum.* The artist shows many tasks and portrays the way these were shared by men, women, and children. *(Landschaftsverband Rheinland/Rheinisches Landesmuseum, Bonn)*

chapter

13 EUROPE IN THE MIDDLE AGES, 850–1400

Chapter Preview

Political Developments
• How did medieval rulers overcome internal divisions and external threats, and work to create larger and more stable territories?

Revival and Reform in the Christian Church
• How did the Christian church enhance its power and create new institutions and religious practices?

The Crusades
• What were the motives, course, and consequences of the Crusades?

The Changing Life of the People
• What was life like for the common people of medieval Europe, and how were the lives of nobles and townspeople different?

The Culture of the Middle Ages
• What were the primary new cultural institutions and forms developed in medieval Europe?

Crises of the Later Middle Ages
• Why has the late Middle Ages been seen as a time of calamity and crisis?

The Italian Renaissance humanist Francesco Petrarch (1304–1374) coined the term *Middle Ages* to describe the period in European history from the end of the Roman Empire until his own time. Petrarch believed that his own age was a golden age marked by intellectual and cultural brilliance that recaptured the cultural splendor of ancient Roman civilization. Between the Roman world and the Renaissance, Petrarch believed, were the "Middle Ages," a time of Gothic barbarism and intellectual stagnation. Petrarch's terminology and time divisions have been widely adapted, but he had it wrong about barbarism and stagnation. Europeans developed new political and economic structures in the medieval period and displayed enormous intellectual energy and creative vitality.

One of the concepts that became more widely used was, in fact, the notion of "Europe." Classical geographers used the term *Europe* to distinguish this landmass from Africa and Asia, but in the medieval period the idea that there was a distinctive European culture began to take shape. While the peoples living there did not define themselves as European for centuries, a European identity began to be forged in the medieval period. That identity was shaped by interactions with other parts of the world and by Europeans' own expansion in this era.

POLITICAL DEVELOPMENTS

How did medieval rulers overcome internal divisions and external threats, and work to create larger and more stable territories?

Petrarch dated the beginning of the Middle Ages to the fifth century, the time of the fall of the Roman Empire in the West. The growth of Germanic kingdoms such as those of the Merovingians and Carolingians (see page 182) are thus generally viewed as the beginning of "medieval" politics in Europe. After a period of disruption in the ninth and tenth centuries, rulers built on Carolingian models to restore order and create new systems of law and justice.

Feudalism and Manorialism

vassal *A knight who has sworn loyalty to a particular lord. Vassal is derived from a Celtic word meaning "servant."*

fief *A portion of land, the use of which was given by a lord to a vassal in exchange for the latter's oath of loyalty.*

feudalism *A medieval European political system that defines the military obligations and relations between a lord and his vassals and involves the granting of fiefs.*

manorialism *The economic system that governed rural life in medieval Europe, in which the landed estates of a lord were worked by the peasants under his jurisdiction in exchange for his protection.*

serf *A peasant who lost his freedom and became permanently bound to the landed estate of a lord.*

The large-scale division of Charlemagne's empire was accompanied by a decentralization of power at the local level. Civil wars weakened the power and prestige of kings who could do little about domestic violence. Likewise, the great invasions of the ninth century, especially the Viking invasions (see page 353), weakened royal authority. The Frankish kings could do little to halt the invaders, and the local aristocracy had to assume responsibility for defense. Common people turned for protection to the strongest power, the local counts, whom they considered their rightful rulers. Thus, in the ninth and tenth centuries great aristocratic families increased their authority.

The most powerful nobles were those able to gain the allegiance of warriors, often symbolized in an oath-swearing ceremony of homage and fealty that grew out of earlier Germanic oaths of loyalty. In this ceremony, a warrior (knight) swore his loyalty as a **vassal**—from a Celtic term meaning "servant"—to the more powerful individual, who became his lord. In return for the vassal's loyalty, aid, and military assistance, the lord promised him protection and material support. This support might be a place in the lord's household but was more likely land of the vassal's own, called a **fief** (*feudum* in Latin). The fief might contain forests, churches, and towns. The fief theoretically still belonged to the lord, and the vassal only had the use of it. Peasants living on a fief produced the food and other goods necessary to maintain the knight.

Though historians debate this, fiefs appear to have been granted extensively first by Charles Martel and then by his successors, including Charlemagne and his grandsons. These fiefs went to their most powerful nobles, who often took the title of count. As the Carolingians' control of their territories weakened, the practice of granting fiefs moved to the local level, with lay lords, bishops, and abbots as well as kings granting fiefs. This system, later named **feudalism,** was based on personal ties of loyalty cemented by grants of land rather than on allegiance to an abstract state or governmental system.

Feudalism concerned the rights, powers, and lifestyles of the military elite. **Manorialism** involved the services of the peasant class. The two were linked. The economic power of the warrior class rested on landed estates, which were worked by peasants. Peasants needed protection, and lords demanded something in return for that protection. Free farmers surrendered themselves and their land to the lord's jurisdiction. The land was given back to them to farm, but they were tied to the land by various payments and services. Those obligations varied from place to place, but certain practices became common everywhere. The peasant had to give the lord a percentage of the annual harvest, pay a fine to marry someone from outside the lord's estate, and pay a fine—usually the best sheep or cow owned—to inherit property. Most significant, the peasant lost his freedom and became a **serf,** part of the lord's permanent labor force, bound to the land and unable to leave it without the lord's permission. With large tracts of land and a small pool of labor, the most profitable form of capital was not land but laborers.

● **Homage and Fealty** Although the rite of entering a feudal relationship varied widely across Europe and sometimes was entirely verbal, we have a few illustrations of it. Here the vassal kneels before the lord, places his clasped hands between those of the lord, and declares, "I become your man." Sometimes the lord handed over a clump of earth, representing the fief, and the ceremony concluded with a kiss, symbolizing peace between them. *(Osterreichische Nationalbibliothek)*

The transition from freedom to serfdom was slow, depending on the degree of political order in a given region. By the year 800, though, perhaps 60 percent of the population of western Europe had been reduced to serfdom. While there were many economic levels within this serf class, from the highly prosperous to the desperately poor, all had lost their freedom.

Invasions and Migrations

From the moors of Scotland to the mountains of Sicily, there arose in the ninth century the prayer, "Save us, O God, from the violence of the Northmen." The Northmen, also known as Normans or Vikings, were pagan Germanic peoples from Norway, Sweden, and Denmark who had remained beyond the sway of the Christianizing and civilizing influences of the Carolingian Empire. Some scholars believe that the name *Viking* derives from the Old Norse word *vik*, meaning "creek." A Viking, then, was a pirate who waited in a creek or bay to attack passing vessels.

Viking assaults began around 800, and by the mid-tenth century the Vikings had brought large sections of continental Europe and Britain under their sway. In the east, they pierced the rivers of Russia as far as the Black Sea. In the west, they established permanent settlements on Iceland and short-lived ones in Greenland and Newfoundland in Canada (see Map 13.1).

The Vikings were superb seamen with advanced methods of boatbuilding. Propelled either by oars or by sails, deckless, and about sixty-five-feet long, a Viking ship could carry between forty and sixty men—quite enough to harass an isolated monastery or village. Against these ships navigated by thoroughly experienced and utterly fearless sailors, the Carolingian Empire, with no navy, was helpless. At first the Vikings attacked and sailed off laden with booty. Later, on returning, they settled down and colonized the areas they had conquered.

Along with the Vikings, groups of central European steppe peoples known as Magyars also raided villages in the late ninth century, taking plunder and captives and forcing leaders to pay tribute in an effort to prevent further looting and destruction. Moving westward, small bands of Magyars on horseback reached as far as Spain and the Atlantic coast. They subdued northern Italy, compelled Bavaria and Saxony to pay tribute, and penetrated even into the Rhineland and Burgundy. People thought of them as returning Huns, so the Magyars came to be known as Hungarians. They settled in the area that is now Hungary, became Christian, and in the eleventh century allied with the papacy.

From the south, the Muslims also began new encroachments, concentrating on the two southern peninsulas, Italy and Spain. In Italy the Muslims held Sicily, then drove northward and sacked Rome in 846. Most of Spain had remained under their domination since the eighth century. Expert seamen, they sailed around the Iberian Peninsula and braved the dangerous shoals and winds of the Atlantic coast. They also attacked Mediterranean settlements along the coast of Provence.

Chronology

ca. 800–950	Viking, Magyar, and Muslim attacks on Europe
1066–1087	Reign of William the Conqueror
1075–1122	Investiture controversy
1085–1248	Reconquista, the Christian reconquest of Spain from Muslims
1086	*Domesday Book*
1095–1270	Crusades
1180–1270	Height of construction of cathedrals in France
1215	Magna Carta
1225–1274	Life of Saint Thomas Aquinas, author of *Summa Theologica*
1309–1376	Papacy in Avignon
1315–1322	Famine in northern Europe
ca. 1337–1453	Hundred Years' War
1347	Black Death arrives in Europe
1358	Jacquerie peasant uprising in France
1378–1417	Great Schism
1431	Joan of Arc declared a heretic and burned at the stake

Viking, Magyar, and Muslim attacks accelerated the development of feudalism. Lords capable of rallying fighting men, supporting them, and putting up resistance to the invaders did so. They also assumed political power in their territories. Weak and defenseless people sought the protection of local strongmen. From the perspective of a person in what had been Charlemagne's empire, this was a period of chaos.

People in other parts of Europe might have had a different opinion, however. In Muslim Spain scholars worked in thriving cities, and new crops such as cotton and sugar enhanced ordinary people's lives. In eastern Europe states such as Moravia and Hungary became strong kingdoms. A Viking point of view might be the most positive, for by 1100 descendents of the Vikings not only ruled their homelands in Denmark, Norway, and Sweden, but also ruled northern France (a province known as Normandy), England, Sicily, Iceland, and Kievan Rus, with an outpost in Greenland and occasional voyages to North America.

MAP 13.1 **Invasions and Migrations of the Ninth Century** Vikings, Magyars, and Muslims all moved into central and western Europe in the ninth century, and Viking ships also sailed the rivers of Russia and the northern Atlantic ocean

● **The Bayeux Tapestry** William's conquest of England was recorded in thread on a narrative embroidery panel measuring 231 feet by 19 inches. In this scene, two nobles and a bishop acclaim Harold Godwinson, William's rival, as king of England. The nobles hold a sword, symbol of military power, and the bishop holds a stole, symbol of clerical power. Harold himself holds a scepter and an orb, both symbols of royal power. The embroidery provides an important historical source for the clothing, armor, and lifestyles of the Norman and Anglo-Saxon warrior class. It eventually ended up in Bayeux in northern France, where it is displayed in a museum today, and is incorrectly called a "tapestry," which is a different kind of needlework. *(Tapisserie de Bayeux et avec autorisation spéciale de la Ville de Bayeux)*

The Restoration of Order

The eleventh century witnessed the beginnings of political stability in western Europe. Foreign invasions gradually declined, and in some parts of Europe rulers began to strengthen and extend their authority, creating more unified states out of the feudal system. Medieval rulers had common goals. To increase public order, they wanted to establish an effective means of communication with all peoples. They also wanted more revenue and efficient bureaucracies. The solutions they found to these problems laid the foundations for modern national states.

Political developments in England, France, and Germany provide good examples of the beginnings of the national state in the central Middle Ages. Under the pressure of Viking invasions in the ninth and tenth centuries, the seven kingdoms of Anglo-Saxon England united under one king. At the same time, England was divided into local shires, or counties, each under the jurisdiction of a sheriff appointed by the king. The kingdom of England, therefore, had a political head start on the rest of Europe.

When Edward the Confessor (r. 1042–1066) died, his cousin, Duke William of Normandy, claimed the English throne and won it by defeating his Anglo-Saxon rival at the Battle of Hastings. As William the Conqueror (r. 1066–1087) subdued the rest of the country, he distributed land to his Norman followers and required all feudal lords to swear an oath of allegiance to him as king. He retained the Anglo-Saxon institution of sheriff. The sheriff had the responsibility of catching criminals, collecting taxes, and raising soldiers for the king when ordered.

In 1085 William decided to conduct a systematic survey of the entire country to determine how much wealth there was and who had it. Groups of royal officials or judges were sent to every part of England. A priest and six local people swore an oath to answer truthfully. Because they swore (Latin, *juror*), they were called **jurors,** and from this small body of local people, the jury system in English-speaking countries gradually evolved. The records collected from the entire country, called *Domesday*

jurors *In William the Conqueror's reign, a priest and six local people who swore an oath to answer truthfully all questions about their wealth.*

Book, provided William and his descendants with vital information for governing the country.

In 1128 William's granddaughter Matilda married Geoffrey of Anjou. Their son, who became Henry II of England, inherited the French provinces of Normandy, Anjou, and Touraine in northwestern France. When Henry married the great heiress Eleanor of Aquitaine in 1152, he claimed lordship over Aquitaine, Poitou, and Gascony in southwestern France as well. The histories of England and France were thus closely intertwined in the central Middle Ages.

In the early twelfth century France consisted of a number of nearly independent provinces, each governed by its local ruler. The work of unifying France began under Philip II (r. 1180–1223), called "Augustus" because he vastly enlarged the territory of the kingdom. By the end of his reign, Philip was effectively master of northern France. His descendants acquired important holdings in southern France, and by 1300 most of the provinces of modern France had been added to the royal domain through diplomacy, marriage, war, and inheritance.

In central Europe, the German king Otto I (r. 936–973) defeated many other lords to build up his power. The basis of Otto's power was an alliance with and control of the church. Otto asserted the right to control church appointments. Bishops and abbots had to perform feudal homage for the lands that accompanied the church office. This practice, later called **lay investiture,** led to a grave crisis in the eleventh century (see page 360). German rulers were not able to build up centralized power. Under Otto I and his successors, a sort of confederacy (a weak union of strong principalities), later called the Holy Roman Empire, developed in which the emperor shared power with princes, dukes, counts, archbishops, and bishops.

Frederick Barbarossa (r. 1152–1190) of the house of Hohenstaufen tried valiantly to make the Holy Roman Empire a united state. He made alliances with the great lay princes and even compelled the great churchmen to become his vassals. Unfortunately, Frederick did not concentrate his efforts and resources in one area. He became embroiled in the affairs of Italy, hoping to cash in on the wealth Italian cities had gained through trade. He led six expeditions into Italy, but his brutal methods provoked revolts, and the cities, allied with the papacy, defeated him in 1176. Frederick was forced to recognize the autonomy of the cities. Meanwhile, back in Germany, Frederick's absence allowed the princes and other rulers of independent provinces to consolidate their power.

lay investiture   *The selection and appointment of church officials by secular authorities.*

Law and Justice

Throughout Europe in the twelfth and thirteenth centuries, the law was a hodge-podge of customs, feudal rights, and provincial practices. Kings wanted to blend these elements into a uniform system of rules acceptable and applicable to all their peoples. In France and England, kings successfully contributed to the development of national states through the administration of their laws.

The French king Louis IX (r. 1226–1270) was famous in his time for his concern for justice. Each French province, even after being made part of the kingdom of France, retained its unique laws and procedures, but Louis IX created a royal judicial system. He established the Parlement of Paris, a kind of supreme court that welcomed appeals from local administrators and from the courts of feudal lords throughout France.

Under Henry II (r. 1154–1189), England developed and extended a **common law**—a law common to and accepted by the entire country. No other country in medieval Europe did so. Each year Henry sent out *circuit judges* (royal officials who traveled in a given circuit or district) to hear civil and criminal cases. Wherever the king's judges sat, there sat the king's court. Slowly, the king's court gained jurisdiction over all property disputes and criminal actions.

common law   *A law that originated in, and was applied by, the king's court.*

Proving guilt or innocence in criminal cases could pose a problem. Where there was no specific accuser, the court sought witnesses, then looked for written evidence. If the judges found neither and the suspect had a bad reputation in the community, the person went to trial by ordeal. He or she was bound hand and foot and dropped into a lake or river. Because water was supposed to be a pure substance, it would reject anything foul or unclean. Thus the innocent person would sink and the guilty person float. Because God determined guilt or innocence, a priest had to be present to bless the water. Henry disliked the system because the clergy controlled the procedure and because many suspicious people seemed to beat the system and escape punishment, but he had no alternative. Then in 1215 the church's Fourth Lateran Council forbade priests' participation in such trials, effectively ending them. Royal justice was desacralized. In the course of the thirteenth century, the king's judges adopted the practice of calling on twelve people to decide the accused's guilt or innocence. Trial by jury was only gradually accepted; medieval Europeans had more confidence in the judgment of God than in that of ordinary people.

Henry's son John (r. 1199–1216) met with serious disappointment. He lost the French province of Normandy to Philip Augustus in 1204 and spent the rest of his reign trying to win it back. Saddled with heavy debt from his father and brother Richard (r. 1189–1199), John tried to squeeze more money from nobles and town-dwellers, which created an atmosphere of resentment.

When John's military campaign failed in 1214, it was clear that the French lands that had once belonged to the English king were lost for good. His ineptitude as a soldier in a culture that idealized military glory turned the people against him. The barons revolted and in 1215 forced him to attach his seal to Magna Carta—the "Great Charter," which became the cornerstone of English justice and law.

Magna Carta signifies the principle that the king and the government shall be under the law and that everyone, including the king, must obey the law. If a government is to be legitimate, the theory emerged, then government must operate according to the *rule of law*. Some clauses of Magna Carta contain the germ of the ideas of *due process of law* and the right to a fair and speedy trial. A person may not be arbitrarily arrested and held indefinitely in prison without being accused of crime and brought to trial. Every English king in the Middle Ages reissued Magna Carta as evidence of his promise to observe the law. Centuries later, ideas of the rule of law and due process had global consequences.

> **Primary Source:**
> **Magna Carta: The Great Charter of Liberties**
> *Learn what rights and liberties the English nobility, on behalf of all free Englishmen, forced King John to grant them in 1215.*

REVIVAL AND REFORM IN THE CHRISTIAN CHURCH

How did the Christian church enhance its power and create new institutions and religious practices?

The eleventh century witnessed the beginnings of a remarkable religious revival. Monasteries remodeled themselves, and new religious orders were founded. After a century of corruption and decadence, the papacy reformed itself. The popes worked to clarify church doctrine and codify church law. Religion structured people's daily lives and the yearly calendar. Christianity expanded into Europe's northern and eastern regions, and Christian rulers expanded their holdings in Muslim Spain.

Monastic Reforms

The Viking, Magyar, and Muslim invaders attacked and ransacked many monasteries across Europe. Some religious communities fled and dispersed. In the period of political disorder that followed the disintegration of the Carolingian Empire, many religious houses fell under the control and domination of local feudal lords. Powerful laymen appointed themselves as abbots but kept their wives or mistresses. They took for themselves the lands and goods of monasteries, spending monastic revenues and selling monastic offices. The level of spiritual observance and intellectual activity declined.

An opportunity for reform came in 909, when William the Pious, duke of Aquitaine, established the abbey of Cluny in Burgundy. Duke William declared that the monastery was to be free from any feudal responsibilities to him or any other lord, its members subordinate only to the pope. The first two abbots of Cluny set very high standards of religious behavior and stressed strict observance of *The Rule of Saint Benedict*. Cluny gradually came to stand for clerical celibacy and the suppression of *simony* (the sale of church offices). In a disorderly world, Cluny represented religious and political stability. Laypersons placed lands under Cluny's custody and monastic houses under its jurisdiction for reform.

Deeply impressed laypeople showered gifts on monasteries with good reputations, but with this wealth came lay influence. And as the monasteries became richer, the lifestyle of the monks grew increasingly luxurious. Monastic observance and spiritual fervor declined. Soon fresh demands for reform were heard. The result was the founding of new religious orders in the late eleventh and early twelfth centuries.

The best representative of the new reforming spirit was the Cistercian order. The Cistercians combined a very simple liturgical life, a radical rejection of the traditional feudal sources of income (such as the possession of mills and serfs), and many innovative economic practices. The Cistercians' dynamic growth and rapid expansion had a profound impact on European society.

Throughout the Middle Ages, social class defined the kinds of religious life open to women and men in Europe. Kings and nobles often established convents for their daughters, sisters, aunts, or aging mothers. Entrance was restricted to women of the founder's class. (See the feature "Individuals in Society: Hildegard of Bingen.") Monks and nuns came into the convent or monastery as children.

The pattern of life within individual monasteries varied widely from house to house and from region to region. One central activity, however, was performed everywhere. Daily life centered on the *liturgy* or *Divine Office,* psalms, and other prayers, which monks and nuns prayed seven times a day and once during the night. Prayers were offered for peace, rain, good harvests, the civil authorities, the monks' and nuns' families, and their benefactors. Monastic patrons in turn lavished gifts on the monasteries, which often became very wealthy, controlling large tracts of land and the peasants who farmed them.

In the thirteenth century the growth of cities provided a new challenge for the church. Many urban people thought that the church did not fulfil their spiritual needs. They turned instead to heresies, many of which, somewhat ironically, denied the value of material wealth. Combating heresy became a principal task of new types of religious orders, most prominently the Dominicans and Franciscans, who preached, ministered to city dwellers, and also staffed the papal Inquisition, a special court designed to root out heresy. Dominicans and Franciscans also acted as missionaries in border areas of Europe, and beginning in the sixteenth century would be important agents of the spread of Christianity into European colonies around the world.

Papal Reforms

Serious efforts at papal reform began under Pope Leo IX (r. 1049–1054). He traveled widely, holding councils that issued decrees against violence, simony, and clerical marriage. Although celibacy had technically been an obligation for ordination since the fourth century, in the tenth and eleventh centuries probably a majority of European priests were married or living with a woman.

A church council produced another reform—removing the influence of Roman aristocratic factions in papal elections. Since the eighth century the priests of the

Hildegard of Bingen

The tenth child of a lesser noble family, Hildegard (1098–1179) was given when eight years old as an oblate to an abbey in the Rhineland, where she learned Latin and received a good education. She spent most of her life in various women's religious communities, two of which she founded herself. When she was a child, she began having mystical visions, often of light in the sky, but told few people about them. In middle age, however, her visions became more dramatic: "And it came to pass . . . when I was 42 years and 7 months old, that the heavens were opened and a blinding light of exceptional brilliance flowed through my entire brain. And so it kindled my whole heart and breast like a flame, not burning but warming . . . and suddenly I understood of the meaning of expositions of the books."* She wanted the church to approve of her visions and wrote first to St. Bernard of Clairvaux, who answered her briefly and dismissively, and then to Pope Eugenius, who encouraged her to write them down. Her first work was *Scivias* (Know the Ways of the Lord), a record of her mystical visions that incorporates vast theological learning (see the illustration).

Obviously possessed of leadership and administrative talents, Hildegard left her abbey in 1147 to found the convent of Rupertsberg near Bingen. There she produced *Physica* (On the Physical Elements) and *Causa et Curae* (Causes and Cures), scientific works on the curative properties of natural elements; poems; a mystery play; and several more works of mysticism. She carried on a huge correspondence with scholars, prelates, and ordinary people. When she was over fifty, she left her community to preach to audiences of clergy and laity, and she was the only woman of her time whose opinions on religious matters were considered authoritative by the church.

Hildegard's visions have been explored by theologians and also by neurologists, who judge that they may have originated in migraine headaches, as she reports many of the same phenomena that migraine sufferers do: auras of light around objects, areas of blindness, feelings of intense doubt and intense euphoria. The interpretations that she develops come from her theological insight and learning, however, not her illness. That same insight also emerges in her music, which is what she is best known for today. Eighty of her compositions survive—a huge number for a medieval composer—most of them written to be sung by the nuns in her convent, so they have strong lines for female voices. Many of her songs and chants

In one of her visions, Hildegard saw the Synagogue (the building where Jews worship) metaphorically as a very tall woman who holds in her arms Moses with the stone tablets of the Ten Commandments. *(Rheinisches Bildarchiv, Koln)*

have been recorded recently by various artists and are available on compact disk, as downloads, and on several websites.

Questions for Analysis

1. Why do you think Hildegard might have kept her visions secret? Why do you think she sought church approval for them?

2. In what ways might Hildegard's vision of Synagogue have been shaped by her own experiences? How does this vision compare with other ideas about the Jews that you have read about in this chapter?

*From *Scivias*, trans. Mother Columba Hart and Jane Bishop, *The Classics of Western Spirituallity* (New York/Mahwah: Paulist Press, 1990).

major churches around Rome had constituted a special group, called a "college," that advised the pope. They were called "cardinals," from the Latin *cardo,* or "hinge." They were the hinges on which the church turned. The Lateran Synod of 1059 decreed that these cardinals had the sole authority and power to elect the pope and that they would govern the church when the office was vacant.

By 1073 the reform movement was well advanced. That year, Cardinal Hildebrand was elected as Pope Gregory VII, and reform took on a political character. Gregory believed that the pope, as the successor of Saint Peter, was the vicar of God on earth and that papal orders were the orders of God. He insisted that the church should be completely free of lay control, and in 1075 he ordered clerics who accepted investiture from laymen to be deposed, and laymen who invested clerics to be *excommunicated*—cut off from the sacraments and the Christian community. The rulers of Europe immediately protested this restriction of their power.

The strongest reaction came from Henry IV of the Holy Roman Empire. Gregory excommunicated church officials who supported Henry, and suspended him from the emperorship. In January 1077 Henry arrived at the pope's residence in Canossa in northern Italy and, according to legend, stood outside in the snow for three days seeking forgiveness. As a priest, Gregory was obliged to grant absolution and readmit the emperor into the Christian community. Although the emperor, the most powerful ruler in Europe, bowed before the pope, Henry actually won a victory—albeit a temporary one. He regained the emperorship and authority over his subjects, but the controversy encouraged German nobles to resist any expansion in the emperor's power. The nobles gained power, subordinating knights and reducing free men and serfs to servile status. When the investiture issue was finally settled in 1122 by a compromise, the nobility held the balance of power in Germany.

Popular Religion

Religion was not simply a matter of institutions and officials in medieval Europe, but of everyday practice. Apart from the land, the weather, and local legal and social conditions, religion had the greatest impact on the daily lives of ordinary people. Religious practices varied widely from country to country and even from province to province. But nowhere was religion a one-hour-a-week affair. Most people in medieval Europe were Christian, but there were small Jewish communities scattered in many parts of Europe, as well as Muslims in the Iberian peninsula, Sicily, other Mediterranean islands, and southeastern Europe.

For Christians, the village church was the center of community life—social, political, and economic as well as religious—with the parish priest in charge of a host of activities. Every Sunday and on holy days, the villagers stood at Mass or squatted on the floor (there were no chairs), breaking the painful routine of work. The feasts that accompanied baptisms, weddings, funerals, and other celebrations were commonly held in the churchyard. Popular religion consisted largely of rituals heavy with symbolism. Before slicing a loaf of bread, the pious woman tapped the sign of the cross on it with her knife. Before planting, the village priest customarily went out and sprinkled the fields with water, symbolizing refreshment and life. Everyone participated in village processions. The entire calendar was designed with reference to Christmas, Easter, and Pentecost, events in the life of Jesus and his disciples.

Along with days marking events in the life of Jesus, the Christian calendar was filled with saints' days. **Saints** were individuals who had lived particularly holy lives and were honored locally or more widely for their connection with the divine. The cult of the saints, which developed in a rural and uneducated environment, represents a central feature of popular culture in the Middle Ages. People believed that the saints possessed supernatural powers that enabled them to perform miracles, and the saint became the special property of the locality in which his or her relics rested. Relics such as bones, articles of clothing, the saint's tears, saliva, and even the dust from the

saints *Individuals who had lived particularly holy lives and were consequently accorded great honor by medieval Christians. Saints were believed to possess the power to work miracles and were frequently invoked for healing and protection.*

saint's tomb were enclosed in the church altar. In return for the saint's healing and support, peasants would offer the saint prayers, loyalty, and gifts.

People had a strong sense of the presence of God. They believed that God rewarded the virtuous with peace, health, and material prosperity and punished sinners with disease, poor harvests, and war. Sin was caused by the Devil, who lurked everywhere and constantly incited people to evil deeds.

Increasing suspicion and hostility marked relations between religious groups throughout the Middle Ages, but there were also important similarities in the ways Christians, Jews, and Muslims in Europe understood and experienced their religions. In all three traditions, every major life transition was marked by a ceremony that included religious elements. Weddings often involved religious officials, and religious ceremonies welcomed children into the community. Death was marked by religious rituals, and the living had obligations to the dead, including prayers and special mourning periods, in all three religions.

The Expansion of Latin Christendom

The eleventh and twelfth centuries not only saw reforms in monasticism and the papacy, but also an expansion of Christianity into Scandinavia, the Baltic lands, eastern Europe, and Spain that had profound cultural consequences. Wars of expansion, the establishment of new Christian bishoprics, and the vast migration of colonists, together with the papal emphasis on a unified Christian world, brought about the gradual Europeanization of the frontier.

Latin Christian influences entered Scandinavia and the Baltic lands primarily through the creation of dioceses. This took place in Denmark in the tenth and eleventh centuries, and the institutional church spread rather quickly due to the support offered by the strong throne. Dioceses were established in Norway and Sweden in the eleventh century, and in 1164 Uppsala, long the center of the pagan cults of Odin and Thor, became a Catholic archdiocese.

Otto I (see page 356) planted a string of dioceses along his northern and eastern frontiers, hoping to pacify the newly conquered Slavs in eastern Europe. Frequent Slavic revolts illustrate the people's resentment of German lords and clerics and indicate that the church did not easily penetrate the region.

The church also moved into central Europe, first in Bohemia in the tenth century and from there into Poland and Hungary in the eleventh century. In the twelfth and thirteenth centuries thousands of settlers poured into eastern Europe. They settled in Silesia, Mecklenburg, Bohemia, Poland, Hungary, and Transylvania. New immigrants were German in descent, name, language, and law. Hundreds of small market towns populated by these newcomers supplied the needs of the rural countryside. Larger towns such as Cracow and Riga engaged in long-distance trade and gradually grew into large urban centers.

● **Almohad Banner** This finely worked embroidered banner is typical of Muslim style; it incorporates Arabic lettering on the edges and includes no representation of the human form. The Almohads were a strict Muslim dynasty from North Africa that had ruled about half of Spain in the twelfth century. In 1212 King Alfonso VIII of Castile won a decisive victory over Almohad forces at Las Navas de Tolosa, and Christian holdings in Spain increased. *(Institut Amatller d'Art Hispanic)*

The Iberian peninsula was another area of Christian expansion. About 950 Caliph Abd al-Rahman III (912–961) of the Umayyad Dynasty of Córdoba ruled most of the Iberian Peninsula. Christian Spain consisted of the small kingdoms of Castile, León, Catalonia, Aragon, Navarre, and Portugal. When civil wars erupted among Rahman's descendants, though, Muslim lands were split among several small kingdoms, and the Christian reconquest was made easier.

Fourteenth-century clerics used the term **reconquista** (reconquest) to describe what they called a sacred and patriotic crusade to wrest Spain from "alien" Muslim hands. This religious myth became part of Spanish national psychology. The reconquest took several centuries, but by 1248 Christians held all of the peninsula save for the small state of Granada.

As the Christians advanced, they changed the face of Spanish cities, transforming mosques into cathedrals and, in the process, destroying Muslim art—just as the Muslims, in the eighth century, had destroyed the pagan temples they found. The reconquista also meant the establishment of the Roman institutional church throughout Spain. Behind the advancing Christian armies came immigrants who settled in the cities that were depopulated with the expulsion of Muslims.

reconquista *A fourteenth-century term used to describe the Christian crusade to wrest Spain back from the Muslims; clerics believed it was a sacred and patriotic mission.*

Toward a Christian Society

By about 1300 frontier areas of northern and eastern Europe and Spain shared a broad cultural uniformity with the core regions of western Christendom: France, Germany, England, and Italy. The papal reform movement of the eleventh century had increased the prestige of the papacy and loyalty to it. Loyalty meant, on the local level, following the Roman liturgy, which led to a broad uniformity of religious practice across Europe.

During the reign of Pope Innocent III (1198–1216), papal directives and legates flowed to all parts of Europe. The papacy was recognized as the nerve center of a homogeneous Christian society. Europeans identified themselves as Christians and even described themselves as belonging to "the Christian race." As in the Islamic world, religion had replaced tribal and political structures as the essence of culture.

Migration and colonization, however, had a dark side. At first, legal and cultural pluralism existed: native peoples remained subject to their traditional laws, and newcomers lived under the laws of the countries from which they had come. Then, in the fourteenth century, economic tensions following the great famine and the Black Death (see pages 374–375) caused ethnic and "national" tensions to surface and multiply. In frontier regions immigrants settled in the towns, and native-born people lived in the countryside. Success in competition for openings in the guilds and for ecclesiastical offices came to be based on blood descent. Intermarriage was forbidden. Guild regulations were explicitly racist, with protectionist laws for some, exclusionist rules for others. Rulers of the Christian kingdoms of Spain passed legislation discriminating against Muslims and Jews living under Christian rule. Perhaps the harshest racial laws were in Ireland, imposed by the ruling English on the native Irish, who were denied access to the courts and basic rights and liberties.

THE CRUSADES

What were the motives, course, and consequences of the Crusades?

The expansion of Christianity in the Middle Ages was not limited to Europe, but extended to the eastern Mediterranean in what were later termed **Crusades.** Crusades in the late eleventh and early twelfth centuries were wars sponsored by the papacy for the recovery of the Holy Land from the Muslims. The word *crusade* was not actually used at the time and did not appear in English until the late sixteenth century. It means

Crusades *Holy wars sponsored by the papacy for the recovery of the Holy Land from the Muslims in the late eleventh and early twelfth centuries.*

MAP 13.2 **The Routes of the Crusades** The Crusaders took many different sea and land routes on their way to Jerusalem, often crossing the lands of the Byzantine Empire, which led to conflict with eastern Christians. The Crusader kingdoms in the East lasted only briefly.

literally "taking the cross," from the cross that soldiers sewed on their garments as a Christian symbol. At the time people going off to fight simply said they were taking "the way of the cross" or "the road to Jerusalem." Although people of all ages and classes participated in the Crusades, so many knights did so that crusading became a distinctive feature of the upper-class lifestyle. In an aristocratic, military society, men coveted reputations as Crusaders; the Christian knight who had been to the Holy Land enjoyed great prestige.

Background of the Crusades

In the eleventh century the papacy had strong reasons for wanting to launch an expedition against Muslims in the East. It had been involved in the bitter struggle over church reform and lay investiture. If the pope could muster a large army against the enemies of Christianity, his claim to be leader of Christian society in the West would be strengthened. Moreover, in 1054 a serious theological disagreement had split the Greek church of Byzantium and the Roman church of the West. The pope believed that a crusade would lead to strong Roman influence in Greek territories and eventually the reunion of the two churches.

In 1071 at Manzikert in eastern Anatolia, Turkish soldiers defeated a Greek army and occupied much of Asia Minor. The emperor at Constantinople appealed to the West for support. Shortly afterward, the holy city of Jerusalem fell to the Turks. Pilgrimages to holy places in the Middle East became very dangerous, and the papacy claimed to be outraged that the holy city was in the hands of unbelievers. Since the Muslims had held Palestine since the eighth century, the papacy actually feared that the Seljuk Turks would be less accommodating to Christian pilgrims than the previous Muslim rulers had been.

In 1095 Pope Urban II called for a great Christian holy war against the infidels. He urged Christian knights who had been fighting one another to direct their energies against the true enemies of God, the Muslims. At the same time Crusaders could acquire spiritual merit and earn themselves a place in paradise. Ideas about pilgrimage, holy warfare, and the threat to Christendom were not new; Urban tied them all together.

The Course of the Crusades

Thousands of people of all classes joined the crusade. Although most of the Crusaders were French, pilgrims from many regions streamed southward from the Rhineland, through Germany and the Balkans. Of all of the developments of the High Middle Ages, none better reveals Europeans' religious and emotional fervor and the influence of the reformed papacy than the extraordinary outpouring of support for the First Crusade.

The First Crusade was successful, mostly because of the dynamic enthusiasm of the participants. The Crusaders had little more than religious zeal. They knew little of the geography or climate of the Middle East. Although there were several counts with military experience, the Crusaders could never agree on a leader. Lines of supply were never set up. Starvation and disease wracked the army, and the Turks slaughtered hundreds of noncombatants. Nevertheless, convinced that "God wills it," the war cry of the Crusaders, the army pressed on and in 1099 captured Jerusalem. Although the Crusaders fought bravely, Arab disunity was a chief reason for their victory. At Jerusalem, Edessa, Tripoli, and Antioch, Crusader kingdoms were founded on the Western feudal model (see Map 13.2).

Primary Source:
Annals
Read a harrowing, firsthand account of the pillage of Constantinople by Western Crusaders on April 13, 1204.

Between 1096 and 1270, the crusading ideal was expressed in eight papally approved expeditions to the East. Despite the success of the First Crusade, none of the later ones accomplished very much. During the Fourth Crusade (1202–1204), careless preparation and inadequate financing had disastrous consequences for Latin-Byzantine relations. In April 1204 the Crusaders and Venetians stormed Constantinople; sacked the city, destroying its magnificent library; and grabbed thousands of relics, which were later sold in Europe. The Byzantine Empire, as a political unit, never recovered from this destruction. The empire splintered into three parts and soon consisted of little more than the city of Constantinople. Moreover, the assault of one Christian people on another—when one of the goals of the crusade was reunion of the Greek and Latin churches—made the split between the churches permanent and discredited the entire crusading movement.

Much of medieval warfare consisted of the besieging of towns and castles. Help could not enter nor could anyone leave; the larger the number of besiegers, the greater was the chance the fortification would fall. Women swelled the numbers of besiegers. Women assisted in filling with earth the moats surrounding fortified places so that ladders and war engines could be brought close. In war zones some women concealed their sex by donning chain mail and helmets and fought with the knights.

In the late thirteenth century Turkish armies gradually conquered all other Muslim rulers and then turned against the Crusader states. In 1291 their last stronghold, the port of Acre, fell in a battle that was just as bloody as the first battle for Jerusalem two centuries earlier. Knights then needed a new battlefield for military actions, which some found in Spain, where the rulers of Aragon and Castile continued fighting Muslims until 1492.

Consequences of the Crusades

The Crusades provided an outlet for nobles' dreams of glory. Wars of foreign conquest had occurred before the Crusades, as the Norman Conquest of England in 1066 illustrates (see page 377), but for many knights migration began with the taking of the cross. The Crusades introduced some Europeans to Eastern luxury goods, but their immediate cultural impact on the West remains debatable. By the late eleventh century strong economic and intellectual ties with the East had already been made. The Crusades were a boon to Italian merchants, however, who profited from outfitting military expeditions as well as from the opening of new trade routes and the establishment of trading communities in the Crusader states.

The Crusades proved to be a disaster for Jewish-Christian relations. In the eleventh century Jews played a major role in the international trade between the Muslim Middle East and the West. Jews also lent money to peasants, townspeople, and nobles. When the First Crusade was launched, many poor knights had to borrow from Jews to equip themselves for the expedition. Debt bred resentment. Hostility to Jews was further enhanced by Christian beliefs that they engaged in the ritual murder of Christians to use their blood in religious rituals. Such accusations led to the killing of Jewish families and sometimes entire Jewish communities, sometimes by burning people alive in the synagogue or Jewish section of town.

Legal restrictions on Jews gradually increased. Jews were forbidden to have Christian servants or employees, to hold public office, to appear in public on Christian holy days, or to enter Christian parts of town without a badge marking them as Jews.

The Crusades also left an inheritance of deep bitterness in Christian-Muslim relations. Each side dehumanized the other, viewing those who followed the other religion as unbelievers. (See the feature "Listening to the Past: An Arab View of the Crusades" on pages 384–385.) Whereas Europeans perceived the Crusades as sacred religious movements, Muslims saw them as expansionist and imperialistic. The ideal of a sacred mission to conquer or convert Muslim peoples entered Europeans' consciousness and became a continuing goal. When in 1492 Christopher Columbus sailed west, hoping to reach India, he used the language of the Crusades in his diaries, which show that he was preoccupied with the conquest of Jerusalem (see Chapter 15). Columbus wanted to establish a Christian base in India from which a new crusade against Islam could be launched.

●●●●●●●●●●●●●●●

THE CHANGING LIFE OF THE PEOPLE

What was life like for the common people of medieval Europe, and how were the lives of nobles and townspeople different?

In the late ninth century medieval intellectuals described Christian society as composed of those who pray (the monks), those who fight (the nobles), and those who work (the peasants). This image of society became popular in the Middle Ages, especially among people who were worried about the changes they saw around them. They asserted that the three orders had been established by God and that every person had been assigned a fixed place in the social order.

The tripartite model does not fully describe medieval society, however. There were degrees of wealth and status within each group. The model does not take townspeople and the emerging commercial classes into consideration. It completely excludes those who were not Christian, such as Jews, Muslims, and pagans. Those who used the model, generally bishops and other church officials, ignored the fact that each of these groups was made up of both women and men; they spoke only of warriors, monks, and farmers. Despite—or perhaps because of—these limitations, the model of the three orders was a powerful mental construct. We can use it to organize our investigation of life in the Middle Ages, though we can broaden our categories to include groups and issues that medieval authors did not. (See page 358 for discussion of the life of monks—"those who pray.")

Those Who Work

The men and women who worked the land in the twelfth and thirteenth centuries made up the overwhelming majority of the population, probably more than 90 percent. The evolution of localized feudal systems into more centralized states had relatively little impact on the daily lives of peasants except when it involved warfare. While only nobles fought, their battles often destroyed the houses, barns, and fields of ordinary people, who might also be killed either directly or as a result of the famine and disease that often accompanied war. People might seek protection in the local castle during times of warfare, but typically they worked and lived without paying much attention to the political developments underway there.

This lack of attention went in the other direction as well. Since villagers did not perform what were considered "noble" deeds, the aristocratic monks and clerics who wrote the records that serve as historical sources did not spend time or precious writing materials on them. So it is more difficult to find information on the vast majority of Europeans who were peasants than on the small group at the top of society.

Medieval theologians lumped everyone who worked the land into the category of "those who work," but in fact there were many levels of peasants, ranging from complete slaves to free and very rich farmers. Slaves were found in western Europe in the central Middle Ages, but in steadily declining numbers. That the word *slave* derives from *Slav* attests to the widespread trade in men and women from the Slavic areas. Legal language differed considerably from place to place, and the distinction between slave and serf was not always clear. Both lacked freedom—the power to do as they wished—and both were subject to the arbitrary will of one person, the lord. A serf, however, could not be bought and sold like an animal or an inanimate object, as a slave could.

The serf was required to perform labor services on the lord's land. The number of workdays varied, but it was usually three days a week except in the planting or harvest seasons, when it increased. Serfs frequently had to pay arbitrary levies, as for marriage or inheritance. The precise amounts of tax paid to the lord depended on local custom and tradition. A free person had to do none of these things. For his or her landholding, rent had to be paid to the lord, and that was often the sole obligation. A free person could move and live as he or she wished.

Serfdom was a hereditary condition. A person born a serf was likely to die a serf, though many serfs did secure their freedom. More than anything else, the economic revival that began in the eleventh century (see pages 368–371) advanced the cause of freedom for serfs. The revival saw the rise of towns, increased land productivity, the growth of long-distance trade, and the development of a money economy. With the advent of a money economy, serfs could save money and, through a third-person intermediary, use it to buy their freedom. Many energetic and hard-working serfs acquired their freedom through this method of manumission in the High Middle Ages.

The thirteenth century witnessed enormous immigration to many parts of Europe that previously had been sparsely settled. Immigration and colonization provided the opportunity for freedom and social mobility.

Another opportunity for increased personal freedom, or at least for a reduction in traditional manorial obligations and dues, was provided by the reclamation of wasteland and forestland in the eleventh and twelfth centuries. Marshes and fens were drained and slowly made arable. This type of agricultural advancement frequently improved the peasants' social and legal condition.

In the Middle Ages most European peasants, free and unfree, lived on a manor, the estate of a lord (see page 352). The manor was the basic unit of medieval rural organization and the center of rural life. The arable land of the manor was divided into two sections. The *demesne,* or home farm, was cultivated by the peasants for the lord. The other, usually larger, section was held by the peasantry. All the arable land, both the lord's and the peasants', was divided into strips, and the strips belonging to any

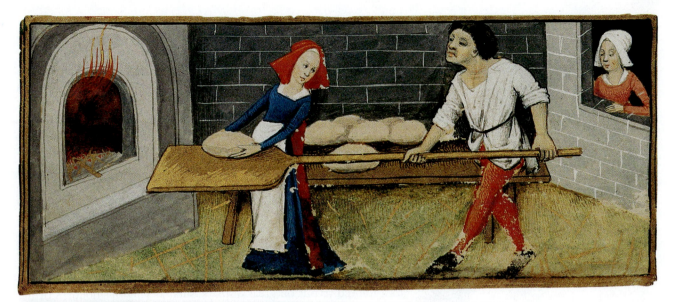

● **Baking Bread** Bread and beer or ale were the main manorial products for local consumption. While women dominated the making of ale and beer, men and women cooperated in the making and baking of bread—the staple of the diet. Most people did not have ovens in their own homes because of the danger of fire, but used the communal manorial oven, which, like a modern pizza oven, could bake several loaves at once. *(Bibliothèque nationale de France)*

given individual were scattered throughout the manor. All peasants cooperated in the cultivation of the land, working it as a group. All shared in any disaster as well as in any large harvest.

The peasants' work was typically divided according to gender. Men were responsible for clearing new land, plowing, and caring for large animals, and women were responsible for the care of small animals, spinning, and food preparation. Both sexes harvested and planted, though often there were gender-specific tasks within each of these major undertakings. Women and men worked in the vineyards and in the harvest and preparation of crops needed by the textile industry—flax and plants used for dyeing cloth.

Scholars have recently spent much energy investigating the structure of medieval peasant households. It appears that in western and central Europe a peasant household consisted of a simple nuclear family: a married couple alone or with a couple of children, or a widow or widower with children. The typical household numbered about five people, and blended households with half-siblings and step-parents were common, as death frequently took a first spouse and the survivor remarried.

The mainstay of the diet for peasants everywhere—and for all other classes—was bread. The diet of those living in an area with access to a river, lake, or stream was supplemented with fish, which could be preserved by salting. In many places, severe laws against hunting and trapping in the forests restricted deer and other game to the king and nobility. Except for the rare chicken or illegally caught wild game, meat appeared on the table only on the great feast days of the Christian year: Christmas, Easter, and Pentecost. Some scholars believe that by the mid-thirteenth century, there was a great increase in the consumption of meat generally. If so, this improvement in diet is evidence of an improved standard of living.

Those Who Fight

The nobility, though a small fraction of the total population, strongly influenced all aspects of medieval culture—political, economic, religious, educational, and artistic.

● **Saint Maurice** Certain individuals were held up to young men as models of ideal chivalry. One of these was Saint Maurice (d. 287), a soldier apparently executed by the Romans for refusing to renounce his Christian faith. He first emerges in the Carolingian period, and later he was held up as a model knight and declared a patron of the Holy Roman Empire and protector of the imperial (German) army in wars against the pagan Slavs. Until 1240 he was portrayed as a white man, but after that he was usually represented as a black man, as in this sandstone statue from Magdeburg Cathedral (ca. 1250). We have no idea why this change happened. Who commissioned this statue? Who carved it? Did an actual person serve as the model, and if so what was he doing in Magdeburg? *(Image of the Black Project, Harvard University/ Hickey-Robertson, Houston)*

chivalry *A code of conduct that governed the conduct of a knight, characterized by the virtues of bravery, generosity, honor, graciousness, mercy, and gallantry toward women.*

Despite political, scientific, and industrial revolutions, the nobility continued to hold real political and social power in Europe down to the nineteenth century.

Members of the nobility enjoyed a special legal status. A nobleman was free personally and in his possessions. He was limited only by his military obligation to king, duke, or prince. As the result of his liberty, he had certain rights and responsibilities. He raised troops and commanded them in the field. He held courts that dispensed a sort of justice. Sometimes he coined money for use within his territories. As lord of the people who settled on his lands, he made political decisions affecting them, resolved disputes among them, and protected them in time of attack. The liberty and privileges of the noble were inheritable, perpetuated by blood and not by wealth alone.

As a vassal a noble was required to fight for his lord or for the king when called on to do so. By the mid-twelfth century, this service was limited in most parts of western Europe to forty days a year. The noble was obliged to attend his lord's court on important occasions when the lord wanted to put on great displays, such as religious holidays or the marriage of a son or daughter.

Originally, most knights focused solely on military skills, but gradually a different ideal of knighthood emerged, usually termed **chivalry.** Chivalry was a code of conduct originally devised by the clergy to transform the crude and brutal behavior of the knightly class. It may have originated in oaths administered to Crusaders in which fighting was declared to have a sacred purpose and knights vowed loyalty to the church as well as to their lords. Other qualities gradually became part of chivalry: bravery, generosity, honor, graciousness, mercy, and eventually gallantry toward women. The chivalric ideal—and it was an ideal, not a standard pattern of behavior—created a new standard of masculinity for nobles, in which loyalty and honor remained the most important qualities, but graceful dancing and intelligent conversation were not considered unmanly.

Until the late thirteenth century, when royal authority intervened, a noble in France or England had great power over the knights and peasants on his estates. He maintained order among them and dispensed justice to them. The quality of life on the manor and its productivity were related in no small way to the temperament and decency of the lord—and his lady.

Women played a large and important role in the functioning of the estate. They were responsible for the practical management of the household's "inner economy"—cooking, brewing, spinning, weaving, caring for yard animals. When the lord was away for long periods, his wife became the sole manager of the family properties. Often the responsibilities of the estate fell permanently to her when she became a widow.

Towns and Cities

The rise of towns and the growth of a new business and commercial class was a central part of Europe's recovery after the disorders of the tenth century. The growth of towns was made possible by several factors: a rise in population; increased agricultural output, which provided an adequate food supply for new town dwellers; and a minimum of peace and political stability, which allowed merchants to transport and sell goods. The development of towns was to lay the foundations for Europe's transformation, centuries later, from a rural agricultural society into an urban industrial society—a change with global implications. In their backgrounds and abilities, townspeople represented diversity and change. Their occupations and their preoccupations were different from those of the feudal nobility and the laboring peasantry. Medieval towns had a few characteristics in common. Walls enclosed the town. (The terms *burgher* and *bourgeois* derive from the Old English and Old German words *burg, burgh, borg,* and *borough* for "a walled or fortified place.") The town had a marketplace. It was likely to have a mint for the coining of money and a court to settle disputes. In each town, many people inhabited a small, cramped area. As population increased, towns rebuilt their walls, expanding the living space to accommodate growing numbers.

The history of towns in the eleventh through thirteenth centuries consists largely of merchants' efforts to acquire liberties. In the Middle Ages *liberties* meant special privileges. For the town dweller, liberties included the privilege of living and trading on the lord's land. The most important privilege a medieval townsperson could gain was personal freedom. It gradually developed that an individual who lived in a town for a year and a day, and was accepted by the townspeople, was free of servile obligations and servile status. More than anything else, perhaps, the personal freedom that came with residence in a town contributed to the emancipation of many serfs in the central Middle Ages. Liberty meant citizenship, and, unlike foreigners and outsiders of any kind, a full citizen of a town did not have to pay taxes and tolls in the market. Obviously, this exemption increased profits.

In the acquisition of full rights of self-government, the **merchant guilds** played a large role. Medieval people were long accustomed to communal enterprises. In the late tenth and early eleventh centuries, those who were engaged in foreign trade joined together in merchant guilds; united enterprise provided them greater security and less risk of losses than did individual action. At about the same time, the artisans and craftsmen of particular trades formed their own guilds. These were the butchers, bakers, and candlestick makers. Members of the **craft guilds** determined the quality, quantity, and price of the goods produced and the number of apprentices and journeymen affiliated with the guild. Formal membership in guilds was generally limited to men, but women worked less formally in guild shops.

By the late eleventh century, especially in the towns of the Low Countries (modern Netherlands, Belgium, and Luxembourg) and northern Italy, the leaders of the merchant guilds were rich and powerful. They constituted an oligarchy in their towns, controlling economic life and bargaining with kings and lords for political independence and full rights of self-government.

Medieval cities served, above all else, as markets. In some respects the entire city was a marketplace. The place where a product was made and sold was typically the merchant's residence. Usually the ground floor was the scene of production. A window or

merchant guilds *Associations of merchants and traders organized to provide greater security and minimize loss in commercial ventures.*

craft guilds *Associations of artisans and craftsmen organized to regulate the quality, quantity, and price of the goods produced as well as the number of affiliated apprentices and journeymen.*

● **Medieval City Street**   This illumination shows a street scene of a medieval town with a barber, cloth merchants, and an apothecary all offering their wares and services on the ground floor of their household-workshops. *(Bibliothèque nationale de France)*

door opened from the main workroom directly onto the street, and passersby could look in and see the goods being produced. The merchant's family lived above the business on the second or third floor. As the business and the family expanded, the merchant built additional stories on top of the house.

Most medieval cities developed haphazardly. There was little town planning. Air and water pollution presented serious problems. Many families raised pigs for household consumption in sties next to their houses. Horses and oxen, the chief means of transportation and power, dropped tons of dung on the streets every year. It was universal practice in the early towns to dump household waste, both animal and human, into the road in front of one's house. The stench must have been abominable. Lack of space, air pollution, and sanitation problems bedeviled urban people in medieval times, as they do today. Still, people wanted to get into medieval cities because they represented opportunities for economic advancement, social mobility, and improvement in legal status.

The Expansion of Long-Distance Trade

The growth of towns went hand-in-hand with a remarkable expansion of trade, as artisans and craftsmen manufactured goods for local and foreign consumption. Most trade centered in towns and was controlled by professional traders. The transportation of goods involved serious risks. Shipwrecks were common. Pirates infested the sea-lanes, and robbers and thieves roamed almost all of the land routes. Since the risks were so great, merchants preferred to share them. A group of people would thus pool some of their capital to finance an expedition to a distant place. When the ship or caravan returned and the goods brought back were sold, the investors would share the profits. If disaster struck the caravan, an investor's loss was limited to the amount of that individual's investment.

The Italian cities, especially Venice, led the West in trade in general and completely dominated the Asian market. In 1082 Venice made an important commercial treaty with the Byzantine Empire, gaining significant trading privileges in Constantinople. The sacking of that city during the Fourth Crusade (see page 364) brought Venice vast trading rights. Venice was ideally located at the northwestern end of the Adriatic Sea, with easy access to the transalpine land routes as well as the Adriatic and Mediterranean sea-lanes. The markets of North Africa, Byzantium, and Russia and the great fairs of Ghent in Flanders and Champagne in France provided commercial opportunities that Venice quickly seized. Venetian ships carried salt from the Venetian lagoon, pepper and other spices from North Africa, and slaves, silk, and purple textiles from the East to northern and western Europe. Wealthy European consumers had greater access to foreign luxuries, and their tastes became more sophisticated.

Merchants from other cities in northern Italy such as Florence and Milan were also important traders, and they developed new business procedures that facilitated the movement of goods and money. The towns of Bruges, Ghent, and Ypres in Flanders were also leaders in long-distance trade and built up a vast industry in the manufacture of cloth. This was made easier by Flanders' geographical situation. Just across the Channel from England, Flanders had easy access to English wool.

Wool was the cornerstone of the English medieval economy. Population growth in the twelfth century and the success of the Flemish and Italian textile industries created foreign demand for English wool. The production of English wool stimulated Flemish manufacturing, and the expansion of the Flemish cloth industry in turn spurred the production of English wool. The availability of raw wool also encouraged the development of domestic cloth manufacture within England, and commercial families in these towns grew fabulously rich.

In much of northern Europe, the **Hanseatic League** (known as the Hansa for short), a mercantile association of towns formed to achieve mutual security and exclusive trading rights, controlled trade. During the thirteenth century perhaps two hundred

Hanseatic League *A mercantile association of towns that allowed for mutual protection and security.*

cities from Holland to Poland joined the league, but Lübeck always remained the dominant member. The ships of the Hansa cities carried furs, wax, copper, fish, grain, timber, and wine. These goods were exchanged for finished products, mainly cloth and salt, from western cities. At cities such as Bruges and London, Hanseatic merchants secured special trading concessions exempting them from all tolls and allowing them to trade at local fairs. Hanseatic merchants established foreign trading centers, which they called "factories." The term *factory* was subsequently used in the seventeenth and eighteenth centuries to mean business offices and places in Asia and Africa where goods were stored and slaves held before being shipped to Europe or the Americas. (See Table 9.1 on page 237 for the size of the trans-Saharan slave trade.)

These developments added up to what is often called the **commercial revolution.** In giving the transformation this name, historians point not only to an increase in the sheer volume of trade and in the complexity and sophistication of business procedures, but also to the new attitude toward business and making money. Some even detect a "capitalist spirit" in which making a profit is regarded as a good thing in itself, regardless of the uses to which that profit is put.

commercial revolution *The transformation of the economic structure of Europe, beginning in the eleventh century, from a rural, manorial society to a more complex mercantile society.*

The commercial revolution created a great deal of new wealth, which did not escape the attention of kings and other rulers. Wealth could be taxed, and through taxation kings could create strong and centralized states. In the years to come, alliances with the middle classes were to enable kings to defeat feudal powers and aristocratic interests and to build the states that came to be called "modern."

The commercial revolution also provided the opportunity for thousands of serfs to improve their social position. The slow but steady transformation of European society from almost completely rural and isolated to relatively more sophisticated constituted the greatest effect of the commercial revolution that began in the eleventh century.

THE CULTURE OF THE MIDDLE AGES

What were the primary new cultural institutions and forms developed in medieval Europe?

Just as the first strong secular states emerged in the thirteenth century, so did the first universities. This was no coincidence. The new bureaucratic states and the church needed educated administrators, and universities were a response to this need. This period also gave rise to new styles of architecture and literature.

Universities and Scholasticism

Since the time of the Carolingian Empire, monasteries and cathedral schools had offered the only formal instruction available. Monasteries were located in rural environments and geared to religious concerns. In contrast, schools attached to cathedrals and run by the bishop and his clergy were frequently situated in bustling cities, and in the eleventh century in Bologna and other Italian cities wealthy businessmen established municipal schools. Inhabited by people of many backgrounds and "nationalities," cities stimulated the growth and exchange of ideas. In the course of the twelfth century, cathedral schools in France and municipal schools in Italy developed into universities.

The beginnings of the universities in Europe owe at least one central idea to the Islamic world. As we have seen, features in the structure of Muslim higher education bear striking parallels to later European ones (see page 214). The most significant of these developments was the **college,** which appeared in Europe about a century after its Muslim counterpart, the madrasa, in the Islamic world. First at Paris, then at Oxford in England, universities began as collections of colleges, privately endowed residences for the lodging of poor students. A medieval university was a corporation, an abstract juristic or legal entity with rights and personality. Islamic law accepted only

college *A university was made up of a collection of these privately endowed residences for the lodging of poor students.*

an actual physical person as having a legal personality. Europeans adapted their legal principles to Muslim ideas of the college, and the notion of the university emerged in the West.

The growth of the University of Bologna coincided with a revival of interest in Roman law. The study of Roman law as embodied in Justinian's *Code* had never completely died out in the West, but this sudden burst of interest seems to have been inspired by Irnerius (d. 1125), a great teacher at Bologna. Irnerius not only explained the Roman law of Justinian's *Code* but also applied it to difficult practical situations.

At Salerno, interest in medicine had persisted for centuries. Greek and Muslim physicians there had studied the use of herbs as cures and experimented with surgery. The twelfth century ushered in a new interest in Greek medical texts and in the work of Arab and Greek doctors.

In the first decades of the twelfth century, students converged on Paris. These young men crowded into the cathedral school of Notre Dame and spilled over into the area later called the Latin Quarter—whose name probably reflects the Italian origin of many of the students. The cathedral school's international reputation had already drawn to Paris scholars from all over Europe. One of the most famous of them was Peter Abélard (1079–1142). Fascinated by logic, which he believed could be used to solve most problems, Abélard used a method of systematic doubting in his writing and teaching. As he put it, "By doubting we come to questioning, and by questioning we perceive the truth." Other scholars merely asserted theological principles; Abélard discussed and analyzed them.

Scholastics *Medieval professors who developed a method of thinking, reasoning, and writing in which questions were raised and authorities cited on both sides of a question.*

In northern Europe—at Paris and later at Oxford and Cambridge in England—associations or guilds of professors organized universities. University faculties grouped themselves according to academic disciplines, or schools—law, medicine, arts, and theology. The professors, known as schoolmen or **Scholastics,** developed a method of thinking, reasoning, and writing in which questions were raised and authorities cited on both sides of a question. The goal of the Scholastic method was to arrive at definitive answers and to provide a rational explanation for what was believed on faith.

Thirteenth-century Scholastics devoted an enormous amount of time to collecting and organizing knowledge on all topics. These collections were published as *summa,* or reference books. There were summa on law, philosophy, vegetation, animal life, and theology. Saint Thomas Aquinas (1225–1274), a professor at Paris, produced the most famous collection, the *Summa Theologica,* which deals with a vast number of theological questions.

Primary Source:
Summa Theologica: **On Free Will**
This selection from Thomas Aquinas, on the question of free will, shows a synthesis of Aristotelian logic and Christian theology.

At all universities, the standard method of teaching was the *lecture*—that is, a reading. The professor read a passage from the Bible, Justinian's *Code,* or one of Aristotle's treatises. He then explained and interpreted the passage; his interpretation was called a *gloss.* Students wrote down everything. Because books had to be copied by hand, they were extremely expensive, and few students could afford them. Examinations were given after three, four, or five years of study, when the student applied for a degree. Examinations were oral and very difficult. If the candidate passed, he was awarded the first, or bachelor's, degree. Further study, about as long, arduous, and expensive as it is today, enabled the graduate to try for the master's and doctor's degrees. Degrees were technically licenses to teach. Most students, however, did not become teachers. They staffed the expanding royal and papal administrations.

Cathedrals

As we have seen, religious devotion was expressed through daily rituals, holiday ceremonies, and the creation of new institutions such as universities and religious orders. People also wanted permanent visible representations of their piety, and both church and city leaders wanted physical symbols of their wealth and power. These aims found their outlet in the building of tens of thousands of churches, chapels, abbeys, and, most spectacularly, **cathedrals** in the twelfth and thirteenth centuries. A cathedral is the church of a bishop and the administrative headquarters of a diocese, a church district headed by a bishop. The word comes from the Greek word *kathedra,* meaning seat, because the bishop's throne, a symbol of the office, is located in the cathedral.

Between 1180 and 1270 in France alone, eighty cathedrals, about five hundred abbey churches, and tens of thousands of parish churches were constructed. All these churches displayed a new architectural style. Fifteenth-century critics called the new style **Gothic** because they mistakenly believed that the fifth-century Goths invented it. It actually developed partly in reaction to the earlier Romanesque style, which resembled ancient Roman architecture. Cathedrals, abbeys, and village churches testify to the deep religious faith and piety of medieval people.

The inspiration for the Gothic style originated in the brain of Suger, abbot of Saint-Denis, who had decided to reconstruct the old Carolingian church at his monastery. The basic features of Gothic architecture—the pointed arch, the ribbed vault, and the flying buttress—allowed unprecedented interior lightness. From Muslim Spain, Islamic methods of ribbed vaulting seem to have heavily influenced the building of Gothic churches. Since the ceiling of a Gothic church weighed less than that of a

cathedral *A church, headed by a bishop, which forms the administrative center of a diocese. From the Greek term* kathedra, *meaning "seat," since the cathedral housed the throne of the bishop.*

Gothic *The term for the architectural and artistic style that prevailed in Europe from the mid-twelfth to the sixteenth century.*

● **Notre Dame Cathedral, Paris (begun 1163), View from the South**   This view offers a fine example of the twin towers (*left*), the spire, the great rose window over the south portal, and the flying buttresses that support the walls and the vaults. Like hundreds of other churches in medieval Europe, it was dedicated to the Virgin. With a nave rising 226 feet, Notre Dame was the tallest building in Europe. (*David R. Frazier/Photo Researchers, Inc.*)

Romanesque church, the walls could be thinner. Stained-glass windows were cut into the stone, so that the interior, Suger exulted, "would shine with the wonderful and uninterrupted light of most sacred windows, pervading the interior beauty."[1]

Cathedrals served secular as well as religious purposes. The sanctuary containing the altar and the bishop's chair belonged to the clergy, but the rest of the church belonged to the people. In addition to marriages, baptisms, and funerals, there were scores of feast days on which the entire town gathered in the cathedral for festivities. Local guilds met in the cathedrals to arrange business deals and to plan recreational events and the support of disabled members. Magistrates and municipal officials held political meetings there. Pilgrims slept there, lovers courted there, and traveling actors staged plays there. First and foremost, however, the cathedral was intended to teach the people the doctrines of Christian faith through visual images. Architecture became the servant of theology.

Troubadour Poetry

While amateur musicians played for peasant festivities, professional musicians and poets performed and composed at the courts of nobles and rulers in medieval Europe. In southern Europe, especially in the area of southern France known as Provence, poets who called themselves **troubadours** wrote and sang lyric verses celebrating love, desire, beauty, and gallantry. The word *troubadour* comes from the Provençal word *trobar,* which in turn derives from the Arabic *taraba,* meaning "to sing" or "to sing poetry." Troubadour songs had a variety of themes. Men sang about "courtly love," the pure love a knight felt for his lady, whom he sought to win by military prowess and patience; about the love a knight felt for the wife of his feudal lord; or about carnal desires seeking satisfaction. Some poems exalted the married state, and others idealized adulterous relationships; some were earthy and bawdy, and others advised young girls to remain chaste in preparation for marriage.

Troubadours certainly felt Hispano-Arabic influences. In the eleventh century Christians of southern France were in intimate contact with the Arabized world of Andalusia, where reverence for the lady in a "courtly" tradition had long existed. Troubadour poetry represents another facet of the strong Muslim influence on European culture and life.

troubadours *Medieval poets in southern Europe who wrote and sang lyrical verses devoted to the themes of love, desire, beauty, and gallantry.*

CRISES OF THE LATER MIDDLE AGES

Why has the late Middle Ages been seen as a time of calamity and crisis?

During the later Middle Ages, the last book of the New Testament, the book of Revelation, inspired thousands of sermons and hundreds of religious tracts. The book of Revelation deals with visions of the end of the world, with disease, war, famine, and death. It is no wonder this part of the Bible was so popular. Between 1300 and 1450 Europeans experienced a frightful series of shocks: climate change, economic dislocation, plague, war, social upheaval, and increased crime and violence. Death and preoccupation with death make the fourteenth century one of the most wrenching periods of history in Europe.

The Great Famine and the Black Death

Economic difficulties originating in the later thirteenth century were fully manifest by the start of the fourteenth. In the first decade, the countries of northern Europe experienced considerable price inflation. The costs of grain, livestock, and dairy products rose sharply. Severe weather, which historical geographers label the Little Ice Age, made a serious situation frightful. An unusual number of storms brought torrential rains, ruining the wheat, oat, and hay crops on which people and animals almost everywhere depended. Population had steadily increased in the twelfth and thirteenth centuries. The amount of food yielded, however, did not match the level of population growth. Bad weather had disastrous results. Poor harvests—one in four was likely to be poor—led to scarcity and starvation. Almost all of northern Europe suffered a terrible famine in the years 1315 to 1322. Famine had dire social consequences: peasants were forced to sell or mortgage their lands for money to buy food; the number of vagabonds, or homeless people, greatly increased, as did petty crime. An undernourished population was ripe for the Grim Reaper, who appeared in 1347 in the form of the **Black Death** (see Map 13.3).

Plague symptoms were first described in 1331 in southwestern China, part of the Mongol Empire. Plague-infested rats accompanied Mongol armies and merchant caravans carrying silk, spices, and gold across central Asia in the 1330s. Then they stowed away on ships, carrying the disease to the ports of the Black Sea by the 1340s. In October 1347 Genoese ships traveling from the Crimea in southern Russia brought the bubonic plague to Messina, from which it spread across Sicily and up into Italy. By late spring of 1348 southern Germany was attacked. Frightened French authorities chased a galley bearing the disease from the port of Marseilles, but not before plague had

Black Death   *The bubonic plague that first struck Europe in 1347. It spread either in the bubonic form by flea bites or in the pneumonic form directly from the breath of one person to another. In less virulent forms, the disease reappeared many times until the early eighteenth century.*

MAP 13.3   **The Course of the Black Death in Fourteenth-Century Europe**   The bubonic plague followed trade routes as it spread into and across Europe, carried by rats on board ship and in merchants' bags and parcels. A few cities that took strict quarantine measures were spared.

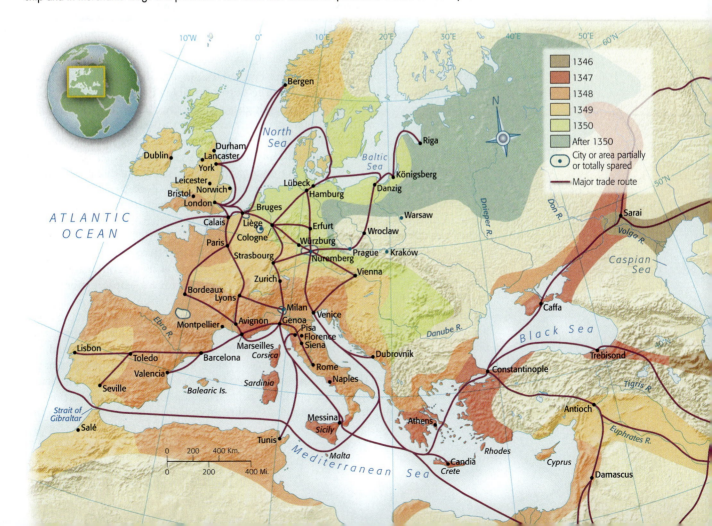

● **Procession of Saint Gregory** According to the *Golden Legend,* a thirteenth-century collection of saints' lives, the bubonic plague ravaged Rome when Gregory I was elected pope (r. 590–604). He immediately ordered special prayers and processions around the city. Here, as people circle the walls, new victims fall (center). The architecture, the cardinals, and the friars all indicate that this painting dates from the fourteenth, not the sixth, century. *(Musée Condé, Chantilly/Art Resource, NY)*

infected the city. In June 1348 two ships entered the Bristol Channel and introduced it into England. All Europe felt the scourge of this horrible disease.

Most historians and almost all microbiologists identify the disease that spread in the fourteenth century as the bubonic plague, caused by the bacillus *Yersinia pestis.* The disease normally afflicts rats. Fleas living on the infected rats drink their blood; the bacteria that cause the plague multiply in the flea's gut; and the flea passes them on to the next rat it bites by throwing up into the bite. Usually the disease is limited to rats and other rodents, but at certain points in history—perhaps when most rats have been killed off—the fleas have jumped from their rodent hosts to humans and other animals. The bacillus could also be transmitted directly from person to person through coughing.

Urban conditions were ideal for the spread of disease. Narrow streets filled with mud, refuse, and human excrement were as much cesspools as thoroughfares. Dead animals and sore-covered beggars greeted the traveler. Houses whose upper stories projected over the lower ones eliminated light and air. And extreme overcrowding was commonplace. Standards of personal hygiene remained frightfully low. Fleas and body lice were universal afflictions: one more bite did not cause much alarm. But if that nibble came from a bacillus-bearing flea, an entire household or area was doomed.

The classic symptom of the bubonic plague was a growth the size of a nut or an apple in the armpit, in the groin, or on the neck. This was the boil, or *bubo,* that gave the disease its name and caused agonizing pain. If the bubo was lanced and the pus thoroughly drained, the victim had a chance of recovery. The secondary stage was the appearance of black spots or blotches caused by bleeding under the skin. Finally, the victim began to cough violently and spit blood. This stage, indicating the presence of thousands of bacilli in the bloodstream, signaled the end, and death followed in two or three days.

Physicians could sometimes ease the pain but had no cure. Most people—lay, scholarly, and medical—believed that the Black Death was caused by some "vicious property in the air" that carried the disease from place to place. When ignorance was joined to fear and ancient bigotry, savage cruelty sometimes resulted. Many people believed that the Jews had poisoned the wells of Christian communities and thereby infected the drinking water. This charge led to the murder of thousands of Jews across Europe.

Because population figures for the period before the arrival of the plague do not exist for most countries and cities, only educated guesses can be made about mortality rates. Of a total English population of perhaps 4.2 million, probably 1.4 million died of the Black Death in its several visits. Densely populated Italian cities endured incredible losses. Florence lost between one-half and two-thirds of its population when the plague visited in 1348. The disease recurred intermittently in the 1360s and 1370s and reappeared many times down to the early 1700s.

Economic historians and demographers sharply dispute the impact of the plague on the economy in the late fourteenth century. The traditional view that the plague had a disastrous effect has been greatly modified. Many parts of Europe suffered from overpopulation in the early fourteenth century. Population decline brought increased demand for labor, which meant greater mobility among peasant and working classes. Wages rose, providing better distribution of income. Per capita wealth among those who survived increased, and some areas experienced economic prosperity as a long-term consequence of the plague.

The psychological consequences of the plague were profound. It is not surprising that some people sought release in orgies and gross sensuality, while others turned to the severest forms of asceticism and frenzied religious fervor. Groups of *flagellants,* men and women who whipped and scourged themselves as penance for their and society's sins, believed that the Black Death was God's punishment for humanity's wickedness.

The Hundred Years' War

The plague ravaged populations in Asia, North Africa, and Europe; in western Europe a long international war added further death and destruction. England and France had engaged in sporadic military hostilities from the time of the Norman Conquest in 1066, and in the middle of the fourteenth century these became more intense. From 1337 to 1453, the two countries intermittently fought one another in what was the longest war in European history, ultimately dubbed the Hundred Years' War though it actually lasted 116 years.

The Hundred Years' War had both distant and immediate causes. The immediate cause of the war was a dispute over who would inherit the French throne. The English claimed Aquitaine as an ancient feudal inheritance. In 1329 England's King Edward III (r. 1327–1377) paid homage to Philip VI (r. 1328–1350) for Aquitaine. French policy, however, was strongly expansionist, and in 1337 Philip, determined to exercise full jurisdiction there, confiscated the duchy. Edward III maintained that the only way he could exercise his rightful sovereignty over Aquitaine was by assuming the title of king of France. As the grandson and eldest surviving male descendant of Philip the Fair, he believed he could rightfully make this claim.

More distant causes included economic factors involving the wool trade and the control of Flemish towns. The wool trade between England and Flanders was the cornerstone of both countries' economies; they were closely interdependent. Flanders was a fief of the French crown, and the Flemish aristocracy was highly sympathetic to

● **Siege of the Castle of Mortagne near Bordeaux (1377)** Medieval warfare usually consisted of small skirmishes and attacks on castles. This miniature of a battle in the Hundred Years' War shows the French besieging an English-held castle, which held out for six months. Most of the soldiers use longbows, although at the left two men shoot primitive muskets above a pair of cannon. Painted in the late fifteenth century, the scene reflects military technology available at the time it was painted, not the time of the actual siege. (© British Library Board. All Rights Reserved. MS royal 14e. iv f.23)

the monarchy in Paris. But the wealth of Flemish merchants and cloth manufacturers depended on English wool, and Flemish burghers strongly supported the claims of Edward III.

The Hundred Years' War was popular because it presented unusual opportunities for wealth and advancement. Poor and unemployed knights were promised regular wages. Great nobles expected to be rewarded with estates. Royal exhortations to the troops before battles repeatedly stressed that, if victorious, the men might keep whatever they seized. The war, fought almost entirely in France and the Low Countries, consisted mainly of a series of random sieges and cavalry raids. During the war's early stages, England was highly successful, using longbows fired by foot soldiers and early cannons against French mounted knights. By 1419 the English had advanced to the walls of Paris. But the French cause was not lost. Though England scored the initial victories, France won the war.

The ultimate French success rests heavily on the actions of an obscure French peasant girl, Joan of Arc, whose vision and work revived French fortunes and led to victory. Born in 1412 to well-to-do peasants, Joan of Arc grew up in a pious household. During adolescence she began to hear voices, which she later said belonged to Saint

Michael, Saint Catherine, and Saint Margaret. In 1428 these voices told her that the dauphin (the uncrowned King Charles VII) had to be crowned and the English expelled from France. Joan went to the French court and secured the support of the dauphin for her relief of the besieged city of Orléans.

Joan arrived before Orléans on April 28, 1429. Seventeen years old, she knew little of warfare and believed that if she could keep the French troops from swearing and frequenting brothels, victory would be theirs. On May 8 the English, weakened by disease and lack of supplies, withdrew from Orléans. Ten days later, Charles VII was crowned king at Reims. These two events marked the turning point in the war.

In 1430 England's allies, the Burgundians, captured Joan and sold her to the English. The French did not intervene. The English wanted Joan eliminated for obvious political reasons, but sorcery (witchcraft) was the charge at her trial. Witch persecution was increasing in the fifteenth century, and Joan's wearing of men's clothes appeared not only aberrant but indicative of contact with the Devil. In 1431 the court condemned her as a heretic, and she was burned at the stake in the marketplace at Rouen. A new trial in 1456 rehabilitated her name. In 1920 she was canonized, and today she is revered as the second patron saint of France.

The relief of Orléans stimulated French pride and rallied French resources. As the war dragged on, loss of life mounted, and money appeared to be flowing into a bottomless pit, demands for an end increased in England. Slowly the French reconquered Normandy and finally ejected the English from Aquitaine. At the war's end in 1453, only the town of Calais remained in English hands.

The long war had a profound impact on the political and cultural lives of the two countries. Most notably, it stimulated the development of the English Parliament. Between 1250 and 1450, representative assemblies from several classes of society flourished in many European countries, but only the English Parliament became a powerful national body. Edward III's constant need for money to pay for the war compelled him to summon it many times, and its representatives slowly built up their powers.

In England and France the war promoted *nationalism*—the feeling of unity and identity that binds together a people who speak the same language, have a common ancestry and customs, and live in the same area. In the fourteenth century nationalism largely took the form of hostility toward foreigners. Both Philip VI and Edward III drummed up support for the war by portraying the enemy as an alien, evil people. Perhaps no one expressed this national consciousness better than Joan of Arc when she exulted that the enemy had been "driven out of *France.*"

Challenges to the Church

In times of crisis or disaster, people of all faiths have sought the consolation of religion. While local clergy eased the suffering of many, a dispute over who was the legitimate pope weakened the church as an institution. In 1309, pressure by the French monarchy led the popes to move their court to Avignon in southern France, the location of the papal summer palace. Not surprisingly, all the Avignon popes were French, and they concentrated on bureaucratic and financial matters to the exclusion of spiritual objectives.

In 1376, one of the French popes returned to Rome, and when he died there several years later Roman citizens demanded an Italian pope who would remain in Rome. The cardinals elected Urban VI, but his tactless, arrogant, and bullheaded manner caused them to regret their decision. The cardinals slipped away from Rome and declared Urban's election invalid because it had come about under threats from the Roman mob. They elected a French cardinal, who took the name Clement VII (r. 1378–1394) and set himself up at Avignon in opposition to Urban. There were thus two popes, a situation that was later termed the **Great Schism.**

Great Schism *The period from 1378 to 1417 during which the Western Christian church had two popes, one in Rome and one in Avignon.*

The powers of Europe aligned themselves with Urban or Clement along strictly political lines. France recognized the Frenchman, Clement; England, France's historic enemy, recognized Urban. The scandal provoked horror and vigorous cries for reform. The common people—hard-pressed by inflation, wars, and plague—were thoroughly confused about which pope was legitimate. The schism weakened the religious faith of many Christians.

A first attempt to heal the schism led to a threefold schism, but finally, because of the pressure of the Holy Roman emperor Sigismund, a great council met at Constance (1414–1418). The council eventually deposed the three schismatic popes and elected a new leader, who took the name Martin V (1417–1431). Martin dissolved the council, and the schism was over. Nothing was done about reform, however, though many people hoped the council would address this. In the later fifteenth century the papacy concentrated on Italian problems to the exclusion of universal Christian interests.

Peasant and Urban Revolts

In 1358, when French taxation for the Hundred Years' War fell heavily on the poor, the frustrations of the French peasantry exploded in a massive uprising called the **Jacquerie,** after a supposedly happy agricultural laborer, Jacques Bonhomme (Good Fellow). Recently hit by plague and experiencing famine in some areas, peasants erupted in anger and frustration. Crowds swept through the countryside, slashing the throats of nobles, burning their castles, raping their wives and daughters, and killing or maiming their horses and cattle. Artisans, small merchants, and parish priests joined the peasants. Urban and rural groups committed terrible destruction, and for several weeks the nobles were on the defensive. Then the upper class united to repress the revolt with merciless ferocity. Thousands of the "Jacques," innocent as well as guilty, were cut down.

The Peasants' Revolt in England in 1381, involving perhaps a hundred thousand people, was probably the largest single uprising of the entire Middle Ages. The causes of the rebellion were complex and varied from place to place. In general, though, the thirteenth century had witnessed the steady commutation of labor services for cash rents, and the Black Death had drastically cut the labor supply. As a result, peasants demanded higher wages and fewer manorial obligations. Their lords countered with a law freezing wages and binding workers to their manors. Unable to climb higher, the peasants found release for their economic frustrations in revolt. But economic grievances combined with other factors. The south of England, where the revolt broke out, had been subjected to frequent and destructive French raids. The English government did little to protect the south, and villages grew increasingly scared and insecure. Moreover, decades of aristocratic violence, much of it perpetrated against the weak peasantry, had bred hostility and bitterness.

The straw that broke the camel's back in England was the reimposition of a head tax on all adult males. Beginning with assaults on the tax collectors, the uprising in England followed much the same course as had the Jacquerie in France. Castles and manors were sacked; manorial records were destroyed. Many nobles, including the archbishop of Canterbury, who had ordered the collection of the tax, were murdered. Urban discontent merged with rural violence. Apprentices and journeymen, frustrated because the highest positions in the guilds were closed to them, rioted.

The boy-king Richard II (r. 1377–1399) met the leaders of the revolt, agreed to charters ensuring the peasants' freedom, tricked them with false promises, and then proceeded to crush the uprising with terrible ferocity. Although the nobility tried to restore ancient duties of serfdom, virtually a century of freedom had elapsed, and the commutation of manorial services continued. Rural serfdom had disappeared in England by 1550.

Jacquerie   *A massive uprising by French peasants in 1358 protesting heavy taxation.*

Conditions in England and France were not unique. In Florence in 1378 the *ciompi*, or poor propertyless workers, revolted. Serious social trouble occurred in Lübeck, Brunswick, and other German cities. In Spain in 1391 massive uprisings in Seville and Barcelona took the form of vicious attacks on Jewish communities. Rebellions and uprisings everywhere revealed deep peasant and working-class frustration and the general socioeconomic crisis of the time.

Chapter Summary

To assess your mastery of this chapter, go to
bedfordstmartins.com/mckayworld

Key Terms

vassal
fief
feudalism
manorialism
serf
jurors
lay investiture
common law
saints
reconquista
Crusades
chivalry
merchant guilds
craft guilds
Hanseatic League
commercial revolution
college
Scholastics
cathedral
Gothic
troubadours
Black Death
Great Schism
Jacquerie

• How did medieval rulers overcome internal divisions and external threats, and work to create larger and more stable territories?

As Charlemagne's empire broke down, a new form of decentralized government, later known as feudalism, emerged. Local strongmen provided what little security existed. No European political power was strong enough to put up effective resistance to external attack, which came from many directions. Vikings from Scandinavia carried out raids for plunder along the coasts and rivers of Europe and traveled as far as Iceland, Greenland, North America, and Russia. In many places they set up permanent states, as did the Magyars, who came into Europe from the east. The end of the great invasions signaled the beginning of profound changes in European society. As domestic disorder slowly subsided, rulers began to develop new institutions of government and legal codes that enabled them to assert their power over lesser lords and the general population.

• How did the Christian church enhance its power and create new institutions and religious practices?

The eleventh century witnessed the beginnings of a religious revival. Monasteries remodeled themselves, and new religious orders were founded. After a century of corruption and decadence, the papacy reformed itself. The popes worked to clarify church doctrine and codify church law. Religion structured people's daily lives and the yearly calendar. Christianity expanded into Europe's northern and eastern regions, and Christian rulers expanded their holdings in Muslim Spain.

• What were the motives, course, and consequences of the Crusades?

A papal call to retake the holy city of Jerusalem led to the Crusades, nearly two centuries of warfare between Christians and Muslims. The enormous popular response to papal calls for crusading reveals the influence of the reformed papacy and a new sense that war against the church's enemies was a duty of nobles. The Crusades were initially successful, and small Christian states were established in the Middle East. These did not last very long, however, and other effects of the Crusades were disastrous. Jewish communities in Europe were regularly attacked; relations between the Western and Eastern Christian churches were poisoned by the Crusaders' attack on Constantinople; and Christian-Muslim relations became more uniformly hostile than they had been earlier.

• What was life like for the common people of medieval Europe, and how were the lives of nobles and townspeople different?

The performance of agricultural services and the payment of rents preoccupied peasants throughout the Middle Ages. Though peasants led hard lives, the reclamation of wasteland and forestlands, migration to frontier territory, or flight to a town offered a means of social mobility. Nobles were a tiny fraction of the total population, but they exerted great power over all aspects of life. Aristocratic values and attitudes, often described as chivalry, shaded all aspects of medieval culture. Medieval cities recruited people from the countryside with the promise of greater freedom and new possibilities. Cities provided economic opportunity, which, together with the revival of long-distance trade and a new capitalistic spirit, led to greater wealth, a higher standard of living, and upward social mobility for many people. Merchants and artisans formed guilds to protect their means of livelihood. Not everyone in medieval cities shared in the prosperity, however, for many residents lived hand-to-mouth on low wages.

• What were the primary new cultural institutions and forms developed in medieval Europe?

The towns that became centers of trade and production in the High Middle Ages developed into cultural and intellectual centers. Trade brought in new ideas as well as merchandise, and in many cities a new type of educational institution—the university—emerged from cathedral and municipal schools. Universities developed theological, legal, and medical courses of study based on classical models and provided trained officials for the new government bureaucracies. Economic growth meant that merchants, nobles, and guild masters had disposable income they could spend on artistic products and more elaborate consumer goods. They supported the building of churches and cathedrals as visible symbols of their Christian faith and their civic pride; cathedrals in particular grew larger and more sumptuous, with high towers, stained-glass windows, and multiple altars. University education was in Latin and limited to men, but the High Middle Ages also saw the creation of new types of vernacular literature. Poems, songs, and stories were written down in local dialects and celebrated things of concern to ordinary people. In this, the troubadours of southern France led the way, using Arabic models to create romantic stories of heterosexual love.

• Why has the late Middle Ages been seen as a time of calamity and crisis?

In the fourteenth and fifteenth centuries bad weather brought poor harvests, which contributed to the international economic depression and fostered disease. The Black Death caused enormous population losses, with social, psychological, and economic consequences. The Hundred Years' War devastated much of the French countryside and bankrupted England. When peasant frustrations exploded in uprisings, the frightened nobility crushed the revolts. But events had heightened social consciousness among the poor.

Suggested Reading

Bartlett, Robert. *The Making of Europe: Conquest, Colonization and Cultural Change, 950–1350.* 1993. A broad survey of many of the developments traced in this chapter.

Bennett, Judith M. *A Medieval Life: Cecelia Penifader of Brigstock, c. 1297–1344.* 1998. An excellent brief introduction to all aspects of medieval village life from the perspective of one woman, designed for students.

Brooke, Rosalind, and Christopher Brooke. *Popular Religion in the Middle Ages.* 1984. A readable synthesis of material on the beliefs and practices of ordinary Christians.

Glick, Leonard B. *Abraham's Heirs: Jews and Christians in Medieval Europe.* 1999. Provides information on many aspects of Jewish life and Jewish-Christian relations.

Herlihy, David. *The Black Death and the Transformation of the West,* 2d ed. 1997. A fine treatment of the causes and cultural consequences of the disease that remains the best starting point for study of the great epidemic.

Koch, H. W. *Medieval Warfare.* 1978. A beautifully illustrated book covering strategy, tactics, armaments, and costumes of war.

Lawrence, C. H. *Medieval Monasticism: Forms of Religious Life in Western Europe in the Middle Ages.* 1988. Provides a solid introduction to monastic life as it was practiced.

Madden, Thomas. *The New Concise History of the Crusades.* 2005. A highly readable brief survey by the preeminent American scholar of the Crusades.

Sawyer, Peter, ed. *The Oxford Illustrated History of the Vikings.* 1997. Provides a sound account of the Vikings by an international team of scholars.

Shahar, Shulamit. *The Fourth Estate: A History of Women in the Middle Ages,* 2d ed. 2003. Analyzes attitudes toward women and provides information on the lives of women in many situations, including nuns, peasants, noblewomen, and townswomen, in Western Europe between the twelfth and the fifteenth centuries.

Tellenbach, Gerd. *The Church in Western Europe from the Tenth to the Twelfth Century.* 1993. A very good survey by an expert on the investiture controversy.

Tuchman, Barbara. *A Distant Mirror: The Calamitous Fourteenth Century.* 1978. Written for a general audience, the book remains a vivid description of this tumultuous time.

Notes

1. E. Panofsky, trans. and ed., *Abbot Suger on the Abbey Church of St.-Denis and Its Art Treasures* (Princeton, N.J.: Princeton University Press, 1946), p. 101.

Listening to the PAST

An Arab View of the Crusades

The Crusades helped shape the understanding that Arabs and Europeans had of each other and all subsequent relations between the Christian West and the Arab world. To medieval Christians, the Crusades were papally approved military expeditions for the recovery of holy places in Palestine; to the Arabs, these campaigns were "Frankish wars" or "Frankish invasions" for the acquisition of territory.

Early in the thirteenth century, Ibn Al-Athir (1160–1223), a native of Mosul, an important economic and cultural center in northern Mesopotamia (modern Iraq), wrote a history of the First Crusade. He relied on Arab sources for the events he described. Here is his account of the Crusaders' capture of Antioch.

The power of the Franks first became apparent when in the year 478/1085–86* they invaded the territories of Islam and took Toledo and other parts of Andalusia [in Spain]. Then in 484/1091 they attacked and conquered the island of Sicily and turned their attention to the African coast. Certain of their conquests there were won back again but they had other successes, as you will see.

In 490/1097 the Franks attacked Syria. This is how it all began: Baldwin, their King, a kinsman of Roger the Frank who had conquered Sicily, assembled a great army and sent word to Roger saying: "I have assembled a great army and now I am on my way to you, to use your bases for my conquest of the African coast. Thus you and I shall become neighbors."

Roger called together his companions and consulted them about these proposals. "This will be a fine thing for them and for us!" they declared, "for by this means these lands will be converted to the Faith!" At this Roger raised one leg and farted loudly, and swore that it was of more use than their advice. "Why?" "Because if this army comes here it will need quantities of provisions and fleets of ships to transport it to Africa, as well as reinforcements from my own troops. Then,

if the Franks succeed in conquering this territory they will take it over and will need provisioning from Sicily. This will cost me my annual profit from the harvest. If they fail they will return here and be an embarrassment to me here in my own domain." . . .

He summoned Baldwin's messenger and said to him: "If you have decided to make war on the Muslims your best course will be to free Jerusalem from their rule and thereby win great honor. I am bound by certain promises and treaties of allegiance with the ruler of Africa." So the Franks made ready to set out to attack Syria.

Another story is that the Fatimids of Egypt were afraid when they saw the Seljuqids extending their empire through Syria as far as Gaza, until they reached the Egyptian border and Atsiz invaded Egypt itself. They therefore sent to invite the Franks to invade Syria and so protect Egypt from the Muslims.† But God knows best.

When the Franks decided to attack Syria they marched east to Constantinople, so that they could cross the straits and advance into Muslim territory by the easier, land route. When they reached Constantinople, the Emperor of the East refused them permission to pass through his domains. He said: "Unless you first promise me Antioch, I shall not allow you to cross into the Muslim empire." His real intention was to incite them to attack the Muslims, for he was convinced that the Turks, whose invincible control over Asia Minor he had observed, would exterminate every one of them. They accepted his conditions and in 490/1097 they crossed the Bosphorus at Constantinople. . . . They . . . reached Antioch, which they besieged.

When Yaghi Siyan, the ruler of Antioch, heard of their approach, he was not sure how the Christian people of the city would react, so he made the Muslims go outside the city on their own to dig trenches, and the next day sent the Christians out alone to continue the task. When they were ready to return

---

*Muslims traditionally date events from Muhammad's hegira, or emigration, to Medina, which occurred in 622 according to the Christian calendar.

†Although Muslims, Fatimids were related doctrinally to the Shi'ites, but the dominant Sunni Muslims considered the Fatimids heretics.

Miniature showing heavily armored knights fighting Muslims.
(*Bibliothèque nationale de France*)

home at the end of the day he refused to allow them. "Antioch is yours," he said, "but you will have to leave it to me until I see what happens between us and the Franks." "Who will protect our children and our wives?" they said. "I shall look after them for you." So they resigned themselves to their fate, and lived in the Frankish camp for nine months, while the city was under siege.

Yaghi Siyan showed unparalleled courage and wisdom, strength and judgment. If all the Franks who died had survived they would have overrun all the lands of Islam. He protected the families of the Christians in Antioch and would not allow a hair of their heads to be touched.

After the siege had been going on for a long time the Franks made a deal with . . . a cuirass-maker called Ruzbih whom they bribed with a fortune in money and lands. He worked in the tower that stood over the riverbed, where the river flowed out of the city into the valley. The Franks sealed their pact with the cuirass-maker, God damn him! and made their way to the water-gate. They opened it and entered the city. Another gang of them climbed the tower with their ropes. At dawn, when more than 500 of them were in the city and the defenders were worn out after the night watch, they sounded their trumpets. . . . Panic seized Yaghi Siyan and he opened the city gates and fled in terror, with an escort of thirty pages. His army commander arrived, but when he discovered on

enquiry that Yaghi Siyan had fled, he made his escape by another gate. This was of great help to the Franks, for if he had stood firm for an hour, they would have been wiped out. They entered the city by the gates and sacked it, slaughtering all the Muslims they found there. This happened in jumada I (491/April/May 1098). . . .

It was the discord between the Muslim princes . . . that enabled the Franks to overrun the country.

Questions for Analysis

1. From the Arab perspective, when did the crusade begin?

2. How did Ibn Al-Athir explain the Crusaders' expedition to Syria?

3. Why did Antioch fall to the Crusaders?

4. The use of dialogue in historical narrative is a very old device dating from the Greek historian Thucydides (fifth century B.C.E.). Assess the value of Ibn Al-Athir's dialogues for the modern historian.

Sources: P. J. Geary, ed., *Readings in Medieval History* (Peterborough, Ontario: Broadview Press, 1991), pp. 443–444; E. J. Costello, trans., *Arab Historians of the Crusades* (Berkeley and Los Angeles: University of California Press, 1969).

The Sistine Chapel. Michelangelo's frescoes in the Sistine Chapel in the Vatican were commissioned by the pope. The huge ceiling includes biblical scenes, and the far wall shows a dramatic and violent Last Judgment. *(Vatican Museum)*

chapter

14

EUROPE IN THE RENAISSANCE AND REFORMATION, 1350–1600

Chapter Preview

Renaissance Culture
• What were the major cultural developments of the Renaissance?

Social Hierarchies
• What were the key social hierarchies in Renaissance Europe, and how did ideas about hierarchy shape people's lives?

Politics and the State in the Renaissance (ca. 1450–1521)
• How did the nation-states of western Europe evolve in this period?

The Protestant Reformation
• What were the central ideas of Protestant reformers, and why were they appealing to various groups across Europe?

The Catholic Reformation
• How did the Catholic Church respond to the new religious situation?

Religious Violence
• What were the causes and consequences of religious violence, including riots, wars, and witch-hunts?

While the Four Horsemen of the Apocalypse seemed to be carrying war, plague, famine, and death across northern Europe, a new culture was emerging in southern Europe. The fourteenth century witnessed the beginnings of remarkable changes in many aspects of Italian intellectual, artistic, and cultural life. Artists and writers thought that they were living in a new golden age, but not until the sixteenth century was this change given the label we use today—the **Renaissance,** from the French version of a word meaning rebirth. That word was first used by the artist and art historian Giorgio Vasari (1511–1574) to describe the art of "rare men of genius" such as his contemporary Michelangelo. Through their works, Vasari judged, the glory of the classical past had been reborn—or perhaps even surpassed—after centuries of darkness. The word *Renaissance* came to be used not just for art, but for many aspects of life of the period. The new attitude had a slow diffusion out of Italy, with the result that the Renaissance "happened" at different times in different parts of Europe: Italian art of the fourteenth through the early sixteenth century is described as "Renaissance," and so is English literature of the late sixteenth century, including Shakespeare's plays and poetry.

At the same time that Vasari was describing a break with the past in art, religious reformers were carrying out an even more dramatic change. In 1500 there was one Christian church in western Europe to which all Christians at least nominally belonged. Fifty years later there were many, as a result of a religious reform movement that gained wide acceptance and caused Christianity to break into many divisions. This movement, termed the **Protestant Reformation,** looked back to the early Christian church for its inspiration, and many of its reforming ideas had been advocated for centuries. There were thus strong elements of continuity, but it was still a radical change. Along with the Renaissance, the Reformation is often seen as a key element in the creation of the "modern" world.

Renaissance *A French word, translated from the Italian* rinascita, *first used by art historian and critic Giorgio Vasari (1511–1574), meaning rebirth of the culture of classical antiquity. English-speaking students adopted the French term.*

Protestant Reformation *A reform movement that began in the early sixteenth century that rejected the institutionalization of Christianity that characterized the Roman Catholic Church and emphasized individual salvation by grace through faith alone.*

RENAISSANCE CULTURE

What were the major cultural developments of the Renaissance?

The Renaissance was characterized by self-conscious awareness among fourteenth- and fifteenth-century Italians, particularly scholars and writers known as humanists, that they were living in a new era. Their ideas influenced education and were spread through the new technology of the printing press. Interest in the classical past and in the individual also shaped Renaissance art in terms of style and subject matter.

Economic and Political Context

The cultural achievements of the Renaissance rest on the economic and political developments of earlier centuries. Economic growth laid the material basis for the Italian Renaissance, and ambitious merchants gained political power to match their economic power. They then used their money and power to buy luxuries and hire talent.

The first artistic and literary manifestations of the Italian Renaissance appeared in Florence, which possessed enormous wealth because Florentine merchants and bankers had acquired control of papal banking toward the end of the thirteenth century. From their position as tax collectors for the papacy, Florentine mercantile families began to dominate European banking on both sides of the Alps, setting up offices in major European and North African cities. The profits from loans, investments, and money exchanges that poured back to Florence were pumped into urban industries. Such profits contributed to the city's economic vitality and allowed banking families to control the city's politics and culture.

In the twelfth century many Italian cities, including Florence, won their independence from local feudal nobles. The nobles frequently moved into the cities, marrying into rich commercial families and starting their own businesses. This merger of the northern Italian feudal nobility and the commercial elite created a powerful oligarchy that ruled the city and surrounding countryside. In the thirteenth century the common people in many cities revolted against oligarchic rule, but these revolts generally resulted in a greater concentration of power rather than a more broadly based government.

> **Primary Source:**
> **The Practice of Commerce**
> *Get advice from an experienced Florentine merchant before planning your next overland business trip to Cathay!*

Many cities in Italy became **signori,** in which one man ruled and handed down the right to rule to his son. In the fifteenth century the signori in many cities and the most powerful merchant oligarchs in others transformed their households into courts. They built magnificent palaces in the centers of cities and required all political business be done there. They became **patrons** of the arts, hiring architects to design and build these palaces, artists to fill them with paintings and sculptures, and musicians and composers to fill them with music. The Medici rulers of Florence, for example, who made their money in banking and trade, supported an academy for scholars and a host of painters, sculptors, poets, and architects. Courtly culture afforded signori and oligarchs the opportunity to display and assert their wealth and power.

signori *An Italian word used to describe the rulers of city-states and the states ruled by these men.*

patrons *Wealthy individuals who provide financial support to scholars, painters, sculptors, poets, and/or architects.*

In the fifteenth century five powers dominated the Italian peninsula: Venice, Milan, Florence, the Papal States, and the kingdom of Naples (see Map 14.1 on page 404). The major Italian powers competed furiously among themselves for territory and tried to extend their power over smaller city-states. The large cities used diplomacy, spies, paid informers, and any other available means to get information that could be used to advance their ambitions. While the states of northern Europe were moving toward centralization and consolidation, the world of Italian politics resembled a jungle where the powerful dominated the weak.

In one significant respect, however, the Italian city-states anticipated future relations among competing European states after 1500. Whenever one Italian state appeared to gain a predominant position within the peninsula, other states combined to establish a *balance of power* against the major threat. In the formation of these alliances, Renaissance Italians invented the machinery of modern diplomacy: permanent embassies with resident ambassadors in capitals where political relations and commercial ties needed continual monitoring.

The resident ambassador was one of the great political achievements of the Italian Renaissance, but diplomacy did not prevent invasions of Italy, which began in 1494. Italy became the focus of international ambitions and the battleground of foreign armies, and the Italian cities suffered severely from continual warfare. Thus the failure of the city-states to form some type of federal system, to consolidate, or at least to establish a common foreign policy led to centuries of subjugation by outside invaders. Italy was not to achieve unification until 1870.

Intellectual Change

The Renaissance was a self-conscious intellectual movement. The realization that something new and unique was happening first came to writers in the fourteenth century, especially to the poet and humanist Francesco Petrarch (1304–1374). For Petrarch, the Germanic migrations had caused a sharp cultural break with the glories of Rome and inaugurated what he called the "Dark Ages." Along with many of his contemporaries, Petrarch believed that he was witnessing a new golden age of intellectual achievement.

Petrarch and other poets, writers, and artists showed a deep interest in the ancient past, in both the physical remains of the Roman Empire and classical Latin texts. The study of Latin classics became known as the *studia humanitates,* usually translated as "liberal studies" or the "liberal arts." All programs of study contain an implicit philosophy, which in the case of the liberal arts is generally known as **humanism.** Humanism emphasized human beings, their achievements, interests, and capabilities. Whereas medieval writers looked to the classics to reveal God, Renaissance humanists studied the classics to understand human nature.

Renaissance humanists retained a Christian perspective, however: men (and women, though to a lesser degree) were made in the image and likeness of God. Humanists generally rejected classical ideas that were opposed to Christianity, or they sought through reinterpretation an underlying harmony between the pagan and secular and the Christian faith.

Interest in human achievement led humanists to emphasize the importance of the individual. Groups such as families, guilds, and religious organizations continued to provide strong support for the individual and to exercise great social influence. Yet in the Renaissance, artists and intellectuals, unlike their counterparts in the Middle Ages, prized their own uniqueness. This attitude of **individualism** stressed the full development of one's special capabilities and talents. (See the feature "Individuals in Society: Leonardo da Vinci.")

Chronology

1434–1494	Medici family in power in Florence
1450s	Invention of movable metal type in Germany
1469	Marriage of Isabella of Castile and Ferdinand of Aragon
1513	Niccolò Machiavelli, *The Prince*
1521	Diet of Worms
1521–1555	Charles V's wars against Valois kings
1525	Peasant revolts in Germany
1527	Henry VIII of England asks Pope Clement VII to annul his marriage to Catherine of Aragon
1536	John Calvin, *The Institutes of the Christian Religion*
1540	Founding of the Society of Jesus (Jesuits)
1545–1563	Council of Trent
1555	Peace of Augsburg
1558–1603	Reign of Elizabeth in England
1560–1660	Height of European witch-hunt
1568–1578	Civil war in the Netherlands
1572	Saint Bartholomew's Day massacre
1598	Edict of Nantes

humanism   *A term first used by Florentine rhetorician Leonard Bruni as a general word for "the new learning"; the critical study of Latin and Greek literature with the goal of realizing human potential.*

individualism   *A basic feature of the Italian Renaissance stressing personality, uniqueness, genius, and self-consciousness.*

One of the central preoccupations of the humanists was education and moral behavior. Humanists taught that a life active in the world should be the aim of all educated individuals and that education was not simply for private or religious purposes, but to benefit the public good.

Humanists put their ideas into practice. They opened schools and academies in Italian cities and courts in which pupils began with Latin grammar and rhetoric, went on to study Roman history and political philosophy, and then learned Greek in order to study Greek literature and philosophy. These classics, humanists taught, would provide models of how to write clearly, argue effectively, and speak persuasively, important skills for future diplomats, lawyers, military leaders, businessmen, and politicians. Gradually humanist education became the basis for intermediate and advanced education for a large share of middle- and upper-class men.

Humanists were ambivalent about education for women. While they saw the value of exposing women to classical models of moral behavior and reasoning, they also thought that a program of study that emphasized eloquence and action was not proper for women, whose sphere was private and domestic. Humanists never established schools for girls, though a few women of very high social status did gain a humanist education from private tutors. The ideal Renaissance woman looked a great deal more like her medieval counterpart than did the Renaissance man.

Secularism

No Renaissance book on any topic has been more widely read than the short political treatise *The Prince* by Niccolò Machiavelli (1469–1527). The subject of *The Prince* (1513) is political power: how the ruler should gain, maintain, and increase it. The prince should combine the cunning of a fox with the ferocity of a lion to achieve his goals. Asking rhetorically whether it is better for a ruler to be loved or feared, Machiavelli writes, "It will naturally be answered that it would be desirable to be both the one and the other; but as it is difficult to be both at the same time, it is much more safe to be feared than to be loved, when you have to choose between the two."[1]

Unlike medieval political theorists, Machiavelli maintained that the ruler should be concerned with the way things actually are rather than aiming for an ethical ideal. The sole test of a good government is whether it is effective—whether the ruler increases his power. Machiavelli did not advocate amoral behavior, but he believed that political action cannot be restricted by moral considerations. Nevertheless, on the basis of a crude interpretation of *The Prince,* the word *Machiavellian* entered the language as a synonym for the politically devious, corrupt, and crafty, indicating actions in which the end justifies the means.

● **Bennozzo Gozzoli: Procession of the Magi, 1461** This segment of a huge fresco covering three walls of a chapel in the Medici palace in Florence shows members of the Medici family and other contemporary individuals in a procession accompanying the biblical three wise men as they brought gifts to the infant Jesus. Reflecting the self-confidence of his patrons, Gozzoli places several members of the Medici family at the head of the procession, accompanied by their grooms. *(Scala/Art Resource, NY)*

The Prince *A 1513 treatise by Machiavelli on ways to gain, keep, and expand power; because of its subsequent impact, probably the most important literary work of the Renaissance.*

Leonardo da Vinci

Leonardo da Vinci, *Lady with an Ermine.* The enigmatic smile and smoky quality of this portrait can be found in many of Leonardo's works. *(Czartoryski Museum, Krakow/The Bridgeman Art Library)*

What makes a genius? An infinite capacity for taking pains? A deep curiosity about an extensive variety of subjects? A divine spark as manifested by talents that far exceed the norm? Or is it just "one percent inspiration and ninety-nine percent perspiration," as Thomas Edison said? To most observers, Leonardo da Vinci was one of the greatest geniuses in the history of the Western world. In fact, Leonardo was one of the individuals that the Renaissance label "genius" was designed to describe: a special kind of human being with exceptional creative powers.

Leonardo (who, despite the title of a recent best-seller, is always called by his first name) was born in Vinci, near Florence, the illegitimate son of Caterina, a local peasant girl, and Ser Piero da Vinci, a notary public. Caterina later married another native of Vinci. When Ser Piero's marriage to Donna Albrussia produced no children, he and his wife took in Leonardo. Ser Piero secured Leonardo's apprenticeship with the painter and sculptor Andrea del Verrocchio in Florence. In 1472, when Leonardo was just twenty years old, he was listed as a master in Florence's "Company of Artists."

Leonardo's most famous portrait, *Mona Lisa,* shows a woman with an enigmatic smile that Giorgio Vasari described as "so pleasing that it seemed divine rather than human." The portrait, probably of the young wife of a rich Florentine merchant (her exact identity is hotly debated), may actually be the best-known painting in the history of art. One of its competitors in that designation would be another work of Leonardo's, *The Last Supper,* which has been called "the most revered painting in the world."

Leonardo's reputation as a genius does not rest simply on his paintings, however, which are actually few in number, but rather on the breadth of his abilities and interests. In these, he is often understood to be the first "Renaissance man," a phrase we still use for a multi-talented individual. He wanted to reproduce what the eye can see, and he drew everything he saw around him, including executed criminals hanging on gallows as well as the beauties of nature. Trying to understand how the human body worked, Leonardo studied live and dead bodies, doing autopsies and dissections to investigate muscles and circulation. He carefully analyzed the effects of light, using his analysis to paint strong contrasts of light and shadow, and he experimented with perspective.

Leonardo used his drawings as the basis for his paintings and also as a tool of scientific investigation. He drew plans for hundreds of inventions, many of which would become reality centuries later, such as the helicopter, tank, machine gun, and parachute. He was hired by one of the powerful new rulers in Italy, Duke Ludovico Sforza of Milan, to design practical things that the duke needed, including weapons, fortresses, and water systems, as well as to produce works of art. Leonardo left Milan when Sforza was overthrown in war and spent the last years of his life painting, drawing, and designing for the pope and the French king.

Leonardo experimented with new materials for painting and sculpture, some of which worked and some of which did not. The experimental method he used to paint *The Last Supper* caused the picture to deteriorate rapidly, and it began to flake off the wall as soon as it was finished. Leonardo actually regarded it as never quite completed, for he could not find a model for the face of Christ that would evoke the spiritual depth he felt it deserved. His gigantic equestrian statue in honor of Ludovico's father, Duke Francesco Sforza, was never made. The clay model collapsed, and only notes survived. He planned to write books on many subjects but never finished any of them, leaving only notebooks. Leonardo once said that "a painter is not admirable unless he is universal." The patrons who supported him—and he was supported very well— perhaps wished that his inspirations would have been a bit less universal in scope, or at least accompanied by more perspiration.

Questions for Analysis

1. In what ways do the notion of a genius and the notion of a Renaissance man support one another? In what ways do they contradict one another? Which seems a better description of Leonardo?

2. Has the idea of artistic genius changed since the Renaissance? If so, how?

Sources: Giorgio Vasari, *Lives of the Artists,* vol. 1, trans. G. Bull (London: Penguin Books, 1965); S. B. Nuland, *Leonardo da Vinci* (New York: Lipper/Viking, 2000).

Primary Source:
The Prince: Power Politics During the Italian Renaissance
Learn from the man himself what it means to be "Machiavellian."

secularism *An attitude that tends to find the ultimate explanation of everything and the final end of human beings in what reason and the senses can discover, rather than in any spiritual or transcendental belief.*

Machiavelli's *The Prince* is often seen as a prime example of another aspect of the Renaissance, secularism. Secularism involves a basic concern with the material world instead of with the eternal world of spirit. A secular way of thinking tends to find the ultimate explanation of everything and the final end of human beings within the limits of what the senses can discover. Even though medieval business people ruthlessly pursued profits and medieval monks fought fiercely over property, the dominant ideals focused on the otherworldly, on life after death. Renaissance people often had strong and deep spiritual interests, but in their increasingly secular society, attention was concentrated on the here and now. The rich, social-climbing residents of Venice, Florence, and Rome came to see life more as an opportunity to be enjoyed than as a painful pilgrimage to the City of God.

Church leaders did little to combat the new secular spirit. In the fifteenth and early sixteenth centuries, the papal court and the households of the cardinals were just as worldly as those of great urban patricians. Renaissance popes beautified the city of Rome, patronized artists and men of letters, and expended enormous enthusiasm and huge sums of money. Pope Julius II (1503–1513) tore down the old Saint Peter's Basilica and began work on the present structure in 1506. Michelangelo's dome for Saint Peter's is still considered his greatest architectural work.

Despite their interest in secular matters, however, few people (including Machiavelli) questioned the basic tenets of the Christian religion. The thousands of pious paintings, sculptures, processions, and pilgrimages of the Renaissance period prove that strong religious feeling persisted.

Christian Humanism

Christian humanists *Scholars from northern Europe who, in the later years of the fifteenth century, developed programs for broad social reform based on concepts set forth in the Renaissance and on the ideals of the Christian faith.*

In the last quarter of the fifteenth century, students from the Low Countries, France, Germany, and England flocked to Italy, imbibed the "new learning," and carried it back to their countries. Northern humanists, often called Christian humanists, interpreted Italian ideas about and attitudes toward classical antiquity, individualism, and humanism in terms of their own traditions. Christian humanists had profound faith in the power of the human intellect and thought that human nature was capable of improvement through education. They developed a program for broad social reform based on Christian ideals.

The Englishman Thomas More (1478–1535) envisioned a society that would bring out this inherent goodness in his revolutionary book *Utopia* (1516). *Utopia*, whose title means both "a good place" and "nowhere," describes an ideal community on an island somewhere off the mainland of the New World. All children receive a good education, primarily in the Greco-Roman classics, and learning does not cease with maturity, for the goal of all education is to develop rational faculties. Adults divide their days between manual labor or business pursuits and intellectual activities. Because profits from business and property are held in common, there is absolute social equality. Citizens of Utopia lead an ideal, nearly perfect existence because they live by reason; their institutions are perfect.

Contrary to the long-prevailing view that vice and violence existed because people themselves were basically corrupt, More maintained that society's flawed institutions, especially private property, were responsible for corruption and war. According to More, the key to improvement and reform of the individual was reform of the social institutions that molded the individual. His ideas were profoundly original in the sixteenth century.

Better known by contemporaries than Thomas More was the Dutch humanist Desiderius Erasmus (1466?–1536) of Rotterdam. His fame rested largely on his exceptional knowledge of Greek and the Bible. Erasmus's long list of publications includes *The Education of a Christian Prince* (1504), a book combining idealistic and practical suggestions for the formation of a ruler's character through the careful study

● **The Print Shop** This sixteenth-century engraving captures the busy world of a print shop: On the left, men set pieces of type, and an individual wearing glasses checks a copy. At the rear, another applies ink to the type, while a man carries in fresh paper on his head. At the right, the master printer operates the press, while a boy removes the printed pages and sets them to dry. The well-dressed figure in the right foreground may be the patron checking to see whether his job is done. *(Giraudon/Art Resource, NY)*

of Plutarch, Aristotle, Cicero, and Plato; *The Praise of Folly* (1509), a satire of worldly wisdom and a plea for the simple and spontaneous Christian faith of children; and, most important, a critical edition of the Greek New Testament (1516). For Erasmus, education was the key to moral and intellectual improvement, and true Christianity is an inner attitude of the spirit, not outward actions.

The Printed Word

The fourteenth-century humanist Petrarch and the sixteenth-century humanist Erasmus had similar ideas about many things, but the immediate impact of their ideas was very different because of one thing: the printing press with movable metal type. The ideas of Petrarch were spread slowly from person to person by hand copying. The ideas of Erasmus were spread quickly through print, in which hundreds or thousands of identical copies could be made in a short time. Print shops were gathering places for those interested in new ideas.

Printing with movable metal type developed in Germany in the middle of the fifteenth century as a combination of existing technologies. (While printing with movable type was invented in China [see page 335], movable *metal* type was actually developed in the thirteenth century in Korea, though it was tightly controlled by the monarchy and did not have the broad impact that printing did in Europe. Historians have speculated whether German printers somehow learned of the Korean invention, but there is no evidence that they did.) Several metal-smiths, most prominently Johan Gutenberg, transformed the metal stamps used to mark signs on jewelry into type that could be covered with ink and used to mark symbols onto a surface. This type could be rearranged for every page and so used over and over. The printing revolution was also enabled by the ready availability of paper, which was made using techniques that had originated in China and spread into Europe from Muslim Spain.

The effects of the invention of movable-type printing were not felt overnight. Nevertheless, within a half century of the publication of Gutenberg's Bible of 1456, movable type had brought about radical changes. Historians estimate that somewhere between 8 million and 20 million books were printed in Europe before 1500, many more than the number of books produced in all of Western history up to that point. Printing transformed both the private and the public lives of Europeans. It gave hundreds or even thousands of people identical books, so that they could more easily discuss the ideas that the books contained with one another in person or through letters.

Government and church leaders both used and worried about printing. They printed laws, declarations of war, battle accounts, and propaganda, and they also attempted to censor or ban books and authors whose ideas they thought were wrong, though these efforts were rarely effective.

Printing also stimulated the literacy of laypeople and eventually came to have a deep effect on their private lives. Although most of the earliest books and pamphlets dealt with religious subjects, printers produced anything that would sell: professional reference sets, historical romances, biographies, and how-to manuals for the general public. They discovered that illustrations increased a book's sales, so they published both history and pornography full of woodcuts and engravings. Single-page broadsides and flysheets allowed great public events and "wonders" such as comets and two-headed calves to be experienced vicariously by the stay-at-home. Since books and other printed materials were read aloud to illiterate listeners, print bridged the gap between the written and oral cultures.

Art and the Artist

No feature of the Renaissance evokes greater admiration than its artistic masterpieces. In Renaissance Italy powerful urban groups and individuals commissioned works of art. Wealthy merchants and bankers and popes and princes spent vast sums on the arts as a means of glorifying themselves and their families. Patrons varied in their level of involvement as a work progressed; some simply ordered a specific subject or scene, while others oversaw the work of the artist or architect very closely, suggesting themes and styles and demanding changes while the work was in progress.

The content and style of Renaissance art were often different from those of the Middle Ages. The individual portrait emerged as a distinct artistic genre. Rather than reflecting a spiritual ideal, as medieval painting and sculpture tended to do, Renaissance portraits showed human ideals, often portrayed in a more realistic style. The sculptor Donatello (1386–1466) revived the classical figure, with its balance and self-awareness. In architecture, Filippo Brunelleschi (1377–1446) looked to the classical past for inspiration, designing a dome for the cathedral in Florence and a hospital for orphans and foundlings in which all proportions were carefully thought out to achieve a sense of balance and harmony.

As the fifteenth century advanced, classical themes and motifs, such as the lives and loves of pagan gods and goddesses, figured increasingly in painting and sculpture. Religious topics, such as the Annunciation of the Virgin and the Nativity, remained popular among both patrons and artists, but frequently the patron had himself and his family portrayed in the scene.

In the fifteenth century the center of the new art shifted from Florence to Rome, where wealthy cardinals and popes wanted visual expression of the church's and their own families' power and piety. Michelangelo went to Rome about 1500 and began the series of statues, paintings, and architectural projects from which he gained an international reputation: the Pietà, Moses, the redesigning of the Capitoline Hill in central Rome, and, most famously, the ceiling and altar wall of the Sistine Chapel. Pope Julius II, who commissioned the Sistine Chapel, demanded that Michelangelo work as fast as he could and frequently visited the artist at his work with suggestions and criticisms. Michelangelo complained in person and by letter about the pope's meddling, but his reputation did not match the power of the pope, and he kept working. Raphael Sanzio (1483–1520), another Florentine, got the commission for

● **Sandro Botticelli: Primavera, or Spring (ca. 1482)** Venus, the Roman goddess of love, is flanked on her left by Flora, goddess of flowers and fertility, and on her right by the Three Graces, goddesses of banquets, dance, and social occasions. Above, Venus's son Cupid, the god of love, shoots darts of desire, while at the far right the wind god Zephyrus chases the nymph Chloris. Botticelli captured the ideal for female beauty in the Renaissance: slender, with pale skin, a high forehead, red-blond hair, and sloping shoulders. *(Digital image © The Museum of Modern Art/Licensed by Scala/Art Resource, NY)*

frescoes in the papal apartments, and in his relatively short life he painted hundreds of portraits and devotional images, becoming the most sought-after artist in Europe.

Praising their talents, Vasari described both Michelangelo and Raphael as "divine" and "rare men of genius." This adulation of the artist had led many historians to view the Renaissance as the beginning of the concept of the artist as genius. In the Middle Ages, people believed that only God created, albeit through individuals; the medieval conception recognized no particular value in artistic originality. Renaissance artists and humanists came to think that a work of art was the deliberate creation of a unique personality, of an individual who transcended traditions, rules, and theories. A genius had a peculiar gift, which ordinary laws should not inhibit.

Whether in Italy or northern Europe, most Renaissance artists trained in the workshops of older artists. Though they might be "men of genius," artists were still expected to be well-trained in proper artistic techniques and stylistic conventions, for the notion that artistic genius could show up in the work of an untrained artist did not emerge until the twentieth century. By the later sixteenth century formal artistic "academies" were also established to train artists. Like universities, artistic workshops and academies were male-only settings in which men of different ages came together for training and created bonds of friendship, influence, patronage, and sometimes intimacy. Several women did become well-known as painters during the Renaissance, but they were trained by their painter fathers and often quit painting when they married.

● **Artemisia Gentileschi: Esther Before Ahaseurus (ca. 1630)** In this oil painting, Gentileschi shows an Old Testament scene of the Jewish woman Esther who saved her people from being killed by her husband, King Ahaseurus. This deliverance is celebrated in the Jewish holiday of Purim. Both figures are in the elaborate dress worn in Renaissance courts. Typical of a female painter, Artemisia Gentileschi was trained by her father. She mastered the dramatic style favored in the early seventeenth century and became known especially for her portraits of strong biblical and mythological heroines. *(Image copyright © The Metropolitan Museum of Art/Art Resource, NY)*

Women were not alone in being excluded from the institutions of Renaissance culture. Though a few "rare men of genius" such as Leonardo or Michelangelo emerged from artisanal backgrounds, most scholars and artists came from families with at least some money. Renaissance culture did not influence the lives of most people in cities and did not affect life in the villages at all. A small, highly educated minority of literary humanists and artists created the culture of and for an exclusive elite. The Renaissance maintained, or indeed enhanced, a gulf between the learned minority and the uneducated multitude that has survived for many centuries.

SOCIAL HIERARCHIES

What were the key social hierarchies in Renaissance Europe, and how did ideas about hierarchy shape people's lives?

The division between educated and uneducated people was only one of many social hierarchies evident in the Renaissance. Every society has social hierarchies; in ancient Rome, for example, there were patricians and plebians (see page 105). Such hierarchies are to some degree descriptions of social reality, but they are also idealizations—

that is, they describe how people *imagine* their society to be, without all the messy reality of social-climbing merchants or groups that do not fit the standard categories. Social hierarchies in the Renaissance built on those of the Middle Ages but also developed new features that contributed to modern social hierarchies.

Race

Renaissance people did not use the word *race* the way we do, but often used *race, people,* and *nation* interchangeably for ethnic, national, and religious groups—the French race, the Jewish nation, the Irish people, and so on. They did make distinctions based on skin color that provide some of the background for later conceptualizations of race, but these distinctions were interwoven with other characteristics when people thought about human differences.

Ever since the time of the Roman republic, a few black Africans had lived in western Europe. They had come, along with white slaves, as the spoils of war. Even after the collapse of the Roman Empire, Muslim and Christian merchants continued to import them. Unstable political conditions in many parts of Africa enabled enterprising merchants to seize people and sell them into slavery. Local authorities afforded them no protection. Long tradition, moreover, sanctioned the practice of slavery. The evidence of medieval art attests to the continued presence of Africans in Europe throughout the Middle Ages and to Europeans' awareness of them.

Beginning in the fifteenth century sizable numbers of black slaves entered Europe. By the mid-sixteenth century blacks, slave and free, constituted roughly 3 percent of the Portuguese population. In the Iberian Peninsula African slaves intermingled with the people they lived among and sometimes intermarried. Cities such as Lisbon had significant numbers of people of mixed African and European descent.

Although blacks were concentrated in the Iberian Peninsula, there were some Africans in other parts of Europe as well. Black servants were much sought after; aristocrats had their portraits painted with their black pageboys to indicate their wealth and, in the case of noblewomen, to highlight their fair skin (see Gozzoli's *Procession of the Magi* on page 390, in which the Medici rulers of Florence are shown with a black groom). In Renaissance Spain and Italy, blacks performed as dancers, as actors and actresses in courtly dramas, and as musicians, sometimes making up full orchestras.

Africans were not simply amusements at court. In Portugal, Spain, and Italy, slaves supplemented the labor force in virtually all occupations—as servants, agricultural laborers, craftsmen, and seamen on ships. Agriculture in Europe did not involve large plantations, so large-scale agricultural slavery did not develop there; African slaves formed the primary work force on the sugar plantations set up by Europeans on the Atlantic islands in the late fifteenth century, however (see page 446).

Until the voyages down the African coast in the late fifteenth century, Europeans had little concrete knowledge of Africans and their cultures. They perceived Africa as a remote place, the home of strange people isolated by heresy and Islam from superior European civilization. Africans' contact, even as slaves, with Christian Europeans could only "improve" the blacks, they believed. The expanding slave trade only reinforced negative preconceptions about the inferiority of black Africans.

Class

The notion of class—working class, middle class, upper class—did not exist in the Renaissance. By the thirteenth century, however, and even more so by the fifteenth, the idea of a changeable hierarchy based on wealth, what would later come to be termed "social class," was emerging alongside the medieval concept of orders (see page 365). This was particularly true in towns. Most residents of towns were technically members of the "third estate," that is "those who work" rather than "those who fight" and "those who pray." However, this group now included wealthy merchants

● **Vittore Carpaccio: Black Laborers on the Venetian Docks (detail)** Enslaved and free blacks, besides working as gondoliers on the Venetian canals, served on the docks. Here, seven black men careen—clean, caulk, and repair—a ship. Carpaccio's reputation as one of Venice's outstanding painters rests on his eye for details of everyday life. *(Gallerie dell'Accademia, Venice/Scala/Art Resource, NY)*

who oversaw vast trading empires, held positions of political power, and lived in splendor that rivaled the richest nobles.

The development of a hierarchy of wealth did not mean an end to the hierarchy of orders, however, and even poorer nobles still had higher status than merchants. If this had not been the case, wealthy Italian merchants would not have bothered to buy noble titles and country villas, nor would wealthy English and Spanish merchants have been eager to marry their daughters and sons into often impoverished noble families. The nobility maintained its status in most parts of Europe not by maintaining rigid boundaries, but by taking in and integrating the new social elite of wealth.

Gender

debate about women *A discussion, which began in the later years of the fourteenth century, that attempted to answer fundamental questions of gender and define the role of women in society.*

Renaissance people would not have understood the word *gender* to refer to categories of people, but they would have easily grasped the concept. Toward the end of the fourteenth century learned men (and a few women) began what was termed the **"debate about women"** (*querelle des femmes*), a debate about women's character and nature that would last for centuries. Misogynist critiques of women from both clerical and secular authors denounced females as devious, domineering, and demanding. In answer, several authors compiled long lists of famous and praiseworthy women exemplary for their loyalty, bravery, and morality. Some writers, including a few women who had gained a humanist education, were not only interested in defending women, but also in exploring the reasons behind women's secondary status—that is, why the great philosophers, statesmen, and poets had generally been men. In this they were anticipating recent discussions about the "social construction of gender" by six hundred years.

Beginning in the sixteenth century, the debate about women also became one about female rulers, sparked primarily by dynastic accidents in many countries, including Spain, England, France, and Scotland, which led to women serving as advisers to child kings or ruling in their own right. There were no successful rebellions against female rulers simply because they were women, but in part this was because female rulers, especially Queen Elizabeth I of England, emphasized qualities regarded as masculine—physical bravery, stamina, wisdom, duty—whenever they appeared in public.

Ideas about women's and men's proper roles determined the actions of ordinary men and women even more forcefully. The dominant notion of the "true" man was that of the married head of household, so men whose class and age would have normally conferred political power but who remained unmarried were sometimes excluded from ruling positions. Actual marriage patterns in Europe left many women unmarried until quite late in life, but this did not lead to greater equality. If they worked for wages, and many women did, women earned about half to two-thirds of what men did even for the same work. Of all the ways in which Renaissance society was hierarchically arranged—class, age, level of education, rank, race, occupation—gender was regarded as the most "natural" and therefore the most important to defend.

● **Italian City Scene** In this detail from a fresco, the Italian painter Lorenzo Lotto captures the mixing of social groups in a Renaissance Italian city. The crowd of men in the right foreground includes wealthy merchants in elaborate hats and colorful coats. Two mercenary soldiers (carrying a sword and a pike) wear short doublets and tight hose stylishly slit to reveal colored undergarments, while boys play with toy weapons at their feet. Clothing like that of the soldiers, which emphasized the masculine form, was frequently criticized for its expense and its "indecency." At the left, women sell vegetables and bread, which would have been a common sight at any city marketplace. *(Scala/Art Resource, NY)*

POLITICS AND THE STATE IN THE RENAISSANCE (CA. 1450–1521)

How did the nation-states of western Europe evolve in this period?

The High Middle Ages had witnessed the origins of many of the basic institutions of the modern state. Sheriffs, inquests, juries, circuit judges, professional bureaucracies, and representative assemblies all trace their origins to the twelfth and thirteenth centuries. The linchpin for the development of states, however, was strong monarchy. Beginning in the fifteenth century rulers utilized aggressive methods to build up their governments. They began the work of reducing violence, curbing unruly nobles, and establishing domestic order. They emphasized royal majesty and royal sovereignty and insisted on the respect and loyalty of all subjects.

France

The Hundred Years' War left France drastically depopulated, commercially ruined, and agriculturally weak (see page 379). Nonetheless, the ruler whom Joan of Arc had seen crowned at Reims, Charles VII (r. 1422–1461), revived the monarchy and France. He reorganized the royal council, giving increased influence to middle-class men, and strengthened royal finances through such taxes as the *gabelle* (on salt) and the *taille* (land tax). These taxes remained the Crown's chief sources of income until the Revolution of 1789. By establishing regular companies of cavalry and archers— recruited, paid, and inspected by the state—Charles created the first permanent royal army. By 1453 French armies had expelled the English from French soil except in Calais. His son Louis XI (r. 1461–1483), called the "Spider King" because of his treacherous character, improved upon Charles's army and used it to stop aristocratic brigandage, curb urban independence, and conquer the largest remaining noble holding on France's borders.

Two further developments strengthened the French monarchy. The marriage of Louis XII (r. 1498–1515) and Anne of Brittany added the large western duchy of Brittany to the state. Then the French king Francis I and Pope Leo X reached a mutually satisfactory agreement about church and state powers in 1516. The new treaty, the Concordat of Bologna, approved the pope's right to receive the first year's income of new bishops and abbots. In return, Leo X recognized the French ruler's right to select French bishops and abbots. French kings thereafter effectively controlled the appointment and thus the policies of church officials in the kingdom.

England

English society suffered severely in the fourteenth and fifteenth centuries. Population, decimated by the Black Death, continued to decline. Between 1455 and 1471 adherents of the ducal houses of York and Lancaster waged civil war, commonly called the **Wars of the Roses** because the symbol of the Yorkists was a white rose and that of the Lancastrians a red one. The chronic disorder hurt trade, agriculture, and domestic industry, and the authority of the monarchy sank lower than it had been in centuries.

The Yorkist Edward IV (r. 1461–1483) began establishing domestic tranquility. He succeeded in defeating the Lancastrian forces and after 1471 began to reconstruct the monarchy and consolidate royal power. Henry VII (r. 1485–1509) of the Welsh house of Tudor worked to restore royal prestige, to crush the power of the nobility, and to establish order and law at the local level. Because the government halted the long period of anarchy, it won the key support of the merchant and agricultural upper middle

Wars of the Roses *An exhausting conflict in fifteenth-century England between the ducal houses of York (represented by a white rose) and Lancaster (represented by a red rose). The war lasted from 1455 until 1471 and ended with a victory of the Yorkist forces led by Edward IV.*

class. Edward IV and subsequently the Tudors, excepting Henry VIII, conducted foreign policy on the basis of diplomacy, avoiding expensive wars. Thus the English monarchy did not depend on Parliament for money, and the Crown undercut that source of aristocratic influence.

Henry VII did summon several meetings of Parliament in the early years of his reign, primarily to confirm laws, but the center of royal authority was the royal council, which governed at the national level. There Henry VII revealed his distrust of the nobility: very few great lords were among the king's closest advisers, who instead were lesser landowners and lawyers. They were, in a sense, middle class. The royal council handled any business the king put before it—executive, legislative, and judicial. For example, the council conducted negotiations with foreign governments and secured international recognition of the Tudor dynasty through the marriage in 1501 of Henry VII's eldest son Arthur to Catherine of Aragon, the daughter of Ferdinand and Isabella of Spain.

Secretive, cautious, and thrifty, Henry VII rebuilt the monarchy. He encouraged the cloth industry and built up the English merchant marine. English exports of wool and the royal export tax on that wool steadily increased. Henry crushed an invasion from Ireland and secured peace with Scotland through the marriage of his daughter Margaret to the Scottish king. When Henry VII died in 1509, he left a country at peace both domestically and internationally, a substantially augmented treasury, and the dignity and role of the royal majesty much enhanced.

Spain

While England and France laid the foundations of unified nation-states during the Renaissance, Spain remained a conglomerate of independent kingdoms. Even the wedding in 1469 of the dynamic and aggressive Isabella of Castile and the crafty and persistent Ferdinand of Aragon did not bring about administrative unity. Rather, their marriage constituted a dynastic union of two royal houses, not the political union of two peoples, though they did pursue a common foreign policy.

Ferdinand and Isabella were able to exert their authority in ways similar to the rulers of France and England, however. They curbed aristocratic power by excluding aristocrats and great territorial magnates from the royal council, and instead appointed only men of middle-class background. The council and various government boards recruited men trained in Roman law, which exalted the power of the Crown. They also secured from the Spanish pope Alexander VI the right to appoint bishops in Spain and in the Hispanic territories in America, enabling them to establish the equivalent of a national church. In 1492 their armies conquered Granada, the last territory held by Arabs in southern Spain.

There still remained a sizable and, in the view of the majority of the Spanish people, potentially dangerous minority, the Jews. When the kings of France and England had expelled the Jews from their kingdoms, many had sought refuge in Spain. During the long centuries of the reconquista, Christian kings had renewed Jewish rights and privileges; in fact, Jewish industry, intelligence, and money had supported royal power. While Christians of all classes borrowed from Jewish moneylenders and while all who could afford them sought Jewish physicians, a strong undercurrent of resentment of Jewish influence and wealth festered.

In the fourteenth century anti-Semitism in Spain was aggravated by fiery anti-Jewish preaching, by economic dislocation, and by the search for a scapegoat during the Black Death. Anti-Semitic pogroms swept the towns of Spain; one scholar estimates that 40 percent of the Jewish population was killed or forced to convert.[2] Those converted were called *conversos* or **New Christians.** Conversos were often well-educated and held prominent positions in government, the church, medicine, law, and business.

New Christians *The translation of the Spanish word* conversos, *referring to Spanish Jews who converted to Christianity in the fourteenth century in order to avoid persecution.*

● **Felipe Bigarny: Ferdinand and Isabella** In these wooden sculptures, the Burgundian artist Felipe Bigarny portrays Ferdinand and Isabella as paragons of Christian piety, kneeling at prayer. Ferdinand is shown in armor, a symbol of his military accomplishments and masculinity. Isabella wears a simple white head covering rather than something more elaborate to indicate her modesty, a key virtue for women, though her actions and writings indicate that she was more determined and forceful than Ferdinand. *(Capilla Real, Granada/Laurie Platt Winfrey, Inc.)*

Such successes bred resentment. Aristocratic grandees resented their financial dependence; the poor hated the converso tax collectors; and churchmen doubted the sincerity of their conversions. Queen Isabella shared these suspicions, and she and Ferdinand received permission from Pope Sixtus IV to establish an Inquisition to "search out and punish converts from Judaism who had transgressed against Christianity by secretly adhering to Jewish beliefs and performing rites of the Jews."[3] Investigations and trials began immediately, as officials of the Inquisition looked for conversos who showed any sign of incomplete conversion, such as not eating pork.

Recent scholarship has carefully analyzed documents of the Inquisition. Most conversos identified themselves as sincere Christians; many came from families that had received baptism generations before. In response, officials of the Inquisition developed a new type of anti-Semitism. A person's status as a Jew, they argued, could not be changed by religious conversion, but was in their blood and was heritable, so Jews could never be true Christians. In what were known as "purity of the blood" laws, having pure Christian blood became a requirement for noble status. Ideas about Jews developed in Spain were important components in European concepts of race, and discussions of "Jewish blood" later expanded into notions of the "Jewish race."

Shortly after the conquest of Granada, Isabella and Ferdinand issued an edict expelling all practicing Jews from Spain. Of the community of perhaps 200,000 Jews, 150,000 fled. Absolute religious orthodoxy and "purity of blood" served as the theoretical foundation of the Spanish national state.

The Habsburgs

War and diplomacy were important ways that states increased their power in sixteenth-century Europe, but so was marriage. Because almost all of Europe was ruled by hereditary dynasties—the papal states and a few cities being the exceptions—claiming and holding resources involved shrewd marital strategies, for it was far cheaper to gain land by inheritance than by war. Royal and noble sons and daughters were important tools of state policy.

The benefits of an advantageous marriage stretched across generations, a process that can be seen most dramatically with the Habsburgs. The Holy Roman emperor Frederick III, a Habsburg who was the ruler of most of Austria, acquired only a small amount of territory—but a great deal of money—with his marriage to Princess Eleonore of Portugal in 1452. He arranged for his son Maximilian to marry Europe's most prominent heiress, Mary of Burgundy, in 1477; she inherited the Netherlands, Luxembourg, and the county of Burgundy in what is now eastern France. Through this union with the rich and powerful duchy of Burgundy, the Austrian house of Habsburg, already the strongest ruling family in the empire, became an international power. The marriage of Maximilian and Mary angered the French, however, who considered Burgundy French territory, and inaugurated centuries of conflict between the Austrian house of Habsburg and the kings of France. Within the empire, German principalities that resented Austria's pre-eminence began to see that they shared interests with France.

Maximilian learned the lesson of marital politics well, marrying his son and daughter to the children of Ferdinand and Isabella, the rulers of Spain, much of southern Italy, and eventually the Spanish New World empire. His grandson Charles V (1500–1558) fell heir to a vast and incredibly diverse collection of states and peoples, each governed in a different manner and held together only by the person of the emperor (see Map 14.1 and page 410). Charles was convinced that it was his duty to maintain the political and religious unity of Western Christendom. This conviction would be challenged far more than Charles ever anticipated.

THE PROTESTANT REFORMATION

What were the central ideas of Protestant reformers, and why were they appealing to various groups across Europe?

Calls for reform in the church came from many quarters in early-sixteenth-century Europe—from educated laypeople such as Christian humanists and urban residents, from villagers and artisans, and from church officials themselves. This dissatisfaction helps explain why the ideas of Martin Luther, an obscure professor from a new and not very prestigious German university, found a ready audience. Within a decade of his first publishing his ideas (using the new technology of the printing press), much of central Europe and Scandinavia had broken with the Catholic Church, and even more radical concepts of the Christian message were being developed and linked to calls for social change.

Criticism of the Church

Sixteenth-century Europeans were deeply pious. Despite—or perhaps because of—the depth of their piety, many people were also highly critical of the Roman Catholic Church and its clergy. Papal conflicts with rulers and the Great Schism badly damaged the prestige of church leaders. Humanists denounced corruption in the church, the superstitions of the parish clergy, and the excessive rituals of the monks. Many ordinary

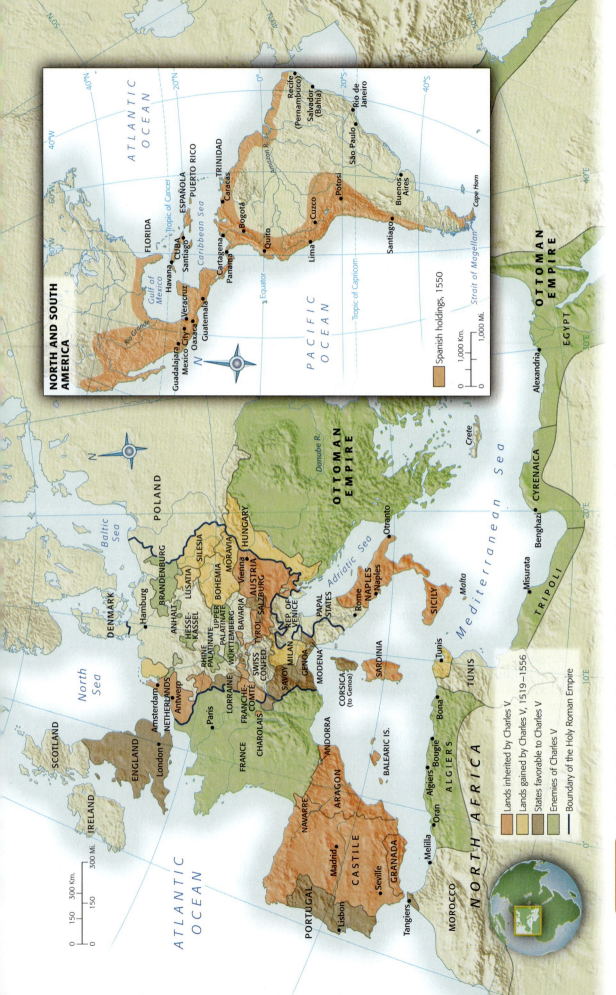

NORTH AND SOUTH AMERICA

ATLANTIC OCEAN

PACIFIC OCEAN

Spanish holdings, 1550

Guadalajara · Mexico City · Oaxaca · Guatemala · Veracruz · Havana · Santiago · CUBA · FLORIDA · PUERTO RICO · ESPAÑOLA · TRINIDAD · Caracas · Cartagena · Panamá · Bogotá · Quito · Lima · Cuzco · Potosí · Santiago · Buenos Aires · São Paulo · Rio de Janeiro · Salvador (Bahia) · Recife (Pernambuco) · Cape Horn

Gulf of Mexico · Caribbean Sea · Rio Grande · Amazon R. · Equator · Tropic of Cancer · Tropic of Capricorn · Strait of Magellan

1,000 Km. · 1,000 Mi.

ATLANTIC OCEAN

North Sea · Baltic Sea · Mediterranean Sea · Adriatic Sea

SCOTLAND · IRELAND · ENGLAND · London · DENMARK · Hamburg · POLAND · BRANDENBURG · ANHALT · HESSE-KASSEL · LUSATIA · SILESIA · MORAVIA · BOHEMIA · Vienna · AUSTRIA · SALZBURG · HUNGARY · OTTOMAN EMPIRE · Danube R. · NETHERLANDS · Amsterdam · Antwerp · RHINE PALATINATE · UPPER PALATINATE · WÜRTTEMBERG · BAVARIA · TYROL · SWISS CONFED. · MILAN · GENOA · MODENA · REP. OF VENICE · PAPAL STATES · Rome · NAPLES · Naples · Otranto · Crete · Paris · LORRAINE · FRANCHE-COMTÉ · CHAROLAIS · SAVOY · FRANCE · CORSICA (to Genoa) · SARDINIA · SICILY · Malta · Misurata · CYRENAICA · Benghazi · TRIPOLI · ANDORRA · NAVARRE · ARAGON · CASTILE · GRANADA · Madrid · Seville · PORTUGAL · Lisbon · Tangiers · BALEARIC IS. · Melilla · Oran · Algiers · Bougie · ALGIERS · Bona · TUNIS · Tunis · NORTH AFRICA · MOROCCO · EGYPT · Alexandria

Lands inherited by Charles V
Lands gained by Charles V, 1519–1556
States favorable to Charles V
Enemies of Charles V
Boundary of the Holy Roman Empire

300 Mi. · 300 Km. · 150

MAP 14.1 **The Global Empire of Charles V** Charles V exercised theoretical jurisdiction over more European territory than anyone since Charlemagne. He also claimed authority over large parts of North and South America, though actual Spanish control was weak in much of this area.

people agreed. Court records, bishops' visitations of parishes, and even popular songs and printed images show widespread **anticlericalism,** or opposition to the clergy.

In the early sixteenth century critics of the church concentrated their attacks on three disorders—clerical immorality, clerical ignorance, and clerical absenteeism. Charges of clerical immorality were aimed at a number of priests who were drunkards, neglected the rule of celibacy, gambled, or indulged in fancy dress. Charges of clerical ignorance applied to barely literate priests who delivered poor quality sermons and who were obviously ignorant of the Latin words of the Mass.

In regard to absenteeism, many clerics, especially higher ecclesiastics, held several *benefices* (or offices) simultaneously—a practice termed *pluralism*—but seldom visited the benefices, let alone performed the spiritual responsibilities those offices entailed. Instead, they collected revenues from all of them and hired a poor priest, paying him just a fraction of the income to fulfill the spiritual duties of a particular local church.

There was also local resentment of clerical privileges and immunities. Priests, monks, and nuns were exempt from civic responsibilities, such as defending the city and paying taxes. Yet religious orders frequently held large amounts of urban property, in some cities as much as one-third. City governments were increasingly determined to integrate the clergy into civic life. This brought city leaders into opposition with bishops and the papacy, which for centuries had stressed the independence of the church from lay control and the distinction between members of the clergy and laypeople.

Martin Luther

By itself, widespread criticism of the church did not lead to the dramatic changes of the sixteenth century. Those resulted from the personal religious struggle of a German university professor, Martin Luther (1483–1546). Luther's middle-class father wanted him to be a lawyer, but a sense of religious calling led him to join the Augustinian friars, an order whose members often preached, taught, and assisted the poor. Luther was ordained a priest in 1507 and after additional study earned a doctorate of theology. From 1512 until his death in 1546, he served as professor of the Scriptures at the new University of Wittenberg.

Martin Luther was a very conscientious friar. His scrupulous observance of the religious routine, frequent confessions, and fasting, however, gave him only temporary relief from anxieties about sin and his ability to meet God's demands. Through his study of Saint Paul's letters in the New Testament, he gradually arrived at a new understanding of Christian doctrine. His understanding is often summarized as "faith alone, grace alone, Scripture alone." He believed that salvation and justification come through faith. Faith is a free gift of God, not the result of human effort. God's word is revealed only in Scripture, not in the traditions of the church.

At the same time Luther was engaged in scholarly reflections and professorial lecturing, Pope Leo X authorized a special St. Peter's indulgence to finance his building plans in Rome. An **indulgence** was a document, signed by the pope or another church official, that substituted for penance. The archbishop who controlled the area in which Wittenberg was located, Albert of Mainz, was an enthusiastic promoter of this indulgence sale. He received a share of the profits in order to pay off a debt from a wealthy banking family, a debt he had incurred in order to purchase a papal dispensation allowing him to become the bishop of several other territories as well. Albert's indulgence sale, run by a Dominican friar who mounted an advertising blitz, promised that the purchase of indulgences would bring full forgiveness for one's own sins or release from purgatory for a loved one. One of the slogans—"As soon as coin in coffer rings, the soul from purgatory springs"—brought phenomenal success.

Luther was severely troubled that many people believed that they had no further need for repentance once they had purchased indulgences. He wrote a letter to Archbishop Albert on the subject and enclosed in Latin "Ninety-five Theses on the Power

anticlericalism *A widespread sentiment in the early sixteenth century characterized by resentment of clerical immorality, ignorance, and absenteeism. An important cause of the Protestant Reformation.*

> **Primary Source:**
> **Table Talk**
> *Read Martin Luther in his own words, speaking out forcefully and candidly—and sometimes with humor—against Catholic institutions.*

indulgence *A papal statement granting remission of a priest-imposed penalty for sin (no one knew what penalty God would impose after death).*

● **The Folly of Indulgences** In this woodcut from the early Reformation, the church's sale of indulgences is viciously satirized. With one claw in holy water, another resting on the coins paid for indulgences, and a third stretched out for offerings, the church, in the form of a rapacious bird, writes out an indulgence with excrement. The creature's head and gaping mouth represent Hell, with foolish Christians inside, others being cooked in a pot above, and a demon delivering the pope in a three-tiered crown and holding the keys to Heaven, a symbol of papal authority. Illustrations such as this, often printed as single-sheet broadsides and sold very cheaply, clearly conveyed criticism of the church to people who could not read. *(Kunstsammlungen der Veste Coburg)*

Diet of Worms *An assembly of the Estates of the Holy Roman Empire convened by Charles V in the German city of Worms. It was here that Martin Luther refused to recant his writings.*

Protestant *Originally meaning "a follower of Luther," this term came to be generally applied to all non-Catholic Christians.*

of Indulgences." His argument was that indulgences undermined the seriousness of the sacrament of penance and competed with the preaching of the Gospel. After Luther's death, biographies reported that the theses were also posted on the door of the church at Wittenberg Castle on October 31, 1517. Such an act would have been very strange—they were in Latin and written for those learned in theology, not for normal churchgoers—but it has become a standard part of Luther lore. In any case, Luther intended the theses for academic debate, but by December 1517 they had been translated into German and were read throughout the Holy Roman Empire.

Luther was ordered to come to Rome, which he was able to avoid because of the political situation in the Holy Roman Empire. The pope ordered him to recant many of his ideas, and Luther publicly burned the papal letter. In this highly charged atmosphere, the twenty-one-year-old emperor Charles V held his first diet (assembly of the Estates of the empire) in the German city of Worms. Charles summoned Luther to appear before the **Diet of Worms.** When ordered to recant, Luther replied in language that rang all over Europe:

Unless I am convinced by the evidence of Scripture or by plain reason—for I do not accept the authority of the Pope or the councils alone, since it is established that they have often erred and contradicted themselves—I am bound by the Scriptures I have cited and my conscience is captive to the Word of God. I cannot and will not recant anything, for it is neither safe nor right to go against conscience. God help me. Amen.[4]

Protestant Thought and Its Appeal

As he developed his ideas, Luther gathered followers, who came to be called Protestants. The word **Protestant** derives from a "protest" drawn up by a small group of reforming German princes in 1529. At first *Protestant* meant "a follower of Luther" but with the appearance of many protesting sects, it became a general term applied to all non-Catholic western European Christians.

Protestants agreed on many things. First, how is a person to be saved? Traditional Catholic teaching held that salvation is achieved by both faith and good works. Protestants held that salvation comes by faith alone, irrespective of good works or the sacraments. God, not people, initiates salvation. (See the feature "Listening to the Past: Martin Luther, *On Christian Liberty*" on pages 422–423.) Second, where does religious authority reside? Christian doctrine had long maintained that authority rests both in the Bible and in the traditional teaching of the church. For Protestants, authority rests in the Bible alone. For a doctrine or issue to be valid, it had to have a scriptural basis. Third, what is the church? Protestants held that the church is a spiritual *priesthood of all believers,* an invisible fellowship not fixed in any place or person, which differed markedly from the Roman Catholic practice of a clerical, hierarchical institution headed by the pope in Rome. Fourth, what is the highest form of Christian life? The medieval church had stressed the superiority of the monastic and religious life over the secular. Luther disagreed and argued that every person should serve God in his or her individual calling.

Pulpits and printing presses spread Luther's message all over Germany. By the time of his death, people of all social classes had become Lutheran. What was the immense appeal of Luther's religious ideas and those of other Protestants?

Educated people and humanists were much attracted by Luther's ideas. He advocated a simpler personal religion based on faith, a return to the spirit of the early church, the centrality of the Scriptures in the liturgy and in Christian life, and the abolition of elaborate ceremonies—precisely the reforms the Christian humanists had been calling for. His insistence that everyone should read and reflect on the Scriptures attracted the literate and thoughtful middle classes partly because Luther appealed to their intelligence. This included many priests and monks, who became clergy in the new Protestant churches. Luther's ideas also appealed to townspeople who envied the church's wealth and resented paying for it. After cities became Protestant, the city council taxed the clergy and placed them under the jurisdiction of civil courts.

Scholars in many disciplines have attributed Luther's fame and success to the invention of the printing press, which rapidly reproduced and made known his ideas. Many printed works included woodcuts and other illustrations, so that even those who could not read could grasp the main ideas. Hymns such as "A Mighty Fortress Is Our God" (which Luther wrote) were also important means of conveying central points of doctrine. Equally important was Luther's incredible skill with language; his linguistic skill, together with his translation of the New Testament into German in 1523, led to the acceptance of his dialect of German as the standard version of German.

Luther lived in a territory ruled by a noble—the Elector of Saxony—and he also worked closely with political authorities, viewing them as fully justified in reforming the church in their territories. He instructed all Christians to obey their secular rulers, whom he saw as divinely ordained to maintain order. Individuals may have been convinced of the truth of Protestant teachings by hearing sermons, listening to hymns, or reading pamphlets, but a territory became Protestant when its ruler, whether a noble or a city council, brought in a reformer or two to reeducate the territory's clergy, sponsored public sermons, and confiscated church property. This happened in many of the states of the empire during the 1520s and then moved beyond the empire to Denmark-Norway and Sweden.

In the sixteenth century the practice of religion remained a public matter. The ruler determined the official form of religious practice in his (or occasionally her) jurisdiction. Almost everyone believed that the presence of a faith different from that of the majority represented a political threat to the security of the state. Few believed in religious liberty; those with different ideas had to convert or leave.

The Radical Reformation and the German Peasants' War

Some individuals and groups rejected the idea that church and state needed to be united, and sought to create a voluntary community of believers as they understood it to have existed in New Testament times. In terms of theology and spiritual practices, these individuals and groups varied widely, though they are generally termed "radicals" for their insistence on a more extensive break with the past. Some adopted the baptism of believers—for which they were given the title of "Anabaptists" or rebaptizers by their enemies—while others saw all outward sacraments or rituals as misguided. Some groups attempted communal ownership of property, living very simply and rejecting anything they thought unbiblical. Some reacted harshly to members who deviated, but others argued for complete religious toleration and individualism.

Religious radicals were met with fanatical hatred and bitter persecution. Protestants and Catholics all saw—quite correctly—that the radicals' call for the separation of church and state would lead ultimately to the secularization of society. Radicals were either banished or cruelly executed by burning, beating, or drowning. Their community spirit and the edifying example of their lives, however, contributed to the survival of radical ideas. Later, the Quakers, with their gentle pacifism; the Baptists, with their emphasis on inner spiritual light; the Congregationalists, with their democratic church organization; and in 1787 the authors of the U.S. Constitution, with their opposition to the "establishment of religion" (state churches), would all trace their origins, in part, to the radicals of the sixteenth century.

In the early sixteenth century the economic condition of the peasantry varied from place to place but was generally worse than it had been in the fifteenth century and was deteriorating. Peasants demanded limitations on the new taxes and services their noble landlords were imposing. They peasants believed that their demands conformed to the Scriptures and cited Luther as a theologian who could prove that they did.

Luther wanted to prevent rebellion. Initially he sided with the peasants, blasting the lords for robbing their subjects. But when rebellion broke out, the peasants who expected Luther's support were soon disillusioned. Freedom for Luther meant independence from the authority of the Roman church; it did *not* mean opposition to legally established secular powers. Firmly convinced that rebellion would hasten the end of civilized society, he wrote the tract *Against the Murderous, Thieving Hordes of the Peasants:* "Let everyone who can smite, slay, and stab [the peasants], secretly and openly, remembering that nothing can be more poisonous, hurtful or devilish than a rebel."[5] The nobility ferociously crushed the revolt. Historians estimate that more than seventy-five thousand peasants were killed in 1525.

The German Peasants' War of 1525 greatly strengthened the authority of lay rulers. Not surprisingly, the Reformation lost much of its popular appeal after 1525, though peasants and urban rebels sometimes found a place for their social and religious ideas in radical groups. Peasants' economic conditions did moderately improve, however. For example, in many parts of Germany, enclosed fields, meadows, and forests were returned to common use.

The Reformation and Marriage

Luther and other Protestants believed that a priest's or nun's vows of celibacy went against human nature and God's commandments. Luther married a former nun, Katharina von Bora (1499–1532), who quickly had several children. Most other Protestant reformers also married, and their wives had to create a new and respectable role for themselves—pastor's wife—to overcome being viewed as simply a new type of priest's concubine. They were living demonstrations of their husband's convictions about the superiority of marriage to celibacy, and they were expected to be models of wifely obedience and Christian charity.

Protestants did not break with medieval Scholastic theologians in their idea that women were to be subject to men. Women were advised to be cheerful rather than grudging in their obedience, for in doing so they demonstrated their willingness to follow God's plan. Men were urged to treat their wives kindly and considerately, but also to enforce their authority, through physical coercion if necessary. Both continental and English marriage manuals use the metaphor of breaking a horse for teaching a wife obedience, though laws did set limits on the husband's power to do so. A few women took Luther's idea about the priesthood of all believers to heart and wrote religious pamphlets and hymns, but no sixteenth-century Protestants officially allowed women to hold positions of religious authority. Monarchs such as Elizabeth I of England and female territorial rulers of the states of the Holy Roman Empire did determine religious policies, however.

Catholics viewed marriage as a sacramental union that, if validly entered into, could not be dissolved. Protestants saw marriage as a contract in which each partner promised the other support, companionship, and the sharing of mutual goods. Marriages in which spouses did not comfort or support one another endangered their own souls

● **Lucas Cranach the Elder: Martin Luther and Katharina von Bora** Cranach painted this double marriage portrait to celebrate Luther's wedding in 1525 to Katharina von Bora, a former nun. The couple quickly became a model of the ideal marriage, and many churches wanted their portraits. More than sixty similar paintings, with slight variations, were produced by Cranach's workshop and hung in churches and wealthy homes. *(Uffizi, Florence/Scala/Art Resource, NY)*

and the surrounding community, and most Protestants came to allow divorce. Divorce remained rare, however, as marriage was such an important social and economic institution.

The Reformation generally brought the closing of monasteries and convents, and marriage became virtually the only occupation for upper-class Protestant women. Women in some convents recognized this and fought the Reformation, or argued that they could still be pious Protestants within convent walls. Most nuns left, however, and we do not know what happened to them. The Protestant emphasis on marriage made unmarried women (and men) suspect, for they did not belong to the type of household regarded as the cornerstone of a proper, godly society.

The Reformation and German Politics

Criticism of the church was widespread in Europe in the early sixteenth century, and calls for reform came from many areas. Yet such movements could be more easily squelched by the strong central governments of Spain, France, and England. The Holy Roman Empire, in contrast, included hundreds of largely independent states. The authority of the emperor was far less than that of the monarchs of western Europe, and local rulers continued to exercise great power.

Luther's ideas appealed to German rulers for a variety of reasons. Though Germany was not a nation, people did have an understanding of being German because of their language and traditions. Luther frequently used the phrase "we Germans" in his attacks on the papacy. Luther's appeal to national feeling influenced many rulers. Some German rulers were sincerely attracted to Lutheran ideas, but material considerations swayed many others to embrace the new faith. The rejection of Roman Catholicism and adoption of Protestantism would mean the legal confiscation of lush farmlands, rich monasteries, and wealthy shrines. Thus many political authorities in the empire used the religious issue to extend their financial and political power and to enhance their independence from the emperor.

Charles V, elected as emperor in 1521, must share blame with the German princes for the disintegration of imperial authority in the empire. He neither understood nor took an interest in the constitutional problems of Germany, and he lacked the material resources to oppose Protestantism effectively there. Throughout his reign, he was preoccupied with his Flemish, Spanish, Italian, and American territories. Moreover, the expansion of the Ottoman Empire prevented him from acting effectively against the Protestants; the Ottoman Turks threatened Habsburg lands in southeastern Europe at just the point that the Reformation began, and in 1529 were even besieging Vienna.

Five times between 1521 and 1555, Charles V went to war with the Valois kings of France. The cornerstone of French foreign policy in the sixteenth and seventeenth centuries was the desire to keep the German states divided. Thus Europe witnessed the paradox of the Catholic king of France supporting the Lutheran princes in their challenge to his fellow Catholic, Charles V. The Habsburg-Valois Wars advanced the cause of Protestantism and promoted the political fragmentation of the German Empire.

Finally, in 1555, Charles agreed to the Peace of Augsburg, which officially recognized Lutheranism. Each prince was permitted to determine the religion of his territory. Most of northern and central Germany became Lutheran; the south remained Roman Catholic. The Peace of Augsburg ended religious war in Germany for many decades. His hope of uniting his empire under a single church dashed, Charles V abdicated in 1556, transferring power over his Spanish and Netherlandish holdings to his son Philip and his imperial power to his brother Ferdinand.

The Spread of the Protestant Reformation

States within the Holy Roman Empire and the kingdom of Denmark-Norway were the earliest territories to accept the Protestant Reformation, but by the later 1520s religious change came to England, France, and eastern Europe. In all these areas, a second generation of reformers built on earlier ideas to develop their own theology and plans for institutional change.

As on the continent, the Reformation in England had economic as well as religious causes. As elsewhere, too, Christian humanists had for decades been calling for the purification of the church. However, the impetus for England's break with Rome was the ruler's desire for a new wife. When the personal matter of the divorce of King Henry VIII (r. 1509–1547) became enmeshed with political issues, a complete break with Rome resulted.

In 1527, after eighteen years of marriage, Henry's wife, Catherine of Aragon, had failed to produce a male child, and Henry claimed that only a male child could prevent a disputed succession. Henry had also fallen in love with a lady at court, Anne Boleyn. So Henry petitioned Pope Clement VII for an annulment of his marriage to Catherine. When the pope procrastinated in granting the annulment, Henry decided to remove the English church from papal authority.

Henry used Parliament to legalize the Reformation in England and to make himself the supreme head of the Church of England. Some opposed the king and were

● **Allegory of the Tudor Dynasty**   The unknown creator of this work intended to glorify the virtues of the Protestant succession; the painting has no historical reality. Enthroned Henry VIII (r. 1509–1547) hands the sword of justice to his Protestant son Edward VI (r. 1547–1553). At left the Catholic Queen Mary (r. 1553–1558) and her husband Philip of Spain are followed by Mars, god of war, signifying violence and civil disorder. At right the figures of Peace and Plenty accompany the Protestant Elizabeth I (r. 1558–1603), symbolizing England's happy fate under her rule. *(Yale Center for British Art, Paul Mellon Collection/The Bridgeman Art Library)*

beheaded, among them Thomas More, the king's chancellor and author of *Utopia* (see page 392). When Anne Boleyn failed twice to produce a male child, Henry VIII charged her with adulterous incest and in 1536 had her beheaded. His third wife, Jane Seymour, gave Henry the desired son, Edward, but she died in childbirth. Henry went on to three more wives.

Between 1535 and 1539, under the influence of his chief minister Thomas Cromwell, Henry decided to dissolve the English monasteries because he wanted their wealth. Hundreds of properties were sold to the middle and upper classes, strengthening the upper classes and tying them to the Tudor dynasty. Henry's motives combined personal, political, social, and economic elements. What about everyday English people? Recent scholarship points out that people rarely "converted" from Catholicism to Protestantism overnight. People responded to an action of the Crown that was played out in their own neighborhood—the closing of a monastery, the ending of masses for the dead—with a combination of resistance, acceptance, and collaboration.

Loyalty to the Catholic Church was particularly strong in Ireland. Ireland had been claimed by English kings since the twelfth century, but in reality the English had firm control of only the area around Dublin known as the Pale. In 1536, on orders from London, the Irish parliament, which represented only the English landlords and the people of the Pale, approved the English laws severing the church from Rome. The (English) ruling class adopted the new reformed faith, but most of the Irish people remained Roman Catholic. Irish armed opposition to the Reformation led to harsh repression by the English, thus adding religious antagonism to the ethnic hostility that had been a feature of English policy toward Ireland for centuries (see page 362).

In the short reign of Henry's sickly son, Edward VI (r. 1547–1553), strongly Protestant ideas exerted a significant influence on the religious life of the country. The equally brief reign of Mary Tudor (r. 1553–1558) witnessed a sharp move back to Catholicism. The devoutly Catholic daughter of Catherine of Aragon, Mary rescinded the Reformation legislation of her father's reign and restored Roman Catholicism. Mary's marriage to her cousin Philip of Spain, son of the emperor Charles V, proved highly unpopular in England, and her execution of several hundred Protestants further alienated her subjects. During her reign, many Protestants fled to the continent. Mary's death raised to the throne her sister Elizabeth (r. 1558–1603) and inaugurated the beginning of religious stability.

Elizabeth, Henry's daughter with Anne Boleyn, had been raised a Protestant, but at the start of her reign sharp differences existed in England. On the one hand, Catholics wanted a Roman Catholic ruler. On the other hand, a vocal number of returning exiles wanted all Catholic elements in the Church of England eliminated. The latter, because they wanted to "purify" the church, were called "Puritans." Shrewdly, Elizabeth chose a middle course between Catholic and Puritan extremes. She referred to herself as the "supreme governor of the Church of England," which allowed Catholics to remain loyal to her without denying the pope. She required her subjects to attend church or risk a fine, but did not interfere with their privately held beliefs. The Anglican Church, as the Church of England was called, moved in a moderately Protestant direction.

Calvinism

In 1509, while Luther was preparing for a doctorate at Wittenberg, John Calvin (1509–1564) was born in Noyon in northwestern France. As a young man he studied law, which had a decisive impact on his mind and later thought. In 1533 he experienced a religious crisis, as a result of which he converted to Protestantism. Calvin believed that God had specifically selected him to reform the church. Accordingly, he accepted an invitation to assist in the reformation of the city of Geneva. There, beginning in 1541, Calvin worked assiduously to establish a Christian society ruled by God through civil magistrates and reformed ministers. Geneva, "a city that was a church," became the model of a Christian community for sixteenth-century Protestant reformers.

To understand Calvin's Geneva, it is necessary to understand Calvin's ideas. These he embodied in *The Institutes of the Christian Religion,* first published in 1536 and definitively issued in 1559. The cornerstone of Calvin's theology was his belief in the absolute sovereignty and omnipotence of God and the total weakness of humanity. Before the infinite power of God, he asserted, men and women are as insignificant as grains of sand.

Calvin did not ascribe free will to human beings because that would detract from the sovereignty of God. Men and women cannot actively work to achieve salvation; rather, God in his infinite wisdom decided at the beginning of time who would be saved and who damned. This viewpoint constitutes the theological principle called **predestination.** Many people consider the doctrine of predestination, which dates back to Saint Augustine and Saint Paul, to be a pessimistic view of the nature of God. But "this terrible decree," as even Calvin called it, did not lead to pessimism or fatalism. Rather, predestination served as an energizing dynamic, convincing people that hardships were part of the constant struggle against evil.

predestination *Calvin's teaching that, by God's decree, some persons are guided to salvation and others to damnation; that God has called us not according to our works but according to his purpose and grace.*

Calvin aroused Genevans to a high standard of morality. In the reformation of the city, the Genevan Consistory also exercised a powerful role. This body of laymen and pastors was assembled "to keep watch over every man's life [and] to admonish amiably those whom they see leading a disorderly life."[6] Although all municipal governments in early modern Europe regulated citizens' conduct, none did so with the severity of Geneva's Consistory under Calvin's leadership. Absence from sermons, criticism of ministers, dancing, card playing, family quarrels, and heavy drinking were all investigated and punished by the Consistory.

Religious refugees from France, England, Spain, Scotland, and Italy visited Calvin's Geneva. Subsequently, the Reformed church of Calvin served as the model for the Presbyterian church in Scotland, the Huguenot church in France, and the Puritan churches in England and New England.

The Calvinist ethic of the "calling" dignified all work with a religious aspect. Hard work, well done, was pleasing to God. This doctrine encouraged an aggressive, vigorous activism. These factors, together with the social and economic applications of Calvin's theology, made Calvinism the most dynamic force in sixteenth- and seventeenth-century Protestantism.

THE CATHOLIC REFORMATION

How did the Catholic Church respond to the new religious situation?

Between 1517 and 1547 Protestantism made remarkable advances. Nevertheless, the Roman Catholic Church made a significant comeback. After about 1540 no new large areas of Europe, other than the Netherlands, accepted Protestant beliefs (see Map 14.2). Many historians see the developments within the Catholic Church after the Protestant Reformation as two interrelated movements, one a drive for internal reform linked to earlier reform efforts, and the other a Counter-Reformation that opposed Protestants intellectually, politically, militarily, and institutionally. In both movements, the papacy, new religious orders, and the Council of Trent that met from 1545 to 1563 were important agents.

The Reformed Papacy and the Council of Trent

Renaissance popes and advisers were not blind to the need for church reforms, but they resisted calls for a general council representing the entire church, fearing loss of power, revenue, and prestige. This changed beginning with Pope Paul III (1534–1549), and the papal court became the center of the reform movement rather than its chief opponent. The lives of the pope and his reform-minded cardinals, abbots, and bishops were models of decorum and piety.

In 1542 Pope Paul III established the Sacred Congregation of the **Holy Office,** with jurisdiction over the Roman Inquisition, a powerful instrument of the Catholic Reformation. The Inquisition was a committee of six cardinals with judicial authority over all Catholics and the power to arrest, imprison, and execute. Within the Papal States, the Inquisition effectively destroyed heresy (and some heretics).

Pope Paul III also called an ecumenical council, which met intermittently from 1545 to 1563 at Trent, an imperial city close to Italy. It was called not only to reform the church but also to secure reconciliation with the Protestants. Lutherans and Calvinists were invited to participate, but their insistence that the Scriptures be the sole basis for discussion made reconciliation impossible.

Nonetheless, the decrees of the Council of Trent laid a solid basis for the spiritual renewal of the Catholic Church. It gave equal validity to the Scriptures and to tradition

Holy Office *An official Roman Catholic agency founded in 1542 to combat international doctrinal heresy and to promote sound doctrine on faith and morals.*

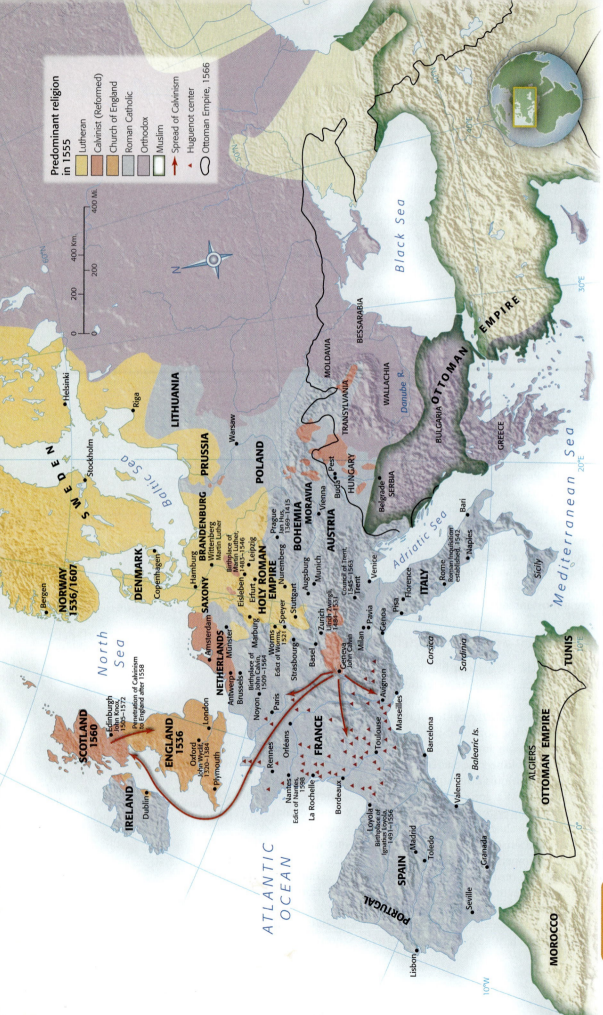

Predominant religion in 1555

- Lutheran
- Calvinist (Reformed)
- Church of England
- Roman Catholic
- Orthodox
- Muslim
- → Spread of Calvinism
- ▲ Huguenot center
- ◯ Ottoman Empire, 1566

400 Mi.

400 Km.

200

200

N

Black Sea

OTTOMAN EMPIRE

BESSARABIA

MOLDAVIA

WALLACHIA

TRANSYLVANIA

Danube R.

BULGARIA OTTOMAN

SERBIA

GREECE

Adriatic Sea

Mediterranean Sea

Helsinki

Riga

LITHUANIA

PRUSSIA

Warsaw

POLAND

MORAVIA

BOHEMIA

Prague • Jan Hus, 1369–1415

AUSTRIA

Budapest Vienna

HUNGARY

Belgrade

Bari

Naples

Sicily

Sardinia

TUNIS

Baltic Sea

SWEDEN

Stockholm

Bergen

NORWAY 1536/1607

DENMARK

Copenhagen

Hamburg

SAXONY

BRANDENBURG

Wittenberg • Martin Luther

Eisleben • Birthplace of Martin Luther, 1483–1546

Erfurt

Leipzig

Nuremberg

Augsburg

Munich

Stuttgart

Speyer

Worms • Edict of Worms, 1521

Marburg

HOLY ROMAN EMPIRE

Zurich • Ulrich Zwingli, 1484–1531

Basel

Strasbourg

Geneva • John Calvin

Milan Pavia

Venice

Trent • Council of Trent, 1545–1563

Genoa

Pisa

Florence

Rome • Roman Inquisition established, 1542

ITALY

Corsica

North Sea

SCOTLAND 1560

Edinburgh • John Knox, 1505–1572

Penetration of Calvinism to England after 1558

IRELAND

Dublin

ENGLAND 1536

Oxford • John Wyclif, 1320–1384

London

Plymouth

NETHERLANDS

Amsterdam

Münster

Antwerp

Brussels

Rennes

Noyon • Birthplace of John Calvin, 1509–1564

Paris

Orléans

FRANCE

Nantes • Edict of Nantes, 1598

La Rochelle

Bordeaux

Toulouse

Avignon

Marseilles

Barcelona

Balearic Is.

Valencia

Loyola • Birthplace of Ignatius Loyola, 1491–1556

Madrid

Toledo

SPAIN

PORTUGAL

Lisbon

Seville

Granada

ATLANTIC OCEAN

ALGIERS

OTTOMAN EMPIRE

MOROCCO

MAP 14.2 **Religious Divisions in Europe** The Reformation shattered the religious unity of Western Christendom. The situation was even more complicated than a map of this scale can show. Many cities within the Holy Roman Empire, for example, accepted a different faith than did the surrounding countryside; Augsburg, Basel, and Strasbourg were all Protestant, though surrounded by territory ruled by Catholic nobles.

as sources of religious truth and authority. It reaffirmed the seven sacraments and the traditional Catholic teaching on transubstantiation. It tackled the disciplinary matters that had disillusioned the faithful, requiring bishops to reside in their own dioceses, suppressing pluralism and simony, and forbidding the sale of indulgences. Clerics who kept concubines were to give them up. In a highly original decree, the council required every diocese to establish a seminary for the education and training of the clergy. Seminary professors were to determine whether candidates for ordination had *vocations,* genuine callings to the priesthood. This was a novel idea, since from the time of the early church, parents had determined their sons' (and daughters') religious careers. Finally, great emphasis was laid on preaching and instructing the laity, especially the uneducated. One decision had especially important social consequences for laypeople. The Council of Trent stipulated that for a marriage to be valid, consent (the essence of marriage) as given in the vows had to be made publicly before witnesses, one of whom had to be the parish priest. Trent thereby ended the widespread practice of secret marriages in Catholic countries. The decrees of the Council of Trent laid a solid basis for the spiritual renewal of the church. For four centuries the doctrinal and disciplinary legislation of Trent served as the basis for Roman Catholic faith, organization, and practice.

New Religious Orders

The establishment of new religious orders within the church reveals a central feature of the Catholic Reformation. Most of these new orders developed in response to one crying need: to raise the moral and intellectual level of the clergy and people. Education was a major goal of the two most famous orders.

The Ursuline order of nuns, founded by Angela Merici (1474–1540), attained enormous prestige for the education of women. The daughter of a country gentleman, Angela Merici worked for many years among the poor, sick, and uneducated around her native Brescia in northern Italy. In 1535 she established the first women's religious order concentrating exclusively on teaching young girls, with the goal of re-Christianizing society by training future wives and mothers. After receiving papal approval in 1565, the Ursulines rapidly spread to France and the New World.

The Society of Jesus, or **Jesuits,** founded by Ignatius Loyola (1491–1556), played a powerful international role in strengthening Catholicism in Europe and spreading the faith around the world. While recuperating from a severe battle wound in his legs, Loyola studied a life of Christ and other religious books and decided to give up his military career and become a soldier of Christ. The first Jesuits, whom Loyola recruited primarily from the wealthy merchant and professional classes, saw the Reformation as a pastoral problem, its causes and cures related not to doctrinal issues but to people's spiritual condition. Reform of the church, as Luther and Calvin understood that term, played no role in the future the Jesuits planned for themselves. Their goal was "to help souls." The Society of Jesus developed into a highly centralized, tightly knit organization. In addition to the traditional vows of poverty, chastity, and obedience, professed members vowed to go anywhere the pope said they were needed. They attracted many recruits and achieved phenomenal success for the papacy and the reformed Catholic Church, carrying Christianity to India and Japan before 1550 and to Brazil, North America, and the Congo in the seventeenth century. Within Europe the Jesuits brought southern Germany and much of eastern Europe back to Catholicism. Jesuit schools adopted the modern humanist curricula and methods, educating the sons of the nobility as well as the poor. As confessors and spiritual directors to kings, Jesuits exerted great political influence.

● **Teresa of Ávila.** Teresa of Ávila (1515–1582) was a Spanish nun who began to experience mystical visions that led her to reform convents, making them stricter and less hierarchical. This seventeenth-century enamelwork shows one of her visions, of an angel piercing her heart. Teresa founded new religious houses, seeing these as answers to the Protestant takeover of Catholic churches. She became a saint and in 1970 was the first woman declared a Doctor of the Church, a title given to a theologian of outstanding merit. *(By gracious permission of Catherine Hamilton Kappauf)*

Jesuits *Members of the Society of Jesus, founded by Ignatius Loyola and approved by the papacy in 1540, whose goal was the spread of the Roman Catholic faith through humanistic schools and missionary activity.*

RELIGIOUS VIOLENCE

What were the causes and consequences of religious violence, including riots, wars, and witch-hunts?

In 1559 France and Spain signed the Treaty of Cateau-Cambrésis, which ended the long conflict known as the Habsburg-Valois Wars. However, over the next century religious differences led to riots, civil wars, and international conflicts. Especially in France and the Netherlands, Protestants and Catholics used violent actions as well as preaching and teaching against other, for each side regarded the other as a poison in the community that would provoke the wrath of God. Catholics and Protestants alike feared people of other faiths, whom they often saw as agents of Satan. Even more, they feared those who were explicitly identified with Satan: witches living in their midst. This era was the time of the most virulent witch persecutions in European history, as both Protestants and Catholics tried to make their cities and states more godly.

French Religious Wars

The costs of the Habsburg-Valois Wars, waged intermittently through the first half of the sixteenth century, forced the French to increase taxes and borrow heavily. King Francis I's treaty with the pope (see page 400) gave the French crown a rich supplement of money and offices, and also a vested financial interest in Catholicism. Significant numbers of French people, however, were attracted to the "reformed religion," as Calvinism was called. Initially, Calvinism drew converts from among reform-minded members of the Catholic clergy, the industrious middle classes, and artisan groups. Many French Calvinists (called "Huguenots") lived in major cities such as Paris, Lyons, and Rouen. When Henry II died in 1559, perhaps one-tenth of the population had become Calvinist.

Huguenots *French Calvinists, many of whom lived in the major cities of Paris, Lyons, and Rouen.*

The feebleness of the French monarchy was the seed from which the weeds of civil violence sprang. The three weak sons of Henry II who occupied the throne could not provide the necessary leadership, and they were often dominated by their mother, Catherine de' Medici. The French nobility took advantage of this monarchical weakness. Just as German princes in the Holy Roman Empire had adopted Lutheranism as a means of opposition to Emperor Charles V, so French nobles frequently adopted the reformed religion as a religious cloak for their independence. Armed clashes between Catholic royalist lords and Calvinist antimonarchical lords occurred in many parts of France. Both Calvinists and Catholics believed that the others' books, services, and ministers polluted the community. Preachers incited violence, and religious ceremonies such as baptisms, marriages, and funerals triggered it.

Calvinist teachings called the power of sacred images into question, and mobs in many cities took down and smashed statues, stained-glass windows, and paintings. Though it was often inspired by fiery Protestant sermons, this **iconoclasm** is an example of men and women carrying out the Reformation themselves, rethinking the church's system of meaning and the relationship between the unseen and the seen. Catholic mobs responded by defending images, and crowds on both sides killed their opponents, often in gruesome ways.

iconoclasm *The destruction of a religious symbol or monument. During the Reformation, images of the saints, stained-glass windows, and paintings were destroyed by Protestants on the ground that they violated the biblical command against "graven images."*

A savage Catholic attack on Calvinists in Paris on August 24, 1572 (Saint Bartholomew's Day), followed the usual pattern. The occasion was the marriage ceremony of the king's sister Margaret of Valois to the Protestant Henry of Navarre, which was intended to help reconcile Catholics and Huguenots. Instead Huguenot wedding guests in Paris were massacred, and other Protestants were slaughtered by mobs. Religious violence spread to the provinces, where thousands were killed. This **Saint Bartholomew's Day massacre** led to a civil war that dragged on for fifteen years. Agriculture in many areas was destroyed; commercial life declined severely; and starvation and death haunted the land.

Saint Bartholomew's Day massacre *A savage 1572 Catholic attack on Calvinists in Paris that led to a long civil war.*

What ultimately saved France was a small group of moderates of both faiths called **politiques** who believed that only the restoration of a strong monarchy could reverse the trend toward collapse. The politiques also favored accepting the Huguenots as an officially recognized and organized pressure group. The death of Catherine de' Medici, followed by the assassination of King Henry III, paved the way for the accession of Henry of Navarre (the unfortunate bridegroom of the St. Bartholomew's Day massacre), a politique who became Henry IV (r. 1589–1610).

Henry's willingness to sacrifice religious principles to political necessity saved France. He converted to Catholicism but also issued the **Edict of Nantes,** which granted liberty of conscience and liberty of public worship to Huguenots in 150 fortified towns. The reign of Henry IV and the Edict of Nantes prepared the way for French absolutism in the seventeenth century by helping restore internal peace in France.

The Netherlands Under Charles V

In the Netherlands, what began as a movement for the reformation of the church developed into a struggle for Dutch independence. Emperor Charles V had inherited the seventeen provinces that compose present-day Belgium and the Netherlands (see page 403). In the Netherlands as elsewhere, corruption in the Roman church and the critical spirit of the Renaissance provoked pressure for reform, and Lutheran ideas took root. Charles V had grown up in the Netherlands, however, and he was able to limit their impact. But Charles V abdicated in 1556 and transferred power over the Netherlands to his son Philip, who had grown up in Spain. Protestant ideas spread.

By the 1560s Protestants in the Netherlands were primarily Calvinists. Calvinism's intellectual seriousness, moral gravity, and emphasis on any form of labor well done appealed to middle-class merchants and financiers and working-class people. Whereas Lutherans taught respect for the powers that be, Calvinism tended to encourage opposition to "illegal" civil authorities.

In the 1560s Spanish authorities attempted to suppress Calvinist worship and raised taxes, which sparked riots and a wave of iconoclasm. Philip II sent twenty thousand Spanish troops under the duke of Alva to pacify the Low Countries. Alva interpreted "pacification" to mean the ruthless extermination of religious and political dissidents. On top of the Inquisition, he opened his own tribunal, soon called the "Council of Blood." On March 3, 1568, fifteen hundred men were executed.

For ten years, civil war raged in the Netherlands between Catholics and Protestants and between the seventeen provinces and Spain. Eventually the ten southern provinces—the Spanish Netherlands (the future Belgium)—came under the control of the Spanish

● **Giorgio Vasari: Massacre of Coligny and the Huguenots (1573)** The Italian artist Vasari depicts the Saint Bartholomew's Day massacre in Paris, one of many bloody events in the religious wars that accompanied the Reformation. Here Admiral Coligny, a leader of the French Protestants (called Huguenots) is hurled from a window while his followers are slaughtered. This fresco was commissioned by Pope Gregory XIII to decorate a hall in the Vatican Palace in Rome. Both sides used visual images to win followers and celebrate their victories. *(Vatican Palace/Scala/Art Resource, NY)*

politiques *A group of moderate Catholics and Huguenots who sought to end the religious violence in France by restoring a strong monarchy and granting official recognition to the Huguenots.*

Edict of Nantes *A declaration issued in 1598 by Henry IV which granted liberty of conscience and liberty of public worship to Huguenots in 150 fortified French towns.*

Union of Utrecht *A treaty signed in 1579 that united the seven northern provinces of the Netherlands (all of which were Protestant) into a single political unity. This led to their declaration of independence from Catholic Spain in 1581.*

Habsburg forces. The seven northern provinces, led by Holland, formed the **Union of Utrecht** and in 1581 declared their independence from Spain. The north was Protestant; the south remained Catholic. Philip did not accept this, and war continued. England was even drawn into the conflict, supplying money and troops to the United Provinces. (Spain launched the Spanish Armada, an unsuccessful invasion of England in response.) Hostilities ended in 1609 when Spain agreed to a truce that recognized the independence of the United Provinces.

The Great European Witch-Hunt

The relationship between the Reformation and the upsurge in trials for witchcraft that occurred at roughly the same time is complex. Increasing persecution for witchcraft actually began before the Reformation in the 1480s, but it became especially common about 1560. Religious reformers' extreme notions of the Devil's powers and the insecurity created by the religious wars contributed to this increase. Both Protestants and Catholics tried and executed witches, with church officials and secular authorities acting together.

The heightened sense of God's power and divine wrath in the Reformation era was an important factor in the witch-hunts, but other factors were also significant. In the later Middle Ages, many educated Christian theologians, canon lawyers, and officials added a demonological component to existing ideas about witches. For them, the essence of witchcraft was making a pact with the Devil that required the witch to do the Devil's bidding. Witches were no longer simply people who used magical power to do harm and get what they wanted, but rather people used by the Devil to do what *he* wanted. Some demonological theorists also claimed that witches were organized in an international conspiracy to overthrow Christianity.

Trials involving this new notion of witchcraft as diabolical heresy began in Switzerland and southern Germany in the late fifteenth century, became less numerous in the early decades of the Reformation when Protestants and Catholics were busy fighting each other, and then picked up again about 1560, spreading to much of western Europe and to European colonies in the Americas. Scholars estimate that during the sixteenth and seventeenth centuries somewhere between 100,000 and 200,000 people were officially tried for witchcraft, and between 40,000 and 60,000 were executed. While the trials were secret, executions were not, and the list of charges were read out for all to hear.

Though the gender balance varied widely in different parts of Europe, between 75 and 85 percent of those tried and executed were women. Ideas about women, and the roles women actually played in society, were thus important factors shaping the

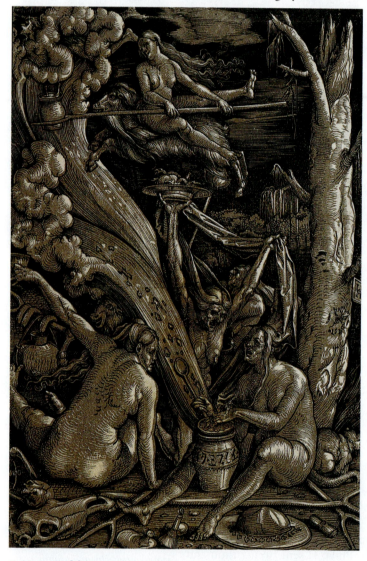

● **Hans Baldung Grien: Witches' Sabbat (1510)** In this woodcut, Grien combines learned and popular beliefs about witches: they traveled at night, met at sabbats (or assemblies), feasted on infants (in dish held high), concocted strange potions, and had animal "familiars" that were really demons (here a cat). Grien also highlights the sexual nature of witchcraft by portraying the women naked and showing them with goats, which were common symbols of sexuality. *(Germanisches Nationalmuseum Nürnberg)*

witch-hunts. Some demonologists expressed virulent **misogyny,** or hatred of women, viewing women as weaker and so more likely to give in to the Devil.

Most witch trials began with a single accusation in a village or town. Individuals accused someone they knew of using magic to spoil food, make children ill, kill animals, raise a hailstorm, or do other types of harm. Tensions within families, households, and neighborhoods often played a role in these accusations. Suspects were questioned and tortured by legal authorities, and often implicated others. The circle of the accused grew, sometimes into a much larger hunt that historians have called a "witch panic." Panics were most common in the part of Europe that saw the most witch accusations in general—the Holy Roman Empire, Switzerland, and parts of France. Most of this area consisted of very small governmental units that were jealous of each other and, after the Reformation, were divided by religion. The rulers of these small territories often felt more threatened than did the monarchs of western Europe, and they saw persecuting witches as a way to demonstrate their piety and concern for order.

Panics often occurred after some type of climatic disaster, such as an unusually cold and wet summer, and they came in waves. In large-scale panics a wider variety of suspects were taken in—wealthier people, children, a greater proportion of men. Mass panics tended to end when it became clear to legal authorities, or to the community itself, that the people being questioned or executed were not what they understood witches to be, or that the scope of accusations was beyond belief. Some from their community might be in league with Satan, they thought, but not this type of person and not as many as this.

Similar skepticism led to the gradual end of witch-hunts in Europe. Even in the sixteenth century a few individuals questioned whether witches could ever do harm, make a pact with the Devil, or engage in the wild activities attributed to them. Doubts about whether secret denunciations were valid or torture would ever yield a truthful confession gradually spread among the same type of religious and legal authorities who had so vigorously persecuted witches. Prosecutions for witchcraft became less common and were gradually outlawed. The last official execution for witchcraft in England was in 1682, though the last one in the Holy Roman Empire was not until 1775.

misogyny *A negative attitude toward women as a group. The fact that between 75 and 85 percent of the victims in the witchcraft trials of the sixteenth and seventeenth centuries were women is indicative of the misogynistic attitude that characterized European society.*

Chapter Summary

Key Terms

Renaissance
Protestant Reformation
signori
patrons
humanism
individualism
The Prince
secularism
Christian humanists
debate about women
Wars of the Roses
New Christians
anticlericalism
indulgence
Diet of Worms
Protestant
predestination
Holy Office
Jesuits
Huguenots
iconoclasm
Saint Bartholomew's Day massacre
politiques
Edict of Nantes
Union of Utrecht
misogyny

> To assess your mastery of this chapter, go to
> **bedfordstmartins.com/mckayworld**

• **What were the major cultural developments of the Renaissance?**

The Italian Renaissance rested on the phenomenal economic growth of Italian city-states, such as Florence, in which merchant oligarchs held political power. The Renaissance was characterized by self-conscious awareness among fourteenth- and fifteenth-century Italians, particularly scholars and writers known as humanists, that they were living in a new era. Key to this attitude was a serious interest in the Latin classics, a belief in individual potential, and a more secular attitude toward life. Humanists opened schools for boys and young men to train them for an active life of public service, but they had doubts about whether humanist education was appropriate for women. As humanism spread to northern Europe, religious concerns became more pronounced, and Christian humanists set out plans for the reform of church and society. Their ideas were spread to a much wider audience than those of early humanists because of the development of the printing press with movable metal type, which revolutionized communication. Interest in the classical past and in the individual also shaped Renaissance art in terms of style and subject matter.

• **What were the key social hierarchies in Renaissance Europe, and how did ideas about hierarchy shape people's lives?**

Social hierarchies in the Renaissance built on those of the Middle Ages, but also developed new features that contributed to the modern social hierarchies of race, class, and gender. Black Africans entered Europe in sizable numbers for the first time since the collapse of the Roman Empire, and Europeans fit them into changing understandings of ethnicity and race. The medieval hierarchy of orders based on function in society intermingled with a new hierarchy based on wealth, with new types of elites becoming more powerful. The Renaissance debate about women led many to discuss women's nature and proper role in society, a discussion sharpened by the presence of a number of ruling queens in this era.

• **How did the nation-states of western Europe evolve in this period?**

With taxes provided by business people, kings in western Europe established greater peace and order, both essential for trade. Feudal monarchies gradually evolved in the direction of nation-states. In Spain, France, and England, rulers also emphasized royal dignity and authority, and they utilized Machiavellian ideas to ensure the preservation and continuation of their governments. Like the merchant oligarchs and signori of Italian city-states, Renaissance monarchs manipulated culture to enhance their power.

• **What were the central ideas of Protestant reformers, and why were they appealing to various groups across Europe?**

The Catholic Church in the early sixteenth century had serious problems, and many individuals and groups had long called for reform. This background of discontent helps explain why Martin Luther's ideas found such a ready audience. Luther and other Protestants developed a new understanding of Christian doctrine that emphasized faith, the power of God's grace, and the centrality of the Bible. Protestant ideas were attractive to educated people and urban residents, and they spread rapidly through preaching, hymns, and the printing press. Some reformers developed more radical ideas about infant baptism, the ownership of property, and the separation between church and state. Both Protestants and Catholics regarded these as dangerous, and radicals were banished or executed. The German Peasants' War, in which Luther's ideas were linked to calls for social and economic reform, was similarly put down harshly. The Protestant reformers did not break with medieval ideas about the proper gender hierarchy, though they did elevate the status of marriage and viewed orderly households as the key building blocks of society. The progress of the Reformation was shaped by the political situation in the Holy Roman Empire, in which decentralization allowed the Reformation to spread. In England the political issue of the royal succession triggered the break with Rome, and a Protestant church was established. Protestant ideas also spread into France and eastern Europe. In all these areas, a second generation of reformers, the most important of whom was John Calvin, developed their own theology and plans for institutional change.

• How did the Catholic Church respond to the new religious situation?

The Roman Catholic Church responded slowly to the Protestant challenge, but by the 1530s the papacy was leading a movement for reform within the church instead of blocking it. Catholic doctrine was reaffirmed at the Council of Trent, and reform measures such as the opening of seminaries for priests and a ban on holding multiple church offices were introduced. New religious orders such as the Jesuits and the Ursulines spread Catholic ideas through teaching, and in the case of the Jesuits through missionary work.

• What were the causes and consequences of religious violence, including riots, wars, and witch-hunts?

Religious differences led to riots, civil wars, and international conflicts in the later sixteenth century. In France and the Netherlands, Calvinist Protestants and Catholics used violent actions against one another, and religious differences mixed with political and economic grievances. Long civil wars resulted, which in the case of the Netherlands became an international conflict. War ended in France with the Edict of Nantes in which Protestants were given some civil rights, and in the Netherlands with a division of the country into a Protestant north and Catholic south. The era of religious wars was also the time of the most extensive witch persecutions in European history, as both Protestants and Catholics tried to rid their cities and states of people they regarded as linked to the Devil.

(continued on page 424)

Listening to the PAST

Martin Luther, *On Christian Liberty*

The idea of liberty or freedom has played a powerful role in the history of human society and culture, but the meaning and understanding of liberty has undergone continual change and interpretation. In the Roman world, where slavery was a basic institution, liberty meant the condition of being a free man, independent of obligations to a master. In the Middle Ages, possessing liberty meant having special privileges or rights that other persons or institutions did not have. A lord or a monastery, for example, might speak of his or its liberties, and citizens in London were said to possess the "freedom of the city," which allowed them to practice trades and own property without interference. Likewise, the first chapter of Magna Carta (1215), often called the "Charter of Liberties," states: "Holy Church shall be free and have its rights entire and its liberties inviolate," meaning that the English church was independent of the authority of the king.

The idea of liberty also has a religious dimension, and the reformer Martin Luther formulated a classic interpretation of liberty in his treatise On Christian Liberty *(sometimes translated as* On the Freedom of a Christian*), arguably his finest piece. Written in Latin for the pope but translated immediately into German and published widely, it contains the main themes of Luther's theology: the importance of faith, the relationship of Christian faith and good works, the dual nature of human beings, and the fundamental importance of Scripture. Luther writes that Christians were freed through Christ, not by their own actions, from sin and death.*

Christian faith has appeared to many an easy thing; nay, not a few even reckon it among the social virtues, as it were; and this they do because they have not made proof of it experimentally, and have never tasted of what efficacy it is. For it is not possible for any man to write well about it, or to understand well what is rightly written, who has not at some time tasted of its spirit, under the pressure of tribulation; while he who has tasted of it, even to a very small extent, can never write, speak, think, or hear about it sufficiently. . . .

I hope that . . . I have attained some little drop of faith, and that I can speak of this matter, if not with more elegance, certainly with more solidity. . . .

A Christian man is the most free lord of all, and subject to none; a Christian man is the most dutiful servant of all, and subject to everyone.

Although these statements appear contradictory, yet, when they are found to agree together, they will do excellently for my purpose. They are both the statements of Paul himself, who says, "Though I be free from all men, yet have I made myself a servant unto all" (I Cor. 9:19), and "Owe no man anything but to love one another" (Rom. 13:8). Now love is by its own nature dutiful and obedient to the beloved object. Thus even Christ, though Lord of all things, was yet made of a woman; made under the law; at once free and a servant; at once in the form of God and in the form of a servant.

Let us examine the subject on a deeper and less simple principle. Man is composed of a twofold nature, a spiritual and a bodily. As regards the spiritual nature, which they name the soul, he is called the spiritual, inward, new man; as regards the bodily nature, which they name the flesh, he is called the fleshly, outward, old man. The Apostle speaks of this: "Though our outward man perish, yet the inward man is renewed day by day" (II Cor. 4:16). The result of this diversity is that in the Scriptures opposing statements are made concerning the same man, the fact being that in the same man these two men are opposed to one another; the flesh lusting against the spirit, and the spirit against the flesh (Gal. 5:17).

We first approach the subject of the inward man, that we may see by what means a man becomes justified, free, and a true Christian; that is, a spiritual, new, and inward man. It is certain that absolutely none among outward things, under whatever name they may be reckoned, has any influence in producing Christian righteousness or liberty, nor, on the other hand, unrighteousness or slavery. This can be shown by an easy argument.

What can it profit to the soul that the body should be in good condition, free, and full of life, that it should eat, drink, and act according to its pleasure, when even the most impious slaves of every kind of vice are prosperous in these matters? Again, what harm

On effective preaching, especially to the uneducated, Luther urged the minister "to keep it simple for the simple." *(Church of St. Marien, Wittenberg/The Bridgeman Art Library)*

can ill health, bondage, hunger, thirst, or any other outward evil, do to the soul, when even the most pious of men, and the freest in the purity of their conscience, are harassed by these things? Neither of these states of things has to do with the liberty or the slavery of the soul.

And so it will profit nothing that the body should be adorned with sacred vestment, or dwell in holy places, or be occupied in sacred offices, or pray, fast, and abstain from certain meats, or do whatever works can be done through the body and in the body. Something widely different will be necessary for the justification and liberty of the soul, since the things I have spoken of can be done by an impious person, and only hypocrites are produced by devotion to these things. On the other hand, it will not at all injure the soul that the body should be clothed in profane raiment, should dwell in profane places, should eat and drink in the ordinary fashion, should not pray aloud, and should leave undone all the things above mentioned, which may be done by hypocrites.

. . . One thing, and one alone, is necessary for life, justification, and Christian liberty; and that is the most Holy Word of God, the Gospel of Christ, as He says, "I am the resurrection and the life; he that believeth in me shall not die eternally" (John 9:25), and also, "If the Son shall make you free, ye shall be free indeed" (John 8:36), and "Man shall not live by bread alone, but by every word that proceedeth out of the mouth of God" (Matt. 4:4).

Let us therefore hold it for certain and firmly established that the soul can do without everything except the Word of God, without which none at all of its wants is provided for. But, having the Word, it is rich and wants for nothing, since that is the Word of life, of truth, of light, of peace, of justification, of salvation, of joy, of liberty, of wisdom, of virtue, of grace, of glory, and of every good thing. . . .

But you will ask, "What is this Word, and by what means is it to be used, since there are so many words of God?" I answer, "The Apostle Paul (Rom. 1) explains what it is, namely the Gospel of God, concerning His Son, incarnate, suffering, risen, and glorified

through the Spirit, the Sanctifier." To preach Christ is to feed the soul, to justify it, to set it free, and to save it, if it believes the preaching. For faith alone, and the efficacious use of the Word of God, bring salvation. "If thou shalt confess with thy mouth the Lord Jesus, and shalt believe in thine heart that God hath raised Him from the dead, thou shalt be saved" (Rom. 9:9); . . . and "The just shall live by faith" (Rom. 1:17). . . .

But this faith cannot consist of all with works; that is, if you imagine that you can be justified by those works, whatever they are, along with it. . . . Therefore, when you begin to believe, you learn at the same time that all that is in you is utterly guilty, sinful, and damnable, according to that saying, "All have sinned, and come short of the glory of God" (Rom. 3:23). . . . When you have learned this, you will know that Christ is necessary for you, since He has suffered and risen again for you, that, believing on Him, you might by this faith become another man, all your sins being remitted, and you being justified by the merits of another, namely Christ alone.

. . . [A]nd since it [faith] alone justifies, it is evident that by no outward work or labour can the inward man be at all justified, made free, and saved; and that no works whatever have any relation to him. . . . Therefore the first care of every Christian ought to be to lay aside all reliance on works, and strengthen his faith alone more and more, and by it grow in knowledge, not of works, but of Christ Jesus, who has suffered and risen again for him, as Peter teaches (I Peter 5).

Questions for Analysis

1. What did Luther mean by liberty?

2. Why, for Luther, was Scripture basic to Christian life?

Source: Luther's Primary Works, ed. H. Wace and C. A. Buchheim (London: Holder and Stoughton, 1896). Reprinted in *The Portable Renaissance Reader,* ed. James Bruce Ross and Mary Martin McLaughlin (New York: Penguin Books, 1981), pp. 721–726.

Suggested Reading

Bossy, John. *Christianity in the West, 1500–1700.* 1985. A lively, brief overview.

Earle, T. F., and K. J. P. Lowe, eds. *Black Africans in Renaissance Europe.* 2005. Includes essays discussing many aspects of ideas about race and the experience of Africans in Europe.

Ertman, Thomas. *The Birth of Leviathan: Building States and Regimes in Medieval and Early Modern Europe.* 1997. A good introduction to the creation of nation-states.

Grafton, Anthony, and Lisa Jardine. *From Humanism to the Humanities: Education and the Liberal Arts in Fifteenth and Sixteenth Century Europe.* 1986. Discusses humanist education and other developments in Renaissance learning.

Hale, J. R. *The Civilization of Europe in the Renaissance.* 1994. Provides a comprehensive treatment of the period, arranged thematically.

Holmes, George, ed. *Art and Politics in Renaissance Italy.* 1993. Treats the art of Florence and Rome against a political background.

Hsia, R. Po-Chia. *The World of Catholic Renewal, 1540–1770.* 1998. Situates the Catholic Reformation in a global context and provides coverage of colonial Catholicism.

Levack, Brian. *The Witchhunt in Early Modern Europe,* 3d ed. 2007. Provides a good introduction and helpful bibliographies to the vast literature on witchcraft.

Lindbergh, Carter. *The European Reformations.* 1996. Provides a thorough discussion of the Protestant Reformation and some discussion of Catholic issues.

Man, John. *Gutenberg Revolution: The Story of a Genius and an Invention That Changed the World.* 2002. Presents a rather idealized view of Gutenberg, but has good discussions of his milieu and excellent illustrations.

Nauert, Charles. *Humanism and the Culture of Renaissance Europe.* 1995. Provides a thorough introduction to humanism throughout Europe.

Oberman, Heiko. *Luther: Man Between God and the Devil.* 1989. Provides a thorough grounding in Luther's thought.

Wiesner-Hanks, Merry E. *Women and Gender in Early Modern Europe,* 3d ed. 2008. Discusses all aspects of women's lives and ideas about gender.

Notes

1. C. E. Detmold, trans., *The Historical, Political, and Diplomatic Writings of Niccolò Machiavelli* (Boston: J. R. Osgood, 1882), pp. 54–55.

2. See B. F. Reilly, *The Medieval Spains* (New York: Cambridge University Press, 1993), pp. 198–203.

3. B. Netanyahu, *The Origins of the Inquisition in Fifteenth Century Spain* (New York: Random House, 1995), p. 921.

4. Quoted in E. H. Harbison, *The Age of Reformation* (Ithaca, N.Y.: Cornell University Press, 1963), p. 52.

5. Quoted ibid., p. 284.

6. Ibid., p. 137.

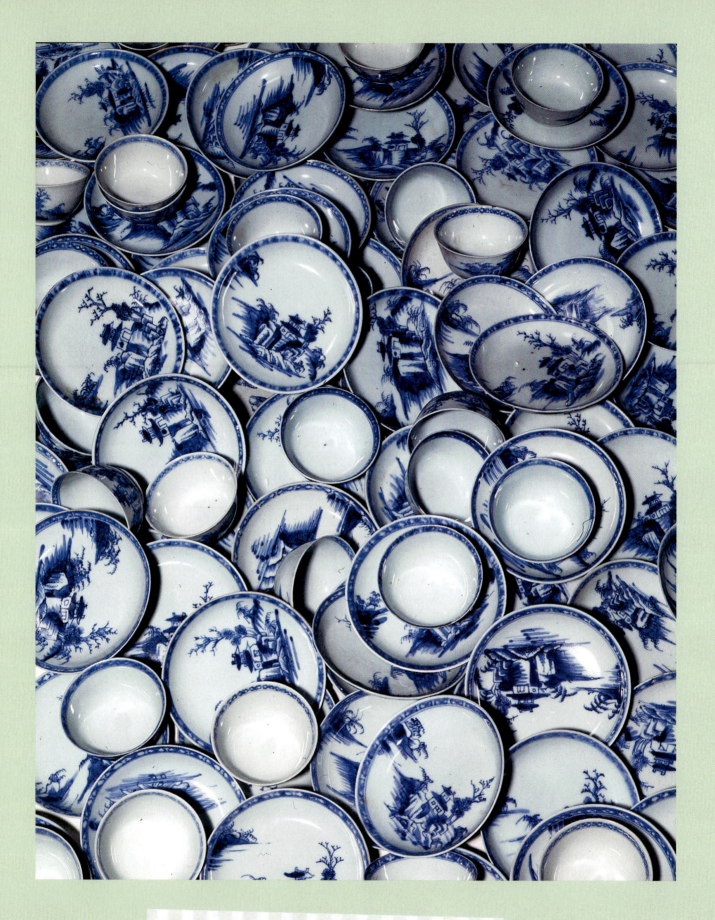

Porcelain from a Seventeenth-Century Chinese Ship's Cargo, recovered from the sea, which was intended for European markets. *(Christie's Images)*

15 THE ACCELERATION OF GLOBAL CONTACT

Prior to 1500 Europeans were relatively marginal players in a centuries-old trading system that linked Africa, Asia, and Europe. Elite classes everywhere prized Chinese porcelains and silks, while wealthy members of the Celestial Kingdom, as China called itself, wanted ivory and black slaves from East Africa and exotic goods and peacocks from India. African people wanted textiles from India and cowrie shells from the Maldive Islands. Europeans craved spices and silks, but they had few desirable goods to offer their trading partners.

The locus of these desires and commercial exchanges was the Indian Ocean. Arab, Persian, Turkish, Indian, black African, Chinese, and European merchants and adventurers fought each other for the trade that brought great wealth. They also jostled with Muslim scholars, Buddhist teachers, and Christian missionaries, who competed for the religious adherence of the peoples of the Malay Archipelago, Sumatra, Java, Borneo, and the Philippine Islands. The ancient civilizations of Africa, the Americas, Asia, and Southeast Asia confronted each other, and those confrontations sometimes led to conquest, exploitation, and profound social change.

The European search for better access to Southeast Asian spices led to a new overseas empire in the Indian Ocean and the accidental discovery of the Western Hemisphere. Within a short time, South and North America had joined a worldwide web. Europeans came to dominate trading networks and political empires of truly global proportions. The era of "globalization" had begun. Global contacts created new forms of cultural exchange, assimilation, conversion, and resistance. Europeans sought to impose their cultural values on the people they encountered and struggled to comprehend the peoples and societies they found. The Age of Discovery laid the foundations for the modern world as we know it today.

THE INDIAN OCEAN: HUB OF AN AFRO-EURASIAN TRADING WORLD

What were the distinctive features of Southeast Asian cultures and trade, and what was the impact of Islam and Christianity on Southeast Asian peoples?

Covering 20 percent of the earth's total ocean area, the Indian Ocean is the globe's third-largest waterway (after the Atlantic and Pacific). The Chinese called this vast region the Southern Ocean. Arabs, Indians, and Persians described it as "the lands below the winds," meaning the seasonal monsoons that carried ships across the ocean. Moderate and predictable, the monsoon winds blow from the west or south between April and August and from the northwest or northeast between December and March. Only in the eastern periphery, near the Philippine Islands, is there a dangerous typhoon belt—whirlwinds bringing tremendous rains and possible tornadoes.

High temperatures and abundant rainfall all year round contribute to a heavily forested environment. Throughout Southeast Asia, forests offer "an abundance and diversity of forms (of trees) . . . without parallel anywhere else in the world."[1] The abundance of bamboo, teak, mahogany, and other woods close to the waterways made the area especially favorable for maritime activity.

Peoples and Cultures

From at least the first millennium B.C.E., the peoples of Southeast Asia have been open to waterborne commerce. With trade came settlers from the Malay Peninsula (the southern extremity of the Asian continent), India, China, and East Africa, resulting in

● **Agricultural Work in Southeast Asia** Using a water buffalo (a common draft animal in Southeast Asia), a man plows a rice field, while a woman husks rice in this Filipino scene from the early eighteenth century. Their house is on stilts as protection against floods. *(Bibliothèque nationale de France)*

an enormous variety of languages, cultures, and religions. In spite of this diversity, certain sociocultural similarities connected the region.

First, by the fifteenth century, the peoples of what we call Indonesia, Malaysia, the Philippines, and the many islands in between all spoke languages of the Austronesian family, reflecting continuing interactions among the peoples speaking them. Second, a common environment led to a diet based on rice, fish, palms, and palm wine. Rice, harvested by women, is probably indigenous to the region, and it formed the staple of the diet from Luzon in the Philippines westward to Java, Sumatra, Siam (Thailand), and Vietnam. The seas provided many varieties of fish, crabs, and shrimp. Everywhere fishing, called "the secondary industry" (after commerce), served as the chief male occupation, well ahead of agriculture. Lacking grasslands, Southeast Asia has no pastoral tradition, no cattle or sheep, and thus meat and milk products from these animals played a small role in the diet. Animal protein came mostly from chickens and from pigs, which were raised almost everywhere and were the center of feasting. Cucumbers, onions, and gourds supplemented the diet, and fruits—coconuts, bananas, mangoes, limes, and pineapples (after they were introduced from the Americas)—substituted for vegetables. Sugar cane grew in profusion. It was chewed as a confectionery and used as a sweetener.[2]

In comparison to India, China, or even Europe (after the Black Death), Southeast Asia was sparsely populated. People were concentrated in port cities and in areas of intense rice cultivation. The seventeenth and eighteenth centuries witnessed slow but steady population growth, while the nineteenth century, under European colonial rule, witnessed very rapid expansion. Almost all Southeast Asian people married at a young age (about twenty). Marriage practices varied greatly from Indian, Chinese, and European ones, reflecting marked differences in the status of women.

The important role played by women in planting and harvesting rice gave them authority and economic power. Because of women's reproductive role, daughters had a high value. In contrast to India, China, the Middle East, and Europe, in Southeast Asia the more daughters a man had, the richer he was. At marriage the groom paid the bride (or sometimes her family) a sum of money called **bride wealth,** which remained under her control. This practice was in sharp contrast to the Chinese, Indian, and European dowry, which came under the husband's control. Unlike the Chinese practice, a married couple usually resided in the wife's village. Property was administered jointly, in contrast to the Chinese principle and Indian practice that wives had no say in the disposal of family property. All children, regardless of gender, inherited equally, and when Islam arrived in the region, the rule that sons receive double the inheritance of daughters was never implemented.

Although rulers commonly had multiple wives or concubines, the vast majority of ordinary people were monogamous. In contrast to most parts of the world except Africa, Southeast Asian peoples regarded premarital sexual activity with indulgence, and no premium was placed on virginity at marriage. Divorce was easy if a pair proved incompatible; common property and children were divided. Divorce carried no social stigma, and either the woman or the man could initiate it.[3]

Chronology

1450–1650	Age of Discovery
1492	Columbus lands on San Salvador
1511	Portuguese capture Malacca from Muslims
1518	Atlantic slave trade begins
1520	Spaniards defeat Aztec army
1532	Pizarro arrives in Peru and defeats Inca Empire
1542	First Jesuit, Saint Francis Xavier, arrives in Malacca
1547	Oviedo, *General History of the Indies*
1550–1700	Disease leads to 80 percent population decline in American Southeast
1570–1630	Worldwide commercial boom
1571	Spanish missionaries arrive in Southeast Asia
1602	Dutch East India Company established
1635	Tokugawa Shogunate closes Japan to trade; Japanese expel Spanish and Portuguese missionaries

bride wealth *A Southeast Asian custom whereby at marriage the groom paid the bride or her family a sum of money that remained under her control.*

Religious Revolutions

Diversity—by district, community, village, and even individual—characterized religious practice in Southeast Asia. People practiced a kind of animism, believing that spiritual powers inhabited natural objects. To survive and prosper, a person had to know how to please, appease, and manipulate those forces. To ensure human fertility, cure sickness, produce a good harvest, safeguard the living, and help the dead attain a contented afterlife, the individual propitiated the forces by providing sacrificial offerings or feasts. For example, in the Philippines and eastern Indonesia, certain activities were forbidden during the period of mourning following death, but great feasting then followed. Exquisite clothing, pottery, and jewelry were buried with the corpse to ensure his or her status in the afterlife. In Borneo, Cambodia, Burma, and the Philippines, slaves were sometimes killed to serve their deceased owners. Death rituals, like life rituals, had enormous variation in Southeast Asia.

Throughout the first millennium C.E., Hindu and Buddhist cults, Confucianists, and Jewish, Christian, and Muslim traders and travelers carried their beliefs to Southeast Asia. Beginning in the late thirteenth century, Muslim merchants established sizable trading colonies in the ports of northern Sumatra, eastern Java, Champa, and the east coast of the Malay Peninsula (see Map 15.1). Once the ruler of Malacca, the largest port city in Indonesia, accepted Islam, Muslim businessmen controlled commercial transactions there; the saying went that these transactions were "sealed with a handshake and a glance at heaven." The very name *Malacca* derives from the Arabic *malakat,* meaning "market," an apt description for this center of Indian Ocean trade. Islamic success continued from 1400 to 1650. Rulers of the port states on the spice route to northern Java and the Moluccas (Maluku), and those on the trading route to Brunei in Borneo and Manila in the Philippines, adhered to the faith of Allah.

With the arrival of the Portuguese (see page 439) and their capture of Malacca in 1511, fierce competition ensued between Muslims and Christians. The mid-sixteenth century witnessed the galvanized energy of the Counter-Reformation in Europe and the expansion of the Ottoman Empire through southwestern Asia and southeastern Europe. From Rome the first Jesuit, Saint Francis Xavier (1506–1552), reached Malacca in 1542. Likewise, Suleiman the Magnificent and his successors sent proselytizers. After the Spanish occupation of Manila in the Philippines in 1571, the Spanish crown flooded Southeast Asia with missionaries. Unlike Southeast Asian animism, Islam and Christianity insisted on an exclusive path to salvation: the renunciation of paganism and some outward sign of membership in the new faith.

What was the reaction of Southeast Asian peoples to these religions? How did adherents of the Middle Eastern religions spread their faith? Southeast Asians saw Muslims and Christians as wealthy, powerful traders and warriors. Thus native peoples believed that the foreigners must possess some secret ability to manipulate the spirit world. A contemporary Spaniard wrote that Southeast Asians believed

● **Woman Offering Betel** In Southeast Asia, betel served as the basic social lubricant. A combination of the betel nut, leaf, and lime, betel sweetened the breath and relaxed the mind; it was central to the rituals of lovemaking; and it was offered on all important social occasions, such as birth, marriage, and death. (Leiden University Library, ms. Or. 8655)

● **Palepai, or Ship Cloth (woven cotton textile, Sumatra, nineteenth century)** In Southeast Asian society, where the sea permeated so many aspects of life and culture, it is natural that it would influence art. Produced for millennia, ship cloths—depicting fabulous sailing vessels with multiple decks, birds, and animals—signified the transition from one social or spiritual state to another. They were displayed by the aristocracy only on important occasions, such as weddings or the presentation of a first grandchild to maternal grandparents. *(Museum of Fine Arts, Boston, The William E. Nickerson Fund No. 2 [1980.172]. Indonesian, Dutch colonial rule, mid-19th century, cotton plain weave, discontinuous supplementary weft patterning, 73.7 x 382.3 cm. © 2008 Museum of Fine Arts, Boston)*

"that paradise and successful (business) enterprises are reserved for those who submit to the religion of the Moros (Muslims) of Brunei[;] . . . they are the richer people." Southeast Asians also were impressed by Muslim and European ships and firearms. The foreigners seemed to have a more ruthless view of war than the natives (perhaps because they had no place to retreat to). As the Muslims and Christians fought for commercial superiority throughout the sixteenth century, indigenous peoples watched closely, "partly for reasons of self-preservation, partly that they might adopt the spiritual and practical techniques of the winners."[4]

Christian priests and Muslim teachers quickly learned the locals' languages and translated their Scriptures into those languages. The instruction of rulers and the educated into either faith was by memorization of the catechism, or sacred texts; teaching the masses was oral—they were expected to learn the basic prayers and customs of the new faiths. The Muslims and Christians differed in one fundamental strategy: whereas the Christians relied on a celibate clergy who defined the new community through baptism, the Muslims often married locally and accepted Southeast Asian cultures. No Asian was ordained a priest or served as catechist before 1700. By contrast, the Muslims showed little of the iconoclastic zeal for the destruction of pagan idols, statues, and temples that the Christians did. The Muslims did face a major obstacle, however: the indigenous peoples' attachment to pork, the main meat source and the central dish in all feasting.

Acceptance of one of the prophetic religions varied with time and place. Coastal port cities on major trade routes had "substantial" numbers of Muslims, and rulers of the port states of Sumatra, the Malay Peninsula, northern Java, and the Moluccas identified themselves as Muslims. By 1700 most rural and urban people had abandoned pork and pagan practices, adopted Islamic dress, submitted to circumcision, and considered themselves part of the international Muslim community. In the Philippines Islam achieved some success, especially in the south. But Magellan's military conquest, the enormous enthusiasm of the Jesuit missionaries, and the vigorous support of the Spanish crown led to the Christianization of most of the islands. As elsewhere, whether individuals conformed to Muslim or Christian standards was another

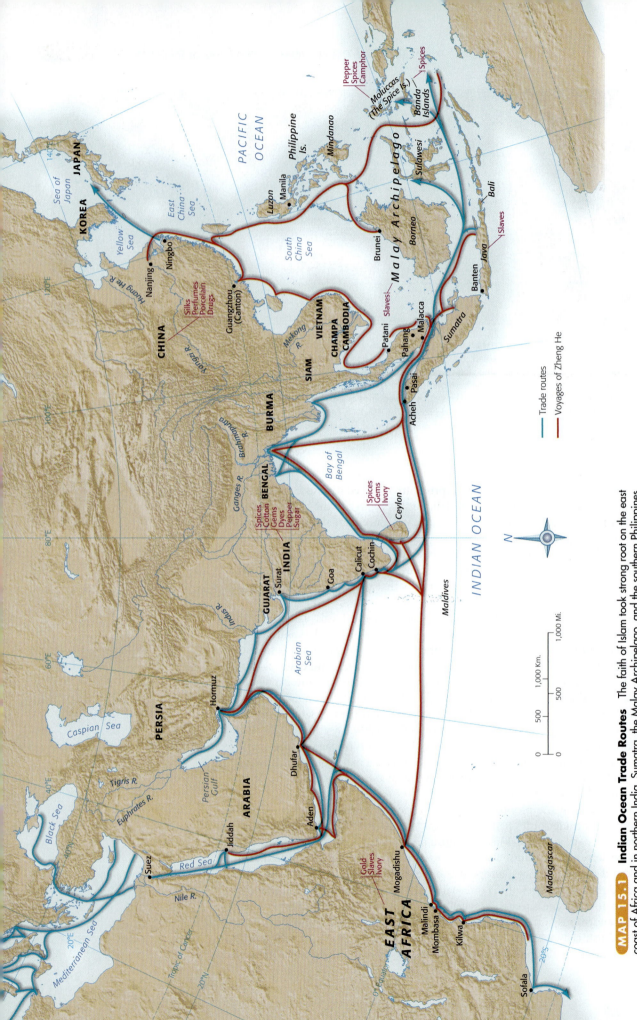

MAP 15.1 **Indian Ocean Trade Routes** The faith of Islam took strong root on the east coast of Africa and in northern India, Sumatra, the Malay Archipelago, and the southern Philippines. In the sixteenth and seventeenth centuries, Christianity competed with Islam for the adherence of peoples on all the Indian Ocean islands. (*Source: Some data from The Times Atlas of World History, 3d ed., page 146.*)

Trade routes

Voyages of Zheng He

PACIFIC OCEAN

JAPAN

KOREA

Sea of Japan

Yellow Sea

Nanjing

Ningbo

East China Sea

CHINA

Silks
Perfumes
Porcelain
Drugs

Guangzhou (Canton)

Huang He R.

Yangzi R.

South China Sea

Philippine Is.

Luzon

Manila

Mindanao

Brunei

Borneo

Sulawesi

Bali

Java

Banten

Slaves

Malay Archipelago

Sumatra

Malacca

Pahang

Patani

Slaves

Acheh

Pasai

Moluccas (The Spice Is.)

Pepper
Spices
Camphor

Banda Islands

Spices

VIETNAM

CHAMPA

CAMBODIA

SIAM

Mekong R.

BURMA

BENGAL

Brahmaputra R.

Ganges R.

Spices
Cotton
Gems
Dyes
Pepper
Sugar

Bay of Bengal

Spices
Gems
Ivory

Ceylon

INDIA

GUJARAT

Surat

Goa

Calicut

Cochin

Indus R.

PERSIA

Caspian Sea

Hormuz

Persian Gulf

Tigris R.

Euphrates R.

ARABIA

Arabian Sea

Dhufar

Aden

Jiddah

Red Sea

Suez

Nile R.

Black Sea

Mediterranean Sea

Maldives

INDIAN OCEAN

EAST AFRICA

Mogadishu

Gold
Slaves
Ivory

Malindi

Mombasa

Kilwa

Sofala

Madagascar

N

1,000 Mi.

1,000 Km.

500

500

0

0

140°E

120°E

100°E

80°E

60°E

40°E

20°E

Equator

Tropic of Cancer

20°N

20°S

matter. Recent scholars speak of the "adherence" of peoples in the sixteenth century to Islam, rather than their "conversion." Still, the official acceptance of one of the two Scripture-based religions by more than half the people of Southeast Asia has had lasting importance. Today Indonesia has the largest Muslim population in the world.

Trade and Commerce

Since Han and Roman times, seaborne trade between China (always the biggest market for Southeast Asian goods), India, the Middle East, and Europe had flowed across the Indian Ocean. From the seventh through the thirteenth centuries, the volume of this trade steadily increased. In the late fourteenth century, with the European and West Asian populations recovering from the Black Death, demand for Southeast Asian goods accelerated.

Other developments stimulated the market for Southeast Asian goods. The collapse of the Central Asian overland caravan route, the famous Silk Road, gave a boost to traffic originating in the Indian Ocean and flowing up the Red Sea to Mediterranean ports. Chinese expansion into Vietnam and Burma increased the population of the Celestial Kingdom and the demand for exotic goods. Above all, the seven voyages of the Chinese admiral Zheng He in 1405 launched for Southeast Asia the "age of commerce." (See the feature "Individuals in Society: Zheng He.")

In the fifteenth century Malacca became the great commercial entrepôt on the Indian Ocean. To Malacca came Chinese porcelains, silks, and camphor (used in the manufacture of many medications, including those to reduce fevers); pepper, cloves, nutmeg, and raw materials such as sappanwood and sandalwood from the Moluccas; sugar from the Philippines; and Indian printed cotton and woven tapestries, copper weapons, incense, dyes, and opium (which already had a sizable market in China). Muslim merchants in other port cities, such as Patani on the Malay Peninsula, Pasai in Sumatra, and Demak in Java, shared in this trade. They also exchanged cowrie shells from the Maldive Islands. These shells were in enormous demand throughout Africa as symbols of wealth and status, as decoration, and as a medium of currency in African trade. Muslim businessmen in Southeast Asia thus had dealings with their coreligionists in the East African ports of Mogadishu, Kilwa, and Sofala.

Merchants at Malacca stockpiled goods in fortified warehouses while waiting for the next monsoon. Whereas the wealth of cities in Mughal India rested mainly on agriculture, that of Malacca and other Southeast Asian cities depended on commerce. In all of Asia, Malacca, with its many mosques and elegant homes, enjoyed the reputation of being a sophisticated city, full of "music, ballads, and poetry."[5]

EUROPEAN DISCOVERY, RECONNAISSANCE, AND EXPANSION

How and why did Europeans undertake ambitious voyages of expansion that would usher in a new era of global contact?

Europe was by no means isolated before the voyages of exploration and the "discovery" of the New World; Europeans were aware of and in contact with the riches of the Indian Ocean trading world. From the time of the Crusades, Italian merchants brought the products of the East to luxury markets in Europe eager for silks, spices, porcelain, and other fine goods. But because they did not produce many products desired by Eastern elites, Europeans were relatively modest players in trade beyond its borders. Their limited role was reduced even further in the mid-fourteenth century, when the Black Death, combined with the ravages of the Mongol warlord Tamerlane, led to a collapse in trade routes and commercial markets.

From these lows, however, Europeans would soon undertake new and unprecedented expansion. As population and trade recovered, new European players entered the scene, eager to spread Christianity and to undo Italian dominance of trade with the East. A century after the plague, Iberian explorers began the overseas voyages that helped create the modern world, with staggering consequences for their own continent and the rest of the planet.

Causes of European Expansion

European expansion had multiple causes. The European market was eager for luxury goods from the East and for spices in particular. The spices not only added flavor to the monotonous European diet, but they also served as perfumes, medicines, and dyes. Apart from a desire for trade goods, religious fervor was another important catalyst for expansion. The passion and energy ignited by the Iberian reconquista encouraged the Portuguese and Spanish to continue the Christian crusade. Since organized Muslim polities such as the Ottoman Empire were too strong to defeat, Iberians turned their attention to non-Christian peoples elsewhere.

Individual explorers combined these motivations in unique ways. Christopher Columbus was a devout Christian who was increasingly haunted by messianic obsessions in the last years of his life. As Bartholomew Diaz put it, his own motives were "to serve God and His Majesty, to give light to those who were in darkness and to grow rich as all men desire to do." When Vasco da Gama reached the port of Calicut, India, in 1498 and a native asked what the Portuguese wanted, he replied, "Christians and spices."[6] The bluntest of the Spanish conquistadors, Hernando Cortés, announced as he prepared to conquer Mexico, "I have come to win gold, not to plow the fields like a peasant."[7]

Eagerness for exploration could be heightened by a lack of opportunity at home. After the reconquista, young men of the Spanish upper classes found their economic and political opportunities greatly limited. The ambitious turned to overseas trade to seek their fortunes.[8] A desire for glory and the urge to explore motivated many as well.

Whatever the reasons, the voyages were made possible by the growth of government power. Individuals did not possess the massive sums needed to explore vast oceans and control remote continents. The Spanish monarchy was stronger than before and in a position to support foreign ventures. In Portugal explorers looked to Prince Henry the Navigator (1394–1460) for financial support and encouragement. Like voyagers, monarchs shared a mix of motivations, from desire to please God to desire to win glory and profit from trade.

For ordinary sailors, life at sea was dangerous, overcrowded, unbearably stench-ridden, filled with hunger, and ill-paid. For months at a time, 100 to 120 people lived and worked in a space of between 150 and 180 square meters. Horses, cows, pigs, chickens, rats, and lice accompanied them on the voyages. As one scholar concluded, "traveling on a ship must have been one of the most uncomfortable and oppressive experiences in the world."[9]

Why did men choose to join these miserable crews? They did so to escape poverty at home, to continue a family trade, to win a few crumbs of the great riches of empire, or to find a better life as illegal immigrants in the colonies. Moreover, many orphans and poor boys were placed on board as young pages and had little say in the decision. Women also paid a price for the voyages of exploration. Left alone for months or years at a time and frequently widowed, sailors' wives struggled to feed their families. The widow of a sailor lost on Magellan's 1519 voyage had to wait until 1547 to collect her husband's salary from the Crown.[10]

The people who stayed at home had a powerful impact on the process. Court coteries and factions influenced a monarch's decisions and could lavishly reward individuals or cut them out of the spoils of empire. Then there was the public: the small

Primary Source:

The Agreement with Columbus of April 17 and 30, 1492

Read the contract signed by Columbus and his royal patrons, and see what riches he hoped to gain from his expedition.

Individuals IN SOCIETY

Zheng He

In 1403 the Chinese emperor Yongle ordered his coastal provinces to build a vast fleet of ships, with construction centered at Longjiang near Nanjing; the inland provinces were to provide wood and float it down the Yangzi River. Thirty thousand shipwrights, carpenters, sailmakers, ropers, and caulkers worked in a frenzy. As work progressed, Yongle selected a commander for the fleet. The emperor chose Zheng He (1371–1433), despite fearing that he was too old (thirty-five) for so politically important an expedition. The decision rested on Zheng He's unquestioned loyalty, strength of character, energy, ability, and eloquence. These qualities apparently were expected to compensate for Zheng He's lack of seamanship.

The southwestern province of Yunnan had a large Muslim population, and Zheng He was born into that group. When the then prince Zhi Di defeated the Mongols in Yunnan, Zheng He's father was killed in the related disorder. The young boy was taken prisoner and, as was the custom, castrated. Raised in Zhi Di's household, he learned to read and write, studied Confucian writings, and accompanied the prince on all military expeditions. By age twenty, Zheng He was not the soft, effeminate stereotype of the eunuch; rather he was "seven feet tall and had a waist five feet in circumference. His cheeks and forehead were high . . . [and] he had glaring eyes . . . [and] a voice loud as a bell. . . . He was accustomed to battle." Zheng He must have made an imposing impression. A devout Muslim, he persuaded the emperor to place mosques under imperial protection after a period of persecution. On his travels, he prayed at mosques at Malacca and Hormuz. Unable to sire sons, he adopted a nephew. In Chinese history, he was the first eunuch to hold such an important command.

The first fleet, composed of 317 ships, including junks, supply ships, water tankers, warships, transports for horses, and patrol boats, and carrying twenty-eight thousand sailors and soldiers, represents the largest naval force in world history before World War I. Because it bore tons of beautiful porcelains, elegant silks, lacquer ware, and exquisite artifacts to be exchanged for goods abroad, it was called the "treasure fleet."

Between 1405 and 1433, Zheng He led seven voyages, which combined the emperor's diplomatic, political, geographical, and commercial goals (see Map 15.1). Yongle wanted to secure China's hegemony over tributary states and collect pledges of loyalty

Zheng He, voyager to India, Persia, Arabia, and Africa. *(From Lo Monteng, The Western Sea Cruises of Eunuch San Pao, 1597)*

from them. To gain information on winds, tides, distant lands, and rare plants and animals, Zheng He sailed as far west as Egypt. Smallpox epidemics had recently hit China, and one purpose of his voyages was to gather pharmacological products; an Arab text on drugs and therapies was secured and translated into Chinese. He also brought back a giraffe and mahogany, a wood ideal for ships' rudders because of its hardness.

Just before his death, Zheng He recorded his accomplishments on stone tablets. The expeditions had unified "seas and continents . . . the countries beyond the horizon from the ends of the earth have all become subjects . . . and the distances and routes between distant lands may be calculated," implying that China had accumulated considerable geographical information. From around the Indian Ocean, official tribute flowed to the Ming court. A vast immigration of Chinese people into Southeast Asia, sometimes called the Chinese diaspora, followed the expeditions. Immigrants carried with them Chinese culture, including social customs, diet, and practical objects of Chinese technology—calendars, books, scales for weights and measures, and musical instruments. With legends collected about him and monuments erected to him, Zheng He became a great cult hero.

Questions for Analysis

1. What do the voyages of the treasure fleet tell us about China in the fifteenth century?
2. What was Zheng He's legacy?

Source: Louise Levathes, *When China Ruled the Seas: The Treasure Fleet of the Dragon Throne, 1405–1433* (New York: Oxford University Press, 1996).

number of people who could read were a rapt audience for tales of fantastic places and unknown peoples. Scholars have frequently described the European discoveries as a manifestation of Renaissance curiosity about the physical universe—the desire to know more about the geography and peoples of the world. Fernández de Oviedo's *General History of the Indies* (1547), a detailed eyewitness account of plants, animals, and peoples, was widely read. Indeed, the elite's desire for the exotic goods brought by overseas trade helped stimulate the whole process of expansion.

Technological Stimuli to Exploration

Technological developments in shipbuilding, weaponry, and navigation provided another impetus for European expansion. Since ancient times, most seagoing vessels had been narrow, open boats called *galleys* propelled largely by slaves or convicts manning the oars. Though well suited to the placid waters of the Mediterranean, galleys could not withstand the rough winds and uncharted shoals of the Atlantic. The need for sturdier craft, as well as population losses caused by the Black Death, forced the development of a new style of ship that would not require much manpower to sail.

In the course of the fifteenth century, the Portuguese developed the **caravel,** a small, light, three-masted sailing ship. Though somewhat slower than the galley, the caravel held more cargo. Its triangular lateen sails and sternpost rudder also made the caravel a much more maneuverable vessel. When fitted with cannon, it could dominate larger vessels.

Great strides in cartography and navigational aids were also made in this period. The magnetic compass enabled sailors to determine their direction and position at sea. Around 1410 Arab scholars reintroduced Europeans to **Ptolemy's *Geography.*** Written in the second century C.E. by a Hellenized Egyptian, the work synthesized the geographical knowledge of the classical world. It also treated the idea of latitude and longitude. The astrolabe, an instrument invented by the ancient Greeks and perfected by Muslim navigators, was used to determine the altitude of the sun and other celestial bodies. It permitted mariners to plot their latitude, or position north or south of the equator.

Although it showed the world as round, Ptolemy's work also contained crucial errors. Unaware of the Americas, he showed the world as much smaller than it is, so that Asia appeared not very distant from Europe to the west. Based on this work, cartographers fashioned new maps that combined classical knowledge with the latest information from mariners. First the Genoese and Venetians, and then the Portuguese and Spanish, took the lead in these advances.[11]

Much of the new technology that Europeans used in their voyages was borrowed from the East. For example, gunpowder, the compass, and the sternpost rudder were all Chinese inventions. The lateen sail, which allowed European ships to tack against the wind, was a product of the Indian Ocean trade world and was brought to the Mediterranean on Arab ships. Navigational aids, such as the astrolabe, were also acquired from others, and advances in cartography drew on the rich tradition of Judeo-Arabic mathematical and astronomical learning in Iberia.

The Portuguese Overseas Empire

At the end of the fourteenth century Portugal was a small and poor nation on the margins of European life whose principal activities were fishing and subsistence farming. It would have been hard to predict Portugal's phenomenal success overseas in the next two centuries. Yet Portugal had a long history of seafaring and navigation. Blocked from access to western Europe by Spain, the Portuguese turned to the Atlantic and North Africa, whose waters they knew better than other Europeans. Nature also favored the Portuguese: winds blowing along their coast offered passage to Africa, its Atlantic islands, and, ultimately, Brazil.

General History of the Indies *A fifty-volume firsthand description of the natural plants, animals, and peoples of Spanish America. Oviedo was a former colonial administrator who was named Historian of the Indies by the King of Spain in 1532.*

caravel *A small, maneuverable, three-mast sailing ship developed by the Portuguese in the fifteenth century. The caravel gave the Portuguese a distinct advantage in exploration and trade.*

Ptolemy's *Geography* *A second century C.E. work that synthesized the classical knowledge of geography and treated the concepts of longitude and latitude. The work was reintroduced to Europeans in 1410 by Arab scholars and provided a template for later geographical scholarship.*

In the early phases of Portuguese exploration, Prince Henry, a younger son of the king, played a leading role. A nineteenth-century scholar dubbed Henry "the Navigator" because of his support for the study of geography and navigation and for the annual expeditions he sponsored down the western coast of Africa. Although he never personally participated in voyages of exploration, Henry's involvement ensured that Portugal did not abandon the effort despite early disappointments.

The objectives of Portuguese policy included aristocratic desires for martial glory, the historic Iberian crusade to Christianize Muslims, and the quest to find gold, slaves, an overseas route to the spice markets of India, and the mythical king Prester John. Portugal's conquest of Ceuta, an Arab city in northern Morocco, in 1415 marked the beginning of European exploration and control of overseas territory. In the 1420s, under Henry's direction, the Portuguese began to settle the Atlantic islands of Madeira (ca. 1420) and the Azores (1427). In 1443 the Portuguese founded their first African commercial settlement at Arguim in present-day Mauritania. By the time of Henry's death in 1460, his support for exploration was vindicated by thriving sugar plantations on the Atlantic islands and new access to gold.

In the fifteenth century most of the gold that reached Europe came from the Sudan in West Africa and from the Akan peoples living near the area of present-day Ghana. Muslim caravans brought the gold north across the Sahara to Mediterranean ports. Then the Portuguese muscled in on this commerce in gold. Under King John II (r. 1481–1495) the Portuguese established trading posts and forts on the gold-rich Guinea coast and penetrated into the African continent all the way to Timbuktu (see Map 15.2). By 1500 Portugal controlled the flow of African gold to Europe. The golden century of Portuguese prosperity had begun.

Still the Portuguese pushed farther south down the west coast of Africa. In 1487 Bartholomew Diaz rounded the Cape of Good Hope at the southern tip, but storms and a threatened mutiny forced him to turn back. On a later expedition in 1497 Vasco da Gama commanded a fleet of four ships in search of a sea route to the Indian Ocean trade. Da Gama's ships rounded the Cape and sailed up the east coast of Africa. With the help of an Indian guide, da Gama sailed across the Arabian Sea to the port of Calicut in India. Overcoming local hostility, he returned to Lisbon with spices and samples of Indian cloth. He had failed to forge any trading alliances with local powers, but he had proved the possibility of lucrative trade with the East via the Cape route.

King Manuel (r. 1495–1521) promptly dispatched thirteen ships under the command of Pedro Alvares Cabral, assisted by Diaz, to set up trading posts in India. Half the fleet was lost on the return voyage, but the six spice-laden vessels that dropped anchor in Lisbon harbor in July 1501 more than paid for the entire expedition. Thereafter, a Portuguese convoy set out for passage around the Cape every March. Lisbon became the entrance port for Asian goods into Europe—but this was not accomplished without a fight.

Muslims (of Middle Eastern, Indian, Southeast Asian, and Chinese ethnic backgrounds) had controlled the Indian Ocean trade for centuries. With the Portuguese

● **Nocturnal** An instrument for determining the hour of night at sea by finding the progress of certain stars around the polestar (center aperture). *(National Maritime Museum, London)*

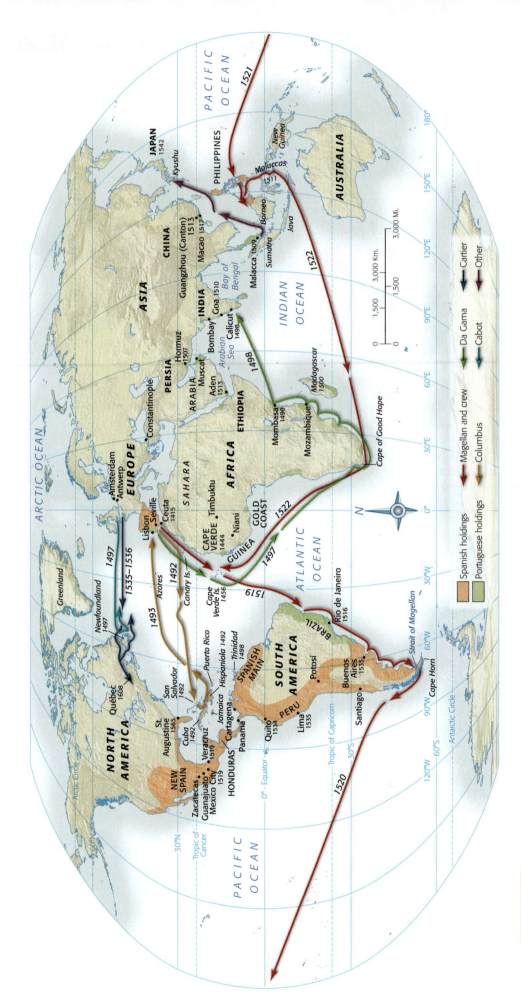

MAP 15.2 **European Exploration and Conquest, Fifteenth and Sixteenth Centuries**
The voyages of discovery marked another phase in the centuries-old migrations of European peoples. Consider the major contemporary significance of each of the voyages depicted on the map.

● **Pepper Harvest**   To break the monotony of their bland diet, Europeans had a passion for pepper, which—along with cinnamon, cloves, nutmeg, and ginger—was the main object of the Asian trade. Since one kilo of pepper cost 2 grams of silver at the place of production in the East Indies and from 10 to 14 grams of silver in Alexandria, Egypt, 14 to 18 grams in Venice, and 20 to 30 grams at the markets of northern Europe, we can appreciate the fifteenth-century expression "as dear as pepper." Here natives fill vats, and the dealer tastes a peppercorn for pungency. *(Bibliothèque nationale de France)*

entry into the region, the brisk Muslim trade was violently disrupted as the Portuguese sank or plundered every Muslim spice ship they met. In 1511 Afonso de Albuquerque, whom the Portuguese crown had named governor of India (1509–1515), captured Malacca, the great Indian Ocean trading entrepôt. Thereafter Portuguese commercial wealth gradually increased, and the Portuguese dominated the European spice market. Albuquerque's bombardment of Goa, Calicut, and Malacca laid the foundations for Portuguese imperialism in the sixteenth and seventeenth centuries.

In March 1493, between the voyages of Diaz and da Gama, Spanish ships under a triumphant Genoese mariner named Christopher Columbus (1451–1506), in the service of the Spanish crown, entered Lisbon harbor. Spain also had begun the quest for an empire.

The Problem of Christopher Columbus

Christopher Columbus is a controversial figure in history—glorified by some as the brave discoverer of America, vilified by others as a cruel exploiter of Native Americans. It is important to put him into the context of his own time. First, what kind of man was Columbus, and what forces or influences shaped him? Second, in sailing westward from Europe, what were his goals? Third, did he achieve his goals, and what did he make of his discoveries?

In his dream of a westward passage to the Indies, the Genoese Columbus embodied centuries-old Italian traditions of involvement with Eastern trade. Columbus was also very knowledgeable about the sea. He had worked as a mapmaker, and he was familiar with such fifteenth-century Portuguese navigational developments as *portolans*—written

● **Intercontinental Exchange**
In 1515 an Indian prince sent the king of Portugal a splendid gift—the first Indian rhinoceros to reach Europe since the fall of the Roman Empire. The subject of a famous engraving by the painter Albrecht Dürer and reproduced repeatedly by minor artists for the next two centuries, a drawing of the exotic rhinoceros must have made an excellent conversation piece for European hosts and their guests. *(Luisa Ricciarini)*

descriptions of the courses along which ships sailed, showing bays, coves, capes, ports, and the distances between these places—and the use of the compass as a nautical instrument. As he implied in his *Journal,* he had acquired not only theoretical but also practical experience: "I have spent twenty-three years at sea and have not left it for any length of time worth mentioning, and I have seen everything from east to west [meaning he had been to England] and I have been to Guinea [north and west Africa]."[12] Although some of Columbus's geographical information, such as his measurement of the distance from Portugal west to Japan as 2,760 miles when it is actually 12,000, proved inaccurate, his successful thirty-three-day voyage to the Caribbean owed a great deal to his seamanship.

Columbus was also a deeply religious man. He had witnessed the Spanish reconquest of Granada and shared fully in the religious and nationalistic fervor surrounding that event. Like the Spanish rulers and most Europeans of his age, Columbus understood Christianity as a missionary religion that should be carried to places where it did not exist. He viewed himself as a divine agent: "God made me the messenger of the new heaven and the new earth of which he spoke in the Apocalypse of St. John . . . and he showed me the post where to find it."[13]

What was the object of this first voyage? Columbus wanted to find a direct ocean trading route to Asia. Rejected by the Portuguese in 1483 and by Ferdinand and Isabella of Spain in 1486, the project finally won the backing of the Spanish monarchy in 1492. Inspired by the stories of Marco Polo, Columbus dreamed of reaching the court of the Great Khan (not realizing that the Ming Dynasty had overthrown the Mongols in 1368). Based on Ptolemy's *Geography* and other texts, he expected to pass the islands of Japan and then land on the east coast of China.

How did Columbus interpret what he had found, and in his mind did he achieve what he had set out to do? On October 12 he landed in the Bahamas, which he christened San Salvador. Columbus believed he had found some small islands off the east coast of Cipangu (Japan). On encountering natives of the islands, he gave them some beads and "many other trifles of small value," pronouncing them delighted with these gifts and eager to trade. In a letter he wrote to Ferdinand and Isabella on his return to Spain, Columbus described the natives as handsome, peaceful, and primitive people whose body painting reminded him of the Canary Islands natives. He concluded that they would make good slaves and could quickly be converted to Christianity. (See the feature "Listening to the Past: Columbus Describes His First Voyage" on pages 458–459.)

Columbus received reassuring reports—via hand gestures and mime—of the presence of gold and of a great king in the vicinity. From San Salvador, Columbus sailed southwest, believing that this course would take him to Japan or the coast of China. He landed on Cuba on October 28. Deciding that he must be on the mainland near the coastal city of Quinsay (Hangzhou), he sent a small embassy inland with letters from Ferdinand and Isabella and instructions to locate the grand city. The expedition included an Arabic-speaker to serve as interpreter with the khan.

The landing party, however, found only small villages with simple peoples. Confronted with this disappointment, Columbus apparently gave up on his aim to meet the Great Khan. Instead, he focused on trying to find gold or other valuables among the peoples he had discovered. In January, confident that gold would later be found, he headed back to Spain. News of his voyage spread rapidly across Europe.[14]

Over the next decades, the Spanish confirmed Columbus's change of course by adopting the model of conquest and colonization they had already introduced in the Canary Islands rather than one of exchange with equals (as envisaged for the Mongol khan). On his second voyage, Columbus forcibly subjugated the island of Hispaniola, enslaved its indigenous peoples, and laid the basis for a system of land grants tied to their labor service. Columbus himself, however, had little interest in or capacity for governing. Revolt soon broke out against him and his brother on Hispaniola. A royal expedition sent to investigate returned the brothers to Spain in chains. Columbus was quickly cleared of wrongdoing, but he did not recover his authority over the territories. Instead, they came under royal control.

Columbus was very much a man of his times. To the end of his life in 1506, he believed that he had found small islands off the coast of Asia. He never realized the scope of his achievement: to have found a vast continent unknown to Europeans, except for a fleeting Viking presence centuries earlier. He could not know that the scale of his discoveries would revolutionize world power, raising issues of trade, settlement, government bureaucracy, and the rights of native and African peoples.

New World Conquest

In 1519, the year Magellan departed on his worldwide expedition, a brash and determined Spanish **conquistadore** ("conqueror") named Hernando Cortés (1485–1547) crossed from Hispaniola in the West Indies to mainland Mexico in search of gold. Accompanied by six hundred men, seventeen horses, and ten cannon, Cortés was to launch the conquest of Aztec Mexico.

Cortés landed at Veracruz in February 1519. From there he led a march to Tenochtitlán (now Mexico City), capital of the sophisticated **Aztec Empire** ruled by Montezuma II (r. 1502–1520). Larger than any European city of the time, the capital was the heart of a civilization with advanced mathematics, astronomy, and engineering, with a complex social system, and with oral poetry and historical traditions.

The Spaniards arrived in the capital when the Aztecs were preoccupied with harvesting their crops. According to a later Spanish account, the timing was ideal. A series of natural phenomena, signs, and portents seemed to augur disaster for the Aztecs. A comet was seen in daytime, and two temples were suddenly destroyed, one by lightning unaccompanied by thunder. These and other apparently inexplicable events had an unnerving and demoralizing effect on Montezuma.

Even more important was the empire's internal weakness. The Aztec state religion, the sacred cult of Huitzilopochtli, necessitated constant warfare against neighboring peoples to secure captives for religious sacrifice and laborers for agricultural and infrastructural work. When Cortés landed, recently defeated tribes were not yet fully integrated into the empire. Increases in tribute provoked revolt, which led to reconquest, retribution, and demands for higher tribute, which in turn sparked greater resentment

conquistadore *Spanish for "conqueror," the term refers to Spanish soldier-explorers, such as Hernando Cortés and Francisco Pizarro, who sought to conquer the New World for the Spanish crown.*

Aztec Empire *A Native American civilization that possessed advanced mathematical, astronomical, and engineering technology. Its capital, Tenochtitlán (now the site of Mexico City), was larger than any contemporary European city. Conquered by Cortés in 1520.*

● **Doña Marina Translating for Hernando Cortés During His Meeting with Montezuma** In April 1519 Doña Marina (or La Malinche as she is known in Mexico) was among twenty women given to the Spanish as slaves. Fluent in Nahuatl and Yucatec Mayan (spoken by a Spanish priest accompanying Cortés), she acted as an interpreter and diplomatic guide for the Spanish. She had a close personal relationship with Cortés and bore his son in 1522. Doña Marina has been seen variously as a traitor to her people, as a victim of Spanish conquest, and as the founder of the Mexican people. She highlights the complex interaction between native peoples and the Spanish and the role women often played as cultural mediators between the two sides. (The Granger Collection, New York)

and fresh revolt. When the Spaniards appeared, the Totonacs greeted them as liberators, and other subject peoples joined them against the Aztecs.[15]

Montezuma himself refrained from attacking the Spaniards as they advanced toward his capital and welcomed Cortés and his men into Tenochtitlán. Historians have often condemned the Aztec ruler for vacillation and weakness. But he relied on the advice of his state council, itself divided, and on the dubious loyalty of tributary communities. When Cortés—with incredible boldness—took Montezuma hostage, the emperor's influence over his people crumbled.

Later, in retaliation for a revolt by the entire population of Tenochtitlán that killed many Spaniards, Montezuma was executed. Afterwards, the Spaniards escaped from the city and inflicted a crushing defeat on the Aztec army at Otumba near Lake Texcoco on July 7, 1520. After this victory Cortés began the systematic conquest of Mexico.

Inca Empire *The Peruvian empire that was at its peak from 1438 until 1532.*

More amazing than the defeat of the Aztecs was the fall of the remote **Inca Empire** perched at 9,800 to 13,000 feet above sea level. (The word *Inca* refers both to the people who lived in the valleys of the Andes Mountains in present-day Peru and to their ruler.) The borders of this vast and sophisticated empire were well fortified, but the Inca neither expected foreign invaders nor knew of the fate of the Aztec Empire to the north. The imperial government, based in the capital city of Cuzco, commanded loyalty from the people, but at the time of the Spanish invasion it had been embroiled in a civil war over succession. The Inca Huascar had been fighting his half-brother Atauhualpa for five years over the crown.

Francisco Pizarro (ca. 1475–1541), a conquistador of modest Spanish origins, landed on the northern coast of Peru on May 13, 1532, the very day Atauhualpa won the decisive battle. The Spaniard soon learned about the war and its outcome. As

Pizarro advanced across the steep Andes toward Cuzco, Atauhualpa was proceeding to the capital for his coronation. Like Montezuma in Mexico, Atauhualpa was kept fully informed of the Spaniards' movements and accepted Pizarro's invitation to meet in the provincial town of Cajamarca. Intending to extend a peaceful welcome to the newcomers, Atauhualpa and his followers were unarmed. The Spaniards captured him and collected an enormous ransom in gold. Instead of freeing the new emperor, however, they executed him on trumped-up charges.

Decades of violence ensued, marked by Incan resistance and internal struggles among Spanish forces for the spoils of empire. By the 1570s the Spanish crown had succeeded in imposing control. With Spanish conquest, a new chapter opened in European relations with the New World.

THE IMPACT OF CONTACT

What was the impact of European conquest on the peoples and ecologies of the New World?

In the sixteenth and seventeenth centuries, following Columbus's voyages, substantial numbers of Spaniards crossed the Atlantic for ports in the Caribbean, the Spanish Main, and present-day Argentina. Thousands of Portuguese sailed for Brazil. The ships on which they traveled were not as large as the so-called Indiamen going to the Indian Ocean; the latter had larger carrying capacities and were expected to return with tons of spices, pepper, sugar, and gold. Only half the migrants, merchants, missionaries, royal officials, soldiers, wives, concubines, and slaves reached American (or Indian Ocean) ports. Poor health, poor shipboard hygiene, climatic extremes, rancid food, and putrid water killed the other half.[16] Those who reached America, however, eventually had an enormous impact not only there but also on the whole world.

Colonial Administration

Having seized the great Amerindian and Andean ceremonial centers in Mexico and Peru, the Spanish conquistadors proceeded to subdue the main areas of Native American civilization in the New World. Columbus, Cortés, and Pizarro claimed the lands they had "discovered" for the Spanish crown. How were these lands to be governed?

According to the Spanish theory of absolutism, the Crown was entitled to exercise full authority over all imperial lands. In the sixteenth century the Crown divided Spain's New World territories into four **viceroyalties,** or administrative divisions. New Spain, with its capital at Mexico City, consisted of Mexico, Central America, and present-day California, Arizona, New Mexico, and Texas. Peru, with its viceregal seat at Lima, originally consisted of all the lands in continental South America but later was reduced to the territory of modern Peru, Chile, Bolivia, and Ecuador. New Granada, with Bogotá as its administrative center, included present-day Venezuela, Colombia, Panama, and, after 1739, Ecuador. La Plata, with Buenos Aires as its capital, consisted of Argentina, Uruguay, and Paraguay. Within each territory a *viceroy,* or imperial governor, had broad military and civil authority as the Spanish sovereign's direct representative. The viceroy presided over the **audiencia,** twelve to fifteen judges who served as an advisory council and as the highest judicial body.

From the early sixteenth century to the beginning of the nineteenth, the Spanish monarchy acted on the mercantilist principle that the colonies existed for the financial benefit of the mother country. The mining of gold and silver was always the most important industry in the colonies. The Crown claimed the **quinto,** one-fifth of all precious metals mined in the Americas. Gold and silver yielded the Spanish monarchy 25 percent of its total income. In return, Spain shipped manufactured goods to the New World and discouraged the development of native industries.

viceroyalties *The name for the four administrative units of Spanish possessions in the Americas: New Spain, Peru, New Granada, and La Plata.*

audiencia *Presided over by the viceroy, the twelve to fifteen judges who served as an advisory council and as the highest judicial body.*

quinto *One-fifth of all precious metals mined in the Americas that the Crown claimed as its own.*

The Portuguese governed their colony of Brazil in a similar manner. After the union of the Portuguese and Spanish crowns in 1580, Spanish administrative forms were introduced. Local officials called *corregidores* held judicial and military powers. Mercantilist policies placed severe restrictions on Brazilian industries that might compete with those of Portugal. In the seventeenth century the use of black slave labor made possible the cultivation of coffee, cotton, and sugar. In the eighteenth century Brazil produced one tenth of the world's sugar.

The Columbian Exchange

Columbian Exchange *The exchange of animals, plants, and diseases between the Old and the New Worlds.*

The Age of Discovery led to the migration of peoples, which in turn led to an exchange of fauna and flora—of animals, plants, and diseases, a complex process known as the **Columbian Exchange.** Spanish and Portuguese immigrants to the Americas wanted the diet with which they were familiar, so they searched for climatic zones favorable to those crops. Everywhere they settled they brought and raised wheat—in the highlands of Mexico, the Rio de la Plata, New Granada (in northern South America), and Chile. By 1535 Mexico was exporting wheat. Grapes did well in parts of Peru and Chile. It took the Spanish longer to discover areas where suitable soil and adequate rainfall would nourish olive trees, but by the 1560s the coastal valleys of Peru and Chile were dotted with olive groves. Columbus had brought sugar plants on his second voyage; Spaniards also introduced rice and bananas from the Canary Islands, and the Portuguese carried these items to Brazil. All plants and trees had to be brought from Europe, but not all plants arrived intentionally. In clumps of mud on shoes and in the folds of textiles came the seeds of immigrant grasses.

Apart from wild turkeys and game, Native Americans had no animals for food; apart from alpacas and llamas, they had no animals for travel or to use as beasts of burden. On his second voyage in 1493 Columbus introduced horses, cattle, sheep, dogs, pigs, chickens, and goats. The multiplication of these animals proved spectacular. The horse enabled the Spanish conquerors and the Amerindians to travel faster and farther and to transport heavy loads.

The Spanish and Portuguese returned to Europe with maize (corn), white potatoes, and many varieties of beans, squash, pumpkins, avocados, and tomatoes. Because maize grows in climates too dry for rice and too wet for wheat, gives a high yield per unit of land, and has a short growing season, it proved an especially important crop for Europeans. So too did the nutritious white potato, which slowly spread from west to east—to Ireland, England, and France in the seventeenth century; and to Germany, Poland, Hungary, and Russia in the eighteenth. Ironically, the white potato reached New England from old England in 1718.

Spanish Settlement and Indigenous Population Decline

In the sixteenth century perhaps two hundred thousand Spaniards immigrated to the New World. Mostly soldiers and adventurers unable to find employment in Spain, they came for profits. After assisting in the conquest of the Aztecs and the subjugation of the Incas, these men carved out vast estates in temperate grazing areas and imported Spanish sheep, cattle, and horses for the kinds of ranching with which they were familiar. In coastal tropic areas unsuited for grazing the Spanish erected huge plantations to supply sugar for the European market. Around 1550 silver was discovered in present-day Bolivia and Mexico. How were the cattle ranches, sugar plantations, and silver mines to be worked? The conquistadors first turned to the Amerindians.

encomienda system *The Spanish system whereby the Crown granted the conquerors the right to employ groups of Amerindians in a town or area as agricultural or mining laborers or as tribute payers; it was a disguised form of slavery.*

The Spanish quickly established the **encomienda system,** in which the Crown granted the conquerors the right to employ groups of Amerindians as agricultural or mining laborers or as tribute payers. Laboring in the blistering heat of tropical cane fields or in the dark, dank, and dangerous mines, the Amerindians died in staggering numbers.

Students of the history of medicine have suggested another crucial explanation for indigenous population losses: disease. Having little or no resistance to diseases brought from the Old World, the inhabitants of the highlands of Mexico and Peru, especially, fell victim to smallpox, typhus, influenza, and other diseases. According to one expert, smallpox caused "in all likelihood the most severe single loss of aboriginal population that ever occurred."[17] (The old belief that syphilis was a New World disease imported to Europe by Columbus's sailors has been discredited by the discovery of pre-Columbian skeletons in Europe bearing signs of the disease.)

Although disease was a leading cause of death, there were many others, including malnutrition and starvation as people were forced to neglect their own fields. Many indigenous peoples also died through outright violence.[18] According to the Franciscan missionary Bartolomé de Las Casas (1474–1566), the Spanish maliciously murdered thousands:

To these quiet Lambs . . . came the Spaniards like most c(r)uel Tygres, Wolves and Lions, enrag'd with a sharp and tedious hunger; for these forty years past, minding nothing else but the slaughter of these unfortunate wretches, whom with divers kinds of torments neither seen nor heard of before, they have so cruelly and inhumanely butchered, that of three millions of people which Hispaniola itself did contain, there are left remaining alive scarce three hundred persons.[19]

Las Casas's remarks concentrate on the Caribbean islands, but the death rate elsewhere was also overwhelming.

The Franciscan, Dominican, and Jesuit missionaries who accompanied the conquistadors and settlers played an important role in converting the Amerindians to Christianity, teaching them European methods of agriculture, and inculcating loyalty to the Spanish crown. In terms of numbers of people baptized, missionaries enjoyed phenomenal success, though the depth of the Amerindians' understanding of Christianity remains debatable. Missionaries, especially Las Casas, asserted that the Amerindians had human rights, and through Las Casas's and others' persistent pressure the emperor Charles V abolished the worst abuses of the encomienda system in 1531.

For colonial administrators the main problem posed by the astronomically high death rate was the loss of a subjugated labor force. As early as 1511 King Ferdinand of Spain observed that the Amerindians seemed to be "very frail" and that "one black could do the work of four Indians."[20] Thus was born an absurd myth and the new tragedy of the Atlantic slave trade.

Primary Source:
General History of the Things of New Spain
Read an account of the Spanish conquest of the Aztec Empire, compiled from eyewitness testimony by the Aztecs themselves.

NEW GLOBAL ECONOMIES, FORCED MIGRATIONS, AND ENCOUNTERS

How was the era of global contact shaped by new commercial empires, cultural encounters, and forced migrations?

The centuries-old Afro-Eurasian trade world was forever changed by the European voyages of discovery and their aftermath. For the first time, a truly global economy emerged in the sixteenth and seventeenth centuries, and it forged new links among far-flung peoples, cultures, and societies. The ancient civilizations of Europe, Africa, the Americas, Asia, and Southeast Asia confronted each other in new and rapidly evolving ways, and those confrontations sometimes led to conquest, exploitation, and profound social and cultural change.

Sugar and Slavery

Throughout the Middle Ages slavery was deeply entrenched in the Mediterranean. The bubonic plague, famines, and other epidemics created severe shortages of agricultural and domestic workers throughout Europe, encouraging Italian merchants to buy slaves from the Black Sea region and the Balkans. Renaissance merchants continued the slave trade despite papal threats of excommunication. The Genoese set up colonial stations in the Crimea and along the Black Sea; according to an international authority on slavery, these outposts were "virtual laboratories" for the development of slave plantation agriculture in the New World.[21] This form of slavery had nothing to do with race; almost all slaves were white. Black African slavery entered the European picture and took root in South and then North America after the 1453 Ottoman capture of Constantinople halted the flow of white slaves. Mediterranean Europe, cut off from its traditional source of slaves, then turned to sub-Saharan Africa, which had a long history of slave trading.

sugar   *Originally from the South Pacific, sugar quickly became a demanded luxury in Europe. Sugar plants were brought to the New World by Columbus and became the primary crop for export. The desire for workers on sugar plantations, particularly in Brazil, led to a tremendous increase in the African slave trade.*

Native to the South Pacific, **sugar** was taken in ancient times to India, where farmers learned to preserve cane juice as granules that could be stored and shipped. From there, sugar traveled to China and the Mediterranean, where islands like Crete, Sicily, and Cyprus had the necessary warm and wet climate. When Genoese and other Italians colonized the Canary Islands and the Portuguese settled on the Madeira Islands, sugar plantations came to the Atlantic. In this stage of European expansion, "the history of slavery became inextricably tied up with the history of sugar."[22] Originally sugar was an expensive luxury that only the very affluent could afford, but population increases and monetary expansion in the fifteenth century led to an increasing demand for it.

Resourceful Italians provided the capital, cane, and technology for sugar cultivation on plantations in southern Portugal, Madeira, and the Canary Islands. Meanwhile, in

● **A New World Sugar Refinery, Brazil**   Sugar, a luxury in great demand in Europe, was the most important and most profitable plantation crop in the New World. This image shows the processing and refinement of sugar on a Brazilian plantation. Sugar cane was grown, harvested, and processed by African slaves who labored under brutal and ruthless conditions to generate enormous profits for plantation owners. *(The Bridgeman Art Library/Getty Images)*

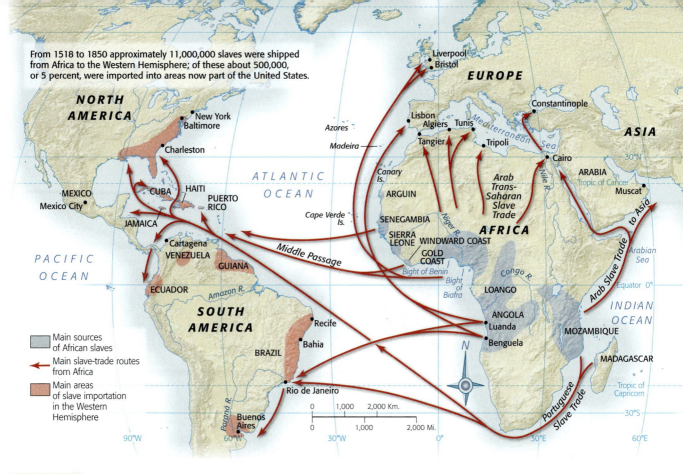

From 1518 to 1850 approximately 11,000,000 slaves were shipped from Africa to the Western Hemisphere; of these about 500,000, or 5 percent, were imported into areas now part of the United States.

Main sources of African slaves

→ **Main slave-trade routes from Africa**

Main areas of slave importation in the Western Hemisphere

MAP 15.3 **The African Slave Trade** Decades before the discovery of America, Greek, Russian, Bulgarian, Armenian, and then black slaves worked the plantation economies of southern Italy, Sicily, Portugal, and Mediterranean Spain—thereby serving as models for the American form of slavery.

the period 1490 to 1530, Portuguese traders brought between three hundred and two thousand black slaves to Lisbon each year (see Map 15.3), where they performed most of the manual labor and constituted 10 percent of the city's population. From there slaves were transported to the sugar plantations of Madeira, the Azores, and the Cape Verde Islands. Sugar and the small Atlantic islands gave New World slavery its distinctive shape. Columbus himself, who spent a decade in Madeira, brought sugar plants on his voyages to "the Indies."

In Africa, where slavery was entrenched (as it was in the Islamic world, southern Europe, and China), African kings and dealers sold black slaves to European merchants who participated in the transatlantic trade. The Portuguese brought the first slaves to Brazil; by 1600 four thousand were being imported annually. After its founding in 1621, the Dutch West India Company, with the full support of the government of the United Provinces, transported thousands of Africans to Brazil and the Caribbean. In the late seventeenth century, with the chartering of the Royal African Company, the English got involved. Altogether, traders from all these countries brought around twelve million African slaves to the West Indies and North America.

European sailors found the Atlantic passage cramped and uncomfortable, but conditions for African slaves were lethal. Before 1700, when slavers decided it was better business to improve conditions, some 20 percent of slaves died on the voyage.[23] The most common cause of death was from dysentery induced by poor-quality food and water, intense crowding, and lack of sanitation. Men were often kept in irons during the passage, while women and girls were fair game for sailors. To increase profits, slave traders packed several hundred captives on each ship. One slaver explained that he removed his boots before entering the slave hold because he had to crawl over their packed bodies.[24]

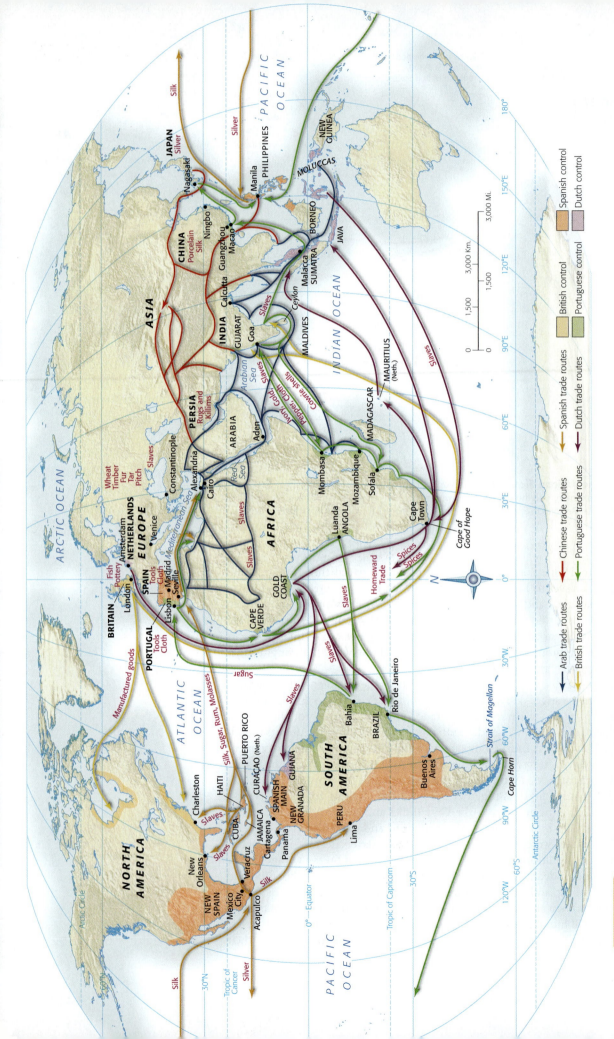

MAP 15.4 **Seaborne Trading Empires in the Sixteenth and Seventeenth Centuries** By the mid-seventeenth century, trade linked all parts of the world except for Australia. Notice that trade in slaves was not confined to the Atlantic but involved almost all parts of the world.

Spanish control
Dutch control
British control
Portuguese control

Arab trade routes
British trade routes
Chinese trade routes
Portuguese trade routes
Spanish trade routes
Dutch trade routes

0   1,500   3,000 Km.
0   1,500   3,000 Mi.

The eighteenth century witnessed the peak of the Atlantic slave trade. In 1790 there were 757,181 blacks in a total U.S. population of 3,929,625. In Brazil during the same decade, blacks numbered about 2 million in a total population of 3.25 million.

Global Trade Networks

The Europeans' discovery of the Americas and their exploration of the Pacific for the first time linked the entire world by intercontinental seaborne trade. That trade brought into being three successive European commercial empires: the Portuguese, the Spanish, and the Dutch.

In the sixteenth century, naval power and shipborne artillery gave Portugal hegemony over the sea route to India. To Lisbon the Portuguese fleet brought spices, which the Portuguese paid for with textiles produced at Gujarat and Coromandel in India and with gold and ivory from East Africa (see Map 15.4). From their fortified bases at Goa on the Arabian Sea and at Malacca on the Malay Peninsula, ships of Malabar teak carried goods to the Portuguese settlement at Macao in the South China Sea. From Macao, loaded with Chinese silks and porcelains, Portuguese ships sailed to the Japanese port of Nagasaki and to the Philippine port of Manila, where Chinese goods were exchanged for Spanish (that is, Latin American) silver. Throughout Asia, the Portuguese traded in slaves—black Africans, Chinese, and Japanese. To India the Portuguese exported horses from Mesopotamia and copper from Arabia; from India they exported hawks and peacocks for the Chinese and Japanese markets.

Across the Atlantic, Portuguese Brazil provided most of the sugar consumed in Europe in the sixteenth and early seventeenth centuries. African slave labor produced sugar on Brazilian plantations, and Portuguese merchants controlled both the slave trade between West Africa and Brazil and the commerce in sugar between Brazil and Portugal. The Portuguese were the first worldwide traders, and Portuguese was the language of the Asian maritime trade.

Spanish possessions in the New World constituted basically a land empire, and in the sixteenth century the Spaniards devised a method of governing that empire (see page 443). But across the Pacific, the Spaniards also built a seaborne empire, centered at Manila in the Philippines, which had been "discovered" by Ferdinand Magellan in 1521. Between 1564 and 1571, the Spanish navigator Miguel Lopez de Legazpi sailed from Mexico and through a swift and almost bloodless conquest took over the Philippine Islands. Legazpi founded Manila, which served as the transpacific bridge between Spanish America and the extreme Eastern trade.

Chinese silk, sold by the Portuguese in Manila for American silver, was transported to Acapulco in Mexico, from which it was carried overland to Veracruz for re-export to Spain. Because hostile Pacific winds prohibited direct passage from the Philippines to Peru, large shipments of silk also arrived at Acapulco for transport to Peru (see Map 15.4). Spanish merchants could never satisfy the European demand for silk, so huge amounts of bullion went from Acapulco to Manila. For example, in 1597, 12 million pesos of silver, almost the total value of the transatlantic trade, crossed the Pacific. After about 1640, the Spanish silk trade declined because it could not compete with Dutch imports.

Stimulated by a large demand for goods in Europe, India, China, and Japan, a worldwide commercial boom occurred from about 1570 to 1630. In Japan the gradual decline of violence, unification, and the development of marketing networks led to a leap in orders for foreign products: textiles from India, silks and porcelains from China, raw materials and spices from Southeast Asia; enslaved humans from Africa. The Japanese navy expanded, and Japanese mines poured out vast quantities of silver that paid for those wares. Then, in 1635, maritime trade stopped when the Tokugawa Shogunate closed the islands to trade and forbade merchants to travel abroad under penalty of death.

● **The Port of Banten in Western Java** Influenced by Muslim traders and emerging in the early sixteenth century as a Muslim kingdom, Banten evolved into a thriving entrepôt. The city stood on the trade route to China; as this Dutch engraving suggests, in the seventeenth century the Dutch East India Company used Banten as an important collection point for spices purchased for sale in Europe. *(Archives Charmet/The Bridgeman Art Library)*

age of commerce *A period of heavy trading from 1570 to 1630 in which Southeast Asia exchanged its spices and other raw materials for textiles from India, silver from the Americas and Japan, and silk, ceramics, and manufactures from China.*

China, with a population increase, urban growth, and a rare period of government-approved foreign trade, also underwent international commercial expansion. China wanted raw materials, sugar, and spices from Southeast Asia; ivory and slaves from Africa; and cotton cloth from India. Merchants in Mughal India conducted a huge long-distance trade extending as far north as Poland and Russia. India also sought spices from the Moluccas, sugar from Vietnam and the Philippines, and rice and raw materials from Southeast Asia. In this early modern **age of commerce,** Southeast Asia exchanged its pepper, spices, woods, resin, pearls, and sugar for textiles from India; silver from the Americas and Japan; and silk, ceramics, and manufactures from China. The Southeast Asian merchant marine also expanded. The European demand for Indian pepper, Southeast Asian nutmeg and cloves, and Chinese silks and porcelains was virtually insatiable. But Europeans offered nothing that Asian peoples wanted. Therefore, Europeans had to pay for their purchases with silver or gold—hence the steady flow of specie from Mexico and South America to Asia.

In the latter half of the seventeenth century, the worldwide Dutch seaborne trade predominated. The Dutch Empire was built on spices. In 1599 a Dutch fleet returned to Amsterdam carrying 600,000 pounds of pepper and 250,000 pounds of cloves and nutmeg. Those who had invested in the expedition received a profit of 100 percent. The voyage led to the establishment in 1602 of the Dutch East India Company, founded with the stated intention of capturing the spice trade from the Portuguese.

The Dutch fleet, sailing from the Cape of Good Hope and avoiding the Portuguese forts in India, steered directly for the Sunda Strait in Indonesia (see Map 15.4). The Dutch wanted direct access to and control of the Indonesian sources of spices. In return for assisting Indonesian princes in local squabbles and disputes with the

Portuguese, the Dutch won broad commercial concessions. Through agreements, seizures, and outright war, they gained control of the western access to the Indonesian archipelago. Gradually, they acquired political domination over the archipelago itself. Exchanging European manufactured goods—armor, firearms, linens, and toys—the Dutch soon had a monopoly on the very lucrative spice trade.[25] The seaborne empires of Portugal, Spain, and Holland paved the way for the eighteenth-century mercantilist empires of France and Great Britain.

The Chinese and Japanese Discovery of the West

Why did Europeans, rather than Chinese, take the lead in exploring parts of the globe distant from their native countries? In the fifteenth century China was obviously the largest geographical power in Asia. Chinese sailors had both the theoretical maritime knowledge and the practical experience of long-distance ocean travel (see page 435). In 1435 the Chinese knew some of the Pacific Ocean, all of the Indian Ocean, the Arabian Sea, and the Red Sea. Europeans knew little more than the Mediterranean Sea and the Atlantic Ocean along the northwestern coast of Africa. About 1500 China had a population between 65 million and 80 million, whereas the population of Spain was only about 6.5 million, barely one-tenth of China's. The emperors' wealth was more than double that of the kings of Spain and France combined.

Europeans, as we have seen, sailed to the Americas and Asia seeking spices, gold, and trade. Was Chinese culture hostile to trade and foreign commerce? According to traditional scholarship, Chinese Confucian teaching disparaged commerce and merchants. In the orthodox Confucian ordering of social classes—scholars, farmers, artisans, and merchants—merchants ranked lowest. Moreover, Confucian belief held that trade encouraged competition, competition led to social mobility and change, and change promoted disorder in society. But whatever theoretical ideas the Chinese literati may have had about merchants, Western observers took a different view. One later expert on China wrote that the Chinese had "a singular penchant for trade"[26]; another writer commented that the Chinese were "a race of traders than whom there has not been in the world a shrewder and a keener." Following Zheng He's voyages (see page 435), tens of thousands of Chinese emigrated to the Philippines, where they acquired commercial dominance of Luzon by 1600. Thus hostility to trade and commerce does not explain China's failure to expand.

Rather, internal and domestic difficulties offer better explanations. In the fifteenth century Mongol pressures on China's northern border forced the emperors to focus on domestic security rather than foreign exploration. The emperor Zhengtong (r. 1436–1449 and 1457–1464) held that overseas expeditions brought little visible return. At a time when he was forced to conserve resources for the army, he stopped maritime expeditions, closed China's borders, and forbade foreign travel (the last law was widely flouted). Administrative disorder also aggravated imperial financial difficulties. At the time when the "new monarchs" of Europe (see page 400) were reducing disorderly elements in their societies and centralizing their administrations, Chinese emperors were losing domestic control and threatened by strong foreign invaders. The failure to utilize rich maritime knowledge opened China's vast coastline first to Japanese pirates and then to persistent and aggressive European traders.

The desire to Christianize pagan peoples was a major motive in Europeans' overseas expansion. In 1582 the Jesuit Matteo Ricci (1552–1610) settled at Macao on the mouth of the Canton River. Like the Christian monks who had converted the Germanic tribes of early medieval Europe, Ricci sought first to convert the emperor and elite groups and then, through gradual assimilation, to win the throngs of Chinese. He tried to present Christianity to the Chinese in Chinese terms. He understood the Chinese respect for learning and worked to win converts among the scholarly class. When Ricci was admitted to the Imperial City at Beijing (Peking), he addressed the emperor Wanli:

Primary Source:
Journals: Matteo Ricci
This story about Jesuit missionaries in China provides an interesting look at the nexus of religion and politics in the early seventeenth century.

Li Ma-tou [Ricci's name transliterated into Chinese], your Majesty's servant, comes from the Far West, addresses himself to Your Majesty with respect, in order to offer gifts from his country. Despite the distance, fame told me of the remarkable teaching and fine institutions with which the imperial court has endowed all its peoples. I desired to share these advantages and live out my life as one of Your Majesty's subjects, hoping in return to be of some small use.[27]

Ricci presented the emperor with two clocks, one of them decorated with dragons and eagles in the Chinese style. The emperor's growing fascination with clocks gave Ricci the opportunity to display other examples of Western technology. He instructed court scholars about astronomical equipment and the manufacture of cannon and drew for them a map of the world—with China at its center. These inventions greatly impressed the Chinese intelligentsia. Over a century later, a Jesuit wrote, "The Imperial Palace is stuffed with clocks, . . . watches, carillons, repeaters, organs, spheres, and astronomical clocks of all kinds—there are more than four thousand pieces from the best masters of Paris and London."[28] The Chinese first learned about Europe from the Jesuits.

But the Christians and the Chinese did not understand one another. Because the Jesuits served the imperial court as mathematicians, astronomers, and cartographers, the Chinese emperors allowed them to remain in Beijing. The Jesuits, however, were primarily interested in converting the Chinese to Christianity. The missionaries thought that by showing the pre-eminence of Western science, they were demonstrating the superiority of Western religion. This was a relationship that the Chinese did not acknowledge. They could not accept a religion that required total commitment and taught the existence of an absolute. Only a small number among intellectual elites became Christians. Most Chinese were hostile to the Western faith. They accused Christians of corrupting Chinese morals because they forbade people to honor their ancestors—and corruption of morals translated into disturbing the public order. They also accused Christians of destroying Chinese sanctuaries, of revering a man (Christ) who had been executed as a public criminal, and of spying on behalf of the Japanese. In the mid-eighteenth century the emperor forbade Christianity and expelled the missionaries.

The Christian West and the Chinese world learned a great deal from each other. The Jesuits probably were "responsible for the rebirth of Chinese mathematics in the seventeenth and eighteenth centuries," and Western contributions stimulated the Chinese development of other sciences.[29] From the Chinese, Europeans got the idea of building bridges suspended by chains. The first Western experiments in electrostatics and magnetism in the seventeenth century derived from Chinese models. Travel accounts about Chinese society and customs had a profound impact on Europeans, making them more sensitive to the beautiful diversity of peoples and manners.

Initial Japanese contacts with Europeans paralleled those of the Chinese. In 1542 Portuguese merchants arrived in Japan. They vigorously supported Christian missionary activity, and in 1547 the Jesuit missionary Saint Francis Xavier landed at Kagoshima, preached widely, and in two years won many converts. From the beginning, however, the Japanese government feared that native converts might have conflicting political loyalties. Divided allegiance could encourage Euro-

● **Kangnido Map (1684)** Diplomatic relations between Korea and the Ming Chinese court brought Korean scholars in touch with Chinese thought. This Korean map of the world is probably based on a Chinese model. *(© British Library Board. All rights reserved. From Lee Chan,* Hanguk ui ko chido/Yi Chan cho *[Old Maps of Korea], 1997)*

pean invasion of the islands—the Japanese authorities had the example of the Philippines, where Spanish conquest followed missionary activity.

Convinced that European merchants and missionaries had contributed to the civil disorder that the regime was trying to eradicate, the Japanese government decided to expel the Spanish and Portuguese and to close Japan to all foreign influence. A decree of 1635 was directed at the commissioners of the port of Nagasaki, a center of Japanese Christianity:

If there is any place where the teachings of the padres (Catholic priests) is practiced, the two of you must order a thorough investigation. . . . If there are any Southern Barbarians (Westerners) who propagate the teachings of the padres, or otherwise commit crimes, they may be incarcerated in the prison.[30]

In 1639 an imperial memorandum decreed, "Hereafter entry by the Portuguese galeota [galleon or large oceangoing warship] is forbidden. If they insist on coming [to Japan], the ships must be destroyed and anyone aboard those ships must be beheaded."[31]

When tens of thousands of Japanese Christians made a stand on the peninsula of Shimabara, the Dutch lent the Japanese government cannon. The Protestant Dutch hated Catholicism, and as businessmen they hated the Portuguese, their great commercial rivals. Convinced that the Dutch had come only for trade and did not want to proselytize, the imperial government allowed them to remain. But Japanese authorities ordered them to remove their factory-station from Hirado on the western tip of Kyushu to the tiny island of Deshima, which covered just 2,100 square feet. The government limited Dutch trade to one ship a year, watched the Dutch very closely, and required Dutch officials to pay an annual visit to the capital to renew their loyalty. The

● **Arrival of the Nanbanjin or "Southern Barbarians"** Just as wealthy eighteenth-century Europeans craved Chinese silken wallpaper because of its "exotic" quality, so rich Japanese decorated their homes with screens depicting the "strange" Westerners; the gold leaf suggests the screen's great value. In the central panel, a Portuguese ship captain (shaded by a parasol carried by a black servant) arrives in the port of Nagasaki. Black porters carry boxes of goods and rare animals as gifts "to sweeten up" Japanese merchants. They are received by tall, black-robed Jesuits. Europeans were called "barbarians" because of what the Japanese perceived as their terrible manners and the stench they emitted from a meat-based diet and lack of bathing. (Michael Holford)

Japanese also compelled the Dutch merchants to perform servile acts that other Europeans considered humiliating.

Long after Christianity ceased to be a possible threat to the Japanese government, the fear of Christianity sustained a policy of banning Western books on science and religion. Until well into the eighteenth century, Japanese intellectuals were effectively cut off from Western development, and Japanese opinions of Westerners were not high.

The Worldwide Economic Effects of Spanish Silver

The economic effects of exchange between Spain and China were perhaps even more important than the cultural ones. Silver mined in the Americas played a major role in both European and Asian economic development in the sixteenth and seventeenth centuries. In 1545, at an altitude of fifteen thousand feet, the Spanish discovered an incredible source of silver at Potosí (in present-day Bolivia) in territory conquered from the Inca Empire. The frigid place where nothing grew had not been settled. A half-century later, 160,000 people lived there, making it about the size of the city of London. In the second half of the sixteenth century Potosí yielded perhaps 60 percent of all the silver mined in the world. From Potosí and the mines at Zacatecas and Guanajuato in Mexico, huge quantities of precious metals poured forth, destined for the port of Seville in Spain.

The mining of gold and silver became the most important industry in the colonies. The Crown claimed the quinto, one-fifth of all precious metals mined in South America. Gold and silver yielded the Spanish monarchy 25 percent of its total income. Spanish predominance, however, proved temporary.

In the sixteenth century Spain experienced a steady population increase, creating a sharp rise in the demand for food and goods. Spanish colonies in the Americas also represented a demand for products. Since Spain had expelled some of the best farmers and businessmen—the Muslims and Jews—in the fifteenth century, the Spanish economy was suffering and could not meet the new demands. Prices rose. Because the cost of manufacturing cloth and other goods increased, Spanish products could not compete in the international market with cheaper products made elsewhere. The textile industry was badly hurt. Prices spiraled upward faster than the government could levy taxes to dampen the economy. (Higher taxes would have cut the public's buying power; with fewer goods sold, prices would have come down.)

Did the flood of silver bullion from America cause the inflation? Prices rose most steeply before 1565, but bullion imports reached their peak between 1580 and 1620. Thus there is no direct correlation between silver imports and the inflation rate. Did the substantial population growth accelerate the inflation rate? It may have done so. After 1600, when the population pressure declined, prices gradually stabilized. One fact is certain: the price revolution severely strained government budgets. Several times between 1557 and 1647, Spain's King Philip II and his successors repudiated the state debt, thereby undermining confidence in the government and leading the economy into a shambles.

As Philip II paid his armies and foreign debts with silver bullion, Spanish inflation was transmitted to the rest of Europe. Between 1560 and 1600, much of Europe experienced large price increases. Prices doubled and in some cases quadrupled. Spain suffered most severely, but all European countries were affected. People who lived on fixed incomes, such as the continental nobles, were badly hurt because their money bought less. Those who owed fixed sums of money, such as the middle class, prospered: in a time of rising prices, debts had less value each year. Food costs rose most sharply, and the poor fared worst of all.

And what of Asia? What economic impact did the Spanish and Portuguese discoveries have on Asian societies and on world trade? Some recent scholars argue that the key to understanding world trade in the sixteenth and early seventeenth centuries is not Europe, where hitherto most research has focused, but China. Within China the overissue of paper money had by 1450 reduced the value of that medium of currency to virtually nothing. Gold was too valuable for ordinary transactions. So the Ming government shifted to a silver-based currency. The result was that China was the main buyer of world silver—that is, China exchanged its silks and porcelains for silver.

While the mines of South America and Mexico poured out silver, so too did Japanese mines, shipping to Manila and Macao perhaps two hundred tons a year. American and Japanese silver had a profound impact on China. On the one hand, it contributed to the rise of a merchant class that converted to a silver zone. On the other hand, the Ming Dynasty, by allowing the payment of taxes in silver instead of the traditional rice, weakened its financial basis. As the purchasing power of silver declined in China, so did the value of silver taxes. This development led to a fiscal crisis that helped bring down the Ming Dynasty and contributed to the rise of the Qing.

Beyond China itself, Chinese imports of silver had crucial global ramifications: "When silver from Mexico and Japan entered the Ming Empire in great quantity, the value of silver began to decline and inflation set in, for as the metal became more abundant its buying power diminished."[32] This inflationary trend affected the values of commodities across the world. From a global perspective, the economic impact of China on the West was thus greater than any European influence on China or the rest of Asia.[33]

At the heart of world trade was not Europe, but China. The silver market drove world trade, with the Americas and Japan being the mainstays on the supply side and China dominating the demand side. Europeans were only the middlemen in the trade among Europe, the New World, and China.

Chapter Summary

To assess your mastery of this chapter, go to
bedfordstmartins.com/mckayworld

• What were the distinctive features of Southeast Asian cultures and trade, and what was the impact of Islam and Christianity on Southeast Asian peoples?

Prior to Columbus's voyages, well-developed trade routes linked the peoples and products of Africa, Asia, and Europe. The Indian Ocean was the center of the Afro-Eurasian trade world, ringed by cosmopolitan commercial cities such as Mombasa, Malacca, and Macao. Rice and seafood were staples of the diet, and women gained prestige from their role in rice cultivation. Southeast Asia's traditional animist beliefs were challenged in the sixteenth and seventeenth centuries by the arrival of Christian missionaries and Muslim teachers. Eventually, more than half the area's population accepted one of these two religions.

• How and why did Europeans undertake ambitious voyages of expansion that would usher in a new era of global contact?

Originally, Europeans played a minor role in the Afro-Eurasian trading world, since they did not produce many products desired by Eastern elites. In the sixteenth and seventeenth centuries, Europeans for the first time gained access to large parts of the globe. European peoples had the intellectual curiosity, driving ambition, and material incentive to challenge their marginal role in

Key Terms

bride wealth
General History of the Indies
caravel
Ptolemy's *Geography*
conquistadore
Aztec Empire
Inca Empire
viceroyalties
audiencia
quinto
Columbian Exchange
encomienda system
sugar
age of commerce

the pre-existing trade world. The revived monarchies of the sixteenth century now possessed sufficient resources to back ambitious seafarers like Christopher Columbus and Vasco da Gama.

• What was the impact of European conquest on the peoples and ecologies of the New World?

In the New World, Europeans discovered territories wholly unknown to them and forcibly established new colonies. European intrusion into the Americas led to the subjugation of native peoples for use in American silver and gold mines, along with the establishment of political and ecclesiastical administrations to govern the new territories. The resulting Columbian Exchange decimated native populations and fostered exchange of myriad plant, animal, and viral species. The spread of American plants, especially maize and potatoes, improved the diets of Asian, African, and European peoples and contributed to an almost worldwide population boom beginning in the mid-seventeenth century. Europeans carried smallpox and other diseases to the Americas, along with new weapons of war and economic exploitation, causing a massive population decline among Native American peoples.

• How was the era of global contact shaped by new commercial empires, cultural encounters, and forced migrations?

Exploration and exploitation contributed to a more sophisticated standard of living in Europe, in the form of spices and Asian luxury goods, and to terrible inflation resulting from the influx of South American silver and gold. Governments, the upper classes, and the peasantry were badly hurt by the resulting inflation. Meanwhile, the middle class of bankers, shippers, financiers, and manufacturers prospered for much of the seventeenth century.

Other consequences of European expansion had global proportions. Indian Ocean trade, long dominated by Muslim merchants operating from autonomous city-ports, increasingly fell under the control of Portuguese, and later Dutch, merchants. In China the lure of international trade encouraged the development of the porcelain and silk industries, as well as the immigration of thousands of Chinese people to Southeast Asia. In Japan the Indian Ocean trade in spices, silks, and Indian cotton prompted the greater exploitation of Japanese silver mines to yield the ore with which to pay for foreign goods. Both Chinese and Japanese leaders rebuffed efforts by Christian missionaries to spread their faith. Most tragically, the slave trade took on new proportions of scale and intensity as many millions of Africans were transported to labor in horrific conditions in the mines and plantations of the New World.

Suggested Reading

Crosby, Alfred W. *The Columbian Exchange: Biological and Cultural Consequences of 1492,* 30th anniversary ed. 2003. An innovative and highly influential account of the environmental impact of Columbus's voyages.

Davis, David B. *Slavery and Human Progress.* 1984. A moving and authoritative account of New World slavery.

Fernández-Armesto, Felip. *Columbus.* 1992. An excellent biography of Christopher Columbus.

Frederickson, George M. *The Arrogance of Race: Historical Perspectives on Slavery, Racism, and Social Inequality.*

1988. Analyzes the social and economic circumstances associated with the rise of plantation slavery.

Greenblatt, Stephen. *Marvelous Possessions: The Wonder of the New World.* 1991. Describes the cultural impact of New World discoveries on Europeans.

Northrup, David, ed. *The Atlantic Slave Trade.* 1994. Collected essays by leading scholars on many different aspects of the slave trade.

Pérez-Mallaína, Pablo E. *Spain's Men of the Sea: Daily Life on the Indies Fleet in the Sixteenth Century.* 1998. A description of recruitment, daily life, and career paths for ordinary sailors and officers in the Spanish fleet.

Pomeranz, Kenneth, and Steven Topik. *The World That Trade Created: Society, Culture and the World Economy, 1400 to the Present.* 1999. The creation of a world market presented through rich and vivid stories of merchants, miners, slaves, and farmers.

Restall, Matthew. *Seven Myths of Spanish Conquest.* 2003. A re-examination of common ideas about why and how the Spanish conquered native civilizations in the New World.

Scammell, Geoffrey V. *The World Encompassed: The First European Maritime Empires, c. 800–1650.* 1981. A detailed overview of the first European empires, including the Italian city-states, Portugal, and Spain.

Subrahamanyam, Sanjay. *The Career and Legend of Vasco da Gama.* 1998. A probing biography that places Vasco da Gama in the context of Portuguese politics and society.

Notes

1. A. Reid, *Southeast Asia in the Age of Commerce, 1450–1680.* Vol. 1: *The Land Under the Winds* (New Haven, Conn.: Yale University Press, 1988), p. 2.
2. Ibid., pp. 3–20.
3. Ibid., pp. 146–155.
4. A. Reid, *Southeast Asia in the Age of Commerce, 1450–1680.* Vol. 2: *Expansion and Crisis* (New Haven, Conn.: Yale University Press, 1993), pp. 133–192; the quotation is on p. 151.
5. Ibid., Chaps. 1 and 2, pp. 1–131.
6. Quoted in C. M. Cipolla, *Guns, Sails, and Empires: Technological Innovation and the Early Phases of European Expansion, 1400–1700* (New York: Minerva Press, 1965), p. 132.
7. Quoted in F. H. Littell, *The Macmillan Atlas: History of Christianity* (New York: Macmillan, 1976), p. 75.
8. See C. R. Phillips, *Ciudad Real, 1500–1750: Growth, Crisis, and Readjustment in the Spanish Economy* (Cambridge, Mass.: Harvard University Press, 1979), pp. 103–104, 115.
9. Ibid., p. 134.
10. Ibid., p. 19.
11. Scammell, *The World Encompassed: The First European Trade Empires, c. 800–1650* (London: Methuen, 1981), p. 207.
12. Quoted in F. Maddison, "Tradition and Innovation: Columbus' First Voyage and Portuguese Navigation in the Fifteenth Century," in *Circa 1492: Art in the Age of Exploration,* ed. J. A. Levenson (Washington, D.C.: National Gallery of Art, 1991), p. 69.
13. Quoted in R. L. Kagan, "The Spain of Ferdinand and Isabella," in *Circa 1492: Art in the Age of Exploration,* ed. J. A. Levenson (Washington, D.C.: National Gallery of Art, 1991), p. 60.
14. Peter Hulme, *Colonial Encounters: Europe and the Native Caribbean, 1492–1797* (London and New York: Methuan, 1986), pp. 22–31.
15. G. W. Conrad and A. A. Demarest, *Religion and Empire: The Dynamics of Aztec and Inca Expansionism* (New York: Cambridge University Press, 1993), pp. 67–69.
16. A. J. R. Russell-Wood, *The Portuguese Empire, 1415–1808: A World on the Move* (Baltimore: Johns Hopkins University Press, 1998), pp. 58–59.
17. Quoted in A. W. Crosby, *The Columbian Exchange: Biological and Cultural Consequences of 1492* (Westport, Conn.: Greenwood, 1972), p. 39.
18. Ibid., pp. 35–59.
19. Quoted in C. Gibson, ed., *The Black Legend: Anti-Spanish Attitudes in the Old World and the New* (New York: Knopf, 1971), pp. 74–75.
20. Quoted in L. B. Rout, Jr., *The African Experience in Spanish America* (New York: Cambridge University Press, 1976), p. 23.
21. C. Verlinden, *The Beginnings of Modern Colonization,* trans. Y. Freccero (Ithaca, N.Y.: Cornell University Press, 1970), pp. 5–6, 80–97.
22. This section leans heavily on D. B. Davis, *Slavery and Human Progress* (New York: Oxford University Press, 1984), pp. 54–62; the quotation is on p. 58.
23. Herbert S. Klein, "Profits and the Causes of Mortality," in David Northrup, ed., *The Atlantic Slave Trade* (Lexington, Mass.: D. C. Heath and Co., 1994), p. 116.
24. Malcolm Cowley and Daniel P. Mannix, "The Middle Passage," in David Northrup, ed., *The Atlantic Slave Trade* (Lexington, Mass.: D. C. Heath and Co., 1994), p. 101.
25. Parry, *The Age of Reconnaissance* (Berkeley: University of California Press, 1981), Chaps. 12, 14, and 15.
26. Arthur Henderson Smith, *Village Life in China: A Study in Sociology* (New York: F.H. Revell Co., 1899), p. 49.
27. Quoted in S. Neill, *A History of Christian Missions* (New York: Penguin Books, 1977), p. 163.
28. Quoted in C. M. Cipolla, *Clocks and Culture: 1300–1700* (New York: W. W. Norton, 1978), p. 86.
29. J. Gernet, *A History of Chinese Civilization* (New York: Cambridge University Press, 1982), p. 458.
30. Quoted in A. J. Andrea and J. H. Overfield, *The Human Record,* vol. 1 (Boston: Houghton Mifflin, 1990), pp. 406–407.
31. Quoted ibid., p. 408.
32. Quoted in D. O. Flynn and A. Giráldez, "Born with a 'Silver Spoon': The Origin of World Trade in 1571," *Journal of World History* 6 (Fall 1985): 203.
33. Ibid., pp. 217–218.

Listening to the
PAST

Columbus Describes His First Voyage

On his return voyage to Spain in January 1493, Christopher Columbus composed a letter intended for wide circulation and had copies of it sent ahead to Isabella and Ferdinand and others when the ship docked at Lisbon. Because the letter sums up Columbus's understanding of his achievements, it is considered the most important document of his first voyage.

Since I know that you will be pleased at the great success with which the Lord has crowned my voyage, I write to inform you how in thirty-three days I crossed from the Canary Islands to the Indies, with the fleet which our most illustrious sovereigns gave me. I found very many islands with large populations and took possession of them all for their Highnesses; this I did by proclamation and unfurled the royal standard. No opposition was offered.

I named the first island that I found "San Salvador," in honour of our Lord and Saviour who has granted me this miracle. . . . When I reached Cuba, I followed its north coast westwards, and found it so extensive that I thought this must be the mainland, the province of Cathay.* . . . From there I saw another island eighteen leagues eastwards which I then named "Hispaniola."† . . .

Hispaniola is a wonder. The mountains and hills, the plains and meadow lands are both fertile and beautiful. They are most suitable for planting crops and for raising cattle of all kinds, and there are good sites for building towns and villages. The harbours are incredibly fine and there are many great rivers with broad

channels and the majority contain gold.‡ The trees, fruits and plants are very different from those of Cuba. In Hispaniola there are many spices and large mines of gold and other metals.§ . . .

The inhabitants of this island, and all the rest that I discovered or heard of, go naked, as their mothers bore them, men and women alike. A few of the women, however, cover a single place with a leaf of a plant or piece of cotton which they weave for the purpose. They have no iron or steel or arms and are not capable of using them, not because they are not strong and well built but because they are amazingly timid. All the weapons they have are canes cut at seeding time, at the end of which they fix a sharpened stick, but they have not the courage to make use of these, for very often when I have sent two or three men to a village to have conversation with them a great number of them have come out. But as soon as they saw my men all fled immediately, a father not even waiting for his son. And this is not because we have harmed any of them; on the contrary, wherever I have gone and been able to have conversation with them, I have given them some of the various things I had, a cloth and other articles, and received nothing in exchange. But they have still remained incurably timid. True, when they have been reassured and lost their fear, they are so ingenuous and so liberal with all their possessions that no one who has not seen them would believe it. If one asks for anything they have they never say no. On the contrary, they offer a share to anyone with demonstrations of heartfelt affection, and they are immediately content with any small thing, valuable or valueless, that is given them. I forbade the men to give them bits of broken crockery, fragments of glass or tags of laces, though if they could get them they fancied them the finest jewels in the world.

I hoped to win them to the love and service of their Highnesses and of the whole Spanish nation and to

---

*Cathay is the old name for China. In the log-book and later in this letter Columbus accepts the native story that Cuba is an island that they can circumnavigate in something more than twenty-one days, yet he insists here and later, during the second voyage, that it is in fact part of the Asiatic mainland.

†Hispaniola is the second largest island of the West Indies; Haiti occupies the western third of the island, the Dominican Republic the rest.

‡This did not prove to be true.

§These statements are also inaccurate.

Columbus's map of Hispaniola. Would this small, vague sketch of Hispaniola (now Haiti and the Dominican Republic) have been of much use to explorers after Columbus? *(Col. Duke of Alba, Madrid/Institut Amatller d'Art Hispanic)*

persuade them to collect and give us of the things which they possessed in abundance and which we needed. They have no religion and are not idolaters; but all believe that power and goodness dwell in the sky and they are firmly convinced that I have come from the sky with these ships and people. In this belief they gave me a good reception everywhere, once they had overcome their fear; and this is not because they are stupid—far from it, they are men of great intelligence, for they navigate all those seas, and give a marvellously good account of everything—but because they have never before seen men clothed or ships like these. . . .

In all these islands the men are seemingly content with one woman, but their chief or king is allowed more than twenty. The women appear to work more than the men and I have not been able to find out if they have private property. As far as I could see whatever a man had was shared among all the rest and this particularly applies to food. . . . In another island, which I am told is larger than Hispaniola, the people have no hair. Here there is a vast quantity of gold, and from here and the other islands I bring Indians as evidence.

In conclusion, to speak only of the results of this very hasty voyage, their Highnesses can see that I will give them as much gold as they require, if they will render me some very slight assistance; also I will give them all the spices and cotton they want. . . . I will also bring them as much aloes as they ask and as many slaves, who will be taken from the idolaters. I believe also that I have found rhubarb and cinnamon and there will be countless other things in addition. . . .

So all Christendom will be delighted that our Redeemer has given victory to our most illustrious King and Queen and their renowned kingdoms, in this great matter. They should hold great celebrations and render solemn thanks to the Holy Trinity with many solemn prayers, for the great triumph which they will have, by the conversion of so many peoples to our holy faith and for the temporal benefits which will follow, for not only Spain, but all Christendom will receive encouragement and profit.

This is a brief account of the facts.
Written in the caravel off the Canary Islands.‖
15 February 1493

At your orders
THE ADMIRAL

Questions for Analysis

1. How did Columbus explain the success of his voyage?

2. What was Columbus's view of the Native Americans he met?

3. Evaluate his statements that the Caribbean islands possessed gold, cotton, and spices.

4. Why did Columbus cling to the idea that he had reached Asia?

Source: J. M. Cohen, ed. and trans., *The Four Voyages of Christopher Columbus* (Penguin Classics, 1958), pp. 115–123. Copyright © J. M. Cohen, 1958. Reproduced by permission of Penguin Books, Ltd.

‖Actually, Columbus was off Santa Maria in the Azores.

Hyacinthe Rigaud: Louis XIV, King of France and Navarre (1701). Louis XIV is surrounded by the symbols of his power: the sword of justice, the scepter of power, and the crown. The vigor and strength of the king's stocking-covered legs contrast with the age and wisdom of his lined face. *(Scala/Art Resource, NY)*

chapter

16 ABSOLUTISM AND CONSTITUTIONALISM IN EUROPE, CA. 1589–1725

Chapter Preview

Seventeenth-Century Crisis and Rebuilding
• What were the common crises and achievements of seventeenth-century European states?

Absolutism in France and Spain
• How and why did Louis XIV of France lead the way in forging the absolute state, and why did Spain experience decline in the same period?

Absolutism in Eastern Europe: Austria, Prussia, and Russia
• How did Austrian, Prussian, and Russian rulers in eastern Europe build absolute monarchies—monarchies that proved even more durable than that of Louis XIV?

Constitutionalism
• How and why did the constitutional state triumph in Holland and England?

The seventeenth century was a period of crisis and transformation in Europe. Agricultural and manufacturing slumps meant that many people struggled to feed themselves and their families. After a long period of growth, population rates stagnated or even fell. Religious and dynastic conflicts led to almost constant war, visiting violence and destruction on ordinary people.

The demands of war reshaped European states. Armies grew larger than they had been since the time of the Roman Empire. To pay for these armies, governments greatly increased taxes. They also created new bureaucracies to collect the taxes and to foster economic activity that might increase state revenue. Despite numerous obstacles, European states succeeded in gathering more power during this period. What one historian described as the long European "struggle for stability" that originated with the Reformation in the early sixteenth century was largely resolved by 1680.[1] Thus at the same time that powerful governments were emerging and evolving in Asia—such as the Qing Dynasty in China, the Tokugawa Shogunate in Japan, and the Mughal Empire in India—European rulers also increased the power of the central state.

Important differences existed, however, in terms of which authority within the state possessed sovereignty—the Crown or privileged groups. Between roughly 1589 and 1715 two basic patterns of government emerged in Europe: absolute monarchy and the constitutional state. Almost all subsequent European governments have been modeled on one of these patterns, which have also influenced greatly the rest of the world in the past three centuries.

SEVENTEENTH-CENTURY CRISIS AND REBUILDING

What were the common crises and achievements of seventeenth-century European states?

Historians often refer to the seventeenth century as an "age of crisis." After the economic and demographic growth of the sixteenth century, Europe faltered into stagnation and retrenchment. This was partially due to climate changes beyond anyone's control, but it also resulted from bitter religious divides, increased governmental pressures, and war. Overburdened peasants and city-dwellers took action to defend themselves, sometimes profiting from elite conflicts to obtain relief. In the long run, however, governments proved increasingly able to impose their will on the populace. This period witnessed a spectacular growth in army size as well as new forms of taxation, government bureaucracies, and increased state sovereignty.

moral economy *A historian's term for an economic perspective in which the needs of a community take precedence over competition and profit.*

Economic and Demographic Crisis

European rural society lived on the edge of subsistence. Because of the crude technology and low crop yield, peasants were constantly threatened by scarcity and famine. In the seventeenth century a period of colder and wetter climate, dubbed by historians as a "little ice age," meant a shorter farming season. A bad harvest created dearth; a series of bad harvests could lead to famine. Recurrent famines significantly reduced the population of early modern Europe. Most people did not die of outright starvation, but rather of diseases brought on by malnutrition and exhaustion. Facilitated by the weakened population, outbreaks of bubonic plague continued in Europe until the 1720s.

Industry also suffered. While the evidence does not permit broad generalizations, it appears that the output of woolen textiles, one of the most important European manufactures, declined sharply in the first half of the seventeenth century. Food prices were high, wages stagnated, and unemployment soared. This economic crisis was not universal: it struck various regions at different times and to different degrees. In the middle decades of the century, Spain, France, Germany, and England all experienced great economic difficulties.

The urban poor and peasants were the hardest hit. When the price of bread rose beyond their capacity to pay, they frequently took action. In towns they invaded bakers' shops to seize bread and resell it at a "just price." In rural areas they attacked convoys taking grain away to the cities. Women often led these actions, since their role as mothers gave them some impunity in authorities' eyes. Historians have labeled this vision of a world in which community needs predominate over competition and profit a **moral economy.**

● **Estonia in the 1660s** The Estonians were conquered by German military nobility in the Middle Ages and reduced to serfdom. The German-speaking nobles ruled the Estonian peasants with an iron hand, and Peter the Great reaffirmed their domination when Russia annexed Estonia (see Map 16.4 on page 476). *(Time Life Pictures/Getty Images)*

The Return of Serfdom in the East

While economic and social hardship were common across Europe, important differences existed between east and west. In the west the demographic losses of the Black Death allowed peasants to escape from serfdom, and a small number of peasants in each village owned both enough land to feed themselves and the livestock and ploughs necessary to work their land. In eastern Europe seventeenth-century peasants had largely lost their ability to own land independently. Unlike those in the west, eastern European peasants had unsuccessfully countered efforts by noble lords to increase their exploitation in the labor shortages following the Black Death. Eastern lords triumphed because they made their kings and princes issue laws that restricted the right of their peasants to move to take advantage of better opportunities elsewhere. In Prussian territories by 1500, the law required that runaway peasants be hunted down and returned to their lords. Moreover, lords steadily took more and more of their peasants' land and arbitrarily imposed heavier and heavier labor obligations. By the early 1500s lords in many territories could command their peasants to work for them without pay for as many as six days a week.

The gradual erosion of the peasantry's economic position was bound up with manipulation of the legal system. The local lord was also the local prosecutor, judge, and jailer. There were no independent royal officials to provide justice or uphold the common law.

Between 1500 and 1650 the consolidation of serfdom in eastern Europe was accompanied by the growth of estate agriculture, particularly in Poland and eastern Germany. As economic expansion and population growth resumed after 1500, eastern lords had powerful economic incentives to increase the production of their estates, and they succeeded in squeezing sizable surpluses out of the impoverished peasants. These surpluses were sold to foreign merchants, who exported them to the growing cities of wealthier western Europe.

Finally, with the approval of weak kings, the landlords systematically undermined the medieval privileges of the towns and the power of the urban classes. For example, eastern towns also lost their medieval right of refuge and were compelled to return runaways to their lords. The population of the towns and the urban middle classes declined greatly. This development both reflected and promoted the supremacy of noble landlords in most of eastern Europe in the sixteenth century.

The Thirty Years' War

In the first half of the seventeenth century, the fragile balance of life was violently upturned by the ravages of the Thirty Years' War (1618–1648). The Holy Roman Empire was a confederation of hundreds of principalities, independent cities, duchies, and other polities loosely united under an elected emperor. The uneasy truce between Catholics and Protestants created by the Peace of Augsburg of 1555 deteriorated as the faiths of various

Chronology

ca. 1400–1650	Re-emergence of serfdom in eastern Europe
1533–1584	Reign of Ivan the Terrible in Russia
1589–1610	Reign of Henry IV in France
1598–1613	"Time of Troubles" in Russia
1602	Dutch East India Company founded
1620–1740	Growth of absolutism in Austria and Prussia
1642–1649	English civil war, which ends with execution of Charles I
1643–1715	Reign of Louis XIV in France
1652	Nikon reforms Russian Orthodox Church
1653–1658	Military rule in England under Oliver Cromwell
1660	Restoration of English monarchy under Charles II
1665–1683	Jean-Baptiste Colbert applies mercantilism to France
1670	Charles II agrees to re-Catholicize England in secret agreement with Louis XIV
1670–1671	Cossack revolt led by Stenka Razin
ca. 1680–1750	Construction of baroque palaces
1682–1725	Reign of Peter the Great in Russia
1683–1718	Habsburgs defend Vienna; win war with Ottoman Turks
1685	Edict of Nantes revoked
1688–1689	Glorious Revolution in England
1701–1713	War of the Spanish Succession

Labels on main map:

NORWAY
SWEDEN
FINLAND
SCOTLAND
Edinburgh
North Sea
ESTONIA
LIVONIA
RUSSIA
IRELAND
Dublin
ENGLAND
Baltic Sea
See Inset
DENMARK
Copenhagen
Vilna
London
UNITED PROVINCES
Amsterdam
Danzig
PRUSSIA
POLAND-LITHUANIA
Magdeburg
Berlin
Vistula R.
Warsaw
ATLANTIC OCEAN
Antwerp
Essen
Cologne
SPANISH NETHERLANDS
Rhine R.
SAXONY
SILESIA
Dnieper R.
Paris
Seine R.
LOWER PALATINATE
UPPER PALATINATE
Prague
BOHEMIA
MORAVIA
Nantes
Metz
Loire R.
BAVARIA
Augsburg
Vienna
AUSTRIA
FRANCE
FRANCHE-COMTÉ
Salzburg
SALZBURG
STYRIA
Buda
Pest
MOLDAVIA
JEDISAN
Zurich
SWITZERLAND
TYROL
Trent
CARINTHIA
CARNIOLA
HUNGARY
TRANSYLVANIA
BESSARABIA
Geneva
SAVOY
Rhône R.
PIEDMONT
MILAN
REPUBLIC OF VENICE
Venice
CROATIA
SLAVONIA
Belgrade
WALLACHIA
Danube R.
Black Sea
GENOA
BOSNIA
SERBIA
Ebro R.
SPAIN
Tagus R.
TUSCANY
PAPAL STATES
Corsica (to Genoa)
Adriatic Sea
HERZEGOVINA
MONTENEGRO
BULGARIA
OTTOMAN EMPIRE
Rome
Sardinia
NAPLES
Naples
Constantinople
Balearic Is.
Aegean Sea
Palermo
Sicily
Mediterranean Sea
GREECE
Athens
Crete (to Rep. Of Venice)

Inset map (Denmark):

North Sea
SWEDEN
JUTLAND
Copenhagen
DENMARK
55°N
Baltic Sea
SCHLESWIG
WISMAR
POMERANIA
Lübeck
Hamburg
BREMEN
MECKLENBURG
VERDEN
Elbe R.
BRANDENBURG
10°E
15°E

Legend:

Austrian Habsburg lands
Spanish Habsburg lands
Other German states
Swedish lands by 1648
Ottoman Empire and tributary states
Boundary of the Holy Roman Empire

0   150   300 Km.
0   150   300 Mi.

MAP 16.1 **Europe After the Thirty Years' War** Which country emerged from the Thirty Years' War as the strongest European power? What dynastic house was that country's major rival in the early modern period?

areas shifted. Lutheran princes felt compelled to form the **Protestant Union** (1608), and Catholics retaliated with the Catholic League (1609). Each alliance was determined that the other should make no religious or territorial advance. Dynastic interests were also involved; the Spanish Habsburgs strongly supported the goals of their Austrian relatives—the unity of the empire and the preservation of Catholicism within it.

The war is traditionally divided into four phases. The first, or Bohemian, phase (1618–1625) was characterized by civil war in Bohemia between the Catholic League and the Protestant Union. In 1620 Catholic forces defeated Protestants at the Battle of the White Mountain. The second, or Danish, phase of the war (1625–1629)—so called because of the leadership of the Protestant king Christian IV of Denmark (r. 1588–1648)—witnessed additional Catholic victories. The Catholic imperial army led by Albert of Wallenstein swept through Silesia, north to the Baltic, and east into Pomerania, scoring smashing victories. Habsburg power peaked in 1629. The emperor issued the Edict of Restitution, whereby all Catholic properties lost to Protestantism since 1552 were restored, and only Catholics and Lutherans were allowed to practice their faiths.

The third, or Swedish, phase of the war (1630–1635) began with the arrival in Germany of the Swedish king Gustavus Adolphus (r. 1594–1632). The ablest administrator of his day and a devout Lutheran, he intervened to support the empire's Protestants. The French chief minister, Cardinal Richelieu, subsidized the Swedes, hoping to weaken Habsburg power in Europe. Gustavus Adolphus won two important battles but was fatally wounded in combat. The final, or French, phase of the war (1635–1648) was prompted by Richelieu's concern that the Habsburgs would rebound after the death of Gustavus Adolphus. Richelieu declared war on Spain and sent military as well as financial assistance. Finally, in October 1648 peace was achieved.

The 1648 **Peace of Westphalia** that ended the Thirty Years' War marked a turning point in European history. Conflicts fought over religious faith ended. The treaties recognized the independent authority of more than three hundred German princes (see Map 16.1), reconfirming the emperor's severely limited authority. The Augsburg agreement of 1555 became permanent, adding Calvinism to Catholicism and Lutheranism as legally permissible creeds. The north German states remained Protestant; the south German states, Catholic.

The Thirty Years' War was probably the most destructive event for the central European economy and society prior to the twentieth century. Perhaps one-third of urban residents and two-fifths of the rural population died, leaving entire areas depopulated. Trade in southern German cities, such as Augsburg, was virtually destroyed. Agricultural areas suffered catastrophically. Many small farmers lost their land, allowing nobles to enlarge their estates and consolidate their control.[2]

Seventeenth-Century State-Building: Common Obstacles and Achievements

In this context of economic and demographic depression, monarchs began to make new demands on their people. Traditionally, historians have distinguished sharply between the "absolutist" governments of France, Spain, Central Europe, and Russia and the constitutional monarchies of England and the Dutch Republic. Whereas absolutist monarchs gathered all power under their personal control, constitutional monarchs were obliged to respect laws passed by representative institutions. More recently, historians have emphasized commonalities among these powers. Despite their political differences, absolutist and constitutional states shared common projects of protecting and expanding their frontiers, raising new taxes, and consolidating central control.

Rulers who wished to increase their authority encountered formidable obstacles. Some were purely material. Without paved roads, telephones, or other modern

Protestant Union *An alliance formed by Lutheran princes in the Holy Roman Empire that eventually led to the Thirty Years' War.*

Peace of Westphalia *The name of a series of treaties that concluded the Thirty Years' War in 1648.*

technology, it took weeks to convey orders from the central government to the provinces. Rulers also suffered from a lack of information about their realms, making it impossible to police and tax the population effectively. Local power structures presented another serious obstacle. Nobles, the church, the legislative corps, town councils, guilds, and other bodies held legal privileges, which could not easily be rescinded. In some kingdoms, many people spoke a language different from the Crown's, further diminishing their willingness to obey its commands.

Nonetheless, over the course of the seventeenth century both absolutist and constitutional governments achieved new levels of central control. This increased authority focused in four areas in particular: greater taxation, growth in armed forces, larger and more efficient bureaucracies, and the increased ability to compel obedience from their subjects. Over time, centralized power added up to something close to **sovereignty**. A state may be termed sovereign when it possesses a monopoly over the instruments of justice and the use of force within clearly defined boundaries. In a sovereign state, no system of courts, such as ecclesiastical tribunals, competes with state courts in the dispensation of justice; and private armies, such as those of feudal lords, present no threat to central authority. While seventeenth-century states did not acquire total sovereignty, they made important strides toward that goal.

sovereignty *The exercise of complete and autonomous authority over a political body. The rulers of early modern states strove to achieve sovereignty, in competition with traditional power-holders like noble estates, the church, and town councils.*

ABSOLUTISM IN FRANCE AND SPAIN

How and why did Louis XIV of France lead the way in forging the absolute state, and why did Spain experience decline in the same period?

In the Middle Ages jurists held that as a consequence of monarchs' coronation and anointment with sacred oil, they ruled "by the grace of God." Law was given by God; kings discovered or "found" the law and acknowledged that they must respect and obey it. In the absolutist state, kings amplified these claims, asserting that, as they were chosen by God, they were responsible to God alone. They claimed exclusive power to make and enforce laws, denying any other institution or group the authority to check their power. Historians have been debating since his reign how successfully Louis XIV and other absolutist monarchs realized these claims.

The Foundations of Absolutism: Henry IV, Sully, and Richelieu

Louis XIV's absolutism had long roots. In 1589 his grandfather Henry IV (r. 1589–1610), the founder of the Bourbon dynasty, acquired a devastated country. Civil wars between Protestants and Catholics had wracked France since 1561. Poor harvests had reduced peasants to starvation, and commercial activity had declined drastically. "Henri le Grand" (Henry the Great), as the king was called, promised "a chicken in every pot" and inaugurated a remarkable recovery.

He did so by keeping France at peace during most of his reign. Although he had converted to Catholicism, he issued the Edict of Nantes, allowing Protestants the right to worship in 150 traditionally Protestant towns throughout France. He sharply lowered taxes and instead charged royal officials an annual fee to guarantee heredity in their offices. He also improved the infrastructure of the country, building new roads and canals and repairing the ravages of years of civil war. Yet despite his efforts at peace, Henry was murdered in 1610 by François Ravaillac, a Catholic zealot, setting off a national crisis.

After the death of Henry IV his wife, the queen-regent Marie de' Medici, headed the government for the child-king Louis XIII (r. 1610–1643). In 1628 Armand Jean du Plessis—Cardinal Richelieu (1585–1642)—became first minister of the French crown. Richelieu's maneuvers allowed the monarchy to maintain power within Europe and within its own borders despite the turmoil of the Thirty Years' War.

Cardinal Richelieu's political genius is best reflected in the administrative system he established to strengthen royal control. He extended the use of **intendants,** commissioners for each of France's thirty-two districts who were appointed directly by the monarch, to whom they were solely responsible. They recruited men for the army, supervised the collection of taxes, presided over the administration of local law, checked up on the local nobility, and regulated economic activities in their districts. As the intendants' power increased under Richelieu, so did the power of the centralized French state.

Under Richelieu, the French monarchy also acted to repress Protestantism. Louis personally supervised the siege of La Rochelle, fourth largest of the French Atlantic ports and a major commercial center with strong ties to Protestant Holland and England. After the city fell in October 1628, its municipal government was suppressed. Protestants retained the right of public worship, but the Catholic liturgy was restored. The fall of La Rochelle was one step in the removal of Protestantism as a strong force in French life.

Richelieu did not aim to wipe out Protestantism in the rest of Europe, however. His main foreign policy goal was to destroy the Catholic Habsburgs' grip on territories that surrounded France. Consequently, Richelieu supported Habsburg enemies, including Protestants. In 1631 he signed a treaty with the Lutheran king Gustavus Adolphus promising French support against the Habsburgs in the Thirty Years' War. For the French cardinal, interests of state outweighed religious considerations.

Richelieu's successor as chief minister for the next boy-king, Louis XIV, was Cardinal Jules Mazarin (1602–1661). Along with the regent, Queen Mother Anne of Austria, Mazarin continued Richelieu's centralizing policies. His struggle to increase royal revenues to meet the costs of war led to the uprisings of 1648–1653 known as the **Fronde.** A *frondeur* was originally a street urchin who threw mud at the passing carriages of the rich, but the word came to be applied to the many individuals and groups who opposed the policies of the government. The most influential of these groups were the robe nobility—court judges—and the sword nobility—the aristocracy. During the first of several riots, the queen mother fled Paris with Louis XIV. As the rebellion continued, civil order broke down completely. In 1651 Anne's regency ended with the declaration of Louis as king in his own right. Much of the rebellion died away, and its leaders came to terms with the government.

The conflicts of the Fronde had significant results for the future. The twin evils of noble factionalism and popular riots left the French wishing for peace and for a strong monarch to reimpose order. This was the legacy that Louis XIV inherited when he assumed personal rule in 1661. Humiliated by his flight from Paris, he was determined to avoid any recurrence of rebellion.

Louis XIV and Absolutism

In the reign of Louis XIV (r. 1643–1715), the longest in European history, the French monarchy reached the peak of absolutist development. In the magnificence of his court and the brilliance of the culture that he presided over, the "Sun King" dominated his age. Religion, Anne, and Mazarin all taught Louis the doctrine of the **divine right of kings:** God had established kings as his rulers on earth, and they were answerable ultimately to God alone. Kings were divinely anointed and shared in the sacred nature of divinity; however, they could not simply do as they pleased. They had to obey God's laws and rule for the good of the people.

Louis worked very hard at the business of governing. He ruled his realm through several councils of state and insisted on taking a personal role in many of the councils' decisions. He selected councilors from the recently ennobled or the upper middle

intendants *Commissioners for each of France's thirty-two administrative districts. Appointed by and answering directly to the monarch, they were key elements in Richelieu's plan to centralize the French state.*

Fronde *A series of violent uprisings during the minority of Louis XIV triggered by oppressive taxation and growing royal authority; the last attempt of the French nobility to resist the king by arms.*

divine right of kings *The doctrine that kings were established in their rule by God and were accountable only to God. In such a system, the will of God and that of the king become inseparable. Characteristic of absolute monarchies.*

class because he wanted "people to know by the rank of the men who served him that he had no intention of sharing power with them."[3]

Despite increasing financial problems, Louis never called a meeting of the Estates General. The nobility therefore had no means of united expression or action. Nor did Louis have a first minister; he kept himself free from worry about the inordinate power of a Richelieu.

In 1682 Louis moved his court to the newly renovated palace at Versailles, requiring all great nobles to spend part of the year in attendance on him there. Since the king controlled the distribution of offices, pensions, and other benefits, nobles vied to win his favor through elaborate rituals of court etiquette. (See the feature "Listening to the Past: The Court at Versailles" on pages 490–491.) The grandeur of the palace and its gardens broadcast the king's glory to visiting dignitaries, and Versailles was soon copied by would-be absolutist monarchs across Europe.

Although personally tolerant, Louis hated division within the realm and insisted that religious unity was essential to his royal dignity and to the security of the state. He thus pursued the policy of Protestant repression launched by Richelieu. In 1685 Louis revoked the Edict of Nantes, by which his grandfather Henry IV had granted liberty of conscience to French Huguenots. The new law ordered the destruction of Huguenot churches, the closing of schools, the Catholic baptism of Huguenots, and the exile of Huguenot pastors who refused to renounce their faith. The result was the departure of some of his most loyal and industrially skilled subjects.

Despite his claims to absolute authority, there were multiple constraints on Louis's power. In practice he governed through collaboration with nobles, who maintained tremendous prestige and authority in their ancestral lands. He achieved new centralized authority by reaffirming the traditional privileges of the nobility, while largely excluding them from active involvement in government.

Financial and Economic Management Under Louis XIV: Colbert

France's ability to build armies and fight wars depended on a strong economy. Fortunately for Louis, his controller general, Jean-Baptiste Colbert (1619–1683), proved himself a financial genius. His central principle was that the wealth and the economy of France should serve the state. To this end he rigorously applied mercantilist policies to France.

mercantilism *A system of economic regulations aimed at increasing the power of the state.*

Mercantilism is a collection of governmental policies for the regulation of economic activities by and for the state. In seventeenth- and eighteenth-century economic theory, a nation's international power was thought to be based on its wealth, specifically its gold supply. To accumulate gold, a country always had to sell more goods abroad than it bought. Colbert thus insisted that France should be self-sufficient, able to produce within its borders everything French subjects needed.

Colbert supported old industries and created new ones, focusing especially on textiles, the most important sector of the economy. Colbert enacted new production regulations, created guilds to boost quality standards, and encouraged foreign craftsmen to immigrate to France. To encourage the purchase of French goods, he abolished many domestic tariffs and raised tariffs on foreign products. In 1664 Colbert founded the Company of the East Indies with (unfulfilled) hopes of competing with the Dutch for Asian trade.

Colbert also hoped to make Canada—rich in untapped minerals and some of the best agricultural land in the world—part of a vast French empire. He sent four thousand peasants from western France to Quebec, whose capital was founded in 1608 under Henry IV. Subsequently, the Jesuit Jacques Marquette and the merchant Louis Joliet sailed down the Mississippi River and claimed possession of the land on both sides as far south as present-day Arkansas. In 1684 French explorers continued

● **Rubens: The Death of Henri IV and the Proclamation of the Regency (1622–1625)**   In 1622 the regent Marie de' Medici commissioned Peter Paul Rubens to paint a cycle of paintings depicting her life. This one portrays two distinct moments: the assassination of Henry IV (shown on the left ascending to Heaven), and Marie's subsequent proclamation as regent. The other twenty-three canvasses in the cycle similarly glorify Marie, a tricky undertaking given her unhappy marriage to Henry IV and her tumultuous relationship with her son Louis XIII, who removed her from the regency in 1617. As in this image, Rubens frequently resorted to allegory and classical imagery to elevate the events of Marie's life. *(Réunion des Musées Nationaux/Art Resource, NY)*

down the Mississippi to its mouth and claimed vast territories and the rich delta for Louis XIV. The area was called, naturally, "Louisiana."

During Colbert's tenure as controller general, Louis was able to pursue his goals without massive tax increases and without creating a stream of new offices. The constant pressure of warfare after Colbert's death, however, undid many of his economic achievements.

Louis XIV's Wars

Louis XIV wrote that "the character of a conqueror is regarded as the noblest and highest of titles." In pursuit of the title of conqueror, he kept France at war for thirty-three of the fifty-four years of his personal rule. François le Tellier (later, marquis de Louvois), Louis's secretary of state for war, equaled Colbert's achievements in the economic realm. Louvois created a professional army in which the French state, rather than private nobles, employed the soldiers. The French army grew in size from roughly 125,000 men in the Thirty Years' War (1630–1648) to 250,000 during the Dutch War (1672–1678) and 340,000 during the War of the League of Augsburg (1688–1697).[4] Uniforms and weapons were standardized and a rational system of training and promotion devised. Many historians believe that the new loyalty, professionalism, and size of the French army is the best case for the success of absolutism under Louis XIV. Whatever his compromises elsewhere, the French monarch had firm control of his armed forces. As in so many other matters, Louis's model was followed across Europe.

Louis's goal was to expand France to what he considered its "natural" borders and to secure those lands from any threat of outside invasion. His armies managed to expand French borders to include important commercial centers in the Spanish Netherlands and Flanders, as well as all of Franche-Comté between 1667 and 1678. In 1681 Louis seized the city of Strasbourg, and three years later he sent his armies into the province of Lorraine. At that moment the king seemed invincible. In fact, Louis had reached the limit of his expansion. The wars of the 1680s and 1690s brought no additional territories but placed unbearable strains on French resources. Colbert's successors resorted to desperate measures to finance these wars, including devaluation of the currency and new taxes.

Louis's last war was endured by a French people suffering high taxes, crop failure, and widespread malnutrition and death. In 1700 the childless Spanish king Charles II (r. 1665–1700) died, opening a struggle for control of Spain and its colonies. His will bequeathed the Spanish crown and its empire to Philip of Anjou, Louis XIV's grandson (Louis's wife, Maria-Theresa, had been Charles's sister). This testament violated a prior treaty by which the European powers had agreed to divide the Spanish possessions between the king of France and the Holy Roman emperor, both brothers-in-law of Charles II. Claiming that he was following both Spanish and French interests, Louis broke with the treaty and accepted the will.

Peace of Utrecht *A series of treaties, from 1713 to 1715, that ended the War of the Spanish Succession, ended French expansion in Europe, and marked the rise of the British Empire.*

In 1701 the English, Dutch, Austrians, and Prussians formed the Grand Alliance against Louis XIV. War dragged on until 1713. The **Peace of Utrecht,** which ended the war, applied the principle of partition. Louis's grandson Philip remained the first Bourbon king of Spain on the understanding that the French and Spanish crowns would never be united. France surrendered Newfoundland, Nova Scotia, and the Hudson Bay territory to England, which also acquired Gibraltar, Minorca, and control of the African slave trade from Spain (see Map 16.2).

The Peace of Utrecht represented the balance-of-power principle in operation, setting limits on the extent to which any one power—in this case, France—could expand. It also marked the end of French expansion. Thirty-five years of war had brought rights to all of Alsace and some commercial centers in the north. But at what price? In 1714 an exhausted France hovered on the brink of bankruptcy. It is no wonder that when Louis XIV died on September 1, 1715, many subjects felt as much relief as they did sorrow.

The Decline of Absolutist Spain in the Seventeenth Century

As French power was growing, Spanish power was diminishing. By the early seventeenth century the seeds of disaster were sprouting. Between 1610 and 1650 Spanish trade with the colonies fell 60 percent, due to competition from local industries in the colonies and from Dutch and English traders. At the same time, the native Indians and African slaves who toiled in the South American silver mines suffered frightful epidemics of disease. Ultimately, the lodes started to run dry, and the quantity of metal produced steadily declined after 1620.

In Madrid, however, royal expenditures constantly exceeded income. To meet mountainous state debt and declining revenues, the Crown repeatedly devalued the coinage and declared bankruptcy. Given the frequency of state bankruptcies, national credit plummeted.

Seventeenth-century Spain was the victim of its past. It could not forget the grandeur of the sixteenth century and respond to changing circumstances. Although Spain lacked the finances to fight expensive wars, the imperial tradition demanded the revival of war with the Dutch at the expiration of a twelve-year truce in 1622 and a long war with France over Mantua (1628–1659). Spain thus became embroiled in the Thirty Years' War. These conflicts, on top of an empty treasury, brought disaster.

In 1640 Spain faced serious revolts in Catalonia and Portugal. The Portuguese succeeded in regaining independence from Habsburg rule under their new king, John IV (r. 1640–1656). In 1643 the French inflicted a crushing defeat on a Spanish army at Rocroi in what is now Belgium. By the Treaty of the Pyrenees of 1659, which ended

● **Peeter Snayers: Spanish Troops (detail)**   The long wars that Spain fought over Dutch independence, in support of Habsburg interests in Germany, and against France left the country militarily exhausted and financially drained by the mid-1600s. Here Spanish troops—thin, emaciated, and probably unpaid—straggle away from battle. *(Museo Nacional del Prado, Madrid. Photo: José Baztan y Alberto Otero)*

the French-Spanish conflict, Spain was compelled to surrender extensive territories to France.

Spain's decline can also be traced to a failure to invest in productive enterprises. In contrast to the other countries of western Europe, Spain had only a tiny middle class. Public opinion condemned moneymaking as vulgar and undignified. Thousands entered economically unproductive professions: there were said to be nine thousand monasteries in the province of Castile alone. Some three hundred thousand people who had once been Muslims were expelled by Philip III in 1609, significantly reducing the pool of skilled workers and merchants. Those working in the textile industry were forced out of business when the flood of gold and silver produced severe inflation, pushing their production costs to the point where they could not compete in colonial and international markets.[5]

Spanish aristocrats, attempting to maintain an extravagant lifestyle they could no longer afford, increased the rents on their estates. High rents and heavy taxes in turn drove the peasants from the land. Agricultural production suffered, and peasants departed for the large cities, where they swelled the ranks of unemployed beggars. Spain also ignored new scientific methods because they came from heretical nations, Holland and England.

ABSOLUTISM IN EASTERN EUROPE: AUSTRIA, PRUSSIA, AND RUSSIA

How did Austrian, Prussian, and Russian rulers in eastern Europe build absolute monarchies—monarchies that proved even more durable than that of Louis XIV?

The rulers of eastern Europe also labored to build strong absolutist states in the seventeenth century. But they built on social and economic foundations different from those in western Europe, namely serfdom and the strong nobility who benefited from it.

Despite the strength of the nobility, strong kings did begin to emerge in many eastern European lands in the course of the seventeenth century. There were endless

MAP 16.2 **Europe in 1715** The series of treaties commonly called the Peace of Utrecht (April 1713–November 1715) ended the War of the Spanish Succession and redrew the map of Europe. A French Bourbon king succeeded to the Spanish throne. France surrendered to Austria the Spanish Netherlands (later Belgium), then in French hands, and France recognized the Hohenzollern rulers of Prussia. Spain ceded Gibraltar to Great Britain, for which it has been a strategic naval station ever since. Spain also granted to Britain the *asiento*, the contract for supplying African slaves to America.

Legend:
- French Bourbon lands
- Spanish Bourbon lands
- Austrian Habsburg lands
- Prussian lands
- Great Britain
- Boundary of the Holy Roman Empire
- Russian Empire
- Russian gains, by 1725
- Ottoman Empire, 1722

RUSSIAN EMPIRE

Moscow

Smolensk

Kiev

UKRAINE

St. Petersburg

INGRIA

ESTONIA

LIVONIA

Riga

LITHUANIA

POLAND

Warsaw

EAST PRUSSIA

BRANDENBURG-PRUSSIA

Berlin

SILESIA

SAXONY

BOHEMIA

Vistula R.

Oder R.

Don R.

Dnieper R.

Dniester R.

CRIMEA

Black Sea

MOLDAVIA

WALLACHIA

TRANSYLVANIA

HUNGARY

Pest
Buda

Danube R.

BULGARIA

SERBIA

Belgrade

BOSNIA

HERZEGOVINA

MONTENEGRO

ALBANIA

Constantinople

OTTOMAN EMPIRE

Aegean Sea

GREECE

N O R W A Y

Oslo

S W E D E N

KINGDOM OF DENMARK

DENMARK

Baltic Sea

North Sea

HANOVER

UNITED NETHERLANDS

Utrecht

HOLY ROMAN EMPIRE

PALATINATE

LORRAINE

Strasbourg

Rhine R.

BAVARIA

AUSTRIA

Vienna

CROATIA

SLAVONIA

REPUBLIC OF VENICE

Adriatic Sea

SWITZERLAND

SAVOY

MILAN

MODENA

GENOA

Po R.

TUSCANY

PAPAL STATES

Rome

KINGDOM OF NAPLES

Naples

Sicily (Savoy)

Sardinia (Austria)

Corsica (Genoa)

Mediterranean Sea

GREAT BRITAIN

SCOTLAND

Edinburgh

ENGLAND

London

Thames R.

IRELAND

Dublin

North Sea

FRANCE

Paris

Seine R.

Loire R.

Rhône R.

Garonne R.

Toulouse

Marseilles

CATALONIA

Minorca (Gr. Br.)

Balearic Is.

Ebro R.

SPAIN

Madrid

Duero R.

Tagus R.

GIBRALTAR (Gr. Br.)

PORTUGAL

Lisbon

ATLANTIC OCEAN

300 Mi.
300 Km.
150
150
0

N

wars, and in this atmosphere of continuous military emergency monarchs found ways to reduce the political power of the landlord nobility. Cautiously leaving the nobles as unchallenged masters of their peasants, eastern monarchs gradually monopolized political power.

There were important variations on the absolutist theme in eastern Europe. The royal absolutism created in Prussia was stronger and more effective than that established in Austria. As for Russia, it developed its own form of absolutism, which was quite different from that of France or even Prussia.

The Austrian Habsburgs

Like all of central Europe, the Habsburgs emerged from the Thirty Years' War impoverished and exhausted. Their efforts to destroy Protestantism in the German lands and to turn the weak Holy Roman Empire into a real state had failed. Although the Habsburgs remained the hereditary emperors, real power lay in the hands of a bewildering variety of separate political jurisdictions. Defeat in central Europe encouraged the Habsburgs to turn away from a quest for imperial dominance and to focus inward and eastward in an attempt to unify their diverse holdings. If they could not impose Catholicism in the empire, at least they could do so in their own domains.

Habsburg victory over Bohemia during the Thirty Years' War was an important step in this direction. Ferdinand II (r. 1619–1637) drastically reduced the power of the **Bohemian Estates,** the largely Protestant representative assembly. He also confiscated the landholdings of Protestant nobles and gave them to loyal Catholic nobles and to the foreign aristocratic mercenaries who led his armies. After 1650 a large portion of the Bohemian nobility was of recent origin and owed everything to the Habsburgs.

Bohemian Estates   *The largely Protestant representative body of the different estates in Bohemia. Significantly reduced in power by Ferdinand II.*

With the help of this new nobility, the Habsburgs established direct rule over Bohemia. The condition of the enserfed peasantry worsened substantially: three days per week of unpaid labor—the *robot*—became the norm. Protestantism was also stamped out. The reorganization of Bohemia was a giant step toward creating absolutist rule.

Ferdinand III (r. 1637–1657) continued to build state power. He centralized the government in the hereditary German-speaking provinces, which formed the core Habsburg holdings. For the first time, a permanent standing army was ready to put down any internal opposition.

The Habsburg monarchy then turned east toward the plains of Hungary, which had been divided between the Ottomans and the Habsburgs in the early sixteenth century. Between 1683 and 1699 the Habsburgs pushed the Ottomans from most of Hungary and Transylvania. The recovery of all the former kingdom of Hungary was completed in 1718.

The Hungarian nobility, despite its reduced strength, effectively thwarted the full development of Habsburg absolutism. Throughout the seventeenth century Hungarian nobles rose in revolt against attempts to impose absolute rule. They never triumphed decisively, but neither were they crushed the way the nobility in Bohemia had been in 1620. In 1703, with the Habsburgs bogged down in the War of the Spanish Succession (see page 470), the Hungarians rose in one last patriotic rebellion under Prince Francis Rákóczy.

Rákóczy and his forces were eventually defeated, but the Habsburgs agreed to restore many of the traditional privileges of the aristocracy in return for Hungarian acceptance of hereditary Habsburg rule. Thus Hungary, unlike Austria and Bohemia, was never fully integrated into a centralized, absolute Habsburg state.

Despite checks on their ambitions in Hungary, the Habsburgs made significant achievements in state-building elsewhere by forging consensus with the church and the nobility. A sense of common identity and loyalty to the monarchy grew among elites in Habsburg lands, even to a certain extent in Hungary. German became the language of the common culture, and zealous Catholicism helped fuse a collective identity. Vienna became the political and cultural center of the empire. By 1700 it was a thriving city with a population of one hundred thousand, with its own version of Versailles, the royal palace of Schönbrunn.

Prussia in the Seventeenth Century

In the fifteenth and sixteenth centuries, the Hohenzollern family had ruled parts of eastern Germany as the imperial electors of Brandenburg and the dukes of Prussia, but they had little real power. Although the **elector of Brandenburg** enjoyed the right to help choose the Holy Roman emperor, nothing would suggest that the Hohenzollern territories would come to play an important role in European affairs.

When he came to power in 1640, the twenty-year-old Frederick William, later known as the "Great Elector," was determined to unify his three provinces and enlarge them by diplomacy and war. These provinces were Brandenburg; Prussia, inherited in 1618; and scattered holdings along the Rhine, inherited in 1614 (see Map 16.3). Each was inhabited by German-speakers, but each had its own estates. Although the estates had not met regularly during the chaotic Thirty Years' War, taxes could not be levied without their consent. The estates of Brandenburg and Prussia were dominated by the nobility and the landowning classes, known as the **Junkers.**

elector of Brandenburg *One of the electors of the Holy Roman Empire, hereditarily held by the Hohenzollern family. Frederick William was able to use and expand the office, ultimately resulting in the consolidation of the Prussian state.*

Junkers *The nobility of Brandenburg and Prussia. Reluctant allies of Frederick William in his consolidation of the Prussian state.*

MAP 16.3 **The Growth of Austria and Brandenburg-Prussia to 1748** Austria expanded to the southwest into Hungary and Transylvania at the expense of the Ottoman Empire. It was unable to hold the rich German province of Silesia, however, which was conquered by Brandenburg-Prussia.

Frederick William profited from ongoing European war and the threat of Tatar invasion to argue for the need for a permanent standing army. In 1660 he persuaded Junkers in the estates to accept taxation without consent in order to fund an army. They agreed to do so in exchange for reconfirmation of their own privileges, including authority over the serfs. Opposition from the towns was crushed ruthlessly.

Thereafter, the estates' power declined rapidly, for the Great Elector had both financial independence and superior force. State revenue tripled during his reign, and the army expanded drastically. In 1688 a population of one million supported a peacetime standing army of thirty thousand. In 1701 the elector's son, Frederick I, received the elevated title of king of Prussia (instead of elector) as a reward for aiding the Holy Roman emperor in the War of the Spanish Succession.

The Consolidation of Prussian Absolutism

Frederick William I, "the Soldiers' King" (r. 1713–1740), completed his grandfather's work, eliminating the last traces of parliamentary estates and local self-government. It was he who truly established Prussian absolutism and transformed Prussia into a military state. Frederick William was intensely attached to military life. He always wore an army uniform, and he lived the highly disciplined life of the professional soldier. Years later he summed up his life's philosophy in his instructions to his son: "A formidable army and a war chest large enough to make this army mobile in times of need can create great respect for you in the world, so that you can speak a word like the other powers."[6]

The king's power grab brought him into considerable conflict with the Junkers; yet, in the end, he successfully enlisted the Prussian nobility to lead his growing army. A new compromise was worked out whereby the proud nobility commanded the peasantry in the army as well as on the estates.

Penny-pinching and hard-working, Frederick William achieved results. Prussia, twelfth in Europe in population, had the fourth largest army by 1740. The Prussian army was the best in Europe, astonishing foreign observers with its precision, skill, and discipline. Frederick William and his ministers also built an exceptionally honest and conscientious bureaucracy to administer the country and foster economic development.

Nevertheless, Prussians paid a heavy and lasting price for the obsessions of their royal drillmaster. Civil society became rigid and highly disciplined. As a Prussian minister later summed up, "To keep quiet is the first civic duty."[7] Thus the policies of Frederick William I combined with harsh peasant bondage and Junker tyranny to lay the foundations for a highly militaristic country.

The Mongol Yoke and the Rise of Moscow

In the thirteenth century the Kievan principality was conquered by the Mongols, a group of nomadic tribes from present-day Mongolia who had come together under Chinggis Khan

● **A Prussian Giant Grenadier**   Frederick William I wanted tall, handsome soldiers. He dressed them in tight bright uniforms to distinguish them from the peasant population from which most soldiers came. He also ordered several portraits of his favorites from his court painter, J. C. Merk. Grenadiers wore the miter cap instead of an ordinary hat so that they could hurl their heavy grenades unimpeded by a broad brim. *(The Royal Collection © 2007, Her Majesty Queen Elizabeth II)*

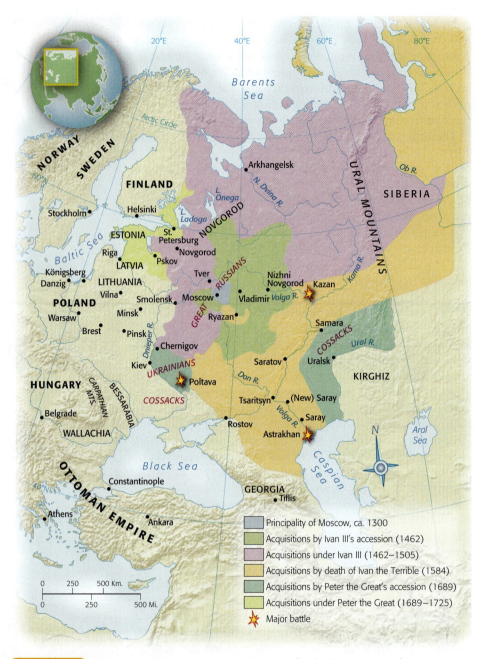

■	Principality of Moscow, ca. 1300
■	Acquisitions by Ivan III's accession (1462)
■	Acquisitions under Ivan III (1462–1505)
■	Acquisitions by death of Ivan the Terrible (1584)
■	Acquisitions by Peter the Great's accession (1689)
■	Acquisitions under Peter the Great (1689–1725)
✦	Major battle

 **MAP 16.4** **The Expansion of Russia to 1725** After the disintegration of the Kievan state and the Mongol conquest, the princes of Moscow and their descendants gradually extended their rule over an enormous territory.

Mongol Yoke *The two-hundred-year rule of the Mongol khan over the former territories of Kievan Rus, a medieval state centered in the city of Kiev and comprising portions of modern-day Ukraine, Russia, and Belarussia. This period is considered a prelude to the rise of absolutist Russia.*

(1162–1227). The two-hundred-year period of rule under the Mongol khan (king), known as the **Mongol Yoke,** set the stage for the rise of absolutist Russia.

The Mongols forced the Slavic princes to submit to their rule and to give them tribute and slaves. Beginning with Alexander Nevsky in 1252, the princes of Moscow became particularly adept at serving the Mongols. They loyally put down popular uprisings and collected the khan's taxes. As reward, the princes of Moscow emerged as hereditary great princes. Eventually the Muscovite princes were able to destroy the other princes who were their rivals for power. Ivan III (r. 1462–1505) consolidated power around Moscow and won Novgorod, almost reaching the Baltic Sea (see Map 16.4).

By about 1480 Ivan III felt strong enough to stop acknowledging the khan as his supreme ruler. To legitimize their new authority, he and his successors declared themselves *autocrats,* meaning that, like the khans, they were the sole source of power. Yet also like the khans, they needed the cooperation of the local elites. The highest ranking nobles or **boyars** enabled them to rule with an extremely limited government apparatus.

Another source of legitimacy lay in Moscow's claim to the political and religious inheritance of the Byzantine Empire. After the fall of Constantinople to the Turks in 1453, the princes of Moscow asserted themselves as the heirs of both the caesars and Orthodox Christianity, the one true faith. (The title **tsar,** first taken by Ivan IV in 1533, is a contraction of *caesar.*) Ivan's marriage to the daughter of the last Byzantine emperor further enhanced the aura of Moscow's imperial inheritance.

boyars *The highest ranking members of the Russian nobility.*

tsar *The Slavic word for* caesar; *Ivan III initiated this title for the absolute ruler of Russia.*

Tsar and People to 1689

Developments in Russia took a chaotic turn with the reign of Ivan IV (r. 1533–1584), the famous "Ivan the Terrible." Ivan's reign was characterized by endless wars and violent purges. He was successful in defeating the remnants of Mongol power, adding

● **Saint Basil's Cathedral, Moscow** With its sloping roofs and colorful onion-shaped domes, Saint Basil's is a striking example of powerful Byzantine influences on Russian culture. According to tradition, an enchanted Ivan the Terrible blinded the cathedral's architects to ensure that they would never duplicate their fantastic achievement, which still dazzles the beholder in today's Red Square. *(George Holton/ Photo Researchers)*

● **Gustaf Cederstrom: The Swedish Victory at Narva** This poignant re-creation focuses on the contrast between the Swedish officers in handsome dress uniforms and the battered Russian soldiers laying down their standards in surrender. Charles XII of Sweden scored brilliant, rapid-fire victories over Denmark, Saxony, and Russia, but he failed to make peace with Peter while he was ahead and eventually lost Sweden's holdings on the Baltic coast. (© The National Museum of Fine Arts, Stockholm)

service nobility *Those upon whom a non-hereditary noble title was bestowed as a result of their military service to Ivan IV.*

Cossacks *Free groups and outlaw armies living on the steppes bordering Russia from the fourteenth century onward. Their numbers were increased by runaway peasants during the time of Ivan the Terrible.*

vast new territories to the realm and laying the foundations for the huge, multiethnic Russian empire. After the sudden death of his beloved wife Anastasia (of the Romanov family), Ivan jailed and executed any he suspected of opposing him. Many victims were from the leading boyar families, and their families, friends, servants, and peasants were also executed. Their large estates were broken up, with some of the land added to the tsar's domain and the rest given to the lower **service nobility,** a group of newly made nobles who served in the tsar's army.

Ivan also took strides toward making all commoners servants of the tsar. As a result, growing numbers fled toward wild, recently conquered territories to the east and south. There they joined the numbers of free peoples and outlaw armies known as **Cossacks.**

Simultaneously, urban traders and artisans were also bound to their towns and jobs so that the tsar could tax them more heavily. Even the wealthiest merchants had no security in their work or property. These restrictions checked the growth of the Russian middle classes and stood in sharp contrast to developments in western Europe.

Following Ivan's death, Russia entered a chaotic period known as the "Time of Troubles" (1598–1613). While Ivan's relatives struggled for power, the Cossacks and peasants rebelled against nobles and officials. This social explosion from below brought the nobility together. They crushed the Cossack rebellion and elected Ivan's sixteen-year-old grandnephew, Michael Romanov, the new hereditary tsar (r. 1613–1645).

Although the new tsar successfully reconsolidated central authority, social and religious uprisings continued.

Despite the turbulence of the period, the Romanov tsars made several important achievements during the second half of the seventeenth century. After a long war, Russia gained a large mass of Ukraine from weak and decentralized Poland in 1667 (see Map 16.4) and completed the conquest of Siberia by the end of the century. Territorial expansion was accompanied by growth of the bureaucracy and the army. The great profits from Siberia's natural resources, especially furs, funded the Romanov's bid for great power status.

The Reforms of Peter the Great

Heir to the first efforts at state-building, Peter the Great (r. 1682–1725) embarked on a tremendous campaign to accelerate and complete these processes. A giant for his time at six feet seven inches, and possessing enormous energy and willpower, Peter was determined to continue the tsarist tradition of territorial expansion. After 1689 Peter ruled independently for thirty-six years, only one of which was peaceful.

Fascinated by foreign technology, the tsar led a group of 250 Russian officials and young nobles on an eighteen-month tour of western Europe. Traveling unofficially to avoid diplomatic ceremonies, Peter worked with his hands at various crafts and met with foreign kings and experts. He was particularly impressed with the growing power of the Dutch and the English, and he considered how Russia could profit from their example.

Suffering initial defeat in war with Sweden in 1701, Peter responded with measures designed to increase state power, strengthen his armies, and gain victory. He required every nobleman to serve in the army or in the civil administration—for life. Since a more modern army and government required skilled technicians and experts, Peter created schools and universities to produce them. Peter established an interlocking military-civilian bureaucracy with fourteen ranks, and he decreed that all had to start at the bottom and work toward the top. Some people of non-noble origins rose to high positions in this embryonic meritocracy. Drawing on his experience abroad,

> **Primary Source:**
> **Edicts and Decrees**
> *Read a selection of Peter the Great's decrees, and find out how he wished to modernize—and westernize—Russia.*

● **Peter the Great in 1723** This compelling portrait by Grigory Musikiysky captures the strength and determination of the warrior tsar after more than three decades of personal rule. In his hand Peter holds the scepter, symbol of royal sovereignty, and across his breastplate is draped an ermine fur, a mark of honor. In the background are the battleships of Russia's new Baltic fleet and the famous St. Peter and St. Paul Fortress that Peter built in St. Petersburg. *(The Bridgeman Art Library)*

Peter searched out talented foreigners and placed them in his service. These measures gradually combined to make the army and government more powerful and efficient.

Peter also greatly increased the service requirements of commoners. He established a regular standing army of more than two hundred thousand peasant-soldiers commanded by noble officers. Taxes on peasants increased threefold during Peter's reign. Serfs were arbitrarily assigned to work in the growing number of factories and mines that serviced the military.

Peter's new war machine was able to crush Sweden's small army in Ukraine at Poltava in 1709, one of the most significant battles in Russian history. Russia's victory was conclusive in 1721, and Estonia and present-day Latvia (see Map 16.4) came under Russian rule for the first time. The cost was high—warfare consumed 80 to 85 percent of all revenues. But Russia became the dominant power in the Baltic and very much a European Great Power.

After his victory at Poltava, Peter channeled enormous resources into building a new western-style capital on the Baltic to rival the great cities of Europe. Originally a desolate and swampy Swedish outpost, the magnificent city of St. Petersburg was designed to reflect modern urban planning with wide, straight avenues, buildings set in a uniform line, and large parks. Each summer, twenty-five to forty thousand peasants were sent to labor in St. Petersburg without pay.

There were other important consequences of Peter's reign. For Peter, modernization meant westernization, and both Westerners and Western ideas flowed into Russia for the first time. He required nobles to shave their heavy beards and wear Western clothing, previously banned in Russia. He required them to attend parties where young men and women would mix together and freely choose their own spouses. From these efforts a new class of Western-oriented Russians began to emerge.

CONSTITUTIONALISM — *How and why did the constitutional state triumph in Holland and England?*

constitutionalism *A form of government in which power is limited by law and balanced between the authority and power of the government on the one hand, and the rights and liberties of the subject or citizen on the other hand.*

While France, Prussia, Russia, and Austria developed the absolutist state, England and Holland evolved toward **constitutionalism,** which is the limitation of government by law. Constitutionalism also implies a balance between the authority and power of the government, on the one hand, and the rights and liberties of the subjects, on the other.

A nation's constitution may be written or unwritten. It may be embodied in one basic document, occasionally revised by amendment, like the Constitution of the United States. Or it may be only partly formalized and include parliamentary statutes, judicial decisions, and a body of traditional procedures and practices, like the English and Dutch constitutions. Whether written or unwritten, a constitution gets its binding force from the government's acknowledgment that it must respect that constitution—that is, that the state must govern according to the laws.

Absolutist Claims in England (1603–1649)

In 1588 Queen Elizabeth I of England exercised very great personal power. A rare female monarch, Elizabeth was able to maintain control over her realm in part by refusing to marry and submit to a husband. She was immensely popular with her people, but left no immediate heir to continue her legacy.

In 1603 Elizabeth's Scottish cousin James Stuart succeeded her as James I (r. 1603–1625). King James was well educated and had thirty-five years' experience as king of Scotland. But he was not as interested in displaying the majesty of monarchy as Elizabeth had been. Urged to wave at the crowds who waited to greet their new ruler, James complained that he was tired and threatened to drop his breeches "so they can cheer at my arse."[8]

James's greatest problem, however, stemmed from his belief that a monarch has a divine (or God-given) right to his authority and is responsible only to God. James went so far as to lecture the House of Commons: "There are no privileges and immunities which can stand against a divinely appointed King." Such a view ran directly counter to the long-standing English idea that a person's property could not be taken away without due process of law. James I and his son Charles I considered such constraints intolerable and a threat to their divine-right prerogative. Consequently, at every Parliament between 1603 and 1640, bitter squabbles erupted between the Crown and the articulate and legally minded Commons. Charles I's attempt to govern without Parliament (1629–1640) and to finance his government by arbitrary nonparliamentary levies brought the country to a crisis.

Religious Divides

Religious issues also embittered relations between the king and the House of Commons. In the early seventeenth century increasing numbers of English people felt dissatisfied with the Church of England established by Henry VIII and reformed by Elizabeth. Many **Puritans** believed that the Reformation had not gone far enough. They wanted to "purify" the Anglican Church of Roman Catholic elements—elaborate vestments and ceremonials, bishops, and even the giving and wearing of wedding rings.

James I responded to such ideas by declaring, "No bishop, no king." For James, bishops were among the chief supporters of the throne. His son and successor, Charles I, further antagonized religious sentiments. Not only did he marry a Catholic princess, but he also supported the heavy-handed policies of the Archbishop of Canterbury William Laud (1573–1645). In 1637 Laud attempted to impose two new elements on church organization in Scotland: a new prayer book, modeled on the Anglican *Book of Common Prayer,* and bishoprics, which the Presbyterian Scots firmly rejected. The Scots therefore revolted. To finance an army to put down the Scots, King Charles was compelled to summon Parliament in November 1640.

Charles had ruled from 1629 to 1640 without Parliament, financing his government through extraordinary stopgap levies considered illegal by most English people. For example, the king revived a medieval law requiring coastal districts to help pay the cost of ships for defense, but he levied the tax, called "ship money," on inland as well as coastal counties. Most members of Parliament believed that such taxation without consent amounted to despotism. Consequently, they were not willing to trust the king with an army. Moreover, many supported the Scots' resistance to Charles's religious innovations and had little wish for military action against them. Accordingly, this Parliament, called the "Long Parliament" because it sat from 1640

Puritans *Members of a sixteenth- and seventeenth-century reform movement within the Church of England that advocated "purifying" it of Roman Catholic elements, such as bishops, elaborate ceremonials, and the wedding ring.*

● **Puritan Occupations** These twelve engravings depict typical Puritan occupations and show that the Puritans came primarily from the artisan and lower middle classes. The governing classes and peasants adhered to the traditions of the Church of England. *(Visual Connection Archive)*

to 1660, enacted legislation that limited the power of the monarch and made arbitrary government impossible.

In 1641 the Commons passed the Triennial Act, which compelled the king to summon Parliament every three years. The Commons impeached Archbishop Laud and then went further and threatened to abolish bishops. King Charles, fearful of a Scottish invasion—the original reason for summoning Parliament— reluctantly accepted these measures.

The next act in the conflict was precipitated by the outbreak of rebellion in Ireland, where English governors and landlords had long exploited the people. In 1641 the Catholic gentry of Ireland led an uprising in response to a feared invasion by anti-Catholic forces of the British Long Parliament.

Without an army, Charles I could neither come to terms with the Scots nor respond to the Irish rebellion. After a failed attempt to arrest parliamentary leaders, Charles left London for the north of England. There, he recruited an army drawn from the nobility and its cavalry staff, the rural gentry, and mercenaries. The parliamentary army was composed of the militia of the city of London and country squires with business connections.

New Model Army *The parliamentary army, under the command of Oliver Cromwell, that fought the army of Charles I in the English civil war.*

The English civil war (1642–1649) pitted the power of the king against that of the Parliament. After three years of fighting, Parliament's **New Model Army** defeated the king's armies at the battles of Naseby and Langport in the summer of 1645. Charles, though, refused to concede defeat. Both sides jockeyed for position, waiting for a decisive event. This arrived in the form of the army under the leadership of Oliver Cromwell, a member of the House of Commons and a devout Puritan. In 1647 Cromwell's forces captured the king and dismissed members of the Parliament who opposed his actions. In 1649 the remaining representatives, known as the "Rump Parliament," put Charles on trial for high treason. Charles was found guilty and beheaded on January 30, 1649, an act that sent shock waves around Europe.

Puritanical Absolutism in England: Cromwell and the Protectorate

With the execution of Charles, kingship was abolished. A *commonwealth,* or republican government, was proclaimed. Theoretically, legislative power rested in the surviving members of Parliament, and executive power was lodged in a council of state. In fact, the army that had defeated the king controlled the government, and Oliver Cromwell controlled the army. Though called the **Protectorate,** the rule of Cromwell (1653–1658) constituted military dictatorship.

Protectorate *The military dictatorship established by Oliver Cromwell following the execution of Charles I.*

The army prepared a constitution, the Instrument of Government (1653), that invested executive power in a lord protector (Cromwell) and a council of state. The instrument provided for triennial parliaments and gave Parliament the sole power to raise taxes. But after repeated disputes, Cromwell dismissed Parliament in 1655, and the instrument was never formally endorsed. Cromwell continued the standing army and proclaimed quasi-martial law. He divided England into twelve military districts, each governed by a major general. Reflecting Puritan ideas of morality, Cromwell's state forbade sports, kept the theaters closed, and rigorously censored the press.

On the issue of religion, Cromwell favored some degree of toleration, and the Instrument of Government gave all Christians except Roman Catholics the right to practice their faith. Cromwell had long associated Catholicism in Ireland with sedition and heresy. In September of the year that his army came to power, it crushed a rebellion at Drogheda and massacred the garrison. After Cromwell's departure for England, atrocities worsened. The English banned Catholicism in Ireland, executed priests, and confiscated land from Catholics for English and Scottish settlers. These brutal acts left a legacy of Irish hatred for England.

● **Cartoon of 1649: "The Royall Oake of Brittayne"** Chopping down this tree signifies the end of royal authority, stability, the Magna Carta, and the rule of law. As pigs graze (representing the unconcerned common people) being fattened for slaughter, Oliver Cromwell, with his feet in Hell, quotes Scripture. This is a royalist view of the collapse of Charles I's government and the rule of Cromwell. *(Courtesy of the Trustees of the British Museum)*

Cromwell adopted mercantilist policies similar to those of absolutist France. He enforced a Navigation Act (1651) requiring that English goods be transported on English ships. The navigation act was a great boost to the development of an English merchant marine and brought about a short but successful war with the commercially threatened Dutch. Cromwell also welcomed the immigration of Jews because of their skills, and they began to return to England after four centuries of absence.

The Protectorate collapsed when Cromwell died in 1658 and his ineffectual son succeeded him. Fed up with military rule, the English longed for a return to civilian government and, with it, common law and social stability. By 1660 they were ready to restore the monarchy.

The Restoration of the English Monarchy

The Restoration of 1660 brought to the throne Charles II (r. 1660–1685), eldest son of Charles I, who had been living on the Continent. Both houses of Parliament were also restored, together with the established Anglican church. The Restoration failed to resolve two serious problems, however. What was to be the attitude of the state toward Puritans, Catholics, and dissenters from the established church? And what was to be the relationship between the king and Parliament?

To answer the first question, Parliament enacted the **Test Act** of 1673 against those outside the Church of England, denying them the right to vote, hold public office, preach, teach, attend the universities, or even assemble for meetings. But these restrictions could not be enforced. When the Quaker William Penn held a meeting of his Friends and was arrested, the jury refused to convict him.

Test Act *Legislation, passed by the English parliament in 1673 designed to secure the position of the Anglican Church. It sought to suppress the influence of Puritans, Catholics, and other dissenters by denying them the right to vote, preach, assemble, hold public office, and attend or teach at the universities.*

In politics Charles II was determined "not to set out in his travels again," which meant that he intended to avoid exile by working well with Parliament. This intention did not last, however. Finding that Parliament did not grant him an adequate income, Charles entered into a secret agreement with his cousin Louis XIV. The French king would give Charles two hundred thousand pounds annually, and in return Charles would relax the laws against Catholics, gradually re-Catholicize England, and convert to Catholicism himself. When the details of this treaty leaked out, a great wave of anti-Catholic sentiment swept England.

When James II (r. 1685–1688) succeeded his brother, the worst English anti-Catholic fears were realized. In violation of the Test Act, James appointed Roman Catholics to positions in the army, the universities, and local government. When these actions were challenged in the courts, the judges, whom James had appointed, decided for the king. The king was suspending the law at will and appeared to be reviving the absolutism of his father and grandfather. He went further. Attempting to broaden his base of support with Protestant dissenters and nonconformists, James issued a declaration of indulgence granting religious freedom to all.

Seeking to prevent the return of Catholic absolutism, a group of eminent persons offered the English throne to James's Protestant daughter Mary and her Dutch husband, Prince William of Orange. In December 1688 James II, his queen, and their infant son fled to France and became pensioners of Louis XIV. Early in 1689 William and Mary were crowned king and queen of England.

The Triumph of England's Parliament: Constitutional Monarchy and Cabinet Government

The English call the events of 1688 and 1689 the "Glorious Revolution" because it replaced one king with another with a minimum of bloodshed. It also represented the destruction, once and for all, of the idea of divine-right monarchy. William and Mary accepted the English throne from Parliament and in so doing explicitly recognized the supremacy of Parliament. The revolution of 1688 established the principle that sovereignty, the ultimate power in the state, was divided between king and Parliament and that the king ruled with the consent of the governed.

The men who brought about the revolution framed their intentions in the Bill of Rights, which was formulated in direct response to Stuart absolutism. Law was to be made in Parliament; once made, it could not be suspended by the Crown. Parliament had to be called at least once every three years. The independence of the judiciary was established, and there was to be no standing army in peacetime. Protestants could possess arms but the Catholic minority could not. Additional legislation granted freedom of worship to Protestant dissenters and required that the English monarch always be Protestant.

Second Treatise of Civil Government *A work of political philosophy published by John Locke in 1690 that argued government's only purpose was to defend the natural rights of life, liberty, and property.*

The Glorious Revolution and the concept of representative government found its best defense in political philosopher John Locke's *Second Treatise of Civil Government* (1690). Locke (1632–1704) maintained that a government that oversteps its proper function—protecting the natural rights of life, liberty, and property—becomes a tyranny. By "natural" rights Locke meant rights basic to all men because all have the ability to reason. (His idea that there are natural or universal rights equally valid for all peoples and societies was especially popular in colonial America.) Under a tyrannical government, the people have the natural right to rebellion. On the basis of this link, he justified limiting the vote to property owners. (American colonists also appreciated his arguments that Native Americans had no property rights since they did not cultivate the land and, by extension, no political rights because they possessed no property.)

The events of 1688 and 1689 did not constitute a democratic revolution. The revolution placed sovereignty in Parliament, and Parliament represented the upper classes.

● **Jan Steen: The Christening Feast** As the mother, surrounded by midwives, rests in bed (*rear left*) and the father proudly displays the swaddled child, thirteen other people, united by gestures and gazes, prepare the celebratory meal. Very prolific, Steen was a master of warm-hearted domestic scenes. In contrast to the order and cleanliness of many seventeenth-century Dutch genre paintings, Steen's more disorderly portrayals gave rise to the epithet "a Jan Steen household," meaning an untidy house. *(Wallace Collection, London/The Bridgeman Art Library)*

The age of aristocratic government lasted at least until 1832 and in many ways until 1928, when women received full voting rights.

The Dutch Republic in the Seventeenth Century

In the late sixteenth century the seven northern provinces of the Netherlands fought for and won their independence from Spain. The independence of the Republic of the United Provinces of the Netherlands was recognized in 1648 in the treaty that ended the Thirty Years' War. In this period, often called the "golden age of the Netherlands," Dutch ideas and attitudes played a profound role in shaping a new and modern worldview. At the same time, the United Provinces was another model of the development of the modern constitutional state.

The government of the United Provinces had none of the standard categories of seventeenth-century political organization. The Dutch were not monarchical but rather fiercely republican. Within each province, an oligarchy of wealthy businessmen called "regents" handled domestic affairs in the local Estates (assemblies). The

States General *The name of the national assembly of the United Provinces of the Netherlands, where the wealthy merchant class held real power; because many issues had to be referred back to the provinces, the United Provinces was a confederation, or weak union of strong states.*

stadholder *The executive officer in each of the United Provinces of the Netherlands; in practice, this position was dominated by the Prince of Orange.*

provincial Estates held virtually all the power. A federal assembly, or **States General,** handled matters of foreign affairs, such as war. But the States General did not possess sovereign authority; all issues had to be referred back to the local Estates for approval. In each province, the estates appointed an executive officer, known as the **stadholder,** who carried out ceremonial functions and was responsible for military defense. Although in theory freely chosen by the Estates and answerable to them, in practice the Princes of Orange were almost always chosen as stadholders. Tensions persisted between supporters of the staunchly republican estates and those of the aristocratic House of Orange. Holland, which had the largest navy and the most wealth, dominated the seven provinces of the republic and the States General.

The political success of the Dutch rested on the phenomenal commercial prosperity of the Netherlands. The moral and ethical bases of that commercial wealth were thrift, frugality, and religious toleration. Although there is scattered evidence of anti-Semitism, Jews enjoyed a level of acceptance and assimilation in Dutch business and general culture unique in early modern Europe. (See the feature "Individuals in Society: Glückel of Hameln.") In the Dutch Republic, toleration paid off: it attracted a great deal of foreign capital and investment.

The Dutch came to dominate the shipping business by putting profits from their original industry—herring fishing—into shipbuilding (see Map 16.5). They boasted the lowest shipping rates and largest merchant marine in Europe, allowing them to undersell foreign competitors. Trade and commerce brought the Dutch the highest standard of living in Europe, perhaps in the world. Salaries were high, and all classes of society ate well. A scholar has described the Netherlands as "an island of plenty in a sea of want." Consequently, the Netherlands experienced very few of the food riots that characterized the rest of Europe.[9]

MAP 16.5 **Seventeenth-Century Dutch Commerce** Dutch wealth rested on commerce, and commerce depended on the huge Dutch merchant marine, manned by perhaps forty-eight thousand sailors. The fleet carried goods from all parts of the globe to the port of Amsterdam.

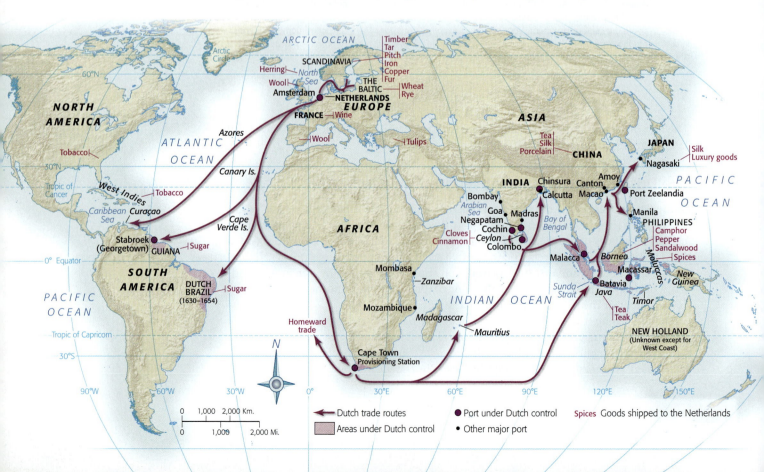

Glückel of Hameln

In 1690 a Jewish widow in the small German town of Hameln* in Lower Saxony sat down to write her autobiography. She wanted to distract her mind from the terrible grief she felt over the death of her husband and to provide her twelve children with a record "so you will know from what sort of people you have sprung, lest today or tomorrow your beloved children or grandchildren came and know naught of their family." Out of her pain and heightened consciousness, Glückel (1646–1724) produced an invaluable source for scholars.

She was born in Hamburg two years before the end of the Thirty Years' War. In 1649 the merchants of Hamburg expelled the Jews, who moved to nearby Altona, then under Danish rule. When the Swedes overran Altona in 1657–1658, the Jews returned to Hamburg "purely at the mercy of the Town Council." Glückel's narrative proceeds against a background of the constant harassment to which Jews were subjected—special papers, permits, bribes—and in Hameln she wrote, "And so it has been to this day and, I fear, will continue in like fashion."

When Glückel was "barely twelve," her father betrothed her to Chayim Hameln. She married at age fourteen. She describes him as "the perfect pattern of the pious Jew," a man who stopped his work every day for study and prayer, fasted, and was scrupulously honest in his business dealings. Only a few years older than Glückel, Chayim earned his living dealing in precious metals and in making small loans on pledges (articles held on security). This work required his constant travel to larger cities, markets, and fairs, often in bad weather, always over dangerous roads. Chayim consulted his wife about all his business dealings. As he lay dying, a friend asked if he had any last wishes. "None," he replied. "My wife knows everything. She shall do as she has always done." For thirty years Glückel had been his friend, full business partner, and wife. They had thirteen children, twelve of whom survived their father, eight then unmarried. As Chayim had foretold, Glückel succeeded in launching the boys in careers and in providing dowries for the girls.

Glückel's world was her family, the Jewish community of Hameln, and the Jewish communities

Gentleness and deep mutual devotion seem to pervade Rembrandt's *The Jewish Bride*. (Rijksmuseum-Stichting Amsterdam)

into which her children married. Social and business activities took her to Amsterdam, Baiersdorf, Bamberg, Berlin, Cleves, Danzig, Metz, and Vienna, so her world was not narrow or provincial. She took great pride that Prince Frederick of Cleves, later king of Prussia, danced at the wedding of her eldest daughter. The rising prosperity of Chayim's businesses allowed the couple to maintain up to six servants.

Glückel was deeply religious, and her culture was steeped in Jewish literature, legends, and mystical and secular works. Above all, she relied on the Bible. Her language, heavily sprinkled with scriptural references, testifies to a rare familiarity with the basic book of Western civilization. The Scriptures were her consolation, the source of her great strength in a hostile world.

Students who would learn about business practices, the importance of the dowry in marriage, childbirth, the ceremony of bris, birthrates, family celebrations, and even the meaning of life can gain a good deal from the memoirs of this extraordinary woman who was, in the words of one of her descendants, the poet Heinrich Heine, "the gift of a world to me."

Questions for Analysis

1. Consider the ways in which Glückel of Hameln was both an ordinary and an extraordinary woman of her times. Would you call her a marginal or a central person in her society?

2. How was Glückel's life affected by the broad events and issues of the seventeenth century?

Source: The Memoirs of Glückel of Hameln (New York: Schocken Books, 1977).

---

*A town immortalized by the Brothers Grimm. In 1284 the town contracted with the Pied Piper to rid it of rats and mice; he lured them away by playing his flute. When the citizens refused to pay, he charmed away their children in revenge.

Chapter Summary

Key Terms

moral economy
Protestant Union
Peace of Westphalia
sovereignty
intendants
Fronde
divine right of kings
mercantilism
Peace of Utrecht
Bohemian Estates
elector of Brandenburg
Junkers
Mongol Yoke
boyars
tsar
service nobility
Cossacks
constitutionalism
Puritans
New Model Army
Protectorate
Test Act
*Second Treatise of Civil
 Government*
States General
stadholder

To assess your mastery of this chapter, go to
bedfordstmartins.com/mckayworld

• *What were the common crises and achievements of seventeenth-century European states?*

Most parts of Europe experienced the seventeenth century as a period of severe economic, social, and military crisis. Across the continent, rulers faced popular rebellions from their desperate subjects, who were pushed to the brink by poor harvests, high taxes, and decades of war. Many forces, including powerful noblemen, the church, and regional and local loyalties, constrained the state's authority. Despite these obstacles, most European states emerged from the seventeenth century with increased powers and more centralized control. Whether they ruled through monarchical fiat or parliamentary negotiation, European governments strengthened their bureaucracies, raised more taxes, and significantly expanded their armies.

• *How and why did Louis XIV of France lead the way in forging the absolute state, and why did Spain experience decline in the same period?*

Under Louis XIV France witnessed the high point of monarchical ambitions in western Europe. The king saw himself as the representative of God on earth, and it has been said that "to the seventeenth century imagination God was a sort of image of Louis XIV."[10] Under Louis's rule, France developed a centralized bureaucracy, a professional army, and a state-directed economy, all of which he personally supervised. Historians now agree that, despite his claims to absolute power, Louis XIV ruled, in practice, by securing the collaboration of high nobles. In exchange for confirmation of their ancient privileges, the nobles were willing to cooperate with the expansion of state power. In Spain, where monarchs made similar claims to absolute power, the seventeenth century witnessed economic catastrophe and a decline in royal capacities.

• *How did Austrian, Prussian, and Russian rulers in eastern Europe build absolute monarchies—monarchies that proved even more durable than that of Louis XIV?*

Within a framework of resurgent serfdom and entrenched nobility, Austrian and Prussian monarchs also fashioned absolutist states in the seventeenth and early eighteenth centuries. These monarchs won absolutist control over standing armies, permanent taxes, and legislative bodies. But they did not question the underlying social and economic relationships. Indeed, they enhanced the privileges of the nobility, which furnished the leading servitors for enlarged armies and growing government bureaucracies. In Russia social and economic trends were similar to those in Austria and Prussia. Unlike those two states, however, Russia had a long history of powerful princes. Tsar Peter the Great succeeded in tightening up Russia's traditional absolutism and modernizing it by reforming the army, the bureaucracy, and the defense industry. In Russia and throughout eastern Europe war and the needs of the state in times of war weighed heavily in the triumph of absolutism.

• How and why did the constitutional state triumph in Holland and England?

Holland and England defied the general trend toward absolute monarchy. While Holland prospered under a unique republican confederation of separate provinces, England—fortunately shielded from continental armies and military emergencies by its navy and the English Channel—evolved into the first modern constitutional state. After 1688, power was divided between king and Parliament, with Parliament enjoying the greater share. The Bill of Rights marked an important milestone in world history, although the framers left to later generations the task of making constitutional government work.

Suggested Reading

Benedict, Philip, and Myron P. Gutmann, eds. *Early Modern Europe: From Crisis to Stability.* 2005. A helpful introduction to the many facets of the seventeenth-century crisis.

Burke, Peter. *The Fabrication of Louis XIV.* 1992. Explains the use of architecture, art, medals, and other symbols to promote the king's image.

Collins, James B. *The State in Early Modern France.* 1995. A detailed and well-argued survey of French administration from Louis XIII to Louis XVI.

Elliott, John H. *Richelieu and Olivares.* 1984. A comparison of the chief ministers of France and Spain that also reveals differences and similarities in the countries they led.

Gaunt, Peter, ed. *The English Civil War: The Essential Readings.* 2000. A collection showcasing leading historians' interpretations of the civil war.

Hagen, William W. *Ordinary Prussians: Brandenburg Junkers and Villagers, 1500–1840.* 2002. Provides a fascinating encounter with the people of a Prussian estate.

Hughes, Lindsey, ed. *Peter the Great and the West: New Perspectives.* 2001. Essays by leading scholars on the reign of Peter the Great and his opening of Russia to the West.

Ingrao, Charles W. *The Habsburg Monarchy, 1618–1815,* 2d ed. 2000. An excellent synthesis of the political and social development of the Habsburg empire in the early modern period.

Lincoln, W. Bruce. *Sunlight at Midnight: St. Petersburg and the Rise of Modern Russia.* 2001. Captures the spirit of Peter the Great's new northern capital.

McKay, Derek. *The Great Elector: Frederick William of Brandenburg-Prussia.* 2001. Examines the formative years of Prussian power.

Parker, Geoffrey. *The Thirty Years War,* 2d ed. 1997. The standard account of the Thirty Years' War.

Schama, Simon. *The Embarrassment of Riches: An Interpretation of Dutch Culture in the Golden Age.* 1987. A lengthy but vivid and highly readable account of Dutch culture in the seventeenth century, including a chapter on the mania for speculation on the tulip market.

Notes

1. The classic study Theodore K. Rabb, *The Struggle for Stability in Early Modern Europe* (Oxford: Oxford University Press, 1975).
2. H. Kamen, "The Economic and Social Consequences of the Thirty Years' War," *Past and Present* 39 (April 1968): 44–61.
3. Quoted in J. Wolf, *Louis XIV* (New York: W. W. Norton, 1968), p. 146.
4. John A. Lynn, "Recalculating French Army Growth," in *The Military Revolution Debate: Readings on the Military Transformation of Early Modern Europe,* ed. Clifford J. Rogers (Boulder, Colo.: Westview Press, 1995), p. 125.
5. J. H. Elliott, *Imperial Spain, 1469–1716* (New York: Mentor Books, 1963), pp. 306–308.
6. Ibid., p. 43.
7. Quoted in Hans Rosenberg, *Bureaucracy, Aristocracy, and Autocracy* (Cambridge, Mass.: Harvard University Press, 1958), p. 40.
8. For a revisionist interpretation, see J. Wormald, "James VI and I: Two Kings or One?" *History* 62 (June 1983): 187–209.
9. S. Schama, *The Embarrassment of Riches: An Interpretation of Dutch Culture in the Golden Age* (New York: Alfred A. Knopf, 1987), pp. 165–170; quotation is on p. 167.
10. C. J. Friedrich and C. Blitzer, *The Age of Power* (Ithaca, N.Y.: Cornell University Press, 1957), p. 112.

Listening to the PAST

The Court at Versailles

Although the Duc de Saint-Simon (1675–1755) was a soldier, courtier, and diplomat, his enduring reputation rests on The Memoirs *(1788), his eyewitness account of the personality and court of Louis XIV. A nobleman of extremely high status, Saint-Simon resented Louis's high-handed treatment of the ancient nobility and his promotion of newer nobles and the bourgeoisie. The Memoirs, excerpted here, remains a monument of French literature and an indispensable historical source, partly for its portrait of the court at Versailles.*

Very early in the reign of Louis XIV the Court was removed from Paris, never to return. The troubles of the minority had given him a dislike to that city; his enforced and surreptitious flight from it still rankled in his memory; he did not consider himself safe there, and thought cabals would be more easily detected if the Court was in the country, where the movements and temporary absences of any of its members would be more easily noticed. . . . No doubt that he was also influenced by the feeling that he would be regarded with greater awe and veneration when no longer exposed every day to the gaze of the multitude.

His love-affair with Mademoiselle de la Vallière, which at first was covered as far as possible with a veil of mystery, was the cause of frequent excursions to Versailles. . . . The visits of Louis XIV becoming more frequent, he enlarged the *château* by degrees till its immense buildings afforded better accommodation for the Court than was to be found at St. Germain, where most of the courtiers had to put up with uncomfortable lodgings in the town. The Court was therefore removed to Versailles in 1682, not long before the Queen's death. The new building contained an infinite number of rooms for courtiers, and the King liked the grant of these rooms to be regarded as a coveted privilege.

He availed himself of the frequent festivities at Versailles, and his excursions to other places, as a means of making the courtiers assiduous in their attendance and anxious to please him; for he nominated beforehand those who were to take part in them, and could thus gratify some and inflict a snub on others. He was conscious that the substantial favours he had to bestow were not nearly sufficient to produce a continual effect; he had therefore to invent imaginary ones, and no one was so clever in devising petty distinctions and preferences which aroused jealousy and emulation. The visits to Marly later on were very useful to him in this way; also those to Trianon [Marly and Trianon were small country houses], where certain ladies, chosen beforehand, were admitted to his table. It was another distinction to hold his candlestick at his *coucher* [preparations for going to bed]; as soon as he had finished his prayers he used to name the courtier to whom it was to be handed, always choosing one of the highest rank among those present. . . .

Not only did he expect all persons of distinction to be in continual attendance at Court, but he was quick to notice the absence of those of inferior degree; at his *lever* [formal rising from bed in the morning], his *coucher*, his meals, in the gardens of Versailles (the only place where the courtiers in general were allowed to follow him), he used to cast his eyes to right and left; nothing escaped him, he saw everybody. If any one habitually living at Court absented himself he insisted on knowing the reason; those who came there only for flying visits had also to give a satisfactory explanation; any one who seldom or never appeared there was certain to incur his displeasure. If asked to bestow a favour on such persons he would reply haughtily: "I do not know him"; of such as rarely presented themselves he would say, "He is a man I never see"; and from these judgements there was no appeal.

He always took great pains to find out what was going on in public places, in society, in private houses, even family secrets, and maintained an immense number of spies and tale-bearers. These were of all sorts; some did not know that their reports were carried to him; others did know it; there were others, again, who used to write to him directly, through channels which he prescribed; others who were admitted by the back-stairs and saw him in his private room. Many a man in all ranks of life was ruined by these methods, often very unjustly, without ever being able to discover the

Louis XIV was extremely proud of the gardens at Versailles and personally led ambassadors and other highly ranked visitors on tours of the extensive palace grounds. *(Erich Lessing/Art Resource, NY)*

reason; and when the King had once taken a prejudice against a man, he hardly ever got over it. . . .

No one understood better than Louis XIV the art of enhancing the value of a favour by his manner of bestowing it; he knew how to make the most of a word, a smile, even of a glance. If he addressed any one, were it but to ask a trifling question or make some commonplace remark, all eyes were turned on the person so honored; it was a mark of favour which always gave rise to comment. . . .

He loved splendour, magnificence, and profusion in all things, and encouraged similar tastes in his Court; to spend money freely on equipages [the king's horse carriages] and buildings, on feasting and at cards, was a sure way to gain his favour, perhaps to obtain the honour of a word from him. Motives of policy had something to do with this; by making expensive habits the fashion, and, for people in a certain position, a necessity, he compelled his courtiers to live beyond their income, and gradually reduced them to depend on his bounty for the means of subsistence. This was a plague which, once introduced, became a scourge to the whole country, for it did not take long to spread to Paris, and thence to the armies and the provinces; so that a man of any position is now estimated entirely according to his expenditure on his table and other luxuries. This folly, sustained by pride and ostentation, has already produced widespread confusion; it threatens to end in nothing short of ruin and a general overthrow.

Questions for Analysis

1. What was the role of etiquette and ceremony at the court of Versailles? How could Louis XIV use them in everyday life at court to influence and control nobles?

2. How important do you think Louis's individual character and personality were to his style of governing? What challenges might this present to his successors?

3. Do you think Saint-Simon is an objective and trustworthy recorder of life at court? Why?

Source: F. Arkwright, ed., *The Memoirs of the Duke de Saint Simon,* vol. 5 (New York: Brentano's, n.d.), pp. 271–274, 276–278.

Voltaire, the Renowned Enlightenment Thinker, leans forward on the left to exchange ideas and witty conversation with Frederick the Great, king of Prussia.
(Bildarchiv Preussischer Kulturbesitz/Art Resource, NY)

17 TOWARD A NEW WORLDVIEW IN THE WEST, 1540–1789

The intellectual developments of the seventeenth and eighteenth centuries created the modern worldview that the West continues to hold—and debate—to this day. In the seventeenth century fundamentally new ways of understanding the natural world emerged. In the nineteenth century scholars hailed these achievements as a "scientific revolution" that produced modern science as we know it. The new science created in the seventeenth century entailed the search for precise knowledge of the physical world based on the union of experimental observations with sophisticated mathematics.

In the eighteenth century philosophers extended the use of reason from nature to human society. They sought to bring the light of reason to bear on the darkness of prejudice, outmoded traditions, and ignorance. Self-proclaimed members of an "Enlightenment" movement, they wished to bring the same progress to human affairs as their predecessors had brought to the understanding of the natural world. While the scientific revolution ushered in modern science, the Enlightenment created concepts of human rights, equality, progress, universalism, and tolerance that still guide Western societies today.

While many view the scientific revolution and the Enlightenment as bedrocks of the achievement of Western civilization, others have seen a darker side. For these critics, the mastery over nature permitted by the scientific revolution threatens to overwhelm the earth's fragile equilibrium, and the belief in the universal application of "reason" can lead to arrogance and intolerance, particularly intolerance of other people's spiritual values. Such vivid debates about the legacy of these intellectual and cultural developments testifies to their continuing importance in today's world.

THE SCIENTIFIC REVOLUTION
What was revolutionary in new attitudes toward the natural world?

The emergence of modern science was a development of tremendous long-term significance. A noted historian has said that the scientific revolution was "the real origin both of the modern world and the modern mentality."[1] With the scientific revolution Western society began to acquire its most distinctive traits.

Scientific Thought in 1500

Since developments in astronomy and physics were at the heart of the scientific revolution, one must begin with the traditional European conception of the universe. The practitioners of the scientific revolution did not consider their field *science* but rather **natural philosophy,** and their intention was philosophical: to ask fundamental questions about the nature of the universe, its purpose, and how it functioned. In the early 1500s natural philosophy was still based primarily on the ideas of Aristotle, the great Greek philosopher of the fourth century B.C.E. Medieval theologians such as Thomas Aquinas brought Aristotelian philosophy into harmony with Christian doctrines. According to the revised Aristotelian view, a motionless earth was fixed at the center of the universe. Around it moved ten separate transparent crystal spheres. In the first eight spheres were embedded, in turn, the moon, the sun, the five known planets, and the stars. Then followed two spheres added during the Middle Ages to account for slight changes in the positions of the stars over the centuries. Beyond the tenth sphere was Heaven, with the throne of God and the souls of the saved. Angels kept the spheres moving in perfect circles. Human beings were at the center of the universe, forming the critical link in a "great chain of being" that stretched from the throne of God to the most lowly insect on earth.

Aristotle's views also dominated thinking about physics and motion on earth. Aristotle had distinguished sharply between the celestial spheres and the earth. The celestial spheres consisted of a perfect, incorruptible "quintessence," or fifth essence. The earth was composed of four imperfect, changeable elements. The "light" elements (air and fire) naturally moved upward, while the "heavy" elements (water and earth) naturally moved downward. These natural directions of motion did not always prevail, however, for elements were often mixed together and could be affected by an outside force such as a human being. Aristotle and his followers also believed that a uniform force moved an object at a constant speed and that the object would stop as soon as that force was removed.

natural philosophy *An early modern term for the study of the nature of the universe, its purpose and how it functioned; it encompassed what today we would call science.*

The Copernican Hypothesis

The first great departure from the medieval system came from Nicolaus Copernicus (1473–1543). As a young man Copernicus studied church law and astronomy in various European universities. He saw how professional astronomers still depended for their calculations

● **The Aristotelian Universe as Imagined in the Sixteenth Century** A round earth is at the center, surrounded by spheres of water, air, and fire. Beyond this small nucleus, the moon, the sun, and the five planets were embedded in their own rotating crystal spheres, with the stars sharing the surface of one enormous sphere. Beyond, the heavens were composed of unchanging ether. *(Image Select/Art Resource, NY)*

on the second century B.C.E. work of Ptolemy. Copernicus felt that Ptolemy's cumbersome and occasionally inaccurate rules detracted from the majesty of a perfect Creator. He preferred an old Greek idea being discussed in Renaissance Italy: that the sun, rather than the earth, was at the center of the universe. Finishing his studies and returning to a church position in East Prussia, Copernicus worked on his hypothesis from 1506 to 1530. Never questioning the Aristotelian belief in crystal spheres or the idea that circular motion was most perfect and divine, Copernicus theorized that the stars and planets, including the earth, revolved around a fixed sun. Yet fearing ridicule, Copernicus did not publish his *On the Revolutions of the Heavenly Spheres* until 1543, the year of his death.

The **Copernican hypothesis** brought sharp attacks from religious leaders, especially Protestants, who objected to the idea that the earth moved but the sun did not. Martin Luther noted that the theory was counter to the Bible: "as the Holy Scripture tells us, so did Joshua bid the sun stand still and not the earth."[2] John Calvin also condemned Copernicus. Catholic reaction was milder at first. The Catholic Church had never held to literal interpretations of the Bible and did not declare the Copernican hypothesis false until 1616.

This slow reaction also reflected the slow progress of Copernicus's theory. Other events were almost as influential in creating doubts about traditional astronomy. In 1572 a new star appeared and shone very brightly for almost two years. The new star, which was actually a distant exploding star, made an enormous impression. It seemed to contradict the idea that the heavenly spheres were unchanging and therefore perfect. In 1577 a new comet suddenly moved through the sky, cutting a straight path across the supposedly impenetrable crystal spheres. It was time, as a typical scientific writer put it, for "the radical renovation of astronomy."[3]

Chronology

ca. 1540–1690	Scientific revolution
1543	Copernicus, *On the Revolutions of the Heavenly Spheres*
1564–1642	Life of Galileo
1571–1630	Life of Kepler
1662	Royal Society of London founded
1687	Newton, *Principia* and law of universal gravitation
1690	Locke, *Essay Concerning Human Understanding*
ca. 1690–1780	Enlightenment
1694–1778	Life of Voltaire
1700–1789	Growth of book publishing
1720–1780	Rococo style in art and decoration
1740–1786	Reign of Frederick the Great of Prussia
ca. 1750–1790	Enlightened absolutists
1751–1765	Diderot and d'Alembert, *Encyclopedia*
1762	Rousseau, *The Social Contract*
1762–1796	Reign of Catherine the Great of Russia
1780–1790	Reign of Joseph II of Austria

From Brahe to Galileo

One astronomer who agreed was Tycho Brahe (1546–1601). Born into a Danish noble family, Brahe was an imposing man who had lost a piece of his nose in a duel and replaced it with a special bridge of gold and silver alloy. He established himself as Europe's leading astronomer with his detailed observations of the new star of 1572. For twenty years he meticulously observed the stars and planets with the naked eye in the most sophisticated observatory of his day. His limited understanding of mathematics prevented him, however, from making much sense out of his mass of data. Part Ptolemaic, part Copernican, he believed that all the planets except earth revolved around the sun and that the entire group of sun and planets revolved in turn around the earth-moon system.

It was left to Brahe's assistant, Johannes Kepler (1571–1630), to rework Brahe's observations. A brilliant mathematician, Kepler eventually moved beyond his belief that the universe was built on mystical mathematical relationships and a musical harmony of the heavenly bodies.

Copernican hypothesis *The idea that the sun, not the earth, was the center of the universe; this had tremendous scientific and religious implications.*

Primary Source:
Letter to the Grand Duchess Christina
Read Galileo's passionate defense of his scientific research against those who would condemn it as un-Christian.

experimental method *The approach, first developed by Galileo, that the proper way to explore the workings of the universe was through repeatable experiments rather than speculation.*

law of inertia *A law formulated by Galileo that stated that rest was not the natural state of an object. Rather, an object continues in motion forever unless stopped by some external force.*

Kepler formulated three famous laws of planetary motion. First, building on Copernican theory, he demonstrated in 1609 that the orbits of the planets around the sun are elliptical rather than circular. Second, he demonstrated that planets do not move at a uniform speed in their orbits. Third, in 1619 he showed that the time a planet takes to make its complete orbit is precisely related to its distance from the sun. Kepler's contribution was monumental. Whereas Copernicus had speculated, Kepler proved mathematically the precise relations of a sun-centered (solar) system. His work demolished the old system of Aristotle and Ptolemy, and in his third law he came close to formulating the idea of universal gravitation.

While Kepler was unraveling planetary motion, a young Florentine named Galileo Galilei (1564–1642) was challenging the old ideas about motion. Like Kepler and so many early scientists, Galileo was a poor nobleman first marked for a religious career. Instead his fascination with mathematics led to a professorship in which he examined motion and mechanics in a new way. His great achievement was the elaboration of the **experimental method.** That is, rather than speculate about what might or should happen, Galileo conducted controlled experiments to find out what actually *did* happen.

In some of these experiments Galileo measured the movement of a rolling ball across a surface that he constructed, repeating the action again and again to verify his results. In his famous acceleration experiment, he showed that a uniform force—in this case, gravity—produced a uniform acceleration. Through another experiment, he formulated the **law of inertia.** Rest was not the natural state of objects. Rather, an object continues in motion forever unless stopped by some external force. Aristotelian physics was in shambles. In the tradition of Brahe, Galileo also applied the experimental method to astronomy. On hearing details about the invention of the telescope in Holland, Galileo made one for himself. He wrote in 1610 in *Siderus Nuncius:*

By the aid of a telescope anyone may behold [the Milky Way] in a manner which so distinctly appeals to the senses that all the disputes which have tormented philosophers through so many ages are exploded by the irrefutable evidence of our eyes, and we are freed from wordy disputes upon the subject. For the galaxy is nothing else but a mass of innumerable stars planted together in clusters.[4]

Reading these famous lines, one feels a crucial corner in Western civilization being turned. No longer should one rely on established authority. A new method of learning and investigating was being developed, one that proved capable of great extension. A historian investigating documents of the past, for example, is not so different from a Galileo studying stars and rolling balls.

Galileo was employed in Florence by the Medici grand dukes of Tuscany, and his work eventually angered some theologians. In 1624 Pope Urban

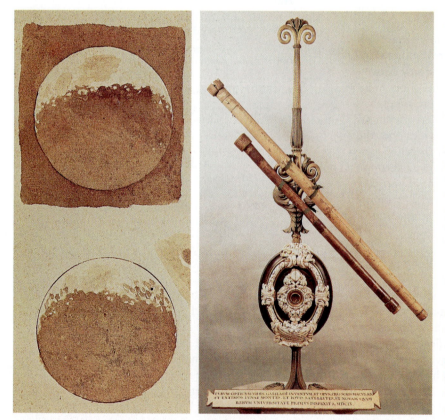

● **Galileo's Paintings of the Moon** When Galileo published the results of his telescopic observations of the moon, he added these paintings to illustrate the marvels he had seen. Galileo made two telescopes, which are shown here. The larger one magnifies fourteen times, the smaller one twenty times. *(Biblioteca Nazionale Centrale, Florence/Art Resource, NY; Museum of Science, Florence/Art Resource, NY)*

VIII ruled that Galileo could write about different possible systems of the world as long as he did not presume to judge which one actually existed. After the publication in Italian of his *Dialogue on the Two Chief Systems of the World* in 1632, which lampooned Aristotle and Ptolemy and defended Copernicus, Galileo was tried for heresy by the papal Inquisition. Imprisoned and threatened with torture, the aging Galileo recanted, "renouncing and cursing" his Copernican errors.

Newton's Synthesis

The accomplishments of Kepler, Galileo, and others had taken effect by about 1640. The old astronomy and physics were in ruins, and several fundamental breakthroughs had been made. But the new findings failed to explain which forces controlled the movement of the planets and objects on earth. That challenge was taken up by the English scientist Isaac Newton (1642–1727). Newton was born into lower English gentry and attended Cambridge University. A genius who spectacularly united the experimental and theoretical-mathematical sides of modern science, Newton was far from being the perfect rationalist eulogized by later centuries. Like many other practitioners of the new science, Newton was both intensely religious and fascinated by alchemy.

He arrived at some of his most basic ideas about physics in 1666 at age twenty-four but was unable to prove them mathematically. In 1684, after years of studying optics, Newton returned to physics for eighteen extraordinarily intensive months. The result was his towering accomplishment, a single explanatory system that could integrate the astronomy of Copernicus, as corrected by Kepler's laws, with the physics of Galileo and his predecessors. Newton did this through a set of mathematical laws that explain motion and mechanics. These laws of dynamics are complex, and it took scientists and engineers two hundred years to work out all their implications. Nevertheless, the key feature of the Newtonian synthesis was the **law of universal gravitation.** According to this law, every body in the universe attracts every other body in the universe in a precise mathematical relationship, whereby the force of attraction is proportional to the quantity of matter of the objects and inversely proportional to the square of the distance between them. The whole universe—from Kepler's elliptical orbits to Galileo's rolling balls—was unified in one majestic system. Newton's synthesis prevailed until the twentieth century.

law of universal gravitation
A law stating that every body in the universe attracts every other body in the universe in a precise mathematical relationship, with the force of attraction being proportional to the quantity of matter of the objects and inversely proportional to the square of the distance between them.

Causes of the Scientific Revolution

The scientific revolution drew on long-term developments in European culture. The first was the development of the medieval university. By the fourteenth and fifteenth centuries leading universities included professorships of mathematics, astronomy, and physics within their faculties of philosophy. Although the prestige of the new fields was low, critical thinking was now applied to scientific problems by a permanent community of scholars. And an outlet existed for the talents of a Galileo or a Newton: all the great pathfinders either studied or taught at universities.

Second, the Renaissance also stimulated scientific progress. The recovery of ancient texts showed that classical mathematicians had their differences; Europeans were forced to try to resolve these ancient controversies by means of their own efforts. Renaissance patrons played a role in funding scientific investigations as well as artistic projects, as the Medicis of Florence did for Galileo.

The navigational problems of long sea voyages in the age of overseas expansion were a third factor in the scientific revolution. As early as 1484 the king of Portugal appointed a commission of mathematicians to perfect tables to help seamen find their latitude. Navigational problems were also critical in the development of many new scientific instruments, such as the telescope, barometer, thermometer, pendulum clock, microscope, and air pump. Better instruments, which permitted more accurate observations, often led to important new knowledge.

The fourth factor in the scientific revolution was the development of better ways of obtaining knowledge about the world. Two important thinkers, Francis Bacon (1561–1626) and René Descartes (1596–1650), were influential in describing and advocating for improved scientific methods based on experimentation and mathematical reasoning.

The English politician and writer Francis Bacon was the greatest early propagandist for the new scientific method. Bacon argued that the researcher who wants to learn more about leaves or rocks should not speculate but rather should collect many specimens and then compare and analyze them. General principles will then emerge. Bacon's contribution was to formalize the empirical method, which had already been used by Brahe and Galileo, into the general theory of inductive reasoning known as **empiricism.**

empiricism *A theory of inductive reasoning that calls for acquiring evidence through observation and experimentation rather than reason and speculation.*

The French philosopher René Descartes was a genius who made his first great discovery in mathematics. As a twenty-three-year-old soldier serving in the Thirty Years' War, he experienced a life-changing intellectual vision one night in 1619. Descartes saw that there was a perfect correspondence between geometry and algebra and that geometrical, spatial figures could be expressed as algebraic equations and vice versa. A major step forward in the history of mathematics, Descartes's discovery of analytic geometry provided scientists with an important new tool.

Descartes's highest achievement was to develop his initial vision into a whole philosophy of knowledge and science. He decided it was necessary to doubt everything that could reasonably be doubted and then, as in geometry, to use deductive reasoning from self-evident principles to ascertain scientific laws. Descartes's reasoning ultimately reduced all substances to "matter" and "mind"—that is, to the physical and the spiritual. His view of the world as consisting of two fundamental entities is known as **Cartesian dualism.**

Cartesian dualism *The premise of René Descartes that all of reality could ultimately be reduced to mind and matter.*

Bacon's inductive experimentalism and Descartes's deductive, mathematical reasoning are combined in the modern scientific method, which emerged in the late seventeenth century. Neither man's extreme approach was sufficient by itself. Bacon's inability to appreciate the importance of mathematics and his obsession with practical results revealed the limitations of antitheoretical empiricism. Likewise, some of Descartes's positions—he believed, for example, that it was possible to deduce the whole science of medicine from first principles—demonstrated the inadequacy of dogmatic rationalism. The modern scientific method has joined precise observations and experimentalism with the search for general laws that may be expressed in rigorously logical, mathematical language.

Science and Society

The rise of modern science had many consequences, some of which are still unfolding. First, it created a new social group—the international **scientific community.** Members of this community were linked by common interests and shared values as well as by the journals and learned scientific societies founded in the later seventeenth and the eighteenth centuries. Their success depended on making new discoveries, and science became competitive. Second, as governments intervened to support research, the new scientific community became closely tied to the state and its agendas. National academies of science were created under state sponsorship in London in 1662, Paris in 1666, Berlin in 1700, and later across Europe. At the same time, scientists developed a critical attitude toward established authority that would inspire thinkers to question traditions in other domains as well.

scientific community *The new international group of scholars with shared values and professional institutions that emerged in the years following the scientific revolution.*

Some things did not change. Scholars have recently analyzed representations of femininity and masculinity in the scientific revolution and have noted that nature was often depicted as a female whose veil of secrecy needed to be stripped away and penetrated by male experts. (In the same time period, the Americas were similarly depicted as a female terrain whose fertile lands needed to be controlled and impregnated by male colonists.) New "rational" methods for approaching nature did not question traditional inequalities between the sexes. Women were largely excluded from academies and then refused membership into scientific communities because they lacked academic credentials. (This continued for a long time. Marie Curie, the first person to win two Nobel prizes, was rejected by the French Academy of Science in 1911 because she was a woman.[5])

There were, however, some exceptions. In Italy, universities and academies did offer posts to women, attracting some foreigners spurned at home. Other women worked as makers of wax anatomical models and as botanical and zoological illustrators. Women were also very much involved in informal scientific communities, attending salons, participating in scientific experiments, and writing learned treatises. Some female intellectuals were recognized as full-fledged members of the philosophical dialogue. In England, Margaret Cavendish, Anne Conway, and Mary Astell all contributed to debates about Descartes's mind-body dualism, among other issues. Descartes himself conducted an intellectual correspondence with the princess Elizabeth of Bohemia, of whom he stated: "I attach more weight to her judgement than to those messieurs the Doctors, who take for a rule of truth the opinions of Aristotle rather than the evidence of reason."[6]

The scientific revolution had few consequences for economic life and mass living standards until the late eighteenth century. True, improvements in the techniques of navigation facilitated overseas trade, but science had relatively few practical economic applications. Thus the scientific revolution was first and foremost an intellectual revolution. For more than a hundred years its greatest impact was on how people thought and believed.

● **Metamorphoses of the Caterpillar and Moth**
Maria Sibylla Merian (1647–1717), the stepdaughter of a Dutch painter, became a celebrated scientific illustrator in her own right. Her finely observed pictures of insects in the South American colony of Surinam introduced many new species, shown in their various stages of development. For Merian, science was intimately tied with art: she not only painted but also bred caterpillars and performed experiments on them. Her two-year stay in Surinam, accompanied by a teenage daughter, was a daring feat for a seventeenth-century woman. (*Bildarchiv Preussischer Kulturbesitz/Art Resource, NY*)

THE ENLIGHTENMENT

How did the new worldview affect the way people thought about society and human relations?

The scientific revolution was the single most important factor in the creation of the new worldview of the eighteenth-century **Enlightenment.** This worldview, which has played a large role in shaping the modern mind, grew out of a rich mix of diverse and often conflicting ideas. Despite the diversity, three central concepts stand at the core of Enlightenment thinking. The most important and original idea was that the methods of natural science could be used to examine and understand all aspects of life. This was what intellectuals meant by *reason,* a favorite word of Enlightenment thinkers.

Enlightenment *An eighteenth-century intellectual movement whose three central concepts were the use of reason, the scientific method, and progress.*

rationalism *The general opinion among Enlightenment thinkers that nothing should be accepted on faith and that everything should be subjected to secular critical examination.*

progress *The goal of Enlightenment thinkers to create better societies and better people by discarding outmoded traditions and embracing rationalism.*

skepticism *The premise, enunciated most clearly by the French Huguenot Pierre Bayle, that nothing could be known beyond all doubt.*

Nothing was to be accepted on faith. Everything was to be submitted to **rationalism**, a secular, critical way of thinking. A second important Enlightenment concept was that the scientific method was capable of discovering the laws of human society as well as those of nature. Thus was social science born. Its birth led to the third key idea, that of **progress.** Armed with the proper method of discovering the laws of human existence, Enlightenment thinkers believed they could help create better societies and better people. Their belief was strengthened by some modest improvements in economic and social life during the eighteenth century.

The Emergence of the Enlightenment

The generation that came of age between the publication of Newton's *Principia* in 1687 and the death of Louis XIV in 1715 tied the knot between the scientific revolution and a new outlook on life. Talented writers of that generation popularized hard-to-understand scientific achievements for the educated elite.

A new generation came to believe that the human mind is capable of making great progress. Medieval and Reformation thinkers had been concerned primarily with sin and salvation. The humanists of the Renaissance had emphasized worldly matters, but their inspiration was the wisdom of the past. Enlightenment thinkers came to believe that, at least in science and mathematics, their era had gone far beyond antiquity. Progress, at least intellectual progress, was very possible.

Some writers of the later seventeenth century came to draw antireligious implications from the scientific revolution. In the wake of the devastation wrought by the Thirty Years' War, some people asked whether ideological conformity in religious matters was really necessary. Others skeptically asked if religious truth could ever be known with absolute certainty and concluded that it could not. This was a new development because many seventeenth-century scientists, like Isaac Newton, believed that their work exalted God and helped explain his creation to fellow believers.

The most famous skeptic was Pierre Bayle (1647–1706), a French Huguenot who found refuge in the Netherlands. Bayle critically examined past religious beliefs and persecutions in his *Historical and Critical Dictionary* (1697). He concluded that nothing can ever be known beyond all doubt, a view known as **skepticism.** His *Dictionary* was reprinted frequently in the Netherlands and in England and was found in more private libraries of eighteenth-century France than any other book.

The rapidly growing travel literature on non-European lands and cultures was another cause of uncertainty. In the wake of the great discoveries, Europeans were learning that the peoples of China, India, Africa, and the Americas all had their own very different beliefs and customs. Europeans shaved their faces and let their hair grow. Turks shaved their heads and let their beards grow. In Europe a man bowed before a woman to show respect. In Siam a man turned his back on a woman when he met

● **Popularizing Science** The frontispiece illustration of *Conversations on the Plurality of Worlds* by Bernard de Fontenelle (1657–1757) invites a nonscientific audience to share the pleasures of astronomy with an elegant lady and an entertaining teacher. The drawing shows the planets revolving around the sun. *(By permission of the Syndics of Cambridge University Library)*

her because it was disrespectful to look directly at her. Countless similar examples discussed in the travel accounts helped change the perspective of educated Europeans. They began to look at truth and morality in relative, rather than absolute, terms.

A final cause and manifestation of European intellectual turmoil was John Locke's *Essay Concerning Human Understanding* (1690). Locke's essay brilliantly set forth a new theory about how human beings learn. Rejecting Descartes's view that people are born with certain basic ideas, Locke insisted that all ideas are derived from experience. The human mind at birth is like a blank tablet, or **tabula rasa,** on which the environment writes the individual's understanding and beliefs. Human development is therefore determined by education and social institutions. Along with Newton's *Principia,* Locke's *Essay Concerning Human Understanding* was a key intellectual inspiration of the Enlightenment.

tabula rasa *Literally, a "blank tablet." It is incorporated into Locke's belief that all ideas are derived from experience and that the human mind at birth is like a blank tablet on which the environment writes the individual's understanding and beliefs.*

The Philosophes and the Public

By the time Louis XIV died in 1715, many elements of the new worldview had been assembled. Yet Christian Europe was still strongly attached to its traditional beliefs, as witnessed by the powerful revival of religious orthodoxy in the first half of the eighteenth century. By the outbreak of the American Revolution in 1775, however, a large portion of western Europe's educated elite had embraced the new ideas. This acceptance was the work of the **philosophes,** a group of influential intellectuals who proclaimed that they were bringing knowledge and reason to the world.

Philosophe is the French word for "philosopher," and it was in France that the Enlightenment reached its highest development. There were at least three reasons for this. First, French was the international language of the educated classes, and France was still Europe's wealthiest and most populous country. Second, although censorship existed in France, it was not as thorough as in eastern and east-central Europe. Philosophes like the baron de Montesquieu (1689–1755) used satire and double meanings to spread their message. Third, French philosophes made it their goal to reach a larger audience of elites, many of whom were joined together in the eighteenth-century concept of the "republic of letters"—an imaginary transnational realm of educated critical thinkers.

philosophes *Intellectuals in France who proclaimed that they were bringing the light of knowledge and reason to their fellow creatures in the Age of Enlightenment.*

The influence of writers like Montesquieu on the enlightened public can be seen in the results of his political writing. Disturbed by royal absolutism under Louis XIV and inspired by the example of the physical sciences, Montesquieu set out to apply the critical method to the problem of government. *The Spirit of Laws* (1748) was a complex comparative study of republics, monarchies, and despotisms—a pioneering inquiry in the emerging social sciences. Showing that forms of government were shaped by history, geography, and customs, Montesquieu focused on the conditions that would promote liberty and prevent tyranny. He argued for a **separation of powers,** with political power divided and shared by a variety of classes and estates holding unequal rights and privileges. Admiring greatly the English balance of power among the king, the houses of Parliament, and the independent courts, Montesquieu believed that in France the thirteen high courts—the *parlements*—were frontline defenders of liberty against royal despotism. Apprehensive about the uneducated poor, Montesquieu was no democrat, but his theory of separation of powers had a great impact on the constitutions of the United States in 1789 and of France in 1791.

separation of powers *The belief, developed by a French philosophe that political power in society should be dispersed and shared rather than focused in a single individual or institution.*

The most famous and in many ways most representative philosophe was François Marie Arouet, who was known by the pen name Voltaire (1694–1778). In his long career, this son of a comfortable middle-class family wrote more than seventy witty volumes, hobnobbed with royalty, and made a fortune in shrewd business speculations. His early career, however, was turbulent, and he was twice arrested for insulting noblemen. Voltaire moved to England for three years to escape his enemies and came to share Montesquieu's enthusiasm for English institutions.

**Primary Source:
Treatise on Toleration**
Voltaire makes a powerful argument for cultural and religious tolerance.

Returning to France, Voltaire had the great fortune of meeting Gabrielle-Emilie Le Tonnelier de Breteuil, marquise du Châtelet (1706–1749), an intellectually gifted woman from the high aristocracy with a passion for science. Inviting Voltaire to live in her country house at Cirey in Lorraine and becoming his long-time companion (under the eyes of her tolerant husband), Madame du Châtelet studied physics and mathematics and published scientific articles and translations. Her translation with an accompanying commentary of Newton's *Principia* into French for the first (and only) time was her greatest work. This female intellectual, who had patiently explained Newton's complex mathematical proofs to Europe's foremost philosophe, had no doubt that women's limited scientific contributions in the past were due to limited and unequal education. She once wrote that if she were a ruler "I would reform an abuse which cuts off, so to speak, half the human race. I would make women participate in all the rights of humankind, and above all in those of the intellect."[7]

While living at Cirey, Voltaire wrote works praising England and popularizing English scientific progress. Newton, he wrote, was history's greatest man, for he had used his genius for the benefit of humanity. "It is," wrote Voltaire, "the man who sways our minds by the prevalence of reason and the native force of truth, not they who reduce mankind to a state of slavery by force and downright violence . . . that claims our reverence and admiration."[8] In the true style of the Enlightenment, Voltaire mixed the glorification of science and reason with an appeal for better individuals and institutions.

Yet like almost all of the philosophes, Voltaire was a reformer, not a revolutionary. He pessimistically concluded that the best one could hope for in government was a good monarch, since human beings "are very rarely worthy to govern themselves." Nor did he believe in social and economic equality. The idea of making servants equal to their masters was "absurd and impossible." The only realizable equality, Voltaire thought, was that "by which the citizen only depends on the laws which protect the freedom of the feeble against the ambitions of the strong."[9]

● **Madame du Châtelet** The marquise du Châtelet was fascinated by the new world system of Isaac Newton. She helped spread Newton's ideas in France by translating his *Principia* and by influencing Voltaire, her companion for fifteen years until her death. *(Giraudon/Art Resource, NY)*

Voltaire's philosophical and religious positions were much more radical. His writings challenged the Catholic Church and Christian theology at almost every point. Voltaire clearly believed in God, but his was a distant, deistic God, the great Clockmaker who built an orderly universe and let it run. Above all, Voltaire and most of the philosophes hated religious intolerance, which they believed led to fanaticism and savage, inhuman action. Simple piety and human kindness—as embodied in Christ's commandments to "love God and your neighbor as yourself"—were religion enough, as may be seen in Voltaire's famous essay on religion.

The ultimate strength of the French philosophes lay in their number, dedication, and organization. The philosophes felt they were engaged in a common undertaking. Their greatest and most representative intellectual achievement was, quite fittingly, a group effort—the seventeen-volume *Encyclopedia: The Rational Dictionary of the Sciences, the Arts, and the Crafts,* edited by Denis Diderot (1713–1784) and Jean le Rond d'Alembert (1717–1783). From different circles and with different interests, the two men enlisted coauthors who would examine the rapidly expanding whole of human knowledge and help them demonstrate how to think critically and objectively about all matters. As Diderot said, he wanted the *Encyclopedia* to "change the general way of thinking."[10]

Not every article was daring or original, but the overall effect was little short of revolutionary. Science and industry were exalted, religion and immortality questioned. Intolerance, injustice, and out-of-date social institutions were openly criticized. The encyclopedists were convinced that greater knowledge would make possible economic, social, and political progress and thus greater human happiness. The *Encyclopedia* was widely read throughout western Europe, especially in less-expensive reprint editions. It summed up the new worldview of the Enlightenment.

Urban Culture and the Public Sphere

Enlightenment ideas did not float on thin air. A series of new institutions and practices emerged in the late seventeenth and eighteenth centuries to facilitate the spread of Enlightenment ideas. First, the production and consumption of books grew dramatically in the eighteenth century. Moreover, the types of books people read changed dramatically. The proportion of religious and devotional books published declined after 1750; history and law held constant; the arts and sciences surged.

Reading more books on many more subjects, Europe's educated public increasingly approached reading in a new way. The result was what some scholars have called

● **Selling Books, Promoting Ideas**   This appealing bookshop with its intriguing ads for the latest works offers to put customers "Under the Protection of Minerva," the Roman goddess of wisdom. Large packets of books sit ready for shipment to foreign countries. Book consumption surged in the eighteenth century. *(Musée des Beaux-Arts, Dijon/Art Resource, NY)*

reading revolution *The transition in Europe from a society where literacy consisted of patriarchal and communal reading of religious texts to a society where literacy was commonplace and reading material was broad and diverse.*

salons *Regular social gatherings held by talented and rich Parisian women in their homes, where philosophes and their followers met to discuss literature, science, and philosophy.*

public sphere *An idealized intellectual environment that emerged in Europe during the Enlightenment, where members of society came together as individuals to discuss issues relevant to the society, economics, and politics of the day.*

a "reading revolution." The old style of reading was centered on a core of sacred texts that inspired reverence and taught earthly duty and obedience to God. Reading was patriarchal and communal, with the father of the family slowly reading the text aloud and the audience savoring each word. Now reading involved a broader field of books that constantly changed. Reading became individual and silent, and texts could be questioned. Subtle but profound, the reading revolution ushered in new ways of relating to the written word.

Conversation and debate also played a critical role in the Enlightenment. Paris set the example, and other European cities followed. In Paris a number of talented wealthy women presided over regular social gatherings in their elegant drawing rooms, or **salons.** There they encouraged the exchange of witty, uncensored observations on literature, science, and philosophy. Talented hostesses, or *salonnières*, mediated the public's freewheeling examination of Enlightenment thought. As one philosophe described his Enlightenment hostess and her salon:

She could unite the different types, even the most antagonistic, sustaining the conversation by a well-aimed phrase, animating and guiding it at will. . . . Politics, religion, philosophy, news: nothing was excluded. Her circle met daily from five to nine. There one found men of all ranks in the State, the Church, and the Court, soldiers and foreigners, and the leading writers of the day.[11]

As this passage suggests, the salons created a cultural realm free from dogma and censorship. There a diverse but educated public could debate issues and form its own ideas. Through their invitation lists, salon hostesses brought together members of the intellectual, economic, and social elites. In such an atmosphere, the philosophes, the French nobility, and the prosperous middle classes intermingled and influenced one another. Thinking critically about almost any question became fashionable and flourished alongside hopes for human progress.

Admirers of the salonnières, some philosophes championed greater rights and expanded education for women, claiming that the position and treatment of women were the best indicators of a society's level of civilization and decency.[12] To be sure, for these male philosophes greater rights for women did not mean equal rights, and the philosophes were not particularly disturbed by the fact that elite women remained legally subordinate to men in economic and political affairs. Elite women lacked many rights, but so did most men.

While membership at the salons was restricted to the well-born and well-connected, a number of institutions emerged for the rest of society. Lending libraries served an important function for people who could not afford to buy their own books. The coffeehouses that first appeared in the late seventeenth century became meccas of philosophical discussion. In addition, book clubs, Masonic lodges, and journals all played roles in the creation of a new **public sphere** that celebrated open debate informed by critical reason. The public sphere was an idealized space where members of society came together as individuals to discuss issues relevant to the society, economics, and politics of the day.

What of the common people? Did they participate in the Enlightenment? Philosophes did not direct their message to peasants or urban laborers. They believed that the masses had no time or talent for philosophical speculation and that elevating them would be a long and potentially dangerous process. Deluded by superstitions and driven by violent passions, they thought, the people were like children in need of firm parental guidance. *Encyclopedia* editor d'Alembert characteristically made a sharp distinction between "the truly enlightened public" and "the blind and noisy multitude."[13]

There is some evidence, however, that the people were not immune to the words of the philosophes. At a time of rising literacy, book prices were dropping in cities and towns, and many philosophical ideas were popularized in cheap pamphlets. Moreover,

even illiterate people had access to written material through the practice of public reading. Although they were barred from salons and academies, ordinary people were not wholly isolated from the new ideas in circulation.

Late Enlightenment

After about 1770 a number of thinkers and writers began to attack Enlightenment faith in reason and progress. The most famous of these was the Swiss Jean-Jacques Rousseau (1712–1778), the son of a poor watchmaker who made his way into the world of Paris salons through his brilliant intellect. Appealing but neurotic, Rousseau came to believe that his philosophe friends and the women of the Parisian salons were plotting against him. In the mid-1750s he broke with them, living thereafter as a lonely outsider with his uneducated common-law wife and going in his own highly original direction.

Like other Enlightenment thinkers, Rousseau was passionately committed to individual freedom. Unlike them, however, he attacked rationalism and civilization as destroying, rather than liberating, the individual. Warm, spontaneous feeling had to complement and correct cold intellect. Moreover, the basic goodness of the individual and the unspoiled child had to be protected from the decadent refinements of civilization. Rousseau's ideals greatly influenced the early romantic movement (see pages 682–683), which rebelled against the culture of the Enlightenment.

Rousseau's critique of social mores included an attack on contemporary gender roles. He believed that since nature relegated women to assume a passive role in sexual relations, they should also be passive in social life. Instead, their passion for attending salons and pulling the strings of power had a corrupting effect on both society and politics. Rousseau thus rejected the sophisticated way of life of Parisian elite women, calling on them to abandon their stylish corsets and breast-feed their children.

● **Enlightenment Culture**
Here the seven-year-old Austrian child prodigy Wolfgang Amadeus Mozart (1756–1791) plays his own composition at an "English tea" given by the Princess de Conti near Paris. Mozart's phenomenal creative powers lasted a lifetime, and he produced a vast range of symphonies, operas, and chamber music. (*Réunion des Musées Nationaux/Art Resource, NY*)

Primary Source:
Rousseau Espouses Popular Sovereignty and the General Will
Modern democracies owe much to the political ideas of this French philosopher.

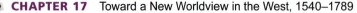

general will *A political concept, first set forth by Jean-Jacques Rousseau, that refers to the collective desires of the citizenry as opposed to individual interests.*

Rousseau's contribution to political theory in *The Social Contract* (1762) would prove enormously influential. His contribution was based on two fundamental concepts: the general will and popular sovereignty. According to Rousseau, the **general will** is sacred and absolute, reflecting the common interests of the people, who have displaced the monarch as the holder of sovereign power. The general will is not necessarily the will of the majority, however. At times the general will may be the authentic, long-term needs of the people as correctly interpreted by a farseeing minority. (The concept has since been used by some dictators who have claimed that they, rather than some momentary majority of the voters, represent the general will.)

As the reading public developed, it joined forces with the philosophes to call for greater freedom of speech. Immanuel Kant (1724–1804), a professor in East Prussia and the greatest German philosopher of his day, posed the question of the age when he published a pamphlet in 1784 entitled *What Is Enlightenment?* Kant answered, "*Sapere Aude!* [dare to know] Have courage to use your own understanding!—that is the motto of enlightenment." He argued that if serious thinkers were allowed to exercise their reason publicly in print, enlightenment would surely follow. Kant was no revolutionary; he also insisted that in their private lives, individuals must obey all laws, no matter how unreasonable, and should be punished for "impertinent" criticism. Kant thus tried to reconcile absolute monarchical authority with a critical public sphere. This balancing act characterized experiments with "enlightened absolutism" in the eighteenth century.

Race and the Enlightenment

In recent years, historians have found in the scientific revolution and the Enlightenment a crucial turning point in European ideas about race. A primary catalyst for new ideas about race was the urge to classify nature unleashed by the scientific revolution's insistence on careful empirical observation. In *The System of Nature* (1735) Swedish botanist Carl von Linné argued that nature was organized into a God-given hierarchy. As scientists developed more elaborate taxonomies of plant and animal species, they also began to classify humans into hierarchically ordered "races" and to investigate the origins of race. The Comte de Buffon argued that humans originated with one species that then developed into distinct races due largely to climactic conditions. According to Immanuel Kant, there were four human races, each of which had derived from an original race of "white brunette" people.

Using the word *race* to designate biologically distinct groups of humans, akin to distinct animal species, was new. Previously, Europeans grouped other peoples into "nations" based on their historical, political, and cultural affiliations, rather than on supposedly innate physical differences. Unsurprisingly, when European thinkers drew up a hierarchical classification of human species, their own "race" was placed at the top. Europeans had long believed they were culturally superior to "barbaric" peoples in Africa and, since 1492, the New World. Emerging ideas about racial difference taught them they were biologically superior as well.

These ideas did not go unchallenged. James Beattie responded directly to claims of white superiority by pointing out that Europeans had started out as savage as nonwhites and that many non-European peoples in the Americas, Asia, and Africa had achieved high levels of civilization. (See the feature "Listening to the Past: Diderot Condemns European Colonialism.")

Scholars are only beginning to analyze links between Enlightenment ideas about race and its notions of equality, progress, and reason. There are clear parallels, though, between the use of science to propagate racial hierarchies and its use to defend social inequalities between men and women. As Rousseau used women's "natural" passivity to argue for their passive role in society, so others used non-Europeans' "natural" inferiority to defend slavery and colonial domination. The new powers of science and reason were thus marshaled to imbue traditional stereotypes with the force of natural law.

THE ENLIGHTENMENT AND ABSOLUTISM

What impact did this new way of thinking have on political developments and monarchical absolutism?

How did the Enlightenment influence politics? To this important question there is no easy answer. Most Enlightenment thinkers outside of England and the Netherlands believed that political change should come from above—from the ruler—rather than from below. It was necessary to educate and "enlighten" the monarch, who could then make good laws and promote human happiness.

Many government officials were attracted to philosophical ideas. They were among the best-educated members of society, and their daily involvement in complex affairs of state made them naturally interested in ideas for reforming human society. Encouraged by these officials, some absolutist rulers of the later eighteenth century tried to govern in an enlightened manner. Yet their actual programs and accomplishments varied greatly. One must closely examine the evolution of monarchical absolutism before judging the significance of what historians have often called the **enlightened absolutism** of the later eighteenth century.

Enlightenment teachings inspired European rulers in small as well as large states in the second half of the eighteenth century. Absolutist princes and monarchs in several west German and Italian states, as well as in Scandinavia, Spain, and Portugal, proclaimed themselves more enlightened. A few smaller states were actually the most successful in making reforms, perhaps because their rulers were not overwhelmed by the size and complexity of their realms. Denmark, for example, carried out extensive land reform in the 1780s that practically abolished serfdom and gave Danish peasants secure tenure on their farms. Yet by far the most influential of the new-style monarchs were in Prussia, Russia, and Austria, and they deserve primary attention.

enlightened absolutism
Term coined by historians to describe the rule of eighteenth-century monarchs who, without renouncing their own absolute authority, adopted Enlightenment ideals of rationalism, progress, and tolerance.

Frederick the Great of Prussia

Frederick II (r. 1740–1786), commonly known as Frederick the Great, built masterfully on the work of his father, Frederick William I (see page 475). Although in his youth he embraced culture and literature rather than the crude life of the barracks, by the time he came to the throne Frederick was determined to use the splendid army that his father had left him. Therefore, when Maria Theresa of Austria inherited the Habsburg dominions upon the death of her father Charles VI, Frederick pounced. He invaded her rich, mainly German province of Silesia in violation of an agreement that had guaranteed her succession. In 1742, as other greedy powers were falling on her lands in the general European War of the Austrian Succession (1740–1748), Maria Theresa was forced to cede almost all of Silesia to Prussia. In one stroke Prussia doubled its population to six million people. Now Prussia unquestionably towered above all the other German states and stood as a European Great Power.

Though successful in 1742, Frederick had to spend much of his reign fighting against great odds to save Prussia from total destruction. When the ongoing competition between Britain and France for colonial empire brought another great conflict in 1756, Maria Theresa fashioned an aggressive alliance with the leaders of France and Russia. During the Seven Years' War (1756–1763), the aim of the alliance was to conquer Prussia and divide its territory. Despite invasions from all sides, Frederick fought with stoic courage. In the end he was miraculously saved: Peter III came to the Russian throne in 1762 and called off the attack against Frederick, whom he greatly admired. The terrible struggle of the Seven Years' War tempered Frederick's interest in territorial expansion and brought him to consider how more enlightened policies for his subjects might also strengthen the state. He tolerantly allowed his subjects to believe as they wished in religious and philosophical matters. He promoted the advancement of knowledge, improving his country's schools and permitting scholars to publish their findings. Moreover, Frederick tried to improve the lives of his subjects more directly. As he wrote his friend Voltaire, "I must enlighten my people, cultivate their manners and morals, and make them as happy as human beings can be, or as happy as the means at my disposal permit."

The legal system and the bureaucracy were Frederick's primary tools. Prussia's laws were simplified, torture of prisoners was abolished, and judges decided cases quickly and impartially. Prussian officials became famous for their hard work and honesty. After the Seven Years' War ended in 1763, Frederick's government energetically promoted the reconstruction of agriculture and industry in his war-torn country. Frederick himself set a good example. He worked hard and lived modestly, claiming that he was "only the first servant of the state." Thus Frederick justified monarchy in terms of practical results and said nothing of the divine right of kings.

Frederick's dedication to high-minded government went only so far, however. While he condemned serfdom in the abstract, he accepted it in practice and did not even free the serfs on his own estates. He accepted and extended the privileges of the nobility, who remained the backbone of the army and the entire Prussian state.

Nor did Frederick listen to thinkers like Moses Mendelssohn (1729–1786), who urged that Jews be given freedom and civil rights. (See the feature "Individuals in Society: Moses Mendelssohn and the Jewish Enlightenment.") The vast majority were confined to tiny, overcrowded ghettos; were excluded by law from most business and professional activities; and could be ordered out of the kingdom at a moment's notice.

Catherine the Great of Russia

Catherine the Great of Russia (r. 1762–1796) was one of the most remarkable rulers of her age, and the French philosophes adored her. Catherine was a German princess from Anhalt-Zerbst, an insignificant principality sandwiched between Prussia and Saxony. Her father commanded a regiment of the Prussian army, but her mother was related to the Romanovs of Russia, and that proved to be Catherine's chance.

At the age of fifteen she was married to the heir to the Russian throne. When her husband Peter III came to power in 1762, his decision to withdraw Russian troops from the coalition against Prussia alienated the army. At the end of six months Catherine and her conspirators deposed Peter III in a palace revolution, and the Orlov brothers murdered him. The German princess became empress of Russia.

Catherine had drunk deeply at the Enlightenment well. Never questioning that absolute monarchy was the best form of government, she set out to rule in an enlightened manner. She had three main goals. First, she worked hard to continue Peter the Great's effort to bring the culture of western Europe to Russia. To do so, she imported Western architects, sculptors, musicians, and intellectuals. She bought many masterpieces of Western art and patronized the philosophes. An enthusiastic letter writer, she corresponded extensively with Voltaire and praised him as the "champion of the human race." When the French government banned the *Encyclopedia,* she offered to publish it in St. Petersburg and sent money to Diderot when he needed it. With these actions, Catherine won good press in the West for herself and for her country. Moreover, this intellectual ruler, who wrote plays and loved good talk, set the tone for the Russian nobility. Peter the Great westernized Russian armies, but it was Catherine who westernized the imagination of the Russian elite.

Catherine's second goal was domestic reform, and she began her reign with sincere and ambitious projects. Better laws were a major concern. In 1767 she appointed a special legislative commission to prepare a new law code. No new unified code was ever produced, but Catherine did restrict the practice of torture and allowed limited religious toleration. She also tried to improve education and strengthen local government. The philosophes applauded these measures and hoped more would follow.

Such was not the case. In 1773 a Cossack soldier named Emelian Pugachev sparked a gigantic uprising of serfs. Proclaiming himself the true tsar, Pugachev issued

Moses Mendelssohn and the Jewish Enlightenment

Lavater (*right*) attempts to convert Mendelssohn, in a painting by Moritz Oppenheim of an imaginary encounter. *(Collection of the Judah L. Magnes Museum, Berkeley)*

In 1743 a small, humpbacked Jewish boy with a stammer left his poor parents in Dessau in central Germany and walked eighty miles to Berlin, the capital of Frederick the Great's Prussia. According to one story, when the boy reached the Rosenthaler Gate, the only one through which Jews could pass, he told the inquiring watchman that his name was Moses and that he had come to Berlin "to learn." The watchman laughed and waved him through. "Go Moses, the sea has opened before you."* Embracing the Enlightenment and seeking a revitalization of Jewish religious thought, Moses Mendelssohn did point his people in a new and uncharted direction.

Turning in Berlin to a learned rabbi he had previously known in Dessau, the young Mendelssohn studied Jewish law and eked out a living copying Hebrew manuscripts in a beautiful hand. But he was soon fascinated by an intellectual world that had been closed to him in the Dessau ghetto. There, like most Jews throughout central Europe, he had spoken Yiddish—a mixture of German, Polish, and Hebrew. Now, working mainly on his own, he mastered German; learned Latin, Greek, French, and English; and studied mathematics and Enlightenment philosophy. Word of his exceptional abilities spread in Berlin's Jewish community (1,500 of the city's 100,000 inhabitants). He began tutoring the children of a wealthy Jewish silk merchant, and he soon became the merchant's clerk and later his partner. But his great passion remained the life of the mind and the spirit, which he avidly pursued in his off hours.

Gentle and unassuming in his personal life, Mendelssohn was a bold thinker. Reading eagerly in Western philosophy since antiquity, he was, as a pious Jew, soon convinced that Enlightenment teachings need not be opposed to Jewish thought and religion. Indeed, he concluded that reason could complement and strengthen religion, although each would retain its integrity as a separate sphere.[†] Developing his idea in his first great work, "On the Immortality of the Soul"

(1767), Mendelssohn used the neutral setting of a philosophical dialogue between Socrates and his followers in ancient Greece to argue that the human soul lived forever. In refusing to bring religion and critical thinking into conflict, he was strongly influenced by contemporary German philosophers who argued similarly on behalf of Christianity. He reflected the way the German Enlightenment generally supported established religion, in contrast to the French Enlightenment, which attacked it. This was the most important difference in Enlightenment thinking between the two countries.

Mendelssohn's treatise on the human soul captivated the educated German public, which marveled that a Jew could have written a philosophical masterpiece. In the excitement, a Christian zealot named Lavater challenged Mendelssohn in a pamphlet to accept Christianity or to demonstrate how the Christian faith was not "reasonable." Replying politely but passionately, the Jewish philosopher affirmed that all his studies had only strengthened him in the faith of his fathers, although he certainly did not seek to convert anyone not born into Judaism. Rather, he urged toleration in religious matters. He spoke up courageously for his fellow Jews and decried the oppression they endured, and he continued to do so for the rest of his life.

Orthodox Jew and German philosophe, Moses Mendelssohn serenely combined two very different worlds. He built a bridge from the ghetto to the dominant culture over which many Jews would pass, including his novelist daughter Dorothea and his famous grandson, the composer Felix Mendelssohn.

Questions for Analysis

1. How did Mendelssohn seek to influence Jewish religious thought in his time?
2. How do Mendelssohn's ideas compare with those of the French Enlightenment?

*H. Kupferberg, *The Mendelssohns: Three Generations of Genius* (New York: Charles Scribner's Sons, 1972), p. 3.

†D. Sorkin, *Moses Mendelssohn and the Religious Enlightenment* (Berkeley: University of California Press, 1996), pp. 8 ff.

MAP 17.1 **The Partition of Poland and Russia's Expansion, 1772–1795** By 1700 Poland had become a weak and decentralized republic with an elected king. All important decisions continued to require the unanimous agreement of all nobles elected to the Polish Diet, which meant that nothing could ever be done to strengthen the state. In 1772 war threatened between Russia and Austria over Russian gains from the Ottoman Empire. To satisfy desires for expansion without fighting, Prussia's Frederick the Great proposed that parts of Poland be divided among Austria, Prussia, and Russia. In 1793 and 1795 the three powers partitioned the remainder, and the ancient republic of Poland vanished from the map.

"decrees" abolishing serfdom, taxes, and army service. Thousands joined his cause, slaughtering landlords and officials over a vast area of southwestern Russia. Pugachev's untrained forces eventually proved no match for Catherine's regular army. Betrayed by his own company, Pugachev was captured and savagely executed.

Pugachev's rebellion put an end to any intentions Catherine might have had about reforming the system. The peasants were clearly dangerous, and her empire rested on noble support. After 1775 Catherine gave the nobles absolute control of their serfs. She extended serfdom into new areas, such as Ukraine. In 1785 she formalized the nobility's privileged position, freeing them from taxes and state service. Under Catherine the Russian nobility attained its most exalted position, and serfdom entered its most oppressive phase.

Catherine's third goal was territorial expansion, and in this respect she was extremely successful. Her armies subjugated the last descendants of the Mongols, the Crimean Tatars, and began conquest of the Caucasus. Her greatest coup by far was the partition

● **Catherine the Great as Equestrian and Miniature of Count Grigory Grigoryevich Orlov** Catherine conspired with her lover, the officer Grigory Orlov, to overthrow her husband Peter III. Grigory and his four officer brothers commanded considerable support among the soldiers stationed in St. Petersburg, who supported the coup. After she became empress, Catherine raised Grigory to the rank of count. Together they had an illegitimate son. *(left: Musée des Beaux-Arts, Chartres/The Bridgeman Art Library; right: State Hermitage Museum, St. Petersburg)*

of Poland (see Map 17.1). When, between 1768 and 1772, Catherine's armies scored unprecedented victories against the Turks and thereby threatened to disturb the balance of power in eastern Europe, Frederick the Great of Prussia obligingly came forward with a deal. He proposed that Turkey be let off easily and that Prussia, Austria, and Russia each compensate itself by taking a gigantic slice of the weakly ruled Polish territory. Catherine jumped at the chance. The first partition of Poland took place in 1772. Two more partitions, in 1793 and 1795, gave all three powers more Polish territory, and the ancient republic of Poland vanished from the map.

The Austrian Habsburgs

In Austria two talented rulers did manage to introduce major reforms, although traditional power politics was more important than Enlightenment teachings. One was Joseph II (r. 1780–1790), a fascinating individual. For an earlier generation of historians, he was the "revolutionary emperor," a tragic hero whose lofty reforms were undone by the landowning nobility. More recent scholarship has revised this romantic interpretation and has stressed how Joseph II continued the state-building work of his mother, the empress Maria Theresa (1740–1780), a remarkable but old-fashioned absolutist.

Emerging from the long War of the Austrian Succession in 1748 with the serious loss of Silesia, Maria Theresa and her closest ministers were determined to introduce reforms that would make the state stronger and more efficient. Three aspects of these reforms were most important. First, Maria Theresa introduced measures aimed at limiting the papacy's political influence in her realm. Second, a series of administrative reforms strengthened the central bureaucracy, minimized provincial differences, and revamped the tax system, taxing even the lands of some nobles. Third, the government sought to improve the lot of the agricultural population, cautiously reducing the power of lords over their hereditary serfs and their partially free peasant tenants.

Coregent with his mother from 1765 onward and a strong supporter of change, Joseph II moved forward rapidly when he came to the throne in 1780. Most notably, Joseph abolished serfdom in 1781, and in 1789 he decreed that all peasant labor obligations be converted into cash payments. This measure was violently rejected not only by the nobility but also by the peasants it was intended to help since they lacked the necessary cash. When a disillusioned Joseph died prematurely at forty-nine, the entire Habsburg empire was in turmoil. His brother Leopold II (r. 1790–1792) canceled Joseph's radical edicts in order to reestablish order. Peasants once again were required to do forced labor for their lords.

The eastern European absolutists of the later eighteenth century combined old-fashioned state-building with the culture and critical thinking of the Enlightenment. In doing so, they succeeded in expanding the role of the state in the life of society. They perfected bureaucratic machines that were to prove surprisingly adaptive and capable of enduring into the twentieth century. Their failure to implement policies we would recognize as humane and enlightened—such as abolishing serfdom—may reveal inherent failures in Enlightenment thinking about equality and social justice, rather than in their execution of an Enlightenment program. The fact that leading philosophes supported rather than criticized Eastern rulers' policies suggests the blinders of the era.

Chapter Summary

Key Terms

natural philosophy
Copernican hypothesis
experimental method
law of inertia
law of universal gravitation
empiricism
Cartesian dualism
scientific community
Enlightenment
rationalism
progress
skepticism
tabula rasa
philosophes
separation of powers
reading revolution
salons
public sphere
general will
enlightened absolutism

To assess your mastery of this chapter, go to
bedfordstmartins.com/mckayworld

• *What was revolutionary in new attitudes toward the natural world?*

Decisive breakthroughs in astronomy and physics in the seventeenth century demolished the imposing medieval synthesis of Aristotelian philosophy and Christian theology. These developments had only limited practical consequences at the time, but the impact of new scientific knowledge on intellectual life was enormous. The emergence of modern science was a distinctive characteristic of Western civilization and became a key element of Western identity.

• *How did the new worldview affect the way people thought about society and human relations?*

Interpreting scientific findings and Newtonian laws in a manner that was both antitradition and antireligion, Enlightenment philosophes extolled the superiority of rational critical thinking. This new method, they believed, promised not just increased knowledge but also the discovery of the fundamental laws of human society. Although they reached differing conclusions when they turned to social and political realities, they did stimulate absolute monarchs to apply reason to statecraft and the search for useful reforms. Above all, the philosophes succeeded in shaping an emerging public opinion and spreading their radically new worldview. During the eighteenth century philosophers drew on scientific principles for new definitions of race, which often justified belief in Western superiority.

• What impact did this new way of thinking have on political developments and monarchical absolutism?

The ideas of the Enlightenment were an inspiration for monarchs, particularly absolutist rulers in central and eastern Europe, who saw in them important tools for reforming and rationalizing their governments. Their primary goal was to strengthen their states and increase the efficiency of their bureaucracies and armies. Enlightened absolutists believed that these reforms would ultimately improve the lot of ordinary people, but this was not their chief concern. With few exceptions, they did not question the institution of serfdom. The fact that leading philosophes supported rather than criticized Eastern rulers' policies suggests some of the limitations of the era.

Suggested Reading

Alexander, John T. *Catherine the Great: Life and Legend.* 1989. The best biography of the famous Russian tsarina.

Beales, Derek. *Joseph II.* 1987. A fine biography of the reforming Habsburg ruler.

Chartier, Roger. *The Cultural Origins of the French Revolution.* 1991. An imaginative analysis of the changing attitudes of the educated public.

Eze, E. Chukwudi, ed. *Race and the Enlightenment: A Reader.* 1997. An invaluable source on the origins of modern racial thinking in the Enlightenment.

Goodman, Dena. *The Republic of Letters: A Cultural History of the Enlightenment.* 1994. An innovative study of the role of salons and salon hostesses in the rise of the Enlightenment.

MacDonagh, Giles. *Frederick the Great.* 2001. An outstanding biography of the Prussian king.

Munck, Thomas. *The Enlightenment: A Comparative History.* 2000. Compares developments in Enlightenment thought in different countries.

Muthu, Sankar. *Enlightenment Against Empire.* 2003. Examines Enlightenment figures' opposition to colonialism.

Outram, Dorinda. *The Enlightenment,* 2d ed. 2006. An outstanding and accessible introduction to Enlightenment debates that emphasizes the Enlightenment's social context and global reach.

Schiebinger, Londa. *The Mind Has No Sex? Women in the Origins of Modern Science.* 1998. Discusses how the new science excluded women.

Shapin, Steven. *The Scientific Revolution.* 2001. A concise and well informed general introduction to the scientific revolution.

Sorkin, David. *Moses Mendelssohn and the Religious Enlightenment.* 1996. A brilliant study of the Jewish philosopher and of the role of religion in the Enlightenment.

Notes

1. H. Butterfield, *The Origins of Modern Science* (New York: Macmillan, 1951), p. viii.
2. Quoted in A. G. R. Smith, *Science and Society in the Sixteenth and Seventeenth Centuries* (New York: Harcourt Brace Jovanovich, 1972), p. 97.
3. Quoted in Butterfield, *The Origins of Modern Science,* p. 47.
4. Ibid., p. 120.
5. L. Schiebinger, *The Mind Has No Sex? Women in the Origins of Modern Science* (Cambridge, Mass.: Harvard University Press, 1989), p. 2.
6. Jacqueline Broad, *Women Philosophers of the Seventeenth Century* (Cambridge: Cambridge University Press, 2003), p. 17.
7. Schiebinger, *The Mind Has No Sex?* p. 64.
8. Quoted in L. M. Marsak, ed., *The Enlightenment* (New York: John Wiley & Sons, 1972), p. 56.
9. Quoted in G. L. Mosse et al., eds., *Europe in Review* (Chicago: Rand McNally, 1964), p. 156.
10. Quoted in P. Gay, "The Unity of the Enlightenment," *History* 3 (1960): 25.
11. Quoted in G. P. Gooch, *Catherine the Great and Other Studies* (Hamden, Conn.: Archon Books, 1966), p. 149.
12. See E. Fox-Genovese, "Women in the Enlightenment," in *Becoming Visible: Women in European History,* 2d ed., ed. R. Bridenthal, C. Koonz, and S. Stuard (Boston: Houghton Mifflin, 1987), esp. pp. 252–259, 263–265.
13. Jean Le Rond d'Alembert, *Eloges lus dans les séances publiques de l'Académie française* (Paris, 1779), p. ix, quoted in Mona Ozouf, "'Public Opinion' at the End of the Old Regime," *The Journal of Modern History* 60, Supplement: Rethinking French Politics in 1788 (September 1988), p. S9.

Listening to the PAST

Diderot Condemns European Colonialism

Europe's global expansion and the travel literature it produced (see Chapter 15) fascinated the philosophes and the reading public. Most travel literature portrayed indigenous peoples as savages, but Enlightenment thinkers often subjected Europeans to unflattering comparisons with indigenous societies in order to criticize European laws and customs.

A small band led by Denis Diderot went further and strongly condemned European conquest and empire building. Diderot wrote many of the unsigned articles in Guillaume Thomas Reynal's History of European Settlements and Commerce in the Two Indies, *a highly critical, banned bestseller. He also reviewed Louis Antoine de Bougainville's* Voyage Around the World *(1771) and in 1772 wrote* Supplement to the Voyage of Bougainville *(published in 1796). In the* Supplement's *second section Diderot uses an imaginary farewell speech by a Tahitian elder to denounce the evils that Bougainville and his companions brought to the island of Tahiti in the South Pacific.*

The Elder's Farewell

. . . You, Bougainville, leader of the ruffians who obey you, pull your ship away swiftly from these shores. We are innocent, we are content, and you can only spoil that happiness. We follow the pure instincts of nature, and you have tried to erase its impression from our hearts. Here, everything belongs to everyone, and you have preached some strange distinction between "yours" and "mine." Our daughters and our wives belong to us all. You shared that privilege with us, and you enflamed them with a frenzy they had never known before. They have become wild in your arms, and you have become deranged in theirs. . . . We are free, but into our earth you have now staked your title to our future servitude. You are neither a god nor a devil. Who are you, then, to make us slaves? Orou, you who understand the language of these men, tell us all, as you have told me, what they have written

on that strip of metal: *This land is ours.* So this land is yours? Why? Because you set foot on it! If a Tahitian should one day land on your shores and engrave on one of your stones or on the bark of one of your trees, *This land belongs to the people of Tahiti,* what would you think then? You are stronger than we are, and what does that mean? When one of the miserable trinkets with which your ship is filled was taken away, what an uproar you made, what revenge you exacted! At that very moment, in the depths of your heart, you were plotting the theft of an entire country! You are not a slave, you would rather die than be one, and yet you wish to make slaves of us. . . . This inhabitant of Tahiti, whom you wish to ensnare like an animal, is your brother. You are both children of Nature. . . .

Leave us to our own customs; they are wiser and more decent than yours. We have no wish to exchange what you call our ignorance for your useless knowledge. Everything that we need and is good for us we already possess. Do we merit contempt because we have not learnt how to acquire superfluous needs? When we are hungry, we have enough to eat. When we are cold, we have enough to wear. You have entered our huts; what do you suppose we lack? Pursue as far as you wish what you call the comforts of life, but let sensible beings stop when they have no more to gain from their labours than imaginary benefits. . . . We have kept our annual and daily labours within the smallest possible limits, because in our eyes nothing is better than leisure. Go back to your own country to agitate and torment yourself as much as you like. But leave us in peace. Do not fill our heads with your false needs and illusory virtues. Look at these men. See how upright, healthy and robust they are. Look at these women. See how they too stand up straight, how healthy, fresh and lovely they are. . . . I can run a league across the plain in less than an hour; your young companions can hardly keep up with me, and yet I'm more than ninety years old.

Woe to this island! Woe to all present Tahitians and to those still to come, from the day of your arrival! We

Painting by Jean-Honoré Fragonard of Denis Diderot, one of the editors of the *Encyclopedia*, the greatest intellectual achievement of the Enlightenment. *(Erich Lessing/Art Resource, NY)*

used to know but one disease, old age, to which men, animals and plants were all equally prey, but you have now brought us a new one [venereal disease]. You have infected our blood. Perhaps we shall be forced to wipe out, with our own hands, some of our daughters, some of our wives and children, those who have lain with your women, and those who have been with your men. . . . A short while ago a young maiden of Tahiti would yield blissfully to the embraces of a Tahitian youth, once she had reached the age of marriage; she would wait impatiently for her mother to lift her veil and expose her breasts; she was proud to stir the desires and attract the amorous glances of a stranger, her relatives, her brother. Without fear or shame, in our presence, in the midst of a circle of innocent Tahitians, to the sound of flutes and between the dances, she welcomed the caresses of the youth whom her young heart and the secret promptings of her senses had selected for her. It was you who first brought the idea of crime and the risk of illness to us.

Our pleasures, once so sweet, are now accompanied with remorse and fear. That man in black [a priest], who stands by your side and listens to me, spoke to our young men; I do not know what he said to our girls, but now they blush and the boys hesitate. If you wish, creep away into the dark forest with the perverse partner of your pleasures, but let the good and simple inhabitants of Tahiti multiply without shame in the light of day under the open sky. What more honest and noble sentiment can you put in the place of the one which we have inspired in them and which nurtures them? When they believe the moment has arrived to enrich the nation and the family with a new citizen, they exalt in it. They eat to live, and to grow; they

grow to multiply, and in that they see neither vice nor shame. Take heed of the effects of your offences. You had hardly arrived among them before they became thieves. You had hardly set foot on our soil before it reeked of blood. The Tahitian who ran to meet you, to greet you, who welcomed you crying, "*taïo,* friend, friend," you killed. And why did you kill him? Because he had been tempted by the glitter of your little serpent's eggs. He offered you his fruits, his wife, his daughter, his hut, and you killed him for a handful of beads which he took without asking. . . .

Go away now, unless your cruel eyes relish the spectacle of death. Go away, leave, and may the guilty seas that spared you on your voyage absolve themselves of their fault and avenge us by swallowing you up before your return.

Questions for Analysis

1. According to the Tahitian elder, in what ways does European expansion and empire building harm Tahitians and other indigenous peoples?

2. What European customs, beliefs, and institutions does Diderot attack through the elder's comparisons of Tahiti and Europe?

Source: Slightly adapted from *Supplement to the Voyage of Bougainville,* in Denis Diderot, *Political Writings,* trans. and ed. John Hope Mason and Robert Wokler (Cambridge: Cambridge University Press, 1992), pp. 41–45. Reprinted with the permission of Cambridge University Press.

Waist Pendant of Benin, Edo Peoples, Nigeria, 16th–19th Centuries. The facial features, the beard, and the ruffled collar are clearly Portuguese, but the braided hair is distinctly African, probably signifying royalty. *(The Metropolitan Museum of Art, Gift of Mr. and Mrs. Klaus G. Perls, 1991 [1991.162.9]. Photograph © 1991 The Metropolitan Museum of Art)*

18 AFRICA AND THE WORLD, CA. 1400–1800

Chapter Preview

Senegambia and Benin
• What different types of economic, social, and political structures were found in Senegambia and Benin?

The Sudan: Songhai, Kanem-Bornu, and Hausaland
• In what ways was the trans-Saharan trade important to the West African kingdoms of Songhai, Kanem-Bornu, and Hausaland?

Ethiopia
• How did the Coptic Christian Church in Ethiopia serve as a unifying force for the society and for the kingdom?

The Swahili City-States
• What was the significance of the Indian Ocean to the political and economic organization of the Swahili city-states?

The African Slave Trade
• What role did slavery play in African societies before European intrusion?

African states and societies of the fifteenth through eighteenth centuries comprised hundreds of ethnic groups and a wide variety of languages, cultures, and kinds of economic and political development. Modern European intrusion into Africa beginning in the fifteenth century led to the transatlantic slave trade, one of the greatest forced migrations in world history. Africa made a substantial, though involuntary, contribution to the building of the West's industrial civilization. In the seventeenth century an increasing desire for sugar in Europe resulted in an increasing demand for slave labor in South America and the West Indies. In the eighteenth century Western technological changes created a demand for cotton and other crops that required extensive human labor. As a result, the West's "need" for African slaves increased dramatically.

SENEGAMBIA AND BENIN

What different types of economic, social, and political structures were found in Senegambia and Benin?

In mid-fifteenth century Africa, a number of kingdoms flourished along the two-thousand-mile west coast between Senegambia and the northeastern shore of the Gulf of Guinea. Because much of that coastal region is covered by tropical rain forest, in contrast to the western Sudan, it is called the West African Forest Region (see Map 18.1). The Senegambian states possessed a homogeneous culture and a common history. For centuries Senegambia—named for the Senegal and Gambia Rivers—served as an important entrepôt for desert caravan contact with North African and Middle Eastern Islamic civilizations. Through the transatlantic slave trade, Senegambia came into contact with Europe and the Americas. Thus Senegambia felt the impact of Islamic culture to the north and of European influences from the maritime West.

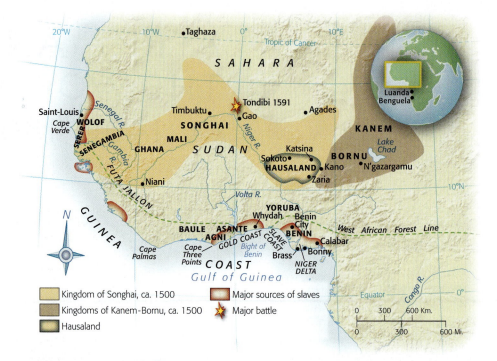

MAP 18.1 **West African Kingdoms and the Slave Trade, ca. 1500–1800** Consider the role that rivers and other geographical factors played in the development of the West African slave trade. Why were Luanda and Benguela the logical Portuguese sources for slaves?

age-grade systems *Among the societies of Senegambia, groups of men and women whom the society initiated into adulthood at the same time.*

oba *The name for the king of Benin.*

The Senegambian peoples spoke Wolof, Serer, and Pulaar, which all belong to the West African language group. Both the Wolof-speakers and the Serer-speakers had clearly defined social classes: royalty, nobility, warriors, peasants, low-caste artisans such as blacksmiths and leatherworkers, and slaves. Slaves were individuals who were pawned for debt, house servants who could not be sold, and people who were acquired through war or purchase. Senegambian slavery varied from society to society but generally was not a benign institution. In some places, slaves were treated as harshly as they would be later in the Western Hemisphere. However, many Senegambian slaves were not considered chattel property to be bought and sold, and some served as royal advisers and enjoyed great power and prestige.[1]

Among Senegambia's stateless societies, where kinship and lineage groups tended to fragment communities, **age-grade systems** evolved. Age-grades were groups of teenage males and females whom the society initiated into adulthood at the same time. Age-grades cut across family ties, created community-wide loyalties, and provided a means of local law enforcement, because each age-grade was responsible for the behavior of all its members.

The typical Senegambian community was a small, self-supporting agricultural village of closely related families. Fields were cut from the surrounding forest, and the average six- to eight-acre farm supported a moderate-size family. Millet and sorghum were the staple grains in northern Senegambia; farther south, forest dwellers cultivated yams as a staple. Village markets for produce exchange offered opportunities for receiving outside news and social diversion. As one scholar has put it, "Life was simple, government largely limited to the settlement of disputes by family heads or elders . . . social life centered on the ceremony accompanying birth, death, and family alliance."[2]

The great forest kingdom of Benin (see Map 18.1) emerged in the fifteenth and sixteenth centuries in what is now southern Nigeria. In the later fifteenth century, the **oba** (or king), Ewuare, a great warrior himself, strengthened his army and pushed Benin's borders as far as the Niger River in the east, westward into Yoruba country, and south to the Gulf of Guinea. During the late sixteenth and seventeenth centuries, the office of the oba evolved from a warrior-kingship to a position of spiritual leadership.

At its height in the late sixteenth century, Benin controlled a vast territory, and European visitors described a sophisticated society. The capital, Benin City, "was a stronghold twenty-five miles in circumference, protected by walls and natural defenses, containing an elaborate royal palace and neatly laid-out houses with verandas and balustrades, and divided by broad avenues and smaller intersecting streets."[3] Visitors also noted that Benin City was kept scrupulously clean and had no beggars and that public security was so effective that theft was unknown. The period also witnessed remarkable artistic creativity in ironwork, carved ivory, and especially bronze portrait busts. Over nine hundred brass plaques survive, providing important information about Benin court life, military triumphs, and cosmological ideas.

In 1485 Portuguese and other Europeans began to appear in Benin in pursuit of trade. Europe's impact on Benin was minimal, however. In the early eighteenth century, tributary states and stronger neighbors nibbled at Benin's frontiers, challenging its power. Benin, however, survived as an independent entity until the British conquered and burned Benin City in 1898.

Women, Marriage, and Work

West Africa's population needs (see page 538) profoundly affected marriage patterns and family structure. Wives and children were highly desired because they could clear and cultivate the land and because they brought prestige, social support, and security in old age. The result was intense competition for women, inequality of access to them, an emphasis on male virility and female fertility, and serious tension between male generations. Polygyny was almost universal; as recently as the nineteenth century two-thirds of rural wives were in polygynous marriages.

Men acquired wives in two ways. First, some couples simply eloped and began unions. More commonly, a man's family compensated the bride's family through the payment of bride wealth for the loss of her reproductive abilities: children; food through her labor; and the culture as she raised her children. Because it took time for a young man to acquire the bride wealth, all but the richest men delayed marriage until about age thirty. Women married at about the onset of puberty.

The easy availability of land in Africa reduced the kinds of generational conflict that occurred in western Europe, where land was scarce. Competition for wives between male generations, however, became "one of the most dynamic and enduring forces in African history."[4] On the one hand, myth and folklore stressed respect for the elderly, and the older men in a community imposed their authority over the younger ones by

Chronology

1400–1600s Salt trade dominates West African economy

ca. 1400–1846 Kanem-Bornu kingdom controls region around Lake Chad

ca. 1440–1550 First Portuguese exploration and settlement along Africa's coasts

ca. 1464–1591 Songhai kingdom dominates the western Sudan

1485 Portuguese and other Europeans first appear in Benin

1492–1528 Muhammad Toure governs and expands kingdom of Songhai

1498 Portuguese explorer Vasco da Gama sails around Africa; Swahili cities' independence begins to decline

ca. 1500–1900 Height of African slave trade

1526 Leo Africanus publishes account of his stay in the Songhai kingdom

1529 Ahmad ibn-Ghazi destroys Ethiopian artistic and literary works and forces conversions to Islam

1541 Portuguese defeat Muslims in Ethiopia

1571–1603 Idris Alooma governs kingdom of Kanem-Bornu

1591 Moroccan army defeats Songhai

1658 Dutch allow importation of slaves into Cape Colony

1680s Famine from Senegambian coast to Upper Nile

1738–1756 Major famine in West Africa

1788 Olaudah Equiano publishes *Travels*

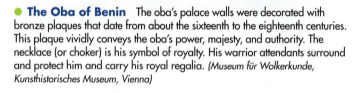

• **The Oba of Benin** The oba's palace walls were decorated with bronze plaques that date from about the sixteenth to the eighteenth centuries. This plaque vividly conveys the oba's power, majesty, and authority. The necklace (or choker) is his symbol of royalty. His warrior attendants surround and protect him and carry his royal regalia. *(Museum für Wolkerkunde, Kunsthistorisches Museum, Vienna)*

including painful rites of initiation into adulthood, such as circumcision. On the other hand, West African societies were not gerontocracies, as few people lived much beyond forty. Young men possessed the powerful asset of their labor, which could easily be turned into independence where so much land was available.

"Without children you are naked" goes a Yoruba proverb, and children were the primary goal of marriage. Just as a man's virility determined his honor, so barrenness damaged a woman's status. A wife's infidelity was considered a less serious problem than her infertility. A woman might have six widely spaced pregnancies in her fertile years; the universal practice of breast-feeding infants for two, three, or even four years may have inhibited conception. Long intervals between births due to food shortages also may have limited pregnancies and checked population growth. Harsh climate, poor nutrition, and infectious diseases also contributed to a high infant mortality rate.

Both nuclear and extended families were common in West Africa. Nuclear families averaged only five or six members, but the household of a Big Man (a local man of power) included his wives, married and unmarried sons, unmarried daughters, poor relations, dependents, and scores of children. Extended families were common among the Hausa and Malinke peoples. On the Gold Coast in the seventeenth century, a well-to-do man's household might number 150 people, in the Kongo region several hundred. Where one family cultivated extensive land, a large household of young adults, children, and slaves probably proved most efficient.

In agriculture men did the heavy work of felling trees and clearing the land; women then planted, weeded, and harvested. Between 1000 and 1400, cassava (manioc), bananas, and plantains came to West Africa from Asia. Cassava became a staple food, but it had little nutritional value. In the sixteenth century the Portuguese introduced maize (corn), sweet potatoes, and new varieties of yams from the Americas.[5] Fish supplemented the diets of people living near bodies of water. According to Olaudah Equiano, the Ibo people in the mid-eighteenth century ate plantains, yams, beans, and Indian corn, along with stewed poultry, goat, or bullock (castrated steer) seasoned with peppers.[6] Such a protein-rich diet was probably exceptional.

Disease posed perhaps the biggest obstacle to population growth. Malaria, spread by mosquitoes and rampant in West Africa (except in cool, dry Cameroon), was the greatest killer, especially of infants. West Africans developed a relatively high degree of immunity to malaria and other parasitic diseases, including hookworm (which enters the body through shoeless feet and attaches itself to the intestines), yaws (contracted by nonsexual contact and recognized by ulcerating lesions), sleeping sickness (the parasite enters the blood through the bite of the tsetse fly; symptoms are enlarged lymph nodes and, at the end, a comatose state), and a mild nonsexual form of syphilis. Acute strains of smallpox introduced by Europeans certainly did not help population growth, nor did venereal syphilis. As in Chinese and European communities in the early modern period, the sick depended on folk medicine. African medical specialists, such as midwives, bone setters, exorcists using religious methods, and herbalists, administered a variety of treatments including herbal medications like salves, ointments, and purgatives. Still, disease was common where the diet was poor and lacked adequate vitamins. Slaves taken to the Americas grew much taller and broader than their African cousins.

Drought, excessive rain, swarms of locusts, and rural wars that prevented the cultivation of land all meant later food shortages and devastating famines that proved another major check on population growth. In the 1680s famine extended from the Senegambian coast to the Upper Nile, and many people sold themselves into slavery for food. In the eighteenth century "slave exports" (see pages 526–539) "peaked during famines, and one ship obtained a full cargo merely by offering food." [7] The worst disaster occurred from 1738 to 1756, when, according to one chronicler, the poor were reduced to cannibalism, an African metaphor for the complete collapse of civilization.[8]

Trade and Industry

As in all premodern societies, West African economies rested on agriculture. There was some trade and industry, but population shortages encouraged local self-sufficiency, slowed transportation, and hindered exchange. There were very few large markets, and their relative isolation from the outside world and failure to attract large numbers of foreign merchants limited technological innovation.

As elsewhere, water was the cheapest method of transportation, and many small dugout canoes and larger trading canoes plied the Niger and its delta region (see Map 18.1). On land West African peoples used pack animals (camels or donkeys) rather than wheeled vehicles; south of the Sahara, only a narrow belt of land was suitable for animal-drawn carts. When traders reached an area infested with tsetse flies, they transferred each animal's load to human porters. Such difficulties in transport severely restricted long-distance trade, so most people relied on the regional exchange of local specialties.

West African communities had a well-organized market system. At informal markets on riverbanks, fishermen bartered fish for local specialties. More formal markets existed within towns and villages or on neutral ground between them. Markets also rotated among neighboring villages on certain days. People exchanged cotton cloth, thread, palm oil, millet, vegetables, and small articles for daily living. Local sellers were usually women; traders from afar were men.

From time immemorial, salt has been one of the most critical trade items. Salt is essential to human health; the Hausa language has more than fifty words for it. The main salt-mining center was at **Taghaza** (see Map 18.1) in the western Sahara. In the most wretched conditions, slaves dug the salt from desiccated lakes and loaded heavy blocks onto camels' backs. **Tuareg** warriors and later Moors (peoples of Berber and

● **Queen Mother and Attendants** As in Ottoman, Chinese, and European societies, so the mothers of African rulers sometimes exercised considerable political power because of their influence on their sons. African kings granted the title "Queen Mother" as a badge of honor. In this figure, the long beaded cap, called "chicken's beak," symbolizes the mother's rank, as do her elaborate neck jewelry and attendants. *(Metropolitan Museum of Art. Gift of Mr. and Mrs. Klaus G. Perls, 1991 [1991.17.111]. Photograph © 1991 The Metropolitan Museum of Art)*

Taghaza *A desolate settlement in the western Sahara; it was the site of the main salt-mining center.*

Tuareg *Along with the Moors, these warriors controlled the north-south trade in salt.*

522

● **Salt Making in the Central Sahara** For centuries camel caravans transported salt south across the Sahara to the great West African kingdoms, where it was exchanged for gold. Here at Tegguida-n-Tessum, Niger, in the central Sahara, salt is still collected by pouring spring water (stored in the larger pools in the background) into the smaller pools dug out of the saline soil. The water leaches out the salt before evaporating in the desert sun, leaving deposits of pure salt behind, which is then shaped into blocks for transport. *(Afrique Photo, Cliché Naud, Paris)*

Cowrie shells *Imported from the Maldive Islands, these served as the medium of exchange in West Africa.*

Arab descent) traded their salt south for gold, grain, slaves, and kola nuts, which were used by Muslims as stimulants or aphrodisiacs. **Cowrie shells,** imported from the Maldive Islands in the Indian Ocean by way of Gujarat (see page 565) and North Africa, served as the medium of exchange. (Shell money continued as a medium long after European intrusion.)

West African peoples engaged in many crafts, such as basket weaving and pottery making. Iron-working, a specialized skill producing articles useful to hunters, farmers, and warriors, became hereditary in individual families; such expertise was regarded as family property. The textile industry had the greatest level of specialization. The earliest fabric in West Africa was made of vegetable fiber. Muslim traders introduced cotton and its weaving in the ninth century, as the fine-quality fabrics found in Mali reveal. By the fifteenth century the Wolof and Malinke regions had professional weavers producing beautiful cloth, but this cloth was too expensive to compete in the Atlantic and Indian Ocean markets after 1500. Women who spun cotton used only a spindle and not a wheel, which slowed output. Women wove on inefficient broadlooms, men on less clumsy but unproductive narrow looms.[9]

THE SUDAN: SONGHAI, KANEM-BORNU, AND HAUSALAND

In what ways was the trans-Saharan trade important to the West African kingdoms of Songhai, Kanem-Bornu, and Hausaland?

The Songhai kingdom, a successor state of Ghana and Mali, dominated the whole Niger region of the western and central Sudan (see Map 18.1). From his capital at Gao, the Songhai king Muhammad Toure (r. 1492–1528) extended his rule as far north as the salt-mining center at Taghaza in the western Sahara and as far east as Agada and Kano. A convert to Islam, Muhammad returned from a pilgrimage to Mecca impressed by what he had seen there. He tried to bring about greater centralization in his own territories by building a strong army, improving taxation procedures, and replacing local Songhai officials with more efficient Arab ones in an effort to substitute royal institutions for ancient kinship ties.

We know little about daily life in Songhai society because of the paucity of written records and surviving artifacts. Some information is provided by Leo Africanus (ca. 1465–1550), a Moroccan captured by pirates and given as a slave to Pope Leo X. Leo Africanus became a Christian, taught Arabic in Rome, and in 1526 published an account of his many travels, including a stay in the Songhai kingdom.

As a scholar, Africanus was naturally impressed by Timbuktu, the second city of the empire, which he visited in 1513. "Here [is] a great store of doctors, judges, priests, and other learned men, that are bountifully maintained at the King's court," he reported.[10] Many of these Islamic scholars had studied in Cairo and other centers of

Muslim learning. They gave Timbuktu a reputation for intellectual sophistication, religious piety, and moral justice.

Songhai under Muhammad Toure seems to have enjoyed economic prosperity. Leo Africanus noted the abundant food supply, which was produced in the southern Savanna and carried to Timbuktu by a large fleet of canoes. The elite had large amounts of money to spend, and expensive North African and European luxuries were much in demand: clothes, copperware, glass and stone beads, perfumes, and horses. The existence of many shops and markets implies the development of an urban culture. At Timbuktu, merchants, scholars, judges, and artisans constituted a distinctive bourgeoisie. The presence of many foreign merchants, including Jews and Italians, gave the city a cosmopolitan atmosphere. Jews largely controlled the working of gold.

Slaves played a very important part in Songhai's economy. On the royal farms scattered throughout the kingdom, slaves produced rice—the staple crop—for the royal granaries. Slaves could possess their own slaves, land, and cattle, but could not bequeath any of this property; the king inherited all of it. Muhammad Toure greatly increased the number of royal slaves. He gave slaves to favorite Muslim scholars, who thus gained a steady source of income. Slaves were also sold at the large market at Gao, where traders from North Africa bought them for resale in Cairo, Constantinople, Lisbon, Naples, Genoa, and Venice.

Despite its considerable economic and cultural strengths, Songhai had serious internal problems. Islam never took root in the countryside, and Muslim officials alienated the king from his people. Muhammad Toure's reforms were a failure. He governed a diverse group of peoples—Tuareg, Malinke, and Fulani, as well as Songhai—who were often hostile to one another, and no cohesive element united them. Finally, the Songhai never developed an effective method of transferring power. Muhammad Toure himself was murdered by one of his sons. His death began a period of political instability that led to the kingdom's slow disintegration.[11]

In 1582 the Moroccan sultanate began to press southward in search of a greater share of the trans-Saharan trade. The Songhai people, lacking effective leadership and believing the desert to be a sure protection against invasion, took no defensive precautions. In 1591 a Moroccan army of three thousand soldiers—many of whom were slaves of European origin equipped with European muskets—crossed the Sahara and inflicted a crushing defeat on the Songhai at Tondibi, spelling the end of the Songhai Empire.

East of Songhai lay the kingdoms of Kanem-Bornu and Hausaland (see Map 18.1). Under the dynamic military leader Idris Alooma (1571–1603), Kanem-Bornu subdued weaker peoples and gained jurisdiction over an extensive area. Well drilled and equipped with firearms, camel-mounted cavalry and a standing army decimated warriors fighting with spears and arrows. Idris Alooma perpetuated a form of feudalism by granting lands to able fighters in return for loyalty and the promise of future military assistance. Meanwhile, agriculture occupied most people, peasants and slaves alike. Kanem-Bornu shared in the trans-Saharan trade, shipping eunuchs and young girls to North Africa in return for horses and firearms. A devout Muslim, Idris Alooma elicited high praise from ibn-Fartura, who wrote a history of his reign called *The Kanem Wars:*

So he made the pilgrimage and visited Medina with delight. . . . Among the benefits which God . . . conferred upon the Sultan Idris Alooma was the acquisition of Turkish musketeers and numerous household slaves who became skilled in firing muskets. . . .

Among the most surprising of his acts was the stand he took against obscenity and adultery, so that no such thing took place openly in his time. Formerly the people had been indifferent to such offences. . . . In fact he was a power among his people and from him came their strength.

The Sultan was intent on the clear path laid down by the Qur'an . . . in all his affairs and actions.[12]

Idris Alooma built mosques at his capital city of N'gazargamu and substituted Muslim courts and Islamic law for African tribunals and ancient customary law. His eighteenth-century successors lacked his vitality and military skills, however, and the empire declined.

Between Songhai and Kanem-Bornu were the lands of the Hausa, an agricultural people who lived in small villages. Hausa merchants, however, carried on a heavy trade in slaves and kola nuts with North African communities across the Sahara, and obscure trading posts evolved into important Hausa city-states like Kano and Katsina, through which Islamic influences entered the region. Kano and Katsina became Muslim intellectual centers and in the fifteenth century attracted scholars from Timbuktu. The Muslim chronicler of the reign of King Muhammad Rimfa of Kano (r. 1463–1499) records that the king introduced the Muslim practices of *purdah,* or seclusion of women; of the *idal-fitr,* or festival after the fast of Ramadan; and of assigning eunuchs to high state offices.[13] As in Songhai and Kanem-Bornu, however, Islam made no strong imprint on the Hausa masses until the nineteenth century.

ETHIOPIA

How did the Coptic Christian Church in Ethiopia serve as a unifying force for the society and for the kingdom?

At the beginning of the sixteenth century, the powerful East African Christian kingdom of Ethiopia extended from Massawa in the north to several tributary states in the south (see Map 18.2). The ruling Solomonic dynasty, however, faced serious troubles. Adal, a Muslim state along the southern base of the Red Sea, began incursions into Ethiopia, and in 1529 the Adal general Ahmad ibn-Ghazi inflicted a disastrous defeat on the Ethiopian emperor Lebna Dengel (r. 1508–1540). Ahmad followed up his victory with systematic devastation of the land, destruction of many Ethiopian artistic and literary works, and the forced conversion of thousands to Islam. Lebna Dengel fled to the mountains and appealed to Portugal for assistance.

In the late twelfth century, tales of Prester John, rumored to be a powerful Christian monarch ruling a vast and wealthy African empire, reached western Europe. The search for Prester John, as well as for gold and spices, spurred the Portuguese to undertake a series of trans-African expeditions. In the 1480s they reached Timbuktu and Mali. Although Prester John was a totally mythical figure, Portuguese emissaries, who by 1508 had reached the Ethiopian capital, triumphantly but mistakenly identified the Ethiopian emperor as Prester John himself.[14] Desirous of converting Ethiopians from Coptic Chris-

● **Saint George in Ethiopian Art** This wall painting of Saint George slaying a dragon resides in the stone-carved Church of St. George at Lalibela, Ethiopia, and attests to the powerful and pervasive Christian influence of Ethiopian culture. *(Galen Frysinger)*

tianity to Roman Catholicism, the Portuguese responded to Lebna Dengel's request for help with a force of musketeers. In 1541 they decisively defeated the Muslims near Lake Tana. No sooner had the Muslim threat ended than Ethiopia encountered three more dangers. The Galla, Cushitic-speaking peoples, moved northward in great numbers, occupying portions of Harar, Shoa, and Amhara. The Ethiopians could not defeat them militarily, and the Galla were not interested in assimilation. For the next two centuries, the two peoples lived together in an uneasy truce. Simultaneous with the Galla migrations was the Ottoman Turks' seizure of Massawa and other coastal cities. Then the Jesuits arrived and attempted to force Roman Catholicism on a proud people whose Coptic form of Christianity long antedated the European version. The overzealous Jesuit missionary Alphonse Mendez tried to revamp the Ethiopian liturgy, rebaptize the people, and replace ancient Ethiopian customs and practices with Roman ones. Since Ethiopian national sentiment was closely tied to Coptic Christianity, violent rebellion and anarchy ensued.

In 1633 the Jesuit missionaries were expelled. For the next two centuries, hostility to foreigners, weak political leadership, and regionalism characterized Ethiopia. Civil conflicts between Galla and Ethiopians erupted continually. The Coptic church, though lacking strong authority, survived as the cornerstone of Ethiopian national identity.

THE SWAHILI CITY-STATES

What was the significance of the Indian Ocean to the political and economic organization of the Swahili city-states?

The word **Swahili,** meaning "People of the Coast," refers to the people living along the East African coast and on the nearby islands. Their history, unlike that of most African peoples, exists in writing. By the eleventh century the Swahili had accepted Islam, and "its acceptance was the factor that marked the acquisition of 'Swahili' identity: Islam gave the society coherent cultural form."[15] Living on the Indian Ocean coast, the Swahili felt the influences of Indians, Indonesians, Persians, and especially Arabs.

Swahili civilization was overwhelmingly maritime. A fertile, well-watered, and intensely cultivated stretch of land no more than ten miles wide extends down the coast: it yielded rice, grains, citrus fruit, and cloves. The region's considerable prosperity, however, rested on trade and commerce. The Swahili acted as middlemen in an Indian Ocean–East African protocapitalism: exchanging ivory, rhinoceros horn, tortoise shells, inlaid ebony chairs, copra (dried coconut meat that yields coconut oil), and inland slaves for Arabian and Persian perfumes, toilet articles, ink, and paper and for Indian textiles, beads, and iron tools. In the fifteenth century the cosmopolitan city-states of Mogadishu, Pate, Lamu, Mombasa, and especially Kilwa enjoyed a worldwide reputation for commercial prosperity and high living standards.[16]

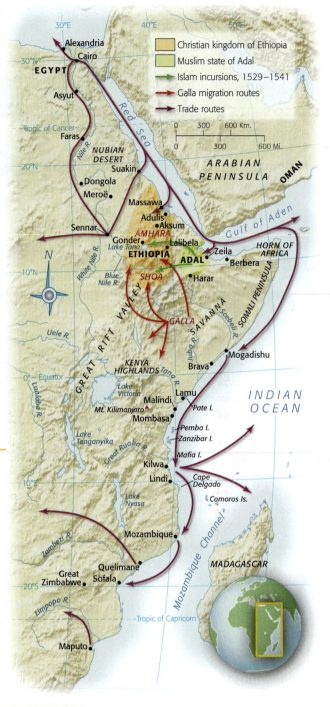

MAP 18.2 **East Africa in the Sixteenth Century** In early modern times, the Christian kingdom of Ethiopia, first isolated and then subjected to Muslim and European pressures, played an insignificant role in world affairs. But the East African city-states, which stretched from Sofala in the south to Mogadishu in the north, had powerfully important commercial relations with Mughal India, China, the Ottoman world, and southern Europe.

Swahili *Meaning "People of the Coast," the term used for the people living along the East African coast and on nearby islands.*

● **Chinese Porcelain Plates**   Embedded in an eighteenth-century Kunduchi pillar tomb, these Chinese plates testify to the enormous Asian-African trade that flourished in the fourteenth to sixteenth centuries. Kunduchi, whose ruins lie north of Dar es Salaam in present-day Tanzania, was one of the Swahili city-states. Why would a Muslim African want a Chinese plate embedded in his tomb? Does it indicate that he was involved in the porcelain trade? *(Werner Forman/Art Resource, NY)*

The arrival of the Portuguese explorer Vasco da Gama (see Map 15.2 on page 438) in 1498 spelled the end of the Swahili cities' independence. Lured by the spice trade, da Gama wanted to build a Portuguese maritime empire in the Indian Ocean. Swahili rulers responded in different ways to Portuguese intrusion. The sultan of Malindi quickly agreed to a trading alliance with the Portuguese. The sultan of Mombasa was tricked into commercial agreements. Still other Swahili rulers totally rejected Portuguese overtures, and their cities were subjected to bombardment. To secure alliances made between 1502 and 1507 the Portuguese erected forts at the southern port cities of Kilwa, Zanzibar, and Sofala. These forts—fortified markets and trading posts—served as the foundation of Portuguese commercial power on the Swahili coast.[17] (See the feature "Listening to the Past: Duarte Barbosa on the Swahili City-States" on pages 542–543.) The better-fortified northern cities, such as Mogadishu, survived as important entrepôts for goods to India.

The Portuguese presence in the south proved hollow, however. Rather than accept Portuguese commercial restrictions, the residents deserted the towns, and the town economies crumbled. Large numbers of Kilwa's people, for example, immigrated to northern cities. The gold flow from inland mines to Sofala slowed to a trickle. Swahili noncooperation successfully prevented the Portuguese from gaining control of the local coastal trade.

In 1589 Portugal finally won an administrative stronghold near Mombasa. Called Fort Jesus, it remained a Portuguese base for over a century. In the late seventeenth century, pressures from the northern European maritime powers—the Dutch, French, and English—aided greatly by Omani Arabs, combined with local African rebellions to bring about the collapse of Portuguese influence in Africa. A Portuguese presence remained only at Mozambique in the far south and Angola on the west coast.

The Portuguese had no religious or cultural impact on the Swahili cities. Their sole effect was the cities' economic decline.

THE AFRICAN SLAVE TRADE

What role did slavery play in African societies before European intrusion?

slave   *A person who is bound in servitude and often traded as property or as a commodity.*

Long before the European intrusion, the exchange of peoples captured in local and ethnic wars within sub-Saharan Africa, the trans-Saharan **slave** trade with the Mediterranean Islamic world beginning in the seventh century, and the slave traffic across the Indian Ocean all testify to the long tradition and continental dimensions of the African slave trade. "Slavery was . . . fundamental to the social, political, and economic order of parts of the northern savanna, Ethiopia and the East African

● **Fort Jesus, Mombasa**   Designed by the Milanese military architect Joao Batista Cairato in traditional European style, and built between 1593 and 1594, this great fortress still stands as a symbol of Portuguese military and commercial power in East Africa and the Indian Ocean in the sixteenth and seventeenth centuries. *(Wolfgang Kaehler Photography)*

coast. . . . Enslavement was an organized activity, sanctioned by law and custom. Slaves were a principal commodity in trade, including the export sector, and slaves were important in the domestic sphere" as concubines, servants, soldiers, and ordinary laborers.[18]

Islamic practices heavily influenced African slavery. African rulers justified enslavement with the Muslim argument that prisoners of war could be sold and that captured peoples were considered chattel, or personal possessions, to be used in any way the owner saw fit. Between 650 and 1600, black as well as white Muslims transported perhaps as many as 4.82 million black slaves across the trans-Saharan trade route.[19] In the fourteenth and fifteenth centuries the rulers and elites of Mali and Benin imported thousands of white slave women, symbols of wealth and status, from the eastern Mediterranean.[20] In 1444, when Portuguese caravels landed 235 slaves at Algarve in southern Portugal, a contemporary observed that they seemed "a marvelous (extraordinary) sight, for, amongst them, were some white enough, fair enough, and well-proportioned; others were less white, like mulattoes; others again were black as Ethiops."[21]

Meanwhile, the flow of black people to Europe, begun during the Renaissance, continued. In the seventeenth and eighteenth centuries, as many as two hundred thousand Africans entered European societies. Some arrived as slaves, others as servants; the legal distinction was not always clear. Eighteenth-century London, for example, had more than ten thousand blacks, most of whom arrived as sailors on Atlantic crossings or as personal servants brought from the West Indies. In England most were

KITCHIN STUFF.

● **Below Stairs** The prints and cartoons of Thomas Rowlandson (1756–1827) testify to the sizable numbers of blacks in eighteenth-century London, where they worked in naval and military as well as domestic service. Here the household cook, maid, and footman relax before the kitchen fire. Interracial marriages were not uncommon. *(Courtesy of the Trustees of the British Museum)*

free, not slaves. Initially, a handsome black was a fashionable accessory, a rare status symbol. Later, English aristocrats considered black servants too ordinary. The duchess of Devonshire offered her mother an eleven-year-old boy, explaining that the duke did not want a Negro servant because "it was more original to have a Chinese page than to have a black one; everybody had a black one."[22] London's black population constituted a well-organized, self-conscious subculture, with black pubs, black churches, and black social groups assisting the black poor and unemployed. Some black people attained wealth and position, the most famous being Francis Barber, the literary giant Samuel Johnson's servant, who inherited Johnson's sizable fortune.

In 1658 the Dutch East India Company began to allow the importation of slaves into the Cape Colony of southern Africa. Over the next century and a half about 75 percent of the slaves brought into the colony came from Dutch East India Company colonies in India and Southeast Asia or from Madagascar, and the remaining 25 percent from Africa. The Dutch East India Company was the single largest slave owner in the Cape Colony, employing its slaves on public works and company farms. Initially, individual company officials collectively owned the most slaves, working them on their wine and grain estates.[23] By about 1740 urban and rural free burghers owned the majority of the slaves. The slave population at the Cape was never large, although from the early 1700s to the 1820s it outnumbered the European free burgher population. When the British ended slavery in the British Empire in 1834, there were only around thirty-six thousand slaves in the Cape Colony.

Some slaves at the Cape served as domestic servants or as semiskilled artisans, but most worked long and hard as field hands and at any other menial or manual forms of labor needed by their European masters. Slave ownership fostered a strong sense of racial and economic solidarity in the white master class. Although in the seventeenth and eighteenth centuries Holland enjoyed a Europe-wide reputation for religious toleration and intellectual freedom (see page 485), in the Cape Colony the Dutch used a strict racial hierarchy and heavy-handed paternalism to maintain control over native peoples and foreign-born slaves.[24]

The Savanna and Horn regions of East Africa experienced a great expansion of the slave trade in the late eighteenth, and first half of the nineteenth centuries. Slave exports from these areas and from the eastern coast amounted to perhaps thirty thousand a year. Why this demand? Merchants and planters wanted slaves to work the sugar plantations on the Mascarene Islands, located east of Madagascar, the clove plantations on Zanzibar and Pemba, and the food plantations along the Kenyan coast. The eastern coast also exported slaves to the Americas, particularly to Brazil. In the late eighteenth and early nineteenth centuries, precisely when the slave trade to North America and the Caribbean declined, the Eastern and Asian markets expanded. Only with colonial conquest by Great Britain, Germany, and Italy after 1870 did suppression of the trade begin. Slavery, of course, persists even today. (See the feature "Global Trade: Slaves" on pages 530–531.)

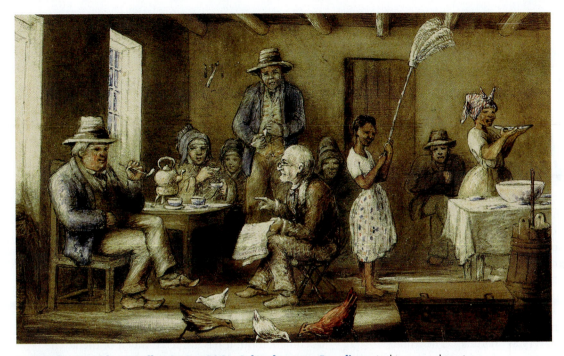

● **Charles Davidson Bell (1813–1882): Schoolmaster Reading**   In this watercolor print, a schoolmaster reads and explains the newspaper *Zuid Afrikaan* (The South African) to the (probably illiterate) household, while black servants cook and fan. Chickens peck for crumbs on the floor. *(William Fehr Collection, IZIKO Museums of Cape Town)*

The Atlantic Slave Trade

Although the trade in African people was a worldwide phenomenon, the Atlantic slave trade involved the largest number of enslaved Africans. This forced migration of millions of human beings, extending from the early sixteenth to the late nineteenth centuries, represents one of the most inhumane, unjust, and shameful tragedies in human history. It also immediately provokes a troubling question: why Africa? Why, in the seventeenth and eighteenth centuries, did enslavement in the Americas become exclusively African?

As we have seen (see page 444), Europeans first used indigenous peoples, the Amerindians, to mine Mexican silver and gold. When they proved ill-suited to the harsh rigors of mining, the Spaniards brought in Africans. Although the Dutch had transported Indonesian peoples to the Cape Colony in South Africa, the cost of transporting Chinese or Pacific island peoples to the Americas was far too great.

One scholar has recently argued that across Europe, a pan-European insider-outsider ideology prevailed. This cultural attitude permitted the enslavement of outsiders but made the enslavement of white Europeans taboo. Europeans could not bear the sight of other Europeans doing plantation slave labor. According to this theory, a similar pan-African ideology did not exist, as Africans had no problem with selling Africans to Europeans.[25] Several facts argue against the validity of this theory. English landlords exploited their Irish peasants with merciless severity; French aristocrats often looked on their peasantry with cold contempt; and Russian boyars treated their serfs with casual indifference and harsh brutality. These and other possible examples contradict the existence of a pan-European ideology or culture that opposed the enslavement of white Europeans. Moreover, the flow of white Slavic slaves from the Balkans into the eastern Mediterranean continued unabated during the same period.

Another theory holds that in the Muslim and Arab worlds by the tenth century, an association had developed between blackness and menial slavery. The Arab word *abd,* or

GLOBAL TRADE

SLAVES

The history of the global slave trade is rife with ironies. The traffic in human persons bought and sold for the profits of their labor cannot decently be compared with that in other commodities; people are not goods. But most societies, with the remarkable exception of the Aborigines in Australia, have treated people as goods and engaged in the slave trade. Those who have been enslaved include captives in war, persons convicted of crimes, persons sold for debt, and persons bought and sold for sex. The ancient Greek philosophers, notably Aristotle, justified slavery as "natural." The Middle Eastern monotheistic faiths—Judaism, Christianity, and Islam—while professing the sacred dignity of each individual, and the Asian religious and sociopolitical ideolo-

gies of Buddhism and Confucianism, while stressing an ordered and harmonious society, all tolerated slavery and urged slaves' obedience to established authorities. Until the Enlightenment of the eighteenth century, most people everywhere accepted slavery as a "natural phenomenon." Nor is it without irony that the Thirteenth Amendment to the U.S. Constitution (ratified in 1865), popularly interpreted as abolishing slavery, allows slavery "as a punishment for crime whereof the party shall have been duly convicted."

Between 1500 and 1900, the transatlantic African slave trade accounted for the largest number of people bought and sold. As such, and because of ample documentation, it has attracted much of the attention of scholars, and it also has tended to identify the institution of slavery with African blacks. From a global perspective, however, the trade was far broader.

The Slave Trade

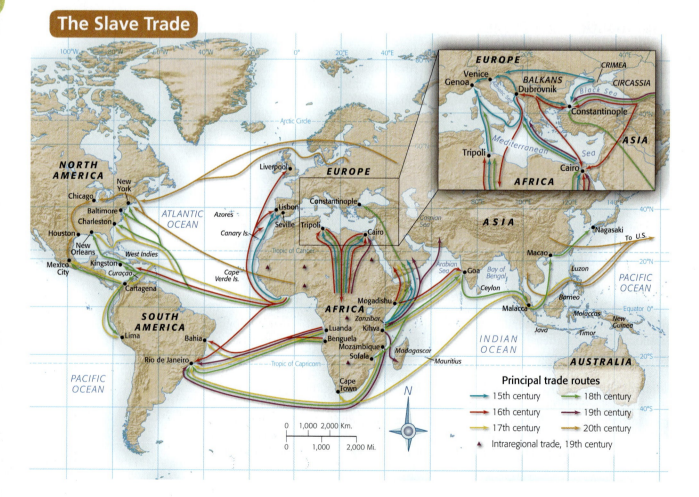

Principal trade routes
- 15th century
- 16th century
- 17th century
- 18th century
- 19th century
- 20th century
- ▲ Intraregional trade, 19th century

530

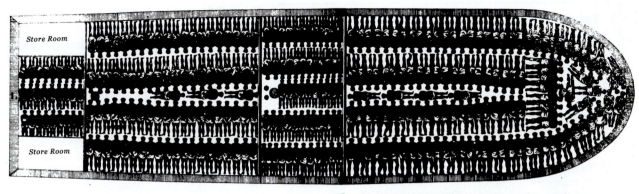

● *The revolting conditions on slave ships sailing to*
● *Caribbean and North American ports pale in*
● *barbarity beside conditions on the southern route*
● *to Brazil, where slaves were literally packed like*
● *sardines in a can.*

Indeed, hundreds of thousands of slaves were white or Asian. The steady flow of women and children from the Crimea, the Caucasus, and the Balkans in the fourteenth to eighteenth centuries for domestic, military, or sexual services in Ottoman lands, Italy, and sub-Saharan Africa; the use of convicts as galley slaves in the Venetian, French, Spanish, and Turkish navies (after the Battle of Lepanto in 1571, ten thousand Christian galley slaves in Turkish service were freed); the enslavement of peoples defeated in war by Aztec, Inca, Sioux, Navajo, and other indigenous peoples of the Americas; the various forms of debt slavery in China and in Russia (where the legal distinction between serf and slave before 1861 was very hazy indeed); the traffic of Indonesian and Pacific Island peoples for slave labor in Dutch South Africa; and the trans-Saharan stream of Africans to Mediterranean ports that continued at medieval rates into the late nineteenth century—all these were different forms of a worldwide practice. Although these forms sometimes had little in common with one another (such as the domestic and military slavery of the Islamic world and the plantation slavery of the Americas), they all involved the buying and selling of human beings who could not move about freely or enjoy the fruits of their labor.

The price of slaves varied widely over time and from market to market, according to age, sex, physical appearance, and buyers' perceptions of the social characteristics of each slave's ethnic background. The Mediterranean and Indian Ocean markets preferred women for domestic service; the Atlantic markets wanted strong young men for mine and plantation work. Changes in supply and demand could lead to great price fluctuations: the arrival of a very large number of slaves in a particular market or the failure of a dealer to appear when expected could drive prices down. We have little solid information on prices for slaves in the Balkans,

Caucasus, or Indian Ocean region. Even in the Atlantic trade, it is difficult to determine, over several centuries, the value of currencies such as the Dutch guilder and the British pound, the cost and insurance on transported slaves, and the cost of goods exchanged for slaves. Yet the grand palazzi of Venice, the gold-encrusted cathedrals of Spain, and the elegant plantation houses of the Southern United States stand as testimony to the vast fortunes made in the slave trade. But how is the human toll measured?

Transformations within societies occurred not only because of local developments but also because of interactions among regions. For example, the virulent racism that in so many ways defines the American experience resulted partly from medieval European habits of dehumanizing the enemy (English versus Irish, German versus Slav, Christian versus Jew and Muslim) and partly from the movement of peoples and ideas all over the globe. American gold prospectors in the 1850s carried the bigotry they had heaped on blacks in the Americas to Australia, where it conditioned attitudes toward Asians and other peoples of color. Racism, like the slave trade, is a global phenomenon.

A final irony exists in the fact that for all the cries for human rights today, the slave trade continues on a broad scale. The ancient Indian Ocean traffic in Indian girls and boys for "service" in the Persian Gulf oil kingdoms and the sale of African children for work in Asia persist. Well-verified British, American, and United Nations reports prove that each year between 1998 and 2000, "criminal elements" brought more than fifty thousand women and children from Latvia, Nigeria, the Philippines, Thailand, China, Russia, and Mexico into the United States to work as sex slaves. They were bought, sold, tricked, and held in captivity, and their labor was exploited for the financial benefit of masters in a global enterprise.

Table 18.1 Estimated Slave Imports by Destination, 1451–1870

DESTINATION	ESTIMATED TOTAL SLAVE IMPORTS
British North America	399,000
Spanish America	1,552,100
British Caribbean	1,665,000
French Caribbean	1,600,200
Dutch Caribbean	500,000
Danish Caribbean	28,000
Brazil	3,646,800
Old World	175,000
	9,566,100

Source: P. D. Curtin, *The Atlantic Slave Trade: A Census* (Madison: University of Wisconsin Press, 1969), p. 268. Used with permission of The University of Wisconsin Press.

"black," had become synonymous with *slave*. Although the great majority of slaves in the Islamic world were white, a racial element existed in Muslim perceptions: not all slaves were black, but blacks were identified with slavery. In Europe, after the arrival of tens of thousands of sub-Saharan Africans in the Iberian Peninsula during the fifteenth century, Christian Europeans also began to make a strong association between slavery and black Africans. Therefore, Africans seemed the "logical" solution to the labor shortage in the Americas.[26] Another important question relating to the African slave trade is this: why were African peoples enslaved in a period when serfdom was declining in western Europe, and when land was so widely available and much of the African continent had a labor shortage? The answer seems to lie in a technical problem related to African agriculture. Partly because of the tsetse fly, which causes sleeping sickness and other diseases, and partly because of easily leached lateritic soils (containing high concentrations of oxides), farmers had great difficulty using draft animals. Tropical soils responded poorly to plowing, and most work had to be done with the hoe. Productivity, therefore, was low. Economists maintain that in most societies, the value of a worker's productivity determines the value of his or her labor. In precolonial Africa, the individual's agricultural productivity was low, so his or her economic value to society was less than the economic value of a European peasant in Europe. Slaves in the Americas were more productive than free producers in Africa. And European slave dealers were very willing to pay a price higher than the value of an African's productivity in Africa.

The incidence of disease in the Americas also helps explain African enslavement. Smallpox took a terrible toll on Native Americans (see page 445), and between 30 and 50 percent of Europeans exposed to malaria succumbed to that sickness. Africans had developed some immunity to both diseases, and in the Americas they experienced the lowest mortality rate of any people, making them, ironically, the most suitable workers for the environment.

The Portuguese "discovered" Brazil in 1500 and founded a sugar colony at Bahia in 1551. Between 1551 and 1575, before the North American traffic began, the Portuguese delivered more African slaves to Brazil than would ever reach British North America (see Table 18.1). Portugal essentially monopolized the slave trade until 1600 and continued to play a large role in the seventeenth century, though the trade was increasingly taken over by the Dutch, French, and English. From 1690 until the House of Commons abolished the slave trade in 1807, England was the leading carrier of African slaves.

Population density and supply conditions along the West African coast and the sailing time to New World markets determined the sources of slaves. As the demand for slaves rose, slavers moved down the West African coast from Senegambia to the more densely populated hinterlands of the Bight of Benin and the Bight of Biafra (see Map 15.3 on page 447). The abundant supply of slaves in Angola, the region south of the Congo River, and the quick passage from Angola to Brazil and the Caribbean established that region as the major coast for Portuguese slavers.

Transatlantic wind patterns partly determined exchange routes. Shippers naturally preferred the swiftest crossing—that is, from the African port nearest the latitude of the intended American destination. Thus Portuguese shippers carried their cargoes

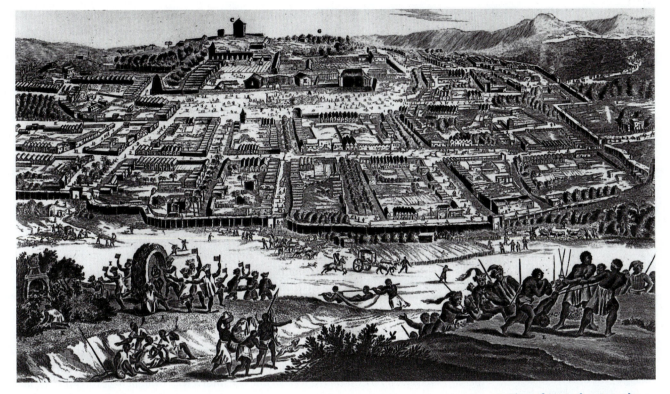

from Angola to Brazil, and British merchants sailed from the Bight of Benin to the Caribbean. The great majority of slaves were intended for the sugar and coffee plantations extending from the Caribbean islands to Brazil.[27] Angola produced 26 percent of all African slaves and 70 percent of all Portuguese slaves. Trading networks extending deep into the interior culminated at two major ports on the Angolan coast, Luanda and Benguela (see Map 18.1). The Portuguese acquired a few slaves through warfare but secured the vast majority through trade with African dealers. Whites did not participate in the inland markets.

Almost all Portuguese shipments went to satisfy the virtually insatiable Brazilian demand for slaves.[28] Here is an excerpt from a Portuguese doctor's 1793 report on conditions in Luanda before the voyage across the Atlantic had begun:

Here takes place the second round of hardships that these unlucky people are forced to suffer . . . their human nature entirely overlooked. The dwelling place of the slave is simply the dirt floor of the compound, and he remains there exposed to harsh conditions and bad weather, and at night there are only a lean-to and some sheds . . . which they are herded into like cattle.

Their food continues scarce as before . . . limited at times to badly cooked beans, at other times to corn. . . .

And when they reach a port . . . , they are branded on the right breast with the coat of arms of the king and nation, of whom they have become vassals. . . . This mark is made with a hot silver instrument in the act of paying the king's duties, and this brand mark is called a carimbo. *. . .*

In this miserable and deprived condition the terrified slaves remain for weeks and months, and the great number of them who die is unspeakable. With some ten or twelve thousand arriving at Luanda each year, it often happens that only six or seven thousand are finally transported to Brazil.[29]

Olaudah Equiano (see the feature "Individuals in Society: Olaudah Equiano") describes the experience of his voyage from Benin to Barbados in the Caribbean:

At last, when the ship we were in had got in all her cargo [of slaves], they made ready with many fearful noises, and we were all put under deck so that we could not see how they managed the vessel. . . . The stench of the hold while we were on the coast was so intolerably loathsome that it was dangerous to remain there for any time, and some of us had been permitted to stay on the deck for the fresh air; but now that the whole ship's cargo were confined together it became absolutely pestilential. The closeness of the place and the heat of the climate, added to the number in the ship, which was so crowded that each had scarcely room to turn himself, almost suffocated us. This produced copious perspirations, so that the air soon became unfit for respiration from a variety of loathsome smells, and brought on a sickness among the slaves, of which many died, thus falling victims to the improvident avarice, as I may call it, of their purchasers. This wretched situation was again aggravated by the galling of the chains, now become insupportable, and the filth of the necessary tubs [of human waste], into which the children often fell and were almost suffocated. The shrieks of the women and the groans of the dying rendered the whole a scene of horror almost inconceivable. Happily perhaps for myself I was soon reduced so low here that it was thought necessary to keep me almost always on deck, and from my extreme youth I was not put in fetters. . . . Two of my wearied countrymen who were chained together (I was near them at the time), preferring death to such a life of misery, somehow made through the nettings and jumped into the sea: immediately another quite dejected fellow, who on account of his illness was suffered to be out of irons, also followed their example. . . . Two of the wretches were drowned, but they got the other and afterwards flogged him unmercifully. . . . The want of fresh air, . . . and the stench of the necessary tubs carried off many. . . . At last we came in sight of the island of Barbados, at which the whites on board gave a great shout and made many signs of joy to us. . . . We soon anchored amongst them off Bridgetown. Many merchants and planters now came on board, though it was in the evening. They put us in separate parcels and examined us attentively. They also made us jump, and pointed to the land, signifying we were to go there. We thought by this we should be eaten by these ugly men, as they appeared to us. . . . They told us we were not to be eaten but to work, and were soon to go on land where we should see many of our country people. This report eased us much; and sure enough soon after we were landed there came to us Africans of all languages.[30]

● **Queen Njiga (also Nzinga) Mbandi Ana de Sousa** Njiga of Ndongo (r. 1624–1629) is the most important female political figure in the history of early modern Angola. She used military force in her expansionist policy and participated fully in the slave trade, but she fiercely resisted Portuguese attempts to control that trade. Here she sits enthroned, wearing her crown (the cross a sign of her Christian baptism) and bracelets, giving an order. She has become a symbol of African resistance to colonial rule. *(Courtesy, Luigi Araldi, Modena)*

**Primary Source:
The Interesting Narrative of Olaudah Equiano: Written by Himself**
Read selections from an ex-slave's autobiography, one of the most influential abolitionist books published in England.

Although the demand was great, Portuguese merchants in Angola and Brazil sought to maintain only a steady trickle of slaves from the African interior to Luanda and across the ocean to Bahia and Rio de Janeiro: a flood of slaves would have depressed the American market. Rio, the port capital through which most slaves passed, commanded the Brazilian trade. Planters and mine operators from the provinces traveled to Rio to buy slaves. Between 1795 and 1808, approximately 10,000 Angolans per year stood in the Rio slave market. In 1810 the figure rose to 18,000; in 1828 it reached 32,000.[31]

The English ports of London, Bristol, and particularly Liverpool dominated the British slave trade. In the eighteenth century Liverpool was the world's greatest slave-trading port. In all three cities, small and cohesive merchant classes exercised great public influence. The cities also had huge stores of industrial products for export, growing shipping industries, and large amounts of ready cash for investment abroad. Merchants generally formed partnerships to raise capital and to share the risks; each voyage was a separate enterprise or venture.

Olaudah Equiano

The transatlantic slave trade was a mass movement involving millions of human beings. It was also the sum of individual lives spent partly or entirely in slavery. Most of those lives remain hidden to us. Olaudah Equiano (1745–1797) represents a rare ray of light into the slaves' obscurity; he is probably the best-known African slave.

Equiano was born in Benin (modern Nigeria) of Ibo ethnicity.* His father, one of the village elders (or chieftains), presided over a large household that included "many slaves," prisoners captured in local wars. All people, slave and free, shared in the cultivation of family lands. One day, when all the adults were in the fields, two strange men and a woman broke into the family compound, kidnapped the eleven-year-old Olaudah and his sister, tied them up, and dragged them into the woods. Brother and sister were separated, and Olaudah was sold several times to various dealers before reaching the coast. As it took six months to walk there, his home must have been far inland. The sea, the slave ship, and the strange appearance of the white crew terrified the boy (see page 534). Equiano's master took him to Jamaica, Virginia, and then to England, where he placed him in the custody of a kind family. They gave him the rudiments of an education, and he was baptized a Christian.

Equiano soon went to sea as a captain's boy (servant), serving in the Royal Navy during the Seven Years' War. On shore at Portsmouth, England, after one battle, Equiano was urged by his master to read, study, and learn basic mathematics. This education served him well, for after a voyage to the West Indies, his master sold him to a Philadelphia Quaker, Robert King, who was a rum and sugar merchant. Equiano worked as a clerk in King's warehouse, as a longshoreman loading and unloading cargo ships, and at sea where he developed good navigational skills; for his work, King paid him. Equiano became an entrepreneur himself, buying and selling small goods in the islands and mainland ports. Determined to buy his freedom, Equiano had amassed enough money by 1766, and King signed the deed of manumission. Equiano was twenty-one years old; he had been a slave for ten years.

He returned to London and used his remaining money to hire tutors to teach him hairdressing, mathematics, and how to play the French horn. When money was scarce, he found work as a merchant seaman, traveling to Portugal, Nice, Genoa, Naples, and Turkey. He participated in an Arctic expedition.

Equiano's *Travels* (1788) reveals a complex and sophisticated man. He had a strong constitution and an equally strong character. His Christian faith undoubtedly sustained him. On the title page of his book, he cited a verse from Isaiah (12:2): "The Lord Jehovah is my strength and my song." The very first thought that came to his mind the day he was freed was a passage from Psalm 126: "I glorified God in my heart, in whom I trusted."

Equiano loathed the brutal slavery he saw in the West Indies and the vicious racism he experienced in the North American colonies. He respected the fairness of Robert King, admired British navigational and industrial technologies, and had many close white friends. He once described himself as "almost an Englishman." He was also involved in the black communities in the West Indies and in London. *Travels* is a well-documented argument for the abolition of slavery and a literary classic that went through nine editions before his death.

Olaudah Equiano spoke to large crowds in the industrial cities of Manchester and Birmingham, arguing that it was in the business interests of manufacturers to support abolition, as Africa was a huge, virtually untapped market for English cloth.

Olaudah Equiano, 1789, dressed as an elegant Englishman, his Bible open to the book of Acts. *(New York Public Library/Art Resource, NY)*

Questions for Analysis

1. How typical was Olaudah Equiano's life as a slave? How atypical?
2. Describe his culture and his sense of himself.

*Recent scholarship has re-examined Equiano's life and raised some questions about his African origins and his experience of the Middle Passage.

Source: Equiano's Travels: The Interesting Narrative of the Life of Olaudah Equiano, ed. Paul Edwards (Portsmouth, N.H.: Heinemann, 1996).

● **Peddlers, Rio de Janeiro (early nineteenth century)**
A British army officer sketched this scene of everyday life in Rio de Janeiro, Brazil. The ability to balance large burdens on the head meant that the hands were free for other use. Note the player (*third from right*) of a musical instrument originating in the Congo. We do not know whether the peddlers were free and self-employed or were selling for their owners. *(From "Views and Costumes of the City and Neighborhood of Rio de Janeiro, Brazil," in Drawings Taken by Lieutenant Chamberlain, During the Years 1819 and 1820* [London: Columbian Press, 1822])

sorting   *A collection or batch of British goods that would be traded for a slave or for a quantity of gold, ivory, or dyewood.*

factory-forts   *Fortified trading posts that were established on the Gold Coast.*

shore trading   *A process for trading goods in which European ships sent boats ashore or invited African dealers to bring traders and slaves out to the ships.*

Slaving ships from Bristol searched the Gold Coast, the Bight of Benin, Bonny, and Calabar. Liverpool's ships drew slaves from Gambia, the Windward Coast, and the Gold Coast. To Africa, British ships carried textiles, gunpowder and flint, beer and spirits, British and Irish linens, and woolen cloth. A collection of goods was grouped together into what was called the **sorting.** An English sorting might include bolts of cloth, firearms, alcohol, tobacco, and hardware; this batch of goods would be traded for an individual slave or a quantity of gold, ivory, or dyewood. Currency was not exchanged; it served as a standard of value and a means of keeping accounts.[32]

European traders had two systems for exchange. First, especially on the Gold Coast, they established **factory-forts.** These fortified trading posts were expensive to maintain but proved useful for fending off European rivals. Second, they used **shore trading,** in which European ships sent boats ashore or invited African dealers to bring traders and slaves out to the ships. The English captain John Adams, who made ten voyages to Africa between 1786 and 1800, described the shore method of trading at Bonny:

This place is the wholesale market for slaves, as not fewer than 20,000 are annually sold here; 16,000 of whom are natives of one nation called Ibo. . . . Fairs where the slaves of the Ibo nation are obtained are held every five or six weeks at several villages, which are situated on the banks of the rivers and creeks in the interior, and to which the African traders of Bonny resort to purchase them.

. . . The traders augment the quantity of their merchandise, by obtaining from their friends, the captains of the slave ships, a considerable quantity of goods on credit. . . . Evening is the period chosen for the time of departure, when they proceed in a body, accompanied by the noise of drums, horns, and gongs. At the expiration of the sixth day, they generally return bringing with them 1,500 or 2,000 slaves, who are sold to Europeans the evening after their arrival, and taken on board the ships. . . .

It is expected that every vessel, on her arrival at Bonny, will fire a salute the instant the anchor is let go, as a compliment to the black monarch who soon afterwards makes his appearance in a large canoe, at which time, all those natives who happen to be alongside the vessel are compelled to proceed in their canoes to a respectful distance, and make way for his Majesty's barge. After a few compliments to the captain, he usually enquires after brother George, meaning the King of England, George III, and hopes he and his family are well. He is not pleased unless he is regaled with the best the ship affords. . . . His power is absolute; and the surrounding country, to a considerable distance, is subject to his dominion.[33]

The shore method of buying slaves allowed the ship to move easily from market to market. The final prices of the slaves depended on their ethnic origin, their availability when the shipper arrived, and their physical health when offered for sale in the West Indies or the North or South American colonies.

Meanwhile, according to one scholar, the northbound trade in slaves across the Sahara "continued without serious disruption until the late nineteenth century, and in a clandestine way and on a much reduced scale it survived well into the twentieth century."[34] The present scholarly consensus is that the trans-Saharan slave trade in the seventeenth and eighteenth centuries was never as important as the transatlantic trade.

Supplying slaves for the foreign market was controlled by a small, wealthy African merchant class, or it was a state monopoly. Gathering a band of raiders and the capital for equipment, guides, tolls, and supplies involved considerable expense. By contemporary standards, slave raiding was a costly operation. Only black African entrepreneurs with sizable capital and labor could afford to finance and direct raiding drives. They exported slaves because the profits on exports were greater than the profits to be made from using labor in the domestic economy:

The export price of slaves never rose to the point where it became cheaper for Europeans to turn to alternative sources of supply, and it never fell to the point where it caused more than a temporary check to the trade. . . . The remarkable expansion of the slave trade in the eighteenth century provides a horrific illustration of the rapid response of producers in an underdeveloped economy to price incentives.[35]

Enslaved African peoples had an enormous impact on the economics of the Portuguese and Spanish colonies of South America and in the Dutch, French, and British colonies of the Caribbean and North America. For example, on the sugar plantations of Mexico and the Caribbean; on the cotton, rice, and tobacco plantations of North America; and in the silver and gold mines of Peru and Mexico, enslaved Africans not only worked in the mines and fields but also filled skilled, supervisory, and administrative positions and performed domestic service. In the United States, African slaves and their descendants influenced many facets of American culture, such as language, music (ragtime and jazz), dance, and diet. Even the U.S. Capitol building, where Congress meets, was built partly by slave labor.[36]

Consequences Within Africa

What economic impact did European trade have on African societies? Africans possessed technology well suited to their environment. Over the centuries, they had cultivated a wide variety of plant foods; developed plant and animal husbandry techniques; and mined, smelted, and otherwise worked a great variety of metals. Apart from firearms, American tobacco and rum, and the cheap brandy brought by the Portuguese, European goods presented no novelty to Africans. They found foreign products desirable because of their low prices. Traders of handwoven Indian cotton textiles, Venetian imitations of African beads, and iron bars from European smelters could undersell African manufacturers. Africans exchanged slaves, ivory, gold, pepper, and animal skins for those goods. Their earnings usually did not remain in Africa. African states eager to expand or to control commerce bought European firearms, although the difficulty of maintaining guns often gave gun owners only marginal superiority over skilled bowmen.[37] The kingdom of Dahomey, however, built its power on the effective use of firearms.

The African merchants who controlled the production of exports gained from foreign trade. Dahomey's king, for example, had a gross income in 1750 of £250,000 from the overseas export of slaves. A portion of his profit was spent on goods that improved his people's living standard. Slave-trading entrepôts, which provided

● **Sapi-Portuguese Saltcellar** Contact with the Sapi people of present-day Sierra Leone in West Africa led sixteenth-century Portuguese traders to commission this ivory saltcellar, for which they brought Portuguese designs. But the object's basic features—a spherical container and separate lid on a flat base, with men, women, and supporting beams below—are distinctly African. An executioner, holding an ax with which he has beheaded five men, stands on the lid. This piece was probably intended as an example of Sapi artistic virtuosity, rather than for practical table use. *(Courtesy, Museo Nazionale Preistorico ed Etnografico, Rome)*

opportunities for traders and for farmers who supplied foodstuffs to towns, caravans, and slave ships, prospered. But such economic returns did not spread very far.[38] International trade did not lead to Africa's economic development. Africa experienced neither technological growth nor the gradual spread of economic benefits in early modern times.

As in the Islamic world (see pages 550–552), women in sub-Saharan Africa also engaged in the slave trade. In Guinea the *signeres,* women slave merchants, acquired considerable riches in the business. One of them, Mae Correia, led a life famous in her region for its wealth and elegance.

The intermarriage of French traders and Wolof women in Senegambia created a *métis,* or mulatto, class. In the emerging urban centers at Saint-Louis, members of this small class adopted the French language, the Roman Catholic faith, and a French manner of life, and they exercised considerable political and economic power. However, European cultural influences did not penetrate West African society beyond the seacoast.

The political consequences of the slave trade varied from place to place. The trade enhanced the power and wealth of some kings and warlords in the short run but promoted conditions of instability and collapse over the long run. In the Congo kingdom, the perpetual Portuguese search for slaves undermined the monarchy, destroyed political unity, and led to constant disorder and warfare; power passed to the village chiefs. Likewise in Angola, which became a Portuguese proprietary colony, the slave trade decimated and scattered the population and destroyed the local economy. By contrast, the military kingdom of Dahomey, which entered into the slave trade in the eighteenth century and made it a royal monopoly, prospered enormously. Dahomey's economic strength rested on the slave trade. The royal army raided deep into the interior, and in the late eighteenth century Dahomey became one of the major West African sources of slaves. When slaving expeditions failed to yield sizable catches and when European demand declined, the resulting depression in the Dahomean economy caused serious political unrest. Iboland, inland from the Niger Delta, from whose great port cities of Bonny and Brass the British drained tens of thousands of slaves, experienced minimal political effects. A high birthrate kept pace with the incursions of the slave trade, and Ibo societies remained demographically and economically strong.

What demographic impact did the slave trade have on Africa? In all, between approximately 1500 and 1900, about 12 million Africans were exported to the Americas, 6 million were exported to Asia, and 8 million were retained within Africa. Table 18.1 and Table 18.2 report the somewhat divergent findings of two careful scholars on the number of slaves shipped to the Americas. Export figures do not include the approximately 10 to 15 percent who died during procurement or in transit.

There is no small irony in the fact that the continent most desperately in need of population, Africa, lost so many millions to the slave trade. Although the British Parliament abolished the slave trade in 1807 and traffic in Africans to Brazil and Cuba gradually declined, *within* Africa the trade continued at the levels of the peak years of the transatlantic trade, 1780–1820. In the later nineteenth century, developing African industries, using slave labor, produced a variety of products for domestic consumption and export. Again, there is irony in the fact that in the eighteenth century, European demand for slaves expanded the trade (and wars) within Africa, yet in the nineteenth century, European imperialists defended territorial aggrandizement by arguing that they were "civilizing" Africans by abolishing slavery. But after 1880, European businessmen (and African governments) did not push abolition; they wanted cheap labor.

Western and American markets wanted young male slaves. Asian and African markets preferred young females. Women were sought for their reproductive value, as sex objects, and because their economic productivity was not threatened by the possibility of physical rebellion, as might be the case with young men. Consequently, two-thirds of those exported to the Americas were male, one-third female. The population on the western coast of Africa became predominantly female; the population in the East African Savanna and Horn regions was predominantly male. The slave trade therefore had significant consequences for the institutions of marriage, slavery itself, and the sexual division of labor. Although Africa's overall population may have shown modest growth from roughly 1650 to 1900, that growth was offset by declines in the Horn and on the eastern and western coasts. While Europe and Asia experienced considerable demographic and economic expansion in the eighteenth century, Africa suffered a decline.[39]

Table 18.2   The Transatlantic Slave Trade, 1450–1900

PERIOD	VOLUME	PERCENTAGE
1450–1600	367,000	3.1
1601–1700	1,868,000	16.0
1701–1800	6,133,000	52.4
1801–1900	3,330,000	28.5
Total	11,698,000	100.0

Source: P. E. Lovejoy, *Transformations in Slavery: A History of Slavery in Africa* (Cambridge: Cambridge University Press, 1983), p. 19. Used with permission.

Chapter Summary

To assess your mastery of this chapter, go to bedfordstmartins.com/mckayworld

• What different types of economic, social, and political structures were found in Senegambia and Benin?

In the early modern world, kingdoms and stateless societies in Africa existed side by side. Stateless, or decentralized, societies oriented around a single village or group of villages without a central capital. The economies of both the kingdoms and the stateless societies were predominantly agricultural and pastoral. The peoples living along the West African coast, in the region known as Senegambia, built their diets around staple grains like millet and sorghum, supplemented by other local foods such as plantains, beans, bananas, and small game like rabbits. Yams were the staple crop in the forest zone to the south, while rice was the principal crop along the Guinea coast. Regional fairs served as sites for the exchange of produce and news and for social interaction. Age-grade systems, which passed on societal norms to successive generations and unified communities, were a common feature of many of these societies. The Wolof-, Serer-, and Pulaar-speaking peoples in Senegambia were also connected to the trans-Saharan caravan trade, which along with goods brought Islamic, and later French, culture to the region.

Key Terms

age-grade systems
oba
Taghaza
Tuareg
cowrie shells
Swahili
slave
sorting
factory-forts
shore trading

• In what ways was the trans-Saharan trade important to the West African kingdoms of Songhai, Kanem-Bornu, and Hausaland?

The Sudanic empires immediately south of the Sahara, such as Songhai, Kanem-Bornu, and Hausaland, were heavily involved in commercial activities, controlling the north-south trans-Saharan trade in gold, salt, cloth, leather, and other items, and the Niger River trade that linked markets the length and breadth of that great river. The two major commodities traded across the vast desert were gold and salt. Islam also came south across the desert, and the rulers of the great West African kingdom of Songhai, and its predecessors Ghana and Mali, were all Muslims. Being part of the Islamic world gave these societies not only commercial links to Europe, the Middle East, and beyond, but also access to some of the most advanced centers of scholarship in the world at the time, like Cairo and Baghdad. Timbuktu, in the heart of West Africa, had its own university. Still, although West African societies experienced strong Islamic influences, Muslim culture affected primarily the royal and elite classes and seldom reached the masses. The West African kingdoms of Benin, Kanem-Bornu, and Hausaland maintained their separate existences for centuries.

• How did the Coptic Christian Church in Ethiopia serve as a unifying force for the society and for the kingdom?

In eastern Africa, Ethiopia had accepted Christianity long before northern and eastern Europe; Ethiopians practiced Coptic Christianity, which shaped their identity. Europeans came to believe that this Christian kingdom in Africa was ruled over by a fabulously wealthy (but totally mythical) Christian monarch named Prester John. The Prester John fable attracted Europeans to Ethiopia for centuries. The myth partly explains why, when the Ethiopians called for European assistance in fighting off Muslim incursions on their borders in the sixteenth century, the Portuguese came to their aid, soundly defeating a Muslim force at Lake Tana in 1541. Jesuit missionaries soon followed and tried to convert Ethiopians to Roman Catholicism, but the Ethiopians fiercely resisted, expelling the Jesuits in 1633. Ethiopia then entered a two-hundred-year period of isolation.

• What was the significance of the Indian Ocean to the political and economic organization of the Swahili city-states?

The wealthy Swahili city-states on the southeastern coast of Africa possessed a Muslim and mercantile culture. They were also predominantly Islamic and have left a written record of their history. A maritime peoples, they were a mixture of African and Arabic, with close ties as well to Persia (Iran), India, and Indonesia. Cities such as Mogadishu, Kilwa, and Sofala communicated in Arabic and acted independently, and their commercial economies were tied to the Indian Ocean trade. The Swahili acted as middlemen and women for the East African link in the vast Indian Ocean trade network. When the Portuguese arrived in the Indian Ocean in the late fifteenth and early sixteenth centuries, they sought to conquer and control this network. Although the Portuguese had little effect on Swahili culture or religion, their presence caused the economic decline or even death of many Swahili cities.

• What role did slavery play in African societies before European intrusion?

Scholars continue to debate the character and extent of African slavery before European intrusion. Many societies had some form of slavery. Generally slaves were obtained as payment for debt, in war, or through simple purchase. Slaves were treated relatively benignly in some societies, serving as wives, house servants, royal guards, or even royal advisers enjoying great prestige. But other slaves suffered under the same harsh and brutal treatment—as field hands, common laborers, sex objects, or miners—as enslaved Africans would experience later in the Western world.

Suggested Reading

Berger, Iris, E. Frances White, and Cathy Skidmore-Heiss. *Women in Sub-Saharan Africa: Restoring Women to History*. 1999. Necessary reading for a complete understanding of African history.

Cooper, Frederick. *Plantation Slavery on the East Coast of Africa*. 1997. Useful study of slavery as practiced in Africa.

Fredrickson, G. M. *Racism: A Short History*. 2002. Contains probably the best recent study of the connection between African slavery and Western racism.

Isichei, Elizabeth. *A History of Christianity in Africa. From Antiquity to the Present*. 1995. Comprehensive survey of Christianity in Africa.

Klein, Martin, and Claire C. Robertson. *Women and Slavery in Africa*. 1997. From perspective that most slaves in Africa were women.

Lovejoy, Paul E. *Transformation in Slavery: A History of Slavery in Africa*. 1983. Essential for an understanding of slavery in an African context.

Manning, P. *Slavery, Colonialism and Economic Growth in Dahomey, 1640–1960.* 1982. An in-depth study of the kingdom of Dahomey, which, after Angola, was the largest exporter of slaves to the Americas.

Middleton, J. *The World of Swahili: An African Mercantile Civilization.* 1992. Introduction to East Africa and the Horn region.

Miers, Suzanne, and Igor Kopytoff. *Slavery in Africa: Historical and Anthropological Perspectives.* 1980. Classic study of slavery in Africa.

Northrup, D. *Africa's Discovery of Europe, 1450–1850.* 2002. Offers a unique perspective on African-European contact.

Pearson, Michael N. *Port Cities and Intruders: The Swahili Coast, India, and Portugal in the Early Modern Era.* 2002. Comprehensive introduction to the Swahili coast and the Indian Ocean trade network.

Powell, Eve Troutt, and John O. Hunwick. *The African Diaspora in the Mediterranean Lands of Islam.* 2002. Important study of Islam and African slave trade.

Robinson, David. *Muslim Societies in African History.* 2004. Valuable introduction to Islam in Africa by a renowned Africanist.

Shell, R. *Children of Bondage: A Social History of the Slave Society at the Cape of Good Hope, 1652–1938.* 1994. A massive study of Cape slave society filled with much valuable statistical data.

Shillington, K. *History of Africa,* 2005. Provides a soundly researched, highly readable, and well-illustrated survey.

Thomas, H. *The Slave Trade.* 1997. Solid, popular account of the transatlantic slave trade.

Thorton, J. *Africa and Africans in the Making of the Atlantic World, 1400–1680.* 1992. Places African developments in an Atlantic context.

Vansina, J. *Kingdoms of the Savanna.* 1966. Classic study of the African Savanna and its peoples.

Notes

1. P. D. Curtin, *Economic Change in Precolonial Africa: Senegambia in the Era of the Slave Trade* (Madison: University of Wisconsin Press, 1975), pp. 34–35; J. A. Rawley, *The Transatlantic Slave Trade: A History*

2. Robert W. July, *Precolonial Africa: An Economic and Social History* (New York: Scribner's, 1975), p. 99.

3. Robert W. July, *A History of the African People* (Prospect Heights, Ill.: Waveland Press, 1998), p. 121.

4. J. Iliffe, *Africans: The History of a Continent* (Cambridge: Cambridge University Press, 2007), pp. 96–97.

5. Ibid., pp. 112–113, 142.

6. *Equiano's Travels: The Interesting Narrative of the Life of Olaudah Equiano,* ed. P. Edwards (Portsmouth, N.H.: Heinemann, 1996), p. 4.

7. Iliffe, *Africans,* p. 137.

8. Ibid., p. 68.

9. Ibid., pp. 86–87.

10. Quoted in R. Hallett, *Africa to 1875* (Ann Arbor: University of Michigan Press, 1970), p. 151.

11. *The Cambridge History of Africa,* vol. 3, *Ca 1050 to 1600,* ed. R. Oliver (Cambridge: Cambridge University Press, 1977), pp. 427–435.

12. A. ibn-Fartura, "The Kanem Wars," in *Nigerian Perspectives,* ed. T. Hodgkin (London: Oxford University Press, 1966), pp. 111–115.

13. "The Kano Chronicle," quoted in *Nigerian Perspectives,* ed. T. Hodgkin (London: Oxford University Press, 1966), pp. 89–90.

14. See A. J. R. Russell-Wood, *The Portuguese Empire: A World on the Move* (Baltimore: Johns Hopkins University Press, 1998), pp. 11–13.

15. J. Middleton, *The World of Swahili: An African Mercantile Civilization* (New Haven, Conn.: Yale University Press, 1992), p. 27.

16. Ibid., pp. 35–38.

17. Russell-Wood, *The Portuguese Empire,* pp. 43–44.

18. P. E. Lovejoy, *Transformations in Slavery: A History of Slavery in Africa* (Cambridge: Cambridge University Press, 1983), p. 19. This section leans heavily on Lovejoy's work.

19. See Table 2.1, "Trans-Saharan Slave Trade, 650–1600," ibid., p. 25.

20. Iliffe, *Africans,* p. 77.

21. Quoted in H. Thomas, *The Slave Trade* (New York: Simon and Schuster, 1997), p. 21.

22. G. Gerzina, *Black London: Life Before Emancipation* (New Brunswick, N.J.: Rutgers University Press, 1995), pp. 29–66, passim; the quotation is on p. 53.

23. C.-H. Shell, *Children of Bondage: A Social History of the Slave Society at the Cape of Good Hope, 1652–1838* (Hanover, N.H.: University Press of New England, 1994), p. 41, fig. 2-1, pp. 149–155, and fig. 5-10.

24. Iliffe, *Africans,* pp. 128–129.

25. See D. Eltis, *The Rise of African Slavery in the Americas* (Cambridge: Cambridge University Press, 2000), Chap. 3; and the review/commentary by J. E. Inikori, *American Historical Review* 106, no. 5 (December 2001): 1751–1753.

26. R. Blackburn, *The Making of New World Slavery: From the Baroque to the Modern, 1492–1800* (New York: Verso, 1998), pp. 79–80.

27. Rawley, *The Transatlantic Slave Trade,* p. 45.

28. Ibid., pp. 41–47.

29. R. E. Conrad, *Children of God's Fire: A Documentary History of Black Slavery in Brazil* (Princeton, N.J.: Princeton University Press, 1983), pp. 20–23.

30. *Equiano's Travels,* pp. 23–26.

31. Rawley, *The Transatlantic Slave Trade,* pp. 45–47.

32. July, *A History of the African People,* p. 171.

33. J. Adams, "Remarks on the Country Extending from Cape Palmas to the River Congo," *Nigerian Perspectives,* ed. T. Hodgkin (London: Oxford University Press, 1966), pp. 178–180.

34. A. G. Hopkins, *An Economic History of West Africa* (New York: Columbia University Press, 1973), p. 83.

35. Ibid., p. 105.

36. J. Thornton, *Africa and Africans in the Making of the Atlantic World* (New York: Cambridge University Press, 1992), pp. 138–142.

37. July, *Precolonial Africa,* pp. 269–270.

38. Hopkins, *An Economic History of West Africa,* p. 119.

39. P. Manning, *Slavery and African Life: Occidental, Oriental, and African Slave Trades* (New York: Cambridge University Press, 1990), pp. 22–23 and Chap. 3, pp. 38–59.

Listening to the
PAST

Duarte Barbosa on the Swahili City-States

The Portuguese linguist Duarte Barbosa made two voyages to India. Arriving first in 1500, he acted for five years as interpreter and translator in Cochin and Cananor in Kerala (in southwestern India on the Malabar Coast) and returned to Lisbon in 1506. On his second visit in 1511, he served the Portuguese government as chief scribe in the factory of Cananor (a factory was a warehouse for the storage of goods, not a manufacturing center) and as the liaison with the local Indian rajah (prince). When Afonso de Albuquerque dismissed Barbosa, he went to Calicut. He returned to Cananor about 1520 and died there in 1545.

On the basis of his trips around the Indian Ocean in 1518, Barbosa completed his Libro des Coisas da India, *a geographical and ethnographic survey of peoples, lands, and commerce from the Cape of Good Hope to China. It was based largely on his personal observations. First published in Italian, the book won wide acclaim in Europe, and modern scholars consider the geographical information in it very accurate.*

Sofala

And the manner of their traffic was this: they came in small vessels named *zambucos* from the kingdoms of Kilwa, Mombasa, and Malindi, bringing many cotton cloths, some spotted and others white and blue, also some of silk, and many small beads, gray, red, and yellow, which things come to the said kingdoms from the great kingdom of Cambay [in Northwest India] in other greater ships. And these wares the said Moors who came from Malindi and Mombasa [purchased from others who bring them hither and] paid for in gold at such a price that those merchants departed well pleased; which gold they gave by weight.

The Moors of Sofala kept these wares and sold them afterwards to the heathen of the Kingdom of Benametapa, who came thither laden with gold which they gave in exchange for the said cloths without weighing it. These Moors collect also great store of ivory which they find hard by Sofala, and this also they sell in the Kingdom of Cambay at five or six cruzados the quintal. They also sell some ambergris, which is brought to them from the Hucicas, and is exceed-

ing good. These Moors are black, and some of them tawny; some of them speak Arabic, but the more part use the language of the country. They clothe themselves from the waist down with cotton and silk cloths, and other cloths they wear over their shoulders like capes, and turbans on their heads. Some of them wear small caps dyed in grain in chequers and other woolen clothes in many tints, also camlets and other silks.

Their food is millet, rice, flesh and fish. In this river as far as the sea are many sea horses, which come out on the land to graze, which horses always move in the sea like fishes; they have tusks like those of small elephants, being whiter and harder, and it never loses color. In the country near Sofala are many wild elephants, exceeding great (which the country-folk know not how to tame), ounces, lions, deer and many other wild beasts. It is a land of plains and hills with many streams of sweet water. . . .

Kilwa

Going along the coast from [the] town of Mozambique, there is an island hard by the mainland which is called Kilwa, in which is a Moorish town with many fair houses of stones and mortar, with many windows after our fashion, very well arranged in streets, with many flat roofs. The doors are of wood, well carved, with excellent joinery. Around it are streams and orchards and fruit-gardens with many channels of sweet water. It has a Moorish king over it. From this place they trade with Sofala, whence they bring back gold, and from here they spread all over . . . the seacoast [which] is well peopled with villages and abodes of Moors.

Before the King our Lord sent out his expedition to discover India the Moors of Sofala, Cuama, Angoya and Mozambique were all subject to the king of Kilwa, who was the most mighty king among them. And in this town was great plenty of gold, as no ships passed towards Sofala without first coming to this island. . . .

This town was taken by force from its king by the Portuguese, as, moved by arrogance, he refused to obey the King our Lord. There they took many prisoners and the king fled from the island, and His

Husuni Kubwa at Kilwa combined a royal palace, a resting place for caravans, and an enclosure for slaves held for later sale. (From Peter S. Garlake, *The Early Islamic Architecture of the East African Coast, Memoir 1 of the British Institute in Eastern Africa, Nairobi, 1966. Original drawing by Peter S. Garlake. Copyright, British Institute in Eastern Africa. Reproduced with permission of BIEA)*

Highness ordered that a fort should be built there, and kept it under his rule and governance. Afterwards he ordered that it should be pulled down, as its maintenance was of no value nor profit to him, and it was destroyed by Antonio de Saldanha. . . .

Malindi

. . . Journeying along the coast towards India, there is a fair town on the mainland lying along a strand, which is named Malindi. It pertains to the Moors and has a Moorish king over it; the which place has many fair stone and mortar houses of many stories, with great plenty of windows and flat roofs, after our fashion. The place is well laid out in streets. The folk are both black and white; they go naked, covering only their private parts with cotton and silk cloths. Others of them wear cloths folded like cloaks and waistbands, and turbans of many rich stuffs on their heads.

They are great barterers, and deal in cloth, gold, ivory, and divers other wares with the Moors and heathen of the great kingdom of Cambay; and to their haven come every year many ships with cargoes of merchandise, from which they get great store of gold, ivory and wax. In this traffic the Cambay merchants make great profits, and thus, on one side and the other, they earn much money. There is great plenty of food in this city, rice, millet, and some wheat which they bring from Cambay, and divers sorts of fruit, inasmuch as there is here abundance of fruit-gardens and

orchards. Here too are plenty of round-tailed sheep, cows and other cattle and great store of oranges, also of hens.

The king and people of this place ever were and are friends of the King of Portugal, and the Portuguese always find in them great comfort and friendship and perfect peace, and there the ships, when they chance to pass that way, obtain supplies in plenty.

Questions for Analysis

1. Locate on a map the city-states that Barbosa discusses.

2. What seems to have impressed Barbosa? What was his attitude toward the various peoples he saw? What Portuguese or Western prejudices do you discern?

3. What was the Portuguese relationship to the Swahili city-states at the time Barbosa saw them?

4. What was the source of Sofala's gold? Of Sofala's and Malindi's ivory? What did Cambay (that is, India) use ivory for?

Source: Basil Davidson, *The African Past: Chronicles from Antiquity to Modern Times* (Boston: Little, Brown, 1964). Copyright © 1964 by Basil Davidson. Reprinted by permission of Curtis Brown, Ltd.

Wedding Procession of Prince Dara-Shikoh, Agra, February 1633. Female musicians ride atop elephants. *(The Royal Collection © 2007, Her Majesty Queen Elizabeth II)*

chapter 19

THE ISLAMIC WORLD POWERS, CA. 1400–1800

Chapter Preview

The Three Turkish Ruling Houses: The Ottomans, Safavids, and Mughals
• How were the three Islamic empires established, and what sorts of governments did they set up?

Cultural Flowering
• What cultural advances occurred under the rule of these three houses?

Non-Muslims Under Muslim Rule
• How did Christians, Jews, Hindus, and other non-Muslims fare under these Islamic states?

Shifting Trade Routes and European Penetration
• How were the Islamic empires affected by the decline in overland trade and the great growth in maritime commerce, and how were European powers able to use trade to make inroads as this period progressed?

Dynastic Decline
• Did any common factors lead to the decline of the Islamic empires in the seventeenth and eighteenth centuries?

After the breakup of the Mongol Empire, new states emerged in south and west Eurasia. By the sixteenth century the Ottoman Empire centered in Anatolia, the Safavid Empire in Persia, and the Mughal Empire in India controlled vast territories from West Africa to Central Asia, from the Balkans to the Bay of Bengal. Their origins were similar (in Turkish tribal polities), and they similarly had to adjust to ruling large sedentary populations. They all adapted to the decline in the supremacy of the mounted archer that resulted from the introduction of firearms.

Lasting almost five hundred years (1453–1918), the Ottoman Empire was one of the largest, best-organized, and most enduring political entities in world history. In Persia the Safavid Dynasty created a Shi'ite state and presided over a brilliant culture. In India the Mughal leader Babur and his successors gained control of much of the Indian subcontinent. Mughal rule inaugurated a period of radical administrative reorganization in India and the flowering of intellectual and architectural creativity. These three states were not allied to each other—the Safavids and Ottomans were divided on theological grounds between Sunni and Shi'ite and competed for control of Mesopotamia. Still they faced similar challenges and responded in similar ways. Culturally they were strongly linked, with ideas, practices, and styles quickly spreading from one society to another.

THE THREE TURKISH RULING HOUSES: THE OTTOMANS, SAFAVIDS, AND MUGHALS

How were the three Islamic empires established, and what sorts of governments did they set up?

Before the Mongols arrived in Central Asia and Persia, another nomadic Central Asian people, the Turks, had gained overlordship in key territories from Anatolia to Delhi in north India. The Turks had been

545

quick to join the Mongols and formed important elements in the armies and administrations of the Mongol states in Persia and Central Asia. In these regions, Turks far outnumbered ethnic Mongols.

As Mongol strength in Persia and Central Asia deteriorated in the late thirteen and fourteenth centuries, the Turks resumed their expansion. In the late fourteenth century, the Turkish leader Tamerlane (1336–1405) built a Central Asian empire from his base in Samarkand, campaigning into India and through Persia to the Black Sea. Tamerlane campaigned continuously from the 1360s till his death in 1405, trying to repeat the achievements of Chinggis Khan. He did not get involved in administering the new territories, but rather appointed lords and let them make use of existing political structures. Thus, when after his death his sons and grandson fought against each other for succession, his empire quickly fell apart, and power devolved to the local level. Sufi orders thrived, and Islam became the most important force integrating the region. It was from the many small Turkish chiefs that the founders of the three main empires emerged.

The Ottoman Turkish Empire

Ottomans *Ruling house of the Turkish empire that lasted from 1453 to 1918.*

Anatolia *The region of modern Turkey.*

The **Ottomans** took their name from Osman (r. 1280–1324), the chief of a band of seminomadic Turks that had migrated into western **Anatolia** during the era when the Mongol Il-khans still held Persia. The Ottomans gradually expanded at the expense of other Turkish statelets and the Byzantine Empire. The Ottoman ruler called himself "border chief," or leader of the *ghazis,* frontier fighters in the *jihad,* or holy war. The earliest Ottoman historical source, a fourteenth-century saga, describes the ghazis as the "instrument of God's religion . . . God's scourge who cleanses the earth from the filth of polytheism . . . God's pure sword."[1] Although temporarily slowed by defeat at the hands of Tamerlane in 1402, the Ottomans quickly reasserted themselves after Tamerlane's death in 1405.

The holy war was intended to subdue, not destroy. The Ottomans built their empire by absorbing the Muslims of Anatolia and by becoming the protector of the Orthodox church and of the millions of Greek Christians in Anatolia and the Balkans. In 1326 they took Bursa in western Anatolia, and in 1352 they gained a foothold in Europe by seizing Gallipoli. Their victories led more men, including recent converts, to join them as ghazi. In 1389 at Kosovo in the Balkans, the Ottomans defeated a combined force of Serbs and Bosnians. In 1396 on the Danube River in modern Bulgaria, they crushed King Sigismund of Hungary, who was supported by French, German, and English knights. After the victories in the Balkans, the Ottomans added to their military through the creation of slave troops (discussed below). These troops were outfitted with guns and artillery and trained to use them effectively.

The reign of Sultan Mehmet II (r. 1451–1481) saw the Ottoman conquest of Constantinople, capital of the Byzantine Empire, which had lasted a thousand years. The Byzantine emperor Constantine IX Palaeologus (r. 1449–1453), with only about ten thousand men, relied on the magnificent system of circular walls and stone fortifications for his defense. Mehmet II had more than one hundred thousand men and a large fleet, but iron chains spanning the harbor kept him out. Turkish ingenuity and Western technology eventually decided the battle. Mehmet's army carried boats over the steep hills to come in behind the chains blocking the harbor, then bombarded the city from the rear. A Transylvanian cannon founder who deserted the Greeks for the Turks cast huge bronze cannon on the spot (bringing raw materials to the scene of military action was easier than moving guns long distances).[2]

Sultan-i-Rum *The name that the Ottoman sultans took as their title; it means "sultan of Rome."*

With the conquest of Constantinople (renamed Istanbul) as a base, the Ottomans quickly absorbed the rest of the Byzantine Empire. They continued to expand through the Middle East and into North Africa in the sixteenth century. Once Constantinople was theirs, the Ottoman sultans considered themselves successors of both the Byzantine and Seljuk emperors, as their title **Sultan-i-Rum** (sultan of Rome) attests.

To begin the transformation of Istanbul into an imperial Ottoman capital, Mehmet ordered the city cleaned up and the walls repaired. He appointed officials to adapt the city administration to Ottoman ways and ordered wealthy residents to participate in building mosques, markets, water fountains, baths, and other public facilities. The population of Istanbul had declined in the decades before the conquest, and warfare, flight, and the sale of many survivors into slavery had decreased the population further. Therefore, Mehmet transplanted to the city inhabitants of other territories, granting them tax remissions and possession of empty houses. He wanted them to start businesses, make the city prosperous, and transform it into a microcosm of the empire.

Gunpowder, invented by the Chinese and adapted to artillery use by the Europeans, played an influential role in the expansion of the Ottoman state. In the first half of the sixteenth century, the Ottomans gained control of shipping in the eastern Mediterranean, eliminated the Portuguese from the Red Sea and Persian Gulf, and supported Andalusian and North African Muslims in their fight against the Spanish reconquista. Under the superb military leadership of Selim (r. 1512–1520), the Ottomans in 1514 turned the Safavids back from Anatolia. The Ottomans also added Syria and Palestine (1516) and Egypt (1517) to the empire, extending their rule across North Africa to Tunisia and Algeria. Selim's rule marks the beginning of four centuries when most Arabs were under Ottoman rule.

Suleiman (r. 1520–1566) extended Ottoman dominion to its widest geographical extent (see Map 19.1). Suleiman's army crushed the Hungarians at Mohács in 1526, killing the king and thousands of his nobles. Three years later, the Turks besieged the Habsburg capital of Vienna. Only an accident—the army's insistence on returning home before winter—prevented Muslim control of all central Europe. The Ottomans' military discipline, ability to coordinate cavalry and infantry, and capability in logistics were usually superior to those of the Europeans.

From the late fourteenth to the early seventeenth century, the Ottoman Empire was a key player in European politics. In 1525 Francis I of France and Suleiman struck an alliance; both believed that only their collaboration could prevent Habsburg hegemony in Europe. The Habsburg emperor Charles V retaliated by seeking an alliance with Safavid Persia. Suleiman renewed the French agreement with Francis's son, Henry II (r. 1547–1559), and the French entente became the cornerstone of Ottoman policy in western Europe. Suleiman also allied with the German Protestant princes, forcing the Catholic Habsburgs to grant concessions to the Protestants. Ottoman pressure proved an important factor in the official recognition of Lutheran Protestants at the Peace of Augsburg in 1555. In addition to the rising tide of Protestantism, the Ottoman threat strengthened the growth of national monarchy in France.

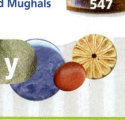

Chronology

1280–1324 Osman, founder of the Ottoman Dynasty

1336–1405 Life of Tamerlane

ca. mid-1400s Coffeehouses become center of Islamic male social life

1453 Ottoman conquest of Constantinople

ca. 1498–1805 Mughal Empire

1501–1722 Safavid Empire

1501–1524 Reign of Shah Ismail

1520–1566 Reign of Ottoman emperor Suleiman I; period of artistic flowering in Ottoman Empire

1520–1558 Hürrem wields influence in Ottoman Empire as Suleiman's wife

1521 Piri Reis, *Book of the Sea,* a navigational map book

1548–1557 Pasha Sinan designs and builds Suleimaniye Mosque in Istanbul

1556–1605 Reign of Akbar in Mughal Empire

1570 Turks take control of Cyprus

1571 First major Ottoman defeat by Christians, at Lepanto

1587–1629 Reign of Shah Abbas; height of Safavid power; carpet weaving becomes major Persian industry

1631–1648 Construction of Taj Mahal under Shah Jahan

1658–1707 Reign of Aurangzeb; Mughal power begins to decline

1668 Bombay leased to British East India Company

1763 Treaty of Paris recognizes British control over much of India

In eastern Europe to the north of Ottoman lands stood the Grand Duchy of Moscow. In the fifteenth century, Ottoman rulers did not regard it as a threat; in 1497 they even gave Russian merchants freedom of trade within the empire. But in 1547 Ivan IV (the Terrible) brought under Russian control the entire Volga region (see Map 19.1). In 1557 Ivan's ally, the Cossack chieftain Dimitrash, tried to take Azov, the northernmost Ottoman fortress. Ottoman plans to recapture the area succeeded in uniting Russia, Persia, and the pope against the Turks.

Though usually victorious on land, the Ottomans did not enjoy complete dominion on the seas. Competition with the Habsburgs and pirates for control of the Mediterranean led the Ottomans to conquer Cyprus in 1570 and settle thousands of Turks from Anatolia there. (Thus began the large Turkish presence on Cyprus that continues to the present day.) In response, Pope Pius V organized a Holy League against the Turks, which had a victory in 1571 at Lepanto with a squadron of more than two hundred Spanish, Venetian, and papal galleys. Still, the Turks remained supreme on land and quickly rebuilt their entire fleet.

To the east, war with Persia occupied the sultans' attention throughout the sixteenth century. Several issues lay at the root of the long and exhausting conflicts:

MAP 19.1 **The Ottoman Empire at Its Height, 1566** The Ottomans, like their great rivals the Habsburgs, rose to rule a vast dynastic empire encompassing many different peoples and ethnic groups. The army and the bureaucracy served to unite the disparate territories into a single state.

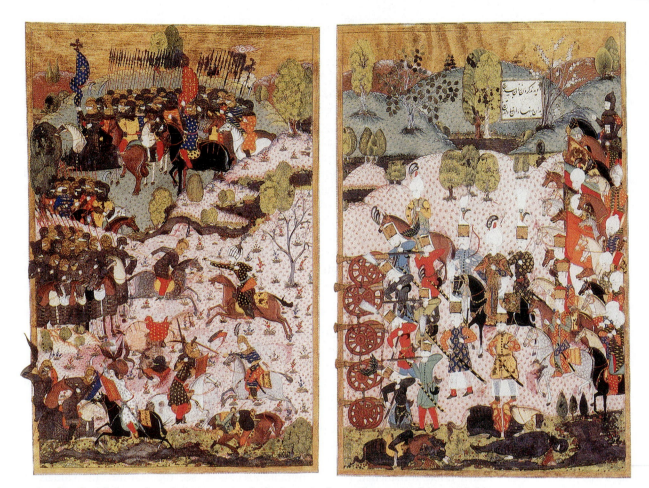

● **Battle of Mohács**   The *Süleymanname* (Book of Suleiman), a biography, contains these wonderful illustrations of the battle that took place in Hungary on August 29, 1526. In the right panel, Suleiman in a white turban sits on a black horse surrounded by his personal guard, while janissaries fire cannon at the enemy. In the left panel, the Europeans are in disarray, in contrast to the Turks' discipline and order. Suleiman inflicted a crushing defeat and absorbed Hungary into the Ottoman Empire. The artist attempted to show the terrain and battle tactics. *(Topkapi Saray Museum, Istanbul)*

religious antagonism between the Sunni Ottomans and the Shi'ite Persians, competition to expand at each other's expense in Mesopotamia, desires to control trade routes, and European alliances. Finally, in 1638, the Ottomans captured Baghdad, and the treaty of Kasr-I-Shirim established a permanent border between the two powers.

The Ottoman political system reached its classic form under Suleiman I. All authority flowed from the **sultan** to his public servants: provincial governors, police officers, military generals, heads of treasuries, viziers. In Turkish history, Suleiman is known as the Lawgiver because of his profound influence on the civil law. He ordered Lütfi Paşa (d. 1562), a poet and juridical scholar of slave origin, to draw up a new general code of laws. This code prescribed penalties for routine criminal acts such as robbery, adultery, and murder. It also sought to reform bureaucratic and financial corruption in areas such as harem intervention in administrative affairs, foreign merchants' payment of bribes to avoid customs duties, imprisonment without trial, and promotion in the provincial administration because of favoritism rather than ability. The legal code also introduced the idea of balanced financial budgets. The head of the religious establishment was given the task of reconciling sultanic law with Islamic law. Suleiman's legal acts influenced many legal codes, including that of the United States. Today, Suleiman's image, along with the images of Solon, Moses, and Thomas Jefferson, appears in the chamber of the U.S. House of Representatives.

sultan   *An Arabic word originally used by the Seljuk Turks to mean authority or dominion; it was used by the Ottomans to connote political and military supremacy.*

devshirme *A process whereby the sultan's agents swept the provinces for Christian youths to become slaves.*

janissaries *Turkish for "recruits"; they formed the elite army corps.*

concubine *A woman who is a recognized spouse but of lower status than a wife.*

Slavery was widespread in the Ottoman empire. Slaves were purchased from Spain, North Africa, and Venice; captured in battle; or drafted through the system known as **devshirme,** by which the sultan's agents compelled Christian families in the Balkans to turn over their boys. As the Ottoman frontier advanced in the fifteenth and sixteenth centuries, Albanian, Bosnian, Wallachian, and Hungarian slave boys filled Ottoman imperial needs. The slave boys were converted to Islam and trained for the imperial civil service and the standing army. The brightest 10 percent entered the palace school, where they learned to read and write Arabic, Ottoman Turkish, and Persian. Other boys were sent to Turkish farms, where they acquired physical toughness in preparation for military service. Known as **janissaries** (Turkish for "recruits"), they formed the elite army corps. Thoroughly indoctrinated and absolutely loyal to the sultan, the janissary slave corps eliminated the influence of old Turkish families and played a central role in Ottoman military affairs in the sixteenth century.

The Ottoman ruling class consisted in part of descendants of Turkish families that had formerly ruled parts of Anatolia and in part of people of varied ethnic origins who rose through the bureaucratic and military ranks, many beginning as the sultan's slaves. All were committed to the Ottoman way: Islamic in faith, loyal to the sultan, and well versed in the Turkish language and the culture of the imperial court. In return for their services to the sultan, they held landed estates for the duration of their lives. The ruling class had the legal right to use and enjoy the profits, but not the ownership, of the land. Since all property belonged to the sultan and reverted to him on the holder's death, Turkish nobles, unlike their European counterparts, did not have a local base independent of the ruler. The absence of a hereditary nobility and private ownership of agricultural land differentiates the Ottoman system from European feudalism.

By the reign of Selim I, the principle was established that the sultan did not contract legal marriage but perpetuated the ruling house through concubinage. A slave **concubine** could have none of the political aspirations or leverage that a native or foreign-born noblewoman had (with a notable exception; see the feature "Individuals in

● **Music in a Garden**
This illustration of a courtly romance depicts several women in a garden, intently listening to a musician, cups of a beverage in their hands. *(Biblioteca Vaticana Apostolica)*

Individuals IN SOCIETY

Hürrem

Hürrem (1505?–1558) was born in the western Ukraine (then part of Poland), the daughter of a Ruthenian priest, and was given the Polish name Aleksandra Lisowska. When Tartars raided, they captured and enslaved her. In 1520 she was given as a gift to Suleiman on the occasion of his accession to the throne. The Venetian ambassador (probably relying on secondhand or thirdhand information) described her as "young, graceful, petite, but not beautiful." She was given the Turkish name Hürrem, meaning "joyful."

Hürrem apparently brought joy to Suleiman. Their first child was born in 1521; by 1525 they had four sons and a daughter; sources note that by that year Suleiman visited no other woman. But he waited eight or nine years before breaking Ottoman dynastic tradition by making Hürrem his legal wife, the first slave concubine so honored. For the rest of her life, Hürrem played a highly influential role in the political, diplomatic, and philanthropic life of the Ottoman state. First, great power flowed from her position as mother of the prince, the future sultan Selim II (r. 1566–1574). Then, as the intimate and most trusted adviser of the sultan, she was Suleiman's closest confidant. He was frequently away in the far-flung corners of his multiethnic empire. Hürrem wrote him long letters filled with her love and longing for him, her prayers for his safety in battle, and political information about affairs in Istanbul, the activities of the grand vizier, and the attitudes of the janissaries. At a time when some people believed that the sultan's absence from the capital endangered his hold on the throne, Hürrem acted as his eyes and ears for potential threats.

Hürrem was the sultan's contact with her native Poland, which sent more embassies to Istanbul than any other power. Through her correspondence with King Sigismund I, peace between Poland and the Ottomans was maintained. When Sigismund II succeeded his father in 1548, Hürrem sent congratulations on his accession, along with two pairs of pajamas (originally a Hindu garment, but commonly worn in southwestern Asia) and six handkerchiefs. By sending the shah of Persia gold-embroidered sheets and shirts she had sewn herself, Hürrem sought to display the wealth of the sultanate and to keep peace between the Ottomans and the Safavids.

The enormous stipend that Suleiman gave Hürrem permitted her to participate in his vast building program. In Jerusalem (in the Ottoman province of Palestine), she founded a hospice for fifty-five pilgrims

Hürrem and her ladies in the harem. *(Bibliothèque nationale de France)*

that included a soup kitchen that fed four hundred pilgrims a day. In Istanbul Suleiman built and Hürrem endowed the Haseki (meaning "royal favorite concubine") mosque complex and a public bath for women near the Women's Market.

Perhaps Hürrem tried to fulfill two functions hitherto distinct in Ottoman political theory: those of the sultan's favorite and mother of the prince. She also performed the conflicting roles of slave concubine and imperial wife. Turks, however, reviled Hürrem and thought she had bewitched Suleiman.

Questions for Analysis

1. Compare Hürrem to other powerful fifteenth- or sixteenth-century women, such as Isabella of Castile, Catherine de' Medici of France, Elizabeth of England, and Mary Queen of Scots.

2. What was Hürrem's "nationality"? What role did it play in her life?

Source: Leslie P. Pierce, *The Imperial Harem: Women and Sovereignty in the Ottoman Empire* (New York: Oxford University Press, 1993).

MAP 19.2 **The Safavid Empire** In the late sixteenth century, the power of the Safavid kingdom of Persia rested on its strong military force, its Shi'ite Muslim faith, and its extraordinarily rich trade in rugs and pottery. Many of the cities on the map, such as Tabriz, Qum, and Shiraz, were great rug-weaving centers.

Society: Hürrem"). When one of the sultan's concubines became pregnant, her status and her salary increased. If she delivered a boy, she raised him until the age of ten or eleven. Then the child was given a province to govern under his mother's supervision. She accompanied him there, was responsible for his good behavior, and worked through imperial officials and the janissary corps to promote his interests. Since succession to the throne was open to all the sultan's sons, at his death fratricide often resulted, and the losers were blinded or executed.

Slave concubinage paralleled the Ottoman development of slave soldiers and slave viziers. All held positions entirely at the sultan's pleasure, owed loyalty solely to him, and thus were more reliable than a hereditary nobility, as existed in Europe. Great social prestige, as well as the opportunity to acquire power and wealth, was attached to being a slave of the imperial household. Suleiman even made it a practice to marry his daughters to top-ranking slave-officials.

The Safavid Theocracy in Persia

After the collapse of Tamerlane's empire in 1405, Persia was controlled by Turkish lords, no single one dominant until 1501 when fourteen-year-old Ismail led a Turkish army to capture Tabriz and declared himself **shah** (king) and a particular Shi'ia sect the official and compulsory religion of his new empire. In the early twenty-first century, Iran remains the only Muslim state in which Shi'ism is the official religion.

The strength of the early **Safavid** state rested on three crucial features. First, it had the loyalty and military support of Turkish Sufis known as **Qizilbash** (a Turkish word meaning "redheads" that was applied to these people because of the red hats they

Primary Source:
Letter to Shah Ismail of Persia
Ottoman sultan Selim I, a Sunni Muslim, threatens war against the Persian shah, his Shia enemy.

shah *Persian word for "king."*

Safavid *The dynasty that encompassed all of Persia and other regions; its state religion was Shi'ism.*

Qizilbash *Nomadic tribesmen who were Sufis and loyal to and supportive of the early Safavid state.*

552

wore). The shah secured the loyalty of the Qizilbash by granting them vast grazing lands, especially on the troublesome Ottoman frontier. In return, the Qizilbash supplied him with troops. Second, the Safavid state utilized the skills of urban bureaucrats and made them an essential part of the civil machinery of government. The third source of Safavid strength was the Shi'ite faith. The Shi'ites claimed descent from Ali, Muhammad's cousin and son-in-law, and believed that leadership among Muslims rightfully belonged to them as the Prophet's descendants. Ismail claimed descent from a line of twelve infallible *imams* (leaders) beginning with Ali and was officially regarded as their representative on earth.

Shi'ism gradually shaped the cultural and political identity of Persia (and later Iran). Recent scholarship asserts that Ismail was not "motivated by cynical notions of political manipulation."[3] He imported Shi'ite *ulama* (scholars outstanding in learning and piety) from other Arab lands to instruct and guide his people, and he persecuted and exiled Sunni ulama. With its puritanical emphasis on the holy law and on self-flagellation in penance for any disloyalty to Ali, the Safavid state represented theocracy triumphant throughout the first half century of its existence.

Safavid power reached its height under Shah Abbas (r. 1587–1629), whose military achievements, support for trade and commerce, and endowment of the arts earned him the epithet "the Great." He moved the capital to Isfahan. He adopted the Ottoman practice of building an army of slaves, primarily captives from the Caucuses (especially Armenians and Georgians), who could serve as a counterweight to the Qizilbash. He increased the use of gunpowder weapons and made alliances with European powers against the Ottomans and Portuguese. In his campaigns against the Ottomans, Shah Abbas captured Baghdad, Mosul, and Diarbakr in Mesopotamia (see Map 19.2).

The Mughal Empire in India

Of the three great Islamic empires of the early modern world, the **Mughal** Empire of India was the largest, wealthiest, and most populous. Extending over 1.2 million square miles at the end of the seventeenth century, with a population between 100 million and 150 million, and with fabulous wealth and resources, the Mughal Empire surpassed Safavid Persia and Ottoman Turkey. Among the Mughal ruler's world contemporaries, only the Ming emperor of China could compare with him.

In 1504 Babur (r. 1483–1530), the Turkish ruler of a small territory in Central Asia, captured Kabul and established a kingdom in Afghanistan. An adventurer who claimed descent from Chinggis Khan and Tamerlane, Babur moved southward into India when he could not expand in Afghanistan. In 1526, with a force of only twelve thousand men, Babur defeated the sultan of Delhi at Panipat. Babur's capture of the cities of Agra and Delhi, key fortresses of the north, paved the way for further conquests in northern India. Although many

● **Persian "Ardabil" Carpet from the Safavid Period**   The Persians were among the first carpet weavers of ancient times and perfected the art over thousands of years. This carpet, reputably from the Safavid shrine at Ardabil, is one of only three signed and dated (around 1539–1540) carpets from the Safavid period, when Persian carpet making was at its zenith. Hand-knotted and hand-dyed, this wool carpet was royally commissioned with a traditional medallion design, consisting of a central sunburst medallion surrounded by radiating pendants. Mosque lamps project from the top and bottom of the medallion. Inscribed on the carpet is an ode by the fourteenth-century poet Hafiz: "I have no refuge in this world other than thy threshold / My head has no resting place other than this doorway." *(Victoria & Albert Museum/The Art Archive)*

Mughal *A term meaning "Mongol," used to refer to the Muslim empire of India, although its founders were primarily Turks, Afghans, and Persians.*

badshah *Persian word for highest ruler; it was the title that Akbar took at the age of thirteen.*

Primary Source:

Akbarnama

These selections from the history of the house of Akbar offer a glimpse inside the policies and religious outlook of the Mughal emperor.

of his soldiers wished to return north with their spoils, Babur decided to stay in India. A gifted writer, Babur wrote an autobiography in Turkish that recounts his military campaigns, describes places and people he encountered, recounts his difficulties giving up wine, and shows his wide-ranging interests in everything from a Turkish general who excelled at leapfrog to his own love of fruit and swimming. He was not particularly impressed by India, complaining that the country lacked good horses, bread, grapes, and meat, and that people were neither kind, friendly, nor clever.

During the reign of Babur's son Humayun (r. 1530–1540 and 1555–1556), the Mughals lost most of their territories in Afghanistan. Humayun went into temporary exile in Persia, where he developed a deep appreciation for Persian art and literature. The reign of Humayun's son Akbar (r. 1556–1605) may well have been the greatest in the history of India. Under his dynamic leadership, the Mughal state took definite form. A boy of thirteen when he became **badshah,** or imperial ruler, Akbar pursued expansionist policies. The Mughal Empire under Akbar eventually included most of the subcontinent north of the Godavari River (see Map 19.3). No kingdom or coalition of kingdoms could long resist Akbar's armies. The once independent states of northern India were forced into a centralized political system under the sole authority of the Mughal emperor.

Akbar replaced Turkish with Persian as the official language of the Mughal Empire. Persian remained the official language until the British replaced it with English in 1835. To govern this vast region, Akbar developed an administrative bureaucracy centered on four co-equal ministers: for finance and revenue; the army and intelligence; the judiciary and religious patronage; and the imperial household, which included roads, bridges, and infrastructure throughout the empire. Under Akbar's Hindu finance minister, Raja Todar Mal, a uniform system of taxes was put in place. In the provinces, imperial governors, appointed by and responsible solely to the emperor, presided over administrative branches modeled on those of the central government. The government, however, rarely interfered in the life of village communities. Whereas the Ottoman sultans and Safavid shahs made extensive use of slaves acquired from non-Muslim lands for military and administrative positions, Akbar used the services of royal princes, nobles, and warrior-aristocrats. Initially these men were Muslims from Central Asia, but to reduce their influence, Akbar vigorously recruited Persians and Hindus. No single ethnic or religious faction could challenge the emperor.

Akbar's descendants extended the Mughal empire further. His son Jahangir (r. 1605–1628) lacked his father's military abilities and administrative genius, but he did succeed in consolidating Mughal rule in Bengal. Jahangir's son Shah Jahan (r. 1628–1658) launched fresh territorial expansion. Faced with dangerous revolts by the Muslims in Ahmadnagar and the resistance of the newly arrived Portuguese in Bengal, Shah Jahan not only crushed them but also strengthened his northwestern frontier. Shah Jahan's son Aurangzeb (r. 1658–1707) deposed his father and confined him for years in a small cell. A puritanically devout and strictly orthodox Muslim, as well as a skillful general and a clever diplomat, Aurangzeb ruled more of India than did any previous badshah, having extended the realm deeper into south India (see Map 19.3).

CULTURAL FLOWERING

What cultural advances occurred under the rule of these three houses?

All three Islamic imperial houses were great patrons and presided over extraordinary artistic flowering. There was much in common across their court cultures, probably because of the common Persian influence on the Turks since the tenth century. In

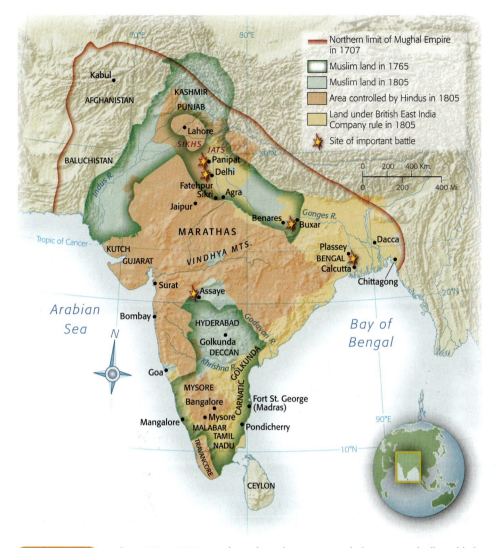

MAP 19.3 **India, 1707–1805** In the eighteenth century, Mughal power gradually yielded to the Hindu Marathas and to the British East India Company.

addition, artistic styles and intellectual and religious trends would spread from one to the other. This was aided by common languages. Persian was used as the administrative language by the Mughals in India, and Arabic was a lingua franca of the entire region because of its centrality in Islam.

One of the arts all three shared was carpets. Carpet designs and weaving techniques demonstrate both cultural integration and local distinctiveness. Turkic migrants carried their weaving traditions with them as they moved but also readily adopted new motifs, especially from Persia. In Anatolia the town of Usak began its rise as a center of commercial carpet production in the fifteenth century. In Safavid Persia, Shah Abbas was determined to improve his country's export trade and built the small cottage business of carpet weaving into a national industry. In the capital city of Isfahan alone, factories employed more than twenty-five thousand weavers, who produced woolen carpets, brocades, and silks of brilliant color, design, and quality. Because the small hands of women and children can tie tinier knots than the large hands of men, women and children have often been used (and exploited) in the manufacture of expensive rugs.

Another art that spread from Persia to both Ottoman and Mughal lands was miniature painting, especially for book illustration. This tradition had been enriched by the many Chinese artists brought to Persia during the Mongol period. There was also an interplay between carpets and miniature painting. The naturalistic reproduction of lotus blossoms, peonies, chrysanthemums, birds, and even dragons, as well as tulips and carnations, appear in both book illustrations and carpets.

Akbar enthusiastically supported artists who produced magnificent paintings and books in the Indo-Persian style. In Mughal India, as throughout the Muslim world, books were regarded as precious objects. Time, talent, and expensive materials went into their production, and they were highly coveted because they reflected wealth, learning, and power. Akbar reportedly possessed twenty-four thousand books when he died. Abu-l-Fazl describes Akbar's library and love of books:

His Majesty's library is divided into several parts. . . . Prose works, poetical works, Hindi, Persian, Greek, Kashmirian, Arabic, are all separately placed. In this order they are also inspected. Experienced people bring them daily and read them before His Majesty, who hears every book from beginning to end . . . and rewards the readers with presents of cash either in gold or silver, according to the number of leaves read out by them. . . . There are no historical facts of past ages, or curiosities of science, or interesting points of philosophy, with which His Majesty, a leader of impartial sages, is unacquainted.[4]

City and Palace Building

In all three empires, strong rulers built capital cities and imperial palaces as visible expressions of dynastic majesty. Europeans called Suleiman "the Magnificent" because of the grandeur of his court. With annual state revenues of about $80 million (at a time when Elizabeth I of England could expect $150,000 and Francis I of France perhaps $1 million) and thousands of servants, he had a lifestyle no European monarch could begin to rival. He used his fabulous wealth to adorn Istanbul with palaces, mosques, schools, and libraries. The building of hospitals, roads, and bridges and the reconstruction of the water systems of the great pilgrimage sites at Mecca and Jerusalem benefited his subjects. Safavid Persia and Mughal India produced rulers with similar ambitions.

The greatest builder under the Ottomans was Pasha Sinan (1491–1588), a Greek-born devshirme recruit who rose to become imperial architect under Suleiman. A contemporary of Michelangelo, Sinan designed 312 public buildings—mosques, schools, hospitals, public baths, palaces, and burial chapels. His masterpieces, the Shehzade and Suleimaniye mosques in Istanbul, which rivaled the Byzantine church of Hagia Sophia, represented solutions to spatial problems unique to domed buildings and expressed the discipline, power, and devotion to Islam that characterized the Ottoman Empire under Suleiman. Istanbul became a prosperous, bustling city of more than a million people.

Shah Abbas made his capital, Isfahan, the jewel of the Safavid empire. A seventeenth-century English visitor described Isfahan's bazaar as "the surprisingest piece of Greatness in Honour of commerce the world can boast of." Besides splendid rugs, stalls displayed pottery and fine china, metalwork of exceptionally high quality, and silks and velvets of stunning weave and design. A city of perhaps 750,000 people, Isfahan contained 162 mosques, 48 schools where future members of the ulama learned the sacred Muslim sciences, 273 public baths, and the vast imperial palace. Private houses had their own garden courts, and public gardens, pools, and parks adorned the wide streets. Tales of the beauty of Isfahan circulated worldwide, attracting thousands of tourists annually in the seventeenth and eighteenth centuries.

Akbar in India was also a great builder. The birth of a long-awaited son, Jahangir, inspired Akbar to build a new city, Fatehpur-Sikri, to symbolize the regime's Islamic

● **Suleimaniye Mosque**   Designed and built (1548–1557) by Sinan, a janissary who became the greatest architect in Ottoman history, and surrounded by madrasas, a hospital, and shops, this mosque asserts the dynasty's power, religious orthodoxy, and the sultan's position as "God's shadow on earth." Suleiman, who financed it, is buried here. *(Robert Frerck/Odyssey/Chicago)*

foundations. He personally supervised the construction of the city, which combined the Muslim tradition of domes, arches, and spacious courts with the Hindu tradition of flat stone beams, ornate decoration, and solidity. According to the historian Abu-l-Fazl, "His Majesty plans splendid edifices, and dresses the work of his mind and heart in the garment of stone and clay."[5] Completed in 1578, the city included an imperial palace, a mosque, lavish gardens, and a hall of worship, as well as thousands of houses for ordinary people. Unfortunately because of its bad water supply, the city was soon abandoned.

Of Akbar's successors, Shah Jahan had the most sophisticated interest in architecture. Because his capital at Agra was cramped, in 1639 he decided to found a new capital city at Delhi. Hindus considered the area especially sacred, and the site reflects their influence. In the design and layout of the buildings, however, Persian ideas predominated, an indication of the numbers of Persian architects and engineers who had flocked to the subcontinent. The walled palace-fortress alone extended over 125 acres. Built partly of red sandstone, partly of marble, it included private chambers for the emperor; mansions for the wives, widows, and concubines of the imperial household; huge audience rooms for the conduct of public business (treasury, arsenal, and military); baths; and vast gardens filled with flowers, trees, and thirty silver fountains spraying water. In 1650, with living quarters for guards, military officials, merchants, dancing girls, scholars, and hordes of cooks and servants, the palace-fortress housed 57,000 people. It also boasted a covered public bazaar (comparable to a modern

● **Isfahan Tiles** The embellishment of Isfahan under Shah Abbas I created an unprecedented need for tiles—as had the rebuilding of imperial Istanbul after 1453, the vast building program of Suleiman the Magnificent, and a huge European demand. Persian potters learned their skills from the Chinese. By the late sixteenth century, Italian and Austrian potters had imitated the Persian and Ottoman tile makers. *(Courtesy of the Trustees of the Victoria & Albert Museum)*

mall), 270 feet long and 27 feet wide, with arcaded shops. It was probably the first roofed shopping center in India, although such centers were common in western Asia. The sight of the magnificent palace left contemporaries speechless, and the words of an earlier poet were inscribed on the walls:

If there is a paradise on the face of the earth,
It is this, it is this.

Beyond the walls, princes and aristocrats built mansions and mosques on a smaller scale. With a population between 375,000 and 400,000, Delhi gained the reputation of being one of the great cities of the Muslim world.

For his palace, Shah Jahan ordered the construction of the Peacock Throne. (See the feature "Listening to the Past: The Weighing of Shah Jahan on His Forty-Second Lunar Birthday" on pages 572–573.) This famous piece was encrusted with emeralds, diamonds, pearls, and rubies. It took seven years to fashion and cost the equivalent of $5 million. It served as the imperial throne of India until 1739, when the Persian warrior Nadir Shah seized it as plunder and carried it to Persia.

Shah Jahan's most enduring monument is the Taj Mahal. Twenty thousand workers toiled eighteen years to build this memorial in Agra to Shah Jahan's favorite wife, who died giving birth to their fifteenth child. One of the most beautiful structures in the world, the Taj Mahal is both an expression of love and a superb architectural blending of Islamic and Indian culture.

Gardens

Many of the architectural masterpieces of this age had splendid gardens attached to them as well. Gardens represent a distinctive and highly developed feature of Persian culture. From the second century, and with the model of the biblical account of the

Garden of Eden (Genesis 2 and 3), a continuous tradition of gardening had existed in Persia. A garden was a walled area with a pool in the center and geometrically laid-out flowering plants, especially roses. "In Arabic, paradise is simply *al janna,* the garden,"[6] and often as much attention was given to flowers as to food crops. First limited to the ruler's court, gardening soon spread among the wealthy citizens. Gardens served not only as centers of prayer and meditation but also as places of revelry and sensuality. A ruler might lounge near his pool as he watched the ladies of his harem bathe in it.

After the Abbasid conquest of Persia in 636–637, formal gardening spread west and east through the Islamic world, as illustrated by the magnificent gardens of Muslim Spain, southern Italy, and later southeastern Europe. The Mongol followers of Tamerlane took landscape architects from Persia back to Samarkand and adapted their designs to nomad encampments. In 1396 Tamerlane ordered the construction of a garden in a meadow, called House of Flowers. When Tamerlane's descendant Babur established the Mughal Dynasty in India, he adapted the Persian garden to the warmer southern climate. Gardens were laid out near palaces, mosques, shrines, and mausoleums, including the Taj Mahal, which had four water channels symbolizing the four rivers of paradise.

Because it represented paradise, the garden played a large role in Muslim literature. Some scholars hold that to understand Arabic poetry, one must study Arabic gardening. The literary genres of flowers and gardens provided basic themes for Hispano-Arab poets and a model for medieval Christian Europe. The secular literature of Muslim Spain, rife with references such as "a garland of verses," influenced the lyric poetry of southern France, the troubadours, and the courtly love tradition.

Gardens, of course, are seasonal. To remind themselves of "paradise" during the cold winter months, rulers, city people, and nomads ordered Persian carpets, which flower all year. Most Persian carpets of all periods use floral patterns and have a formal garden design.

Intellectual and Religious Trends

During the centuries from 1400 to 1800, there were many advances in mathematics, geographical literature, astronomy, medicine, and the religious sciences in the Islamic empires. Building on the knowledge of earlier Islamic writers and stimulated by Ottoman naval power, the geographer and cartographer Piri Reis produced a map incorporating Islamic and Western knowledge that showed all the known world (1513); another of his maps detailed Columbus's third voyage to the New World. Piri Reis's *Book of the Sea* (1521) contained 129 chapters, each with a map incorporating all Islamic (and Western) knowledge of the seas and navigation and describing harbors, tides, dangerous rocks and shores, and storm

● **Polo** Two teams of four on horseback ride back and forth on a grass field measuring 200 by 400 yards, trying to hit a 4½-ounce wooden ball with a 4-foot mallet through the opponents' goal. Because a typical match involves many high-speed collisions among the horses, each player has to maintain a string of expensive ponies in order to change mounts several times during the game. Students of the history of sports believe the game originated in Persia, as shown in this eighteenth-century miniature, whence it spread to India, China, and Japan. Brought from India to England, where it became very popular among the aristocracy in the nineteenth century, polo is a fine example of cross-cultural influences. *(Private Collection)*

areas. Takiyuddin Mehmet (1521–1585), who served as the sultan's chief astronomer, built an observatory at Istanbul. His *Instruments of the Observatory* catalogued astronomical instruments and described an astronomical clock that fixed the location of heavenly bodies with greater precision than ever before.

There were also advances in medicine. Under Suleiman, however, the imperial palace itself became a center of medical science, and the large number of hospitals established in Istanbul and throughout the empire testifies to his support for medical research and his concern for the sick. Abi Ahmet Celebi (1436–1523), the chief physician of the empire, produced a study on kidney and bladder stones and supported the research of the Jewish doctor Musa Colinus ul-Israil on the application of drugs. Celebi founded the first Ottoman medical school, which served as a training institution for physicians of the empire. The sultans and the imperial court relied on a cadre of elite Jewish physicians.

Ottoman physicians made less progress on one of the great scourges of the period, recurrent outbreaks of plague. Muhammed had once said not to go to a country where an epidemic existed but also not to leave a place because an epidemic broke out. As a consequence, when European cities began enforcing quarantines to control the spread of plague, Ottoman rulers dismissed their efforts, leading, some scholars believe, to great loss of life from the plague there.[7]

In the realm of religion, the rulers of all three empires were Muslims and drew legitimacy from their support for Islam, at least among their Muslim subjects. The Sunni-Shi'ia split between the Ottomans and Safavids led to efforts to define and enforce religious orthodoxy on both sides. For the Safavids this entailed suppressing Sufi movements and Sunnis, even marginalizing—sometimes massacring—the original Qizilbash warriors.

Sufi fraternities thrived throughout the Muslim world, even when the states tried to limit them. In India, Sufi orders also influenced non-Muslims. The mystical Bhakti movement among Hindus involved dances, poems, and songs reminiscent of Sufi orders. The development of the new religion of the Sikhs also was influenced by Sufis. The Sikhs traced themselves back to a teacher in the sixteenth century who argued that God did not distinguish between Muslims and Hindus but saw everyone as his children. Sikhs rejected the caste system and forbade alcohol and tobacco, and men did not cut their hair (covering it instead with a turban). The Sikh movement was most successful in northwest India, where Sikh men armed themselves to defend their communities.

Despite all the signs of cultural vitality in the three Islamic empires, none of them adopted the printing press or went through the sorts of cultural expansion associated with it in China and Europe. Until 1729, the Ottoman authorities prohibited printing books in Turkish or Arabic (but Jews, Armenians, and

● **Religious Scholar Filling a Wine Cup** This seventeenth-century Persian painting on paper illustrates four lines of poetry that make fun of a religious scholar who was persuaded to overcome his usual avoidance of wine. *(Freer Gallery of Art, Smithsonian Institution, Washington, D.C., Gift of Charles Lang Freer, F1907.2)*

Greeks could establish presses and print in their own languages). Printing was not banned in Mughal India, but neither did the technology spread, even after Jesuit missionaries printed Bibles in Indian languages beginning in the 1550s. The Islamic authorities in each of these empires did not want to see writings circulate that might unsettle society and religious teachings.

Coffeehouses

In the mid-fifteenth century, a new social convention spread throughout the Islamic world—drinking coffee. Arab writers trace the origins of coffee to Yemen, where the mystical Sufis drank coffee in their *dhiks,* or "devotional services." Sufis sought a trancelike concentration on God to the exclusion of everything else, and the use of coffee helped them stay awake. Most Sufis were not professional holy men but were employed as tradesmen and merchants. Therefore, the use of coffee for pious purposes led to its use as a business lubricant—an extension of hospitality to a potential buyer in a shop. Merchants carried the Yemenite practice to Mecca in about 1490. From Mecca, where pilgrims were introduced to it, drinking coffee spread to Egypt and Syria. In 1555 two Syrians opened a coffeehouse in Istanbul.

Coffeehouses provided a place for conversation and male sociability; there a man could entertain his friends cheaply and more informally than at home. But coffeehouses encountered religious and governmental opposition, which are indistinguishable under the shari'a, or holy law. Opponents of coffeehouses rested their arguments on four grounds: (1) because of its chemical composition, coffee is intoxicating and physically harmful; (2) coffee drinking was an innovation, and therefore a violation of Islamic law; (3) the coffeehouse encouraged political discussions that could be dangerous to the sultan; and (4) patrons of coffeehouses tended to be low types who engaged in immoral behavior, such as gambling, using drugs, soliciting prostitutes, and engaging in sodomy. The musical entertainment that coffeehouses provided, critics said, lent an atmosphere of debauchery. Thus coffeehouses drew the attention of government officials, who were also the guardians of public morality.

● **Turkish Coffeehouse** This sixteenth-century miniature depicts many activities typical of coffeehouses: patrons enter (*upper left*); some sit drinking coffee in small porcelain cups (*center*); the manager makes fresh coffee (*right*). In the center, on a low sofa, men sit reading and talking. At bottom appear activities considered disreputable: musicians playing instruments, others playing games such as backgammon, a board game where moves are determined by rolls of dice. (*Reproduced by kind permission of the Trustees of the Chester Beatty Library, Dublin, Ms 439, folio 9*)

Although debate over the morality of coffeehouses continued through the sixteenth century, the acceptance of them represented a revolution in Islamic life: socializing was no longer confined to the home. Since the medical profession remained divided on coffee's harmful effects, and since the religious authorities could not prove that coffeehouses violated the shari'a, drinking coffee could not be forbidden. In the seventeenth century, coffee and coffeehouses spread to Europe.

NON-MUSLIMS UNDER MUSLIM RULE

How did Christians, Jews, Hindus, and other non-Muslims fare under these Islamic states?

Drawing on Qur'anic teachings, Muslims had long practiced a religious toleration unknown in Christian Europe. On the promise of obedience and the payment of a poll tax, the Muslim rulers guaranteed the lives and property of Christians and Jews. In the case of the Ottomans, this included not only the Christians and Jews who had been living under Muslim rule for centuries, but also the Serbs, Bosnians, Croats, and other Orthodox Christians in the newly conquered Balkans. The Ottoman conqueror of Constantinople, Mehmet, nominated the Greek patriarch as official representative of the Greek population. This and other such appointments recognized non-Muslims as functioning parts of Ottoman society and economy. In 1454 one Jewish resident, Isaac Sarfati, sent a circular letter to his coreligionists in the Rhineland, Swabia, Moravia, and Hungary praising the happy conditions of the Jews under the crescent in contrast to the "great torture chamber" under Christian rulers and urging them to come to Turkey.[8] A massive migration to Ottoman lands followed. When Ferdinand and Isabella of Spain expelled the Jews in 1492, many immigrated to the Ottoman Empire.

Babur and his successors acquired even more non-Muslim subjects with their conquests in India, which had not only Hindus, but substantial numbers also of Jains, Zoroastrians, Christians, and Sikhs. Over time, the number of Indians who converted to Islam increased, but the Mughal rulers did not force conversion. The Ganges plain, the geographical area of the subcontinent most intensely exposed to Mughal rule and for the longest span of time, had, when the first reliable census was taken in 1901, a Muslim population of only 10 to 15 percent. In fact, "in the subcontinent as a whole there is an inverse relationship between the degree of Muslim political penetration and the degree of Islamization."[9]

Akbar went the furthest in promoting Muslim-Hindu accommodation. He celebrated important Hindu festivals, such as Diwali, the festival of lights. He wore his uncut hair in a turban "as a concession to Indian usage and to please his Indian subjects."[10] Twice Akbar married Hindu princesses, one of whom became the mother of his heir, Jahangir. He appointed the Spanish Jesuit Antonio Monserrate (1536–1600) as tutor to his second son, Prince Murad. Hindus eventually totaled 30 percent of the

● **Emperor Akbar and Fatehpur-Sikri** In 1569 Akbar founded the city of Fatehpur-Sikri (the City of Victory) to honor the Muslim holy man Shaykh Salim Chishti, who had foretold the birth of Akbar's son and heir Jahangir. Akbar is shown here seated on the cushion in the center overseeing the construction of the city. The image is contained in the *Akbarnama,* a book of illustrations Akbar commissioned to officially chronicle his reign. *(Victoria & Albert Museum/The Bridgeman Art Library)*

imperial bureaucracy. In 1579 Akbar abolished the **jitza,** the tax on non-Muslims. These actions, especially the abolition of the jitza, infuriated the ulama, and serious conflict erupted between them and the emperor. Ultimately, Akbar issued an imperial decree declaring that the Mughal emperor had supreme authority, even above the ulama, in all religious matters. This statement, resting on a policy of benign toleration, represented a severe defeat for the Muslim religious establishment.

Some of Akbar's successors sided more with the ulama. A combination of religious zeal and financial necessity seems to have prompted Aurangzeb to promote stricter forms of Islam. He appointed censors of public morals in important cities to enforce Islamic laws against gambling, prostitution, drinking, and the use of narcotics. He forbade sati—the self-immolation of widows on their husbands' funeral pyres—and the castration of boys to be sold as eunuchs. He also abolished all taxes not authorized by Islamic law. This measure led to a serious loss of state revenues. To replace them, Aurangzeb in 1679 reimposed the jitza, the tax on non-Muslims.

Regulating Indian society according to Islamic law meant modifying the religious toleration and cultural cosmopolitanism instituted by Akbar. Aurangzeb ordered the destruction of some Hindu temples and tried to curb Sikhism. He required Hindus to pay higher customs duties than Muslims. Out of fidelity to Islamic law, he even criticized his mother's tomb, the Taj Mahal: "The lawfulness of a solid construction over a grave is doubtful, and there can be no doubt about the extravagance involved."[11] Aurangzeb employed more Hindus in the imperial administration than had any previous Mughal ruler, but his religious policy proved highly unpopular with the majority of his subjects.

jitza *A tax on non-Muslims.*

SHIFTING TRADE ROUTES AND EUROPEAN PENETRATION

How were the Islamic empires affected by the decline in overland trade and the great growth in maritime commerce, and how were European powers able to use trade to make inroads as this period progressed?

The economic foundation of all three Islamic empires was agriculture, and taxes on farmers supported the government and armies. Some new crops, including coffee, sugar, and tobacco, became important in this period, but new world crops do not seem to have led to population increases that were as rapid as elsewhere in Eurasia. By 1800, the population of India was about 190 million, that of Safavid lands about 8 million, and that of Ottoman lands about 24 million (the three together thus less than China, about 300 million in 1800).

Trade was also a crucial element in the economies of these three empires. In 1450 all the great highways of international trade were in Muslim hands, and the wealth of the Muslim states rested heavily on commerce. In the early seventeen century, worldwide economic depression and silver shortages had a devastating effect on the East-West overland trade, from which it never recovered. By 1750 the Muslims had lost control of the trade, which probably contributed to the political decline of these empires (discussed below).

European colonial expansion and shifting trade patterns isolated the Ottomans and the Safavids from the centers of growth in the Western Hemisphere and the East Indies. European trade with the Americas, Africa, and Asia by means of the Atlantic also meant that the old southwestern Asian trade routes were bypassed. To try to revive trade with Europe, the Ottomans signed a series of agreements known as **capitulations.** A trade compact signed in 1536 and renewed in 1569 virtually exempted French merchants from Ottoman law and allowed them to travel and buy and sell throughout the sultan's dominions and to pay low customs duties on French imports and exports.

capitulations *A series of agreements that basically surrender the rights of one party. The Ottoman government signed these with European powers and gave them a stranglehold on Ottoman trade and commerce.*

● **Kalamkari Textile from Golconda** Golconda, in southeast India, is the site of a great fortress complex and many palaces, mosques, and Hindu temples that were destroyed in 1687 and left in ruins. This textile is called *kalamkari*, meaning pen or brushed work, and represents a style of design and manufacture unique to the region. Containing a rich variety of Persian, Hindu, and Muslim motifs, this superb example of seventeenth-century painted cotton, depicting various scenes of life in the palace and gardens, suggests the beauty and complexity of Indian textile manufacture. *(The Bridgeman Art Library)*

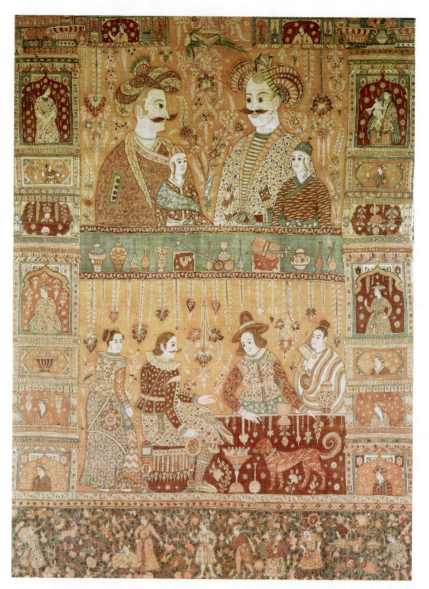

In 1590, in spite of strong French opposition, a group of English merchants gained the right to trade in Ottoman territory in return for supplying the sultan with iron, steel, brass, and tin for his war with Persia. In 1615, as part of a twenty-year peace treaty, the capitulation rights already given to French and English businessmen were extended to the Habsburgs. These capitulations progressively gave European merchants an economic stranglehold on Ottoman trade and commerce.

Whereas trade between Europe and the Ottomans declined as trade routes shifted, direct trade with India expanded greatly. The Mughal period witnessed the growth of a thriving capitalist commercial economy on the Indian subcontinent. Although most people were engaged in agriculture, from which most imperial revenue was derived, a manufacturing industry supported by a money economy and mercantile capitalism expanded.

Block-printed cotton cloth, produced by artisans working at home, was India's chief export. Through an Islamic business device involving advancing payment to artisans, banker-brokers supplied the material for production and the money that the artisans could live on while they worked; the cloth brokers specified the quality, quantity, and design of the finished product. This procedure resembles the later English "domestic" or "putting-out" system (see page 647), for the very good reason that the English took the idea from the Indians. Within India, the demand for cotton cloth, as well as for food crops, was so great that Akbar had to launch a wide-scale road-building campaign. From Gujarat, Indian merchant bankers shipped their cloth worldwide: across the Indian Ocean to Aden and the Muslim-controlled cities on the east coast of Africa; across the Arabian Sea to Muscat and Hormuz and up the Persian Gulf to the cities of Persia; up the Red Sea to the Mediterranean; by sea also to Malacca, Indonesia, China, and Japan; by land across Africa to Ghana on the west coast; and to Astrakhan, Poland, Moscow, and even the Russian cities on the distant Volga River. In many of these places, Indian businessmen had branch offices. All this activity represented enormous trade, which produced fabulous wealth for some Indian merchants. Some scholars have compared India's international trade in the sixteenth century with that of Italian firms, such as the Medici. The Indian trade actually extended over a far wider area. Indian merchants were often devout Hindus, Muslims, Buddhists, or Jains, evidence that undermines the argument of some Western writers, notably Karl Marx (see page 681), that religion retarded Asia's economic development.

European Rivalry for the Indian Trade

Shortly before Babur's invasion of India, the Portuguese under the navigator Pedro Alvares Cabral had opened the subcontinent to Portuguese trade. In 1510 they established the port of Goa on the Arabian Sea as their headquarters and through a policy of piracy and terrorism took control of Muslim shipping in the Indian and Arabian Oceans (see Map 19.3), charging high fees for passage. The Portuguese historian Barrões attempted to justify Portugal's seizure of commercial traffic that the Muslims had long dominated:

It is true that there does exist a common right to all to navigate the seas and in Europe we recognize the rights which others hold against us; but the right does not extend beyond Europe and therefore the Portuguese as Lords of the Sea are justified in confiscating the goods of all those who navigate the seas without their permission.[12]

In short, Western principles of international law should not restrict them in Asia. For almost a century, the Portuguese controlled the spice trade over the Indian Ocean.

In 1602 the Dutch formed the Dutch East India Company with the stated goal of wresting the enormously lucrative spice trade from the Portuguese. The Dutch concentrated their efforts in Indonesia. The scent of fabulous profits also attracted the English. With a charter signed by Queen Elizabeth, eighty London merchants organized the British East India Company. In 1619 Emperor Jahangir granted a British mission important commercial concessions at Surat on the west coast of India. Gifts, medical services, and bribes to Indian rulers enabled the British to set up twenty-seven other coastal forts. Fort St. George on the east coast became the modern city of Madras. In 1668 the city of Bombay—given to England when the Portuguese princess Catherine of Braganza married King Charles II—was leased to the company, marking the virtually total British absorption of Portuguese power in India. In 1690 the company founded a fort that became the city of Calcutta. Thus the three places that later became centers of British economic and political imperialism—Madras, Bombay, and Calcutta (today called Chennai, Mumbai, and Kolkata)—date back to before 1700.

Factory-Fort Societies

The British called their trading post at Surat a **factory-fort** and the term was later used for all European settlements in India. The term did not signify manufacturing; it

factory-fort *A term first used by the British for their trading post at Surat, it was later applied to all European walled settlements in India.*

● **English Factory-Fort at Surat** The factory-fort began as a storage place for goods before they were bought and transported abroad; it gradually expanded to include merchants' residences and some sort of fortification. By 1650 the English had twenty-three factory-forts in India. Surat, in the Gujarat region on the Gulf of Cambay, was the busiest factory-fort and port until it was sacked by the Marathas in 1664. *(Mansell Collection)*

designated the walled compound containing the residences, gardens, and offices of British East India Company officials and the warehouses where goods were stored before being shipped to Europe. The company president exercised political authority over all residents.

Factory-forts existed to make profits from the Asian-European trade, and they evolved into flourishing sources of economic profit. The British East India Company sold silver, copper, zinc, lead, and fabrics to the Indians and bought cotton goods, silks, pepper and other spices, sugar, and opium from them. By the late seventeenth century, the company was earning substantial profits. Profitability increased after 1700 when the company began to trade with China. Some Indian merchants in Calcutta and Bombay made gigantic fortunes from trade within Asia.

Because the directors of the British East India Company in London discouraged all unnecessary expenses and financial risks, they opposed any interference in local Indian politics and even missionary activities. Political instability in India in the early eighteenth century caused the company's factories to evolve into defensive installations manned by small garrisons of native troops (**sepoys**) trained in Western military drill and tactics. When warlords appeared or an uprising occurred, people from the

sepoys *The native Indian troops who were trained as infantrymen.*

surrounding countryside flocked into the fort, and the company factory-forts gradually came to exercise political authority over the territories around them.

Indian and Chinese wares enjoyed great popularity in England and on the European continent in the late seventeenth and early eighteenth centuries. The middle classes wanted Indian textiles, which were colorful, durable, cheap, and washable. The upper classes desired Chinese wallpaper and porcelains and Indian silks and brocades. Europeans had to pay for everything they bought from Asia with precious metals because Asians had little interest in European manufactured articles. Thus there was insistent pressure in England, France, and the Netherlands against the importation of Asian goods because of the fear that the drain of gold would hurt their economies.

The Rise of the British East India Company

The French were the last to arrive in India. In the 1670s the French East India Company established factories at Chandernagore in Bengal, Pondicherry, and elsewhere. Joseph Dupleix (1697–1764), who was appointed governor general at Pondicherry in 1742, made allies of Indian princes and built an army of native troops who were trained as infantrymen.

From 1740 to 1763, Britain and France were almost continually engaged in a tremendous global struggle. India, like North America in the Seven Years' War, became a battlefield and a prize. The French won land battles, but English sea power decided the first phase of the war. Then a series of brilliant victories destroyed French power

● **Taj Mahal at Agra**   This tomb is the finest example of Muslim architecture in India. Its white marble exterior is inlaid with semiprecious stones in Arabic inscriptions and floral designs. The oblong pool reflects the building, which asserts the power of the Mughal Dynasty. *(John Elk/Stock, Boston)*

in southern India. By preventing French reinforcements from arriving, British sea power again proved to be the determining factor, and British jurisdiction soon extended over the important northern province of Bengal. The Treaty of Paris of 1763 recognized British control of much of India, and scholars view the treaty as the beginning of the British Empire in India.

How was the vast subcontinent to be governed? Parliament believed that the British East India Company had too much power and considered the company responsible for the political disorders in India, which were bad for business. The Regulating Act of 1773 created the office of governor general, with an advisory council, to exercise political authority over the territory controlled by the company. The India Act of 1784 required that the governor general be chosen from outside the company, and it made company directors subject to parliamentary supervision.

Implementation of these reforms fell to three successive governors, Warren Hastings, (r. 1774–1785), Lord Charles Cornwallis (r. 1786–1794), and the marquess Richard Wellesley (r. 1797–1805). Hastings sought allies among Indian princes, laid the foundations for the first Indian civil service, abolished tolls to facilitate internal trade, placed the salt and opium trades under government control, and planned a codification of Muslim and Hindu laws. Cornwallis introduced the British style of property relations, in effect converting a motley collection of former Mughal officers, tax collectors, and others into English-style landlords. The result was a new system of landholding in which the rents of tenant farmers supported the landlords. Wellesley was victorious over local rulers who resisted British rule and vastly extended British influence in India. Like most nineteenth-century British governors of India, Wellesley believed that British rule strongly benefited the Indians. With supreme condescension, he wrote that British power should be established over the Indian princes in order

to deprive them of the means of prosecuting any measure or of forming any confederacy hazardous to the security of the British empire, and to enable us to preserve the tranquility of India by exercising a general control over the restless spirit of ambition and violence which is characteristic of every Asiatic government.[13]

DYNASTIC DECLINE

Did any common factors lead to the decline of the Islamic empires in the seventeenth and eighteenth centuries?

By the eighteenth century, all three of the major Islamic empires were on the defensive. They faced some common problems—succession difficulties, financial strain, loss of military superiority—but their circumstances differed in significant ways as well.

The first to fall was the Safavid Empire. Shah Abbas was succeeded by inept rulers whose heavy indulgence in wine and the pleasures of the harem weakened the monarchy and fed the slow disintegration of the state. Shi'ite religious institutions grew stronger. Decline in the military strength of the army encouraged increased foreign aggression. In 1722 the Afghans invaded from the east, seized Isfahan, and were able to repulse an Ottoman invasion from the west. In Isfahan thousands of officials and members of the shah's family were executed. In the following centuries some strong men emerged, but no leader was able to reunite all of Persia.

The Ottoman throne also suffered from a series of weak sultans. In the fifteenth and early sixteenth centuries, Turkish practice guaranteed that the sultans would be forceful men. The sultan's sons gained administrative experience as governors of provinces and military experience on the battlefield as part of their education. After the sultan died, any son who wanted to succeed had to contest his brothers to claim the throne, after which the new sultan would have his defeated brothers executed. Although bloody, this system led to the succession of capable, determined men. After Suleiman's reign, however, this tradition was abandoned. To prevent threats of usurpation, sons of the sultan were brought up in the harem and confined there as adults, denied a role in government. After years of indolence and dissipation, not surprisingly, few of these princes turned out to be strong military leaders. Selim II (r. 1566–1574), whom the Turks called "Selim the Drunkard," left the conduct of public affairs to his vizier while he pursued the pleasures of the harem. Turkish sources attribute his death to a fall in his bath caused by dizziness when he tried to stop drinking. A series of rulers who were incompetent or minor children left power in the hands of leading bureaucratic officials and the mothers of the heirs. Political factions formed around viziers, military leaders, and palace women. In the contest for political favor, the devshirme was abandoned, and political and military ranks were filled by Muslims.

As in parts of Europe, rising population without corresponding economic growth caused serious social problems. A long period of peace in the late sixteenth century and again in the mid-eighteenth century and a decline in the frequency of visits of the plague led to a doubling of the population. The land could not sustain so many people, nor could the towns provide jobs for the thousands of agricultural workers who fled to them. The return of demobilized soldiers aggravated the problem. Inflation, famine, and widespread revolts resulted. The economic center of gravity shifted from the capital to the provinces, and politically the empire began to decentralize as well. Local notables and military men, rather than central officials, exercised political power. Provincial autonomy brought more people into political participation, thus laying a foundation for later nationalism.

Ottoman armies began losing wars and territory along their European borders. The army was depending more on mercenaries, and military technology fell behind. The Ottomans did not keep up with the innovations in drill and command and control that were then transforming European armies. By the terms of the peace treaty with Austria signed at Karlowitz (1699), the Ottomans lost the major European provinces of Hungary and Transylvania, along with the tax revenues they had provided.

In Mughal India the old Turkish practice of letting the heirs fight for the throne persisted, leading to frequent struggles over succession, but also to strong rulers. Yet military challenges proved daunting there as well. After defeating his father and brothers, Aurangzeb pushed the conquest of the south. The stiffest opposition came from the Marathas, a militant Hindu group centered in the western Deccan. From 1681 until his death in 1707, Aurangzeb led repeated sorties through the Deccan. He took many forts and won several battles, but total destruction of the Maratha guerrilla bands eluded him. After his death, they played an important role in the collapse of the Mughal Empire.

Aurangzeb's death led to thirteen years of succession struggles, shattering the empire. His eighteenth-century successors were less successful than the Ottomans in making the dynasty the focus of loyalty. Mughal provincial governors began to rule independently, giving only minimal allegiance to the badshah at Delhi. The Marathas, who pressed steadily northward, constituted the gravest threat to Mughal authority. No ruler could defeat them.

In 1739 the Persian adventurer Nadir Shah invaded India, defeated the Mughal army, looted Delhi, and after a savage massacre carried off a huge amount of treasure, including the Peacock Throne. When Nadir Shah withdrew to Afghanistan, he took with him the Mughal government's prestige. Constant skirmishes between the Afghans and the Marathas for control of the Punjab and northern India ended in 1761 at Panipat, where the Marathas were crushed by the Afghans. At that point, India no longer had any power capable of imposing order on the subcontinent or checking the penetration of the rapacious Europeans.

Chapter Summary

Key Terms

Ottomans
Anatolia
Sultan-i-Rum
sultan
devshirme
janissaries
concubine
shah
Safavid
Qizilbash
Mughal
badshah
jitza
capitulations
factory-fort
sepoys

To assess your mastery of this chapter, go to
bedfordstmartins.com/mckayworld

• *How were the three Islamic empires established, and what sorts of governments did they set up?*

After the decline of the Mongols in Central Asia and Persia, many small Turkic-ruled states emerged. Three of them went on to establish large empires: the Ottomans in Anatolia, the Safavids in Persia, and the Mughals in India. In each case, the state steadily expanded for several generations, though it did eventually run up against foes it could not defeat. All three empires responded to the shift in military technology away from the mounted archer toward the use of gunpowder weapons. The Ottomans in particular made effective use of guns and artillery.

• *What cultural advances occurred under the rule of these three houses?*

The wealth of these empires provided the material basis for a great cultural efflorescence. Royal patronage was especially important in the building of palaces and cities. Other major arts of the period included carpets and book illustrations. Intellectually, this was a fertile period for both natural science and religious speculation. Islam received special protection and support from all three governments, but there were key differences: The Ottomans and Mughals supported the Sunni tradition, the Safavids, the Shi'ite tradition.

• *How did Christians, Jews, Hindus, and other non-Muslims fare under these Islamic states?*

All of the Islamic empires had substantial non-Muslim subjects. The Ottomans ruled over the Balkans, where most of the people were Christian. In India, Muslims were outnumbered by Hindus. Following Islamic teachings, Christians and Jews were not persecuted in these empires, and Hindus in India came to be treated as though they too were "protected" people.

• *How were the Islamic empires affected by the decline in overland trade and the great growth in maritime commerce, and how were European powers able to use trade to make inroads as this period progressed?*

The Islamic regions of Eurasia had been the crossroads of East-West and North-South trade for many centuries, but with the great expansion of European maritime trade in the late fifteenth and sixteenth centuries, trade between Europe and India, China, and Southeast Asia shifted decisively to the maritime route. Indian textiles, much desired in Southeast Asia and China, attracted European businessmen. The inability of Indian leaders in the eighteenth century to resolve their domestic differences led first to British intervention and then to British rule of several parts of the Indian subcontinent.

• Did any common factors lead to the decline of the Islamic empires in the seventeenth and eighteenth centuries?

The eighteenth century saw the destruction of the Safavid Empire and the great decline in the reach of the Mughal Empire. The Ottomans, too, suffered major setbacks in the seventeenth and eighteenth centuries (though they would make a comeback in the nineteenth century). Some of the common problems these empires faced were the end of expansion, difficulties with succession, tendencies toward decentralization, and population growth not matched by economic growth. In India, the Mughals faced not only tendencies toward decentralization but also the appearance of new foes, traders from Europe backed by their governments.

Suggested Reading

Atil, Esin. *The Age of Sultan Suleyman the Magnificent.* 1987. A splendidly illustrated celebration of the man and his times.

Dale, Stephen Frederic. *The Garden of the Eight Paradises: Babur and the Culture of Empire in Central Asia, Afghanistan and India, 1483–1750.* 2004. A scholarly biography that draws on and analyzes Babur's autobiography.

Findley, Carter Vaughn. *The Turks in World History.* 2005. Takes a macro look at the three Islamic empires as part of the history of the Turks.

Finkel, Caroline. *Osman's Dream: A History of the Ottoman Empire.* 2006. A new interpretation that views the Ottomans from their own perspective.

Inalcik, Halil, and Renda Günsel. *Ottoman Civilization.* 2002. A huge, beautifully illustrated, government-sponsored overview, with emphasis on the arts and culture.

Jackson, Peter, and Lawrence Lockhart, eds. *The Cambridge History of Iran,* Vol. 6, *The Timurid and Safavid*

Periods. 1986. A set of essays on the social and cultural as well as political and economic history of Iran by leading scholars.

Lapidus, Ira M. *A History of Islamic Societies,* 2nd ed. 2002. A comprehensive yet lucid survey.

Mukhia, Harbans. *The Mughals of India: A Framework for Understanding.* 2004. A short but thoughtful analysis of the Mughal society and state.

Pierce, Leslie. *The Imperial Harem: Women and Sovereignty in the Ottoman Empire.* 1993. A fresh look at the role of elite women under the Ottomans.

Richards, John F. *The Mughal Empire.* 1993. Offers a coherent narrative history of the period 1526–1720.

Ruthven, Malise, and Azim Nanji. *Historical Atlas of Islam.* 2004. Provides numerous maps illustrating the shifting political history of Islamic states.

Notes

1. Quoted in B. Lewis, *The Muslim Discovery of Europe* (New York: W. W. Norton, 1982), p. 29.

2. W. H. McNeill, *The Pursuit of Power: Technology, Armed Force, and Society Since A.D. 1000* (Chicago: University of Chicago Press, 1982), p. 87.

3. D. Morgan, *Medieval Persia, 1040–1797* (New York: Longman, 1988), pp. 112–113.

4. Quoted in M. C. Beach, *The Imperial Image: Paintings for the Mughal Court* (Washington, D.C.: Freer Gallery of Art, Smithsonian Institution, 1981), pp. 9–10.

5. Quoted in V. A. Smith, *The Oxford History of India* (Oxford: Oxford University Press, 1967), p. 398.

6. J. Goody, *The Culture of Flowers* (Cambridge: Cambridge University Press, 1993), p. 103.

7. See William McNeill, *Plagues and Peoples* (New York: Anchor Books, 1998), pp. 198–199.

8. F. Babinger, *Mehmed the Conqueror and His Times,* trans. R. Manheim (Princeton, N.J.: Princeton University Press, 1978), p. 107.

9. R. M. Eaton, *The Rise of Islam and the Bengal Frontier, 1204–1760* (Berkeley: University of California Press, 1993), p. 115.

10. J. F. Richards, *The New Cambridge History of India: The Mughal Empire* (Cambridge: Cambridge University Press, 1995), p. 45.

11. Quoted in S. K. Ikram, *Muslim Civilization in India* (New York: Columbia University Press, 1964), p. 202.

12. Quoted in K. M. Panikkar, *Asia and Western Domination* (London: George Allen & Unwin, 1965), p. 35.

13. Quoted in W. Bingham, H. Conroy, and F. W. Iklé, *A History of Asia,* vol. 2 (Boston: Allyn and Bacon, 1967), p. 74.

Listening to the
PAST

The Weighing of Shah Jahan on His Forty-Second Lunar Birthday*

In 1799 the nawab (provincial governor) of Oudh in northern India sent to King George III of Great Britain the Padshahnama, *or official history of the reign of Shah Jahan. A volume composed of 239 folios on very high-quality gold-flecked tan paper with forty-four stunningly beautiful paintings illustrating the text, the* Padshahnama *represents both a major historical chronicle of a Mughal emperor's reign and an extraordinary artistic achievement. One of the great art treasures of the world, it now rests in the Royal Library at Windsor.*

All the Mughal emperors had a strong historical sense and the desire to preserve records of their reigns. They brought to India the traditional Muslim respect for books as sources of secular and religious knowledge and as images of their wealth and power. The Padshahnama, *in stressing Shah Jahan's descent from Tamerlane and his right to the throne, in celebrating his bravery and military prowess, and in magnifying his virtues, is one long glorification of Jahan's rule. The Persian scholar and calligrapher Abdul-Hamid Lahawri wrote the text. Many Persian artists painted the illustrations with detailed precision and an exactitude that art historians consider sensitive and faithful to the original.*

Since alms are beneficial for repelling bodily and psychic harm and for attracting spiritual and corporeal benefits, as all peoples, religions, and nations are agreed, His Majesty Arsh-Ashyani [Akbar] established the custom of weighing and had himself weighed twice [a year], once after the end of the solar year and the other after the end of the lunar year. In the solar weighing he was weighed twelve times, first against gold and then eleven other items, while in the lunar weighing he was weighed eight times, first against silver and then seven other items. . . . The amounts from the weighings were given away in alms.

. . . Inasmuch as it benefited the needy, His Majesty Jahanbani [Shah Jahan] has his perfect self weighed twice, and in his generosity he has ordered that gold and silver be used each time. . . .

The lunar weighing ceremony for the end of the forty-third year of the Emperor's life was held. The Emperor, surrounded by a divine aura, was weighed against gold and the other usual things, and the skirt of the world was held out in expectation of gold and silver. On this auspicious day Muhammad-Ali Beg, the ambassador of Iran, was awarded a gold-embroidered robe of honor, a jeweled belt, an elephant, a female elephant, and four large ashrafis, one weighing 400 tolas [a measure of weight, slightly more than two mithcals], the second 300 tolas, the third 200 tolas, and the fourth 100 tolas, and four rupees also of the weights given above, and he was given leave to depart. From the time he paid homage until the time he set out to return he had been given 316,000 rupees in cash and nearly a lac of rupees in goods.

An earlier weighing ceremony of the Emperor Jahangir, on 1 September 1617, was described by the always observant, and usually skeptical, first English ambassador to the Mughal court, Sir Thomas Roe: "Was the Kings Birthday, and the solemnitie of his weighing, to which I went, and was carryed into a very large and beautifull Garden; the square within all water; on the sides flowres and trees. . . . Here attended the Nobilitie, all sitting about it on Carpets, vntill the King came; who at last appeared clothed, or rather loden with Diamonds, Rubies, Pearles, and other precious vanities, so great, so glorious! . . . Suddenly hee entered into the scales, sate like a woman on his legges, and there was put against him many bagges to fit his weight, which were changed sixe times, and they say was siluer, and that I vnderstood his weight to be nine thousand *Rupias,* which are almost one thousand pound sterling."

Another official history of Shah Jahan's reign, the 'Amal-i-Salih, *describes the ceremonial weighing that took place another year.*

*A solar year is the time required for the earth to make one complete revolution around the sun (365 days). A lunar year equals 12 lunar months.

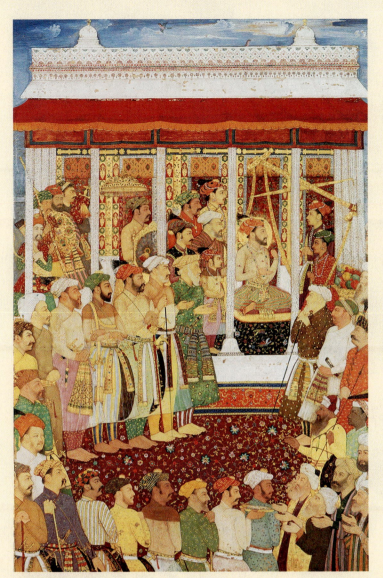

The "Weighing of Shah Jahan," who sits cross-legged on one plate of the scales, as bags of gold and silver wait to be placed on the other side. (The Royal Collection © 2007, Her Majesty Queen Elizabeth II)

Since it is His Majesty's custom and habit to have beggars sought out, and his generous nature is always looking for a pretext to relieve those who are in need, therefore twice a year he sits, like the orient sun in majesty, in the pan of the scale of auspiciousness in the solar and lunar weighing ceremonies. Twice a year by solar and lunar calculation a magnificent celebration and a large-scale banquet is arranged by order of His Majesty. An amount equal to his weight in gold and silver is distributed among the destitute and the poor according to their deservedness and merits. Although this type of alms is not mentioned in the religious law, nonetheless since scholars of this country are all in agreement that such alms are the most perfect type of alms for repelling corporeal and spiritual catastrophes and calamities, therefore this pleasing method was chosen and established by His Majesty Arsh-Ashyani, whose personality was, like the world-illuminating sun, based upon pure effulgence. By this means the poor attained their wishes, and in truth the custom of *aqiqa*—which is an established custom in the law

of the Prophet and his Companions, and in which on the seventh day after birth the equivalent weight of an infant's shaven hair in silver is given in alms, and a sacrificial animal is divided and distributed among the poor—has opened the way to making this custom permissible.

Questions for Analysis

1. Consider Shah Jahan's motives for the practice of ceremonial weighing. Does it have any theological basis?

2. Compare the Mughal practice to something similar in Ottoman, European, and South American societies.

Source: King of the World. The Padshahnama. An Imperial Mughal Manuscript from the Royal Library, Windsor Castle, ed. Milo Cleveland Beach and Ebba Koch, trans. Wheeler Thackston (Washington, D.C.: Azimuth Editions—Sackler Gallery, 1997, pp. 39–43). Reprinted by permission of W. M. Thackston, translator.

Japanese Society. This detail from a seventeenth-century six-panel Japanese screen depicts life in the pleasure quarters, where men and women interacted openly, playing instruments and enjoying games.
(Hikone Castle Museum)

20 CONTINUITY AND CHANGE IN EAST ASIA, CA. 1400–1800

The period from 1400 to 1800 witnessed growth and dynamic change throughout East Asia. Although both China and Japan suffered periods of war, each ended up with expanded territories—Japan taking control of the Ryūkyū Islands to the south and pushing back the Ainu in the north, and Qing China taking control of Mongolia and Tibet. The age of exploration brought New World crops to the region, leading to increased agricultural output and population growth. It also brought new opportunities for foreign trade and new religions, to which the countries of East Asia responded in differing ways. Another link between these countries was the massive Japanese invasions of Korea in the late sixteenth century, which led to war between China and Japan.

In China, the native **Ming Dynasty** (1368–1644) replaced the Mongol Yuan Dynasty (1271–1368). Under the Ming, China saw agricultural reconstruction, remarkable maritime expeditions abroad, commercial expansion, and a vibrant urban culture. Even though many of the Ming emperors were incompetent or perverse, educated men continued to compete avidly for places in the government.

In the early seventeenth century, as the Ming Dynasty fell into disorder, the Manchus put together an efficient state beyond Ming's northeastern border. After they were called in to help suppress peasant rebellions, the Manchus took the throne themselves, founding the Qing Dynasty (1644–1911). The Manchus created a multiethnic empire, adding Taiwan, Mongolia, Tibet, and Xinjiang to their realm. The Qing Empire thus was comparable to the other multinational empires of the early modern world, such as the Ottoman, Russian, and Habsburg empires. In China itself the eighteenth century was a time of peace and prosperity.

In the Japanese islands, the fifteenth century saw the start of civil war that lasted a century. At the end of the sixteenth century, the world seemed to have turned upside down when a commoner, Hideyoshi, became the supreme ruler. His ambitions were grand: he sent his armies to Korea as the first step

Ming Dynasty *The Chinese dynasty in power from 1368 to 1644; it marked a period of agricultural reconstruction, foreign expeditions, commercial expansion, and a vibrant urban culture.*

toward conquering the mainland. He did not succeed in passing on his power to an heir, however. Instead, Tokugawa Ieyasu set up a government that lasted into the nineteenth century. Under this Tokugawa Shogunate (1603–1867), Japan restricted contact with the outside world and social mobility among its own people. Yet Japan thrived, as agricultural productivity increased and a lively urban culture developed.

MING CHINA (1368–1644)

What sort of state and society developed in China after the Mongols were ousted?

The founder of the Ming Dynasty, Zhu Yuanzhang (1328–1398), began life in poverty during the last decades of the Mongol Yuan Dynasty. His home region was hit by drought and then plague in the 1340s, and when he was only sixteen years old, his father, oldest brother, and brother's wife all died, leaving two penniless boys with three bodies to bury. With no relatives to turn to, Zhu Yuanzhang asked a monastery to accept him as a novice. The monastery itself was short of funds, and the monks soon sent Zhu out to beg for food. For three or four years he wandered through central China. Only after he returned to the monastery did he learn to read.

A few years later, in 1351, members of a religious sect known as the Red Turbans rose in rebellion against the government. Red Turban teachings drew on Manichaean ideas about the incompatibility of the forces of good and evil as well as on the cult of the Maitreya Buddha, who according to believers would in the future bring his paradise to earth to relieve human suffering. The Red Turbans met with considerable success, even defeating Mongol cavalry. When Zhu Yuanzhang's temple was burned down in the fighting, Zhu joined the rebels and rose rapidly.

Zhu and his followers developed into brilliant generals, and gradually they defeated one rival after another. In 1356 Zhu took the city of Nanjing and made it his base. In 1368 his armies took Beijing, which the Mongol emperor and his closest followers had vacated just days before. Then forty years old, Zhu Yuanzhang declared himself emperor of the Ming ("Bright") Dynasty. As emperor, he is known as Taizu or the Hongwu emperor.

Taizu started his reign wanting to help the poor. To lighten the weight of government exactions, he ordered a full-scale registration of cultivated land and population so that labor service and taxes could be assessed more fairly. He also tried persuasion. He issued instructions to be read aloud to villagers, telling them to be filial to their parents, live in harmony with their neighbors, work contentedly at their occupations, and refrain from evil.

Although in many ways anti-Mongol, Taizu retained some Yuan practices. One was setting up provinces as the administrative layer between the central government and the prefectures. Another was hereditary service obligations for both artisan and military households. Any family classed as a military household had to supply a soldier at all times, replacing those who were injured, who died, or who deserted.

Garrisons were concentrated along the northern border and near the capital. Each garrison was allocated a tract of land that the soldiers took turns cultivating to supply their own food. Although in theory this system should have supplied the Ming with a large but inexpensive army, the reality was less satisfactory. Garrisons were rarely self-sufficient. Men compelled to become soldiers did not necessarily make good fighting men, and desertion was difficult to prevent. Like earlier dynasties, the Ming turned to non-Chinese northerners for much of its armed forces. Many of the best soldiers in the Ming army were Mongols in Mongol units. Taizu did not try to conquer the Mongols, and Ming China did not extend into modern Inner Mongolia.

Taizu had deeply ambivalent feelings about men of education and sometimes brutally humiliated them in open court, even having them beaten. His behavior was so erratic that most likely he suffered from some form of mental illness. As Taizu became more literate, he realized that scholars could criticize him in covert ways, using phrases that had double meanings or that sounded like words for "bandit," "monk," or the like. Even poems in private circulation could be used as evidence of subversive thoughts. When literary men began to avoid official life, Taizu made it illegal to turn down appointments or to resign from office. He began falling into rages that only the empress could stop, and after her death in 1382 no one could calm him. In 1376 Taizu had thousands of officials killed because they were found to have taken a shortcut in their handling of paperwork related to the grain tax. In 1380 Taizu concluded that his chancellor was plotting to assassinate him. Thousands only remotely connected to him were executed. From then on, Taizu acted as his own chancellor, dealing directly with the heads of departments and ministries.

The next important emperor, called Chengzu or the Yongle emperor (r. 1403–1425), was also a military man. One of Taizu's younger sons, he took the throne by force from his nephew and often led troops into battle against the Mongols. Also like his father, Chengzu was willing to use terror to keep government officials in line.

Early in his reign, Chengzu decided to move the capital from Nanjing to Beijing, which had been his own base as a prince and the capital during Mongol times. Beijing was a planned city, like Chang'an in Sui-Tang times (581–907), and like Chang'an was arranged like a set of boxes within boxes built on a north-south axis. The main outer walls were forty feet high and nearly fifteen miles around, pierced by nine gates. Inside was the Imperial City, with government offices, and within that the palace itself, called the Forbidden City, with close to ten thousand rooms. Because the Forbidden City survives today, people can still see the series of audience halls with vast courtyards between them where attending officials would stand or kneel.

The areas surrounding Beijing were not nearly as agriculturally productive as those around Nanjing. To supply Beijing with grain, the Yuan Grand Canal was broadened, deepened, and supplied with more locks and dams. The 15,000 boats and the 160,000 soldiers of the transport army who pulled loaded barges from the towpaths along the canal became the lifeline of the capital.

Chronology

1368–1644	Ming Dynasty in China
1405–1433	Zheng He's naval expeditions
1407–1420	Construction of Beijing as Chinese capital
16th century	Increased availability of books for general audiences in China
1549	Jesuit missionaries land in Japan
1557	Portuguese set up trading base at Macao
1568–1600	Period of national unification in Japan
1575–1620	Silver shortage in China
1603–1867	Tokugawa Shogunate in Japan
1615	Battle of Osaka leads to persecution of Christians in Japan
1629	Tokugawa government bans actresses from the stage
1639	Japan closes its borders
1644–1911	Qing Dynasty in China
1793	Lord Macartney's diplomatic visit to China

Problems with the Imperial Institution

Ming Taizu had decreed that succession should go to the eldest son of the empress or to the son's eldest son if the son predeceased his father, the system generally followed by earlier dynasties. In Ming times, the flaws in this system became apparent as one mediocre, obtuse, or erratic emperor followed another. There were emperors who refused to hold audiences, who fell into irrational fits, and who let themselves be manipulated by palace ladies.

Because Ming Taizu had abolished the position of chancellor, emperors turned to secretaries and eunuchs to manage the paperwork. Eunuchs were essentially slaves.

● **Forbidden City** The palace complex in Beijing, commonly called the Forbidden City, was built in the early fifteenth century when the capital was moved from Nanjing to Beijing. Audience halls and other important state buildings are arranged on a north-south axis with huge courtyards between them, where officials would stand during ceremonies. *(Reproduced by permission of the Commercial Press [Hong Kong] Limited, from* Daily Life in the Forbidden City.)

Many boys and young men were acquired by dubious means, often from non-Chinese areas in the south, and after they were castrated, they had no option but to serve the imperial family. Zheng He, for instance (see page 599), was taken from Yunnan as a boy of ten by a Ming general assigned the task of securing boys to be castrated. Society considered eunuchs the basest of servants, and Confucian scholars heaped scorn on them. Yet Ming emperors, like rulers in earlier dynasties, often preferred the always compliant eunuchs to high-minded, moralizing civil service officials.

In Ming times, the eunuch establishment became huge. By the late fifteenth century, the eunuch bureaucracy had grown as large as the civil service, each with roughly twelve thousand positions. After 1500, the eunuch bureaucracy grew even more rapidly, and by the mid-sixteenth century, seventy thousand eunuchs were in service throughout the country, ten thousand in the capital. Tension between the two bureaucracies was high. In 1420 Chengzu set up a eunuch-run secret service to investigate cases of suspected corruption and sedition in the regular bureaucracy. Eunuch control over vital government processes, such as appointments, became a severe problem.

Many Ming officials risked their careers and lives trying to admonish emperors. In 1376, when Taizu asked for criticism, one official criticized harsh punishment of officials for minor lapses. Incensed, Taizu had him brought to the capital in chains and let him starve to death in prison. In 1519 when an emperor announced plans to make a tour of the southern provinces, over a hundred officials staged a protest by kneeling in front of the palace. The emperor ordered the officials to remain kneeling for three days, then had them flogged; eleven died. The Confucian tradition celebrated these acts of political protest as heroic. Rarely, however, did they succeed in moving an emperor to change his mind.

Although the educated public complained about the performance of emperors, no one proposed or even imagined alternatives to imperial rule. High officials were forced to find ways to work around uncooperative emperors but were not able to put in place institutions that would limit the damage an emperor could do. Knowing that strong emperors often acted erratically, they came to prefer weak emperors who let them take care of the government. Probably one reason that so many Ming emperors resisted their officials' efforts to manage them was that the officials were indeed trying to keep the emperors engaged in tasks in which they could do relatively little harm.

The Mongols and the Great Wall

The early Ming emperors held Mongol fighting men in awe and feared they might form another great military machine of the sort Chinggis Khan (ca. 1162–1227) had put together two centuries earlier. In fact, in Ming times the Mongols were never united in a pan-Mongol federation. Still, groups of Mongols could and did raid, and twice they threatened the dynasty: in 1449 the khan of the Western Mongols captured the Chinese emperor, and in 1550 Beijing was surrounded by the forces of the khan of the Mongols in Inner Mongolia. Ming officials were very reluctant to grant any privileges to Mongol leaders, such as trading posts along the borders, and wanted the different groups of Mongols to trade only through the envoy system. When trade was finally liberalized in 1570, friction was reduced.

Two important developments shaped Ming-Mongol relations: the building of the Great Wall and closer relations between Mongolia and Tibet. Much of the Ming Great Wall survives today. It extends about 1,500 miles from northeast of Beijing into Gansu province. In the eastern 500 miles, the wall averages about 35 feet high and 20 feet across, with lookout towers every half mile. Much of the way, the wall is faced with brick, which gives it an imposing appearance that greatly impressed the first Westerners who saw it. It was built as a compromise when Ming officials could agree on no other way to manage the Mongol threat.

While China was building the wall, the Mongols were developing strong ties with Tibet, in this period largely ruled by the major Buddhist monasteries. When Tibetan monasteries needed military assistance, they asked competing Mongol leaders for help, and many struggles were decided by Mongol military intervention. Tsong-kha-pa (1357–1419) founded the Yellow Hat or Gelug-pa sect, whose heads later became known as the Dalai Lamas. In 1577 the third Dalai Lama accepted the invitation of Altan Khan to visit Mongolia, and the khan declared Tibetan Buddhism to be the official religion of all the Mongols. The Dalai Lama gave the khan the title "King of Religion," and the khan swore that the Mongols would renounce blood sacrifice. When the third Dalai Lama's reincarnation was found to be the great-grandson of Altan Khan, the ties between Tibet and Mongolia, not surprisingly, became even stronger.

The Examination Life

In sharp contrast to Europe in this era, Ming China had few social barriers. It had no hereditary aristocracy that could have undermined the emperor's absolute power. Although China had no titled aristocracy, it did have an elite whose status was based on a *combination* of wealth, education, family, and government office. Agricultural land remained the most highly prized form of wealth, but antiques, books, paintings and calligraphies, and urban real estate also brought status. China's merchants did not

Primary Source:
On Strange Tales and "On Merchants"
Learn how a Ming official assessed the status of commerce—and merchants—in sixteenth-century China.

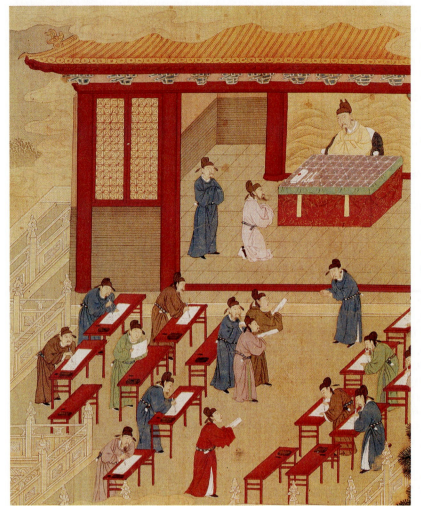

● **Civil Service Examinations** The examinations tested candidates' knowledge of the Confucian canon: rituals, history, poetry, cosmology—all believed to provide the basis for a moral life—and calligraphy. By the eighteenth century, the system was under attack because it failed to select the ablest scholars, the number of candidates had not increased in proportion to population, degrees were sold to the rich, and frequently even successful candidates could not find positions. *(Bibliothèque nationale de France)*

civil service examinations
Highly competitive series of tests held at the prefecture, province, and then capital to select men to become officials.

become a politically articulate bourgeoisie. The politically active class was that of the scholars who Confucianism taught should aid the ruler in running the state. With the possible exception of the Jewish people, no people have respected learning as much as the Chinese. Merchants tried to marry into the scholar class in order to rise in the world.

Thus, despite the harsh and arbitrary ways in which the Ming emperors treated their civil servants, educated men were eager to enter the government. Reversing the policies of the Mongol Yuan Dynasty, the Ming government recruited almost all of its officials through **civil service examinations.** Candidates had to study the Confucian classics and the interpretations of them by the twelfth-century Song scholar Zhu Xi, whose teachings were declared orthodox. To become officials, candidates had to pass examinations at the prefecture, the provincial, and the capital levels. To keep the wealthiest areas from dominating the results, quotas were established for the number of candidates that each province could send on to the capital.

Preparation for the examinations required, in essence, learning a new language—the classical written language was quite different from everyday spoken language—and memorizing long texts. Thus education was best started at four or five, because the young are usually better at both memorization and learning languages. Well-off families hired tutors for their boys as in earlier periods, and schools became increasingly available as well.

Families that for generations had pursued other careers, such as physician or merchant, had more opportunities than ever before to become officials through the exams. (See the feature "Individuals in Society: Tan Yunxian, Woman Doctor.") Clans sometimes operated schools for their members because the clan as a whole would enjoy the prestige of a successful member. Most of those who attended school stayed only a few years, but those who seemed most promising moved on to advanced schools where they would practice essay writing and study the essays of men who had succeeded in the exams.

The examinations at the prefecture level lasted a day and drew hundreds if not thousands of candidates. The government compound would be taken over to give all candidates places to sit and write. The provincial and capital examinations had three sessions spread out over a week. In the first session, candidates wrote essays on passages from the classics. In the second and third sessions, candidates had to write essays on practical policy issues and on a passage from the *Classic of Filial Piety.* In addition, they had to show that they could draft state papers such as edicts, decrees, and judicial

Tan Yunxian, Woman Doctor

Tan Yunxian would have consulted traditional herbals that included sketches of plants of medicinal value and described their uses. (*Sancai tuhui* [Ming Wanli ed.], *caomu 10.53a*)

The grandmother of Tan Yunxian (1461–1554) was the daughter of a physician, and her husband had married into her home to learn medicine himself. At least two of their sons—including Tan Yunxian's father—passed the civil service examination and became officials, raising the social standing of the family considerably. The grandparents wanted to pass their medical knowledge down to someone, and because they found Yunxian very bright, they decided to teach it to her.

Tan Yunxian married and raised four children but also practiced medicine, confining her practice to women. At age fifty she wrote an autobiographical account, *Sayings of a Female Doctor*. In the preface she described how, under her grandmother's tutelage, she had first memorized the *Canon of Problems* and *Canon of the Pulse*. Then when her grandmother had time, she asked her granddaughter to explain particular passages in these classic medical treatises.

Yunxian began the practice of medicine by treating her own children, asking her grandmother to check her diagnoses. When her grandmother was old and ill, she gave Yunxian her notebook of prescriptions and her equipment for making medicines, telling her to study them carefully. Later, Yunxian herself became seriously ill and dreamed of her grandmother telling her on what page of which book to find the prescription that would cure her. When she recovered, she began her medical career in earnest.

Tan's book records the cases of thirty-one patients she treated, most of them women with chronic complaints rather than critical illnesses. Many of the women had what the Chinese classed as women's complaints, such as menstrual irregularities, repeated miscarriages, barrenness, and postpartum fatigue. Some had ailments that men too could suffer, such as coughs, nausea, insomnia, diarrhea, rashes, and swellings. Like other literati physicians, Tan regularly prescribed herbal medications. She also practiced moxibustion. It was thought that burning moxa (dried artemisia) at specified points on the body would, like acupuncture, stimulate the circulation of *qi* (life energy). Because the physician applying the moxa had to touch the patient, male physicians could not perform moxibustion on women.

Tan's patients included working women, and Tan seems to have thought that their problems often sprang from overwork. One woman came to her because she had had vaginal bleeding for three years. When questioned, the woman told Tan that she worked all day with her husband at their kiln making bricks and tiles. Tan Yunxian's diagnosis was overwork, and she gave the woman pills to replenish her yin. A boatman's wife came to her complaining of numbness in her hands. When the woman told Tan that she worked in the wind and rain handling the boat, the doctor advised some time off. Tan Yunxian explained to a servant girl that she had gone back to work too soon after suffering a wind damage fever.

By contrast, when patients came from upper-class families, Tan believed negative emotions were the source of their problems, particularly if a woman reported that her mother-in-law had scolded her or that her husband had recently brought a concubine home. Tan told two upper-class women who had miscarried that they lost their babies because they had hidden their anger, causing fire to turn inward and destabilize the fetus.

Tan Yunxian herself lived a long life, dying at age ninety-three.

Questions for Analysis

1. Why do you think Tan Yunxian treated only women? Why might she have been more effective with women patients than a male physician would have been?

2. What do you think of Tan's diagnoses? Do you think she was able to help many of her patients?

Source: Based on Charlotte Furth, *A Flourishing Yin: Gender in China's Medical History, 960–1665* (Berkeley: University of California Press, 1999), pp. 285–295.

rulings. Reading the dynastic histories was a good way to prepare for the policy issue and state paper questions.

The weeklong provincial examinations were major local events. From five thousand to ten thousand candidates descended on the city and filled up its hostels. Candidates would show up a week in advance to present their credentials and gather the paper, ink, brushes, candles, blankets, and food they needed to survive in their small exam cells. No written material could be taken into the cells, and candidates were searched before being admitted. Anyone caught wearing a cheat-sheet (an inner gown covered with the classics in minuscule script) was thrown out of the exams and banned from the next session as well. Clerks used horns and gongs to begin and end each two-day session. Candidates had time to write rough drafts of their essays, correct them, then copy neat final versions. Tension was high. Sometimes rumors that the examiners had been bribed to leak the questions led to riots in the exam quarters, and knocked-over candles occasionally caused fires.

After the papers were handed in, clerks recopied them and assigned them numbers to preserve anonymity. Proofreaders checked the copying before handing the papers on to the assembled examiners, who divided them up to grade. The grading generally took about twenty days. Most candidates stayed in the vicinity to await the results. Those few who passed (around 2 to 10 percent) were invited to the governor's compound for a celebration. By the time they reached home, most of their friends, neighbors, and relatives had already heard their good news. They could not spend long celebrating, however, because they had to begin preparing for the capital exams, less than a year away.

Life of the People

Everyday life in Ming China followed patterns established in earlier periods. The family remained central to most people's lives, and almost everyone married. Marriages were arranged by parents, commonly when children were in their teens. Because getting a bride could be expensive, a poor man might not be able to afford to marry until his mid-twenties or later. Most women were married by age twenty. Sons were highly desired because they were necessary to continue the family line and to make offerings to ancestors.

Beyond the family, people's lives were shaped by the type of work they did and where they lived. Not only did crops differ north and south, but some regions were much more urbanized than others. In place of the paper money that had circulated in Song and Yuan times, silver ingots came into general use as money. Even agricultural taxes came to be paid in silver rather than grain.

Urban Culture
Large towns and cities proliferated in Ming times and became islands of sophistication in the vast sea of rural villages. Small businesses manufactured textiles, paper, and luxury goods such as silks and porcelains. The southeast became a center for the production of cotton and silks; other areas specialized in the grain and salt trades and in silver. Merchants could make fortunes moving these goods across the country.

Printing was invented in Tang times and had a great impact on the life of the educated elite in Song times, but not until Ming times did it transform the culture of the urban middle classes. By the late Ming period, publishing houses were putting out large numbers of books aimed at general audiences. These included fiction, reference books of all sorts, and popular religious tracts, such as ledgers for calculating the moral value of one's good deeds and subtracting the demerits from bad deeds. To make their books attractive in the marketplace, entrepreneurial book publishers commissioned artists to illustrate them. By the sixteenth century, more and more books were being published in the vernacular language (the language people spoke), espe-

● **Romance** Women were among the most avid readers of the scripts for plays, especially romantic ones like *The Western Chamber,* a story of a young scholar who falls in love with a well-educated girl he encounters by chance. In this scene, the young woman looks up at the moon as her maid looks at its reflection in the pond. Meanwhile, her young lover scales the wall. This multicolor woodblock print, made in 1640, was one of twenty-one made to illustrate the play. *(Museum for East Asian Art, Cologne, Inv.-No. R 61,2 [No. 11]. Photo: Rheinisches Bildarchiv, Cologne)*

cially short stories, novels, and plays. Ming vernacular short stories depicted a world much like that of their readers, full of shop clerks and merchants, monks and prostitutes, students and matchmakers.

The full-length novel appeared during the Ming period. The plots of the early novels were heavily indebted to story cycles developed by oral storytellers over the course of several centuries. *Water Margin* is the episodic story of a band of bandits. *The Romance of the Three Kingdoms* is a work of historical fiction based on the exploits of the generals and statesmen contending for power at the end of the Han Dynasty. *The Journey to the West* is a fantastic account of the Tang monk Xuanzang's travels to India; in this book he is accompanied by a pig and a monkey with supernatural powers. *Plum in the Golden Vase* is a novel of manners about a lustful merchant with a wife and five concubines. Competing publishers brought out their own editions of these novels, sometimes adding new illustrations or commentaries.

The Chinese found recreation and relaxation in many ways. The affluent indulged in an alcoholic drink made from fermented and distilled rice. Once tobacco was introduced, both men and women took up pipes. Plays were very popular. The Jesuit missionary Matteo Ricci, who lived in China from 1583 to 1610, described resident troupes in large cities and traveling troupes that "journey everywhere throughout the length and breadth of the country" putting on plays. The leaders of the troupes would purchase young children and train them to sing and perform. Ricci thought too many people were addicted to these performances:

These groups of actors are employed at all imposing banquets, and when they are called they come prepared to enact any of the ordinary plays. The host at the banquet is usually presented with a volume of plays and he selects the one or several he may like. The guests, between eating and drinking, follow the plays with so much satisfaction that the banquet at times may last for ten hours.[1]

People not only enjoyed listening to plays but also avidly read the play scripts. The love stories and social satires of Tang Xianzu, the greatest of the Ming playwrights, were very popular. One play tells the story of a young man who falls asleep while his meal is cooking. In his dream he sees his whole life: he comes in first in the civil service examinations, rises to high office, is unfairly slandered and condemned to death, then is cleared and promoted. At the point of death, he wakes up, sees that his dinner is nearly ready, and realizes that life passes as quickly as a dream.

Life in the Countryside More than bread in Europe, rice supplied most of the calories of the population in central and south China. (In north China, wheat, made into steamed or baked bread or into noodles, served as the staple of the diet.) Terracing and irrigation of mountain slopes, introduced in the eleventh century, had increased rice harvests. Other innovations also brought good results. Farmers began to stock the rice paddies with fish, which continuously fertilized the rice fields, destroyed malaria-bearing mosquitoes, and enriched the diet. Farmers developed commercial cropping in cotton, sugar cane, and indigo. And new methods of crop rotation allowed for continuous cultivation and for more than one harvest per year from a single field.

The Ming rulers promoted the repopulation and colonization of devastated regions through reclamation of land and massive transfers of people (see Table 20.1). Immigrants received large plots of land and exemption from taxation for many years. Reforestation played a dramatic role in the agricultural revolution. In 1391 the Ming government ordered 50 million trees planted in the Nanjing area. Lumber from the trees was intended for the construction of a maritime fleet. In 1392 each family holding colonized land in Anhui province had to plant two hundred mulberry, jujube, and persimmon trees. In 1396 peasants in the present-day provinces of Hunan and Hubei in central China planted 84 million fruit trees. Historians have estimated that 1 billion trees were planted during Taizu's reign.

What were the social consequences of agricultural development? Increased food production led to steady population growth. Population increase led to the multiplication of markets, towns, and small cities. Larger towns had permanent shops; smaller towns had periodic markets—some every five days, some every ten days, some only once a month. They sold essential goods—pins, matches, oil for lamps, candles, paper, incense, tobacco (after it was introduced from the Americas)—to country people from the surrounding hamlets. The market usually included moneylenders, pawnbrokers, a tearoom, and sometimes a wine shop where tea and rice wine were sold and entertainers performed. Tradesmen carrying their wares on their backs and craftsmen—carpenters, barbers, joiners, locksmiths—moved constantly from market to market. Itinerant salesmen depended on the city market for their wares.

Ming Decline

Beginning in the 1590s the Ming government was beset by fiscal, military, and political problems. The government went nearly bankrupt helping defend Korea against a Japanese invasion (see page 600). Then came a series of natural disasters. Failed harvests, floods, droughts, locusts, and epidemics ravaged one region after another. A "little ice age" brought a drop in average temperatures that shortened the growing season and reduced harvests. In areas where food shortages became critical, gangs of army deserters and laid-off soldiers began scouring the countryside in search of food. Once the gangs had stolen all their grain, hard-pressed farmers joined them just to survive. A former shepherd and postal relay worker became the paramount rebel leader in the north. An ex-soldier became the main leader in the central region between the Huang He (Yellow) and Yangzi Rivers. The Ming government had little choice but to try to increase taxes to deal with these threats, but the last thing people needed was heavier taxes.

Adding to the hardship was a sudden drop in the supply of silver. The Ming economy had come to depend on a large influx of silver from Japan and the New World, which was used to pay for the silk and porcelains exported from China (see pages 601–604). Events in Japan and the Philippines led to disruption of trade. The drop in silver imports led to deflation, which caused real rents to rise. Soon there were riots among urban workers and tenant farmers. In 1642 a group of rebels cut the dikes on the Huang He River, causing massive flooding. A smallpox epidemic soon added to the death toll. In 1644 the last Ming emperor, in despair, took his own life when rebels entered Beijing.

Table 20.1 Land Reclamation in Early Ming China

YEAR	RECLAIMED LAND (IN HECTARES; 1 HECTARE = 2.5 ACRES)
1371	576,000
1373	1,912,000
1374	4,974,000
1379	1,486,000

Source: J. Gernet, *A History of Chinese Civilization*, trans. J. R. Foster (Cambridge: Cambridge University Press, 1982), p. 391. Used with permission.

THE MANCHUS AND QING CHINA (1644–1800)

Did the return of alien rule with the Manchus have any positive consequences for China?

The next dynasty, the **Qing Dynasty,** was founded by the Manchus, a non-Chinese people who were descended from the Jurchens who had ruled north China during the Jin Dynasty (1127–1234), when south China was controlled by the Song. Manchu men shaved the front of their heads and wore their hair in a long braid called a queue.

In the Ming period the Manchus had lived in dispersed communities in what is loosely called Manchuria (the northeast of modern-day China). In the more densely populated southern part of Manchuria, the Manchus lived in close contact with Mongols, Koreans, and Chinese (see Map 20.1). They were not nomads but rather hunters, fishermen, and farmers. Like the Mongols, they were excellent horsemen and archers and had a strongly hierarchical social structure, with elites and slaves. Slaves, often Korean or Chinese, were generally acquired through capture. A Korean visitor described many small Manchu settlements, most no larger than twenty households, supported by fishing, hunting for pelts, collecting pine nuts or ginseng, or growing crops such as wheat, millet, and barley. Villages were often at odds with each other over resources, and men did not leave their villages without arming themselves with bows and arrows or swords. Interspersed among these Manchu settlements were groups of nomadic Mongols who lived in yurts.

The Manchus credited their own rise to Nurhaci (1559–1626). Over several decades, he united the Manchus, then expanded their territories. Like Chinggis Khan, who had reorganized the Mongol armies to reduce the importance of tribal affiliations, Nurhaci created a new social basis for his armies in units called **banners.** Each banner was made up of a set of military companies but included the families and slaves of the soldiers as well. Each company had a hereditary captain, often from Nurhaci's own lineage. Over time new companies and new banners were formed, and by 1644 there were eight each of Manchu, Mongol, and Chinese banners. When new groups were defeated, they were distributed among several banners to lessen their potential for subversion.

Qing Dynasty *The dynasty founded by the Manchus that ruled China from 1644 to 1911.*

banners *Units of the Qing army, composed of soldiers, their families, and slaves.*

The distinguished Ming general Wu Sangui, himself a native of southern Manchuria, was near the eastern end of the Great Wall when he heard that the rebels had captured Beijing. The Manchus proposed to Wu that they join forces and liberate Beijing. Wu opened the gates of the Great Wall to let the Manchus in, and within a couple of weeks they occupied Beijing. When the Manchus made clear that they intended to conquer the rest of the country and take the throne themselves, Wu and many other Chinese generals joined forces with them.

In the summer of 1645, the Manchus ordered all Chinese serving in Manchu armies to shave the front of their heads in the Manchu fashion, presumably to make it easier to recognize whose side they were on. Soon this order was extended to all Chinese men. Because so many of those newly conquered by the Qing refused to shave their hair, Manchu commanders felt justified in ordering the slaughter of defiant cities.

After quelling resistance, the Qing put in place policies and institutions that gave China a respite from war and disorder. Most of the political institutions of the Ming Dynasty were taken over relatively unchanged, including the examination system. Between 1700 and 1800, the Chinese population seems to have nearly doubled, from about 150 million to over 300 million (see Table 20.2). Population growth during the course of the eighteenth century has been attributed to many factors: global warming that extended the growing season, expanded use of New World crops, slowing of the spread of new diseases that had accompanied the sixteenth-century

MAP 20.1 **The Qing Empire** The sheer size of the Qing Empire in China almost inevitably led to its profound cultural influence on the rest of Asia. What geographical and political factors limited the extent of the empire?

expansion of global traffic, and the efficiency of the Qing government in providing relief in times of famine.

Some scholars have recently argued that China's overall standard of living in the mid-eighteenth century was comparable to Europe's and that the standards of China's most developed regions, such as the lower Yangzi region, compared favorably to the most developed regions of Europe at the time, such as England and the Netherlands. Life expectancy, food consumption, and even facilities for transportation were at similar levels. The government in this period had the resources to respond to famines and disasters. Indeed, during the eighteenth century, the treasury was so full that the annual land tax was canceled four times.

Competent and Long-Lived Emperors

For more than a century, China was ruled by only three rulers, each of them hard working, talented, and committed to making the Qing Dynasty a success. Two, the Kangxi and Qianlong emperors, had exceptionally long reigns.

Kangxi (r. 1661–1722) proved adept at meeting the expectations of both the Chinese and the Manchu elites. At age fourteen, he announced that he would begin ruling on his own and had his regent imprisoned. Kangxi could speak, read, and write Chinese and appreciated the value of persuading educated Chinese that the Manchus had a legitimate claim to the Mandate of Heaven. He made efforts to attract Ming loyalists who had been unwilling to serve the Qing. He undertook a series of tours of the south, where Ming loyalism had been strongest, and he held a special exam to select men to compile the official history of the Ming Dynasty.

The Qianlong emperor (r. 1736–1795) put much of his energy into impressing his subjects with his magnificence. He understood that the Qing's capacity to hold their multiethnic empire together rested on their ability to appeal to all those they ruled. Besides Manchu and Chinese, Qianlong learned to converse in Mongolian, Uighur, Tibetan, and Tangut, and he addressed envoys in their own languages. He became as much a patron of Tibetan Buddhism as of Chinese Confucianism. He initiated a massive project to translate the Tibetan Buddhist canon into Mongolian and Manchu and had huge multilingual dictionaries compiled.

To demonstrate to the Chinese scholar-official elite that he was a sage emperor, Qianlong worked on affairs of state from dawn until early afternoon, then turned to reading, painting, and calligraphy. He was ostentatious in his devotion to his mother, visiting her daily and tending to her comfort with all the devotion of the most filial Chinese son. He took several tours down the Grand Canal to the southeast, in part to emulate his grandfather, in part to entertain his mother.

Despite these displays of Chinese virtues, the Qianlong emperor was not fully confident that the Chinese supported his rule, and he was quick to act on any suspicion of anti-Manchu thoughts or actions. During a project to catalogue nearly all the books in China, he began to suspect that some governors were holding back books with seditious content. He ordered full searches for books with disparaging references to the Manchus or to previous alien conquerors. Sometimes passages were deleted or rewritten, but when the entire book was offensive, it was destroyed. So thorough was the proscription that no copies survive of more than two thousand titles.

Table 20.2	Registered Population of China, ca. 1390–1790
ca. 1390	50,000,000
ca. 1685	100,000,000*
ca. 1749	177,495,000
1767	209,840,000
1776	268,238,000
1790	301,487,000

*The catastrophic drop in China's registered population from the time of the Ming-Qing transition to the end of Kangxi's wars with three powerful rebels in 1681 was due to civil wars, foreign invasions, bandit actions, natural disasters, virulent epidemics, and the failure of irrigation systems.

Source: J. D. Spence, *The Search for Modern China* (New York: W. W. Norton, 1991), pp. 93–95.

● **Presenting a Horse to the Emperor** This detail from a 1757 handscroll shows the Qianlong emperor, seated, receiving envoys from the Kazakhs. Note how the envoy, presenting a pure white horse, is kneeling to the ground (performing the kowtow). The artist was Guiseppe Castiglione (1688–1768), an Italian who worked as a painter in Qianlong's court. *(Qing, 1757. Handscroll, ink and colors on paper [45 cm x 2.67 m]. Musée Guimet, Paris/Art Resource, NY)*

Through Qianlong's reign, China remained an enormous producer of manufactured goods and led the way in assembly-line production. The government operated huge textile factories, but there were private firms that were even larger. Hangzhou had a textile firm that gave work to four thousand weavers, twenty thousand spinners, and ten thousand dyers and finishers. The porcelain kilns at Jingdezhen employed division of labor on a large scale and were able to supply porcelain to much of the world. The Qing state benefited from the growth of the economy. The treasury was so full that the Qianlong emperor was able to cancel taxes on several occasions, but when he abdicated in 1796, his treasury had 400 million silver dollars in it.

Imperial Expansion

The Qing Dynasty put together a multiethnic empire that was larger than any earlier Chinese dynasty. Taiwan was acquired in 1683 after Qing armies pursued a rebel there. Mongolia was acquired next. In 1696 Kangxi led an army of eighty thousand men into Mongolia, and within a few years Manchu supremacy was accepted there. Cannon and muskets gave Qing forces military superiority over the Mongols, who were armed only with bows and arrows. Thus the Qing could dominate the steppe cheaply, effectively ending two thousand years of Inner Asian military advantage.

In the 1720s, the Qing established a permanent garrison of banner soldiers in Tibet. By this time, the expanding Qing and Russian empires were nearing each other. In 1689 the Manchu and the Russian rulers approved a treaty—written in Russian, Manchu, Chinese, and Latin—defining their borders in Manchuria and regulating trade. Another treaty in 1727 allowed a Russian ecclesiastical mission to reside in Beijing and a caravan to make a trip from Russia to Beijing once every three years.

The last region to be annexed was Chinese Turkestan (the modern province of Xinjiang). Both the Han and the Tang Dynasties had stationed troops in the region, exercising a loose suzerainty, but neither Song nor Ming had tried to control the area. The Qing won the region in the 1750s through a series of campaigns against Uighur and Dzungar Mongol forces.

Both Tibet and Turkestan were ruled lightly. The local populations kept their own religious leaders and did not have to wear the queue.

JAPAN'S MIDDLE AGES (CA. 1400–1600)

How did Japan change during this period of political instability?

In the twelfth century Japan entered an age dominated by military men, an age that can be compared to Europe's feudal age. The Kamakura Shogunate (1185–1333) had its capital in the east, at Kamakura. It was succeeded by the Ashikaga Shogunate

(1336–1573), which returned the government to Kyoto. The fifteenth century was the great age of Zen-influenced Muromachi culture. The sixteenth century brought civil war that led to massive castle building, rulers of obscure origins who unified the realm, and the invasion of Korea.

Muromachi Culture

The headquarters of the Ashikaga shoguns were on Muromachi Street in Kyoto, and the refined and elegant style that they promoted is often called Muromachi culture. The shoguns patronized Zen Buddhism, the school of Buddhism associated with meditation and mind-to-mind transmission of truth. Because Zen monks were able to read and write Chinese, they often assisted the shoguns in handling foreign affairs. Many of the Kyoto Zen temples in this period had rock gardens. In the garden of Ryoanji, for instance, a temple built in the late fifteenth century, raked white sand surrounds fifteen rocks, but only fourteen of them are visible from any one perspective. Rock gardens were seen as aids to Zen meditation.

Zen ideas permeated the arts. The Silver Pavilion built by the shogun Yoshimasa (r. 1449–1473) epitomizes Zen austerity. A white sand cone constructed in the temple garden was designed to reflect moonlight. Yoshimasa was also influential in the development of the tea ceremony, practiced by warriors, aristocrats, and priests but not women. Aesthetes celebrated the beauty of imperfect objects, such as plain or misshapen cups or pots. Spare monochrome paintings fit into this aesthetic, as did simple asymmetrical flower arrangements.

The shoguns were also patrons of the Nō theater. Nō drama originated in popular forms of entertainment, including comical skits and dances directed to the gods. It was transformed into high art by Zeami (1363–1443), an actor and playwright who also wrote on the aesthetic theory of Nō. Nō was performed on a bare stage with a pine tree painted across the backdrop. One or two actors wearing brilliant brocade robes would perform, using stylized gestures and stances. One actor would wear a mask indicating whether the character he was portraying was male or female, old or young, a god, ghost, or demon. The actors would be accompanied by a chorus and a couple of musicians playing drums and flute. Many of the stories concerned ghosts consumed by jealous passions or desire for revenge. Zeami argued that the most meaningful moments came during silence, when the actor's spiritual presence allowed the audience to catch a glimpse of the mysterious and inexpressible.

Civil War

Civil war began in Kyoto in 1467 as a struggle over succession to the shogunate. Rivals used arson as their chief weapon and burned down temples and mansions, destroying much of the city and its treasures. In the early phases defeated opponents were exiled or allowed to retire to monasteries. As the conflict continued, violence escalated; hostages and prisoners were slaughtered and corpses mutilated. Once Kyoto was laid waste, war spread to outlying areas. When the shogun could no longer protect cities, merchants banded together to hire mercenaries. The Lotus League, a commoner-led religious sect united by faith in the saving power of the Lotus Sutra, set up a commoner-run government that collected taxes and settled disputes. In 1536, during eight days of fighting, the monastery Enryakuji attacked the League and its temples, burned much of the city, and killed men, women, and children thought to be believers.

In these confused and violent circumstances, power devolved to the local level, where warlords, called **daimyo,** built their power bases. Unlike earlier power holders, these new lords were not appointed by the court or shogunate and did not send taxes to absentee overlords. Instead they seized what they needed and used it to build up their territories and recruit more samurai. To raise revenues, they surveyed the land

daimyo *Regional lords in Japan; many had built their power by seizing what they needed and promoting irrigation and trade to raise revenues.*

● **Matsumoto Castle**
Hideyoshi built Matsumoto Castle between 1594 and 1597. Designed to be impregnable, it was surrounded by a moat and had a base constructed of huge stones. In the sixteenth and early seventeenth centuries Spanish and Portuguese missionaries compared Japanese castles favorably to European castles of the period. *(Robert Harding World Imagery)*

and promoted irrigation and trade. Many of the most successful daimyo were self-made men who rose from obscurity.

This was an age of castle building. The castles were built not on mountaintops but on level plains. A castle was surrounded by moats and walls made from huge stones. Inside was a many-storied keep, usually with white plastered walls and tile roofs. Though relatively safe from incendiary missiles, the keeps were vulnerable to Western-style cannon, introduced in the 1570s. Many of the castles had splendid living quarters for the daimyo; leading painters embellished interior sliding doors and screens.

The Victors: Nobunaga and Hideyoshi

The first daimyo to gain a predominance of power was Oda Nobunaga (1534–1582). A samurai of the lesser daimyo class, he built his retainer band from masterless samurai who had been living by robbery and extortion. After he won control of his native province of Owari in 1559, he immediately set out to extend his power and in 1568 seized Kyoto and became the ruler of central Japan. A key achievement was destroying the military power of the great monasteries. He needed to increase revenues, and toward that end he minted coins, the first government-issued money in Japan since 958. He promoted trade by eliminating customs barriers. He opened the little fishing village of Nagasaki to foreign commerce; it soon became Japan's largest port.

In 1582 Nobunaga was forced by one of his vassals to commit suicide. His general and staunchest adherent, Toyotomi Hideyoshi (1537–1598), avenged him and continued the drive toward unification.

Like the Ming founder, Hideyoshi was a peasant's son who rose to power through military service. Hideyoshi succeeded in bringing northern and western Japan under his control. In 1582 he attacked the great fortress at Takamatsu. When direct assault failed, his troops flooded the castle to force its surrender. A successful siege of the town of Kagoshima then brought the southern island of Kyushu under his domination. Hideyoshi soothed the vanquished daimyo as Nobunaga had done—with lands and military positions—but he also required them to swear allegiance and to obey him down to the smallest particular. For the first time in over two centuries, Japan had a single ruler.

Hideyoshi did his best to ensure that future peasants' sons would not be able to rise as he had. His great sword hunt of 1588 collected weapons from farmers, who were no longer allowed to wear swords. Farmers were to remain farmers; they were forbidden to leave their fields to take up trade in the cities. Restrictions were also placed on samurai; they were prohibited from leaving their lord's service or switching occupations.

To improve tax collection, Hideyoshi ordered a survey of the entire country. His agents collected detailed information about each daimyo's lands and about towns, villages, agricultural produce, and industrial output all over Japan. His surveys tied the peasant population to the land and tightened the collection of the land tax.

With the country pacified, Hideyoshi embarked on an ill-fated attempt to conquer Korea and China that ended only with his death.

THE TOKUGAWA SHOGUNATE (1600–1800)

What was life like in Japan during the Tokugawa peace?

On his deathbed, Hideyoshi set up a council of regents to govern during the minority of his infant son. The strongest regent was Hideyoshi's long-time supporter Tokugawa Ieyasu (1543–1616), who ruled vast territories around Edo (modern-day Tokyo). In 1600 at Sekigahara, Ieyasu smashed a coalition of daimyo defenders of the heir and began building his own government. In 1603 he took the title *shogun*. The **Tokugawa Shogunate** that Ieyasu fashioned lasted until 1867. This era is also called the Edo period because the shogunate was located at Edo, starting Tokyo's history as Japan's most important city (see Map 20.2).

Tokugawa Shogunate *The Japanese government founded by Tokugawa Ieyasu that lasted until 1867; it is also called the Edo period because the shogunate was located at Edo*

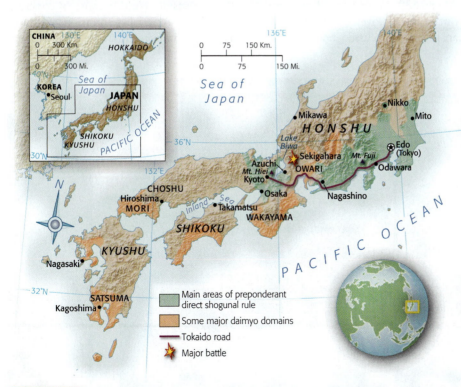

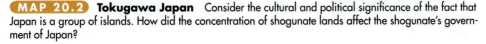

MAP 20.2 **Tokugawa Japan** Consider the cultural and political significance of the fact that Japan is a group of islands. How did the concentration of shogunate lands affect the shogunate's government of Japan?

alternate residence system   *Arrangement in which lords lived in Edo every other year and left their wives and sons there as hostages.*

In the course of the seventeenth century, the Tokugawa shoguns worked to consolidate relations with the daimyo. In a scheme resembling the later residency requirement imposed by Louis XIV in France (see page 467) and Peter the Great in Russia (see page 479), Ieyasu set up the **alternate residence system,** which compelled the lords to live in Edo every other year and to leave their wives and sons there—essentially as hostages. This arrangement had obvious advantages: the shogun could keep tabs on the daimyo, control them through their children, and weaken them financially with the burden of maintaining two residences.

The peace that the Tokugawa Shogunate imposed brought a steady rise in population to about 30 million people by 1800 (making Tokugawa Japan about one-tenth the size of Qing China). As demand for goods grew, so did the number of merchants. To maintain stability, the early Tokugawa shoguns froze social status. Laws rigidly prescribed what each class could and could not do. Nobles, for example, were strictly forbidden, whether by day or by night, to go sauntering through the streets or lanes in places where they had no business to be. Daimyo were prohibited from moving troops outside their frontiers, making alliances, and coining money. Designated dress and stiff rules of etiquette distinguished one class from another. As intended, this stratification protected the Tokugawa shoguns from daimyo attack and inaugurated a long era of peace.

The early Tokugawa shoguns also restricted the construction and repair of castles—symbols, in Japan as in medieval Europe, of feudal independence. Continuing Hideyoshi's policy, the Tokugawa regime enforced a policy of complete separation of samurai and peasants. Samurai were defined as those permitted to carry swords. They had to live in castles (which evolved into castle-towns), and they depended on stipends from their lords, the daimyo. Samurai were effectively prevented from establishing ties to the land, so they could not become landholders. Likewise, merchants and artisans had to live in towns and could not own land. Japanese castle-towns evolved into bustling, sophisticated urban centers.

After 1639, Japan limited its contacts with the outside world because of concerns about both the loyalty of Christian converts and the imperialist ambitions of European powers (discussed below). China remained an important trading partner and

● **Interior of Nijo Castle**   To assert control over the imperial court and the city of Kyoto, Tokugawa Ieyasu built palace-like Nijo Castle there in 1601–1603. He had the sliding doors painted by leading artists of the period, making the castle as elegant as the imperial palace. (*From Fujioka Michio,* Genshoku Nihon no Bijutsu, *Vol. 12:* Shiro to Shoin *[Tokyo: Shogakkan, 1968]*)

● **Daimyo Procession**   Sankin kōtai, or system of alternate residence, meant that some daimyo were always on the road. Travel with retinues between daimyo residences and Edo, the shogun's residence, stimulated construction of roads, inns, and castle towns. As administrative headquarters, Edo functioned as a major consumer center; other castle towns such as Osaka developed as banking and manufacturing centers. *(Tokugawa Art Museum, Nagoya/Tokugawa Reimeikai Foundation)*

source of ideas—Neo-Confucianism gained a stronger hold among the samurai-turned bureaucrats than it had had earlier. Painting in Chinese styles enjoyed great popularity. The Edo period also saw the development of a school of native learning that rejected Buddhism and Confucianism as alien and tried to identify a distinctly Japanese sensibility.

Commercialization

During the civil war period, warfare seems to have promoted social and economic change, much as it had in China during the Warring States Period (403–221 B.C.E.). Trade grew, and greater use was made of coins imported from Ming China. Markets began appearing at river crossings, at the entrances to temples and shrines, and at other places where people congregated. Towns and cities sprang up all around the country, some of them around the new castles. Traders or artisans dealing in a specific product—such as comb makers, sesame oil producers, or metalworkers—began forming guilds. Money-lending was a very profitable business—annual interest rates reached 300 percent. In Kyoto the powerful monastery Enryakuji licensed the money-lenders, in essence running a lucrative protection racket. Foreign trade also flourished, despite chronic problems with pirates who raided the Japanese, Korean, and Chinese coasts (see page 600).

Recent scholarship demonstrates that the Tokugawa era witnessed the foundations of modern Japanese capitalism: the development of a cash economy, the use of money to make more money, the accumulation of large amounts of capital for investment in factory or technological enterprises, the growth of business ventures operating over a national network of roads, and the expansion of wage labor. That these developments occurred simultaneously with, but entirely independent of, similar changes in Europe fascinates and challenges historians.

In most cities, merchant families with special privileges from the government controlled the urban economy. Frequently, a particular family dominated the trade in a particular product; then that family branched out into other businesses. The family of Kōnoike Shinroku provides a typical example. In 1600 he established a sake brewery in the village of Kōnoike (sake is an alcoholic beverage made from fermented rice). By 1604 he had opened a branch office in Edo, and in 1615 he opened an office in Osaka; that same year, he began shipping tax-rice (taxes paid in rice) from western Japan to Osaka. One of Shinroku's sons, Kōnoike Zen'amon, in 1656 founded a banking or money-changing business in Osaka. Forty years later, the Kōnoike family was doing business in thirty-two daimyo domains. Eventually, the Kōnoike banking house

Primary Source:
Common Sense Teachings for Japanese Children and Greater Learning for Women
A Confucian scholar explains how to raise aristocratic Japanese children.

Primary Source:
Some Observations on Merchants
Why lending money to a daimyo is like gambling, and other business insights from early Tokugawa Japan.

made loans to and handled the tax-rice for 110 daimyo families. The Kōnoike continued to expand their businesses. In 1705, with the interest paid from daimyo loans, the Kōnoike bought a tract of ponds and swampland, turned the land into rice paddies, and settled 480 households on the land. Land reclamation under merchant supervision became a typical feature of Tokugawa business practices. Involved by this time in five or six business enterprises, the "house of Kōnoike" had come a long way from brewing sake.

Japanese merchant families also devised distinct patterns and procedures for their business operations. What today is called "Family Style Management Principles" determined the age of appointment or apprenticeship (between eleven and thirteen); the employee's detachment from past social relations and adherence to the norms of a particular family business; salaries; seniority as the basis of promotion, though job performance at the middle rungs determined who reached the higher ranks; and the time for retirement. All employees in a family business were imbued with the "cardinal tenets" of Tokugawa business law: frugality, resourcefulness, and careful accounting. The successful employee also learned appropriate business behavior and a spirit of self-denial. These values formed the basis of what has been called the Japanese "industrious revolution." They help to explain how, after the Meiji Restoration of 1867 (see page 764), Japan was able to industrialize rapidly and compete successfully with the West.

In the seventeenth century, the surplus rural population, together with underemployed samurai and the ambitious and adventurous, thronged to the cities. All wanted a better way of life than could be found in the dull farming villages. Japan's cities grew tremendously: Kyoto became the center for the manufacture of luxury goods like lacquer, brocade, and fine porcelain. Osaka was the chief market, especially for rice. Edo was a center of consumption by the daimyo, their vassals, and government bureaucrats. Both Osaka and Edo reached about a million residents.

These cities needed to import huge quantities of rice. Osaka came to manage most of this rice trade. Other goods—cotton cloth, oil, sugar, salt, paper, and iron ore—also flowed into Osaka. Granted special privileges by the government and having the facilities necessary for large commodity exchange, Osaka became the commercial center of Japan. Wholesalers and brokers were concentrated there. The city was also closely tied to Kyoto, where the emperor and his court resided, creating a big demand for goods and services.

Two hundred fifty towns came into being. Most ranged in size from 3,000 to 20,000 people, but a few, such as Hiroshima, Kagoshima, and Nagoya, had populations between 65,000 and 100,000. In addition, perhaps two hundred transit towns along the roads and highways emerged to service the needs of men traveling on the alternate residence system. In the eighteenth century, perhaps 4 million people, 15 percent of the Japanese population, resided in cities or towns.

The Life of the People in the Edo Period

The Tokugawa shoguns brought an end to civil war by controlling the military. Stripped of power and required to spend alternate years at Edo, many of the daimyo and samurai passed their lives in idle pursuit of pleasure. They spent frantically on fine silks, paintings, concubines, boys, the theater, and the redecoration of their castles. Around 1700 one scholar observed that the entire military class was living "as in an inn, that is, consuming now and paying later."[2] Eighteenth-century Japanese novels, plays, and histories portray the samurai engrossed in tavern brawls and sexual orgies. These frivolities, plus more sophisticated pleasures and the heavy costs of maintaining an alternate residence at Edo, gradually bankrupted the warrior class.

All major cities contained places of amusement for men—teahouses, theaters, restaurants, and houses of prostitution. Desperately poor parents sometimes sold their daughters to entertainment houses (as they did in China and medieval Europe), and

● **Whaling**　Island peoples often depend on the sea for much of their food. In Japan, where whaling is an old and dangerous pursuit, fishermen first snared the whale in huge nets and then harpooned it. Here the banners tell that a whale has been caught. A Japanese proverb holds that "when one whale is caught, it makes seven villages prosperous." The yellowish oil obtained from whale blubber was used for lighting and for the manufacture of soap and candles. *(National Institute of Japanese Literature)*

the most attractive or talented girls, trained in singing, dancing, and conversational arts, became courtesans, later called *geishas,* or "accomplished persons."

The samurai joined the merchants in patronizing the kabuki theater. An art form created by townspeople, kabuki originated in crude, bawdy skits dealing with love and romance. Performances featured elaborate costumes, song, dance, and poetry. Because actresses were thought to corrupt public morals, the Tokugawa government banned them from the stage in 1629. From that time on, men played all the parts. Male actors in female dress and makeup performed as seductively as possible to entice the burly samurai who thronged the theaters. Homosexuality, long accepted in Japan, was widely practiced among the samurai, who pursued the actors and spent profligately on them. Some moralists and bureaucrats complained from time to time, but the Tokugawa government decided to accept kabuki and prostitution as necessary evils. The practices provided employment, gratified the tastes of samurai and townspeople, and diverted former warriors from potential criminal and political mischief. The samurai paid for their costly pleasures in the way their European counterparts did—by fleecing the peasants and borrowing from the merchants.

Cities were also the center for commercial publishing. The reading public eagerly purchased fiction and the scripts for dramas and puppet plays. Ihara Saikaku (1642–1693) wrote stories of the foibles of townspeople in such books as *Five Women Who Loved Love* and *The Life of an Amorous Man.* One of the puppet plays of Chikamatsu

● **Interior View of a Theater**
Complex kabuki plays, which dealt with heroes, loyalty, and tragedy and which included music and dance, became the most popular form of entertainment in Tokugawa Japan for all classes. Movable scenery and lighting effects made possible the staging of storms, fires, and hurricanes. *(TNM Image Archives. Source: http://TnmArchives.jp/)*

Monzaemon (1653–1724) tells the story of the son of a business owner who, caught between duty to his family and love of a prostitute, decides to resolve the situation by double suicide.

Roads needed for the huge processions of daimyo and their retainers coming and going because of the alternate residence system were built or improved to connect every region to Edo. The shogunate prohibited travel by commoners, but they could get passports to take pilgrimages, visit relatives, or seek the soothing waters of medicinal hot springs. Setting out on foot, groups of villagers would travel to such shrines as Ise, often taking large detours to visit Osaka or Edo to sightsee or attend the theater. Older women with daughters-in-law to run their households were among the most avid pilgrims.

According to Japanese tradition, farmers deserved respect. In practice, peasants were often treated callously. It was government policy to tax them to the level of bare subsistence, and official legislation repeatedly redefined their duties. In 1649 every village in Japan received these regulations:

Peasants are people without sense or forethought. Therefore they must not give rice to their wives and children at harvest time, but must save food for the future. They should eat millet, vegetables, and other coarse food instead of rice. Even the fallen leaves of plants should be saved as food against famine. . . . During the seasons of planting and harvesting, however, when the labor is arduous, the food taken may be a little better. . . .

They must not buy tea or sake to drink nor must their wives.

The husband must work in the fields, the wife must work at the loom. Both must do night work. However good-looking a wife may be, if she neglects her household duties by drinking tea or sightseeing or rambling on the hillsides, she must be divorced.

Peasants must wear only cotton or hemp—no silk. They may not smoke tobacco. It is harmful to health, it takes up time, and costs money. It also creates a risk of fire.[3]

During the seventeenth and eighteenth centuries conspicuous consumption by the upper classes led them to increase taxes from 30 or 40 percent of the rice crop to 50 percent. During the eighteenth century peasant protests were chronic. Oppressive taxation provoked eighty-four thousand farmers in the province of Iwaki to revolt in 1739. After widespread burning and destruction, their demands were met. Natural disasters also added to the peasants' misery. In 1783 Mount Asama erupted, spewing volcanic ash that darkened the skies all summer; crop failures led to famine. When famine recurred again in 1787, commoners rioted for five days in Edo, smashing merchants' stores and pouring sake and rice into the muddy streets. The shogunate responded by trying to control the floating population of day laborers without families in the city. At one point they were rounded up and transported to work the gold mines in an island off the north coast, where most of them died within two or three years.

This picture of peasant hardship tells only part of the story, however. Agricultural productivity increased substantially. Peasants who improved their lands and increased their yields continued to pay the same assessed tax and could pocket the surplus as profit. By the early nineteenth century, there existed a large class of relatively wealthy, educated, and ambitious peasant families. Most villages had a dominant family that monopolized the position of headman, who made decisions for the village after consulting a council of elders.

Women in these better-off families were much more likely to learn to read than women in poor peasant families. Girls from middle-level peasant families might have had from two to five years of formal schooling, but they were thought incapable of learning the difficult Chinese characters, so their education focused on moral instruction intended to instill virtue. Daughters of wealthy peasant families learned penmanship, the Chinese classics, poetry, and the proper forms of correspondence, and they rounded out their education with travel.

By the fifteenth and sixteenth centuries, Japan's family and marriage systems had evolved in the direction of a patrilocal, patriarchal system more like China's, and Japanese women had lost the prominent role in high society that they had occupied during the Heian period (794–1185). It became standard for women to move into their husbands' homes, where they occupied positions subordinate both to their husbands and to their mothers-in-law. Elite families stopped dividing their property among all of their children; instead they retained it for the sons alone or increasingly for a single son who would continue the family line. Marriage, which now had greater consequence, also had a more public character and was marked by greater ceremony. Wedding rituals involved both the exchange of betrothal gifts and the movement of the bride from her natal home to her husband's home. She brought with her a trousseau that provided her with clothes and other items she would need for daily life, but not land, which would have given her economic autonomy. On the other hand, her position within her new family was more secure, for it became more difficult for a husband to divorce his wife. She also gained authority within the family. If her husband was away, she managed family affairs. If her husband fathered children with concubines, she was their legal mother.

A peasant wife shared with her husband responsibility for the family's economic well-being. If of poor or middling status, she worked alongside her husband in the fields, doing the routine work while he did the heavy work. If they were farm hands and worked for wages, the wife invariably earned a third or a half less than her husband. Wives of prosperous farmers never worked in the fields, but they reeled silk, wove cloth, helped in any family business, and supervised the maids. When cotton growing spread to Japan in the sixteenth century, women took on the jobs of spinning and weaving it. Whatever their economic status, Japanese women, like women everywhere in the world, tended the children. Families were growing smaller in this period in response to the spread of single-heir inheritance. From studies of household registers, demographic historians have shown that Japanese families restricted the number of children they had by practicing abortion and infanticide, turning to adoption when no heir survived.

How was divorce initiated, and how frequent was it? Customs among the upper class differed considerably from peasant practices. Divorce in samurai society carried a social stigma; it did not among the peasantry. Widows and divorcées of the samurai elite—where female chastity was the core of fidelity—were not expected to remarry. The husband alone could initiate divorce by ordering his wife to leave or by sending her possessions to her natal home. The wife could not prevent divorce or ensure access to her children.

Among the peasant classes, divorce seems to have been fairly common—at least 15 percent in the villages near Osaka in the eighteenth century. A poor woman wanting a divorce could simply leave her husband's home. It was also possible to secure divorce through a temple. If a married woman entered the temple and performed rites there for three years, her marriage bond was dissolved. Sometimes Buddhist temple priests served as divorce brokers: they went to the village headman and had him force the husband to agree to a divorce. News of the coming of temple officials was usually enough to produce a letter of separation.

The Tokugawa period witnessed a major transformation of agriculture, a great leap in productivity and specialization. The rural population increased, but the agricultural population did not; surplus labor was drawn to other employment and to the cities. In fact, Japan suffered an acute shortage of farm labor from 1720 to 1868. In some villages, industry became almost as important as agriculture. At Hirano near Osaka, for example, 61.7 percent of all arable land was sown in cotton. The peasants had a

● **Cottage Industries** Many of the objects Japanese used in everyday life were made at home or in small workshops. These two screens show stages in the production of textiles. Male and female weavers (*left*) and dyers (*right*) worked in the vicinity of other family members, including children and the elderly. (*left: Werner Forman/Corbis; right: Sakamoto Photo Research/Corbis*)

thriving industry: they ginned the cotton locally before transporting it to wholesalers in Osaka. In many rural places, as many peasants worked in the manufacture of silk, cotton, or vegetable oil as in the production of rice.

As the ruling samurai with their fixed stipends became increasingly poorer, the despised merchants grew steadily wealthier. Merchants had no political power, but they accumulated wealth, sometimes great wealth. They also demonstrated the possibility of social mobility and thus the inherent weakness of the regime's system of strict social stratification. By contemporary standards anywhere in the world, the Japanese mercantile class lived very well. In 1705 the shogunate confiscated the property of a merchant in Osaka "for conduct unbecoming a member of the commercial class." In fact, the confiscation was at the urging of influential daimyo and samurai who owed the merchant gigantic debts. The government seized 50 pairs of gold screens, 360 carpets, several mansions, 48 granaries and warehouses scattered around the country, and hundreds of thousands of gold pieces. This merchant possessed fabulous wealth, but other merchants also lived in luxury.

MARITIME TRADE, PIRACY, AND THE ENTRY OF EUROPE INTO THE ASIAN MARITIME SPHERE

How did the sea link the countries of East Asia, and what happened when Europeans entered this maritime sphere?

In the period 1400–1800, maritime trade and piracy connected China and Japan to each other and also to Korea, Southeast Asia, and Europe. All through the period China and Japan traded extensively with each other as well as with Korea. Both Korea and Japan relied on Chinese coinage, and China relied on silver from Japan. During the fifteenth century, China launched overseas expeditions. Japan in the period was a major source of pirates. In the sixteenth century, European traders appeared, eager for Chinese porcelains and silks. Christian missionaries followed, but despite initial successes, they were later banned by the Japanese and then the Chinese governments. Political changes in Europe changed the international makeup of the European traders, from the Portuguese to the Dutch and then the British. By the eighteenth century Chinese tea had become the product in greatest demand.

Zheng He's Voyages

Early in the Ming period, the Chinese government tried to revive the tribute system of the Han (202–220 C.E.) and Tang Dynasties (618–907), when China had dominated East Asia and envoys had arrived from dozens of distant lands. To invite more countries to send missions, the third Ming emperor (Yongle) authorized an extraordinary series of voyages to the Indian Ocean under the command of the Muslim eunuch Zheng He (1371–1433; see also page 435).

Zheng He's father had made the trip to Mecca, and the seven voyages that Zheng led between 1405 and 1433 followed old Arab trade routes. The first of the seven was made by a fleet of 317 ships, of which 62 were huge, 440 feet long. Each expedition involved from twenty thousand to thirty-two thousand men. Their itineraries included stops in Vietnam, Malaysia, Indonesia, Sri Lanka, India, and, in the later voyages, Hormuz (on the coast of Persia) and East Africa (see Map 15.1 on page 432). At each stop, Zheng He went ashore to visit rulers, transmit messages of China's peaceful intentions, and bestow lavish gifts. Rulers were invited to come to China or send envoys and were offered accommodation on the return voyages. Near the Straits of Malacca, Zheng He's fleet battled Chinese pirates, bringing them under control. Zheng He made other shows of force as well, deposing rulers deemed unacceptable in Java, Sumatra, and Sri Lanka.

On the return of these expeditions, the Ming emperor was delighted by the exotic things the fleet brought back, such as giraffes and lions from Africa, fine cotton cloth from India, and gems and spices from Southeast Asia. Ma Huan, an interpreter who accompanied Zheng He, collected data on the plants, animals, peoples, and geography that they encountered and wrote a book titled *The Overall Survey of the Ocean's Shores*. Still, these expeditions were not voyages of discovery; they followed established routes and pursued diplomatic rather than commercial goals.

Why were these voyages abandoned? Officials complained about their cost and modest return. As a consequence, after 1474, all of the remaining ships with three or more masts were broken up and used for lumber. Chinese did not pull back from trade in the South China Sea and Indian Ocean, but the government no longer promoted trade, leaving the initiative to private merchants and migrants.

Piracy and Japan's Overseas Adventures

One goal of Zheng He's expeditions was to suppress piracy, which had become a problem all along the China coast. Already in the thirteenth century social disorder and banditry in Japan had expanded into seaborne banditry, some of it within the Japanese islands, around the Inland Sea, but also in the straits between Korea and Japan. Japanese "sea bandits" would raid the Korean coast, seizing rice and other goods to take back home. In the sixteenth century, bands several hundred strong would attack and loot Chinese coastal cities or hold them ransom. As maritime trade throughout East Asia grew more lively, "sea bandits" also took to attacking ships to steal their cargo. Although the pirates were called the "Japanese pirates" by both the Koreans and the Chinese, pirate gangs in fact recruited from all countries. The Ryūkyūs and Taiwan became major bases.

Possibly encouraged by the exploits of these bandits, Hideyoshi, after his victories in unifying Japan, decided to extend his territory across the seas. In 1590, after receiving congratulations from Korea on his victories, Hideyoshi sent a letter asking the Koreans to allow his armies to pass through their country, declaring that his real target was China: "Disregarding the distance of the sea and mountain reaches that lie in between, I shall in one fell swoop invade Great Ming. I have in mind to introduce Japanese customs and values to the four hundred and more provinces of that country and bestow upon it the benefits of imperial rule and culture for the coming hundred million years."[4] He also sent demands for submission to countries of Southeast Asia and to the Spanish governor of the Philippines.

In 1592 Hideyoshi mobilized 158,000 soldiers and 9,200 sailors for his invasion, and equipped them with muskets and cannon, which had recently been introduced into Japan. His forces overwhelmed Korean defenders and reached Seoul within three weeks and Pyongyang in two months. A few months later, in the middle of winter, Chinese armies arrived to help defend Korea. Japanese forces were pushed back from Pyongyang. A stalemate lasted till 1597; then Hideyoshi sent new troops. This time the Ming army and the Korean navy were more successful in resisting the Japanese. The Korean navy had for years had to defend against Japanese pirates, and was able to keep the Japanese from being able to supply or reinforce their troops. In 1598, after Hideyoshi's death, the Japanese army withdrew. Korea was left devastated. (See the feature "Listening to the Past: Keinen's Poetic Diary of the Korea Campaign" on pages 606–607.)

● **Transport of Chinese Porcelain**   Chinese blue-and-white porcelain, especially the large covered jars shown here, enjoyed enormous popularity in southwestern Asia. This Turkish miniature painting depicts several such pieces, carried for public display in a filigreed cart in a wedding procession; the porcelain was probably part of the bride's dowry. (Topkapi Saray Museum, Istanbul)

Europeans Enter the Scene

In the sixteenth century, Portuguese, Spanish, and Dutch merchants and adventurers began to participate in the East Asian maritime world. The trade between Japan, China, and Southeast Asia was very profitable, and the European traders wanted to carry some of it, as well as carry Asian goods to Europe.

The Portuguese and Dutch were not reluctant to use force to gain control of trade, and they seized outposts many places along the trade routes, including Taiwan. Moreover, they made little distinction between trade, smuggling, and piracy. In 1521 the Ming tried to ban the Portuguese from China. Two years later an expeditionary force commissioned by the Portuguese king to negotiate a friendship treaty defeated its mission by firing on Chinese warships near Guangzhou. In 1557, without informing Beijing, local Chinese officials decided that the way to regulate trade was to allow the Portuguese to build a trading post on uninhabited land near the mouth of the Pearl River. The city they built there—Macao—became the first destination for Europeans going to China until the nineteenth century, and it remained a Portuguese possession until 1999.

European products were not in demand in China, but silver was. Japan had supplied much of China's silver, but with the development of silver mines in the New World, European traders began supplying large quantities of silver to China, which had positive effects in allowing the expansion of the economy.

Chinese were quick to take advantage of the new trading ports set up by European powers. In Batavia harbor, Chinese ships outnumbered those from any other country by two or three to one. Manila, under Spanish control, and Taiwan and Batavia, both under Dutch control, all attracted thousands of Chinese colonists. Local people felt the intrusion of Chinese more than Europeans, and there were riots against Chinese that led to massacres on several occasions.

A side benefit of the appearance of European traders was New World crops. Sweet potatoes, maize, peanuts, tomatoes, chili peppers, tobacco, and other crops were quickly introduced. Sweet potatoes and maize in particular facilitated population growth because they could be grown on land previously thought too sandy or too steep to cultivate. Sweet potatoes became a common poor people's food.

Missionaries

The Spanish and Portuguese kings supported missionary activity, and merchant vessels soon brought Catholic missionaries to East Asia. The first to come were Jesuits, from the order founded by Ignatius Loyola in 1534 to promote Catholic scholarship and combat the Protestant Reformation.

The Jesuit priest Francis Xavier had worked in India and the Indies before China and Japan attracted his attention. After many misadventures, in 1549 he landed on Kyushu, Japan's southernmost island (see Map 20.2). After he was expelled by the local lord, he traveled throughout western Japan as far as Kyoto, proselytizing wherever warlords allowed. He soon made many converts among the poor and even some among the daimyo. Xavier then set his sights on China but died on an uninhabited island off the China coast in 1552.

Other missionaries carried on his work. By 1600 there were three hundred thousand baptized Christians in Japan. Most of them lived on Kyushu, where the shogun's power was weakest and the loyalty of the daimyo most doubtful. In 1615 bands of Christian samurai supported Tokugawa Ieyasu's enemies at the fierce Battle of Osaka. A couple of decades later, thirty thousand peasants in the heavily Catholic area of northern Kyushu revolted. The Tokugawa shoguns thus came to associate Christianity with domestic disorder and insurrection. Accordingly, what had been mild persecution of Christians became ruthless repression after 1639. Foreign priests were expelled or tortured, and thousands of Japanese Christians suffered crucifixion.

● **Dutch in Japan** The Japanese were curious about the appearance, dress, and habits of the Dutch who came to Deshima to trade. In this detail from a long handscroll, Dutch traders are shown interacting with a Japanese samurai in a room with tatami mats on the floor. Note also the Western musical instruments. *(Private Collection/The Bridgeman Art Library)*

Meanwhile, in China the Jesuits concentrated on gaining the linguistic and scholarly knowledge they would need to convert the educated class. The Jesuit Matteo Ricci studied for years in Macao before setting himself up in Nanjing and trying to win over members of the educated class. In 1601 he was given permission to reside in Beijing, where he made several high-placed converts. He also interested Chinese educated men in Western-style geography, astronomy, and Euclidean mathematics.

Ricci and his Jesuit successors believed that Confucianism was compatible with Christianity. Both shared similar concerns for morality and virtue. They viewed making offerings to ancestors as an expression of filial reverence rather than a form of worship. The Franciscan and Dominican mendicant orders that arrived in China in the seventeenth century disagreed. In 1715, religious and political quarrels in Europe led the pope to decide that the Jesuit's accommodating approach was heretical. Angry at this insult, the Kangxi emperor forbade all Christian missionary work in China.

Learning from the West

Although both China and Japan ended up prohibiting Christian missionary work, other aspects of Western culture were seen as impressive and worth learning. The "closed country policy" that Japan instituted in 1639 restricted Japanese from leaving the country and kept European merchants in small enclaves. Still, Japanese interest in Europe did not disappear. Through the Dutch enclave on a tiny island in Nagasaki harbor, a stream of Western ideas and inventions trickled into Japan in the eighteenth century. Western writings, architectural illustrations, calendars, watches, medicine, weapons, and paintings deeply impressed the Japanese. Western portraits and other paintings introduced the Japanese to perspective and shading.

In China, too, both individual scholars and rulers showed an interest in Western learning. The Kangxi emperor frequently discussed scientific and philosophical questions with the Jesuits at court. When he got malaria, he accepted the Jesuit's offer of the medicine quinine. He had translations made of a collection of Western works on mathematics and the calendar. The court was impressed with the Jesuits' skill in astronomy and quickly appointed them to the Board of Astronomy. In 1674, the emperor asked them to re-equip the observatory with European instruments. He and his successors employed Italian painters to make imperial portraits. Qianlong had gardens and palaces built in European designs. Firearms and mechanical clocks also were widely admired. The court established its own clock and watch factory, and in 1673 the emperor insisted that the Jesuits manufacture cannons for him and supervise gunnery practice.

There was also, of course, learning that spread in the opposite direction. Although European anatomy was recognized in both China and Japan as more advanced, medicine was not uniformly better in Europe. One Chinese practice that Europeans adopted was "variolation," an early form of smallpox inoculation. In the early eighteenth century, China enjoyed a positive reputation among the educated in Europe. The Manchu emperors were seen as wise and benevolent rulers. Voltaire wrote of the rationalism of Confucianism and saw advantages to the Chinese political system because the rulers did not put up with parasitical aristocrats or hypocritical priests.

● **Gold-Lacquered Stationery Box** The art of lacquer flourished in Japan during the Middle Ages and Tokugawa period. This lacquer box was made to hold everything one needed to write a letter: paper, brushes, an inkstick, and an inkstone (for grinding the ink and mixing it with water). The box is coated in lacquer and decorated with a landscape scene. *(Tokugawa Art Museum, Nagoya/Tokugawa Reimeikai Foundation)*

Primary Source:

Edict on Trade with Great Britain
Read how the Chinese emperor dismissed Lord Macartney's mission on behalf of Britain's "barbarian merchants."

kowtow *The ritual of kneeling on both knees and bowing one's head to the ground, performed by children to their parents and by subjects to the Chinese ruler.*

● **Porcelain Vase** Among the objects produced in China that were in high demand in Europe in the seventeenth and eighteenth centuries were colorful porcelains. In this period Chinese potters perfected the use of overglaze enamels, which allowed the application of many colors to a single object. Blue, green, yellow, orange, and red all appear on this 18-inch-tall (45.7 cm) vase. *(Image copyright © The Metropolitan Museum/Art Resource, NY)*

British Efforts to Expand Trade with China in the Eighteenth Century

The East Asian maritime world underwent many changes from the sixteenth to the eighteenth centuries. The Japanese pulled back their own traders and limited opportunities for Europeans to trade in Japan. The Qing government limited trading contacts with Europe to Guangzhou in the far south in an attempt to curb piracy. Portugal lost many of its bases to the Dutch. And by the eighteenth century, the British had become as active as the Dutch. In the seventeenth century the British and Dutch sought primarily porcelains and silk, but in the eighteenth century, tea became the commodity in most demand. By the end of the century, tea made up 80 percent of Chinese exports to Europe.

By the late eighteenth century, Britain wanted to renegotiate its relations with China. By then Britain was a great power and did not see why China should be able to dictate the terms of trade. British merchants were permitted to trade only in Guangzhou, even though tea, their principal purchase, was grown mostly in the distant Yangzi Valley (see Map 20.1). They also resented other restrictions imposed on them, such as not being allowed to enter the walled city of Guangzhou, learn Chinese, ride in sedan chairs, or bring women or weapons into the part of the city assigned to them. As British purchases of tea escalated, the balance of trade with China became increasingly lopsided. British merchants, however, could find no goods that Chinese merchants were willing to buy from them.

In the 1790s, King George III sent Lord George Macartney on a mission to China. Macartney was instructed to secure a place for British traders to live near the tea-producing areas, negotiate a commercial treaty, create a desire for British products, arrange for diplomatic representation in Beijing, and open Japan and Southeast Asia to British commerce. He traveled with an entourage of eighty-four and six hundred cases packed with British goods that he hoped would impress the Chinese court and attract trade: clocks, telescopes, knives, globes, plate glass, Wedgwood pottery, landscape paintings, woolen cloth, and carpets. The only member of the British party able to speak Chinese, however, was a twelve-year-old boy who had learned a bit of the language by talking with Chinese passengers on the long voyage.

After Lord Macartney arrived in Guangzhou in 1793, he proceeded overland. Because he would not perform the **kowtow** (kneeling on both knees and bowing his head to the ground), he was denied a formal audience in the palace. He was permitted to meet more informally with the Qianlong emperor at his summer retreat, but no negotiations followed this meeting because Qianlong saw no merit in Macartney's requests. As he pointed out in his formal reply, the Qing Empire "possesses all things in prolific abundance and lacks no product within its own borders"; thus trading with Europe was a kindness, not a necessity.[5] The Qing court was as intent on maintaining the existing system of regulated trade as Britain was intent on doing away with it.

Several members of the Macartney mission wrote books about China on their return, updating European understanding of China. These books, often illustrated, contained descriptions of many elements of Chinese culture and social customs—accounts less rosy than the reports written by the Jesuits a century or two earlier. The British writers, for instance, introduced the idea that Chinese women were oppressed, unable even to sit at the same table with their husbands to eat dinner.

Chapter Summary

To assess your mastery of this chapter, go to
bedfordstmartins.com/mckayworld

• What sort of state and society developed in China after the Mongols were ousted?

After the fall of the Mongols, China was ruled by the native Ming Dynasty for three centuries. The dynasty's founder, who knew poverty firsthand, ruled for thirty years, becoming more paranoid and despotic over time. Very few of his successors were particularly good rulers, yet China in the period thrived in many ways. Population grew. Educational levels were high as more and more men prepared for the civil service examinations. Urban culture was very lively. Novels and short stories written in the vernacular found large audiences.

• Did the return of alien rule with the Manchus have any positive consequences for China?

The Ming suffered a series of disasters, beginning with a Japanese invasion of Korea at the end of the sixteenth century, and in 1644 fell to a force from beyond the Great Wall, the Manchus. The Manchu rulers proved more competent than the Ming emperors and were able to both maintain peace and extend the empire to its maximum extent, bringing Mongolia, Tibet, and Central Asia within the empire. Population grew steadily, probably reaching 300 million or more.

• How did Japan change during this period of political instability?

Japan during the fifteenth and sixteenth centuries was fragmented by civil war. New power holders emerged in the daimyo, who built stone castles to defend their territories. As daimyo attacked and defeated each other, Japan was slowly reunified under Hideyoshi.

• What was life like in Japan during the Tokugawa peace?

After Hideyoshi's death, power was seized by Tokugawa Ieyasu, the founder of the Tokugawa Shogunate. In the seventeenth and eighteenth centuries, Japan reaped the rewards of peace. Steady economic growth and improved agricultural technology swelled the population to approximately 30 million. The samurai were transformed into peaceful city dwellers and civil bureaucrats. The wealth of the business classes grew, and the samurai, dependent on fixed agricultural rents or stipends in rice, fell into debt. The merchants created a lively urban culture, well-depicted in both fiction and the woodblock prints of the "floating world."

• How did the sea link the countries of East Asia, and what happened when Europeans entered this maritime sphere?

In the fifteenth through the eighteenth centuries, maritime trade connected the countries of Asia. Trade between China and Japan was active. Piracy, however, was a perpetual problem. Early in this period, China sent out seven naval expeditions looking to promote diplomatic contacts and trade, which went as far as Africa. In the sixteenth century, European traders arrived in China and Japan. The first traders often acted like pirates, but profitable trading relationships

(continued on page 608)

Keinen's Poetic Diary of the Korea Campaign

*T*he Buddhist priest Keinen (1534?–1611) was ordered in 1597 to accompany the local daimyo on Hideyoshi's second campaign in Korea and spent seven months there. As a Buddhist, he did not revel in military feats but rather deplored the death and suffering that he observed. Adopting the time-honored form of the poetic diary, Keinen ends each day's entry with a short poem. The excerpt quoted here begins about six weeks after he left home.

Eighth month, 4th day. Every one is trying to be the first off the ship; no one wants to lag behind. They fall over each other in trying to get at the plunder, to kill people. It is a sight I cannot bear to see.

> A hubbub rises
> as from roiling clouds and mist
> where they swarm about
> in their rage for the plunder
> of innocent people's goods.

VIII.5. They are burning the houses. As I watched them go up in smoke, I thought that my own existence was like this and was seized by sympathy.

> The "Red Country" is
> what they call it, but black is
> the smoke that rises
> from the burning houses
> where you see flames flying high.

VIII.6. The very fields and hillsides have been put to the fire, not to speak of the forts. People are put to the sword, or they are shackled with chains and bamboo tubes choking the neck. Parents sobbing for their children, children searching for their parents—never before have I seen such a pitiable sight.

> The hills are ablaze
> with the cries of soldiers
> intoxicated
> with their pyrolatry—
> the battleground of demons.

VIII.7. Looking at the various kinds of plunder amassed by them all, I formed a desire for such things. Could I really be like this, I thought, and felt ashamed. How can I attain salvation like this, I thought.

> How ashamed I am!
> For everything that I see
> I form desires—
> a creature of delusions,
> my mind full of attachments.

On the same day, as I exerted myself in reflections on my spiritual state, I felt myself more and more ashamed. And yet the Buddha has vowed not to give weight to the weightiest of evil deeds, not to abandon the most abandoned and intemperate!

> Unless it be through
> reliance on the vow of
> Amida Buddha,
> who could obtain salvation
> with such wicked thoughts as mine?

VIII.8. They are carrying off Korean children and killing their parents. Never shall they see each other again. Their mutual cries—surely this is like the torture meted out by the fiends of hell.

> It is piteous;
> when the four fledglings parted,*
> it must have been thus—
> I see the parents' lament
> over their sobbing children.

VIII.11. As night fell, I saw people's houses go up in smoke. They have lost everything to the fire, all their grain and all their property.

> How wretched it is!
> Smoke lingers still where the grain
> was burned and wasted;
> so that is where I lay my
> head tonight: on the scorched earth.

*An allusion to the proverbial tale of a mother bird's sorrow at her fledglings' departure to the four directions.

VIII.13. His lordship has set up camp about five leagues this side of Namwon. Unless this fortress is taken, our prospects are dubious; so we are to close in and invest it this evening. The word is that fifty or sixty thousand soldiers from Great Ming are garrisoning the place.

We'll solve the challenge
posed even by this fortress
of the Red Country!—
The troops rejoice to hear this,
and they rest their weary feet.

VIII.14. Rain has been falling steadily since the evening. It comes down in sheets, like a waterfall. We have put up a makeshift tent covered with oil paper only, and it is frightening how the rain pours in. It is impossible to sleep. I had to think of the story "The Devil at One Gulp" in *Tales of Ise.*[†] The night described in that tale must have been just like this.

Inexorably,
fearsome torrents beating down
remind me of that
dreadful night when the devil
at one gulp ate his victim.

VIII.15. The fortress is to be stormed before dawn tomorrow. Fascines of bamboo have been distributed to the assault troops. The sun was about to set as they worked their way close in, right up against the edge of the castle's bulwarks, and gunfire opened up from the several siege detachments, accompanied by arrows shot from short-bows. Unthinkable numbers of men were killed. As I saw them dying:

From the fortress, too,
from their short-bows, too.
How many killed? Beyond count
is the number of the dead.

The castle fell to the assault in the course of the night. Lord Hishu's troops were the first inside the walls. Needless to say, he is to get a vermilion-seal letter of commendation.

VIII.16. All in the fortress were slaughtered, to the last man and woman. No prisoners were taken. To be sure, a few were kept alive for exchange purposes.

How cruel! This world
of sorrow and inconstancy
does have one constant—
men and women, young and old
die and vanish; are no more.

Although the Japanese invasion failed, some of the warriors who fought in it were celebrated, like Kato Kiyomasa, shown here fighting a tiger in the hills of Korea. *(Courtesy, Stephen Turnbull)*

VIII.17. Until yesterday they did not know that they would have to die; today, they are transformed into the smoke of impermanence, as is the way of this world of constant change. How can I be unaffected by this!

Look! Everyone, look!
Is this, then, to be called the human condition?—
a life with a deadline,
a life with a limit: today.

Questions for Analysis

1. Which of Keinen's responses can be identified as specifically Buddhist?

2. Does Keinen's use of poetry seem natural, or do you think it seems forced?

3. What would be the purpose of bringing a Buddhist priest opposed to killing on a military campaign?

Source: Sources of Japanese Tradition, by Wm. Theodore de Bary. Copyright © 2001 by Columbia University Press. Reproduced with permission of COLUMBIA UNIVERSITY PRESS in the format Textbook via Copyright Clearance Center.

[†]This is a story of an abduction that ends badly. The lady in question, sequestered in a broken-down storehouse to keep her safe from the elements on a dark and stormy night, is devoured "at one gulp" by an ogre who dwells there.

soon developed. The Chinese economy became so dependent on huge imports of silver acquired through this trade that when supplies were cut off, it caused severe hardship. Trade with Europe brought new world crops and new ideas as well as new trade possibilities. Many of the Catholic missionaries who began to arrive were highly educated and introduced Western science and learning as well as Christianity. Both in Japan and in China, however, the government authorities in the end banned missionary work. Although the shogunate severely restricted trade, some Western scientific ideas and technology entered Japan through the port of Nagasaki. Chinese, too, took an interest in those elements of Western technology and science that seemed superior, such as firearms, clockwork, astronomy, and oil painting.

Suggested Reading

Berry, Mary Elizabeth. *The Culture of Civil War in Kyoto.* 1994. Makes use of diaries and other records to examine how people made sense of violence and social change.

Elman, Benjamin. *A Cultural History of Civil Examinations in Late Imperial China.* 2000. Provides fascinating detail on how the examination system worked.

Elvin, Mark. *The Pattern of the Chinese Past.* 1973. Offers an explanation of China's failure to maintain its technological superiority in terms of a "high-level equilibrium trap."

Keene, Donald. *Yoshimasa and the Silver Pavilion: The Creation of the Soul of Japan.* 2003. A lively introduction to the aesthetic style associated with Zen and its connection to shogunate patrons.

Mote, Frederic *Imperial China* (1999). An overview that analyzes the strengths and weaknesses of both the Ming and Qing Dynasties.

Mungello, David. *The Great Encounter of China and the West, 1500–1800.* 1999. A short but stimulating examination of the various dimensions of the first phase of Chinese-European relations.

Pomeranz, Kenneth. *The Great Divergence: China, Europe, and the Making of the Modern World Economy.* 2000. Argues that the most advanced areas of China were on a par with the most advanced regions of Europe through the eighteenth century.

Totman, Conrad. *A History of Japan.* 2000. An excellent, well-balanced survey.

Vaporis, Constantine Komitos. *Breaking Barriers: Travel and the State in Early Modern Japan.* 1994. An examination of recreational and religious travel.

Waldron, Arthur. *The Great Wall of China: From History to Myth.* 1990. Places the construction of the current Great Wall in the context of Ming-Mongol relations.

Notes

1. L. J. Gallagher, trans., *China in the Sixteenth Century: The Journals of Matthew Ricci: 1583–1610* (New York: Random House, 1953), p. 23.
2. Quoted in D. H. Shively, "Bakufu Versus Kabuki," in *Studies in the Institutional History of Early Modern Japan,* ed. J. W. Hall (Princeton, N.J.: Princeton University Press, 1970), p. 236.
3. Quoted in G. B. Sansom, *A History of Japan, 1615–1867,* vol. 3 (Stanford, Calif.: Stanford University Press, 1978), p. 99.
4. W. T. de Bary et al., eds., *Sources of Japanese Tradition from Earliest Times to 1600* (New York: Columbia University Press, 2001), p. 467.
5. Pei-kai Cheng and M. Lestz, with J. Spence, ed., *The Search for Modern China: A Documentary History* (New York: W.W. Norton, 1999), p. 106

Liberty. The figure of Liberty bears a copy of the Declaration of the Rights of Man in one hand and a pike to defend them in the other, in this painting by the female artist Nanine Vallain. The painting hung in the Jacobin Club until its fall from .power. *(Musée de la Revolution Française, Vizille/The Bridgeman Art Library)*

21 THE REVOLUTION IN POLITICS, 1775–1815

Chapter Preview

Background to Revolution
• *What social, political, and economic factors formed the background to the French Revolution?*

Revolution in Metropole and Colony (1789–1791)
• *What were the immediate events and ideas that sparked the Revolution in France and its Caribbean colony of Saint-Domingue?*

World War and Republican France (1791–1799)
• *How and why did the Revolution take a radical turn at home and in the colonies?*

The Napoleonic Era (1799–1815)
• *What factors explain the rise and fall of Napoleon Bonaparte and his loss of the colony of Saint-Domingue?*

The last years of the eighteenth century were a time of great upheaval. A series of revolutions and revolutionary wars challenged the old order of monarchs and aristocrats. The ideas of freedom and equality, ideas that continue to shape the world, flourished and spread. The revolutionary era began in North America in 1775. Then in 1789 France, the most influential country in Europe, became the leading revolutionary nation. It established first a constitutional monarchy, then a radical republic, and finally a new empire under Napoleon. Inspired by both the ideals of the Revolution and internal colonial conditions, the slaves of Saint-Domingue rose up in 1791. Their rebellion led to the creation of the new independent nation of Haiti in 1805.

The armies of France violently exported revolution beyond the nation's borders in an effort to establish new governments throughout much of Europe. The world of modern domestic and international politics was born.

BACKGROUND TO REVOLUTION

What social, political, and economic factors formed the background to the French Revolution?

The origins of the French Revolution have been one of the most debated topics in history. In order to understand the path to revolution, numerous interrelated factors must be taken into account. These include deep social changes in France, a long-term political crisis that eroded monarchical legitimacy, the impact of new political ideas derived from the Enlightenment, the emergence of a "public sphere" in which such opinions were formed and shared, and, perhaps most important, a financial crisis created by France's participation in expensive overseas wars.

Legal Orders and Social Change

As in the Middle Ages, France's 25 million inhabitants were still legally divided into three orders, or estates—the clergy, the nobility, and everyone else. As the nation's first estate, the clergy numbered about one hundred thousand and had important privileges, including exemption from regular taxes and the ability to tax landowners. The second estate consisted of some four hundred thousand nobles who owned about 25 percent of the land in France. The nobility also enjoyed special privileges associated with their exalted social position, including lighter taxes, exclusive hunting and fishing rights, monopolies on bread-baking and wine-pressing equipment, and the right to wear swords. The third estate was a conglomeration of very different social groups—prosperous merchants, lawyers, and officials along with poorer peasants, urban artisans, and unskilled day laborers—united only by their shared legal status as distinct from the nobility and clergy.

In discussing the origins of the French Revolution, historians long focused on growing tensions between the nobility and the comfortable members of the third estate, the *bourgeoisie* or upper middle class. In this formulation, the French bourgeoisie eventually rose up to lead the entire third estate in a great social revolution that destroyed feudal privileges and established a capitalist order based on individualism and a market economy.

In recent years, a flood of new research has challenged these accepted views. Above all, revisionist historians have questioned the existence of growing conflict between a capitalistic bourgeoisie and a reactionary feudal nobility in eighteenth-century France. Instead, they see both bourgeoisie and nobility as highly fragmented, riddled with internal rivalries. The ancient sword nobility, for example, was separated from the newer robe nobility by differences in wealth, education, and worldview. Differences within the bourgeoisie—between wealthy financiers and local lawyers, for example—were no less profound. Rather than standing as unified blocs against each other, nobility and bourgeoisie formed two parallel social ladders increasingly linked together at the top by wealth, marriage, and Enlightenment culture.

Revisionist historians note that the nobility and the bourgeoisie shared economic interests. Investment in land and government service were the preferred activities of both groups, and the goal of the merchant capitalist was to gain enough wealth to retire from trade, purchase an estate, and live nobly as a large landowner. At the same time, wealthy nobles often acted as aggressive capitalists, investing especially in mining, metallurgy, and foreign trade. In addition, until the Revolution actually began, key sections of both nobility and bourgeoisie were joined in opposition to the government.

Revisionists have clearly shaken the belief that the bourgeoisie and the nobility were locked in growing conflict before the Revolution. Yet they also make clear that the Old Regime had ceased to correspond with social reality by the 1780s. Legally, society was still based on rigid orders inherited from the Middle Ages. In reality, France had already moved far toward being a society based on wealth and education in which an

● **The Three Estates** In this political cartoon from 1789 a peasant of the third estate struggles under the crushing burden of a happy clergyman and a plumed nobleman. The caption—"Let's hope this game ends soon"—sets forth a program of reform that any peasant could understand. (*Réunion des Musées Nationaux/Art Resource, NY*)

A FAUT ESPERER Q'EU JEU LA FINIRA BEN TOT.

l'ituleur en Campagne Ap. 1789.

emerging elite that included both aristocratic and bourgeois notables was frustrated by a bureaucratic monarchy that continued to claim the right to absolute power.

The Crisis of Political Legitimacy

Overlaying these social changes was a century-long political and fiscal struggle between the monarchy and its opponents that was primarily enacted in the law courts. When Louis XIV died, his successor Louis XV (r. 1715–1774) was only five years old. The high courts of France—the parlements—regained the ancient right to evaluate royal decrees publicly in writing before they were registered and given the force of law. The parlements used this power to prevent the king from imposing taxes after a series of wars plunged France into fiscal crisis. The Parlement of Paris asserted that it was acting as the representative of the entire nation when it checked the king's power to levy taxes.

After years of attempting to compromise, Louis XV roused himself to defend his absolutist inheritance. His chancellor, René de Maupeou, abolished the existing parlements, exiled the vociferous members of the Parlement of Paris to the provinces, and began to tax privileged groups. Public opinion sided with the parlements, however, and there was widespread criticism of "royal despotism." The king also came under attack for his many mistresses and lost the sacred aura of God's anointed on earth.

Despite this progressive **desacralization** of the monarchy, its power was still great enough to quell opposition, and Louis XV would probably have prevailed if he had lived long enough, but he died in 1774. The new king, Louis XVI (r. 1774–1792), a shy twenty-year-old with good intentions, yielded in the face of vehement opposition from France's educated elite. He dismissed chancellor Maupeou and recalled the parlements. Louis also waffled on the economy, dismissing controller general Turgot when his attempts to liberalize the economy drew fire. A weakened but unreformed monarchy now faced a judicial opposition that claimed to speak for the entire French nation. The country was drifting toward renewed financial crisis and political upheaval.

The Impact of the American Revolution

Coinciding with the first years of Louis XVI's reign, the American Revolution had an enormous practical and ideological impact on France. French expenses to support the colonists bankrupted the Crown, while the ideals of liberty and equality provided heady inspiration for political reform.

Like the French Revolution, the American Revolution originated in struggles over taxes. The high cost of the Seven Years' War—fought with little financial contribution from the colonies—doubled the British national debt. When the government tried to recoup its losses in increased taxes on the colonies in 1765, the colonists reacted with anger.

Chronology

1775–1783	American Revolution
1786–1789	Financial crisis in France
1789	Feudalism abolished in France; ratification of U.S. Constitution; storming of the Bastille
1789–1799	French Revolution
1790	Burke, *Reflections on the Revolution in France*
1791	Slave insurrection in Saint-Domingue
1792	Wollstonecraft, *A Vindication of the Rights of Woman*
1793	Execution of Louis XVI
1793–1794	Economic controls to help poor in France; Robespierre's Reign of Terror
1794	Robespierre deposed and executed
1794–1799	Thermidorian reaction
1799–1815	Napoleonic era
1804	Haitian republic declares independence
1812	Napoleon invades Russia
1814–1815	Napoleon defeated and exiled

desacralization *The removal (during the reigns of Louis XV and Louis XVI) of the divine sanction that had undergirded the absolutism of Louis XIV.*

The key questions were political rather than economic. To what extent could the home government assert its power while limiting the authority of colonial legislatures? Accordingly, who should represent the colonies, and who had the right to make laws for Americans? The British government replied that Americans were represented in Parliament, albeit indirectly (like most British people themselves), and that the absolute supremacy of Parliament throughout the empire could not be questioned. Many Americans felt otherwise.

In 1773 the dispute reignited after the British government awarded a monopoly on Chinese tea to the East India Company, excluding colonial merchants from a lucrative business. In response, Boston men disguised as Indians held a rowdy "tea party" and threw the company's tea into the harbor. This led to extreme measures. The so-called Coercive Acts closed the port of Boston, curtailed local elections, and expanded the royal governor's power. County conventions in Massachusetts urged that the acts be "rejected as the attempts of a wicked administration to enslave America." Other colonial assemblies joined the protest. In September 1774 the First Continental Congress met in Philadelphia, where the more radical members argued successfully against concessions to the Crown. Compromise was also rejected by the British Parliament, and in April 1775 fighting began at Lexington and Concord.

The fighting spread, and the colonists moved slowly toward open rebellion. The uncompromising attitude of the British government and its use of German mercenaries dissolved long-standing loyalties to the home country. Many "Loyalists" who wished to remain within the empire emigrated to the northern colonies of Canada.

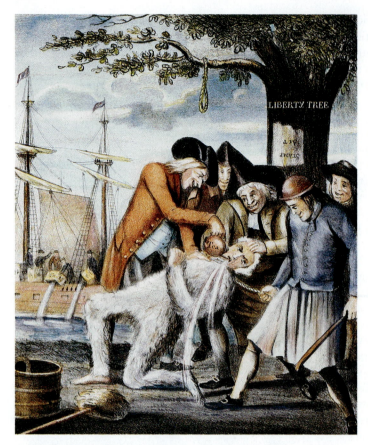

● **Toward Revolution in Boston**　The Boston Tea Party was only one of many angry confrontations between British officials and Boston patriots. On January 27, 1774, an angry crowd seized a British customs collector and tarred and feathered him. This French engraving of 1784 commemorates the defiant and provocative action. *(The Granger Collection, New York)*

Primary Source:
The U.S. Declaration of Independence
Read a selection from Jefferson's famous text, which lays out the Enlightenment principles on which the United States was founded.

On July 4, 1776, the Second Continental Congress adopted the Declaration of Independence. Written by Thomas Jefferson, it boldly listed the tyrannical acts committed by George III (r. 1760–1820) and proclaimed the sovereignty of the American states. It also universalized the traditional rights of English people, stating that "all men are created equal, that they are endowed by their Creator with certain unalienable Rights, that among these are Life, Liberty, and the Pursuit of Happiness." By 1780, all thirteen states had adopted their own written constitutions.

On the international scene, the French wanted revenge for the humiliating defeats of the Seven Years' War. They sympathized with the rebels and supplied guns and gunpowder from the beginning. By 1777 French volunteers were arriving in Virginia, and a dashing young nobleman, the marquis de Lafayette (1757–1834), became one of Washington's most trusted generals. In 1778 the French government offered a formal alliance to the American ambassador in Paris, Benjamin Franklin, and in 1779 and 1780 the Spanish and Dutch declared war on Britain. Catherine the Great of Russia helped organize the League of Armed Neutrality in order to protect neutral shipping rights, which Britain refused to recognize.

Thus by 1780 Great Britain was at war with most of Europe as well as against the thirteen colonies. Outnumbered and suffering severe reverses, a new British government offered peace on generous terms. By the Treaty of Paris of 1783, Britain recognized the independence of the thirteen colonies and ceded vast territory between the

Allegheny Mountains and the Mississippi River to the Americans. In 1787 the Federal Convention met in Philadelphia to draft the new Constitution of the United States.

Europeans who dreamed of a new era were fascinated by the American Revolution. The Americans had begun with a revolutionary defense against tyrannical oppression, and they had been victorious. They had then shown how rational beings could assemble to exercise sovereignty and form a new social contract. All this gave greater reality to the concepts of individual liberty and representative government and reinforced a primary Enlightenment ideal: that a better world was possible.

No country felt the consequences of the American Revolution more directly than France. Hundreds of French officers were inspired by service in America, the marquis de Lafayette chief among them. French intellectuals engaged in passionate analysis of the new federal and state constitutions. Perhaps most importantly, the war's expenses provided the last nail in the coffin for the French treasury.

Financial Crisis

The French Revolution thus had its immediate origins in the king's financial difficulties. Thwarted in its efforts to reform the tax system, the royal government was forced to finance its contribution to the American Revolutionary with borrowed money. As a result, the national debt and the annual budget deficit soared.

By the 1780s, fully 50 percent of France's annual budget went for interest payments on the debt. Another 25 percent went to maintain the military, while 6 percent was absorbed by the king and his court at Versailles. Less than 20 percent of the national budget was available for productive functions, such as transportation and general administration. This was an impossible financial situation.

Louis XVI's minister of finance revived old proposals to impose a general tax on all landed property as well as to form provincial assemblies to administer the tax, and he convinced the king to call an **Assembly of Notables** to gain support for the idea. The notables, mainly important noblemen and high-ranking clergy, opposed the new tax. In exchange for their support, they demanded that control over government spending be given to the provincial assemblies. When the government refused, the notables responded that such sweeping reforms required the approval of the Estates General, the representative body of all three estates, which had not met since 1614.

Assembly of Notables *A consulting body of eminent nobles and clergymen that convened to advise the king of France in 1788 and 1789.*

Facing imminent bankruptcy, the king tried to reassert his authority. He dismissed the notables and established new taxes by decree. The Parlement of Paris promptly declared them null and void. When the king tried to exile the judges, a wave of protest erupted. Frightened investors also refused to advance more loans to the state. Finally, in July 1788, Louis XVI bowed to public opinion and called for a spring session of the Estates General.

REVOLUTION IN METROPOLE AND COLONY (1789–1791)

What were the immediate events and ideas that sparked the Revolution in France and its Caribbean colony of Saint-Domingue?

Although inspired by the ideals of the American Revolution, the French Revolution did not mirror the American example. It was more radical and more complex, more influential and more controversial, more loved and more hated. For Europeans and most of the rest of the world, it was the great revolution of the eighteenth century, *the* revolution that opened the modern era in politics. In turn, the slave insurrection in Saint-Domingue—which ultimately resulted in the second independent republic of the Americas—inspired liberation movements across the world.

The Formation of the National Assembly

Estates General *A legislative body in pre-revolutionary France made up of representatives of each of the three classes, or estates; it was called into session in 1789 for the first time since 1614.*

Once Louis had agreed to hold the **Estates General,** following precedent, he set elections for the three orders. Elected officials from the noble order were primarily conservatives from the provinces, but fully one-third of the nobility's representatives were liberals committed to major changes. The third estate elected lawyers and government officials to represent them, with few delegates representing business or the working poor.

As at previous meetings of the Estates General, local assemblies were to prepare a list of grievances for their representatives to bring to the next electoral level. The petitions for change coming from the three estates showed a surprising degree of consensus. There was general agreement that royal absolutism should give way to a constitutional monarchy in which laws and taxes would require the consent of the Estates General in regular meetings. All agreed that individual liberties should be guaranteed by law and economic regulations loosened. The striking similarities in the grievance petitions of the clergy, nobility, and third estate reflected a shared platform of basic reform among the educated elite.

Yet an increasingly bitter quarrel undermined this consensus: *how* would the Estates General vote, and *who* would lead political reorganization? The Estates General of 1614 had sat as three separate houses. Each house held one vote, despite the fact that the third estate represented the vast majority of France. Given the close ties between them, the nobility and clergy would control all decisions. As soon as the estates were called, the aristocratic Parlement of Paris ruled that the Estates General should once again sit separately. In response to protests from some reform-minded critics, the government agreed that the third estate should have as many delegates as the clergy and the nobility combined but then rendered this act meaningless by upholding voting by separate order.

National Assembly *The first French revolutionary legislature, a constituent assembly made up primarily of representatives of the third estate and a few nobles and clergy who joined them, in session from 1789 to 1791.*

Meeting in May 1789, the estates were almost immediately deadlocked. Delegates of the third estate refused to transact any business until the king ordered the clergy and nobility to sit with them in a single body. Finally, after a six-week war of nerves, a few parish priests began to go over to the third estate, which on June 17 voted to call itself the **"National Assembly."** On June 20 the delegates of the third estate, excluded from their hall because of "repairs," moved to a large indoor tennis court. There they swore the famous Oath of the Tennis Court, pledging not to disband until they had written a new constitution.

The king's response was ambivalent. On June 23 he made a conciliatory speech urging reforms to a joint session, and four days later he ordered the three estates to meet together. At the same time, the vacillating monarch apparently followed the advice of relatives and court nobles who urged him to dissolve the Estates General by force. Belatedly asserting his "divine right" to rule, the king called an army of eighteen thousand troops toward Versailles, and on July 11 he dismissed his finance minister and other liberal ministers.

The Revolt of the Poor and the Oppressed

While delegates of the third estate pressed for political rights, economic hardship gripped the common people. A poor grain harvest in 1788 caused the price of bread to soar, unleashing a classic economic depression of the preindustrial age. Demand for manufactured goods collapsed, and thousands were thrown out of work. By the end of 1789 almost half of the French people were in need of relief. In Paris perhaps 150,000 of the city's 600,000 people were unemployed in July 1789.

Against this background of political and economic crisis, the people of Paris entered decisively onto the revolutionary stage. They believed that they should have steady work and adequate bread at fair prices. They also feared that the dismissal of the king's moderate finance minister would put them at the mercy of aristocratic landowners and grain speculators. As rumors spread that the king's troops would sack the city, angry crowds formed and demanded action. On July 13 the people began to seize arms for the defense of the city, and on July 14 several hundred people marched to the Bastille in search of weapons.

The Bastille, once a medieval fortress, was a detested royal prison. Its panicked governor ordered his men to resist, killing ninety-eight people attempting to enter. Fighting continued until the prison surrendered. The next day a committee of citizens appointed the marquis de Lafayette commander of the city's armed forces. Paris was lost to the king, who was forced to recall the finance minister and disperse his troops. The popular uprising had saved the National Assembly. As the delegates resumed their debates, the countryside sent a radical message. Throughout France peasants began to rise against their lords, ransacking manor houses and burning feudal documents that recorded their obligations. In some areas peasants reinstated traditional village practices, undoing recent enclosures and reoccupying common lands. Fear of vagabonds and outlaws—called the **Great Fear** by contemporaries—seized the countryside and fanned the flames of rebellion. The long-suffering peasants were doing their best to free themselves from manorial rights and exploitation.

In the end, they were successful. On the night of August 4, 1789, the delegates at Versailles agreed to abolish noble privileges—peasant serfdom where it still existed, exclusive hunting rights, fees for justice, village monopolies, and a host of other dues. Thus the French peasantry achieved an unprecedented victory in the early days of revolutionary upheaval. Henceforth, French peasants would seek mainly to protect their achievements. As the Great Fear subsided in the countryside, they became a force for order and stability.

Great Fear *In the summer of 1789, the fear of vagabonds and outlaws that seized the French countryside and fanned the flames of revolution.*

A Limited Monarchy

The National Assembly moved forward. On August 27, 1789, it issued the Declaration of the Rights of Man, which stated, "Men are born and remain free and equal in rights." The declaration also maintained that mankind's natural rights are "liberty, property, security, and resistance to oppression" and that "every man is presumed innocent until he is proven guilty." As for law, "it is an expression of the general will; all citizens have the right to concur personally or through their representatives in its formation. . . . Free expression of thoughts and opinions is one of the most precious rights of mankind: every citizen may therefore speak, write, and publish freely." In short, this clarion call of the liberal revolutionary ideal guaranteed equality before the law, representative government for a sovereign people, and individual freedom. The declaration was disseminated throughout France and Europe and around the world.

Moving beyond general principles to draft a constitution proved difficult. The questions of how much power the king should retain and whether he could veto legislation led to another deadlock. Once again the decisive answer came from the poor—in this instance, the poor women of Paris. Women customarily managed poor families' slender resources. The economic crisis worsened after the fall of the Bastille, as aristocrats fled the country and the luxury market collapsed. Foreign markets also shrunk, and unemployment grew.

On October 5 some seven thousand desperate women marched the twelve miles from Paris to Versailles to demand action. This great crowd invaded the Assembly, "armed with scythes, sticks and pikes." One tough old woman defiantly shouted into the debate, "Who's that talking down there? Make the chatterbox shut up. That's not the point: the point is that we want bread."[1] Hers was the genuine voice of the people, essential to any understanding of the French Revolution.

The women invaded the royal apartments, killed some of the royal bodyguards, and searched for the queen, Marie Antoinette, who was widely despised for her frivolous

Primary Source:
The Declaration of Rights of Man and Citizen
This document, drafted by the National Assembly of France, is an Enlightenment cousin of Jefferson's Declaration.

a Versaille a Versaille. du 5. Octobre 1789.

● **The Women of Paris March to Versailles**   On October 5, 1789, a large group of Parisian market women marched to Versailles to protest the price of bread. For the people of Paris, the king was the baker of last resort, responsible for feeding his people during times of scarcity. The crowd forced the royal family to return with them and to live in Paris, rather than remain isolated from their subjects at court. *(Erich Lessing/Art Resource, NY)*

constitutional monarchy   *A form of government in which the king retains his position as head of state, while the authority to tax and make new laws resides in an elected body.*

and supposedly immoral behavior. The intervention of Lafayette and the National Guard saved the royal family from harm. But the only way to calm the disorder was for the king to live in Paris, as the crowd demanded.

The National Assembly followed the king to Paris, and the next two years, until September 1791, saw the consolidation of the liberal revolution. The National Assembly abolished the nobility as a legal order and pushed forward with the creation of a **constitutional monarchy,** which Louis XVI reluctantly accepted in July 1790. In the final constitution, the king remained the head of state, but lawmaking power was placed in the hands of the National Assembly. New laws broadened women's rights to seek divorce, to inherit property, and to obtain financial support for illegitimate children from fathers, but women were not allowed to hold political office or even vote. The men of the National Assembly believed that civic virtue would be restored if women focused on child rearing and domestic duties.

The National Assembly replaced the patchwork of historic provinces with eighty-three departments of approximately equal size. The jumble of weights and measures that varied from province to province was reformed, leading to the introduction of the metric system in 1793. Monopolies, guilds, and workers' associations were prohibited, and barriers to trade within France were abolished in the name of economic liberty. Thus the National Assembly applied the critical spirit of the Enlightenment in a thorough reform of France's laws and institutions.

The Assembly also imposed a radical reorganization on the country's religious life. It granted religious freedom to French Jews and Protestants. It nationalized the Catholic Church's property, used it as collateral to guarantee a new paper currency, the *assignats* and then sold the property in an attempt to put the state's finances on a solid footing.

Imbued with Enlightenment rationalism, delegates distrusted popular piety and "superstitious religion." Thus they established a national church with priests chosen by voters. The National Assembly forced the Catholic clergy to take a loyalty oath to the new government. The pope formally condemned these actions, and only half of French priests swore the oath. Many sincere Christians, especially those in the countryside, were upset by these changes. The attempt to remake the Catholic Church, like the Assembly's abolition of guilds and workers' associations, sharpened the conflict between the educated classes and the common people that had been emerging in the eighteenth century.

Revolutionary Aspirations in Saint-Domingue

On the eve of the Revolution, French Saint-Domingue—the most profitable of all Caribbean colonies—was even more rife with social tensions than France itself. The island was composed of a variety of social groups who resented and mistrusted one another. The European population included French colonial officials, wealthy plantation owners and merchants, and poor immigrants. Greatly outnumbering the white population were the colony's five hundred thousand slaves, along with a sizable population of free people of African and mixed African European descent. This last group referred to it members as "free coloreds" or *"free people of color."*

free people of color *Free people of African or partly African descent living in the French isles of the Caribbean.*

The political turmoil of the 1780s, with its rhetoric of liberty, equality, and fraternity, raised new challenges and possibilities for each group. For slaves, abolitionist agitation in France and the royal government's attempts to rein in the abuses of slavery led to hope that the mother country might grant them freedom. Free people of color found in such rhetoric the principles on which to base claims for legal and political rights. They hoped for political enfranchisement and to regain legal rights that had been rescinded by colonial administrators. The white elite looked to revolutionary ideals of representative government for the chance to gain control of their own affairs, as had the American colonists before them. The meeting of the Estates General and the Declaration of the Rights of Man and Citizen raised these conflicting colonial aspirations to new levels.

The National Assembly, however, frustrated all of their hopes. It allowed each colony to draft its own constitution, with free rein over decisions on slavery and enfranchisement. After dealing this blow to the aspirations of slaves and free coloreds, the committee also reaffirmed French monopolies over colonial trade, thereby angering planters as well.

Following a failed revolt in Saint-Domingue led by Vincent Ogé, a free man of color, the National Assembly attempted a compromise. It granted political rights to free people of color born to two free parents who possessed sufficient property. The white elite of Saint-Domingue was furious, and the colonial governor refused to enact the legislation. Violence now erupted between groups of whites and free coloreds. The liberal revolution had failed to satisfy contradictory ambitions in the colonies.

WORLD WAR AND REPUBLICAN FRANCE (1791–1799)

How and why did the Revolution take a radical turn at home and in the colonies?

When Louis XVI accepted the National Assembly's constitution in September 1791, a young provincial lawyer and delegate named Maximilien Robespierre (1758–1794) concluded, "The Revolution is over." Robespierre was both right and wrong. He was right in the sense that the most constructive and lasting reforms were in place. Nothing substantial in the way of liberty and fundamental reform would be gained in the next generation. He was wrong in the sense that a much more radical stage lay ahead.

New heroes and new ideologies were to emerge in revolutionary wars and international conflict in which Robespierre himself would play a central role.

Foreign Reactions and the Beginning of War

Revolution in France produced great excitement and a sharp division of opinion in Europe and the United States. Liberals and radicals saw a mighty triumph of liberty over despotism. In Great Britain especially, they hoped that the French example would undo the landed elite's stronghold over Parliament. Conservative leaders, such as Edmund Burke (1729–1797), were deeply troubled by the Revolution. In 1790 Burke published *Reflections on the Revolution in France,* which defended inherited privileges in general and those of the English monarchy and aristocracy in particular. He predicted that thoroughgoing reform like that occurring in France would lead only to chaos and tyranny. Burke's work sparked much debate.

One passionate rebuttal came from a young writer in London, Mary Wollstonecraft (1759–1797). Incensed by Burke's book, Wollstonecraft wrote a blistering, widely read response, *A Vindication of the Rights of Man* (1790). Then she made a daring intellectual leap, developing for the first time the logical implications of natural-law philosophy in her masterpiece, *A Vindication of the Rights of Woman* (1792). To fulfill the still-unrealized potential of the French Revolution and to eliminate sexual inequality, she demanded that

the Rights of Women be respected . . . [and] JUSTICE for one-half of the human race. . . . It is time to effect a revolution in female manners, time to restore to them their lost dignity, and make them, as part of the human species, labor, by reforming themselves, to reform the world.

Wollstonecraft advocated rigorous coeducation, which would make women better wives and mothers, good citizens, and economically independent. Women could manage businesses and enter politics if only men would give them the chance. Wollstonecraft's analysis testified to the power of the Revolution to inspire outside of France. Paralleling ideas put forth independently in France by Olympe de Gouges (1748–1793), a self-taught writer and woman of the people (see the feature "Listening to the Past: Revolution and Women's Rights" on pages 638–639), Wollstonecraft's work marked the birth of the modern women's movement for equal rights.

European rulers, who had at first welcomed the revolution in France as weakening a competing monarchy, realized that their power was also threatened. In June 1791, Louis XVI and Marie-Antoinette were arrested and returned to Paris after trying unsuccessfully to slip out of France. The shock of this arrest led the monarchs of Austria and Prussia to issue the Declaration of Pillnitz in August 1791. This carefully worded statement declared their willingness to intervene in France in certain circumstances and was expected to prevent revolutionary excesses without causing war.

But the crowned heads of Europe misjudged France's revolutionary spirit. The representative body, known as the Legislative Assembly, that convened in October 1791 had new delegates and a different character. Most of the legislators were still prosperous and well-educated, but they were younger and less cautious than their predecessors. Many belonged to a political club called the **Jacobin club,** after the name of the former monastery in which they met. Such clubs had proliferated in Parisian neighborhoods since the beginning of the Revolution, drawing men and women to debate the burning political questions of the day.

The new Legislative Assembly representatives reacted with patriotic fury against the Declaration of Pillnitz. If the kings of Europe were attempting to incite war against France, then "we will incite a war of people against kings. . . . Ten million Frenchmen, kindled by the fire of liberty, armed with the sword, with reason, with eloquence

Jacobin club *In revolutionary France, a political club whose members were a radical republican group.*

● **The Capture of Louis XVI, June 1791** This painting commemorates a dramatic turning point in the French Revolution, the midnight arrest of Louis XVI and the royal family as they tried to flee France in disguise and reach counter-revolutionaries in the Austrian Netherlands. Recognized and stopped at Varennes, the royal family was returned to house arrest in Paris. *(Bibliothèque nationale de France)*

would be able to change the face of the world and make the tyrants tremble on their thrones."[2] In April 1792 France declared war on Francis II, the Habsburg monarch.

France's crusade against tyranny went poorly at first. Prussian forces joined Austria against the French, who broke and fled at their first military encounter with this First Coalition. The road to Paris lay open, and it is possible that only conflict between the eastern monarchs over the division of Poland saved France from defeat.

The Legislative Assembly declared the country in danger, and volunteers rallied to the capital. In this supercharged atmosphere, rumors spread of treason by the king and queen. On August 10, 1792, a revolutionary crowd attacked the royal palace at the Tuileries, while the king and his family fled for their lives to the nearby Legislative Assembly. Rather than offering refuge, the Assembly suspended the king from all his functions, imprisoned him, and called for a new National Convention to be elected by universal male suffrage.

The Second Revolution

second revolution *From 1792 to 1795, the second phase of the French Revolution during which the fall of the French monarchy introduced a rapid radicalization of politics.*

The fall of the monarchy initiated a rapid radicalization of the Revolution, a phase often called the **second revolution.** Louis's imprisonment was followed by the September Massacres. Wild stories that imprisoned aristocrats and priests were plotting with the allied invaders seized the city. Angry crowds invaded the prisons of Paris and slaughtered half the men and women they found. In late September 1792 the new, popularly elected National Convention proclaimed France a republic.

The republic sought to create a new popular culture, fashioning symbols that broke with the past and glorified the new order. Its new revolutionary calendar eliminated saints' days and renamed the days and the months after the seasons of the year, while also adding secular holidays designed to instill a love of nation. These secular celebrations were less successful in villages, where Catholicism was stronger.

Girondists *A group contesting control of the National Convention in France; it was named after a department in southwestern France.*

All members of the National Convention were republicans, and at the beginning almost all belonged to the Jacobin club of Paris. But the Jacobins themselves were increasingly divided into two bitterly opposed groups—the **Girondists,** named after a department in southwestern France that was home to several of their leaders, and **the Mountain,** led by Robespierre and another young lawyer, Georges Jacques Danton. In Paris the National Convention was locked in a life-and-death political struggle between the Mountain and the more moderate Girondists. A majority of the indecisive Convention members, seated in the "Plain" below, floated back and forth between the rival factions.

the Mountain *The radical faction of the National Convention led by Robespierre. So called because its members sat in the uppermost benches on the left side of the assembly hall. The source of the modern division of political ideologies into "Left" and "Right."*

This division emerged clearly after the National Convention overwhelmingly convicted Louis XVI of treason. The Girondists accepted his guilt but did not wish to put the king to death. By a narrow majority, the Mountain carried the day, and Louis was executed on January 21, 1793, on the newly invented guillotine. Both the Girondists and the Mountain were determined to continue the "war against tyranny." The Prussians had been stopped at the Battle of Valmy in September 1792. French armies then invaded Savoy, moved into the German Rhineland, and by November 1792 were occupying the entire Austrian Netherlands (modern Belgium). Everywhere they went French armies of occupation chased the princes, abolished feudalism, and "liberated" the people.

But French armies also lived off the land, requisitioning supplies and plundering local treasures. The liberators looked increasingly like foreign invaders. International tensions mounted. In February 1793 the National Convention, at war with Austria and Prussia, declared war on Britain, Holland, and Spain as well. Republican France was now at war with almost all Europe, a great war that would last almost without interruption until 1815.

Conflict within France added to the turmoil. Peasants in western France revolted against being drafted into the army, and devout Catholics, royalists, and foreign agents encouraged their rebellion. In Paris the National Convention was locked in a life-and-death political struggle between the Girondists and the more moderate Mountain. With the political system bitterly divided, the laboring poor of Paris emerged as the decisive political factor. The laboring poor and the petty traders were often known as the **sans-culottes,** "without breeches," because their men wore trousers instead of the knee breeches of the aristocracy and bourgeoisie. The sans-culottes demanded radical political action to guarantee their daily bread. The Mountain joined with sans-culottes activists in the city government to engineer a popular uprising that forced the Convention to arrest thirty-one Girondist deputies for treason on June 2. All power passed to the Mountain.

sans-culottes *The name for the laboring poor of Paris, so called because the men wore trousers instead of the knee breeches of the aristocracy and middle class; it came to refer to the militant radicals of the city.*

The Convention also formed a Committee of Public Safety to deal with the threats to the Revolution. Led by Robespierre, the committee obtained dictatorial power. Moderates in leading provincial cities, such as Lyons and Marseilles, revolted against excessive central control. The peasant revolt also spread, and the republic's armies were driven back on all fronts. By July 1793 only the areas around Paris and on the eastern frontier were firmly held. Defeat seemed imminent.

The French Revolution

May 5, 1789	Estates General convene at Versailles.
June 17, 1789	Third estate declares itself the National Assembly.
June 20, 1789	Oath of the Tennis Court is sworn.
July 14, 1789	Storming of the Bastille occurs.
July–August 1789	Great Fear ravages the countryside.
August 4, 1789	National Assembly abolishes feudal privileges.
August 27, 1789	National Assembly issues Declaration of the Rights of Man.
October 5, 1789	Women march on Versailles and force royal family to return to Paris.
November 1789	National Assembly confiscates church lands.
July 1790	Civil Constitution of the Clergy establishes a national church. Louis XVI reluctantly agrees to accept a constitutional monarchy.
June 1791	Royal family is arrested while attempting to flee France.
August 1791	Austria and Prussia issue the Declaration of Pillnitz. Slave insurrections break out in Saint-Domingue.
April 1792	France declares war on Austria.
August 1792	Parisian mob attacks the palace and takes Louis XVI prisoner.
September 1792	September Massacres occur. National Convention declares France a republic and abolishes monarchy.
January 1793	Louis XVI is executed.
February 1793	France declares war on Britain, Holland, and Spain. Revolts take place in some provincial cities.
March 1793	Bitter struggle occurs in the National Convention between Girondists and the Mountain.
April–June 1793	Robespierre and the Mountain organize the Committee of Public Safety and arrest Girondist leaders.
September 1793	Price controls are instituted to aid the sans-culottes and mobilize the war effort. British troops invade Saint-Domingue.
1793–1794	Reign of Terror darkens Paris and the provinces.
February 1794	National Convention abolishes slavery in all French territories.
Spring 1794	French armies are victorious on all fronts.
July 1794	Robespierre is executed. Thermidorian reaction begins.
1795–1799	Directory rules.
1795	Economic controls are abolished, and suppression of the sans-culottes begins. Toussaint L'Ouverture named brigadier general.
1797	Napoleon defeats Austrian armies in Italy and returns triumphant to Paris.
1798	Austria, Great Britain, and Russia form the Second Coalition against France.
1799	Napoleon overthrows the Directory and seizes power.

Des Tetes! — du Sang! — la Mort! — à la Lanterne! à la Guillotine! — point de Reine! — Je suis la Deesse de la Liberté! — l'egalité! — que Londres soit brulé! — que Paris soit Libre! — Vive la Guillotine! —

Miss Mary Stokes delt.

A PARIS BELLE.

Pubd Feby 26. 1794, by H. Humphrey No. 18 Old Bond Street

● **Contrasting Visions of the Sans-Culottes** The woman on the left, with her playful cat and calm simplicity, suggests how the French sans-culottes saw themselves as democrats and virtuous citizens. The ferocious sans-culotte harpy on the right, a creation of wartime England's vivid counter-revolutionary imagination, screams for more blood, more death: "I am the Goddess of Liberty! Long live the guillotine!" (Bibliothèque nationale de France)

Total War and the Terror

A year later, in July 1794, the Austrian Netherlands and the Rhineland were once again in the hands of French armies, and the First Coalition was falling apart. This remarkable reversal stemmed from the revolutionary government's success in harnessing, for perhaps the first time in history, the forces of a planned economy, revolutionary terror, and modern nationalism in a total war effort.

Robespierre and the Committee of Public Safety first collaborated with the fiercely patriotic sans-culottes to establish a **planned economy**. Rather than let supply and demand determine prices, the government set maximum allowable prices for key products. The most important was bread. Rationing was introduced, and bakers were permitted to make only the "bread of equality"—a brown bread made of a mixture of all available flours. The poor of Paris may not have eaten well, but at least they ate.

They also worked, mainly to produce arms and munitions for the war effort. The government told craftsmen what to produce, nationalized many small workshops, and requisitioned raw materials and grain. The second revolution and the ascendancy of the sans-culottes had produced an embryonic emergency socialism, which thoroughly frightened Europe's propertied classes and had great influence on the subsequent development of socialist ideology.

planned economy *In response to inflation and high unemployment, Robespierre and the government set maximum prices for products, rather than relying on supply and demand.*

Second, while radical economic measures supplied the poor with bread and the armies with weapons, the **Reign of Terror** (1793–1794) used revolutionary terror to solidify the home front. Special revolutionary courts tried "enemies of the nation" for political crimes. Some forty thousand French men and women were executed or died in prison. Another three hundred thousand suspects were arrested.

The third and perhaps most decisive element in the French republic's victory over the First Coalition was its ability to draw on the explosive power of patriotic dedication to a national mission. An essential part of modern **nationalism,** this commitment was something new in history. With their common identity newly reinforced by the ideas of popular sovereignty and democracy, large numbers of French people were stirred by a common loyalty. They developed an intense emotional commitment to the defense of the nation and saw the war as a life-and-death struggle between good and evil.

The fervor of nationalism combined with the all-out mobilization of resources made the French army virtually unstoppable. After August 1793 all unmarried young men were subject to the draft, resulting in the largest fighting force in the history of European warfare. French armed forces outnumbered their enemies almost four to one.[3] French generals used mass assaults at bayonet point to overwhelm the enemy. "No maneuvering, nothing elaborate," declared the fearless General Hoche. "Just cold steel, passion and patriotism."[4] By spring 1794 French armies were victorious on all fronts. The republic was saved.

Reign of Terror   *The period from 1793 to 1794, during which Robespierre used revolutionary terror to solidify the home front of France. Some 40,000 French men and women were killed during this period.*

nationalism   *Patriotic dedication to a national state and mission; it was a decisive element in the French republic's victory.*

● **Slave Revolt on Saint-Domingue**   Starting in August 1791 the slaves of Saint-Domingue rose in revolt. *(Giraudon/Art Resource, NY)*

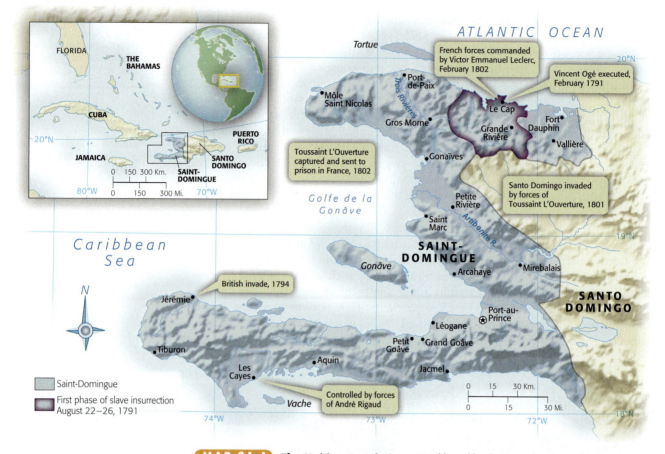

MAP 21.1 **The Haitian Revolution** Neighbored by the Spanish colony of Santo Domingo, Saint-Domingue was the most profitable European colony in the Caribbean. In 1770 the French transferred the capital from Le Cap to Port-au-Prince, which became capital of the newly independent Haïti in 1804. Slave revolts erupted in the north, near Le Cap, in 1791.

Revolution in Saint-Domingue

The second stage of revolution in Saint-Domingue (see Map 21.1) also resulted from decisive action from below. In August 1791 groups of slaves organized a revolt that spread across much of the northern plain. By the end of August the uprising was "10,000 strong, divided into 3 armies, of whom 700 or 800 are on horseback, and tolerably well-armed."[5] During the next month slaves attacked and destroyed hundreds of sugar and coffee plantations.

On April 4, 1792, as war loomed with the European states, the National Assembly issued a decree enfranchising all free blacks and free people of color. This move was intended to gain loyalty against the slave rebellion and stabilize the colony, a vital source of income for the French state.

Less than two years later, on February 4, 1794, the Convention abolished slavery throughout its Caribbean colonies, and in 1795 granted former slaves full political rights. The National Convention was forced to make these concessions when Saint-Domingue came under siege from Spanish and British troops hoping to capture the profitable colony. With former slaves and free colored forces on their side, the French gradually regained control of the island in 1796.

The key leader in the French victory was General Toussaint L'Ouverture (1743–1803), who was named commander of the western province of Saint-Domingue. (See the feature "Individuals in Society: Toussaint L'Ouverture" on page 633.) The increasingly conservative nature of the French government, however, threatened to undo the gains made by former slaves and free people of color. As exiled planters gained a stronger voice in French policymaking, L'Ouverture and other local leaders grew ever more wary of what the future might hold.

The Thermidorian Reaction and the Directory (1794–1799)

With the French army victorious, Robespierre and the Committee of Public Safety relaxed emergency economic controls, but they extended the political Reign of Terror. In March 1794, he wiped out many of his critics as well as long-standing collaborators, including the famous orator Danton. A strange assortment of radicals and moderates in the Convention, knowing that they might be next, organized a conspiracy. They howled down Robespierre when he tried to speak to the National Convention on 9 Thermidor (July 27, 1794). The next day it was Robespierre's turn to face the guillotine.

As Robespierre's closest supporters were also put to death, France unexpectedly experienced a thorough reaction to the violence of the Reign of Terror. In a general way, this **Thermidorian reaction** recalled the early days of the Revolution. The middle-class professionals who had led the liberal revolution of 1789 reasserted their authority, drawing support from their own class, the provincial cities, and the better-off

Thermidorian reaction *The period after the execution of Robespierre in 1794; it was a reaction to the violence of the Reign of Terror.*

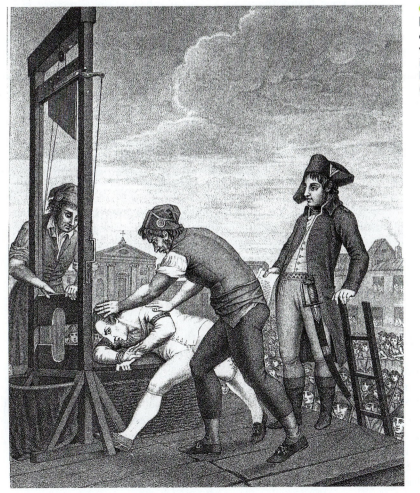

● **The Execution of Robespierre** The guillotine was painted red and was completely wooden except for the heavy iron blade. Large crowds witnessed the executions in a majestic public square in central Paris, then known as the Place de la Revolution and now called the Place de la Concorde (Harmony Square). *(Snark/Art Resource, NY)*

peasants. The National Convention abolished many economic controls, let prices rise sharply, and severely restricted the local political organizations where sans-culottes congregated.

The collapse of economic controls, coupled with runaway inflation, devastated the working poor. After the Convention used the army to suppress protest, the urban poor lost their revolutionary fervor. Excluded and disillusioned, they would have little interest in and influence on politics until 1830. The poor of the countryside turned toward religion as a relief from earthly cares. Rural women, especially, brought back the Catholic Church as the government began to soften its antireligious revolutionary stance.

As for the National Convention, in 1795 its members wrote yet another constitution that they believed would guarantee their economic position and political supremacy. As in previous elections, the mass of the population voted only for electors, whose number was cut back to men of substantial means. Electors then elected the members of a reorganized legislative assembly as well as key officials throughout France. The new assembly also chose a five-man executive—the Directory.

The Directory continued to support French military expansion abroad. War was no longer so much a crusade as a means to meet ever-present, ever-unsolved economic problems. Large, victorious French armies reduced unemployment at home and were able to live off the territories they conquered and plundered.

The unprincipled action of the Directory reinforced widespread disgust with war and starvation. This general dissatisfaction revealed itself clearly in the national elections of 1797, which returned a large number of conservative and even monarchist deputies who favored peace at almost any price. The members of the Directory, fearing for their skins, used the army to nullify the elections and began to govern dictatorially. Two years later Napoleon Bonaparte ended the Directory in a coup d'état and substituted a strong dictatorship for a weak one. The effort to establish stable representative government had failed.

THE NAPOLEONIC ERA (1799–1815)

What factors explain the rise and fall of Napoleon Bonaparte and his loss of the colony of Saint-Domingue?

For almost fifteen years, from 1799 to 1814, France was in the hands of a keen-minded military dictator of exceptional ability. One of history's most fascinating leaders, Napoleon Bonaparte (1769–1821) realized the need to put an end to civil strife in France in order to create unity and consolidate his rule. And he did. But Napoleon saw himself as a man of destiny, and the glory of war and the dream of universal empire proved irresistible. For years he spiraled from victory to victory, but in the end he was destroyed by a mighty coalition united in fear of his restless ambition.

Napoleon's Rule of France

In 1799 when he seized power, young General Napoleon Bonaparte was a national hero. Born in Corsica into an impoverished noble family in 1769, Napoleon left home and became a lieutenant in the French artillery. After a brief and unsuccessful adventure fighting for Corsican independence in 1789, he returned to France as a French patriot and a dedicated revolutionary. Rising rapidly in the new army, Napoleon was placed in command of French forces in Italy and won brilliant victories there in 1796 and 1797. His next campaign, in Egypt, was a failure, but Napoleon returned to France before the fiasco was generally known, and his reputation remained intact.

The Napoleonic Era

November 1799	Napoleon overthrows the Directory.
December 1799	French voters overwhelmingly approve Napoleon's new constitution.
1800	Napoleon founds the Bank of France.
1801	France defeats Austria and acquires Italian and German territories in the Treaty of Lunéville. Napoleon signs the Concordat with the pope.
February 1802	French forces arrive in Saint-Domingue.
March 1802	France signs the Treaty of Amiens with Britain.
August 1802	Napoleon restores slavery in French colonies.
April 1803	Toussaint L'Ouverture dies in France.
January 1804	Jean Jacques Dessalines declares Haitian independence.
March 1804	Napoleonic Code comes into force.
December 1804	Napoleon crowns himself emperor.
May 1805	First Haitian constitution promulgated.
October 1805	Britain defeats the French and Spanish fleet at the Battle of Trafalgar.
December 1805	Napoleon defeats Austria and Russia at the Battle of Austerlitz.
1807	Napoleon redraws the map of Europe in the treaties of Tilsit.
1810	The Grand Empire is at its height.
June 1812	Napoleon invades Russia with 600,000 men.
Fall–Winter 1812	Napoleon makes a disastrous retreat from Russia.
March 1814	Russia, Prussia, Austria, and Britain sign the Treaty of Chaumont, pledging alliance to defeat Napoleon.
April 1814	Napoleon abdicates and is exiled to Elba.
February–June 1815	Napoleon escapes from Elba and rules France until he is defeated at the Battle of Waterloo.

Napoleon soon learned that prominent members of the legislature were plotting against the Directory. Ten years of upheaval and uncertainty had convinced these disillusioned revolutionaries that a strong military ruler was needed to restore order. Together the conspirators and Napoleon organized a takeover. On November 9, 1799, they ousted the Directors, and the following day soldiers disbanded the legislature. Napoleon was named first consul of the republic, and a new constitution consolidating his position was overwhelmingly approved in a plebiscite in December 1799. Republican appearances were maintained, but Napoleon was the real ruler of France.

The essence of Napoleon's domestic policy was to use his great and highly personal powers to maintain order and end civil strife. He did so by working out unwritten agreements with powerful groups in France whereby the groups received favors in return for loyal service. Napoleon's bargain with the solid middle class was codified in the famous Civil Code of 1804, which reasserted two of the fundamental principles of the liberal revolution of 1789: equality of all male citizens before the law and absolute security of wealth and private property. Napoleon and the leading bankers of Paris established the privately owned Bank of France, which served the interests of both the state and the financial oligarchy. Peasants were also appeased when Napoleon defended the gains in land and status they had claimed during the revolution.

At the same time Napoleon perfected a thoroughly centralized state. He consolidated his rule by recruiting disillusioned revolutionaries for the network of ministers, prefects, and centrally appointed mayors that depended on him and came to serve him well. Only former revolutionaries who leaned too far to the left or to the right were excluded.[6] Nor were members of the old nobility slighted. In 1800 and 1802 Napoleon granted amnesty to one hundred thousand émigrés on the condition that they return to France and take a loyalty oath. Members of this returning elite soon occupied many high posts in the expanding centralized state. Napoleon also created a new imperial nobility to reward his most talented generals and officials.

Napoleon applied his diplomatic skills to healing the Catholic Church in France so that it could serve as a bulwark of order and social peace. Napoleon and Pope Pius VII (1800–1823) signed the Concordat of 1801. The pope gained the precious right for French Catholics to practice their religion freely, but Napoleon gained political power: his government now nominated bishops, paid the clergy, and exerted great influence over the church in France.

The domestic reforms of Napoleon's early years were his greatest achievement. Much of his legal and administrative reorganization has survived in France to this day. More generally, Napoleon's domestic initiatives gave the great majority of French people a welcome sense of stability and national unity.

Order and unity had a price: Napoleon's authoritarian rule. Women lost many of the gains they had made in the 1790s. Under the law of the new Napoleonic Code, women were dependents of either their fathers or their husbands, and they could not make contracts or even have bank accounts in their own names. Indeed, Napoleon and his advisers aimed at re-establishing a family monarchy, where the power of the husband and father was as absolute over the wife and the children as that of Napoleon was over his subjects.

Free speech and freedom of the press were continually violated. By 1811 only four newspapers were left, and they were little more than organs of government propaganda. The occasional elections were a farce. Later laws prescribed harsh penalties for political offenses, and people were watched carefully under an efficient spy system. There were about twenty-five hundred political prisoners in 1814.

Napoleon's Expansion in Europe

Napoleon was above all a military man, and a great one. After coming to power in 1799 he sent peace feelers to Austria and Great Britain, the two remaining members of the Second Coalition of 1798. When these overtures were rejected, French armies led by Napoleon decisively defeated the Austrians. In the Treaty of Lunéville (1801), Austria accepted the loss of almost all its Italian possessions, and German territory on the west bank of the Rhine was incorporated into France. The British agreed to the Treaty of Amiens in 1802, allowing France to remain in control of Holland, the Austrian Netherlands, the west bank of the Rhine, and most of the Italian peninsula. The Treaty of Amiens was a diplomatic triumph for Napoleon.

In 1802 Napoleon was secure but driven to expand his power. Aggressively redrawing the map of Germany so as to weaken Austria and encourage the secondary states of southwestern Germany to side with France, Napoleon tried to restrict British trade with all of Europe. He then plotted to attack Great Britain, but his Mediterranean fleet was virtually annihilated by Lord Nelson at the Battle of Trafalgar on October 21, 1805. Invasion of England was henceforth impossible. Renewed fighting had its

● **The Coronation of Napoleon, 1804 (detail)** In this grandiose painting by Jacques-Louis David, Napoleon prepares to crown his wife, Josephine, in an elaborate ceremony in Notre Dame Cathedral. Napoleon, the ultimate upstart, also crowned himself. Pope Pius VII, seated glumly behind the emperor, is reduced to being a spectator. *(Louvre/Réunion des Musées Nationaux/Art Resource, NY)*

advantages, however, for the first consul used the wartime atmosphere to have himself proclaimed emperor in late 1804.

Austria, Russia, and Sweden joined with Britain to form the Third Coalition against France shortly before the Battle of Trafalgar. Actions such as Napoleon's assumption of the Italian crown had convinced both Alexander I of Russia and Francis II of Austria that Napoleon was a threat to their interests and to the European balance of power. Yet they were no match for Napoleon, who scored a brilliant victory over them at the Battle of Austerlitz in December 1805. Alexander I decided to pull back, and Austria accepted large territorial losses in return for peace as the Third Coalition collapsed.

Napoleon then proceeded to reorganize the German states. In 1806 he abolished many of the tiny German states as well as the ancient Holy Roman Empire and established by decree the German Confederation of the Rhine, a union of fifteen German states minus Austria, Prussia, and Saxony. Naming himself "protector" of the confederation, Napoleon firmly controlled western Germany.

Napoleon's intervention in German affairs alarmed the Prussians, who mobilized their armies after more than a decade of peace with France. Napoleon attacked and won two more brilliant victories in October 1806 at Jena and Auerstädt, where the Prussians were outnumbered two to one. The war with Prussia, now joined by Russia, continued into the following spring. After Napoleon's larger armies won another victory, Alexander I of Russia was ready to negotiate the peace. In the subsequent treaties of Tilsit, Prussia lost half of its population, while Russia accepted Napoleon's reorganization of western and central Europe and promised to enforce Napoleon's economic blockade against British goods.

The War of Haitian Independence

Another strong military leader was emerging in the French colonies. Toussaint L'Ouverture increasingly acted as an independent ruler of the western province of Saint-Domingue. This provoked another general, André Rigaud, to set up his own government in the southern peninsula, which had long been more isolated from France than the rest of the colony. Civil war broke out between the two sides in 1799, when L'Ouverture's forces, led by his lieutenant Jean Jacques Dessalines, invaded the south. Victory over Rigaud gave Toussaint control of the entire colony. (See the feature "Individuals in Society: Toussaint L'Ouverture.")

L'Ouverture's victory was soon challenged, however, by Napoleon's arrival in power. Napoleon intended to re-invigorate the Caribbean plantation economy as a basis for expanding French power. He ordered his brother-in-law General Charles-Victor-Emmanuel Leclerc to crush the new regime. In 1802 Leclerc landed in Saint-Domingue. Although Toussaint L'Ouverture cooperated with the French and turned his army over to them, he was arrested and deported, along with his family, to France, where he died in 1803. Jean Jacques Dessalines united the resistance under his command and led them to a crushing victory over the French forces. Of the fifty-eight thousand French soldiers, fifty thousand were lost in combat and to disease. On January 1, 1804, Dessalines formally declared the creation of the new sovereign nation of Haiti, the name used by the pre-Columbian inhabitants of the island. (France's other Caribbean colonies were not granted independence. Napoleon re-established slavery in 1802, and it remained in force until 1848.)

Haiti, the second independent state in the Americas and the first in Latin America, was thus born from the first successful large-scale slave revolt in history. As one recent historian of the Haitian revolution commented:

The insurrection of Saint-Domingue led to the expansion of citizenship beyond racial barriers despite the massive political and economic investment in the slave system at the time. If we live in a world in which democracy is meant to exclude no one, it is in no small part because of the actions of those slaves in Saint-Domingue who insisted that human rights were theirs too.[7]

The Grand Empire and Its End

Grand Empire *Napoleon's name for the European empire over which he intended to rule. This Grand Empire would consist of France, a number of lesser dependent states ruled by his relations, and several major allied states (Austria, Prussia, and Russia).*

Napoleon resigned himself to the loss of Saint-Domingue, but he still maintained imperial ambitions in Europe. Increasingly, he saw himself as the emperor of Europe and not just of France. The so-called **Grand Empire** he built had three parts. The core was an ever-expanding France, which by 1810 included Belgium, Holland, parts of northern Italy, and much German territory on the east bank of the Rhine. Beyond French borders Napoleon established the second part: a number of dependent satellite kingdoms ruled by members of his large family. The third part comprised the independent but allied states of Austria, Prussia, and Russia. After 1806 both satellites and allies were expected to support Napoleon's continental system and to cease trade with Britain.

The impact of the Grand Empire on the peoples of Europe was considerable. In the areas incorporated into France and in the satellites (see Map 21.2), feudal dues and serfdom were abolished. Yet Napoleon put the prosperity and special interests of France first in order to safeguard his power base. Levying heavy taxes in money and men for his armies, he came to be regarded more as a conquering tyrant than as an enlightened liberator. Thus French rule encouraged the growth of reactive

Toussaint L'Ouverture

L ittle is known of the early life of the brilliant military and political leader Toussaint L'Ouverture. He was born in 1743 on a plantation outside Le Cap owned by the Count de Bréda. According to tradition, Toussaint was the eldest son of a captured African prince from modern-day Benin. Toussaint Bréda, as he was then called, occupied a privileged position among slaves. Instead of performing backbreaking labor in the fields, he served his master as a coachman and livestock keeper. He also learned to read and write French and some Latin, but he was always more comfortable in the Creole dialect.

During the 1770s the plantation manager emancipated Toussaint. After being freed, he leased his own small coffee plantation, worked by slaves. A devout Catholic who led a frugal and ascetic life, L'Ouverture impressed others with his enormous physical energy, intellectual acumen, and air of mystery. He married Suzanne Simone, who already had one son, and the couple had another son during their marriage.

Toussaint L'Ouverture entered history in 1791 when he joined the slave uprisings that swept Saint-Domingue. (At some point he took on the cryptic *nom de guerre* "l'ouverture" meaning "the opening.") Toussaint rose to prominence among rebel slaves allied with Spain and by early 1794 controlled his own army. In 1794 he defected to the French side and led his troops to a series of victories against the Spanish. In 1795 France's National Convention promoted L'Ouverture to brigadier general.

Over the next three years L'Ouverture successively eliminated rivals for authority on the island. First he freed himself of the French commissioners sent to govern the colony. With a firm grip on power in the northern province, Toussaint defeated General André Rigaud in 1800 to gain control in the south. His army then marched on the capital of Spanish Santo Domingo on the eastern half of the island, meeting little resistance. The entire island of Hispaniola was now under his command.

With control of Saint-Domingue in his hands, L'Ouverture was confronted with the challenge of building a post-emancipation society, the first of its kind. The task was made even more difficult by the chaos wreaked by war, the destruction of plantations, and bitter social and racial tensions. For L'Ouverture the most pressing concern was to re-establish the plantation economy. Without revenue to pay his army, the gains of the rebellion could be lost. He there-

Equestrian portrait of Toussaint L'Ouverture. (Réunion des Musées Nationaux/Art Resource, NY)

fore encouraged white planters to return and reclaim their property. He also adopted harsh policies toward former slaves, forcing them back to their plantations and restricting their ability to acquire land. When they resisted, he sent troops across the island to enforce submission.

In 1801 L'Ouverture convened a colonial assembly to draft a new constitution that reaffirmed his draconian labor policies. The constitution named L'Ouverture governor for life, leaving Saint-Domingue as a colony in name alone. When news of the constitution arrived in France, an angry Napoleon dispatched General Leclerc to reestablish French control. In June 1802 Leclerc's forces arrested L'Ouverture and took him to France. He was jailed at Fort de Joux in the Jura Mountains near the Swiss border, where he died of pneumonia on April 7, 1803. It was left to his lieutenant, Jean Jacques Dessalines, to win independence for the new Haitian nation.

Questions for Analysis

1. Toussaint L'Ouverture was both slave and slave owner. How did each experience shape his life and actions?

2. Despite their differences, what did Toussaint L'Ouverture and Napoleon Bonaparte have in common? Why did they share a common fate?

MAP 21.2 **Napoleonic Europe in 1810** Only Great Britain remained at war with Napoleon at the height of the Grand Empire. Many British goods were smuggled through Helgoland, a tiny but strategic British possession off the German coast.

Map legend:
- French empire
- Dependent states
- Allied with Napoleon
- At war with Napoleon
- ★ Major battle

400 Mi.
400 Km.
200
200
0
0

Labels on map:

ATLANTIC OCEAN

North Sea

GREAT BRITAIN
London

KINGDOM OF NORWAY AND DENMARK

KINGDOM OF SWEDEN
Stockholm
Copenhagen

Baltic Sea

St. Petersburg

RUSSIAN EMPIRE
Moscow
Borodino 1812
Smolensk
Kiev

Tilsit
Friedland 1807
Königsberg
Danzig

SWEDISH POMERANIA
PRUSSIA
Berlin
Lübeck
Hamburg
Bremen
Elbe R.
Rhine R.
Neman R.

GRAND DUCHY OF WARSAW

SAXONY
WESTPHALIA
Auerstädt 1806
Jena 1806

CONFEDERATION OF THE RHINE
WÜRTTEMBERG
BADEN
BAVARIA
Zurich
SWITZERLAND

Austerlitz 1805
Wagram 1809
Pressburg
Vienna
Buda
Pest

AUSTRIAN EMPIRE

ILLYRIAN PROVINCES

Danube R.

OTTOMAN EMPIRE

Black Sea

Constantinople

Brussels
Waterloo 1815
Paris
Lunéville
Amiens
FRANCE

KINGDOM OF ITALY
Milan
Marengo 1800
Genoa
Marseilles

Corsica
Sardinia
Elba
Rome
Naples
KINGDOM OF NAPLES
Palermo
KINGDOM OF SICILY

Mediterranean Sea

Malta (Gr. Br.)
Ionian Is. (Gr. Br.)
Athens

SPAIN
Madrid
PORTUGAL
Lisbon
GIBRALTAR (Gr. Br.)
Trafalgar 1805

10°W
0°
10°E
20°E
30°E
40°N
50°N
60°N

● **The War in Spain** This unforgettable etching by the Spanish painter Francisco Goya (1746–1828) comes from his famous collection "The Disasters of the War." A French firing squad executes captured Spanish rebels almost as soon as they are captured, an everyday event in a war of atrocities on both sides. Do you think these rebels are "terrorists" or "freedom fighters"? *(Foto Marburg/Art Resource, NY)*

nationalism, for individuals in different lands developed patriotic feelings of their own in opposition to Napoleon's imperialism.

The first great revolt occurred in Spain. In 1808 a coalition of Catholics, monarchists, and patriots rebelled against Napoleon's attempts to make Spain a French satellite with a Bonaparte as its king. Yet Napoleon pushed on, determined to hold his complex and far-flung empire together. In 1810, when the Grand Empire was at its height, Britain still remained at war with France, helping guerrillas in Spain and Portugal. The continental system, organized to exclude British goods from the continent and force that "nation of shopkeepers" to its knees, was a failure. Instead, it was France that suffered economically from Britain's counter-blockade. Perhaps looking for a scapegoat, Napoleon turned on Alexander I of Russia, who in 1811 openly repudiated Napoleon's war of prohibitions against British goods.

Napoleon's invasion of Russia began in June 1812 with a force that eventually numbered 600,000, probably the largest force yet assembled in a single army. Only one-third of this Great Army was French, however; nationals of all the satellites and allies were drafted into the operation. Napoleon reached Smolensk and recklessly pressed on toward Moscow. The great Battle of Borodino that followed was a draw, and the Russians retreated in good order. Alexander ordered the evacuation of Moscow, which then burned in part, and he refused to negotiate. Finally, after five weeks in the abandoned city, Napoleon ordered a retreat, one of the greatest disasters in military history. The Russian army, the Russian winter, and starvation cut Napoleon's army to pieces. When the frozen remnants staggered into Poland and Prussia in December, 370,000 men had died and another 200,000 had been taken prisoner.[8]

Leaving his troops to their fate, Napoleon raced to Paris to raise yet another army. Austria and Prussia deserted Napoleon and joined Russia and Great Britain in the Treaty of Chaumont in March 1814, by which the four powers pledged allegiance to defeat the French emperor. All across Europe patriots called for a "war of liberation" against Napoleon's oppression. Less than a month later, on April 4, 1814, a defeated Napoleon abdicated his throne. The victorious allies granted Napoleon the island of Elba off the coast of Italy as his own tiny state. Napoleon was even allowed to keep his imperial title, and France was required to pay him a yearly income of 2 million francs.

The allies also agreed to the restoration of the Bourbon dynasty under Louis XVIII (r. 1814–1824). The new monarch tried to gain support by issuing the Constitutional Charter, which accepted many of France's revolutionary changes and guaranteed civil liberties. Yet Louis XVIII—old, ugly, and crippled by gout—lacked the glory and magic of Napoleon. Sensing an opportunity, Napoleon staged a daring escape from Elba in February 1815. Landing in France, he issued appeals for support and marched on Paris with a small band of followers. Louis XVIII fled, and once more Napoleon took command. But Napoleon's gamble was a desperate long shot, for the allies were united against him. At the end of a frantic period known as the Hundred Days, they crushed his forces at Waterloo on June 18, 1815, and imprisoned him on the rocky island of St. Helena, off the western coast of Africa. Louis XVIII recommenced his reign. The allies now dealt more harshly with the apparently incorrigible French. As for Napoleon, he took revenge by writing his memoirs, skillfully nurturing the myth that he had been Europe's revolutionary liberator, a romantic hero whose lofty work had been undone by oppressive reactionaries. An era had ended.

Chapter Summary

Key Terms

desacralization
Assembly of Notables
Estates General
National Assembly
Great Fear
constitutional monarchy
free people of color
Jacobin club
second revolution
Girondists
the Mountain
sans-culottes
planned economy
Reign of Terror
nationalism
Thermidorian reaction
Grand Empire

To assess your mastery of this chapter, go to
bedfordstmartins.com/mckayworld

• *What social, political, and economic factors formed the background to the French Revolution?*

The French Revolution was forged by multiple and complex factors. French society had undergone significant transformations during the eighteenth century, which dissolved many economic and social differences among elites without removing the legal distinction between them. These changes were accompanied by political struggles between the monarchy and its officers, particularly in the high law courts. Emerging public opinion focused on the shortcomings of monarchical rule in political and personal terms. With their sacred royal aura severely tarnished, Louis XV and his successor Louis XVI found themselves unable to respond to the financial crises generated by war and public debt. Louis XVI's half-hearted efforts to redress the situation were quickly overwhelmed by demands for fundamental reform.

• *What were the immediate events and ideas that sparked the Revolution in France and its Caribbean colony of Saint-Domingue?*

Forced to call a meeting of the Estates General for the first time since 1614, Louis XVI fell back on the traditional formula of one vote for each of the three orders of society. Debate over the composition of the assembly called forth a bold new paradigm: that the Third Estate in itself constituted the French nation. By 1791 the National Assembly had eliminated Old Regime privileges and had established a constitutional monarchy. Talk in France of liberty, equality, and fraternity raised contradictory aspirations among the wealthy white planters, free people of color, and African slaves of the colony of Saint-Domingue. All looked to the Revolution for a better future, a promise that could not be fulfilled for all.

• How and why did the Revolution take a radical turn at home and in the colonies?

With the execution of the royal couple and the declaration of terror as the order of the day, the French Revolution took an increasingly radical turn from the summer of 1792. Fears of counter-revolutionary conspiracy combined with the outbreak of war convinced many that the Revolution was vulnerable and must be defended against its multiple enemies. In a spiraling cycle of accusations and executions, the Jacobins eliminated political opponents and then factions within their own party. The Directory government that took power after the fall of Robespierre restored political equilibrium at the cost of his platform of social equality. In the colonies, slave revolt and the pressure of war led to the abolition of slavery and the enfranchisement of free people of color and former slaves.

• What factors explain the rise and fall of Napoleon Bonaparte and his loss of the colony of Saint-Domingue?

Wearied by the Directory's weaknesses, conspirators gave Napoleon Bonaparte control of France. His military brilliance, his charisma and determination made him seem ideal to lead France to victory over its enemies. As is so often the case in history, Napoleon's relentless ambitions ultimately led to his downfall. His story is paralleled by that of Toussaint L'Ouverture, another soldier who emerged to the political limelight from the chaos of revolution only to endure exile and defeat.

As complex as its origins are, the legacies of the French Revolution included liberalism, assertive nationalism, radical democratic republicanism, embryonic socialism, self-conscious conservatism, abolitionism, decolonization, and movements for racial and sexual equality. The Revolution also left a rich and turbulent history of electoral competition, legislative assemblies, and even mass politics. Thus the French Revolution presented a range of political options and alternative visions of the future. For this reason, it was truly the revolution in modern European politics.

Suggested Reading

Bell, David A. *The Cult of the Nation in France: Inventing Nationalism, 1680–1800.* 2001. Traces early French nationalism through its revolutionary culmination.

Blanning, T. C. W. *The French Revolutionary Wars (1787–1802).* 1996. A masterful account of the revolutionary wars that also places the French Revolution in its European context.

Broers, Michael. *Europe Under Napoleon.* 2002. Probes Napoleon's impact on the territories he conquered.

Connelly, Owen. *The French Revolution and Napoleonic Era.* 1991. An excellent introduction to the French Revolution and Napoleon.

Desan, Suzanne. *The Family on Trial in Revolutionary France.* 2004. Studies the effects of revolutionary law on the family, including the legalization of divorce.

Dubois, Laurent. *Avengers of the New World: The Story of the Haitian Revolution.* 2004. An excellent and highly readable account of the revolution that transformed the French colony of Saint-Domingue into the independent state of Haiti.

Englund, Steven. *Napoleon: A Political Life.* 2004. A good biography of the French emperor.

(continued on page 640)

Revolution and Women's Rights

The 1789 Declaration of the Rights of Man was a revolutionary call for legal equality, representative government, and individual freedom that excluded women from its manifesto. Among those who saw the contradiction in granting supposedly universal rights to only half the population was Marie Gouze (1748–1793), known to history as Olympe de Gouges. The daughter of a provincial butcher and peddler, she pursued a literary career in Paris after the death of her husband. De Gouges's great work was her "Declaration of the Rights of Woman" (1791). Excerpted here, it called on males to end their oppression of women and to give women equal rights. A radical on women's issues, de Gouges sympathized with the monarchy and criticized Robespierre in print. Convicted of sedition, she was guillotined in November 1793.

. . . Man, are you capable of being just? . . . Tell me, what gives you sovereign empire to oppress my sex? Your strength? Your talents? Observe the Creator in his wisdom . . . and give me, if you dare, an example of this tyrannical empire. Go back to animals, consult the elements, study plants . . . and distinguish, if you can, the sexes in the administration of nature. Everywhere you will find them mingled; everywhere they cooperate in harmonious togetherness in this immortal masterpiece.

Man alone has raised his exceptional circumstances to a principle. . . . [H]e wants to command as a despot a sex which is in full possession of its intellectual faculties; he pretends to enjoy the Revolution and to claim his rights to equality in order to say nothing more about it.

DECLARATION OF THE RIGHTS OF WOMAN AND THE FEMALE CITIZEN

. . . Mothers, daughters, sisters and representatives of the nation demand to be constituted into a national assembly. Believing that ignorance, omission, or scorn for the rights of woman are the only causes of public misfortunes and of the corruption of governments, [the women] have resolved to set forth in a solemn declaration the natural, inalienable, and sacred rights of woman. . . .

I. Woman is born free and lives equal to man in her rights. Social distinctions can be based only on the common utility.

II. The purpose of any political association is the conservation of the natural and imprescriptible rights of woman and man; these rights are liberty, property, security, and especially resistance to oppression.

III. The principle of all sovereignty rests essentially with the nation, which is nothing but the union of woman and man. . . .

IV. Liberty and justice consist of restoring all that belongs to others; thus, the only limits on the exercise of the natural rights of woman are perpetual male tyranny; these limits are to be reformed by the laws of nature and reason.

V. Laws of nature and reason proscribe all acts harmful to society. . . .

VI. The law must be the expression of the general will; all female and male citizens must contribute either personally or through their representatives to its formation; it must be the same for all: male and female citizens, being equal in the eyes of the law, must be equally admitted to all honors, positions, and public employment according to their capacity and without other distinctions besides those of their virtues and talents. . . .

IX. Once any woman is declared guilty, complete rigor is [to be] exercised by the law.

X. No one is to be disquieted for his very basic opinions; woman has the right to mount the scaffold; she must equally have the right to mount the rostrum, provided that her demonstrations do not disturb the legally established public order.

XI. The free communication of thoughts and opinions is one of the most precious rights of woman, since that liberty assures the recognition of children by their fathers. Any female citizen thus may say freely, I am the mother of a child which belongs to you, without being forced by a barbarous prejudice to hide the truth. . . .

XIII. For the support of the public force and the expenses of administration, the contributions of woman and man are equal; she shares all the duties . . . and all the painful tasks; therefore, she must have the same share in the distribution of positions, employment, offices, honors, and jobs. . . .

XVI. No society has a constitution without the guarantee of rights and the separation of powers; the constitution is null if the majority of individuals comprising the nation have not cooperated in drafting it.

XVII. Property belongs to both sexes whether united or separate; for each it is an inviolable and sacred right.

Olympe de Gouges in 1784; aquatint by Madame Aubry (1748–1793). *(Musée de la Ville de Paris, Musée Carnavalet, Paris, France/The Bridgeman Art Library)*

Questions for Analysis

1. On what basis did de Gouges argue for gender equality? Did she believe in natural law?

2. What consequences did "scorn for the rights of woman" have for France, according to de Gouges?

3. Did de Gouges stress political rights at the expense of social and economic rights? If so, why?

Source: Olympe de Gouges, "Declaration of the Rights of Woman," in *Women in Revolutionary Paris, 1789–1795: Selected Documents Translated with Notes and Commentary.* Translated with notes and commentary by Darline Gay Levy, Harriet Branson Applewhite, and Mary Durham Johnson. Copyright © 1979 by the Board of Trustees, University of Illinois. Used with permission of the editors and the University of Illinois Press.

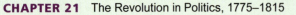

Hunt, Lynn. *Politics, Culture and Class in the French Revolution,* 2d ed. 2004. A pioneering examination of the French Revolution as a cultural phenomenon that generated new festivals, clothing, and songs and even a new calendar.

Landes, John B. *Visualizing the Nation: Gender, Representation, and Revolution in Eighteenth-Century France.* 2001. Analyzes images of gender and the body in revolutionary politics.

Schechter, Ronald. *Obstinate Hebrews: Representations of Jews in France, 1715–1815.* An illuminating study of Jews and attitudes toward them in France from Enlightenment to emancipation.

Sutherland, Donald. *France, 1789–1815.* 1986. An overview of the French Revolution that emphasizes its many opponents as well as its supporters.

Tackett, Timothy. *When the King Took Flight.* 2003. An exciting re-creation of the royal family's doomed effort to escape from Paris.

Notes

1. G. Pernoud and S. Flaisser, eds., *The French Revolution* (Greenwich, Conn.: Fawcett, 1960), p. 61.
2. Quoted in L. Gershoy, *The Era of the French Revolution, 1789–1799* (New York: Van Nostrand, 1957), p. 150.
3. T. Blanning, *The French Revolutionary Wars, 1787–1802* (London: Arnold, 1996), pp. 116–128.
4. 10. Quoted ibid., p. 123.
5. Quoted in Laurent Dubois, *Avengers of the New World: The Story of the Haitian Revolution* (Cambridge: Harvard University Press, 2004), p. 97.
6. I. Woloch, *Napoleon and His Collaborators: The Making of a Dictatorship* (New York: W. W. Norton, 2001), pp. 36–65.
7. Quoted in Laurent Dubois, *Avengers of the New World: The Story of the Haitian Revolution* (Cambridge: Harvard University Press, 2004), p. 3.
8. D. Sutherland, France, *1789–1815: Revolution and Counterrevolution* (New York: Oxford University Press, 1986), p. 420.

Index